AFRICAN NOMADIC ARCHITECTURE

AFRICAN NOMADIC ARCHITECTURE

SPACE, PLACE, AND GENDER

LABELLE PRUSSIN

WITH CONTRIBUTIONS BY AMINA ADAN, PETER A. ANDREWS,
ARLENE FULLERTON, ANDERS GRUM, AND UTA HOLTER

SMITHSONIAN INSTITUTION PRESS
and
THE NATIONAL MUSEUM OF AFRICAN ART
Washington and London

FOR VIC

© 1995 by Labelle Prussin
All rights reserved

ACQUIRING EDITOR: Amy Pastan
MANUSCRIPT EDITOR: Frances Kianka
PRODUCTIION EDITOR: Jack Kirshbaum
DESIGNER: Janice Wheeler
PRODUCTION MANAGER: Ken Sabol

Library of Congress Cataloging-in Publication Data
Prussin, Labelle.
    African nomadic architecture : space, place, and gender / Labelle Prussin.
       p.   cm.
   Includes bibliographical references and index.
   ISBN 1-56098-358-2 (acid-free paper : cloth).
   1. Tents—Africa 2. Architecture. Domestic—Africa
   3. Vernacular architecture—Africa.
I. Title.
NA7461.A1P78 1995
728—dc20   94-43109

British Library Cataloging-in Publication data available
04 03 02 01 00 99 98   5 4 3 2 1

A paperback reissue (1-560989-756-1) of the original cloth edition

The paper used in this publication meets the minimum requirements of the American National Standard for Permanence of Paper for Printed Library Materials Z39.48-1984.

For permission to reproduce any of the illustrations, correspond directly with the sources. Smithsonian Institution Press does not retain reproduction rights for these illustrations individually or maintain a file of addresses for photo sources.

Every effort has been made to reach copyright holders, the author would be pleased to hear from anyone whose rights have been unwittingly infringed.

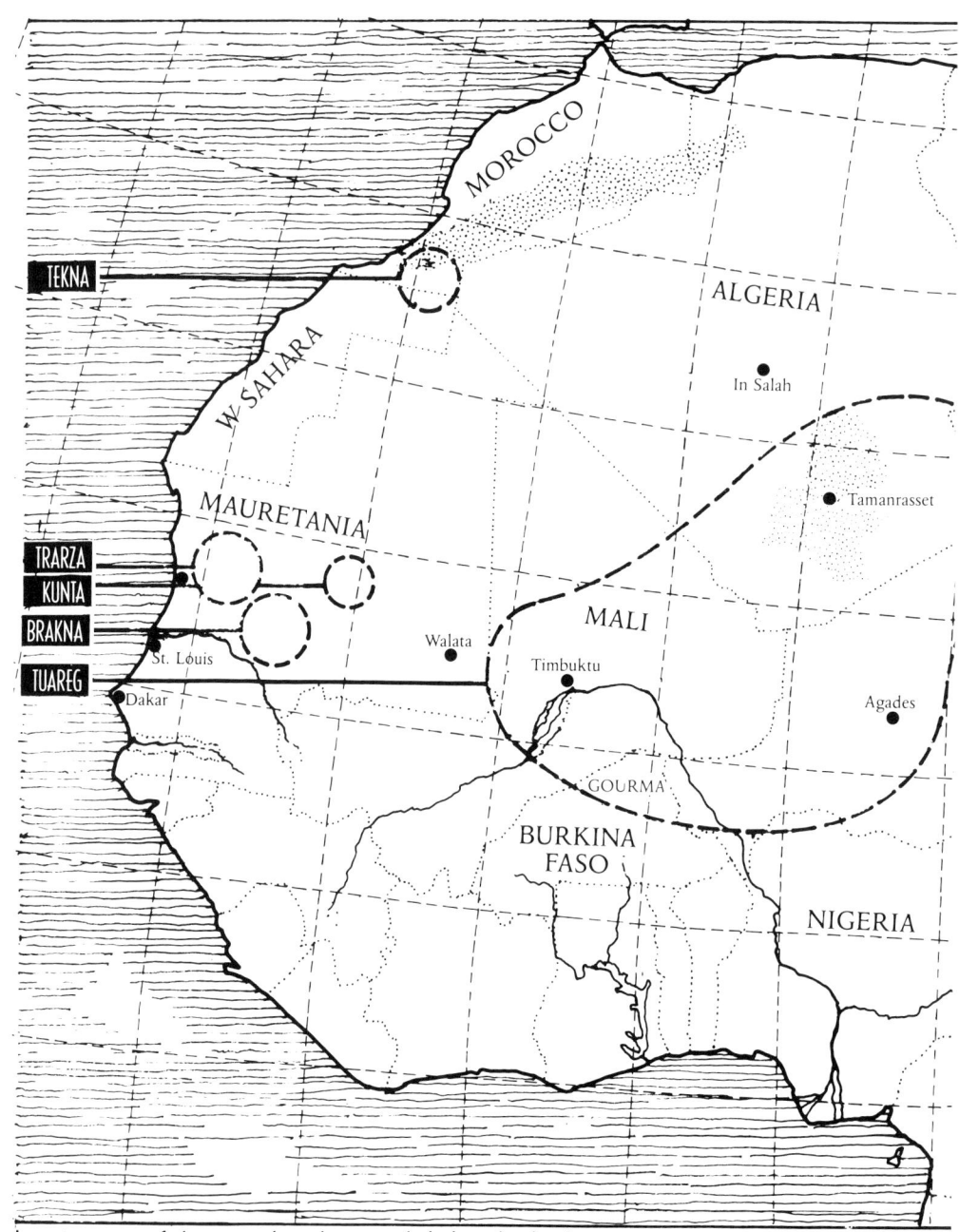

Location map of the nomadic cultures included in this book.

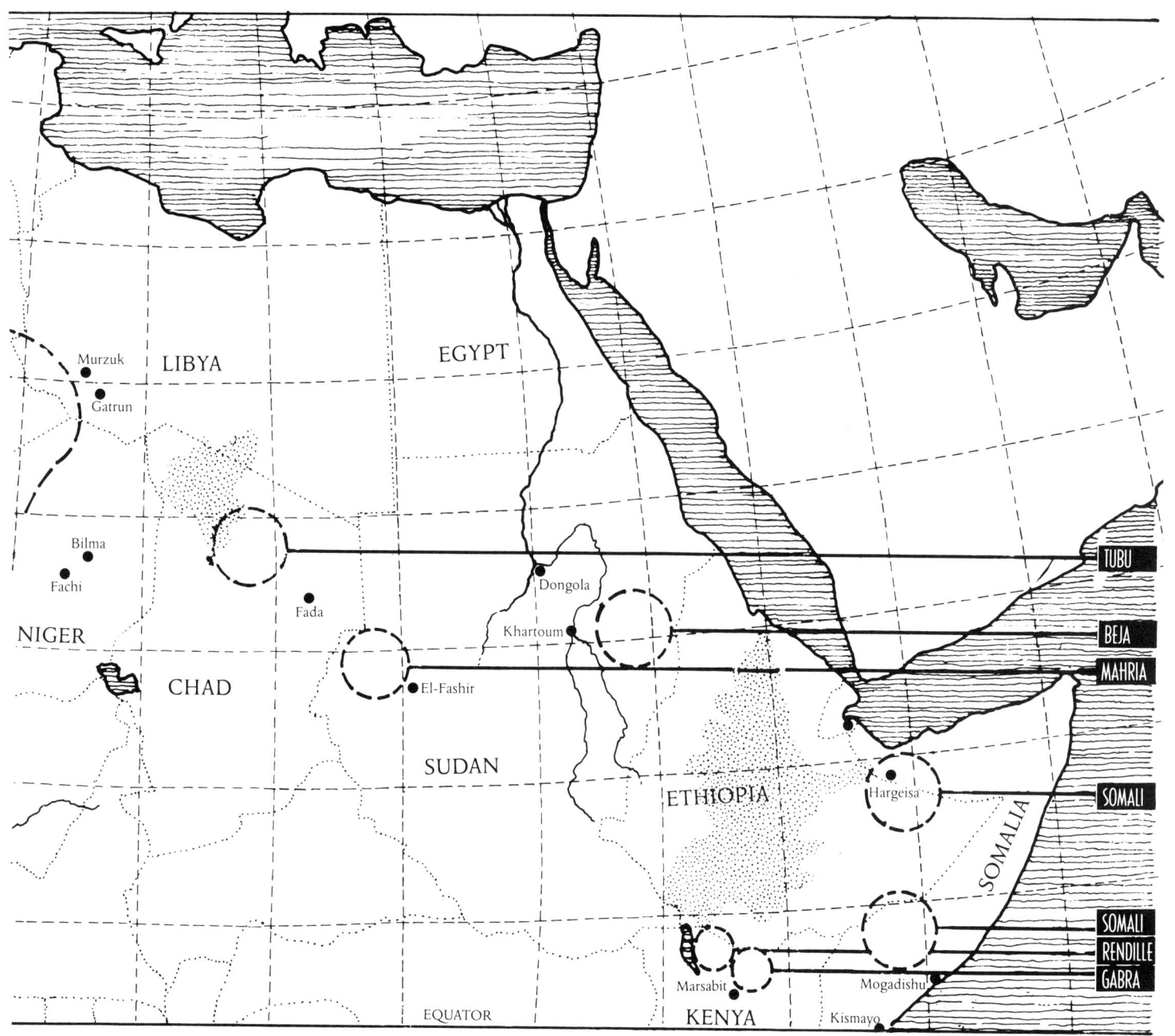

CONTENTS

FOREWORD ix
Robert Farris Thompson

FOREWORD xi
Sylvia H. Williams

ACKNOWLEDGMENTS xii

INTRODUCTION xv

1. THE TENT IN AFRICAN HISTORY 1
Tents as architecture. The Tabernacle. The vernacular tradition. The institutional tradition.
Camels and camel-riding technologies. Litters and palanquins.

2. ENVIRONMENT AND SPACE 20
Topography. Winds and sandstorms. Sun, light, shade, and shadow. Rainfall. Vegetation.
Plant utilization and drought resistance. Palms. Grasses. Acacias. Perception. Spatial ability.
The measure and representation of space. Mobility. Boundaries. Anthropometry. Continuity in space.
The geometry of spatial enclosure.

3. THE CREATIVE PROCESS 44
Technology of transport. Technology of building. Labor value, productivity, and
women's work. Dowries and engendered architecture. Ritual and celebration.
Mnemonics, the acquisition of skills, and play as children's work.

4. THE HASSANIYA-SPEAKING NOMADS: TEKNA, TRARZA, AND BRAKNA 64
Peter A. Andrews and excerpts from Odette Du Puigaudeau in translation
Tents of the Tekna. Arts and customs of the "Moors." The camp. Camel saddlery. Imagery. Birthing.

5. THE TUAREG: KEL AHAGGAR AND KEL FERWAN 88

Based on excerpts from Johannes Nicolaisen and excerpts from Dominique Casajus in translation

Tents and marriage. The Kel Ahaggar marriage ceremony. Marriage ritual and architectural history. Kel Ahaggar tents. Kel Dennek tents. Kel Ferwan tents. Spatial precautions. Palanquins as protection.

6. THE TUBU: NOMADS IN THE EASTERN SAHARA 108

Tubu tents. The Azza. The Tubu marriage ceremony. Saddles and palanquins.

7. MAHRIA TENTS: THE WOMAN'S DOMAIN 124

Uta Holter

The camp. The woman's daily tasks in a mobile camp. The tent as shelter: construction is women's work. The tent as home: furnishings as products of the women's crafts. The tent: woman's domain in the different phases of her life cycle. Future prospects.

8. RENDILLE HABITATION 150

Anders Grum

Settlement patterns. Other settlement types. The house. Furnishings. A new house. Gaalora and Odoola houses. Other house variations.

9. HANDICRAFTS OF THE SOMALI NOMADIC WOMEN 170

Arlene Fullerton and Amina Adan

The *Aqal*. Coverings *(saari)*. Storage things. The *Xeedho*.

10. THE NOMADIC AESTHETIC 186

Environment and space. Inner space. Surfaces. Altars. Container surrogates: palanquins. Gender polarities. Number symbolism, balance, and harmony. Sedentarization.

NOTES 207

BIBLIOGRAPHY 223

ILLUSTRATION CREDITS 233

INDEX 237

FOREWORD

ROBERT FARRIS THOMPSON

Labelle Prussin's *African Nomadic Architecture* gives back to women their own domain and contribution to world architectural history. Rather than give away her plot, revelatory and riveting, allow me to sample some of the gems, of heritage and cultural felicity, which make this text surely one of the classics of twentieth-century architectural history.

The book is, above all, right on time. In the midst of the Western emerald cities of Oz we have crime, greed, and homelessness. The architects of the twenty-first century, almost assuredly, will have to build a way out of a triple crisis of the materialist, capitalist, and idealist modes of intellectual production. Something has to give. Town planners will find that purely Western solutions for the burgeoning refugee and migrant populations are inadequate. The problem cries out for attention to already existing vernacular solutions.

The women builders of the Sahara could teach us a thing or two about housing whole populations on the outskirts of Calcutta, Djakarta, and São Paulo. This is not a romantic call for returning to the plans and elevations of nomadic women builders although the fit between their way of life and the increasingly nomadic nature of populations worldwide presents a compelling parallel.

On the contrary, what I am reminded of, as I read this text, is that some of the richest minds of Western architectural theory have cogently argued the possibility of building *by analogy* with the past, by analogy to farflung programs of architecture, rather than imitating without imagination, fossilizing matters, losing touch with where you are. So what if James Fenimore Cooper in 1836 made fun of Greek revival homes in the following way: "[the] children trundling hoops before the door, beef carried into their kitchens, and smoke issuing . . . from those unclassical objects' chimnies." It meant that the style was *working;* people were living, laboring, and playing in such houses. Classicism, alive with change.

Similarly, if early nineteenth-century America built by analogy with Athens and Rome for American banks and statehouses, perhaps twenty-first-century architects can build by analogy with nomadic women's architecture, where women make inner and outer surfaces of habitat come alive with the lines and colors of textiles. But will this work where snow falls, where populations are dense and urban? Yes, where sheer analogic play comes in and respects both art and practicality, where design and imagination orchestrate permanence of materials and modern heights and spaces.

In a sense, Berber architects of the Atlas Mountains worked out, long ago, just such an equation, giving rise, in the process, to one of the world's richest veins of vernacular building. Recall the kasbahs and ksar of the snow-capped Atlas. Here, in effect, architects, building by analogy with the richness of the women's textiles, lifted up their patterned tents and textiles and turned them into soaring, patterned parapets of clay. These builders let the felicities of women's design come through them, realizing their cities not as "frozen music" but as patterned textiles turned into impressive painted ceilings, especially at Tifnit, impressive patterned towers of clay, especially in the area of Skoura.

Berber vernacular architecture of Morocco is rhythmically and plastically as rich—if not richer—than Le Corbusier's heroic building, the 1955 chapel at Ronchamp, and it connects with the westernmost chapters of Prussin's saga of the Sahara. Why, then, are the towers of Skoura, to say nothing of the tents of the Tuareg, relatively unknown, whereas Ronchamp is a name in art history?

Prussin attacks and decodes all the reasons. One of which is that for want of knowledge about the North African and sub-Saharan canons in architecture, people think Africans are without building—the grass hut vision—and, hence, without culture, and hence one more time, omitted from the handbooks. Part of the problem, Prussin shows, is Western nurturing on the canons of Vitruvius: "durability, propriety, and beauty." There is beauty and propriety galore in Somali and Berber architecture. The catch is: permanence. By Vitruvian standards, architects working in terms of clay or textiles or vellum, no matter how handsomely realized their works, need not apply for inclusion in the canon.

Nonsense, says Prussin. Even lay persons are aware that Mesa Verde, in Amerindian antiquity, or Taos, New Mexico, today, largely built in clay, are as inherently architectural as a cluster of New England frame houses. But, going deeper, in her chapter on the Sahara and the Sahel, Prussin finds that "the tent is a mode of creative expression, a way of reordering a person's relationship with animals and plants, with the earth and the sky, with the rhythms and forces of nature." Again and again she introduces architecture spoken in a woman's voice. She takes the serious reader of world architecture on a safari of one. She connects us to the rich tenting traditions of the Tuareg, Tubu, Mahria, and Somali women: here, as she says, houses move frequently, camels provide transport, marriage rituals set the stage for the creation of art and architecture, and life unfolds in a gender-discrete universe.

The pages on the tent in history are especially germane. She reminds us that Hebrews, like Tuareg, were nomads and that the tabernacle which Yahweh instructed Moses to make was a portable sanctuary set up in the center of the Hebrew encampment. They set up this sacred tent at each stop in the wilderness. She takes us back several millennia to Tassili, realizing, in effect that the rock art there is to African architectural history as the mosaics of Pompeii and Herculaneum are to those seeking to rebuild a history of Greek painting. Caught in the amber of the rock art of Tassili is nothing less than the dawn of the nomadic chapter in black architectural history: "accurate renditions of the nomadic ethnographic present. In the first instance a woman surrounded by herds of cattle, holds what appears to be not a bow but a bentwood frame used in constructing armature tents, much as the Rendille and Somali do. In the second instance the accurate elevations of tent armatures within the four circles (including two persons clearly visible within one) matched my measured drawings of innumerable Gabra, Somali, and Rendille as well as Fulbe pastoral compounds."

In short, this book is important. It stands as a permanent resource for a world in desperate need of alternative traditions as we come to grips with ever-mounting challenges in the housing of nomadic refugees and homeless. Architects will find particularly fascinating the sections where she talks about mnemonics and the acquisition of tectonic skills. The grand summary chapter, "The Nomadic Aesthetic," distills all arguments and puts the Sahara firmly on the map. This is one of those rare books that discovers and defines a whole new field. In the process, Labelle Prussin realizes her own self-set ambition: to reverify the value of private, domestic, women's architecture.

FOREWORD

SYLVIA H. WILLIAMS

In any consideration of architectural history, a discussion of vernacular architecture is almost always conspicuously absent. Similarly, the arts and architecture of African nomadism are at best cursorily included in surveys of African visual traditions. In an effort to correct these omissions, the National Museum of African Art enthusiastically joins the Smithsonian Institution Press as copublisher of Labelle Prussin's *African Nomadic Architecture: Space, Place, and Gender*.

Dr. Prussin, a scholar and architect, has a longstanding and deep interest in the architectural creativity of African nomads, an interest that has been shared by the Museum for several years. In 1986, Dr. Prussin continued her research as the first recipient of a one-year postdoctoral Rockefeller Foundation Residency Fellowship in the Humanities at the National Museum of African Art. During many informal sessions, she opened our eyes and stimulated our curiosity about the built environment, material culture, and collective creativity of nomads. Her association with the Museum continued with Rockefeller Foundation support that, in 1987 and 1988, enabled her to conduct collection research and to explore the possibility of mounting an exhibition. Instead of a static and transitory exhibition, however, the Museum asked Dr. Prussin to consider another medium, film, in which to document permanently the results of her remarkable body of research. Thus, in 1989, Dr. Prussin worked in Kenya developing the concept and script for the film *Nagayati: Arts and Architecture among the Gabra Nomads of Kenya*. Produced by Peter Oud, Film and Photography for Development Work, for the National Museum of African Art, the film documents a Gabra marriage ceremony, during which a new house and its furnishings are created by women who fulfill the roles of designers, builders, owners, and users.

In *African Nomadic Architecture*, Dr. Prussin continues her exemplary scholarship. The reader of this volume will learn about the desert environment and African nomadic life and culture, as those of us at the Museum learned through our rewarding association with Dr. Prussin. We discovered that we were willing to relinquish our familiar preoccupation with permanent, monumental architectural structures. We began to appreciate the ingenuity and complexity of nomadic architecture and to understand how it is inextricably linked to environment and culture. Indeed, we became acutely aware of the contrast between the sensitive relationship that the nomad maintains with nature and Western preoccupation with control of the natural environment. Most important, as revealed in these pages, is Prussin's identification of the three basic elements that distinguish nomadic from sedentary architecture: mobility, gender, and ritual. It is also distinctively an architecture of transformation, motion, and continuity.

Prussin's insights and those of all of the contributors to this important volume have brought to our attention a way of life and collective creativity that is disappearing, and may, if we are not careful, vanish. We are indeed thankful that this volume has been written and that the definition of architecture has thus been expanded and enriched.

ACKNOWLEDGMENTS

Nomadic architecture has always formed part of my greater interest in African architecture, but serious consideration of it began with a National Science Foundation grant in 1985 for fieldwork among the Gabra nomads in northern Kenya. The grant allowed me to become more familiar with, and experience in situ, some of the nomadic cultures in East Africa.

An appointment as a Rockefeller Fellow at the National Museum of African Art in 1987, which had as its mandate the development of new exhibition concepts, provided a rich opportunity to explore the available documentation on African nomadism at both the Library of Congress and the library at the National Museum of African Art. I could not have been successful without the generous support of Sylvia Williams and the immeasurable help provided by Janet Stanley. Some of the ideas and concepts generated by this exposure came together in a preliminary planning conference for an exhibition, again funded by the Rockefeller Foundation. The enthusiasm of its participants in turn provided the impetus for further support from the Rockefeller Foundation to investigate holdings in both European and American museum collections.

Subsequently, the documentation of nomadic holdings in a large number of museum archives introduced me to a vast new world of artifactual riches, and although few of the objects in the holdings have made their way directly into this anthology, all contributed to its overall perspective. I owe a great debt of gratitude to the many directors and curators who welcomed me, gave freely of their time and advice, and opened their reservoir of resources to me: Doran Ross, Museum of Cultural History, University of California at Los Angeles; Pam McCloskey, Seattle Art Museum; Tom Seligman, De Young Museum, San Francisco; Chris Hardin, University Museum, Philadelphia; Christine Gross, Field Museum of Natural History, Chicago; Kathleen K. Skelly and Daniel W. Jones, Jr., who gallantly came to my rescue when my camera failed me at the Peabody Museum, Cambridge, Massachusetts; Enid Schildkraut, American Museum of Natural History; Mary Jo Arnoldi, National Museum of Natural History; Francine Dominique Champault and Francine Ndiaye, Musée de l'Homme, Paris; Roger M. A. Bedaux, Rijksmuseum voor Volkenkunde, Leiden; Lothar Stein and Wolf-Dieter Seiwert, Museum für Völkerkunde, Leipzig; Hans Manndorf and Armand Duchateau, Museum für Völkerkunde, Vienna; Klaus Volprecht, Rautenstrauch-Joest Museum, Cologne; Renate Wente-Lucas, Deutsches Ledermuseum, Offenbach-am-Main; Eike Haberland and Karl Heinz Striedter, Frobenius Institut, Frankfurt-am-Main; Hermann Forkl, Linden-Museum, Stuttgart; John Mack and Julie Hudson, Museum of Mankind, London; Linda Mowat, Pitt-Rivers Museum, Oxford; Keith Nicklin, Horniman Museum, London; Claude Savary, Musée d'Ethnographie, Geneva; and Klaus Ferdinand, Moesgard Forhistorisk Museum, Højbjorg.

Others shared generously of their publications and field experience: Peter Fuchs, Gerhard Göttler, Wolfgang

Creyaufmüller, Ulrich Braukämper, Mette Bovin, and Paul Wilson. French translations would not have been possible without the long-standing support of Norman Skougstad, and for help with Spanish translations I am indebted to Paul Ganapoler.

The architectural emphasis of this anthology is reflected in the illustrations: the choice of line renderings for many of the artifacts (in contrast to exhibition catalogues) and color or black and white photography for architectural environments was a matter of deliberate preference. Credit for illustrative material is noted in the illustration credits, but I would be amiss if I did not extend my special thanks to Richard Mino and Barbara Paxson for their meticulous and prompt response to my cries for help.

A note of thanks is due to the contributors who patiently tolerated my frequent forays into their texts in an attempt to edit and revise the text of subject matter about which they are far more knowledgeable than I can ever hope to be; to the editors at the Smithsonian Institution Press who patiently extended deadlines and suffered my propensity for things visual rather than verbal; to the nameless listeners, friends, and family whose enthusiasm for such an esoteric subject periodically renewed the faltering motivation brought on by occasional despair.

Finally, to the nomads in Africa my debt of gratitude is of a very different kind. To them I owe a sense of awe, humility, and unlimited respect for a native genius, born of necessity, which can turn so little into so much.

INTRODUCTION

> O You! who take the side of the townsman
> And condemn the love of the nomad
> For his limitless horizons!
>
> Is it for their lightness
> That you reproach our tents?
> Have you eulogies only
> For houses of mud and stone?
>
> And on the day of the migration
> When our red camel litters are girthed on the camels
> You would think it a field of anemones,
> Deepening in the rain their richest tones.
>
> EMIR ABD-EL-KADAR   (DAUMAS 1971:6–7)

This book evolved out of field experiences and research for an exhibition on African nomadic arts and architectures proposed to the National Museum of African Art. The exhibition never materialized, but the documentation amassed during its preparatory and planning phases, when set against a backdrop of decades of my own African field experience, brought to light a number of intriguing, innovative, and challenging issues and ideas—as well as dilemmas and paradoxes. The writing and compilation of this anthology turned into an intellectual challenge. Definitions of architecture, conflicting and complementary perspectives on art, craft, and aesthetics emanating from Western and non-Western points of view, the recognition of gender specificity in the creation, recreation, and use of architecture and artifact, and the interfaces between architecture and ritual—all concerns that had engaged my attention in other African architectural contexts—required rethinking in the light of the nomadic condition.

In search of material culture that could be exhibited, I rummaged through the archives of both European and American museums, recording vast numbers of objects and artifacts. As I wandered through the endless museum catacombs, the contrast between what I encountered in the closeted archive and what I experienced in the field was striking: in the main, objects (classified as nomadic) had been collected as single categories or "things," divorced from others and from their situational context. Stored on racks and shelves by material, function, or ethnic group, in locations determined by preservation requirements and the currently accepted museum classification systems, they appeared lifeless and silent in their sterile plastic envelopes. In the field, these objects never exist as discrete, isolated entities but as architectural components which form part of a greater arrangement of things in space. In the field, woven tapestries, textiles and looms, leather pillows, carrying and storage sacks, wooden bedframes and their supports, basketry containers and covers, wooden saddles, assembled by means of metal and leather ties, enveloped in leather and fabric coverings, woven and embroidered room dividers and sleeping backdrops that hang like altar screens, plaited mats and ropes, tent armatures, carved wooden poles, and storage racks bring together a myriad of skills and materials. Interwoven and interdependent, they constitute the building blocks of nomadic architecture. Once removed from their situational context, they become separated in order to be reclassified into categories imposed from without. Amusement turned to frustration when I finally realized that the only nomadic "architecture" I would ever find in the archival collections was that which had been consciously and deliberately assembled as a total entity by a collector familiar with the situational context and knowledgeable about the process used to assemble it.

Exhibitions, perhaps by their very nature, direct attention to discrete objects, to what can be seized immediately by the senses, but our senses are themselves colored by previous cultural experience. When we see objects in an exhibition, we see them detached from the field of meaningful space in which they had existed, much as we may try to restore in some measure the liveliness and exhilaration of the setting that produced them. To be sure, objects do communicate through the visible and tangible qualities of form, color, texture, and size, but the message is greatly enhanced and expanded when they are presented in a field of meaningful space. By focusing on the meaning behind the forms, a book can reintegrate them into a proper gestalt. A book is able, if not to replicate, at least to evoke the spatial dimension that the material objects define—in this case their architectural context. In many instances, the message and its meaning, the language of the artifact, can only be read (and communicated) by restoring discrete "things" or categories to the context from which they were wrenched and reorganizing traditional Western categories into the reality of the field experience.

Only then will be revealed the dignified, heroic, and creative efforts which the human condition is capable of in adapting to the harshest, most fragile, and ephemeral environments.

In a little-known tome that appeared before vernacular architecture had gained respectability, Sibyl Moholy-Nagy (1957:19) wrote: "A people without architecture transmits little of its culture." A corollary to her comment is: can there be a people or a culture without architecture? Decades ago, when conversational cocktail party curiosity turned to my interest in African architecture, the most frequent response was, "I didn't know there was any."

There is something of déjà vu in similar responses to more recent interest in nomadic architecture: can there be a nomadic architecture when the tenets of "durability, convenience or propriety, and beauty" as defined by the Roman engineer Vitruvius continue, overtly or covertly, to underlie contemporary architectural theory and practice? Durability translates into fixity and permanence, but permanence is not necessarily synonymous with sedentarism. A canvas, leather, or mat-covered tent, repaired, maintained, and perpetuated by a repetitive renewal process over time, is often more durable and permanent than a wood frame or an earthen structure. By the same token, we tend to assume that "temporary" is synonymous with "transient." If something moves, we consider it temporary. Although mobility may be its underlying purpose, a movable structure is not necessarily temporary. What is seemingly transitory and ephemeral, processual and only a body of images, is often, by its illusion of stability, more durable than our eroding stone monuments.

Nomadic cultures are, however, elusive, difficult to document and to record. Nation states have always had problems with their nomadic populations and have sought to settle them in order to control them. Nomads do not observe political borders; they do not pay taxes; they are fiercely independent and live outside the cultural pale. They continue to be perceived in the light of the unknown and exotic, leading an ephemeral existence. The nomads of Africa continue to be described in the same romantic, mysterious, exotic light that the European presence, documentation, and reportage had endowed them with over the centuries. The environment itself contributes to this exotic, ethereal, elusive quality: one has only to recall the poetics of nomadism and the desert which are woven through European literature like a thread and absorbed into the painter's canvas in every brush stroke. Objective documentation about African nomadic populations is as elusive as they themselves are in the desert environment.

The study of vernacular architecture, in achieving professional and academic respectability as well as support from the cultures-at-large that created it, while raising a new set of architectural concerns, remains grounded in the traditional theoretical frameworks and value systems which define the field. The architecture of nomadism mandates an innovative approach: its consideration in turn provides a new dimension by redefining the meaning of durability, propriety, and beauty.

More than sixty years ago, Robert Briffault's prodigious and highly controversial work *The Mothers* first appeared. Many may question his sweeping generalizations and farfetched interpretations, but his inquisitive incursions into the byways of anthropology and history merit reconsideration in the context of current concerns with gender. In a chapter on "The Division of Labor" in which he considered "Building," he pointed out that we are not accustomed to think of architecture as a feminine occupation (Briffault 1977). A personal incident of almost forty years ago came to mind. Shortly after I had been admitted to the then very respectable, very male-dominated profession of architecture, two fellow architects, husband and wife, came to dinner. My daughters were already close friends with the wife because she and I had studied and were in practice together, but they had never met her husband. With innocent curiosity, trying to make conversation far beyond her age, my three and a half year old promptly turned to him and asked what he did. He responded: "I am an architect, just like your mother." "Hmm," she replied, "who ever heard of a boy-architect!" Obviously, in the context of her small world of experience, gender role reversal was the norm.

Even after World War II, and despite the acceptance of women into industry during those few years when their services were direly needed, there were few one could turn to for advice or emulation. The search for role models began with Louise Blanchard Bethune and Julia Morgan, but even after having uncovered their prolific repertoires long before others had publicized them, few of us were in a position to benefit from the kinds of social opportunities that led to sponsorship and patronage by the nation's financial elites.

At the height of the growing feminist movement, Doris Cole's small paperback book (1973) appeared. My intrigue with it had less to do with feminist consciousness than with a decade of architectural experience in Africa during which my scholarly appetite for the vernacular had been whetted. Plains Indian women had been building tipis for millennia in the Americas, just as their gender counterparts had been building yurts in Asia and black tents in the Near East and North Africa. It took little thought to make the analogy with the African nomadic women. Here, then, was a new kind of role model!

But was this architecture? Were these nomadic women architects? If I was to use them as role models, not only would the tenets of the discipline require redefinition, but the nature and role of creativity in culture would demand a reinterpretation of Western value systems. For, as Virginia Woolf once pointed out, it is very obvious that the values of women very often differ from those established by the other sex, and it is the masculine values that prevail. To rethink the architectural value system, it would be necessary to pursue the field of creativity within the domestic realm associated with the feminine gender—in contrast to the public realm dominated by the masculine gender.

This approach is not particularly innovative. Nearly a century ago, the sociologist George Simmel (1984: 67) defined culture as a whole in the same terms, affirming that human culture is not asexual, nor does it exist in a domain that lies beyond men and women: with few exceptions, our objective culture is thoroughly male. Edwin Ardener (1975) argued further that dominant groups in society generate and control dominant modes of expression. Women remain muted because their model of reality, their view of the world, cannot be expressed or realized using the terms of the dominant male model. Subdominant groups (and cultures) structure their understanding of the world through the model of the dominant group. As a consequence, women cannot use the male-dominated structures of language to say what they want to say, to give an account of their view of the world.

To be successful in the Western, male-dominated architectural profession, a woman had to learn to design and perform in the "male manner," both on the drawing board and in the field, using a male model of reality. In so doing, the "female" way of designing and its expression often was (and continues to be) sublimated. A good analogy is the left-handed person who, when forced into more culturally acceptable behavior, often becomes ambidextrous—and often more perceptive about both behavioral modes as a consequence. I found from my own experiences in both Africa and the Western world that only when I had successfully mastered design performance in the "male manner" could I return to what was, for me as a woman, a natural architectural design process of integrating components of space and surface, form and function.

To define this process which differs so much from what I was taught and had learned to emulate presupposes two different models of reality, Western and non-Western, and two world views, feminine and masculine. To understand the alternate model of reality and world view involves the examination of their contrasts and convergences. It is a question of engendering and universalizing architecture: the African nomadic setting provides a fertile, even an ideal field in which to do so.

Rarely have the arts and architectures of African nomadism engaged the attention of observer or scholar, in contrast to culture's meticulous attention to monumental and permanent solutions associated with sedentarization. Transient and transformable solutions to the built environment—all adaptive environmental strategies—have never been part of the respectable repertoire of art, architecture, ethnology, or anthropology, nor has the lens of art-artifact and architecture and the built environment been used to understand and explain environmental adaptation. How, then, is one to seek out these contrasts and convergences when the very existence of nomadic architecture has been denied by the world at large? Nomadic architecture has always been outside the pale of Western architectural definition. Even when writing through the lens of his own nomadic heritage, the famed fourteenth-century Near Eastern scholar Ibn Khaldun insisted that "civilization" was possible only with urbanization and sedentarization, because tent architecture is ephemeral. Nomadic architectures, based on "simple structural solutions" and the use of natural materials and resources, could not compete with the priorities the Western world places on high technology. Buckminster Fuller's geodesic domes and Frei Otto's tensile fantasies are welcome, valued members of the architectural realm, but their predecessors in wood, fabric, and leather, "primitive" architectural solutions, have no value until, like a biblical Tent of Meeting, a national pavilion, or a setting for international negotiation, they become a cultural symbol. Only then are they granted historic, albeit ephemeral, respectability.

Architectural history—and its handmaiden, archaeology—has always depended on tangible, fixed, in situ evidence and on recorded visual and/or written verbal documentation for its data base, but the nomadic condition violates its every methodology and skews its every interpretation. Oral traditions in lieu of the written record, eroding and shifting sand dunes in lieu of stone foundations, permeable materials that not only deteriorate rapidly and differentially but become sequentially transformed in time and space are not the raw materials from which the architectural historian or the archaeologist fashions the cloth of history. When the nomadic presence in a specific sedentary cultural context is ignored, the historic interpretation of the sedentary record is itself skewed.

The same rigor which in general has limited field documentation and research of life under such mobile and elusive conditions has specifically militated against involvement by women scholars, and those few who have traveled alone in the desert with the nomads have remained for the most part unsung, unpublished heroines. Over the centuries, most of the available written accounts and descriptions are the result of commercial, military, or colonial interest. As a consequence, the documentation of female productivity and creativity is almost nonexistent for those cultures where men and women move in and control such separate worlds. Museum and private collections accrued in the course of expeditions under such conditions are further skewed because they consisted primarily of artifacts that the male observer had access to and was interested in: tools of warfare, tools essential for economic productivity and the processing of materials valuable for the European market, and "durable," permanent artifacts made of wood and metal.

The domicile has traditionally and universally been the one place in which a woman could create because it has been the only place in which she could exercise control over her environment. In fact, many early women reformers and suffragists, such as Beecher, Gilman, Stowe, Perkins, even Emily Post, sought to address issues of women's rights and equality by attempting to elevate the value of the domestic environment. Theirs was a difficult effort because there is also a need to distinguish what men do and what women do in contrast to the symbolic evaluations given to men and women in society. For example, if what women do as a subdominant group is devalued (i.e., domestic work or "interior design"), then the "nonpermanent" products (such as quilts, weaving, and baskets) that they produce would occupy a lower position in the hierarchy of their aesthetic value system.

Architecture is recognized and acquires "real" value only when it is a purchased commodity or is created with highly valued, reimbursed time and effort. "Nonproductive" labor time and "leisurely" production are corollaries to the devaluation of domestic labor and the assumption that, since domestic labor is unpaid, repetitive, and boring, it is nonproductive and noncreative. Is the house that a nomadic woman creates (her domicile) less valuable, commodity-wise, than the house a man designs, creates, builds, owns, or controls? Social exchanges may take on different forms, but the mobile house is as much real property as the house that is anchored to the ground. As Moore notes (1988:71) in her discussion of economy, dowry, and bridewealth, distinctions made on the basis of the degree and kind of control brides exert over their own marital fortunes and over property transferred at the time of marriage may be more important than the opposition that anthropologists have traditionally drawn between bridewealth and dowry.

For many decades, African art was anonymous art, subsumed by cultural (often erroneously attributed) identity and never documented or recognized in terms of individual creativity. To right such an intellectual error, and perhaps in order to validate African art in a Western construct, for a Western audience and art market, a series of studies that address individual African creativity have appeared. A parallel exists in traditional efforts to attribute individual authorship to architectural monuments, and the search for a cornerstone that designates the master builder. Creativity is perceived to be the exclusive domain of individuality; anonymity, "architecture without architects," is posed in opposition to the "star system" in the creative process.

For the twentieth-century Western mind, the concept of creativity in a collective context is a paradox. A recent, relevant illustration comes from the welcome addition to the growing literature on women in the architectural profession (Berkeley 1989). Its contents remain biographical in nature, focusing on personal experiences, professional reflections, and the accomplishments of individual practitioners who had been able to compete successfully, as individuals, in a world of men.

The debate about individuality and creativity assumes another dimension, one that emphasizes the complexity of the cooperative networks through which art happens, when we think of all the activities, social and otherwise, that must predate the work, for an architectural creation to appear as it finally does (Becker 1982). Every art form and art product rests on an extensive division of labor and a set or system of conventions which can be defined in terms of technological style—the available materials, equipment, training, site response, all of which are inseparable from each other.

Another corollary to the paradox between individual and collective creativity which African art historians have also had to wrestle with is the continuing distinction between arts and crafts. Art is pure form or abstraction; craft is technological process. George Kubler (1962:16) articulated the simple equation more eloquently when he wrote that we are in the presence of a work of art only when it has no preponderant instrumental use, and when its technical and rational foundations are not preeminent. When the technical organization or the rational order of a thing overwhelms our attention, it is an object of use. In dictionary terms, art refers to the conscious arrangement of colors, forms, or other elements in a manner that affects the sense of beauty. It is sensual, not practical. Crafts, on the other hand, are traditionally meant to be useful, and their execution usually involves manual, not inventive, skills. Technique is thus demeaned in favor of "concept" or "personal expression," that is, technological process limits the freedom to create abstractly.

In architecture, the same distinction has been used to segregate "vernacular" or "ethnographic" architecture from the classic, historical model which architectural history bases itself on. This contrast between manual and inventive appears to be peculiarly Western and particularly male. In architecture it is inherently more difficult to separate the technology from the form or the form from the function. Process involves successful structural performance. Technique and workmanship are essential for the creation of a successful form. Technique *is* expression, and mastery *is* meaning. The expression "architectonic" refers specifically to the quintessential fusion or balance of technology, function, form, and decoration which characterizes great architecture.

For the African nomad, life also hangs on the delicate balance maintained between nature and nurture. Ingenious environmental codes of behavior, expressed in highly structured belief systems, safeguard the natural resources on which nomadic existence precariously depends. The world view that structures and unifies the nomadic way of life is based on the profound unity among all created things. It is reflected not only in the political, juridic, and economic aspects of the nomads' lives but in the ways by which they navigate and occupy the space of the desert and structure their material culture.

The nomadic world view and value system also have their own ethnocentric assumptions and indigenous gender ideologies. If political and social status are defined by the occupation of the male head of household, then, as Henrietta Moore suggests (1988: 84), primary value and pastoral wealth is measured by herds and placed on sons rather than daughters. The kinds of movable goods that daughters inherit are not comparable to the durable, permanent goods, the immovable or landed property, that sons receive. When a greater value is placed on livestock inheritance than on artifact inheritance, then women and their creative work become invisible to male pastoralist and Western observer alike.

The dichotomy of gendered worlds (in the sense of exclusion, not contradiction), which structures the public and private domains, further reinforces the invisibility of women's labor. Much of it unfolds within the hidden spaces of the tent's inner reaches. The invisibility of women's creativity in the nomadic context finds a close parallel in the devaluation of crafts and craftspeople among nomads as well as the art-craft dichotomy which characterizes the value systems of the Western world. The devalued roles and relationships between the artisan who produces many of the material artifacts that enter into nomadic architecture and the nomadic clients and patrons of their products are legendary in both myth and reality.

The African deserts are the largest, harshest, and most threatening deserts in the world, and yet, over the years spent traveling in the African milieu, I have found nomadic material culture to be as rich and diverse as that created by its sedentary counterpart and by neighbors in supposedly more favorable environments. Its aesthetic emanates from an ethos unique to its context: rather than being a means by which people separate themselves from their environment, nomadic material culture provides the means whereby people mediate with its special dictates. The tent is a mode of creative expression, a way of reordering a person's relationship with animals and plants, with the earth and the sky, with the rhythms and forces of nature.

The measure of that effort is in their architectural language, spoken in a woman's voice. House is a feminine noun, and the building process that brings it into being is a feminine verb. It derives from a set of singular nomadic phenomena: spatial mobility is inherent in the cultural life-style; nomadic architectures are created by women, and they are the primary producers of the material culture associated with it; the architectural process inherent in mobility unfolds on a stage structured by specific ritual settings for marriage and birthing; and, as others have suggested, men and women live and move in gender-discrete worlds. The four in combination—mobility and architectural process, the woman/wife/mother as producer/owner/user, the ritual that encapsulates fertility and continuity, and the complementarity of discrete, gendered worlds—are the foundation on which the nomadic aesthetic rests.

The desert cuts a swath across the African continent, sweeping from Cap Vert on the Atlantic Ocean to the tip of the Horn of Africa on the Indian Ocean. Only a few among the host of nomadic peoples who inhabit its expanse and engage in pastoralism and transhumance have been included in this anthology: the Hassaniya (Tekna, Trarza, Brakna), the Tuareg, the Tubu, the Mahria, the Somalis, and the Rendille (see location map on endsheets). Among these nomadic cultures, houses move frequently, pack animals (primarily camels) provide transport, marriage rituals set the stage for the creation of both arts and architecture, and life unfolds in a gender-discrete universe. In the course of reviewing their rich range of artifacts and architectures, the difficulties and pitfalls of ascribing particular cultural indicators to specific nomadic cultures became painfully clear to me. The form, material, and style of artifact and architecture used by each were often inseparable from one another. Cultural maps circumscribing nomadic groups in space with discrete boundaries that serve to establish "provenance" become blinders which obscure the complex reality of interaction among nomadic cultures. It is we, with our propensity for compartmentalization and classification, not they, who have circumscribed them on the cultural landscape.

This anthology itself belies the concept of circumscription. In West Africa, for example, Tuareg marriages, involving the creation of a marriage tent, rest on a set of behaviors deriving from Hassaniya building technology, and the architectural components of the tent are often provided by Fulbe- and Hausa-speaking artisans. In the Sudan, Tubu tents are based on Kababish and Mahria building technologies on the one hand, and on Tuareg armature-type tents on the other. In East Africa, Rendille subclans use Gabra tent structures on one hand and Somali armatures on the other in order to define particular clans within their own cultural complex.

Concepts of ethnicity and ethnic identity, often grounded in sedentary cultures, become more difficult to define in the nomadic context. Further, nomads living in essentially similar environments and practicing identical migratory regimes may well possess completely different architectures. At the same time, a particular cultural group may have different kinds of architectures, either in its subgroups or for use at different times of the year, under different circumstances. Yet these various networks of architectural variation also provide us with a potentially viable format for investigating complex, albeit ephemeral, cultural and historic relationships among nomadic cultures in Africa. Cultural interaction and borrowings can provide insights into the historic relationships.

All the contributors to this anthology have, at different times, traveled in the field with "their" nomads. The material culture that they documented has, in turn, swelled the archival collections of European and American museums, and their contributions are a remarkable testament to nomadic diversity in response to what is seemingly a very uniform, albeit harsh, habitat. Their interpretations, equally diverse, are their own, just as the direction, the quality, and the authenticity of this effort are very much the story of my own life: as an architect, as an architectural historian, as a wife, and as a mother. It is precisely the fusion of creativity, intellectual endeavor, emotion, and experience, which I have had to balance in the course of a lifetime of wanderings across a multitude of physical and cultural environments, that explains my unorthodox approach to life.

As an architect, I was always involved in environmental design, interested in creating form, and curious about the ways in which both could be imbued with meaning. I discovered quite early in my professional life that it is not the architect who builds meaning into the design of a building; only its users can imbue it with meaning by repetitive, sensual behaviors. As a maker of things, however, I have also always been aware of the hands-on behavior which imbues meaning into the artifact. The process of creativity provides the actor or actors, men and/or women, with self-identity and self-esteem, with the ability to exercise control over the built environment. When properly exercised and executed, the attendant skills are not only a source of pride and satisfaction in themselves but bring into play the sense of control over the technology, over the medium.

As an architectural historian in search of explanation for the built environment, I found myself seeking, introspectively, the "why" and wherefore of my own creativity.

As a wife and a mother, both gender and continuity were brought into play: I discovered that the creation of things is not an end in itself. Heirlooms that can be used and handed down to posterity validate one's own immortality: the creation of the art form or the architectural form is synonymous with childbirth. The process invokes the African value placed on children for, without children, who will remember me when I die?

Initially this anthology began, not as an attempt to romanticize or glorify domestic labor, but to redress a grievance: to revalidate and reverify the value that has traditionally been placed on productive labor in the private, domestic world of women. It evolved into an effort to understand the field of creativity within the feminine realm—alongside, coexistent with, and often in contrast to the masculine realm. As an attempt to understand the unique qualities of women's arts and architecture by focusing on those situations in which the creation of material culture lies primarily within the feminine, domestic realm, it runs contrary to recent writings which focus on a cultural construct that denigrates those tasks often thought of as "women's work."

Consideration of the architecture of African nomadic cultures has, however, now gone far beyond mere redress: new perspectives have been added to the cultural contexts within which the built environment unfolds. By the same token, the definition of architecture has been broadened and extended, and the issues the new definitions invite may be more relevant for society at large, even though their resolution remains a challenge.

It is hoped that the results of this effort will fire the imagination of a new generation in ways the nomadic experience did for me and my contributors. If it can inspire the adventurous and the curious to search for new directions and new experiences in other worlds, or challenge the young and inquisitive to search for new insights and new interpretations of their own, then it will have been well worth the effort.

AFRICAN NOMADIC ARCHITECTURE

1
THE TENT IN AFRICAN HISTORY

TENTS AS ARCHITECTURE

World history is full of references to nomads and tents, but can one reconstruct an architectural history of such an ephemeral, elusive subject, particularly for the African continent? Efforts to do so have been few and far between. They were motivated by, and served as an introductory background to, more direct, relevant concerns. For example, the earliest serious attempt to write a history of tents (Rhodes 1858) emerged from the author's recognition of a pressing military concern: the development of a more serviceable type of tent for battlefield use.[1] More recent historical and ethnographic overviews (Bidault and Giraud 1946; Faegre 1979) were written in response to the post–World War II European and American resurgence of camping interests and concerns with basic environmental values. Although the most recent historical overview (Drew 1979) was also written as a prelude to the architectural recognition of contemporary tensile architecture, its well-illustrated documentation and the scope of its contents introduced a new theoretical dimension to the subject. By distinguishing vernacular tents from "urban" tents, that is, those symbolic pavilions that served political institutions and military negotiations, Drew established the basis for a new interpretation of tents as architectural phenomena.

Feilberg's cultural history of nomadism (1944) is still the most erudite, ambitious, and remarkably documented history of nomadic architecture. Using extant ethnographic data in support of historic interpretation, he argued for a unilineal architectural evolution from mat-covered, armature frame tents to tensile structures using woven velums, an interpretation that unfortunately continues to be accepted by most scholars who have carried out otherwise successful ethnographic studies of nomadic cultures in the wake of his pioneering work. Tent history is a far richer, more complex amalgam than unilineal explanation allows for: weaving together the threads that could synthesize history and anthropology into a plausible historic reconstruction remains a challenge.

In the overview that follows, it is not my intent to match or supplement already existing historic documentation. Rather, I would like to frame some of the available data into a broader perspective which includes both history and ethnography. The documentation in and of itself provides few physical, concrete insights into the nature of the architectural *process* and the stylistic, technological variations that occur in African tent history. Even so, by using considerable scholarly diligence, it *is* possible to weave the available oral, literary, visual, and ethnographic data into a credible architectural history.

This broader perspective entails distinguishing indigenous tent usage from the tent as a political/religious institutional symbol; it recognizes changes in the nature of desert occupancy and mobility, and acknowledges

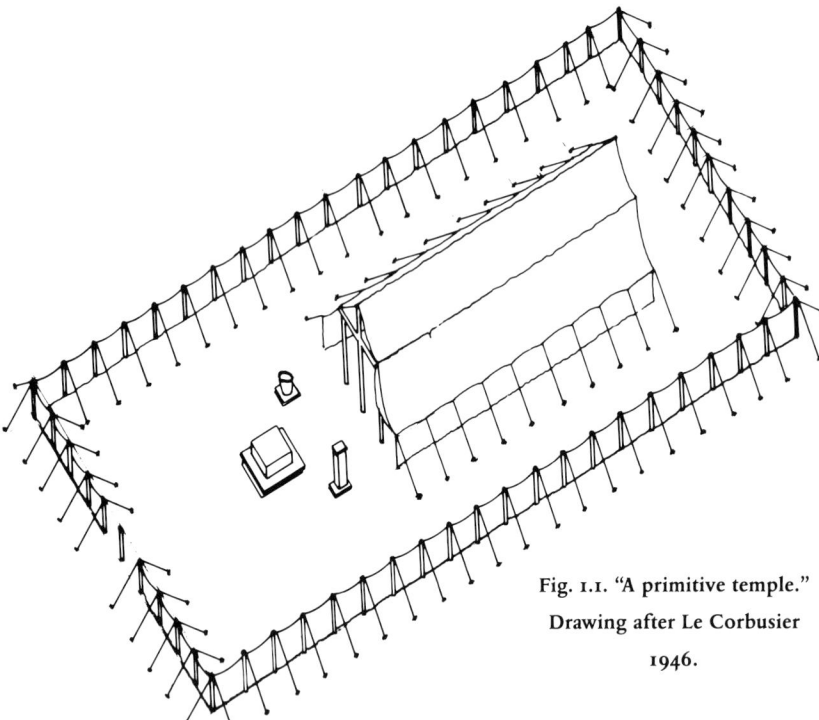

Fig. 1.1. "A primitive temple." Drawing after Le Corbusier 1946.

variations in life-style and social structure wrought by shifts between sedentary and nomadic existence. Because nomadism cannot exist without a technology of transport, this broader perspective involves consideration of the transport technologies upon which nomadism rested and continues to depend. An animal such as the camel became, in itself, an agency of control and a symbol of power in nomadic life. Because women were, and continue to be, the architects of the indigenous built environment in nomadic societies, consideration of the changing role and position of women in such societies is of paramount importance in understanding the relationship between vernacular and institutional tent architecture.

THE TABERNACLE

To illustrate his innovative theories of measure and modular design in the wake of the unfolding twentieth-century rationale for a new architecture, Le Corbusier (1946) chose to use a tent (fig. 1.1). Both the description of this "shelter for a god" and the illustration that accompanied his example of "A primitive temple" were recalled to mind by Edmond Leach's explanatory structuralist text (1976) which suggested using the Old Testament as a structural model. Leach claimed that the reconstruction of the Israelite Tabernacle, as described in the text of the Old Testament, was culturally, architecturally, and archaeologically impossible, although the very precise details of the associated rituals were certainly not imaginary. Further, the meticulously detailed description of the construction of the Ark and the Tabernacle found in the biblical text should be viewed only as a model for the layout of a setting for sacrificial procedure, as a representation of cosmological space. Yet every act, every ritual unfolds in the context of an "environmental memory" embedded with the reality of both physical and spatial parameters. Even when disguised under the cloak of mysticism, a ritual will always have a material referent.[2] If, as Leach suggests, one can consider the biblical texts like the notebook record of a contemporary ethnographer, then it is equally logical to treat the texts as if they were the notebooks of an architectural historian or an ethnoarchaeologist.

The biblical scholarly tradition holds as its central thesis that the Hebrews began as a nomadic people and that their life and literature, poetry and metaphor, imagery, ideals and aspirations continued, long after they had settled, to reflect their origins. The Old Testament, especially its most controversial Book of Exodus, contains innumerable references to tents. It should come as no surprise that the nomadic ideal found quintessential expression in the detailed physical description of the same Tabernacle that Leach so brilliantly analyzed in a ritual context. The Tabernacle that Yahweh instructed Moses to make was a portable sanctuary set up in the center of the Hebrew encampment at each stop in the wilderness—a Tent of Meeting whose plan and structure are easily reconstructed from the detailed biblical descriptions[3] (fig. 1.2). In contrast to historic and contemporary interpretations, as well as Western imageries that cast the Tabernacle in the model of the monumental Temple of Solomon, the reconstruction mirrored Le Corbusier's "primitive temple," but, more intriguingly, it was remarkably close to contemporary Near Eastern black tents and their relatives in North Africa such as the Zemmour tents in the anti-Atlas mountains of Morocco. The assembling of the three tent velums—the "sheets" of linen, woven goats' hair, and tanned rams' skins—remain the basis for many contemporary nomadic

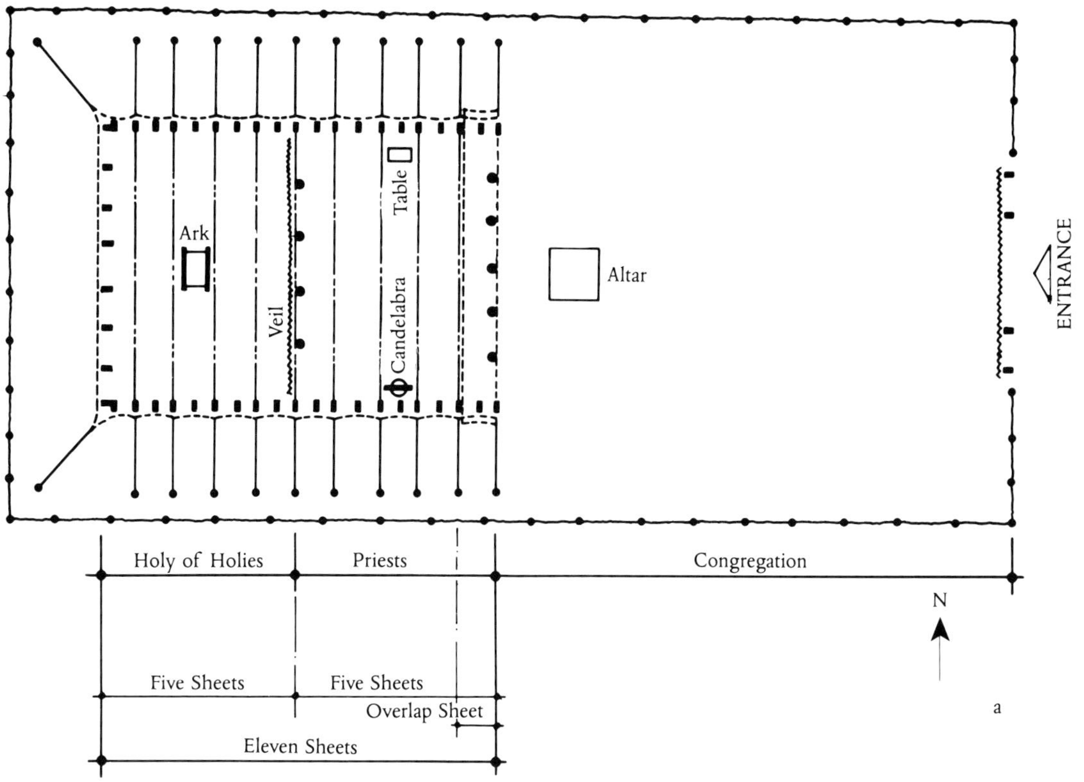

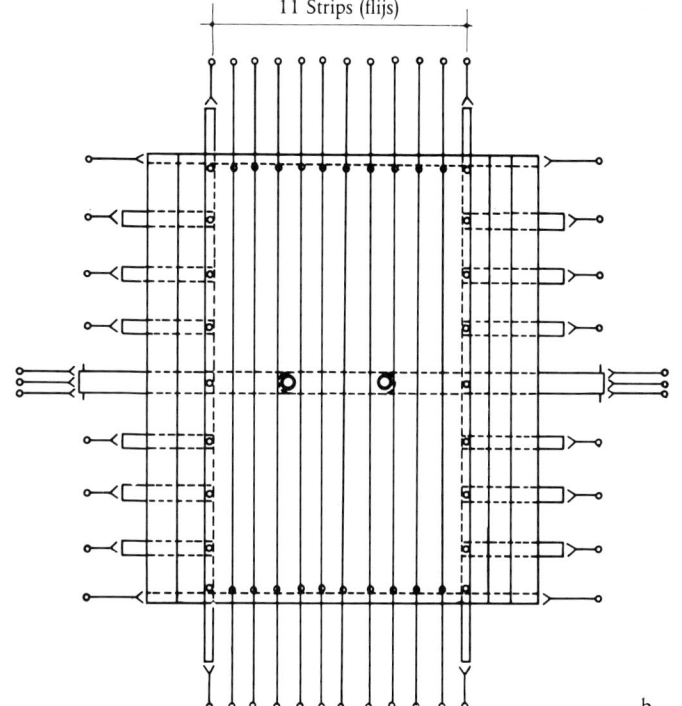

Fig. 1.2. a. Reconstruction of the Tabernacle from descriptive passages in the Book of Exodus. When sewn together, the woven strips ("hangings") created a velum measuring approximately 15 by 20 m. b. Plan of a large Zemmour tent south of the Atlas mountains, Morocco, composed of eleven bands; width 7 m; length 18 m. Drawing after Laoust 1930.

building technologies (evidenced in the chapters that follow) in which several layers of tent linings, often composed of different materials, are used in various ways for different purposes.

Much of the material of the Old Testament originated in the form of poetry, transmitted from generation to generation of bards and singers before being transcribed and translated. The process is not unlike the poetic tradition of many contemporary African nomadic cultures such as the Tuareg and the Somalis. The implication is that one could, with validity and diligence, use what were originally oral traditions to reconstruct architectural evidence and imagery. If collectively held, mutually understood, and ritually reinforced oral traditions are capable of transmitting environmental memories, and if architectonic imagery is its material manifestation, then appropriately interpreted oral traditions afford invaluable insights for the reconstruction of so elusive and ephemeral a subject as a nomadic architecture.

The interpretation of oral traditions (such as those of the Old Testament—the Tabernacle, the Ark, and

The Tent in African History

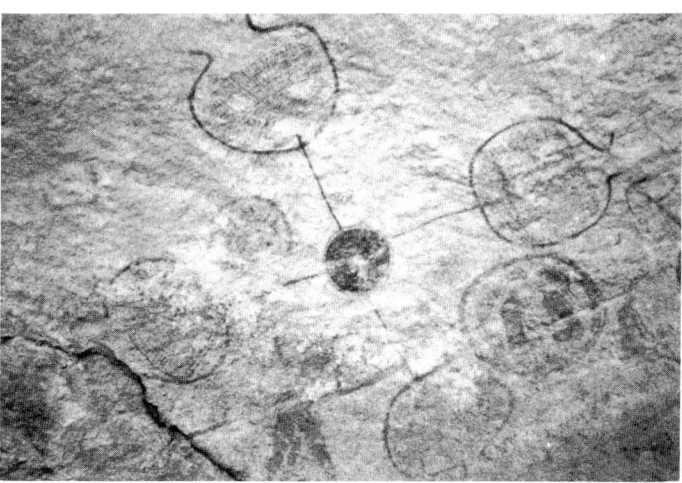

Fig. 1.3. a. Rock painting at Sefar, Tassili n' Ajjer. b. Rock painting, Tassili region, northwest of Djanet, Algeria. c. Rock painting at Sefar, Tassili n' Ajjer.

the Tent of Meeting) which can highlight *change* in architectural imagery over time also introduces a caveat for the interpretation of extant visual evidence. Renderings do not always date from the same period as the original document. Each new edition or recopy of a manuscript reflects the articulated architectural ideals of its own age; each ultimately also reflects the aspirations and values of those with the power to support its creation. By extension, value systems in every age reflect not only social control and power, but the relative position and role of gender at a given point in time.

THE VERNACULAR TRADITION

The rocky mountain massif of Tassili n' Ajjer, in the heart of the Sahara, possesses a wealth of prehistoric rock paintings. Their vibrant variations in style and content, still difficult to trace with precision, nevertheless bear witness to the presence of large and important populations which followed each other over the ages in what is today a seemingly deserted milieu. These remarkable rock paintings remained only images in my mind until, with the opportunity to document tents under construction, the renderings on several of these paintings were intuitively illuminated, much like a satori (fig. 1.3). What had never occurred to me was that they were very accurate renditions of the nomadic ethnographic present. In the first instance (a), a woman, surrounded by herds of cattle, holds what appears to be not a bow, but a bentwood frame used in constructing armature tents, much as the Rendille and the Somalis still do. In the second instance (b), the accurate elevations of tent armatures within the four circles (including two persons clearly visible within one) matched my measured drawings of innumerable Gabra, Somali, and Rendille (as well as Fulbe) pastoral compounds. In the third instance (c), the rectangular tent plan, its entrance, bedstead, and array of baggage clearly defined, matches the measured drawings of contemporary Tubu and Mahria tents. If these representations do in fact reflect the reality of nomadic architecture in a still-undefined, more verdant Saharan time frame when pastoral ancestors had access to the kinds of building resources now utilized further south, then how were they related to those nomadic cultures that continue to build in similar fashion today? The answers to these tantalizing questions depend on much further research, but it is intriguing to dwell on what are probably to date the earliest representations of women builders and their architectural creativity in Africa.

Scholars continue to see the primeval prototype for African armature tents in the *mapalia* (the term is of Punic origin), frequently referred to in Classical literature and represented on a well-preserved Roman North African mosaic dating from the second century A.D.[4] (pl. 1). The reed hut represented on this mosaic has often been invoked as a visual model for the term, but its steep roof profile and exaggerated peak is far more characteristic of sedentary housing, where peaks, often highly ornamented, are strongly emphasized.[5] The difference is clearly evident when the *mapalia* image is compared with, for example, the "beehive" form of armature frame tents which were recorded in the mid-nineteenth century in sub-Saharan Africa and are still an accurate rendering of those that continue to be built to this day by a multitude of African nomadic cultures[6] (fig. 1.4a).

In addition to technological discrepancies, there are differences in the use of materials. Authors have frequently cited the fifth-century B.C. Greek historian Herodotus who described the portable dwellings of rushes and reeds built by the Numidians in the region around Meroe.[7] It seems more likely that the term *mapalia* may have referred to a type of vegetal building which appears in a landscape mosaic of the Upper Nile found in the Temple of Fortuna at Praeneste (1st century B.C.), a barrel-vaulted, sedentary reed structure still to be seen on the banks of the Nile.[8]

Realistically, the term could have referred to a type of light hut, a rural dwelling—perhaps transportable in the course of periodic displacement—in contrast to the solidly built urban architecture. Presumably, the immigrant Numidians who settled on the outskirts of the newly built cities would have maintained the building traditions they were already familiar with (in contrast to Phoenician and Latin stone housing), just as rural migrants to urban centers have done for millennia.[9] A more realistic etymological designation, in the light of the then agricultural-pastoralist symbiosis,

a

b

c

Fig. 1.4. a. Armature tents at Bamba, north of the Niger River Bend, 1854. b. Tuareg tents at Ammalelle (present-day Mali), 1854. c. Contemporary Hadendowa (Beja) tent in the Sudan.

suggests that the Punic term *mapalia* would have subsumed, according to the situation, both the mobile pastoral dwellings and the fixed, agricultural dwellings of the local populations.[10] The *mapalia* could have been built by sedentary agriculturalists as well as nomads.

The northern Tuareg (of Berber descent) are renowned for their skin tents, but again, why and how skin velums came into vernacular use has rarely been considered (fig. 1.4b). Skin tents, in contrast to armature frames which will stand up on their own without depending on a velum for stability, involve a completely different building technology and different building materials and depend on elastic coverings and rigid members. What is particularly relevant to this history, however, is that the early sources cite such tents only in an institutional, not a vernacular, context.

What happens when one considers contemporary building traditions closer to the region Herodotus was describing, for example, that of the indigenous Blemmyes or Beja in Numidia (fig. 1.4c)? The ancient Beja nomadic tribes (the ancestors of the Hadendowa, the Amarar, the Bisharin, and the Beni Amer who currently inhabit a region bounded by Egypt and the Nile on the west and the Red Sea on the east) first came to the attention of the Egyptians in 2500 B.C. (Paul 1954). The first known, unmistakable portrait of a Bejawie occurs on a XIIth Dynasty (1991–1786 B.C.) tomb chapel in Upper Egypt. There was no mention of their nomadic housing, built by interweaving split pieces of palm wood, until the first-century account by the Greek geographer Strabo.[11] Almost a millennium later, one Arab geographer noted that they had tents of animal hair, while another wrote that they had tents of animal skin (Feilberg 1944). Early in the nineteenth century, when Burckhardt (1819) visited the Beja village, "or more properly the encampment," of Atbara, he found tents of woven mats supported on bent poles.[12] His description, albeit vague, is consistent with contemporary Hadendowa building practice (Ausenda 1987). Tracing such a range—and change—in building materials and technologies is not only a challenge to historic architectural reconstruction (and by extension life-style), but a testimony to the complexity and diversity of the nomadic condition.

In sum, using the *mapalia* as an archetype on which to base a history of *all* African nomadic architecture, whether vernacular or institutional, leads to a methodological impasse as well as a theoretical misdirection. A *mapalia* archetype or prototype denies the process of change and the presence of diversity reflected in even the earliest evidence and commentary on African nomadic housing. As even the Tassili frescos reveal, the development of various tent types and structures extended over many centuries and throughout many regions. African tents were not all the same, nor were they necessarily sedentary *or* nomadic—a phenomenon easily understood in the light of the interface between nomadism and sedentarism in Africa today. There is a considerable architectural and technological difference between the interweaving of split pieces of palm wood, the weaving of animal hair, the tanning and stitching of animal skin, and mats woven of palm leaves. Structurally, velums and armatures are not synonymous. An armature can support either a leather or a mat cover, but a true tensile structure cannot be built using mats. Furthermore, the structural performance of reeds, rushes, and stalks differs vastly from that of the acacia and tamarind roots or branches. To compare the description of Herodotus, writing about the Numidians in the fifth century B.C., with those of the Roman historian Corippus, writing about the Byzantine presence in North Africa in the sixth century A.D., is to attribute the same timelessness to African architectural history that Western interpreters of its art history have often been prey to; it denies African history.

THE INSTITUTIONAL TRADITION

World literature abounds with tent references: the Tabernacle and the Tent of Meeting, the royal Assyrian tents of Sennacherib, the military tents of the Roman emperor Trajan, the parasol-roofed tents of Genghis Khan, the tents of Ottoman Turkish rulers in Persian miniatures, the Crusader tents of Charlemagne and Roland in illuminated medieval manuscripts, and the Renaissance Field of the Cloth of Gold, in which the tents of Francis I and Henry VIII served as a quintessential political symbol, are but a few illustrations.

Examples of contemporary usage, equally widespread, occur in religious, military, and political ritual, often serving as a metaphor for the unification of all three functions into a singular symbol of institutional power.

The style of these institutional tents, frequently evolving out of the ethnographic context, in turn became images par excellence of "prestige" architecture, reflecting, indeed invoking and often legitimizing, their ethnographic heritage, a process eloquently described by Ibn Khaldun for the Near East.[13] The acquisition and display of prestigious tent architecture, as much as any other complex of material culture, became a means of articulating competing claims to power by those in authority. The process that Ibn Khaldun described is equally applicable to the African tradition.

The first written evidence for an institutional tent in Africa occurs in the VIth Dynasty correspondence of a Pharaoh (2625–2475 B.C.). Subsequent documents indicate that by 1500 B.C. the tent had become part of Egyptian military life since references to it were all in the context of military campaigns (Drew 1979). The *Annals*, which provide a clear and succinct account of a military campaign, contain several references to royal Egyptian tents, and military tents are well represented on bas reliefs at Ramesseum, Luxor, and Abu Simbel. What they were made of or how they were constructed remains unclear from the bas reliefs.

Two Egyptian terms used in a XIXth Dynasty text (1320–1200 B.C.) suggest that the Libyans (i.e., Nubians), against whom the Egyptians fought, owned and used both mat-covered and leather-covered tents (Feilberg 1944).[14] These same Nubians from the south, who also had a long military tradition, were frequently employed by the Egyptians as auxiliaries and mercenaries, and Nubian captives would presumably also have been pressed into service. It seems feasible that the Egyptian military, finding the southern tent appropriate to their needs, may have adopted, modified, and perhaps even ritualized it.

Deir el-Bahri, part of the Theban temple complex, is best known for its monumental XVIIIth Dynasty temple architecture and Queen Hatshepsut. What is little known, having received only passing reference in Classical literature, is the assumed XXIst Dynasty leather tent which early Egyptian archaeologists discovered amidst the royal mummies in the suggested XIth Dynasty tomb complex (E. Brugsch 1889; H. K. Brugsch 1891).[15] Found folded up in a corner of the funerary chapel, the multicolored leather tent consisted of hundreds of goat or gazelle skins sewn into the form of an elongated cube (fig. 1.5a). Rather like a sarcophagus, the ceiling and its front and sides carried carefully executed colored designs in appliquéd leather. The hieroglyphics inscribed on the leather establish that its female occupant was Princess

Fig. 1.5. a. Leather funerary tent for an Egyptian princess-priestess, Deir el-Bahri, XXIst Dynasty; width 2.40 m; length 2.80 m; height 2.15 m. b. Bas-relief in the Palace of Sennacherib (704–681 B.C.), showing the cross section of an Assyrian officer's tent and, above, two camels. c. Roman leather tents *(papilio)*. Drawings after Brugsch 1889, Pritchard 1959, and Webster 1969.

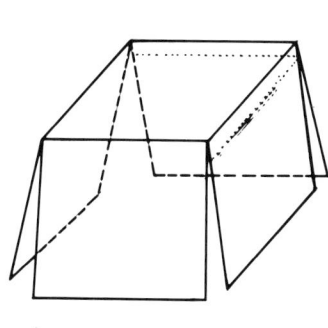

a

b

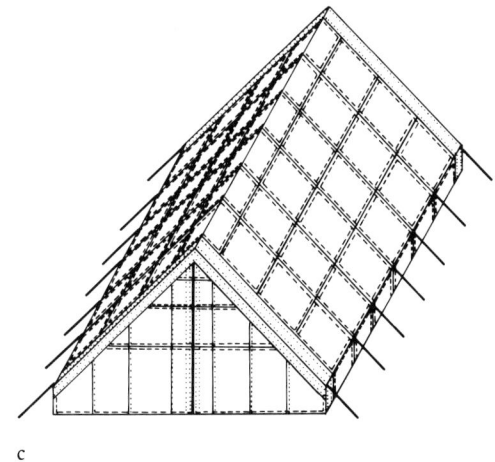

c

Isimkheb, a high priestess, and that it was a funerary symbol of high office.[16] The inscriptions also mention the incense and myrrh from Punt (Upper Egypt, the land of the blacks) used in the funerary offerings. Although how the tent was supported and how it was actually used remain an enigma, its very presence amidst the royal mummies in a funerary chapel raises some intriguing questions. Was the use of a leather tent in a ritual, religious, funerary context related to Egyptian cattle worship, to the Egyptian campaigns in the Nubian south where pastoral populations were prominent, or even more directly to a Beja pastoral heritage?[17] What sparks the imagination is the early religious or ritual association between an Egyptian high priestess and a sarcophagus-shaped leather tent in the context of a pastoral heritage!

Tents were also often mentioned in the accounts of Egyptian campaigns against the Syrians, and the latter unquestionably contributed to military tent traditions. In 1478 B.C., for example, the Egyptians captured the son of the Syrian king of Kadesh in his tent, as well as the tent itself.[18] The representation of Syrian officers' tents on seventh-century B.C. Assyrian bas reliefs not only suggests what the tents looked like, but also that symbolic tent imagery figured in the establishment of Assyrian military primacy over Egypt (fig. 1.5b). What is particularly intriguing is that contemporary Hadendowa (Beja) tents bear a close resemblance to the structure of these ancestral Assyrian tents.

In North Africa the first and second centuries A.D. witnessed a period of extensive Roman colonization and increasing contact with indigenous pastoral tribes.[19] The expansion of Roman settlement networks brought inevitable conflict between pastoralists and immigrant agriculturalists. Major military expeditions against the nomads in turn invoked Berber resistance movements, led to the creation of fortified farms, and resulted in rapidly wrought ecological change. The Berbers were forced south into the desert (Barker 1981). Such major Roman military forays into the Sahara desert would undoubtedly have involved the adaptation and exchange of military fighting styles and their material counterpart, their tents and porterage systems.[20]

The Roman legions also included a number of Syrian guards. Bringing with them the experience essential to a successful Roman military operation in the desert, they were involved in guarding not only Numidian forts but also Mauretanian forts farther west. Logically, they would have brought their military-type tent with them when they joined the Roman marching units in Africa.

When the Roman imperial army went on campaign, the soldiers slept in a *papilio,* a leather tent that could be rolled up into a long sausage shape for transport (fig. 1.5c).[21] The *papilio* consisted of a velum, composed of calfskins or goatskins stitched together in rectangular panels, supported by a central ridgepole and kept taut with guys and triangular cross stays.[22] These tents can be seen in a mosaic of a hunting scene in the House of Isguntus (ca. A.D. 310–330) at Hippo Regius on the Mediterranean coast northwest of Carthage, and in a mosaic of rural scenes, at the entrance to a fortified farm, in the House of Laberii (ca. A.D. 300) at Oudna in Tunisia (fig. 1.6).

When the Roman emperor Augustus discharged his thousands of veterans, he gave them land at the boundary of the empire in exchange for their services: they became soldier-farmers. There was an entire cohort (800 men) of them in Africa (Webster 1969). Policies of setting up "veteran-colonies," the preference of legionnaires to remain in the province they knew after their discharge, or to return to the province where they had been recruited, would explain not only the presence of leather tents on Roman villa mosaics but their subsequent diffusion as well.[23] By the end of the second century, more than half the legionnaires were from Africa.

The military custom of exchanging accoutrements at the end of a battle is also relevant. Gift exchange in the context of the spoils of war was not unique to Rome and North Africa; precedent for it in Egypt and Syria already existed. For example, in A.D. 203, the Numidian king Masinissa received two tents with military equipment, of the same type that Roman consuls were supplied with, as a gift (Feilberg 1944:202, citing Livy). By the sixth century the leather tent apparently was being used extensively by the Numidians.[24]

The arrival of the Arabs in the later seventh century in North Africa stimulated the development of a large

Fig. 1.6. A *papilio* tent on a mosaic at the entrance to a Roman villa, Oudna, Tunisia.

network of major and subsidiary routes: northwest Morocco was linked to the Senegalese coast and the Niger River; Libya was linked to Chad via Murzuk in the Fezzan; and one of the oldest caravan routes in the world, the forty-day route, linked the Nile and El Fashir to the Sudan. A caravan consisting of from a few hundred to several thousand camels involved many nomads, oases, permissions to cross territories, camel changes (where vegetation changed), long periods of time, and the movement of entire families and kin groups.

These routes not only provided the stimulus for the early growth of sub-Saharan city-states and political entities such as the empire of Ghana, but also partly explain an eleventh-century funerary ritual for the king of Ghana. His tomb was not constructed of earth and stone like the walls of his capital, but of an armature framework covered with mats and cloths. The construction of the tomb suggests a nomadic rather than a sedentary heritage.[25] The description suggests that it was an armature framework, not unlike those still used in the region today, that served as a funerary chamber for the king of Ghana.

The eleventh century also witnessed the birth and expansion of the vast Almoravid *jihad* from the far west coast of Africa (what is now Mauretania) into Morocco and southern Spain. The etymology of the word *Almoravid* has traditionally been associated with "the people of the *ribat*" (i.e., citadel), but despite several rigorous archaeological excavations in search of it, the citadel from which the Almoravids reputedly began their advance is yet to be found. In fact, the name Almoravid had no relationship to the building of a fortress or a citadel. Rather, it referred to the unique nomadic fighting tactics employed in waging a holy war.[26]

The Almoravid movement unfolded in the context of both vernacular and institutional tent architectures: family tents, sultan's tents, warrior tents, and tent-mosques. How these may have differed from each other can be gleaned from one of the earliest specific Arabic references to the tent as a political symbol in Africa, a tenth-century account by al-Mas'udi (Feilberg 1944:197). He tells how one grandson of Nizar Ma'ad ("the ancestor of the Arabs of the desert") was given a black tent of animal hair (i.e., a woven tent) and the other a round tent *(kubba)* of red leather. The account reflected an important, obviously symbolic, distinction between a woven animal hair tent (used in the vernacular context) and a round, red leather tent (used in an institutional context). This distinction between a woven animal hair velum and a red leather, possibly parasol-type tent is analogous to the distinction that Ibn Khaldun later made (see note 13) between woven animal hair and finely woven linen fabric.

Similar distinctions can be gleaned from Ibn Battuta's fourteenth-century observations made during his travels in West Africa. The tents *(bait)* of the Berber Berdama who inhabited the region between Gao and Takedda were made in a strange fashion (1853–58, 4:437): "They erect sticks of wood or of rods on which they place the mats; above these they set some interlaced sticks, or a sort of trelliswork which they cover with skins, or better, cotton fabrics." On the other hand (ibid.:443), the sultan (a Berber called Izar, and dressed like a Tuareg) offered him lodging "in one of the tents of the Yanatibun, who are like the *wusfan*" (soldiers of a standing army in Morocco) during his stay at Takedda in the Sahara desert. Ibn Battuta's reference to the "strange fashion" of the tents in this region north of Gao implies that these tents were quite different from those he was familiar with in North Africa (i.e., the Moroccan military tents) and those he subsequently encountered elsewhere in his extensive travels. It is possible that the two kinds of tents he observed bore a close resemblance not only to the nineteenth-century armature tents at Bamba or the leather-covered Tuareg tents at Ammalelle, but to their even earlier representation on Saharan rock paintings (see figs. 1.3, 1.4).

The absence of any archaeological data from Gibraltar during the period of Almoravid occupancy can perhaps also be accounted for by their tent heritage. There is no archaeological evidence to suggest a settlement of any kind or size for the period between the landing of Tariq b. Ziyad's Berber and Moorish contingents at Gibraltar and the construction of the city by the Almohad ruler 'Abdul-Mu'min (Camps 1987). Until the early fourteenth century, Gibraltar was controlled and maintained without fortification or castle, even though it was certainly used as a fortified base (there was a small watchtower) and a place of disembarkation (Norris 1961).

Ibn Khaldun's explanation for the luxurious tents that continued to symbolize political suzeranity among the Arab nations in both Africa and the Orient was not unique to the Arab world. Europe witnessed a similar transformation in which tent imagery was extended to political symbolism in the course of negotiation, exchange, political hierarchy, and military competition. In the Age of Chivalry, tents were frequently exchanged as spoils of war and to cement alliances.[27] Accoutrements of a conquered head of state were often taken over and used, so that the virtue, strength, and courage of the captured enemy could pass to the conqueror. In time, the parasol tent became synonymous with sovereignty.

This particular association turned into an ideograph, an icon for kingship and kingdom which European cartographers applied to the kings of Europe, Asia, and Africa alike. Earlier cartographic convention usually designated kingdoms with a fortress or a castle, but during the sixteenth century it became commonplace to represent kingdoms on a map by a parasol tent. On the Majorican portolan chart, compiled and drawn by Mateus Prunes, the kings of Poland, France, and Spain and the emperor of the Holy Roman Empire, as well as the kings of Guinea, Fez, and Tangiers, are represented in their rich parasol tents emblazoned with heraldic symbols (pl. 2).

The practice of royal peregrination has existed for a long time, both in and out of Africa, and it too has implications for the tent as an institutional symbol.[28] Such travel has always been concerned with the presentation of sovereignty—a slow and systematic exploration of national territory, an itinerant form of government which allowed for the direct control of local institutions. For the contemporary Western mind, this nomadic quality of administration is difficult to visualize, considering our propensity for associating political power and military tactics with the permanent, monumental context of palace, castle, or citadel. African architectural (and urban) history requires a basic shift in architectural reference.

Evidence suggests that royal peregrination was an equally common phenomenon in Africa from Mauretania to southern Libya, Mali, and Niger, and from Ethiopia to the region of Sennar in the Sudan. These various displacements of the court *(harka)* characterized the Almoravid expansion and the subsequent Beni Hassan reconquest of Mauretania. The process of Malian consolidation undertaken by Mansa Musa on his early fourteenth-century pilgrimage to Mecca was precisely such a court peregrination. The formation of the Tuareg Sultanate of Agades, the consolidation of power in the Ethiopian courts, and the later nineteenth-century peregrination of Moulay Hassan all required a continual court displacement in order to maintain political control.[29]

As a regular system of itinerant government, the *harka* permitted the ruling court to maintain direct contact with its far-flung populations, to regulate legal disputes, to facilitate and hasten tax collection, and, where taxes were delinquent, to take repressive action (Aafif 1980–81:161). Imagine the quantities of food, supplies, and pack animals needed for each undertaking, given the mass movement of the court population with its armies, and the duration of the projected "campaigns." The nomadic corvées that were imposed help explain the exchange of both material culture and symbols of political power.

The centuries-long Ethiopian tradition of "moving capitals" and moving camps which characterized the Ethiopian court is recounted in detail by Pankhurst (1982, 1983).[30] In the early seventeenth century, the Portuguese Jesuit missionary Manoel de Almeida wrote of Ethiopia that the emperor's camp was the royal city and capital of the empire. Parasol tents used for ceremonial purposes were a familiar sight at royal courts.[31] The allusions in medieval literature, eyewitness accounts, later Jesuit accounts, and European scholarly accounts testifying to the magnitude, complexity, organization, vitality, and diversity of these royal camps suggest an imagery that defies imagina-

Fig. 1.7. a. View of a village south of Agady in the region of Sennar, 1823. b. A parasol tent at the "Public Procession of the King's Women in Dahomy," 1793.

The Tent in African History

tion.³² The practice continued through the centuries as Parkyns' description of an Abyssinian permanent camp several centuries later (1853, 1:174–75) conveys: "Some (were) bellshaped, some square like an English marquee; some white and others of the black woolen stuff made principally in the southern provinces of Tigre."

Even after the establishment of a fixed capital at Gondar in 1636, royal tents remained in extensive service and much effort continued to be put into their manufacture and transport.³³ The Muslim capital included a number of rich traders, the chief of the "Moors" (who was also the principal merchant in Abyssinia), as well as many weavers, tailors, and persons responsible for the royal tents.

By the end of the eighteenth century, the regions that comprise the modern state of Sudan already had a long history of Muslim sultanates, and the process of territorial consolidation continued, culminating in the conquest of the Funj Sultanate by Muhammed Ali, nominally the Ottoman governor of Egypt. In 1830 M. Cailliaud, a skilled artist who traveled to Meroe and Dongola on behalf of the French government, recorded, in a romantic rendering, the Turkish impact on continuing institutional tent imagery in East Africa. The indigenous village of Agady at the base of the mountains, en route from Sennar, is overshadowed by the Turkish military camp which surrounds the tent of Isma'il Pasha, the Turkish governor's son (fig. 1.7a).

Such Tents of Meeting were also de rigueur in commercial encounters between African royalty and European visitors, and the practice extended down to the West African Guinea Coast, far beyond the traditional pale of tent architecture. Archibald Dalzel, a trader in slaves and ivory and a frequent visitor to the court of the king of Dahomy (present-day Benin), described and rendered one such tent in use (1793:134): "In the center of a spacious 'parade' (i.e., courtyard) was erected a lofty tent, or large umbrella, shaped like a sugar loaf, about fifty feet high, and forty feet wide; it was open below, and rested on a circular range of small iron rails, through which the king could have a view of what passed in the parade. He soon made his appearance, and seated himself, amidst the shouts and acclamations of the people under his tent, on an elegant armed chair, covered with crimson velvet and ornamented with carving and gilding" (fig. 1.7b). Could the presence of such a spectacular parasol tent, so out of context in the coastal rain forest, have been a gift

Fig. 1.8. Guillain's white parasol tent pitched adjacent to the house of Abd-el-Kouri, Somalia, 1856.

from the king's Muslim advisors, or had it been brought by European traders or traders from the north in a commercial gift exchange?[34]

The same parasol tent that had stood for military and political power for so many centuries also served the European explorer on the African continent.[35] Nineteenth-century exploration traveled in the company of military campaigns and commercial ventures, so it comes as no surprise that Guillain, the mid-nineteenth-century explorer who traveled down the east coast of Africa, would choose to illustrate his own white parasol tent in the company of the Somali mat-covered armature frame tents he encountered en route (fig. 1.8).

The tent achieved the ultimate symbolism in the late nineteenth century, at the height of the European age of exploration and expansion in Africa, in the tomb of its most committed and devoted representative, Sir Richard Burton. The deathbed request of the intrepid, brilliant explorer of the African continent was to be interred in a marble replica of his personal parasol fabric tent—an expression of his own immortality using the most ephemeral architectural imagery of all (fig. 1.9). Burton's marble mausoleum, an antithesis of its imagery, brings the circle full turn to the leather funerary tent of Princess Isimkheb which had been fashioned in the shape of a stone sarcophagus!

The references and illustrations cited above are obviously only a brief survey, but perhaps enough to suggest some of the threads that might be woven into a new interpretation and reconstruction of African tent history. For example, the leather tent or canopy has a distinguished institutional genealogy, one that includes not only the Judaic Tent of Meeting and the simulated sarcophagus of an Egyptian high priestess (both in the context of matriliny), but also Roman imperial and military expansion, proto-Berber political symbolism, Islamic proselytizing, and Arab military conquest. It is in these institutional contexts that the ancestral relatives of the leather tent used by northern, noble Tuareg clans must be sought. The adaptation of institutional architectural traditions by indigenous, vernacular populations is one process. It evolves in tandem with the validation, even deification, of vernacular tent traditions by institutional agencies.

CAMELS AND CAMEL-RIDING TECHNOLOGIES

An old proverb refers to the desert as the mother of the camel. Even in these days of mechanized transport and sponsored auto and glider races, it is hard to imagine the Sahara without a camel. More important, any history of African architecture that does not consider the history of camel domestication and transport technology would be woefully askew. The advent of camels in the Sahara marked a watershed in the demographic history of the desert: from an intimidating empty expanse to be crossed, the desert was transformed into a habitable, controllable region that could support nomadic populations. The life of these no-

Fig. 1.9. Sir Richard Burton's marble mausoleum, outside London. Drawing after a photograph.

madic communities depended on and became intricately entwined with the camel. Wealth is still measured by herd size, and transhumance would be impossible without them. Camels play a role in social rituals and customs, are a part of the material culture, and dictate nomadic value systems. Even today, no marriage in the desert is possible without camels. Not only does the camel carry the bride but her house as well. The technology of camel transport is inseparable from tent technology and architecture.

Various authors have addressed the question of camel domestication in Africa, some in greater depth than others, but controversy still surrounds its origin and its history still eludes us.[36] Hypotheses, sometimes colored by the desert experience of their European authors, often rest on the analysis of material evidence for riding technologies. Yet the crucial distinction between no saddles (draft usage), pack saddles (transport), and riding saddles (military usage) is rarely made.

Some scholars assert that camel breeding gradually spread southward from its center in the desert east of Thebes (now Luxor) into the eastern desert of the Sudan (Bulliet 1975). Others conclude that the Egyptians learned to domesticate and breed camels in large numbers for desert work, trade, and warfare from the early desert tribes in the southern Sudan: first the Blemmyes, then the Beja and the Somalis (Epstein 1971, 2:565–67). All agree, however, that in the course of the first millennium B.C. the camel, in response to the needs of Assyrian and Persian conquest strategies, was flourishing.[37]

The earliest renderings of camels in Egypt, and those found on Assyrian wall reliefs of military camps depicting their invasions of Egypt, do not distinguish between riding mounts and pack animals (see fig. 1.5b). On other wall reliefs, it is only captives and other foreigners who rode camels. By the third century B.C., under Ptolemaic rule, camels had come into general use for transport on the desert route between Coptos and the Red Sea, evidenced by many terracotta figurines of loaded camels from both the Hellenistic and Roman periods of Egyptian overrule.

The earliest, frequently cited reference to camels in Roman North Africa comes from an account of the famous battle of Thapsus in 46 B.C. in which Julius Caesar defeated King Juba of Numidia and captured twenty-two camels as booty. There is no clue that might shed light on their use in this military context, but it is generally known that they were initially used as pack animals and for agricultural work (Gauthier-Pilters and Dagg 1981). By the second century A.D., the camel had apparently proven its military worth (evidenced by Emperor Hadrian's establishment of a camel corps), but whether the Roman legions used camels as riding mounts or pack animals is unclear from extant accounts.

Few camels appear on the numerous mosaics of rural scenes in the Roman villas of North Africa, but the context of those that do appear provide the basis for an intriguing, albeit speculative, interpretation. The earliest (on a frieze in the House of the Dionysus Procession at El Djem, ca. A.D. 140–160) shows a camel being ridden by Silenus in the company of wild beasts, on what appears to be a saddle with two side panels (fig. 1.10). Silenus, the oldest of the satyrs, was a primitive deity, a divinity of woodlands and fountains who, it is claimed, prompted Dionysus to invent vine cultivation. The camel-riding Silenus puts one in mind of Ptolemy II Philadelphus who exhibited camels in his famous procession in honor of Dionysus in 274 B.C., but it also recalls the elaborate attribution of the camel as a "dieu du mal," venerated yet feared. Considering the wild animals in whose presence it always appears, the camel must have been perceived as a wild animal, certainly a rural one, perhaps a sacred animal (Foucher 1963:116). Association with Dionysian iconography implies that it was still part of the suburban, indigenous, "unknown" Berber hinterland of Roman Africa.

Subsequent mosaics in the same city dating from the second and early third centuries A.D. also include camels. These mosaics consist of scenes of indigenous populations, agriculture, and the hinterland of the Roman Empire.[38] The scenes add weight to the claim that Emperor Septimius Severus (A.D. 193–211), the founder of Leptis Magna, was instrumental in developing the camel for agricultural use. His Syrian wife, whose background had made her more familiar with the camel's agricultural and military potential, may well have been the instigator.

By the mid-fourth century, life along the North

Fig. 1.10. Silenus riding a camel on a Roman mosaic in the House of the Dionysus Procession, El Djem, Tunisia.

African littoral had changed considerably, and the camel's presence, now frequently documented, seems to have increased almost exponentially.[39] The most remarkable documents from this period are the sculptured scenes of agricultural life in the Tripolitanian hinterland. The majority of them, in which camels are shown as plough animals, occur in the frontier zone of fortified farms which had been settled by soldier-farmers.

A fourth-century Roman mosaic of black camel riders from Tuburbo Maius in Tunisia also documents the presence of black populations in conjunction with these farms.[40] The mosaic of black riders and camels in the midst of wild boars, cattle, and horses, is unfortunately incomplete. While it is impossible to reconstruct who they were or how they were mounted, there is no doubt about the rural context and the association between camels and a black presence.

With Roman agricultural expansion and its aftermath, the role of the camel was extended from a draft to a pack animal. The short-distance routes between settlements previously dictated by horse and chariot could be extended into long-distance routes across the desert, and nomadized Berber populations were able to exploit what had previously been inaccessible terrain.

When the Vandals invaded Africa at the end of the fifth century A.D., the nomadic Berber tribes of the Atlas mountains were already in possession of numerous camel herds, and in the sixth century they were able to resist Roman, Vandal, and Byzantine invasion.[41] They became undisputed masters of the Magreb, using camels to transport supplies and families, for both defensive and offensive military operations but not as a military mount. According to Procopius who described their fifth-century battles with the Vandals, Berber tribesmen arranged their camels in twelve concentric rings, protectively surrounding women and children in the center. In battle, these pack animals were used to form a defensive wall. At the time of the subsequent Byzantine invasion of North Africa, the camel was described as carrying the fortune of the nomad on its back, the infant's cradle, the domestic utensils, and the indigenous woman with food supplies in her arms perched on its summit.

It has been hypothesized that the seventh-century Arab conquest of North Africa was achieved with horses rather than camels (Demougeot 1960), but in fact both were essential for conquest, fulfilling different roles. When the Almoravid leader Sidi Okba b. Nafi undertook his *jihad* from the West African (now Mauretanian) coast toward Kaouar in the late seventh century, his force was said to consist of four hundred horses (i.e., light cavalry), four hundred camels, and eight hundred waterskins. Logic suggests that without the camels (one per horseman) to carry the waterskins (two per camel) needed for survival, the horsemen could never have survived.

In the late sixteenth century, the North African Sa'adian sultan, Al Mansur, attracted by the potential gold revenue, sent five thousand men from Marrakesh across the Sahara to Gao and Timbuktu. This army

The Tent in African History

was dependent on more than ten thousand camels to carry its munitions, food, and water supply, as well as its tents and personal effects (Castries 1923). In the early nineteenth century, the pasha of Tripoli sent a military expedition of two thousand cavalry and five hundred infantry across the Sahara to Bornu. Their transport allowance consisted of one camel for every two infantrymen and two camels for every cavalryman and his horse (Bovill 1970). Horses remain, to this day, the prerogative of military leaders and royalty, but the success of their military operation depended on the pack camel.[42]

Accounts of African transdesert trade, both East and West, always make reference to caravans, but the logistics or technological requirements involved in mounting them have been rarely considered despite their magnitude.[43] The East African caravan trade was as ubiquitous and profitable as the North–West African trade, and the West African caravans must have looked very much like those across the continent in Ethiopia, recorded by J. M. Bernatz with such artistic sensitivity in the early nineteenth century (fig. 1.11). Caravans consisted of far more than merchants and their goods. Entire families and their household goods accompanied them and their nomadic protectors. How these nomadic households moved was graphically portrayed not only on an early undated rock

Fig. 1.11. A salt caravan in the valley of Gugunta, 1852. The illustrator, J. M. Bernatz, accompanied the British Mission to the Court of Shoa.

Fig. 1.12. "March of a nomad horde," Somalia, 1844.

16   African Nomadic Architecture

painting (see fig. 1.13) but on the frontispiece of an early nineteenth-century account from the Ethiopian highlands (fig. 1.12).

LITTERS AND PALANQUINS

These seemingly unrelated vignettes of camel history and transport technology which distinguish between pack saddles and riding saddles, between the camel's use as a pack animal in caravan or migration moves and its use as a military mount in warfare, are particularly relevant to the subject of litters and palanquins, those camel trappings that historically have been an integral part of African tent architecture and mobility (fig. 1.13). Tent history cannot be written without taking them into account. The subject also brings us full circle, albeit metaphorically, to the Ark in the Tabernacle with which this brief historical survey began.

Fieldwork among the Kababish early in the twentieth century led Seligman (1918) to invoke a parallel between the palanquins used by the Kababish in the Sudan and those used by the early Arabs and Semites in which young maidens or warrior queens, seated in litters, led their troops into battle (fig. 1.14a). In certain particulars, the Kababish *otfa* (or *tonkoh*) represents the Ark of the Covenant, and some aspects of the sacredness of the Ark seem to have persisted in the *mahlmal* still held sacred in Egypt and the Near East.[44]

Her suggestion recalls a fourteenth-century account of the interior Beja by al-Maqrizi, which was subsequently recorded by Burckhardt (1819:182): "Their people rear cattle . . . every clan has its priest, who pitches a tent made of feathers, in the shape of a dome, wherein he practices his adorations. . . . On the march, the priest leads his tent upon a camel destined for that sole purpose."

Fig. 1.13. Rock painting, Ayou, Tibesti. The woman on the left is clearly riding in a litter.

The Tent in African History

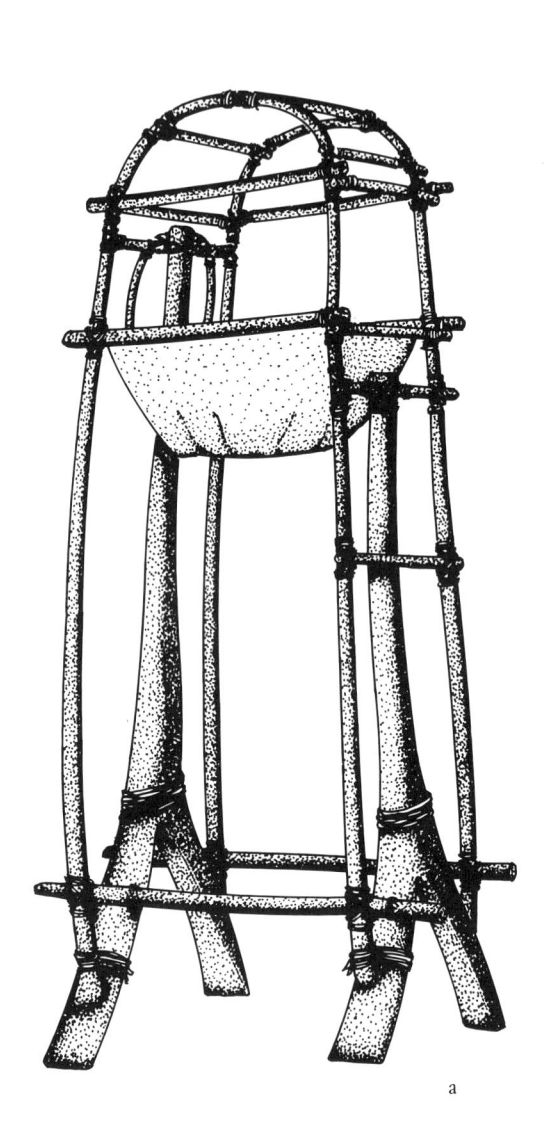

Fig. 1.14. a. Kababish palanquin. Drawing after Seligman 1918. b. A palanquin *(attatich)* commandeered by the French to transport their wounded in skirmishes with the Tuareg in southern Algeria, 1863.

This description also evokes another fourteenth-century military tradition related by Ibn Khaldun (1958, 2:78): "The Rûm (Byzantines), the Gothic rulers in Spain, and many other non-Arab peoples used to employ thrones for the purpose of steadying the battle lines. A throne would be set up for the ruler in the thick of battle.... Flags were run up at the corners of the throne ... (which was) surrounded by and protected by the ruler's entourage, sharpshooters and foot soldiers." He noted further that "the Arabs and most

18   African Nomadic Architecture

other Bedouin nations that move about and employ the techniques of attack and withdrawal, dispose their camels and the pack animals carrying their litters in lines to steady the fighting men."

The *mahlmal, markab, maksar,* or *howdah* of Near Eastern military tactics was used exclusively in times of war; it was a symbol of political suzerainty. Each tribe had its palanquin, which served as a symbol of victory, a banner, a fanfare, a war cry rallying its defenders to battle. Assembled on the camel's back into a fantastic structural splendor, highlighted by its multicolored decorations and ostrich feathers, its superstructure swaying in the wind and sun, this palanquin in which the ruler's daughter sat was a throne, much as the Ark of the Covenant was a throne in the dim past of the Judaic tradition.

The daughter was adorned as a bride, and traditionally, in victory, she was promised to the bravest fighter; in defeat she became a propitiatory victim to the enemy's attacks. Capture of the palanquin by the enemy symbolized defeat. But because the palanquin housed a daughter, embedded in the symbolism was a matrilineal heritage and the material accoutrements of the marriage ritual.

In this same context, the myth of La Kahena, which persists as part of the greater West African Tuareg cultural tradition and embodies the last Berber resistance to the Arab conquest in North Africa, invites close analysis. Little is known about her (much of the speculation has revolved around questions of her Judaic affiliation), but no one disputes her Berber heritage.[45] By the end of the seventh century, the Arabs had easily defeated the Byzantines in their renewed efforts to move westward across North Africa, but the Berber resistance to their expansion persisted. They were held in check for twenty years under the leadership of an enigmatic but well-known, almost mythological figure, a Djerewa woman of the Aures mountains called La Kahena.

It is tempting to indulge the imagination with the background descriptions by al-Maqrizi and Ibn Khaldun. Imagine La Kahena as a powerful warrior, queen of the Aures, head of a resisting Berber (perhaps Judaicized) clan, leading her troops into battle against the Arab invaders. Picture her atop a camel-mounted throne (built up on a pack saddle), in the center of the foray, led by a large idol in wood (Cauvet 1925–26, 2:30). How different would her elaborately decorated palanquin have been from those commandeered by the French in the mid-nineteenth century in their skirmishes with the Tuareg (fig. 1.14b)?

In defeat, her palanquin, a singular political symbol of Berber unity, would have been confiscated or exchanged as part of the spoils of war. But her palanquin was also a metaphor for marriage, a symbol of matriliny, since she had gone out in it as a bride. The exodus that followed her defeat may have looked very much like the early sixteenth-century exodus from the Tuareg city of Agades following its Songhay conquest by Askia Muhammed in 1515 which Barth recorded (1857, 5:461–62): "It is explicitly stated that he drove out five tribes ... and that a considerable number of Berbers, with five hundred *jakhfa* (cages mounted on camels, such as only wealthy people can afford to keep for carrying their wives), left the town." Some of the less elaborate *jakhfa,* which had been built as marriage palanquins, would have looked like those he subsequently recorded.[46] In my mind's eye, the more elegant ones could very well have looked like the noble Tuareg bride's palanquin recorded in the early nineteenth century at a wedding south of Murzuq, Libya[47] (pl. 3).

The reader may be unconvinced by the conjectures, hypotheses, and suggestions that have been drawn from these abbreviated vignettes of history. They barely begin to skim the available sources and deal with vast time spans, complex correlations, and ephemeral material. The intent, however, was not to write a definitive history but only to evoke the possibilities of innovative interpretation that this somewhat engendered and institutionalized perspective offers for the ethnohistorian. Like life itself, is it not possible to address both broad sweeps and intricate details in writing history? Each approach has its own goal and serves a different purpose. It is hoped that the chapters that follow will allay the skepticism of those who may question suppositions seemingly unsupported by evidence.

2
ENVIRONMENT AND SPACE

The nomadic milieu of this anthology, stretching from the Atlantic Ocean on the west, across the continent to the Red Sea, the highlands of Ethiopia, and the Great Rift Valley, consists of a range of environments that travel belt formation across the continent (fig. 2.1). Sometimes the topography is a rocky plateau, sometimes a pebbly plain. In some regions there are huge depressions with dunes of shifting sand *(ergs)*, in others mountainous escarpments. Sometimes the landscape appears almost lunar; sometimes, with the flush of fresh growth, it becomes a veritable carpet of multihued greens created by the diversity of its vegetation. Rainfall, minimal at best, is also notoriously variable, so that rare torrential downpours sporadically interrupt the cloudless atmosphere and, in the wake of rushing water, the dry plains are momentarily transformed into unending lakes.[1]

All would agree that it is browse, forage, and water for animals that are most important for the nomad, since these are critical to herding and pastoral subsistence; and certainly it is these factors that direct and reinforce nomadic patterns of transhumance over space and time. From the perspective of an architect working and designing in an economy of supreme scarcity, the elements of the physical environment most important in determining the form and construction of a nomadic dwelling are also climatic, but involve other, albeit related, concerns, as a little-known ethnographer in a long-forgotten commentary noted (Ferree 1890:147–48): "Climate changes, variations in temperature and rainfall, differences in geologic structure and of animal and vegetable products, the nature of the soil, and the topography of a country—in short, all the factors that constitute environment—are the most important and universal elements." In addition to pointing out the influence of wind, rain, diurnal temperature differentials, and seasonal change on vernacular architecture, the author also noted that the choice of building materials is traceable to climate and geological formation.[2]

The tendency to minimize and downplay the importance and complexity of the natural environment, to which the rapid industrialization and urbanization of the Western world of the post–World War II era led, was berated by two well-known architects in what continues to be a model for any catalogue of human ingenuity in the vernacular tradition (Fitch and Branch 1960). The principles of design that they enumerate serve as the starting point for elaborating on the "structurally brilliant invention of the tent—light in weight, composed of small members and easily erected, dismantled, and packed. At the same time, to judge it by the modern structural criterion of 'the most work from the least material,' the tent (like all tension structures) ranks as a very advanced form of construction" (p. 142).

In architectural terms, structure, form, and space are absolute. Roofs and walls will either stand up or fall down in response to winds and roof loads. They will be constructed of the available material resources, in response to land surfaces and relief, to light and shadow, to temperature, humidity, and evaporation, to radia-

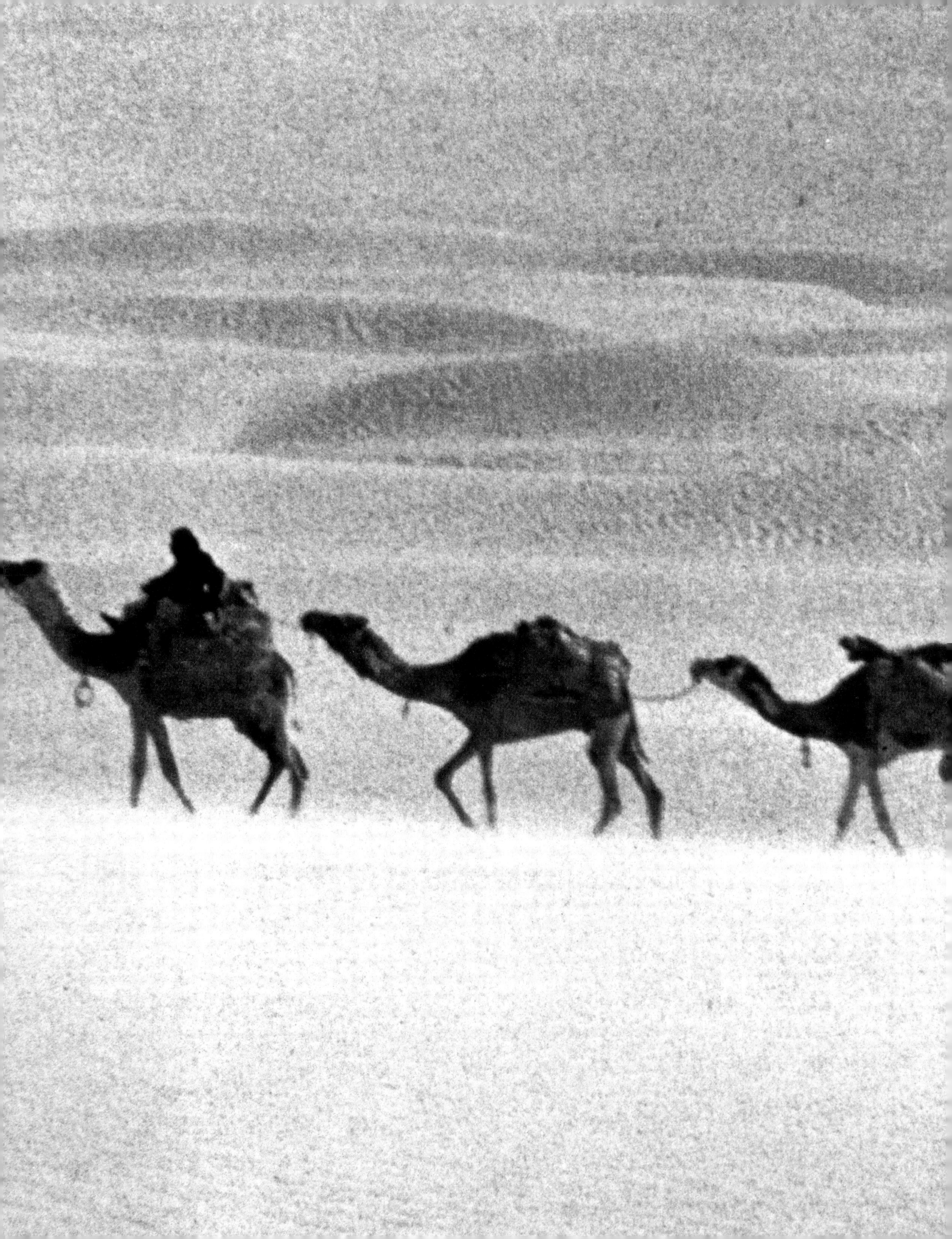

perceptual and psychological phenomenon. Different soil conditions yield different ecological communities of vegetation, and while these, in turn, affect the patterns and strategies of forage and herding, they also account for the different exploitation of natural materials and related, resultant technological skills. There are few geological landmarks in the desert expanse: flanked by the Atlas mountains in the north, the Hoggar, Tibesti, and Ennedi ranges rise dramatically from the Taoudenni, Niger, Chad, and Kufra basins below them (fig. 2.2). In the east, the relatively low, uniform relief is broken by occasional uplands, the Red Sea highlands, and singular volcanic formations.

Mountains and hillocks are seemingly immovable in comparison with the transience of life.[3] These few topographic markers which punctuate uninterrupted sight lines and horizon lines are often encoded in nomadic poetry and myth, becoming psychological anchors for schema of spatial orientation (pl. 4).

WINDS AND SANDSTORMS

In contrast to the documentation on desert rainfall and vegetation, information on winds, windstorms, and sand or dust storms is meager. The former, of major concern to the vested interests of international institutions, governments, and commercial ventures over the decades, has yielded a wealth of valuable data that would serve international strategies and policies relating to desertification and to nomadism. The latter has been overlooked by both geographers and climatologists, despite the fact that the distribution of plants and animals is greatly influenced by the presence or absence of shelter from the wind. Indeed, it is difficult to find geographical atlases with relevant information on winds for this part of the world.

Over much of the year, trade winds, surface winds, and pressure systems combine to create a prevailing pattern of winds from the northeast (fig. 2.3). During the winter months these northeasterlies are characteristic of almost the entire northern half of the continent. During the summer months, the pattern of air movement changes: it is not as uniform, and there is a shift of air masses so that lower southwesterlies prevail in the southeast and the northwesterlies continue to

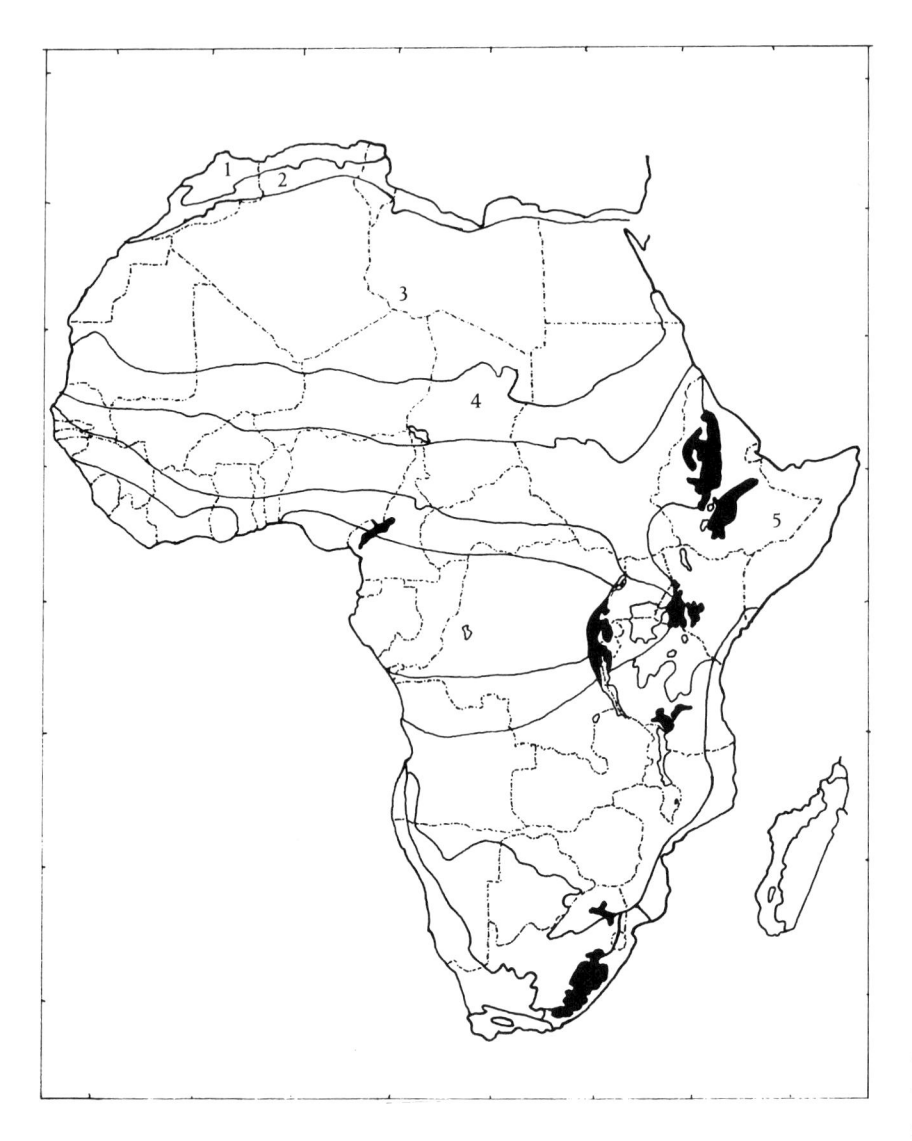

Fig. 2.1. A biogeographic map of plants in Africa. 1. Mediterranean regional center of endemism. 2. Mediterranean-Sahara regional transition zone. 3. Sahara regional transition zone. 4. Sahel regional transition zone. 5. Somali-Masai regional center of endemism. Drawing after White 1983.

tion, in order to satisfy the thermal, physical, social, and psychological requirements that contribute to the character not only of a particular material culture but of a culture at large. Building the bridge between environment and culture is both essential and fundamental if African nomadic architecture is to be understood and appreciated.

TOPOGRAPHY

The desert topography has two basic implications for the nomad. Physically, it is a resource and a precondition for various types of flora, it modifies light and wind conditions, and it mediates the orientation of house sites and settlement patterns. Visually, it is a prevail in the northeast. In the Sahara, winds are most often associated with sandstorms. Sandstorms, essentially phenomena of winter and early spring, are far more frequent than rain, and they often have disastrous effects. During these sandstorms the wind shifts, moving in almost a complete turn. A low pressure area over the Atlantic moves toward the African coast, and the prevailing winter wind from the northeast swings around to the southeast and then to the south. Sooner or later the wind swings into the northwest and then the north, and clear, calm weather returns.

Sandstorms are particularly memorable, as anyone who has experienced the clouds of dust and the sand-laden atmosphere of this dry season phenomenon (*shabali* in the east, *harmattan* in the west) will attest to. Winds and sandstorms are far more frequently mentioned in the oral and written literature, since these phenomena often had dire effects on the traveler attempting to move from one point to another in the desert. The wind begins to assume the proportions of a gale, and streaming wisps of sand race over the ground like trembling nets. This is the moment for decisive action, when shelter must be found as quickly as possible.

The winds and sandstorms, which may have such disastrous effects on people, crops, and domestic animals, are also a critical factor in building orientation and structure, and call for an equally demanding building response. Indeed, the rampant confusion in the ethnographic documentation on the variable orientation of nomadic housing during different seasons of the year is a direct result of our negligence in acknowledging its import. It is also no accident that the structural complexity (and artistic virtuosity) of critical architectural elements reflect this particular wind pattern; that the sturdiest and heaviest artifacts are located on the side of the prevailing winds; that beds and the weight of people on them, which contribute to the structural reinforcement of the windward side, are located precisely in response to wind resistance.[4]

Sandstorms affect visibility and spatial perception in the environment. The senses are enveloped in indescribable ways, obliterating not only the horizon line and the sun, but the most immediate environmental cues so that orientation itself becomes even more dif-

Fig. 2.2. Rising behind the date and dum palms in the Enneri Modrunga region, central Tibesti, are basaltic mountain formations.

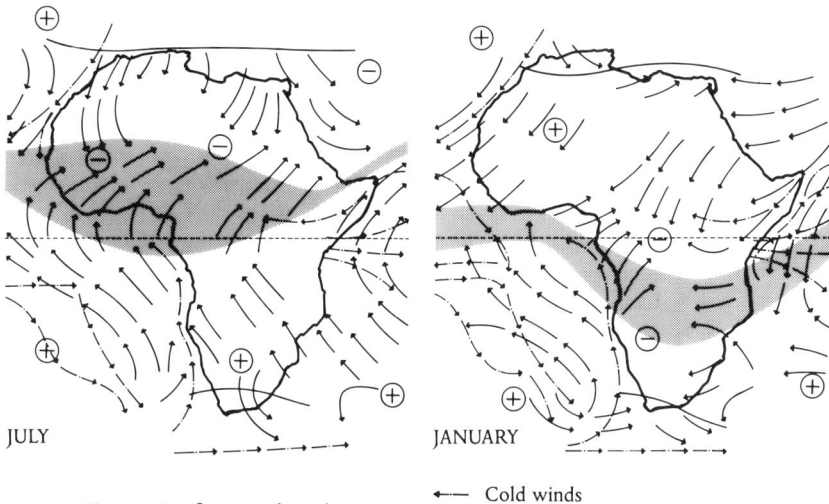

Fig. 2.3. Surface winds and pressure patterns during July and January. Drawing after J. F. Griffiths 1972.

← Cold winds
← Dominant winds
⊖ Low pressures
⊕ High pressures
▓ Zone of intertropical convergences

Environment and Space

ficult.[5] Mirages do even more: they create an entirely fictitious environment, often leading the traveler astray.

The considerable obstacles presented by these sand and windstorms during the daytime hours abate at night. Nights in the desert are crystal clear, even when total darkness prevails during the new moon. Regardless of the time of the month, nowhere else are so many stars so visible with such clarity, brilliance, and sparkle. In a landscape almost devoid of topographic features, this phenomenon explains, at least in part, the role and importance of the lunar calendar in nomadic life. When so much of the nomad's moving activity takes place during the cool hours before the sun has risen, astronomy, on which the nomad depends for navigating the desert, is a sine qua non.

SUN, LIGHT, SHADE, AND SHADOW

The more than ten hours of sunshine that light each day throughout the year in the desert and its adjacent regions are in part the result of the absence of clouds. The absence of a vegetal cover also contributes to greater reflectivity and the intense heat radiation from land surfaces[6] (pl. 5). In response, shade and shadow are eagerly sought out by the nomad desert dweller. Where nature provides the scanty-leafed but spreading branches of an umbrella-type acacia, it becomes the focal point of the transient camp, the men's gathering and meeting place, around which daily life and houses are organized.

The architecture itself creates a pattern of shade and shadow. In the morning, the longest and deepest shadows are cast toward the west by the tents themselves; at midday, there is almost no shade or shadow because the sun is directly overhead; in the late afternoon, the pattern is reversed and the longest shadows are on the east side. Even at night, during the full moon, the light is bright enough to cast long, eerie shadows. It seems more than coincidence that daily household activities respond to this pattern: in the early morning, all the hustle and bustle in preparation for the day's activities unfold adjacent to the western entrance; late in the afternoon in the coolness of evening, the activities (including the material artifacts that accompany them) are moved over into the shade on the east side of the house. In the blinding glare of the midday sun, everyone moves in as close as possible to the tent walls, seeking thermal comfort in the minimal shadow they cast.

The shades and shadows cast by the sun's daily orbit from east to west coincide to a great extent with the direction of the northeastern and southwestern winds; together, they also influence settlement and territorial organization. As so many nomadic camps illustrate, hierarchies of location are organized along a north-south linear axis. House entrances always face west so that the morning activities that unfold in front of them are in the shade and protected from the winds. Camel kraals are often located on the east, immediately behind the houses, in order to divert the winds and minimize the forces on the tent's eastern face. At the same time, windborne human noises that might startle the animals are carried away from them.

RAINFALL

Rainfall is a negligible factor in the architectural context of the desert. Rainfall, which occurs during the wet or "winter" season, comes and goes quickly; evaporation soon follows. Even though it may be torrential, it does not require the sustained shelter that temperate climates respond with. Further, although one might imagine that rainfall would be a critical factor in the encouragement of the vegetal growth, in fact the patterns of woody plant vegetation in the desert are dictated as much by response to groundwater and topography. The system of sandy riverbeds (wadis) and the patterns of the mountain topography are equally important in establishing the patterns of vegetation and the network of oases.

VEGETATION

The desert is always thought of as devoid of vegetation; in reality, the opposite is true. In its cultural context, vegetation is the foundation of every part of an African nomad's existence. Vegetation affects the way in which light is reflected off the surface of the earth and the distance one can see without interruption, that is, the continuity of the horizon line. But the importance of these factors, which enable us to perceive texture, shape, and form as well as distance, is seemingly negligible when compared to its ecological import.

In the past, forestry research has focused primarily on the economic export value of vegetal resources and timbers, on matters of land tenure, on questions of herding practices and pastoralism, and on the agricultural potential of dry season cultivation. More recently, concerns about the gradual encroachment of the desert have brought issues of the ecological balance between pastoralists and their environment into the forefront of scholarly concern. But rarely, if ever, have any of these researches addressed the structural properties inherent in timbers and vegetal resources indigenous to the desert, nor have the structural properties of woody plants used in nomadic building practices ever been studied in detail.[7]

The vegetation in the areas traversed by the nomads in this anthology currently falls into a set of clearly defined parallel belts or zones (White 1983) illustrated in figure 2.1. *Zone 1*, primarily of historical interest to this survey, is essentially a region dominated by montane growth such as the broadleaved oaks, junipers, cypress, cedar, and pine. This montane growth pattern is currently unique on the African continent, although at one time junipers seem to have been far more prevalent in other African montane regions. These trees have provided excellent construction timber for millennia because of their growth pattern. The trunks (and often branches) of these trees grow straight and tall; they continue to be admirably suited for the poles required by the structural support system of North African tents.

In the western part of *Zone 2*, the Argania spinosa (which the Tekna nomads use for their tent poles) dominates the scrub forest and bushland. In much of the eastern region (between Morocco and Tunisia), patches of pine, juniper, and oak forest remain, especially in the mountains. During the centuries of Roman North African settlement, these were the timber species most frequently used for building purposes.

The three climates of *Zone 3*, established on the basis of rainfall distribution, are more or less coincident with three major floristic zones. In the north there are elements of Mediterranean affinity: a few patches of pine, juniper, and oak remain, primarily in the mountains. In the south the flora is tropical, consisting mainly of Acacia tortilis and Panicum turgidum. The central zone contains a mix of the two supported primarily by the rapid runoff in riverbeds.

The original natural vegetation in the north (probably Acacia gummifera and Zizyphus lotus) has almost entirely been replaced by cultivation practices. The original oasis vegetation, which consisted of dum palms and species of Acacia, Maerua, Capparis, and Calotropis procera, has been almost completely replaced by the date palm. Except for certain parts of southern Tunisia, the acacia has tended to disappear in the northern Sahara.

Apart from the oases, the sandy riverbeds are the only desert habitats where trees and large bushes are found. These consist of three main vegetation communities: Hyphaene, Tamarix, and Acacia. The large wadis that radiate from the southwestern slopes of Tibesti support the Hyphaene community which also includes Salvadora persica, Tamarix articulata, Acacia nilotica, and Acacia albida (see fig. 2.2).

Except for the Tamarix and Hyphaene communities on the mountain summits, the large woody plants of the Saharan plains all belong to the acacia communities, forming a very homogeneous belt extending from coastal Mauretania across Tibesti to the East African coast. The most important trees in the acacia communities are the Acacia tortilis (raddiana), Acacia ehrenbergiana, Maerua crassifolia, Balanites aegyptiaca, Capparis decidua, Calotropis procera, Salvadora persica, and Zizyphus mauritiana. The most widespread biogeographic community is composed of Acacia tortilis and the grass Panicum turgidum.[8]

Zone 4, where pastoralism is the main basis of the economy, has commonly come to be known as the Sahel. It is punctuated by the Aïr, Ennedi, and Adrar des Iforas massifs which accommodate the northerly extension of several Sahel species. The wooded grassland is populated by the Acacia tortilis, Commiphora africana, Balanites aegyptiaca, Boscia senegalensis,

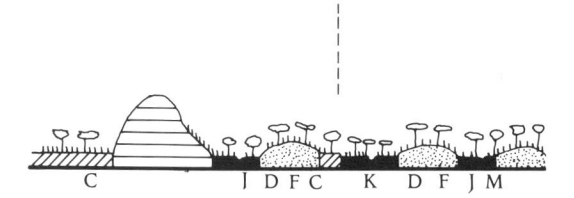

	A	Acacia tortilis
Loams	B	Commiphora africana
Sand Dunes	C	Acacia mellifera
	D	Acacia senegal
	E	Hyphaene thebaica
Wadis	F	Acacia raddiana
	J	Acacia senegal
	K	Acacia arabica
Hills	M	Balanites aegyptiaca

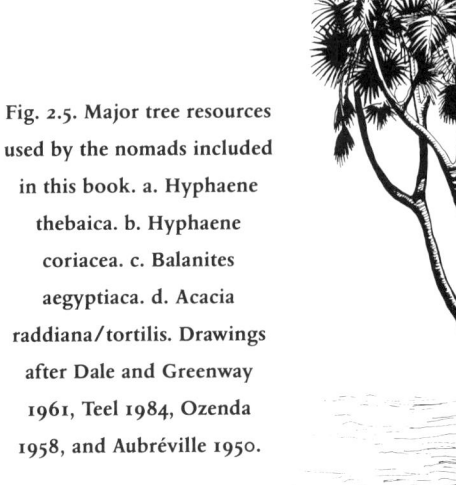

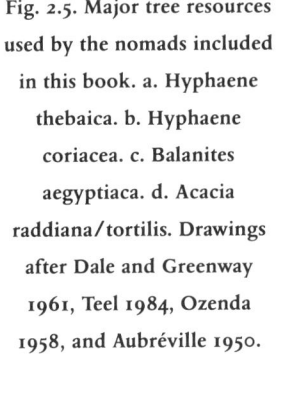

Fig. 2.5. Major tree resources used by the nomads included in this book. a. Hyphaene thebaica. b. Hyphaene coriacea. c. Balanites aegyptiaca. d. Acacia raddiana/tortilis. Drawings after Dale and Greenway 1961, Teel 1984, Ozenda 1958, and Aubréville 1950.

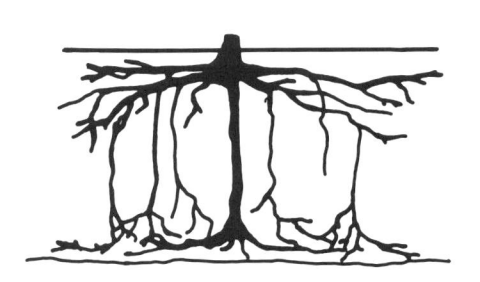

Fig. 2.4. a. Plant preferences for particular topographic conditions. b. Modification of root systems by soil conditions. Drawings after Born 1965 and Kowalski 1971, vol. 2.

and the Maerua crassifolia. Again, the Acacia tortilis is the most abundant, occurring with variations in both the north and south of the zone.

The main vegetation types in *Zone 5* are the Acacia-Commiphora deciduous wooded grassland and the Acacia-Commiphora deciduous bushland. On the slopes of Marsabit mountain, the evergreen and scrub forest consists of Juniperus procera and broadleaved Olea. Except for small stands of dum palm on sites with permanent groundwater at the edge of the Chalbi desert and at the base of Mount Kulal, palms are almost nonexistent.

PLANT UTILIZATION AND DROUGHT RESISTANCE

Many of the species in all five zones have developed mechanisms of drought resistance which enable them to survive and flourish in the arid climates (fig. 2.4). Water-loss reduction, one of these mechanisms, in turn contributes to the remarkable systems of plant utilization employed by the nomads: while the herbaceous plants turn dry and die during the dry season, many of these tree species retain their leaves and fruits throughout the year, making them excellent forage for both man and animal (Bernus 1979, 1980). The trees release humans from dependency on the annual cycle of wet and dry seasons, providing a stability throughout the year unobtainable from annual herbs. Among the trees that are always green are the Salvadora persica, the Balanites aegyptiaca, and the Zizyphus mauritiana. The fruits of various acacias can be used year round. Women's work parties that go out on periodic gathering expeditions will take advantage of the occasion to collect the wood itself for related purposes.

The relationship between harvesting and nomadic building technology is further integrated by a second set of mechanisms, the intensification of water absorption. A common feature of the desert plants mentioned above is the increased efficiency of moisture absorption by means of their extensive root systems. The preponderance of the root system over the aboveground shoot system facilitates the adjustment of the water balance. Additionally, the development of "rain roots" and particularly "sheath roots" among grasses such as the Panicum turgidum guarantees root longevity and survival over long drought periods.

It is perfectly clear from the ethnographic accounts that building technologies and the exploitation of vegetal resources for a range of ethnobotanical uses—indeed, for life itself—are interdependent. Both are contingent upon an intimate, sophisticated knowledge of desert botany. The same woody plants and grasses that make up the ethnobotanical repertoire of nomadic life are also those most commonly used in building and in building-related products (figs. 2.5–2.7).

A striking testimony to nomadic ingenuity and a revelation of the multiple ways in which the available resources are used in the architectural context come from a closer examination of the limited building resources. Construction timber in the desert and its adjacent regions comes from two major families, the palms and the acacias. Conifers and broadleafed deciduous trees such as cypress, pine, and oak, commonly used elsewhere and historically for building, are almost nonexistent in the zones the nomads move in, but the palms and the acacias have been used since time immemorial for a great diversity of purposes.

PALMS

Although palm trunks are never used by the nomads, palm leaves and fronds, particularly those of the dum palm, are utilized for mats and roof coverings. The date palm, usually spared because of its nutritional value, has a reasonably straight trunk but is also unsuitable for most construction requirements: the trunk's cellular structure militates against flat sawing. Fibrous and soft, it cannot carry much weight. Although often used for roof construction in the oases, it cannot be bent, and carving the fibrous texture is well-nigh impossible. The trunk of the dum palm, in contrast, is compact, harder, and stronger, but, because of these same properties, specialized tools are required to cut it. On the other hand, the fibrous quality of the palm leaves make them an extremely exploitable commodity for woven products such as tent mats and basketry. They are far more accessible to nomads without arduous labor, particularly when nomadic camps interact with sedentary oasis dwellers.

GRASSES

One of the remarkable features of the deserts in which the nomads move is the unique symbiotic relationship that obtains among the acacias and particular grasses such as the panicums and asparagus in the southerly reaches of the Sahara and its eastern extensions such as the Chalbi (pl. 6). The existence of this particular characteristic explains the preferential use of these grasses for basketry and mats and the particular technologies associated with them. The artifactual and architectural repertoires reflect the same symbiotic relationship as the natural resources they depend on, especially in those regions where palm is less abundant and access to the oases and its resources is more limited.

ACACIAS

The acacias, which constitute the most widespread and most utilized family of trees, are, as the summary in table 2.1 shows, the most common construction timber resource. Few trees have been utilized by humans in such a broad range of contexts, and, among many of the nomads of Africa, the acacia lies at the

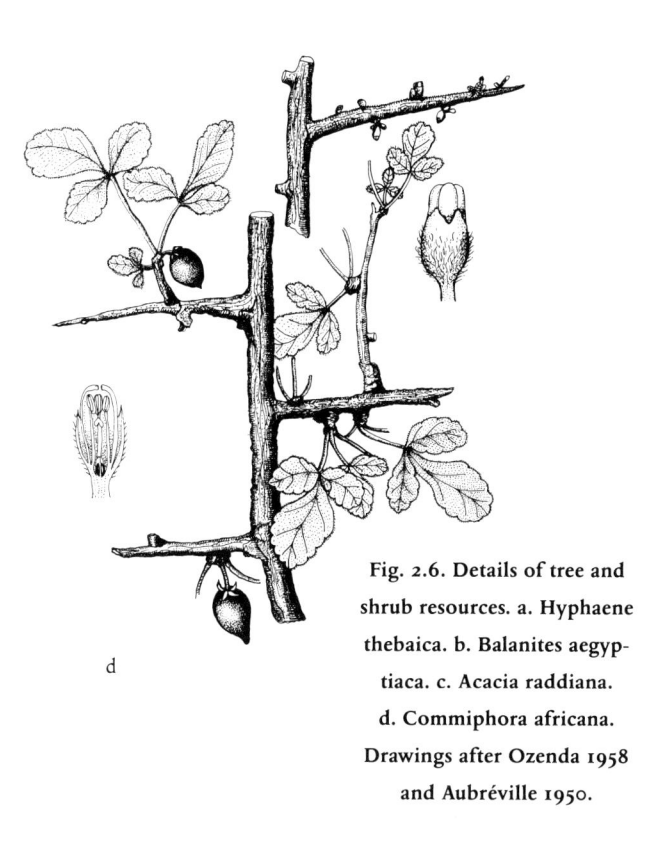

Fig. 2.6. Details of tree and shrub resources. a. Hyphaene thebaica. b. Balanites aegyptiaca. c. Acacia raddiana. d. Commiphora africana. Drawings after Ozenda 1958 and Aubréville 1950.

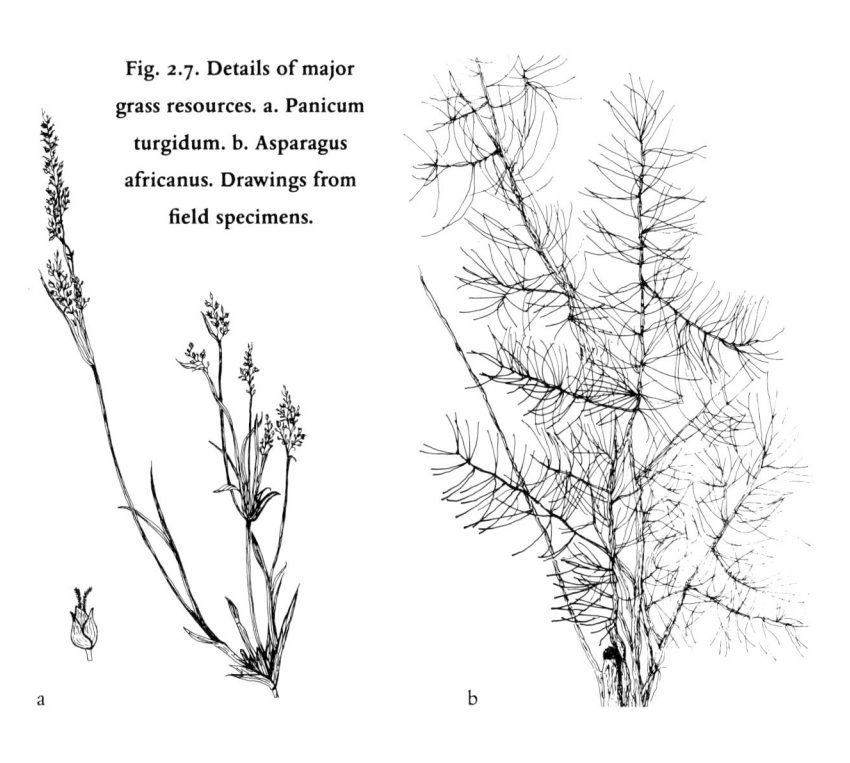

Fig. 2.7. Details of major grass resources. a. Panicum turgidum. b. Asparagus africanus. Drawings from field specimens.

basis of domestic economies. In addition to providing fodder for herds of camels and goats, it is a source of gum arabic, its bark provides the fiber for ropes and basketry, and it is used as fuel and for a wide range of construction purposes, including boat and house building as well as saddle parts. In addition, it is used for a broad spectrum of medicinal purposes, both traditional and contemporary. Leaves and flowers are used for dyes, soaps, and perfumes.[9]

Root systems. The acacia is so widespread because it is so adaptable. Its drought-resistant mechanisms, which surpass those of its community neighbors, allow it to occupy very diverse environments (see fig. 2.4). The acacia's mechanisms of water-loss reduction and the intensification of water absorption derive in part from the unique way in which its root system responds to topographic restraints, soil conditions, rainfall, and groundwater. The spread of subterranean growth is far greater than what is found above ground, namely, its crown. Other factors that account for its prolific presence are the extraordinary growth of its taproot in some environments, its ability to generate a shallow subsurface root system in others, and the hardness of its wood grain. Architectural and artifactual creativity among the nomads rest in particular on the exploitation of its unique root system.

Few treatises on wood and timber consider roots as an exploitable resource, with the possible exception of the fine woodworker who draws upon its unique grain patterns, or the bonsai master who recognizes its inherent role in creating an existential beauty. While all commercial handbooks on wood or timber address the botanical and structural properties of stems or trunks, roots are considered only as appendages to stems.

Root and shoot systems in all woody plants (including acacias) grow differently and serve different purposes in maintaining viable growth; as a consequence, their respective structural properties vary considerably.[10] The cellular structure of roots is denser than the stems and branches that grow above ground, so that the grain more closely approximates that of hardwoods. However, roots are easier to bend than

Environment and Space

Table 2.1

Trees and shrubs

Acacia arabica: bark is used for tanning leather

Acacia bussei: roots are used for bent armatures; camel mats; the bark is woven into water vessels and braided into rope; tanning; fodder; firewood

Acacia ehrenbergiana/seyal: roots and bark are made into rope and cord; the bark is used for tannin, the core for shepherds' staffs

Acacia nilotica: branches used for bed rails; hatchet handles, tent pickets and lateral bars; bark for tannin; pestles; tools

Acacia raddiana: roots are used for bent house arches and tent pickets; wreaths of bent roots are worked into saddles; bark is used for rope; branches are bent into tripod supports; trestles

Acacia senegal: roots are used for shallow bowls

Acacia tortilis: roots and bark are made into rope and cord; roots are used for shepherds' staffs; the core is used for the pommel and cantle of the camel saddle and house poles

Acacia vereck: roots and bark are used for cord; branches for kraals

Argania spinosa: tent poles

Balanites aegyptiaca: tent poles; tanning

Commiphora africana: bed feet; ridgepieces; sections of the camel saddle; carved wooden containers; carved violin bodies (soundboxes)

Commiphora spp.: carved water containers; stools; camel bells

Cordia sinensis Lam.: bent house arches

Hyphaene thebaica: fronds and folioles woven into all kinds of baskets and mats; cordage; sacks

Salvadora persica: trunks are used for poles; branches are bent into arches for barrel-vaulted tents

Tamarix aphylla: straight poles are used for wooden tent structures; wooden saddle frames; roots are used for bent arches

Zizyphus mauritiana: shepherds' staffs; tent pickets

Zizyphus spina christi: kraal fencing; tent poles

Grasses

Asparagus africanus Lam.: bark used to braid basket containers

Panicum turgidum: stems/stalks used for woven windbreaks, bed mats, and mats for tent sidewalls

Sansevieria: mats and rope

---

hardwoods because they have an elongated cellular structure and no appendages; roots do not develop the extensive outer cambium layers (i.e., bark) that characterize stems. Hence they are far more pliable (fig. 2.8). On the other hand, the stems and shoots serve better for vertical loads and carpentered construction systems because they are stiffer and more rigid. Thicker trunk diameters are more easily obtained above ground than below ground and provide a more suitable carving material.

The most intriguing counterpart to the distinction between stems or shoots and roots is the division of labor that attends their respective exploitation. Although there are some exceptions, things that are bent come primarily from the roots; things that are straight or carved come from trunks or stems and branches. All the woodworking the woodworkers, blacksmiths, and carvers undertake make use of branches and stems or trunks above ground; the exploitation of roots below ground for pharmaceutical, nutritional, and most nomadic building purposes is in the hands of women. Bending is in the hands of women; carving is in the hands of men.

Tannin and leather. In the context of nomadism, it would be amiss not to elaborate on another of its long-standing, primary uses, tannin. Among the African nomads, where animal skins are a primary material resource, it would be nearly impossible to transform skins into a utilizable material resource, into leather, without tannin (fig. 2.9). Tannin is most readily obtainable from the bark of various acacia species. Although the technology of tanning is outside the immediate scope of this chapter, the relationship between tanning technologies and vegetal resources is essential for understanding the architectural and transport technologies. This relationship also helps explain the color preference for red, whose dye is obtained from acacia bark, and the pseudo-tanning processes that often enter into the marriage ritual, as discussed in the next chapter.

PERCEPTION

Nomadic acumen in recognizing the most minute features on the landscape, the most subtle changes in color and hue, is remarkable. Skills at tracking, a keen sense of observation, and a wide, vast knowledge of geographic and topographic features, of desert flora

Fig. 2.8. Acacia roots are visually indistinguishable from the tree trunk around which they are being bent.

Fig. 2.9. A goatskin stretched and pegged on the ground.

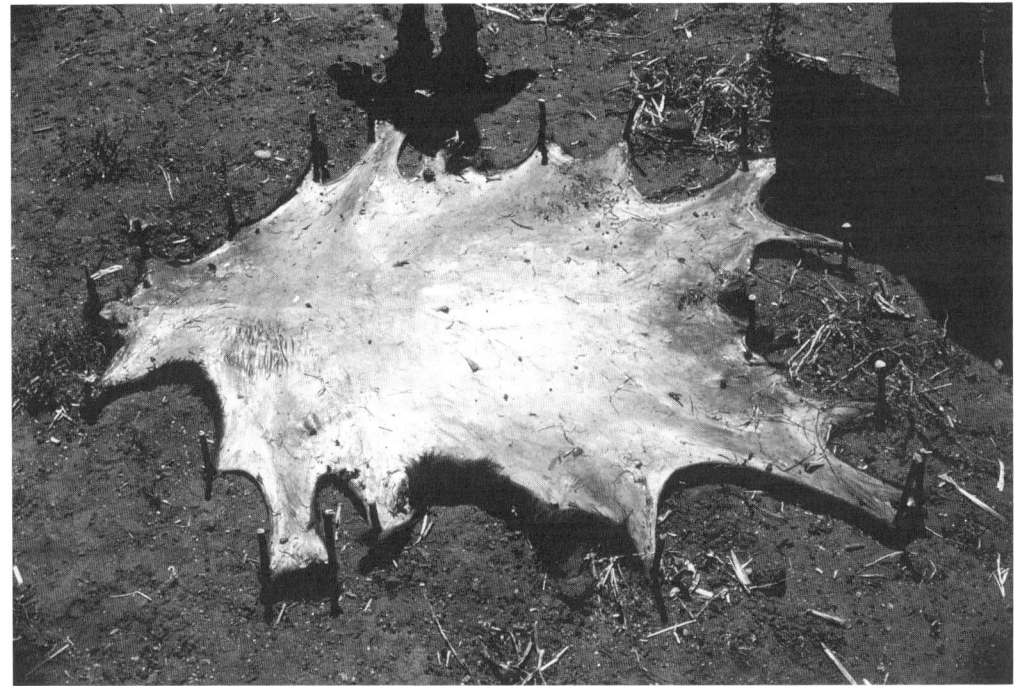

and fauna, coupled with astronomical knowledge, the uncanny sense of where he or she is in space, evoked the admiration of the earliest European travelers.[11]

How do the nomads acquire such an extraordinary knowledge of their environment, and how do they use that knowledge to make decisions, perform tasks, and record and give directions, when seemingly they have maps only in their minds? In normal surroundings, the individual utilizes a redundancy of perceptual cues associated with a knowledge of spatial relations, in a well-established spatial schema that enables him or her to judge the nature of his or her surroundings and to move about them efficiently. In the desert, spatial knowledge comes from a variety of additional sources; direct perceptual experience during navigation becomes a collection of memories from both experience and shared information. The memory of landmarks, route representations, and configural representations are, for the nomad, three very specialized types of spatial knowledge.

We perceive our surroundings as a continuous whole, from near to far, as well as to the side and behind us even when not immediately visible. The principal aspects contributing to the perception of the "ground" on which objects are situated are changes in size, brightness, and surface texture; these changes also enable us to locate objects and thus make judgments as to their distance. When making judgments of distance, however, observers select certain features of the environment as affording clearer, more reliable information than others (Vernon 1970). It is this selective choice that varies with the physical and cultural context.

As we perceive a landscape receding into the distance, receding parallel lines converge as the retinal projection of objects become increasingly smaller with increasing distance; surface texture becomes condensed; clarity of outline and detail, as well as brightness, decrease; color becomes less saturated, changing finally to blue-gray.

Further, texture, brightness, and shadow contribute to the definition of perspective and three-dimensionality. The texture gradient of a receding surface provides a cue to distance: the more textured a surface is, the closer it appears to us. The apparent brightness of an object may be related to its apparent distance: brightly colored objects tend to stand out from the background, and appear to be relatively nearer than when there is little color contrast between them and their background. Shadows (i.e., differences in brightness on different sides of an object) also may contribute to the impression of three dimensions.

Other features of perceived surroundings related to the gradients of linear and aerial perspective are the interposition of objects, the covering of further objects by nearer ones, and height in relation to the level of the eyes (Vernon 1970). But how relevant are these features for the nomad when there are virtually no parallel lines receding in the distance, when there are few nearer objects to cover further objects, and few high points on the horizon? It seems reasonable to assume that particular environmental features assume much greater importance in the nomad's system of spatial orientation. In turn, shadows, color preferences, topographic references, and textural variation serve as the references for conceptual and cultural rationales.[12]

SPATIAL ABILITY

Spatial ability refers to how people represent knowledge about space, how they use and organize spatial information, how they think about space and about objects in space. Obviously such an ability is essential to nomadic survival as well as to architectural aptitude. In Western psychology, one test used to measure such ability is based on the concept of "field-dependence" and "field-independence," terms that refer to how people rely on visual and other information in making judgments about their own orientation and the orientation of objects in space.

In recent decades, this particular test has been used to measure personality traits as well as differences in cognitive, or learning, styles.[13] The test itself involves the use of a bounded field, usually rectangular, and a pair of rods. Subjects are asked to locate the rods as they please on the bounded field. Placing the rods within the bounded field, or in some relationship to the lines that define it, implies field-dependence; placing the rods askew so that they do not relate to the sides of the bounded field, or projecting them beyond it, implies field-independence. These preferences are then related to behavioral patterns and to personality. How applicable is such a test of spatial mobility in a nomadic context, where linear boundaries are so unique and visual representation so limited?

One of the suggested variables that might explain differential spatial ability, developed in the field of cross-cultural psychological research, is ecological adaptation. This hypothesis states that differentiated cognitive styles are facilitated by the nomadic lifestyle which demands a constant reappraisal of the environment and constant perceptual re-articulation of a little-differentiated environment (a snowscape, a savannah, or a desert). The necessity of finding one's way around in a highly uniform terrain must place a great premium on investment in the articulation of space during child development. For example, in a comparative study among the sedentary Temne and the nomadic Eskimo, marked differences were found in field-independence, in articulated concepts of space, and in the linguistic complexity of geometrical-spatial terms (Berry 1992). Similar, even more relevant results were obtained in studies among the children of cattle-keeping Logoli and Gusii agriculturalists in Kenya (Nerlove, Munroe, and Munroe 1971) which demonstrated that greater physical distance from home was related to a higher performance level on an intellective task requiring spatial ability.

The ecological hypothesis is reinforced by another study of field dependence-independence which found that Navajo children were far more field-independent than American children and possessed greater cognitive-perceptual skills such as "disembedding" (the ability to distinguish a scorpion or a snake from its similarly colored background, or a camel or a house from its natural environment), a highly adapted cognitive skill essential for survival in an extremely harsh environment (Dinges and Hollenback 1978). It was also suggested that perhaps language itself, which reflected the tendency to match objects on the basis of form or material rather than size or color, may be the strongest cultural factor for explaining heightened field-independent performance. This particular ability appears to be relevant to weaving completely from memory, in which the duplication of intricate rug patterns (by Navajo and African weavers alike) requires remarkable cognitive abilities in separating individual patterns from the total design. The nomadic building process is also analogous to weaving: the duplication of intricate structural requirements also involves the integration of individual patterns into a total design.

The same studies that argue for an ecological hypothesis not only suggest that nomadic peoples, regardless of the degree of nomadism they engage in, have a more acute spatial ability than do sedentary peoples; they also reveal that in the development of spatial abilities, environmental experience may be one of several unintended learning processes contributing to gender differential in spatial perception. Among the numerous cross-cultural studies that report a difference in cognitive style between males and females (men tend to be more "field-independent" and women more "field-dependent"), the difference is far less marked in nomadic than in sedentary societies. These studies are particularly relevant because of their relationship to problem solving, decision making, and control over the creation and use of their built environment, all of which lie at the basis of architectural design and involve gender-discrete roles in nomadic architecture. When one considers the various aspects of labor and labor time involved, then the relatively greater freedom of women in more nomadic societies, which may result in fewer sex differences in the performance of differentiated tasks (Van Leewen 1978), takes on even more import.

The most persuasive psychological tests are those that argue an ecological model on the basis of reality, rather than a clinical milieu. In a study of the development of gender differences in spatial ability vis-à-vis environmental influences (Archer and Lloyd 1985, citing Sciann), it was found that gender differences, inconsistent in younger children, increased with age. Higher performance on spatial tests was associated with certain kinds of experiences that are relevant not only for spatial tasks but to the gender-specific assignment of these tasks. The ability to judge distances accurately is one such spatial attribute that is greatly improved through experience. As a result, nomads, in reality, would always ultimately achieve a much greater spatial ability than sedentarists; and nomadic women would come close to matching the spatial ability of nomadic men. Perhaps, because their repetitive house building and transport experiences involve, in addition, the approximation of Euclidian space schemata (often used in clinical tests), they might even outmatch their male kin if tested in the field.

While human space perception may be biologically rooted, the level at which it functions in an individual is part of the learning process of acquiring components that make up the cultural milieu in which the individual was raised, that is, human experience from the viewer's perspective (Hallowell 1955). Ultimately it is the viewer, or the subject, who forms the locus of the schemata or code. The directions or paths extending from the subject (the Ego) create the areas and domains of space and their boundaries, but boundaries can be viewed on different levels, extending from one's own anatomy to the furthest reaches of the spatial imagination. Spatially (like temporally) coordinated patterns of behavior are basic to the personal adjustment of all human beings. We use spatial disorientation to measure and define psychosis.

The concept of "space" is often used metaphorically to evoke the idea of an unbounded or unlimited extension in all directions, but the concept is defined and articulated in terms of boundary and direction, which in turn consists of lines, points, or surface planes experienced through the senses, whether these be visual, aural, or tactile.[14] Behavioral and conceptual space cannot exist independently of these physical surfaces or extensions of line which constitute boundaries, but, for many nomads, architecturally defined physical boundaries (as we know them) do not exist.

THE MEASURE AND REPRESENTATION OF SPACE

All human beings define and experience space and its boundaries through movement. Human movement, in turn, links the concept of space to the natural environment—to topography, to the sun, moon, and stars, wind direction—as well as to the built environment and to time. Myths, value and belief systems, and visual, qualitative metaphors may vary from one cultural context to another, but the use of physical metaphors and journeys through space and time to validate themselves in space is common to all cultures. Although the need to order our spatial universe directionally via movement appears to be universal, the choice and interpretation of coordinates and/or axes that define spatial order vary historically and culturally.

Even the most cursory perusal of early Arabic travelers' itineraries (their surface navigations across the deserts of Africa) reveals the extent to which the measure of space was defined by movement in time. For example, the fourteenth-century geographer Ibn Battuta measured distance in temporal stages. "Traveling at a camel's pace," it was the number of days' journey from place to place, that is, point to point, that established his itineraries and his geography.[15] Many centuries later, the French explorer Guillain (1856), traveling on the East African coast, also commented on how his guides estimated the length of the route between two points by the number of days or hours it took to traverse those routes. Recent studies (Gast 1963; Laugel 1957) discuss the importance of "distance-time" correspondences among the Tuareg Kel Ahaggar as indications for water points and the quality of pasturage. The measure and evaluation of distance continue to be made in terms of time, as any visitor to the African desert will quickly discover when they inquire about the distance from one village to another.

The nomadic use of astronomy and topography as guides also evoked frequent commentary by early Arabic as well as European travelers. Caravans traveling from Sijilmassa in southeastern Morocco to the sub-Saharan entrepôts were led by guides who found their way in the desert by observing the stars and the mountains. European travelers on the Mauretanian coast commented on how "all understand well the course of the stars and reason from them pertinently" (Labat 1728, 1:290). En route to Timbuktu, Caillié (1830, 2:361) expressed surprise that "it is by this (the North) star that the Arabs are guided in all their excursions through the desert . . . though without a compass or any instrument for observation, they never go astray." Traveling in southern Algeria in the mid-nineteenth century, Duveyrier (1864:426) observed: "The sun and the stars serve the Tuareg in distinguishing four cardinal directions." Similar observations and praise were voiced by European travelers and explorers traveling in East Africa in the mid-nineteenth century.

Obviously the framework of spatial reference used by Arab travelers and African nomads involved sets of categories (e.g., time and astronomy) for assessing, appraising, and measuring space different from those used by the Western world. But, lest we forget, Western concepts and percepts of space are also culturally and historically defined.[16] Conventions of linear perspective (by which the Western world represents space and which lies at the basis of its visual imagery) by no means define visual reality; it is a particular constructional approach to the representation of pictorial space in the post-Renaissance Western world. Perspective drawing as we know it today was, and still is, absent from various non-Western cultures. One has only to recall not only Islamic and Far Eastern conventions for the representation of space but the world corpus of ethnographic documentation to realize how egocentric the azimuthal systems for representing, measuring, and to some extent defining space and its boundaries are. Cross-cultural as well as historical studies have shown that individuals in other cultures have had, and continue to have, difficulty in perceiving distance in pictures because they have no experience with the reproduction of perspective by converging lines.

Medieval cartographers found a new way of representing space with the development of the azimuthal compass and portolan sea charts (see pl. 2). A portolan sea chart is a systematic mapping method for negotiating sea routes. The portolan consists of a stretch of shoreline (i.e., a boundary line) over which is superimposed a so-called compass rose, a starlike polygon of sixteen points connected by lines, the directional points labeled with the four winds associated with the four cardinal directions. These maps did not provide information about distances; rather they showed *the directions* of space (Edgerton 1976). The Western world assumes that there are "fixed" north-south and east-west axes in the external world (cardinal directions), and we use Euclidean geometry to organize ourselves in space.

In other times and among other cultures, directions in space may not be set by the same fixed coordinates. If fixed axes and geometric grids are less relevant to the nomadic schemata of orientation and of space than to Western, sedentarized cultures, then what is more relevant? Many non-Western cultures, among them the African nomads, use a "hodological" (from the Greek *hodos* = path) system. They do not orient themselves in space according to the physically measurable cardinal directions, but along paths or directions in response to topographic features in the natural environment.

More than half a century ago, a remarkable linguistic study (Brosset 1928) called attention to the fact that Saharan nomads, rather than using cardinal points to orient themselves in space, use "sectors of orientation" whose direction is variable, depending on the position of the observer (fig. 2.10). He observed, first, that, although the words designating the directions of orientation are practically the same in the various regions he traveled, these words generally designate different directions among different culture groups; second, that these indicated directions are not determined by our "objective" cardinal directions; and third, that directions indicated by the same observer using the same word frequently change. In sum, cardinal points and directions are not fixed at infinity as they are for the Western world.

An intriguing example is the etymology of the word *sahel*. The original meaning in literary Arabic is "bank of the sea or river." It was traditionally used to designate the edge of the desert *(sahara)*, but was subsequently extended to gravel plains and the northern margins of the Sahara. Logically, in the south Algerian dialect of Arabic, the term is indeed synonymous with the "south," but in the dialect at Timbuktu it means "north" and for the Reguibat of Morocco it means "west."

How, then, did the term *sahel* acquire its present English and French reference to a semi-arid geographical region of north-central Africa south of the Sahara desert, even though no Arabic-speaking population uses the term in a bioclimatic sense? The birth of its

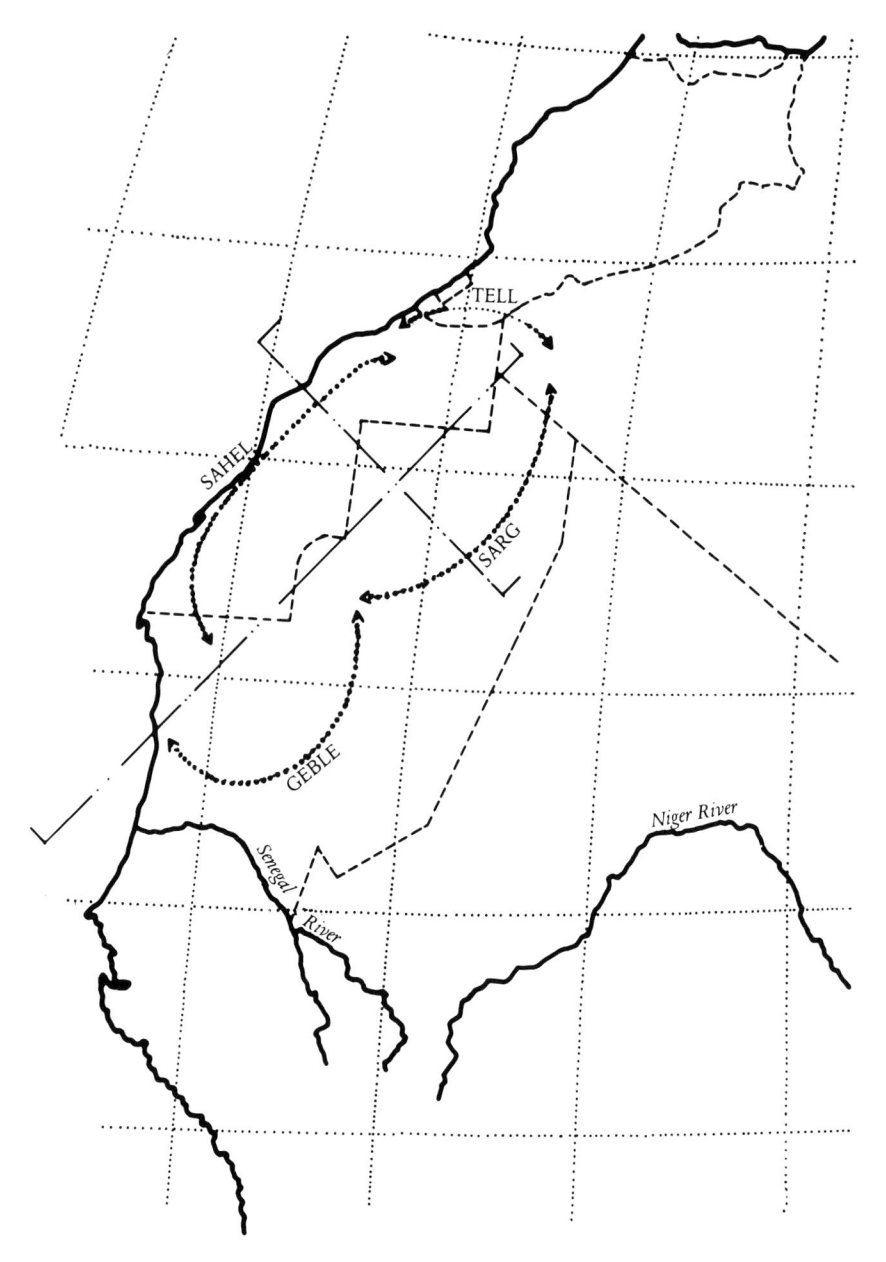

Fig. 2.10. Orientation in space. Drawing after Caro Baroja 1955.

ences in 1900, was not inadvertent; it was the consequence of a different cultural perspective on spatial definition. If Chevalier had arrived from the north (as the explorer Barth had, a half century before), he would have received quite a different response. Imagine the disorientation of a research novice with a newly acquired command of literary Arabic or a localized dialect of it, on arriving in a Saharan country!

The nomadic cultures documented by Brosset were historically involved in caravan trade over various routes across the Sahara desert. Thus, for the Reguibat nomads, *sahel* is the direction of the Atlantic Ocean because their interest and experience lay in two economic poles: Goulimine, Morocco and St. Louis, Senegal. Hence they conceptualized their territory as bounded on the west by the ocean and on the east by a "no-man's land" of vague interest and legendary history. For them, the term *tell* indicates the country where one buys rugs, where one deals in slaves. The direction from St. Louis to Kayes, which their use of the term *geble* indicates, is the country of trade with the Europeans. In principle, the Reguibat nomads establish directions according to the essential routes that govern their economic life.

Among the Tuareg, terms for these variable cardinal points or "sectors of orientation" are equally dependent on the position of the observer (Bernus 1981b). The *sarg* at Timbuktu which sits on the northern bank of the Niger River designates the south, but south of the Niger River, the same term designates the north. Obviously, the regions designated by *sarg* vary according to the observer's reference point.

The African etymology of the term for the direction of Muslim prayer, *kibla,* is related. In literary Arabic, *kibla* = south. For the Syrians, *kibla,* roughly east, was the azimuth of Mecca. In the dialect of the Fezzan, *kibla* = north; in the south Algerian dialect, *kibla* = east-southeast; and at Timbuktu, *kibla* = west. The fortune of the original word, and by extension its use designating the orienting wall that establishes the direction of Mecca for prayer, did an about-face in the course of the subsequent Islamized Arab expansion into Africa.

It is not only the direct experience of the terrain that assists the individual in building up his or her

Western meaning was in a *quid pro quo* (Bernus 1981b, citing Theodore Monod). At the turn of the century, when the botanist Auguste Chevalier arrived in the region of Timbuktu from the south and, pointing north, inquired about the region in the direction of the desert he was told, "It is the *sahel*," that is, the north. The Western adaptation of the name of a geographical direction for a bioclimatic zone, which originated in his note on the subject to the French Academy of Sci-

Fig. 2.11. A camel caravan moving in the desert.

spatial world. This knowledge is also crystallized in language through the customary use of place names, that is, toponymy. Topographic features of prominence on the earth's surface provide one of the most tangible points of reference and are one of the richest sources of village and town names in African history. Under nomadic conditions, where a more dynamic relationship with the natural environment exists, conspicuous land forms such as mountains, hills, ravines, elevated plains, and gullies provide a particularly rich nomenclature because topographic features and wild vegetation constitute the most important attributes of the environment in the nomadic experience of space (Saad 1987).

For example, from Hassaniya (the Arabic dialect with a Berberized vocabulary spoken by the nomads in southern Morocco and Mauretania) come the names of sites such as Atar (*adar* = "the foot" of the mountain); Ouadan (*wadan* = masculine form of the Tuareg *tadant* = Boscia senegalensis, a tree); Tagant (*tagant* = forest, bush); Zemmour (*azemmur* = wild olive tree); Adrar (*adrar* = mountain). In contrast, among the sedentarized agriculturalists in the Sudan who speak the neighboring Soninke language (Azer), it is the social features that determine the etymology of site names. Walata is a Berberization of the Manding *wa-la,* a place *(la)* where a shelter *(wa)* is found. Similarly, Biru, the ancient name of Walata, is the Soninke plural of *bire,* a simple flat roof of straw placed on supports, usually found in markets (Monteil 1949).

MOBILITY

Seafarers acquire spatial knowledge from navigational experience (Thorndyke 1981). Nomadic behavior, like navigational behavior, is also goal-directed, and memory consists of actions in context and in time. Thus navigation in both situations bears comparison. Like the seafarer, nomads gain their sense of direction,

Environment and Space

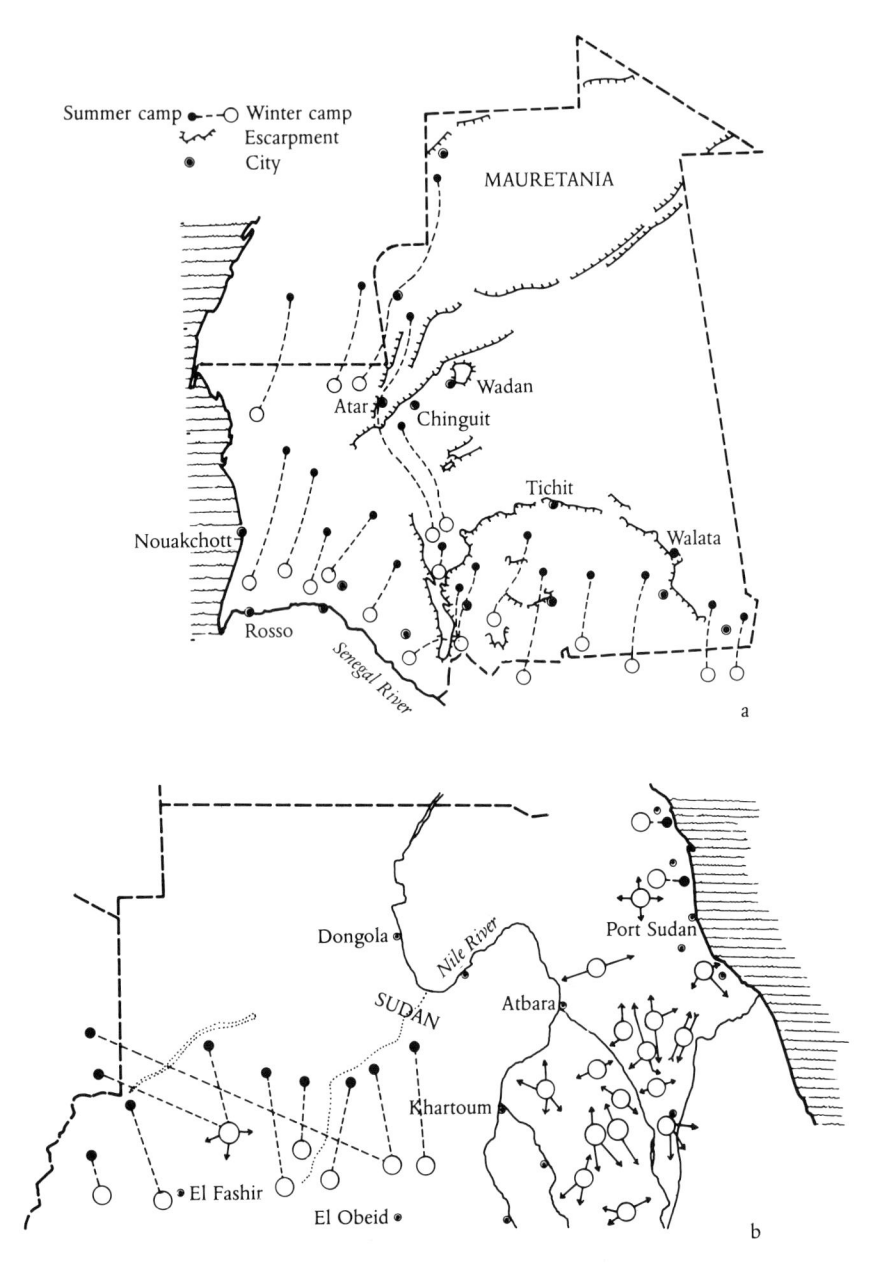

Fig. 2.12. a. Mauretanian transhumance. b. Transhumance in the Nile-Sudan region. Drawings after Toupet and Pitte 1977 and Schiffers 1971–73.

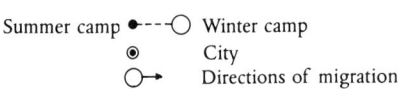

their knowledge about the space around them, from navigational experience. Natural environments on the sea and in the desert seem to have visual similarities. On the sea, there are no fixed landmarks other than the coastline, no topological cues to guide the mariner. The horizon stretches in a seemingly endless line. And wind is as important for the nomad as it is for the seafarer; only the path of the sun from east to west and the changing wind suggest direction. The desert too offers an uninterrupted horizon line in which sand dunes, like ocean waves, are constantly shifting (fig. 2.11). There are few planes offering dark and light contrast among the subtleness of natural colors and hues. But the nomads thus have an advantage over the seafaring mariner: topographic features remain fairly constant over time. Itinerant land-dwellers, in contrast to seafarers, are able to calculate by fixed reference points other than the stars and magnetic north.

The documentation of nomadic cultures the world over acknowledges the importance of pastoral mobility and movement in space (fig. 2.12). With few exceptions, however, there are no studies that specifically address the structuring of their spatial frameworks (Johnson 1978). In addition to the long-distance routes traversed in the course of caravan trade, annual migrations between summer and winter camps are common to nomads. The axes of nomadization are effected not only over vast distances but over constantly changing terrains, in East as well as West Africa, in the Sahel as well as across the Sahara.

A most poignant and dramatic illustration comes from an account by a Rendille elder, Arnirkh Bulyar, of the transhumance of his family's camp over a seventy-one-year period (Grum 1976). In the course of these years between 1903 and 1974, the family camp traveled almost twelve thousand miles in more than 270 periodic moves that extended from the northern shore of Lake Turkana to the Kenya-Somalia border (fig. 2.13). The area they crisscrossed was over a hundred thousand square miles. Distances traveled in each move ranged from seven to one hundred eighty-three miles, and each move involved a number of intermediate stops during which camps had to be pitched and struck.

The majority of the moves were dictated by basic

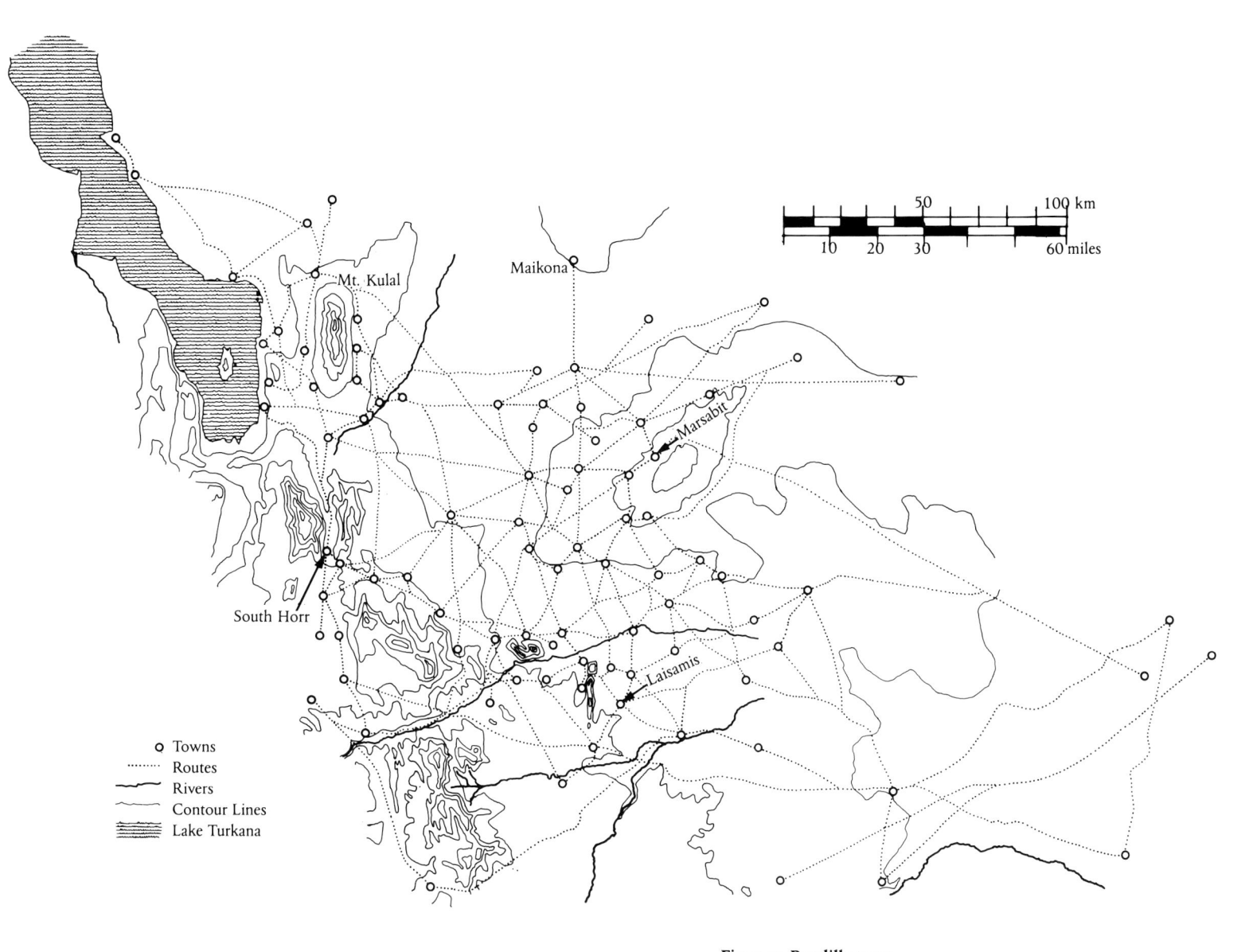

Fig. 2.13. Rendille transhumance over a seventy-five-year period. Drawing after Anders Grum.

herding needs in response to annual seasonal changes —the availability of forage during short and long rainy seasons and dry seasons. Other, time-related social events that dictated moves included rituals *(sorriyo)*, such as circumcision, marriages, and the investiture of elders, and skirmishes with neighboring nomadic groups. The points of reference used by the Rendille elder in describing linear movement on the landscape and the itineraries of the camp were couched primarily in terms of topographic place names: mountains, lakes, valleys, flora, rivers, and water sources.

The documented moves were obviously not one-day moves because, on average, a nomadic camp will move about ten miles a day, so the number of times a camp and its houses were pitched, struck, loaded, and unloaded was far greater than the indicated moves shown on the map. The detailed itineraries for each move reveal almost twelve hundred stopping places over the seventy-one years. Rendille houses were dismantled, reassembled into pack saddles and palanquins, ridden in, disassembled on site, and rebuilt into houses again almost twelve hundred times.[17] The peregrinations of monarchs and courts in European and African history, noted in Chapter 1 above, barely compare with the itineraries of one Rendille family!

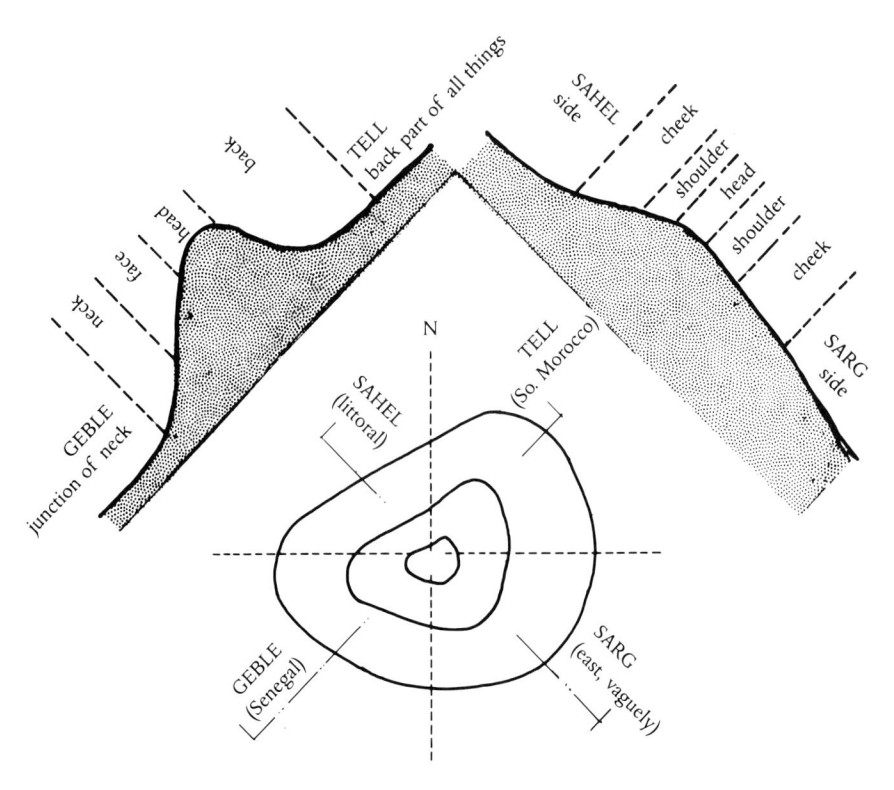

Fig. 2.14. Anthropomorphic orientation to topographic features. Drawing after Monteil 1949.

BOUNDARIES

Although topographic features seemingly represent fixed points in space, they are not forever: rivers dry up, trees fall down and disintegrate, dunes shift, even mountains disappear in the wake of earthquakes. There remains an element of uncertainty in the nomad's mind, more so than in built environments that are fixed in space and able to offer the sedentary dweller environmental cues that remain constant over time, because nomadic existence entails special considerations regarding social and territorial boundaries. For the African nomad, the articulation of spatial boundaries and the delineation of the built form is a recurrent *process,* involving a set of transformations in time. Transportable building systems and a multifunctional repertoire of material goods constantly dissolve and reconstitute building boundaries.

To understand nomadic boundaries, we need to think of the built environment and its spaces in the context of movement: the movement of people, the movement of one's world of material culture. Movement, however, is also an essential part of our cognitive experience. For the nomad, "home" cannot be understood except in terms of journey, just as space is defined by movement. Nomadic built environments consist of a minimal habitat that unfolds in a continuum of repetitive reconstruction and movement through primarily natural environments devoid, for the most part, of built markers. Built boundaries of enclosed space exist only within the narrow confines of the transient, oft-ephemeral "temporary" camp and its transport systems. By comparison, travelers in a sedentary world are only temporarily homeless, yet each time we embark on a journey we carry small articles from home along with us and enact personal rituals in their placement so we can evoke a feeling of temporary security from a "temporary" abode.

ANTHROPOMETRY

Nomads also combine the physical aspects of topographic features endowed with directional names with anthropomorphic associations (fig. 2.14). If one were to draw the plan of a mountain, the sides are named in

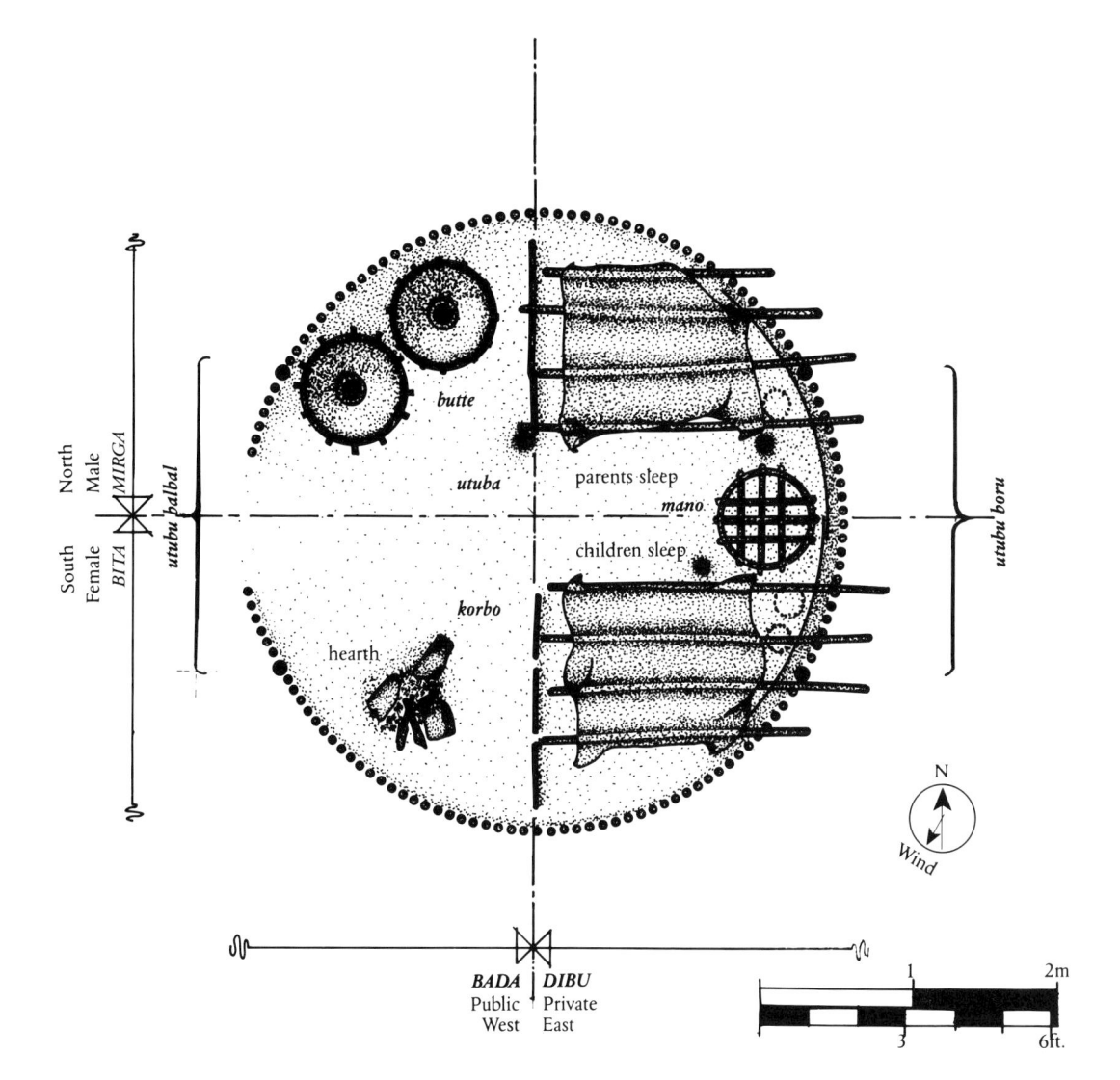

Fig. 2.15. Plan of a Gabra tent illustrating the tight geometry inside the enclosed space. Drawing after field measurements.

relation to the "sectors of orientation" that Brosset pointed out above, rather than the cardinal directions of north, south, east, and west. But these directional planes also carry a set of anthroponyms: "head" for the top of the mountain, two shoulders, face, and back for its upper reaches, the neck for its lower reaches, and, at the base of the mountain, the junction of the neck with the surface plane on the ground and the back of all things.

Given a topographic feature of some sort (e.g., a hill or butte), there is thus a whole nomenclature linking orientation in space (i.e., its directions) to the attributes of the human body. For the Mauretanian nomads, this topographic model is considered as a living being, and as such is always oriented face to the *geble,* back to the *tell.* Cutting a slice through the *geble-tell* axis, the different parts of the hill or butte are named in relation to the direction in question (see fig. 2.10).

The language of African space continues to be expressed in the measures of anthropomorphy. Gast (1963) notes how the Tuareg Kel Ahaggar use the measure of a man with upstretched arms for ascertaining the depth of wells. This same measure, in combination with that of an elbow length, is also applied in the judgment of the length of straw mats that surround the skin tent.

Environment and Space   41

The centricity of the human body, and by extension its symmetries and asymmetries, are essential to psychological well-being and self-identity. Centricity is also built into the nomadic schemata that organize space and its boundary systems. By recognizing that our body is the center and source of the spatial matrix through which we experience the world, we can better appreciate the nature of extensions from it and the reciprocities transacted between body and environment. The body matrix not only gives us our essential knowledge of space and its boundaries but carries with it a palette of meanings, memories, and rhythms that endow architectural space and its boundaries with meaning.

CONTINUITY IN SPACE

Nomadic architecture is a creative *process,* not an end product: nomads constantly recreate and reinforce physical boundaries through social, behavioral mechanisms. The process involves an interface of transport technology and building technology, of the continuity between gender creation of the technology of transport and gender creation of the building technology. These in turn interface with the nature of social use involving both technologies. For example, among a number of African nomadic cultures, the palanquins and houses that constitute bounded built space for the nomads make use of the same architectural elements. The mats, screens, structural poles, and armature ribs that constitute the house are reassembled and transformed into the palanquins within which women and children ride. The elements are collected, processed, and manufactured by women; they are assembled into a house form, struck, and reassembled into a palanquin/litter in which women ride, and are unloaded and reassembled by women. Hence both houses and transport systems are an extension of the gender division of labor in nomadic societies. There is, therefore, a gender division in space and its boundaries which constitutes a continuum from creativity to usage.

Contrary to general thinking, the nomad's home is not temporary. The space it contains is permanent, even though, as a moving volume, it is not fixed permanently in space. Its "permanence" is in the minds and behavior of those who build it, from the repetitive reassemblage and reconstruction of the architectural elements into an almost identical assemblage at each new point in space. The continuity in this process extends from one's hand to the furnishings or immediate relationships between oneself and one's physical environment (e.g., sitting, bending, lying down), to the house, which gets its dimensions from the more extended bodily movements, to the house surrounds, which social interaction determines or dictates, to the landscape of the natural environment beyond.

THE GEOMETRY OF SPATIAL ENCLOSURE

The way in which the awareness of the symmetries of the human body are integrated with topographical space into a geometry of spatial organization is strikingly illustrated in the houses built by the Gabra nomads (fig. 2.15). The mat-covered armature frame tent is a volumetrically bounded space, whose interior is geometrically ordered into a system of quadrangular spaces by using the body matrix as a model to provide the spatial referents so essential to psychological security and mental health.[18] It is, however, a "moving center," a closed circle within which this set of spatial relationships remains constant and in which, as Leach suggested (1976), predictable activities could be controlled and carried out. The closed circle provides, for the nomad, the only place in which constancy (and predictability) can be maintained in a continually changing physical environment. Its tight geometry establishes the controllable dimensions of space so essential to mental health. It is an anthropomorphic framework encoded in the built environment of contained space. The visually perceived surroundings form a kind of framework to which the position of the body and of other objects is related; and the main coordinates of this framework are the horizontal and vertical dimensions of space.

By way of summary, the "enclosure," the tightly bounded container in which one lives during a journey in space, evokes another analogy between seafarer and nomad. In a seagoing vessel, the two foci of existence and experience are *within* the container and the broad limitless expanse of ocean *outside* it. In the nomadic context, the two foci are the house interior with its proximate surroundings and the broad expanse of desert landscape outside it. However, for the nomads, there is a surrogate for the focus on a container, the house-transformed-into-palanquin in which outside space is experienced in transit when the nomadic camp moves from one site to the next. The peripatetic nomadic existence forces us to think about two different, albeit closely related forms of enclosure: the house and the palanquin or litter in which women and small children move. It is no coincidence that the marriage ritual engages both house creation and palanquin creation. It is no coincidence that the technologies brought to bear in both are so closely related.

3
THE CREATIVE PROCESS

The major nineteenth-century architectural theoretician Viollet-le-Duc is familiar to many, but few in this generation have reaped design inspiration from his approach which sought the origins of architecture in the laws of reason. For Viollet-le-Duc, style was the close accord of the imaginative and reasoning faculties—the effort of the active imagination regulated by reason (Hearn 1990:215). To design, he insisted, the architect must before all things take account of the elements that will affect the work: "every part of an edifice or construction should have its *raison d'être*."

Viollet-le-Duc's primary rule regarding materials was to employ each of them in a manner appropriate to its distinctive physical properties. "Composition should have reference to two elements—the material made use of, and the processes that can be applied to it. The first condition of composition is a knowledge of materials and their proper manufacture." In contemporary terms, it is the nature of materials and the act of working with them, the relationship between process and expression, the content of form and the meaning of function that shape and mold the environment. Perfection of technique can, in itself, be an expression of the spiritual.

Viollet-le-Duc's theory was not too distant from the tenets of Islamic architecture in which applied science and technology are inseparable from art. Given the overwhelming Islamic allegiance in the African nomadic world, the analogy seems particularly appropriate. The Arabic word *sina'ah* means both technology and art. It is in turn related to the word for creation *(sun')* (Nasr 1976:249).

The essence of nomadic architecture lies in the process of creation, not the end product. Inherent in this process is the interface between transport technology and building technology, and the continuity in the process which involves labor, that is, the skills involved in its creation and perpetuation, and the behaviors, that is, the rituals that bring it into being. The same components of the built environment are used in both technologies. Saddles, litters and palanquins, structural poles, guy lines, and bentwood arches make use of the same natural resources and architectural elements. The mats, screens, structural poles, and armature ribs that constitute the tent are reassembled and transformed into the palanquins that women and children ride in.

Architecture becomes an assemblage of arts in which the materials and techniques derive from the same natural world that the artist or architect wishes to communicate his or her feelings about. Ensembles of artifacts, ordered in a spatial construct, are sets of transportable components, repetitively and often sequentially transformed in the manner of a sine curve over time. The artifactual repertoire is multifunctional, serving building and transport needs alike, and architectural repertoires consist primarily of natural materials: leather, fabric, woods, and grasses.

The elements are assembled into a house form, struck, and reassembled into a saddle-litter-palanquin in which

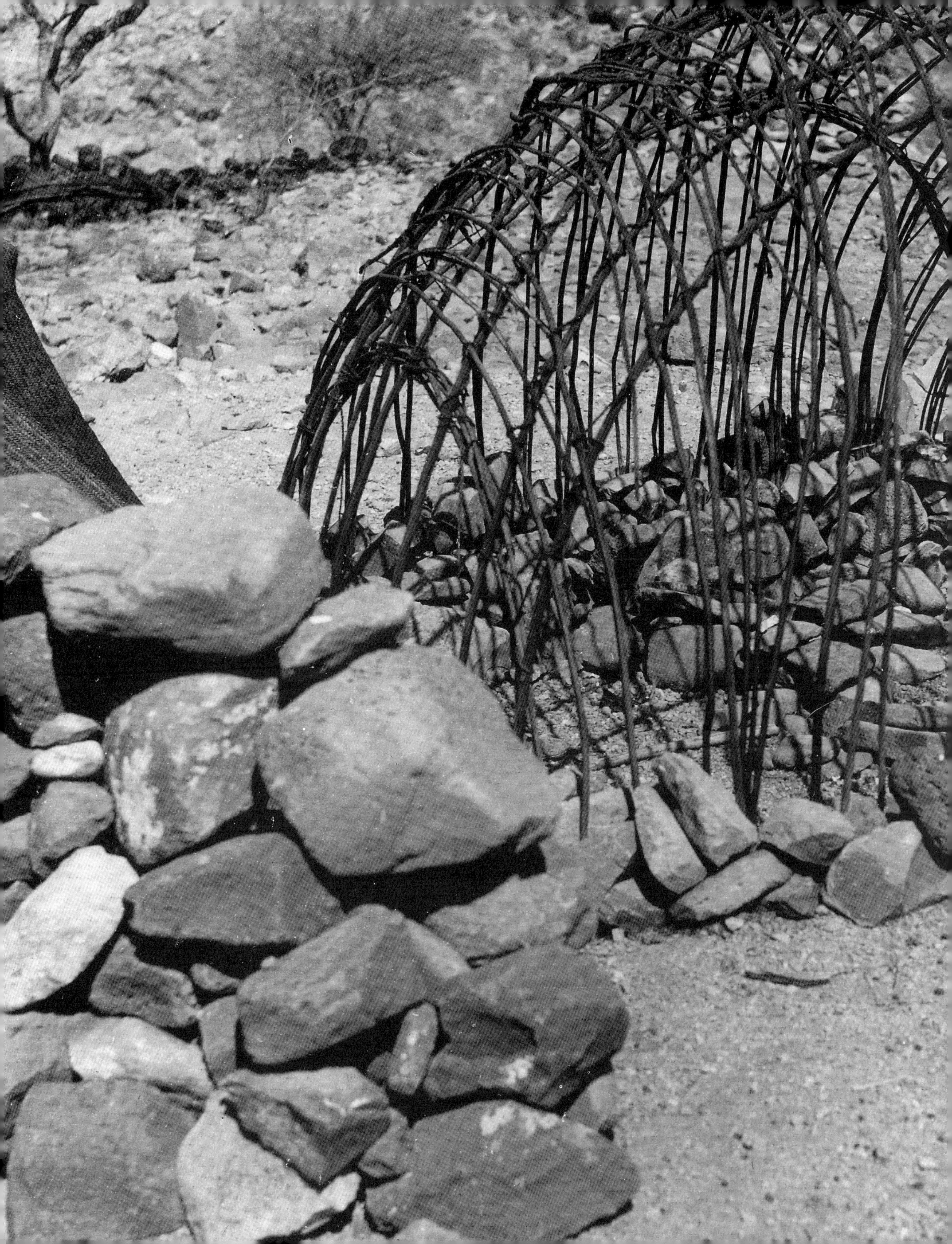

women ride and which women unload and reassemble. The same elements are collected, processed, and manufactured by women. Hence both houses and transport systems are an extension of the gender division of labor. The gender division in space and its boundaries extends, in a continuum, from creativity to use.

The creation of both house and transport are inherent in the rituals of marriage and birthing. The ritual is what endows the built environment with meaning. Belief systems and cosmologies that provide poetic and moral judgments for the rationale of environmental response are in turn expressed through, related to, the ensembles of artifacts and their structure in space, to orientation in space, and to the interface between tent and transport technologies.

Building is a balancing act in which the laws of structure are poised against the laws of gravity. These are easy laws to understand because our own bodies feel the same forces that act upon a building or a saddle. The same principles of construction that hold true for building structure can be applied to the human body and the pack animal. All three are structural systems.

The human structural configuration is determined by the weight and composition of body materials, by gravity and motion. The human body as well as that of animals consists of tensile systems of sinews, a pneumatic system of muscles stretched over a skeletal system of bones in a membrane covering. The basic assumption, the simple logic upon which a building (and a person or animal) is predicated are the forces (the loads and resistance to them) in equilibrium: balance.

Logic suggests that if the same laws operate for the human body, the pack animal, and the building, then there will be a set of coinciding technological and structural principles for all three. This commonality leads me to subsume buildings, transport systems, and human behaviors within one creative process.

Fig. 3.1. a. A Somali tent at Kismayo, Somalia, 1888.
b. The transformation of a Gabra tent (in the background) into its transportable configuration.

TECHNOLOGY OF TRANSPORT

If the Rendille pattern of transhumance is any measure of nomadic life, then the amount of time nomadic families spend moving in space is paramount and transport is a prerequisite. Women spend as much time in and around their vehicles of transport as they do in and around their houses. The saddle-litter-palanquin is a "home" away from home, a "tent within a tent."

Transport technology is a structural challenge to ingenuity and creativity as precisely as building technology is. The same problems must be addressed when transporting a load or enclosing a space: balance, the distribution of forces (i.e., weight or wind), movement, uplift, rigidity. The same limited natural resources are available to the transportation engineer and the building designer: vegetal materials, grasses, leather, and fabrics.

Further, the same gender-discrete skills involved in one design solution are applied to the other, and—indeed, what initially started me on this particular journey and now impels this train of exploratory thought—in many instances, such as among the Gabra, Rendille, and the Somalis, armature tents are transformed, volumetrically and spatially, from transportation systems into building systems (fig. 3.1). The dismantled, packed-for-moving, camel-loaded housing components stand adjacent to or are set against a backdrop of reassembled houses beyond. Structural ties, behavioral and social ties, conceptual and emotional ties link the transport and the building systems.

In pursuing the history of transport technology, I found that, more often than not, historic interpretations were colored by the experiences of those who rode camels but rarely loaded or unloaded them. In historic context, however, the ethnographic overview suggested that it might be more revealing to explore nomadic transport and building technologies by starting with the pack saddle rather than the riding saddle.

This very simple distinction between riding and pack animals is not original. Cauvet (1925–26, 1:558) heuristically implied it when he defined the pack camel ("chameau de bât") as one that is used in the slow transport of heavy merchandise, material, or persons, and reserved the term "chameau de selle" for those that carry one or two persons at a more or less rapid pace without being heavily charged. Others, including the nomads themselves, consider such differences in evaluating the value and performance of the animal.

This particular distinction becomes clearer with the definition of saddle, litter, and palanquin that I have chosen to use. The saddle is the basic framework used to put a load (either baggage or people) on an animal. The litter is a framework above the saddle, a bed, a couch, or a stretcher in which a person can be carried. The palanquin is the armature built up over the litter to support an enclosure such as a canopy. Thus all palanquins are composed of a buildup of parts: (1) the saddle itself; (2) the framework above it, that is, the seat, or the support for the load; and (3) the canopied armatures. Du Puigaudeau's analysis of Hassaniya transport systems (see Chapter 4 below) makes these same distinctions even clearer.

Different usages require different types of harnessing. Historically, there have been three basic types of harnessing technologies: (a) for draft animals; (b) for moving goods (caravans), housing, and belongings (migrations or pilgrimages); and (c) for moving individuals (communication, raids, warfare). Further, if one looks at this tripartite set of functions—draft, pack, and riding—then the historical vignettes in a previous chapter, which may have appeared haphazard to the particular reader, fall more logically into place.

When camels are used as draft animals, their hump presents no problem, but when used as pack or riding animals, then saddle design becomes a challenge because the camel's hump (i.e., its convex back) cannot support a heavy downward load without deforming. A heavy load can be carried only if it is distributed so that the skeletal structure, either through the front legs, hind legs, rib cage, or all of these, bears the brunt of the burden. To carry the burden requires a structure that will straddle its hump in contrast to what is needed when it is used as a draft animal; furthermore, the weight needs to be balanced on both sides in response to the front and back anatomy of the animal. The particular morphology of a dromedary with one hump, whose strength is linked to the forequarters and whose center of gravity is near the axis of the withers, differs from that of a horse or a donkey.

The loading system as well as the anatomy of the animal imposes a system of horizontal and vertical axes which the structure of the saddle must respond to[1] (fig. 3.2). The camel can carry a heavier load than a horse can, but the load is limited by the weight it can rise with and it can carry more weight on its

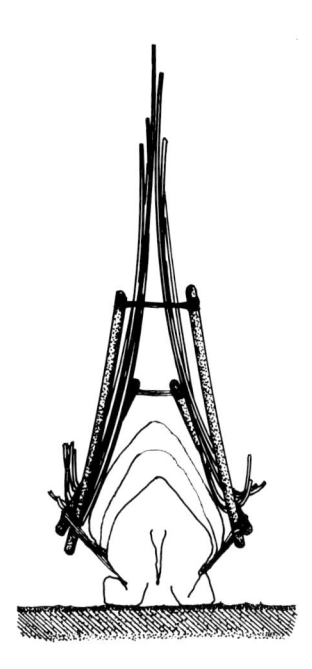

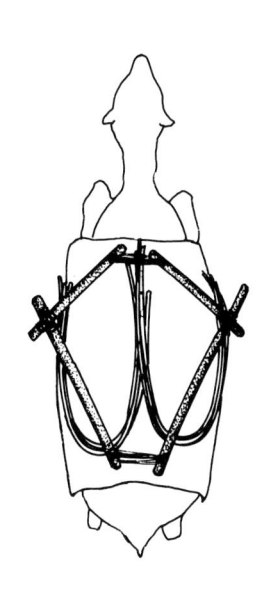

Fig. 3.2. Linear movement, gravity, and balance establish the horizontal and vertical axes on a camel.

withers than on its back. If the load is too heavy, a camel may not be able to raise its hindquarters. Once its hindquarters are up, though, it can always get up on its front legs.

The simplest pack saddle is one composed of only two poles. The two poles, which cross in front of the hump above the withers (representing the tree of the saddle), are held in position by the leather or rope wrapped behind the hump and under the stomach (fig. 3.3a). The two-pole system, when viewed functionally, appears to be a modification of the traditional way of harnessing a draft camel. In Rendille technology, the poles, one on each side of the animal, support a pair of water containers.[2]

What the Somali (and Gabra) pack saddles provide with their two pairs of poles, unlike any other saddles, is a way of transferring the weight from the animal's back down to the ground itself at four points (fig. 3.3b, c). This additional support on the ground not only allows the animal to rise with less weight, but the assemblage of poles making up the pack saddle are crossed at the base and at the top so that the weight is equally distributed, first to the ground and then to the poles; when the thongs around the poles are tightened, they create a pair of rigid triangles straddling the animal. The weight to be carried leans neither in front nor in back, but on the stiff poles that make up the structural triangles. The result is a far more sophisticated structural solution for load distribution than the two-pole system above. It can be compared to a folded parallelogram, adjustable in response to the camel's hump and to the size of the load.

The crossing of two sets of poles is not required when the camel is harnessed as a draft animal. Nor is it required when a horse, a donkey, or a bullock is used to carry loads. The system of adjustable triangulation spanning the camel's hump, which accommodates the particular anatomy of the animal, represents for me an innovative technological leap forward in harnessing the camel as a pack animal.

Among these East African nomads, it is the house, its furnishings, food, and water that constitute the load. In figure 3.3c, the heavier bentwood frames of the Somali *aqal* are slung on both sides of the animal; on rare occasions the lighter framing members will

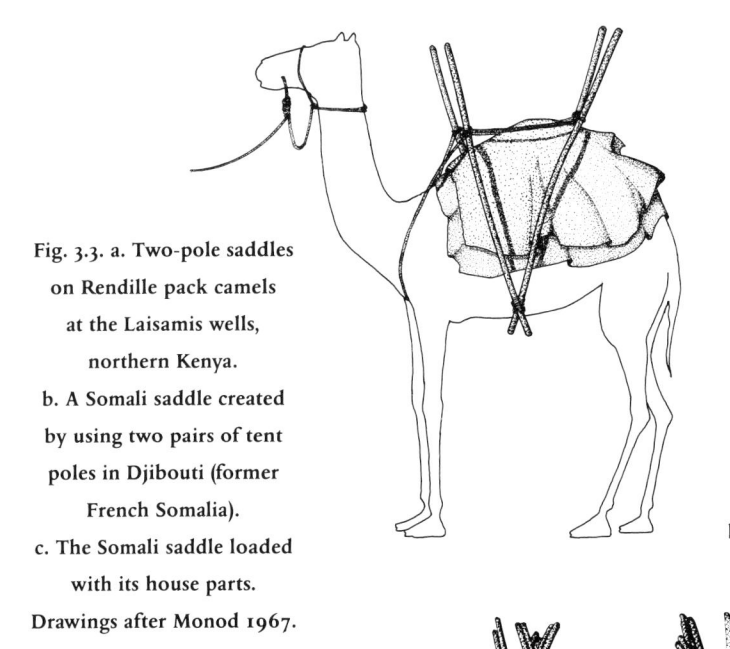

Fig. 3.3. a. Two-pole saddles on Rendille pack camels at the Laisamis wells, northern Kenya.
b. A Somali saddle created by using two pairs of tent poles in Djibouti (former French Somalia).
c. The Somali saddle loaded with its house parts.
Drawings after Monod 1967.

48   African Nomadic Architecture

swing out and above the animal. Among the Rendille and the Gabra (see fig. 3.1b), the house parts ride above the animal, creating a kind of makeshift enclosure. This enclosure is sometimes additionally defined by bending the interior dividing screens of the armature tent over to meet the bent structural members. Somali, Rendille, and Gabra men do not ride camels, and women usually ride them only in the context of a marriage ceremony, when the bentwood members of the armature tent become the framework for a litter. At other times, such litter-palanquins shelter old women, children, and newborn goats during the arduous treks from one site to another.

The prevalent custom of using donkeys as pack animals by some nomads provides additional background for understanding the evolution of transport technology. The northern Tuareg, in particular the Kel Ahaggar and the Dag Rali, saddle their donkeys and use them for riding and pack transport (Nicolaisen 1963:110). In fact, the donkey is generally used for riding by women other than those of aristocratic birth. The bentwood frame *(aruku)*, designed as if it were made to be used for a pack camel, derives from a similar principle (fig. 3.4a). The ends of two bentwood bows are brought and tied together over a pad, so that in fact they could, if necessary, be adjusted to straddle a camel's hump. Tuareg women make them by heating two fresh branches of the Rhus oxyacantha tree over a fire, removing the bark, and bending them into the desired curve with cord. The bent frame is then attached to cushions that rest on the animal's back.

A similar donkey pack saddle is used by the Tekna as well as the nomadic Berbers in southern Libya (Monod 1967) (fig. 3.4b). The two bentwood members are joined across the front and back by two straight, horizontal ties, and another pair of bentwood arches extends out to the sides, forming a kind of cage or litter. These armatures, which rest directly on the donkey's back, accommodate both riding and transport. Not only is the pack donkey saddle thus elaborated into a woman's riding litter, but the bentwood technology used in its creation rests on a woman's skills.

Every subsequent camel saddle design, whether for riding or for carrying loads, bears a structural resem-

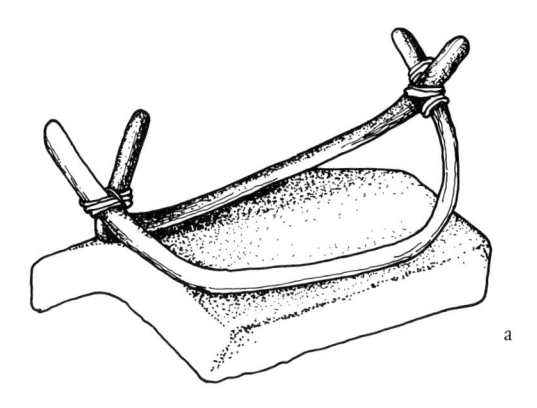

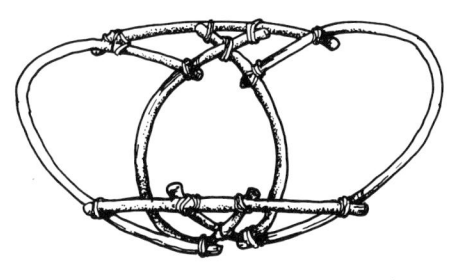

Fig. 3.4. a. A Mauretanian donkey pack saddle. b. A Tekna women's saddle/litter. c. A Tuareg pack saddle from the Tassili region, attached to two cushions of date palm bast. d. A Téda women's pack saddle. Drawings after Monod 1967, Caro Baroja 1955, Nicolaisen 1963, and Chapelle 1957.

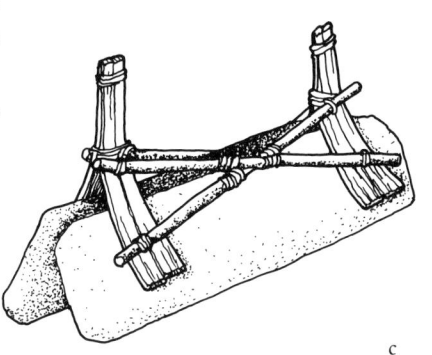

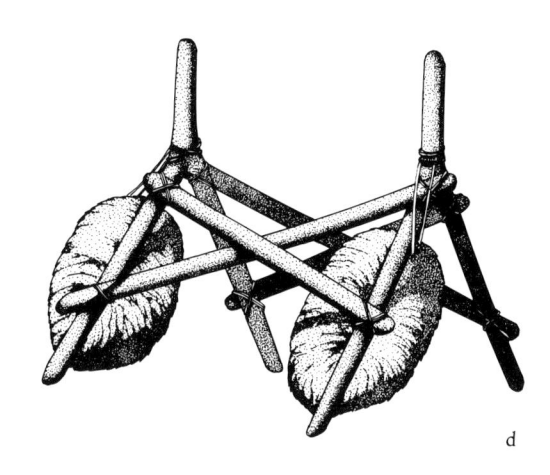

The Creative Process

blance to this basic engineering innovation because it is an offspring. All subsequent litters and palanquins that carry women, as well as goods, consist of a superstructure of one kind or another fastened above this basic design.

The major distinction between the various East African camel saddle structures and those elsewhere is that the framework becomes a permanently assembled entity in its own right; it remains as an assembled unit, and it is the unit that takes on its own symbolic qualities (fig. 3.4c, d). This is done in two ways: in one instance, the forks are composed of two members tied rigidly and solidly together, such as the Tuareg transportation saddle (*tebeyut* or *tkhawit*) made of palm fronds which are only available in the oases. It consists of a frame lashed with thongs, attached to two cushions of date palm bast. In the other instance, a pair of forked poles is substituted, one for the forward part, one for the hinderpart of the hump, in lieu of tying together two pairs of crossed poles or two sets of palm fronds. The forks then need to be tied to each other in order for them to bear any weight. By using wooden members as diagonal crosspieces, the same system of triangulation that provides rigidity to the Somali, Rendille, and Gabra pack saddles is operating for both the Tuareg and the Téda pack camel saddles.[3]

In order to transport the tent and its furnishings, two bentwood frames, through which the mats and the tent poles can be thrust horizontally, are added to the basic armature of the pack saddle (fig. 3.5a). The basic framework used by the Tuareg Kel Ahaggar in southern Algeria and Libya for a canopy comes into being when the same bentwood arches used for the donkey saddle are added to the sides of the structure (fig. 3.5b).

Although northern Tuareg women properly ride donkeys, women of nobility, whether Tuareg or Hassaniya, never ride donkeys; camels are the proper riding animals for them. On top of these various combinations of a pair of naturally or constructed forked poles, more and more elaborate armatures are attached, transforming them into the structural fantasies that characterize the litters and palanquins of wealthier, noble Tuareg women. Among the most complex and intricate basketwork interlace I found was an armature that consisted of three sets of curved bentwood arches: those front and back, those at the sides, and those that rise up vertically. Conceptually, these honor the two sets of horizontal axes and the vertical axis, the three dimensions of volume (fig. 3.5c).

Tristam (1860:68–69) was equally impressed by this same type of palanquin during his travels in the Sahara when he referred to the conspicuous palanquins of the sultan's wives and daughters in their "top-heavy camels, with enormous semicircular hoops across their backs, canopied with white stuff . . . camel-tents . . . formed by three or four wide slips of flexible wood, fastened to the outside of a huge pannier, and then bent over so as to meet the outside of the opposite pannier." Others (Cauvet 1925–26, 1:pls. LXX and LXXI), whose structural complexity I unsuccessfully spent weeks trying to reconstruct, convinced me I was no match for the perceptual acumen or the structural imagination of its creators.

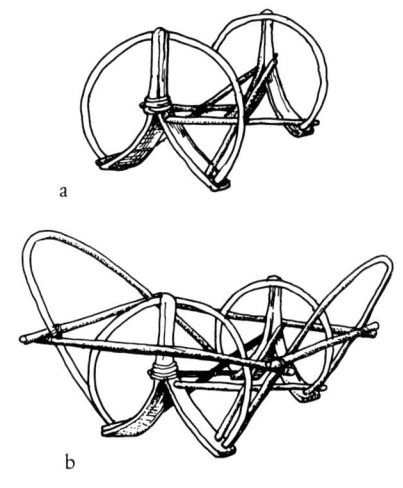

Fig. 3.5. a. Bentwood arches added to the Téda women's pack saddle to transport the tent. b. Basic framework of a Tuareg Kel Ahaggar litter in southern Algeria. c. An "ordinary palanquin *(bassour)* of the simplest model," from Algeria. Drawings after Chapelle 1957 and Cauvet 1925–26, vol. 1.

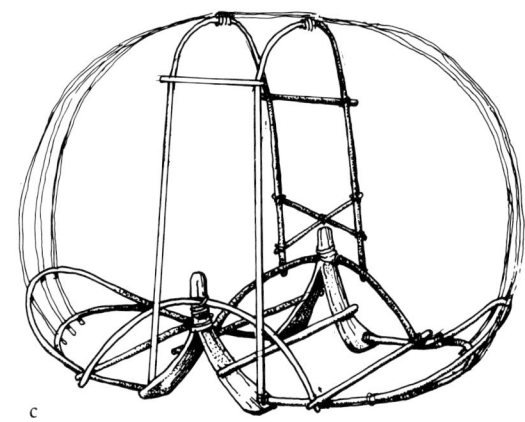

Fig. 3.6. a. Kababish palanquin from the Sudan. b. A Téda women's palanquin. c. A Hassaniya litter. d. The armature of the canopy above it. Drawings after Stein 1981, Chapelle 1957, Domenech 1946, and Monteil 1952.

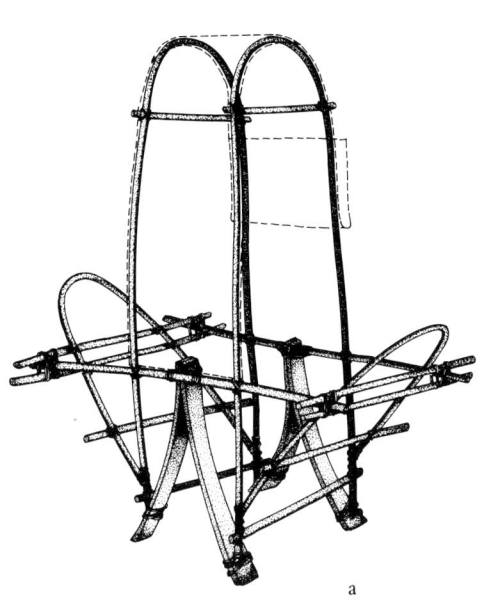

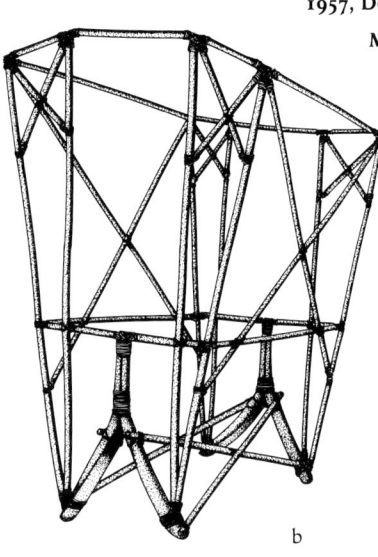

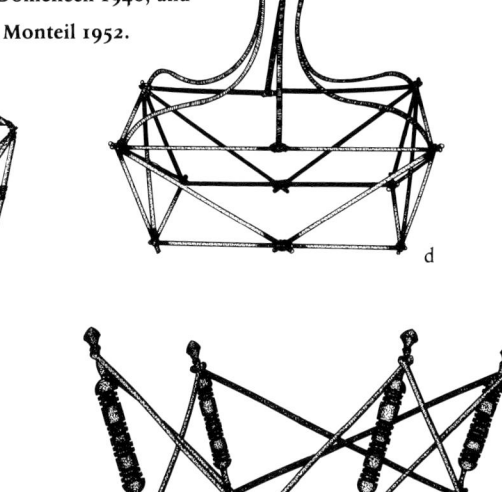

The Kababish palanquin (fig. 3.6a) has a number of points of similarity with the Tuareg palanquin but both depart, in one critical way, from those above: instead of the diagonal bracing that ties the front and rear forks of the saddle together, two pairs of parallel members are used. This critical difference stems from their origin in the traditional riding saddle, a point to which I will return.

The Kababish palanquin differs in a second way. Although the pair of vertical arches rises as high as its Tuareg counterpart, the preponderant use of straight members for reinforcing and the clearly defined square that links the entire armature in tandem suggest another technological innovation: the square is equivalent to a bed, a "bench without feet" (Nachtigal 1971–87, 2:344), over which an arch is formed by fastening bent branches to the long side of the bench.

Palanquin superstructures are built up of two kinds of timbers: straight poles and curved poles. Invariably, the bentwood elements are made from the pliable roots or branches of available trees; the straight poles come from the more rigid sections of trunk and branches of northern hardwood trees. Straight members are processed, often carved, by men; bent members are always made by women.

The assembly of a saddle, whether permanent or temporary, not only requires a perfect knowledge of the camel's anatomy. It also requires a masterly knowledge of knots and the tension of the rawhide stretchers since no metal rivets are used to fasten together the forks and crosspieces. This same knowledge is identical to that used by the woman in fastening together the armature of her tent.

The Téda *adofa* (fig. 3.6b), a palanquin in which the entire framework is composed of straight poles held together with metal fasteners, provides a good illustrative contrast. The square that demarcates the litter recalls the Kababish and the Tuareg palanquins above, but the saddle itself, based on two pairs of diagonals, is seemingly derivative of a pack saddle rather than a riding saddle.

Chapelle (1957:256) has suggested that the artisan who builds it, whoever he might be, may have wanted to imitate the Arab saddle-litter, but did not know

The Creative Process

how, or perhaps did not want to go to the trouble of bending the wood. No information is available on the woods used to fabricate this enormous palanquin cage, but it seems equally reasonable to infer that since these are always fabricated in the Kanem oases by men, neither the resources for bentwood nor the women's skills that dictate alternate styles were available. It appears to be an attempt to emulate, or elaborate on, with unbent poles and straight lines (perhaps in keeping with the same straight poles used in the primary structure of a Tubu tent), the bentwood palanquins of their nomadic neighbors.[4]

The same combined use of straight timbers and bentwood members leads me indirectly back to the palanquin and transport systems used by the Hassaniya (figs. 3.6c, d). The straight, often carved, members used for the litter evolve out of quite a different technology (and gender gestalt) than the canopy armature, constructed of bentwood members, that is attached to it. An even more striking example is the litter illustrated in Chapter 4 below (see fig. 4.12), where the entire canopy structure sits on a litter (constructed very much like a bed in the Sudan) that has been slung across and anchored to the camel's pack saddle. The bentwood arches at the head and foot of the bed echo the same configuration that is attached to the litters above. Conceptually and structurally it evokes the interface between tent and litter: the imagery of the litter as a miniature tent whose main feature continues to be the armature of the bed.

Whether a camel carries a woman, her baggage, or an altar, the same loading problems exist. The model that comes to mind is the Ruala *mahlmal* described by Burckhardt and the *kubba* that accompanies pilgrims to Mecca in which the superstructure extends higher and higher into the air. The higher it extends, the more precarious the ride; but, on the other hand, the taller the armature, the easier it is for those around to see it, so it functions as a banner or standard. It is indeed tempting to suggest that the elaborate framework has, and certainly had in the past, an additional significance, as in the case of the Kababish palanquin recorded by Seligman (see fig. 1.14a), the Tuareg wedding camel recorded by Lyon (see pl. 3), or the very similar one Nachtigal documented among the Awlad Sulayman nomads in the Borku region, Chad.[5]

Balance is equally the key to successful camel riding, as Du Puigaudeau poignantly noted in her early remarks on camel saddlery.[6] Initially camels made poor fighting mounts because pack saddles were insecure platforms.[7] In contrast to pack saddles whose four points of contact divide the weight between withers and the back of the animal, and accommodate a downward thrust, riding saddles had to accommodate the additional force of horizontal thrust, more so under fighting conditions and rapid mobility. In his light saddle, a man is free in all his movements. If thrown off balance, he can leap quickly to the ground, whereas a woman is a prisoner in the shelter of branches and cloth that protect and enclose her. When the animal is used for riding, the saddle must rest on the withers, and an innovative adjustment to the pack saddle, which takes account of the weight of a person in front of the hump and allows for control, speed, and forward thrust, was necessary.

African riding saddles are equally a development from the basic crossed poles of the Somali, Rendille, Gabra pack saddle; they are also derivative of the same pair of forked poles that characterize the simplest pack saddles, but at that point they part company (fig. 3.7). The lightweight Téda riding saddle *(terké)* differs in several ways: instead of diagonally crossing, the connecting members lie parallel to each other, and the pommel is set at a considerable angle to the cantle. This variation reflects the difference between accommodating a rider and accommodating a heavy, inanimate vertical load. The new angle of the pommel was initially in response to the shift in weight from the top of the hump to the withers in front of it. This kind of saddle allows the rider to control the animal at a fast pace without stirrups and reins. The forward thrust of the saddle propels the rider in harmony with the animal's movement.

A man may use this fragile saddle for carrying loads, but it is poorly adapted for this use: it goes out of shape under too heavy a weight, going too deep and pinching the withers. In order to strengthen the saddle, heavier wooden plates (which perform structurally like the diagonal braces of a pack saddle) evolved and were transformed into a seat for a rider. The classic saddle used in the Sudan is no more than a substantial version of the Téda riding saddle with its

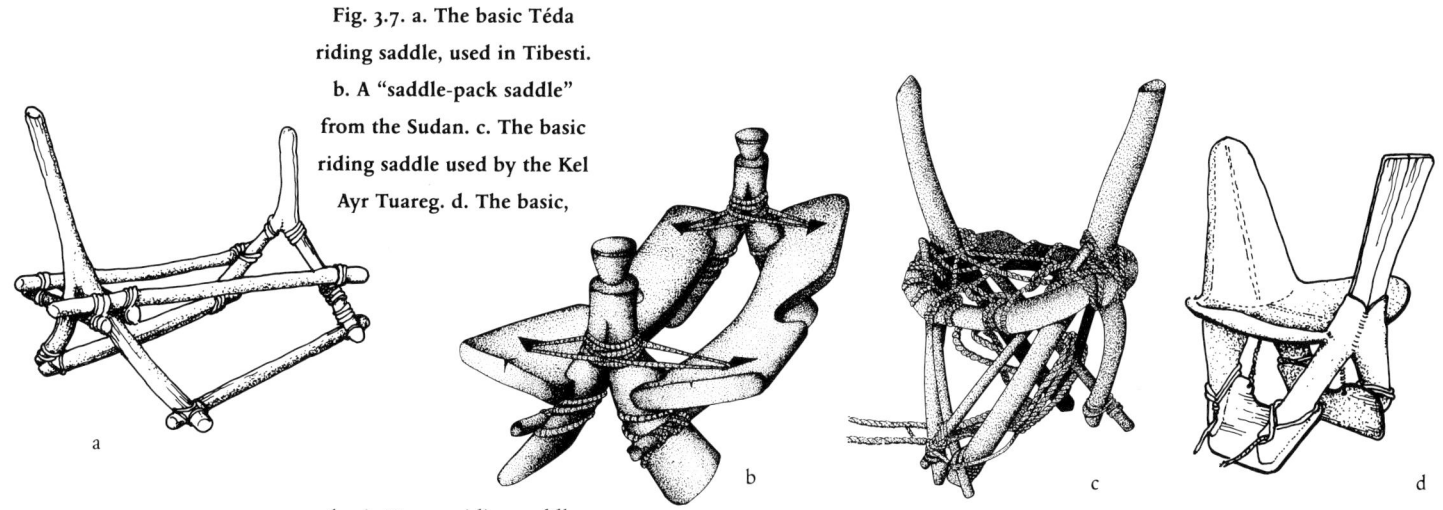

Fig. 3.7. a. The basic Téda riding saddle, used in Tibesti. b. A "saddle-pack saddle" from the Sudan. c. The basic riding saddle used by the Kel Ayr Tuareg. d. The basic, classic Tuareg riding saddle once used more frequently by the Kel Ahaggar Tuareg. Drawings after Le Coeur 1950, Monod 1967, and Nicolaisen 1963.

pair of forked poles tied by means of a set of two parallel bars (Acland 1932).

When al-Omari visited Mali in the fourteenth century, he related that its inhabitants did not know how to saddle their camels even though they rode them (Lewicki 1965:173). His passing remark, in light of the distinction between pack and riding saddles, suggests the rationale for an alternate interpretation for the development of the familiar Tuareg riding saddle.[8]

The simplest, most elementary Tuareg riding saddles (*kantarki* or *delobi*) consist of two forked acacia boughs connected with diagonal members and a bentwood ring for a seat that straddles the hump of the camel (fig. 3.7c). The seat is made of the slender roots of the Acacia raddiana. These roots are bent into a circle, and a net, made of dum palm rope, is pulled taut within the circle for a seat. Logic suggests that this elementary construction is a close cousin of the bentwood donkey saddles above which are also made by the women.

The basic rural riding saddle used by Tuareg herdsmen *(tahyast)* consists of two plates of wood lashed with strips of rawhide and covered with leather (fig. 3.7d). The skin cover is not decorated but serves a structural purpose: laid on wet, the skin shrinks as it dries, solidly pulling the wooden members together into a tight joinery. A sharp eye and close scrutiny will distinguish the same structural principle of a pair of forked poles or a pair of bentwood arches lashed together front and back into a pommel and cantle. Again, it is no more than an elaboration on the earliest pack saddles, donkey or camel.

The far better known, larger, heavier, more elaborate Tuareg riding saddle *(tarik)*, still in use today, is no more than an aristocratic version, in which flat plates have been substituted for bentwood, just as they were in the riding saddle from the Sudan. If one squints a bit, it is easy to visualize the way in which the two curved elements have been brought together in both the pommel and the cantle to terminate in the very well known profile of what has come to be known as the "Croix d'Agadès."[9] It is perhaps no coincidence that the term used by the Tubu *(terké)* for their riding mounts is etymologically so close to the Tuareg term.

TECHNOLOGY OF BUILDING

Nomadic building technologies rest on the same structural principles as their counterpart transport technologies: the equilibrium maintained by balancing the external forces (or loads) with those integral to the building structure. The two pairs of poles are the same poles that perform a critical structural role in house construction, functioning similarly in both the building technology and the transport technology, setting up, in the transposition of one set of structural elements to another, a conceptual synonymity (pl. 7).

In cutting a swath across the African continent, it is possible to trace the same variation in building technology that is possible for transport technology. Although the seemingly limitless stylistic diversity of saddles, litters, and palanquins is matched by the seemingly limitless range of building structures, what is even more startling is the very close relationship between the two technologies. There are a number of parallels between the formal development of saddles, litters, and palanquins and the formal configuration of structural tent types. It is this set of parallels (which ultimately argues for available structural resources and those who exploit them) that dictated the choice of illustrations.

African tents can be broken down structurally into two basic types: tensile structures and armatures. A tensile structure (or, as some would have, a true tent) consists of a center pole (or system of poles) put into compression by stretching a fabric or membrane tautly over it. The tent (a particular type of tensile structure) used by the African nomads rests on the structural interdependence between the pole(s) and the membrane or velum: the poles will not stand up unless the velum is pulled tautly over them; the tautness of the velum (and its support) is a function of the poles below it. Woven fabrics of various kinds function far better than skin velums; not only are they lighter, but because they can be stretched more easily they respond more readily to tensile stress. The armature used by African nomads is an independent structure which can stand up without a taut membrane over it. The mats laid over it are neither structural to any extent nor are they in tension, even though the form or type of mat and its weaving or braiding respond to the demands of the structure.

There is, however, a continuum from the armature in the east and the south to the tensile structure in the north and the west. There is a continuum from a woven velum in the northwest to a leather velum in the west, to an armature using palm leaves, to an armature

Fig. 3.8. a. Danakil tent under construction in 1938, Djibouti. b. The rear reinforcing armature of a Gabra tent.

54   African Nomadic Architecture

using grass matting. It would indeed be tempting to analyze structurally each of these types in detail, taking into account the strength of building materials, the equilibrium achieved in each type of structure, and the external forces acting on it (e.g., winds), but that challenge remains the purview of the engineer.

Rather than overwhelm the reader with the multiple of variations, the chosen illustrations, like those of saddle technology above, serve primarily to suggest a new interpretation. Contrary to those scholars who insist on a simplistic evolutionary sequence from an armature to a tensile structure, it is possible to envision transitions which in some instances went one way, in some instances the other, and in some instances existed (and continue to exist) concurrently.

The armature tent that nomads use stretches as far northeast as former French Somalia. It finds its prototype in the classic "Bantu" hut far south of the desert which so many rural African communities build (Knuffel 1973). The basic construction principle rests on setting up four series of concentric lath arches parallel and perpendicular to each other. The entrance arch, located in one of the four series, is more heavily reinforced. The same procedure is followed by Danakil and Somali builders (fig. 3.8a; see also fig. 9.1). During the course of construction, support poles are used for horizontal resistance as each concentric set of arches goes up. Once the armature is complete and the arches integrated with each other, the armature acts as a unified entity. The support poles are removed, and a central pole is installed within.

There is, however, a critical difference between the stationary Bantu hut and its Somali moving counterpart: it is the rear arch that is heavier, more frequently reinforced, and weighted down with hanging skins and containers in order to resist the fierce northeastern or southwestern winds. The Gabra (and the Rendille), who build a variant on this same basic armature, single out this rear arch structurally and conceptually, linguistically and ritually (fig. 3.8b). Among the Gabra, the *utubu boru* is the first structural component to be put up; it is the wall that receives the ritual marriage containers, that is addressed poetically, and that defines the orientation of the house. The weight and structure of the bed (and its sleeping occupants)

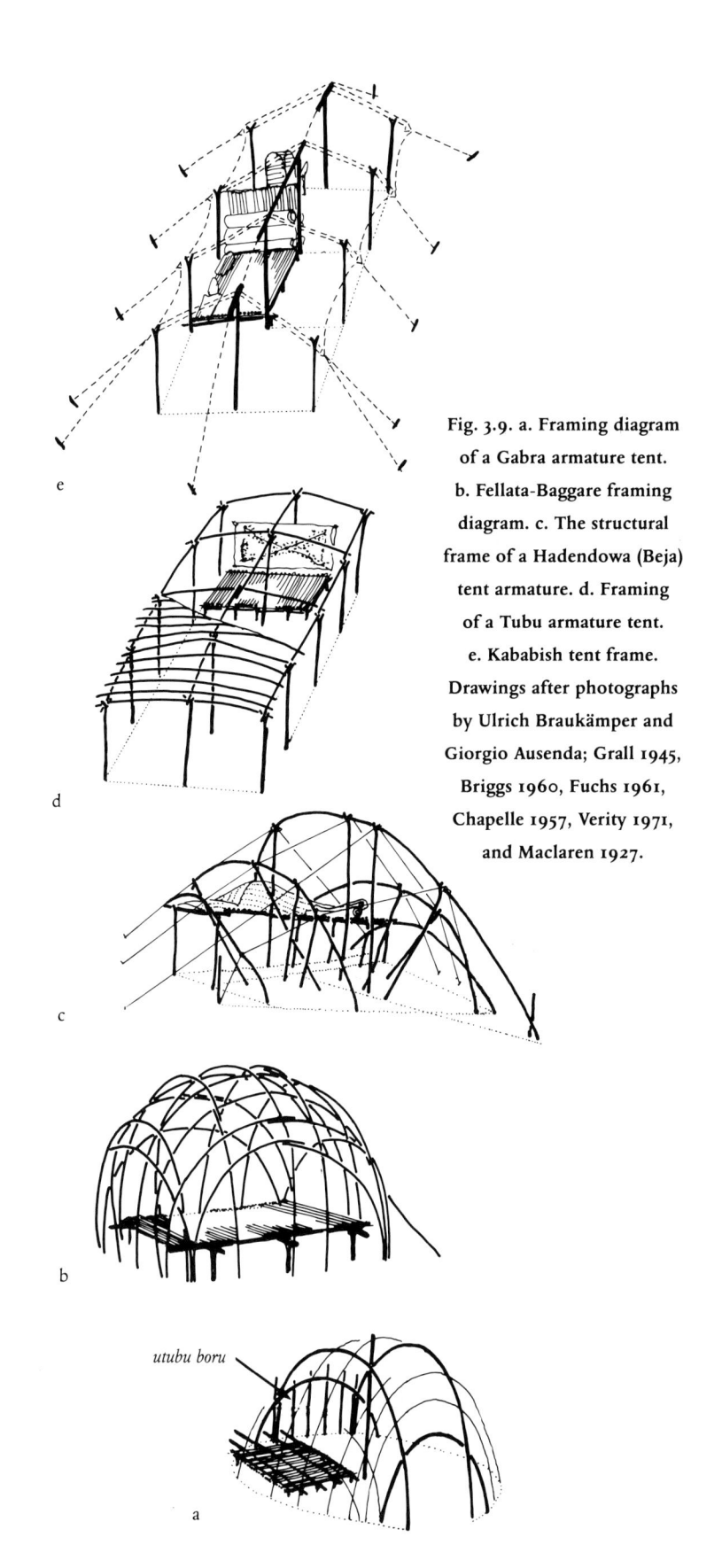

Fig. 3.9. a. Framing diagram of a Gabra armature tent. b. Fellata-Baggare framing diagram. c. The structural frame of a Hadendowa (Beja) tent armature. d. Framing of a Tubu armature tent. e. Kababish tent frame. Drawings after photographs by Ulrich Braukämper and Giorgio Ausenda; Grall 1945, Briggs 1960, Fuchs 1961, Chapelle 1957, Verity 1971, and Maclaren 1927.

The Creative Process

are a critical component in the nomadic efforts to achieve structural stability and wind resistance, and they act in conjunction with the rear reinforcing wall. In the case of the Gabra, bed poles are wedged and tied into the rear wall (fig. 3.9a).

The Fellata-Baggare, who build an armature quite similar to the Somali Danakil above, tie the bedframe resting on its support pickets directly to the armature (fig. 3.9b). As a consequence, the bed is turned into a framework integral with the dome, thus enhancing the stability and equilibrium of the architecture. The horizontal surface of the bed performs the same function as a reinforced vertical wall.

The same poles that establish the frame of the bed and support or increase tension in the armature are used to create the four-pole saddles used to transport the tent and its furnishings. The poles become the structural keys to both the elementary saddle and the architectural assemblage. The bentwood arches in the house become the bentwood armature of the litter framework and occupy the same position in space vis-à-vis other elements, so one could say that the armature of the litter becomes not only a physical but a conceptual synonym to the tent.

The Hadendowa (Beja) tent is, in a bizarre way, a composite between an armature tent and a tensile structure: bentwood arches are used in one dimension, and guy ropes are used to stabilize the structure in the other dimension (fig. 3.9c). In order to compensate for this anomaly, a major bed armature, consisting of forked poles and cross members, is built integrally with the tent armature to provide additional reinforcement to the guy lines and increase resistance to the wind. The long woven mats made by the women and pinned to the guy lines along their long dimension are of little structural value.

The Tubu tent armature is less satisfactory in structural terms than either the domical "beehive" structures or the hybrid Hadendowa tent. The structural poles are not as stable, and because the guy lines (or equivalent bentwood members) which would stabilize the structure are absent, side poles are angled inwards (see fig. 6.5). Among the Tubu, the bed and its assemblage of associated artifacts, including the leather backdrop and the sacks behind it, perform a similar structural function: together, they resist the wind.

Often a proper pack saddle for transport occupies the space immediately behind the bed, so there is still a conceptual association between bed and saddlery, even though the tent poles are not performing the same function. Again, the long woven mats are merely wrapped around and over the tent frame.

Although the Kababish tent (and those of its neighbors in northern Kordofan and southern Dongola) uses a similar system of structural poles along a central axis, it is, in fact a tensile structure, in which a woven velum, consisting of four long strips of camel-hair carpeting, is anchored into the ground by means of a system of guy ropes in both dimensions (Verity 1971; Maclaren 1927). Although the front and side walls may remain open, the back wall, facing the wind, is invariably put up using attractive striped carpets which, like the velum, are spun and woven by women. Against this back wall, centered between the two main poles and their crossbeam *(bahir)* sits the bed, an assemblage of wooden pedestals, bars, and reed mats, often surrounded by wall hangings. Behind it, at the head, is the storeroom for the wife's belongings, including her litter-palanquin. With a little stretch of the imagination, the ensemble can be interpreted as an armature tent within a tensile structure!

In all cases, whether armature frame or tensile structure, the pitching of these tents is always a woman's work. The variations are a result not only of available resources but of the gender-discrete processing or production of the elements of which they consist. The most desirable straight poles, those used for carving, are those found in the northern belts. In the south, where they are scarce and more valuable, bentwood arches, fabricated from the acacia and tamarind roots that women gather in the course of other domestic work, are a logical substitute. On the other hand, the straight poles retain symbolic value; they are a symbol of authority, and, even when unavailable, the system predicated on their use is retained.

This reverse process is perhaps best illustrated by turning, albeit very briefly, to the range of Tuareg tent types and their western and northern Hassaniya affines (fig. 3.10a–e). The leather tents that were traditionally used by the northern Kel Ahaggar, while they appear to be poor structural relatives of those used by the Hassaniya, are in principle a true tensile structure in contemporary engineering terms. But Tuareg women do not weave; they tan leather. Hardwoods are scarce, and acacias, which could be used for arches, are even scarcer on the landscape. In order for the single central pole to remain vertical, and the structure to remain stable and upright, the velum must be taut completely around the perimeter, truly a problem with leather which is less apt to give than a woven velum.

Further south, the Kel Dennek continue to use a leather tarpaulin, but the introduction of two pairs of forked poles changes not only the structural configuration but the interior spatial organization as well: the leather is supported in part by the guy lines which extend over the side poles from the center apex to ground pegs beyond, on the outside. Even if the leather sheet was removed, the structure of poles and guy lines would remain standing.

But the Kel Ahaggar move not only in southern Algeria and Libya, but further south on the other side of the desert, in Mali and Niger. Here, apparently, they build a rather different structure, one that continues to use a leather velum, but the velum is supported by three pairs of posts. The system is similar to those used by other nomadic cultures east of them. There are no guy lines: tension in the leather tarpaulin is maintained by ground pegs to which the velum is directly attached, working in combination with three sets of crossbeams rather than a single pole and ridgepiece.

Some things change; some things remain the same. The introduction of an arch as a substitute for one of the forked poles supporting the central beam does not change the basic structural principle. It is, however, a harbinger of change in the availability of resources and their relevant production skills, which finds ultimate expression in the mat-covered, armature style of a Kel Ferwan tent. The three main bentwood arches are a substitute solution to the three post and beam supports above; the four corner posts are related to the two sets of forked poles which marked the beginning of a transition from a purely tensile structure to an independent armature that can stand completely on its own. But the structure of a Tuareg Kel Ferwan armature tent is in some ways comparable to the Danakil tent with which the story started, and in other ways it is similar to the armature tent built by the Fellata-Baggare cattle herders. Ultimately, it is only by reex-

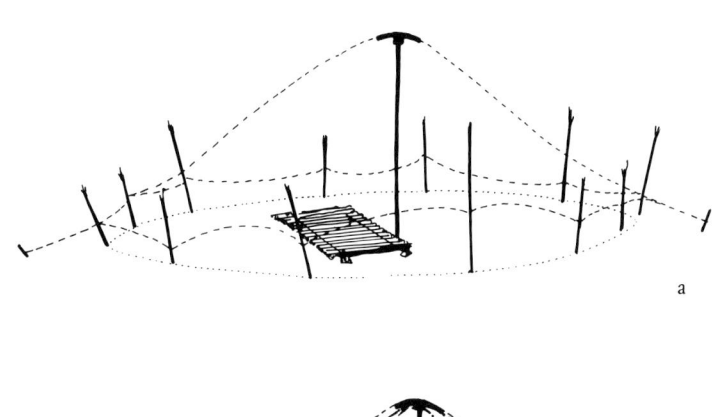

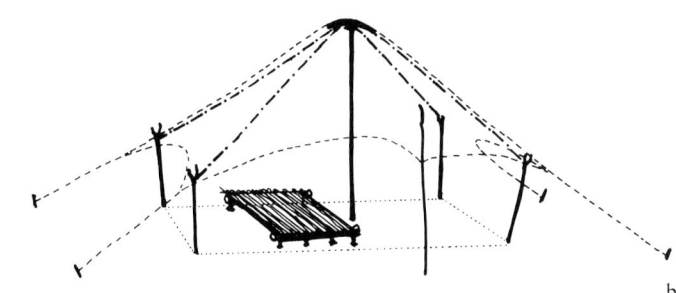

Fig. 3.10. a. Kel Ahaggar leather tent. b. Kel Dennek leather tent. c–d. Kel Ahaggar leather tent framing. e. Kel Ferwan mat-covered armature tent. Drawings based on Nicolas 1950, Foucauld 1951–52, Lhote 1947, and Casajus 1987.

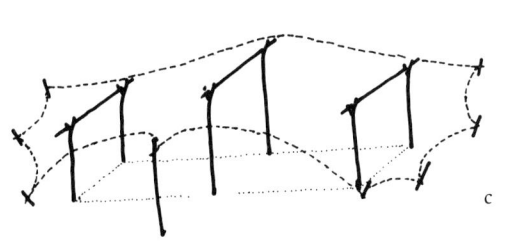

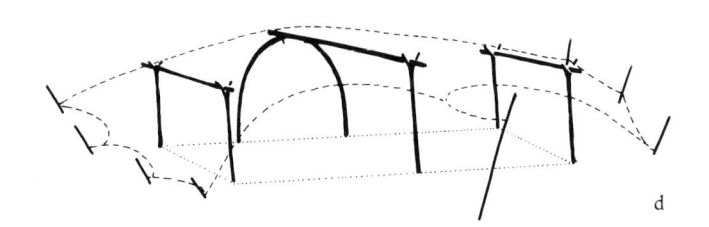

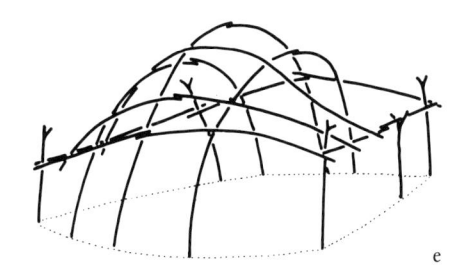

The Creative Process

amining the transport technologies associated with each that the architectural *process* by which it evolved from its prototypical Berber and Hassaniya forebears (who also use only a pair of poles to transport their woven tents) will be clarified.

LABOR VALUE, PRODUCTIVITY, AND WOMEN'S WORK

Most, if not all, of my years of fieldwork in Africa had been spent in the company of men. Men were the guardians, the custodians of both the social structure and the acceptable livelihoods; they were the knowledgeable bearers of the history, the oral traditions, the literature. It was they who granted permission to ask questions, to photograph, to record information. The building traditions I was recording seemed to be primarily in their hands.

Subsequently, in the course of combing through the rather elusive but vast literature on African nomads, I was struck by how many early observers commented on women's building roles, in the course of their travels, in contrast to the paucity of such commentary in more recent accounts. The earliest European account of the Mauretanian nomads in the environs of Isle d'Arguin (near Nouadibou, Mauretania) already mentioned the fact that tents are women's work.[10] A century later the work done by Zenaghe women equally evoked comment.[11] Closer to us in time, Douls wrote (1888:204): "Immediately after morning prayers . . . the women and young girls occupied themselves with striking the tent and loading the camels. The men surveyed the operation."

Duveyrier, the first European to give a scholarly account of the Kel Ahaggar Tuareg, was equally impressed with the extent of Tuareg women's work.[12] Even earlier, Pallme, traveling in the region of Kordofan in the Sudan, had commented on how much more industrious women were than men.[13] Further east on the continent, the Somalis evoked the same reaction (Guillain 1856, 2:427): "Among the Somali, all the work rests on the women: the care and education of the infants, the maintenance of the house, the preparation of food, the cutting of wood, the supply of water, up to the construction of the house are in her department."

In general, with few exceptions, economists tend to dismiss domestic production and home industries as marginal. In the case of nomadic societies, economic studies, and by extension political studies, focus on herding economies and their management by men. Herding is a male occupation. For the most part, women's labor time is part of the reproductive cycle rather than the productive cycle of labor time. The creation of a marriage house, women's work, is culturally perceived as part of the woman's reproductive process, not as a technologically productive process. In general, those parts of the built environment created by women are often considered expendable, perishable, and less valuable. When a door is fabricated by a woodworker out of carved wooden elements, it is recognized as having value, whereas when the door is made of plaited rope by a basketmaker, it carries little architectural value. Yet almost all the labor necessary for the creation, maintenance, and transport of the architecture and its related artifacts continues, to this day, to be in the hands of women (pl. 8).

Neglecting the gender-based allocation of labor is a reflection (or a result) of the cultural value system that accrues to the work: it is equally a reflection of the social and political position of the gender involved in its creation. The Gabra said to me: "Standing is work, sitting is resting." The implication is that whatever is done while sitting is not work. So herding, of course, is work, hard work, because one stands all day, and perhaps house pitching and striking, camel loading and unloading, are also work. But when the manufacture of every furnishing or the transformation of every raw material into a finished artifactual or architectural component is done by women while they are "sitting down," then the perception of women's work carries with it a negative connotation: women do not work.

DOWRIES AND ENGENDERED ARCHITECTURE

The creation of a house and its furnishings in nomadic society is part of the dowry institution: it occurs in the context of marriage. Considered by many as simply a means of insuring a woman's right to inherit a share of the patrimonial property, the institution requires considerable rethinking in light of the nomadic condition where such a major part of women's work enters into its creation. The important distinction to be considered lies in the nature of the inheritance. While animals that are inherited reproduce and herds increase, the house and its furnishings, inherited from mother to daughter, tend to dissipate and disintegrate over time. Is then the nomadic dowry, properly speaking, an inheritance? To the extent that it does give women power and control over the domicile, it is. The key issue, as Moore (1988:52–53) has pointed out, is the relationship between women's productive and reproductive roles. Since the productive role, that is, the production of the domicile, is integral with the reproductive role in domestic, women's work, the architectural and artifactual creative role it involves tends to be ignored or neglected.

The first time I arrived in a nomadic camp, I was startled to discover that there were almost no men about other than the venerable elders lolling under the single shade tree in the distance. Adult men and adolescent boys were absent. Men and boys spend their days largely outside the camp; women and girls stay within it, even though the "work" of each gender may be equally necessary to the productivity and to the maintenance of the social structure.

The daily tasks involved in productive labor are equally divided into masculine and feminine realms, as is the case in much of rural Africa—and the world at large. The work is carried out separately, and skills are transmitted within the tightly defined gender-discrete social interaction. The division of labor by sex and the nature of gender-discrete labor, productivity, and creativity in nomadic society are somehow far more evident and obvious than in sedentary agricultural societies. The responsibilities are more specifically defined along gender lines: who does what, who is responsible for providing what, who speaks to whom, and which gender occupies which space in the course of the day. The very division of the spaces within a tent reflect and echo, as already pointed out, this division of social labor.

But there are two parts to productive labor: the production of raw materials (i.e., their collection) and the processing of these materials. Here, too, the "production" of materials themselves sometimes defines the gender responsibility vis-à-vis processing responsibilities. For example, metalworking is exclusively in the masculine domain, and by extension woodworking with specialized metal tools is equally men's work. But wood and its products (e.g., bark, fiber, leaves) are utilized in many other ways. As a result, the cutting down of heavy timber and the carving of wood, which are in men's hands, and the bending of wood, which relates to stems and roots and is in women's hands, are equally processing responsibilities, but they are defined by collection. One of the striking phenomena that emerged so clearly from the overview of building and transport technology is that wood which is gathered or harvested, particularly roots below ground, is in the realm of women's responsibility; it is part of the more general gathering and harvesting activities that women's parties engage in.

The process of leatherworking (i.e., sewing and tailoring) is equally a function of its production. Tanning is related to herding: women tan goat and sheepskins, while men tan camel and wild animal skins (antelope and giraffe). At the same time, tanning itself is related to the collection of acacia bark (obtained by women) from which tannin is obtained. The various kinds of tanning processes that result from this division of labor have a direct impact on the finished materials used in creating the nomadic architecture, as well as on their "style."

By distinguishing the process of leatherworking from its production, the historical record becomes easier to unravel. Centuries ago, Ibn Khaldun (1958, 2:366) made the distinction between spinning, weaving, and tailoring when he enumerated the "necessary and noble crafts of civilization." While spinning and weaving is necessary to all, tailoring (and embroidery) is a function of sedentary "civilization."[14] Thus embroidery on leather, which is equivalent to silk embroidery and involves "tailoring," is quite distinct from merely tanning it, and traditionally in the Near East embroidery was always in the hands of men. But when "nobility," the written word, and inheritance were functions of matrilineality, gender roles in both process and production assumed a different dimension.

The production of spun fiber and the process of weaving are another case in point which, if analyzed in detail, would surely shed historic light on the preferential use, as well as the changing availability of woven in preference to leather velums among particular nomadic populations. It would give added relevance to the clear distinction made by the "ancestor of the Arabs of the desert" when he gave one of his sons a black tent of animal hair and the other a round tent *(kubba)* of red leather (Feilberg 1944:197, citing al-Masʿudi, A.D. 943).

Ultimately the distinction can be applied to building and transport technologies. The substitution of bent arches for straight poles involves more than a simple structural alternative, more than the mere availability of natural resources; it involves a gender-discrete differentiation between production and process. The substitution of pliable roots gathered, bent, and shaped by women for the straight poles cut and carved by blacksmiths and woodworkers is an equally strong explanation for transitional styles among the Tuareg as the substitution of mats for leather velums. Technological style has more to do with shifts in gender-discrete responsibilities during cultural interaction than with simple "diffusion."

Equally related to the distinction between production and process is the collective nature of one in contrast to the other. The gathering of plants and wild grains, of roots and branches—the processing of materials—involves veritable expeditions by nomadic women. The subsequent production of artifacts, as well as the creation of house and furnishings, also involve collective labor. The labor of maintaining and transporting the entire built environment is likewise a collective process.

In the nomadic world, herding and domesticity, ritual and creativity, are separate and discrete in space. Hence labor prescriptions and practices in each of the two separate, gendered worlds should also be considered in terms of space. Access to resources, the conditions of work, and the distribution of the products of work, all of which reflect this discrete, engendered occupancy pattern, have a spatial as well as a temporal component. Consideration of the relationship of production and processing to space of the "workplace" (i.e., the bush, the camp) suggests that the domicile is as important as the collective nature of the creative process because it represents "control" over space. It follows logically that since so much of the woman's creativity is directed toward setting up the physical requirements for a household, and since the domicile is the scene of both her creativity and control, much of the work involved in transforming the natural environment into a built environment is in her hands.

RITUAL AND CELEBRATION

African nomadic architecture comes into being in the context of the marriage ritual: the architectural process is experienced by the society of women; men look on (pl. 9). The building process is a ritual process, a female ritual process that rigorously excludes male kith and kin, a ritual that patterns women's lives from birth to death. By looking at the marriage ritual, we can focus on the discovery of women's experiences as distinct from men's perception of women's experience. We can discover that world of intimacy, love, and uniquely female bonding which draws women together during every stage of their lives, from childhood through adolescence through courtship, marriage, childbirth and child rearing, death and mourning. It is during the marriage ritual that women reveal their deepest feelings to each other. Most importantly, it is this component of the nomadic marriage ceremony that grants women control.

Historians rarely consider architecture as a handmaiden of ceremony and spectacle, except in very highly charged religious or emotional situations such as the Gothic cathedral, in which the ritual related to the Stations of the Cross establishes the plan, or the Kaaba in which the seven circumambulations around it establish the ideal of the square. In ritual, movement is highly ordered and structured. For example, it is only by pacing and touching the surfaces that articulate space (e.g., the Kaaba at Mecca), by inhaling its good and bad smells, that we come to terms with it, come to know and possess it, make it ours.

The nomadic tent is equally a handmaiden of ceremony and spectacle, and movement in space is inherent in the marriage ritual: the movement of people, of its key actors, and of their entire built world. The creation of the tent is a moving spectacle. There is no better illustration in response to Turner's plea for the need to view celebratory symbols in action, in movement, in becoming, as essentially involved in process (1982:20) than the nomad's tent.

Not only are movements per se tightly prescribed;

Fig. 3.11. a. The ceremonial relocation and reconstruction of a Gabra wedding tent within its kraal. b. Ritual movement during a Gabra age-set transition feast.

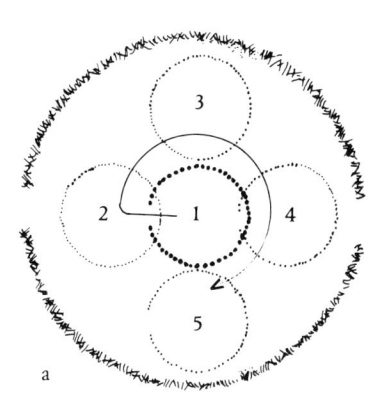

KOLOMPTE TRANSITION FEAST — Galbo phratry, Gabra
A house of *qallu*
B *nabo* of the "young men"
   Manguba (Kommicha becoming Yuba)
   Dambala (becoming Kommicha)
C *nabo* of the elders
   Gurjab (Dabela)
   Affata (Yuba becoming Dabela)
   B1 Jiblo moiety opening
   B2 Lossa moiety opening
   C1 Jiblo moiety opening
   C2 Lossa moiety opening
a. *barchuma* (stool) of the Dabela and Yuba
b. Dabela (*abba dibe*: the drum and its custodian)
c. fire

PROCESSION
1. Gifts of milk in *ghorfa* and tobacco in *katela*; branch of olive tree brought to elders.
2. Young men sing at the Jiblo openings; Women sing at the Lossa openings.
3. Urgessa at fire, while outside the *nabo* young men wait; performed by the *hayu* of Manguba, Dambala and Affata.
4. Sacrifice (sorio) of two ewes.
5. Sacrifice of male goat and lamb. Prior to 6, the hornblower blows his horn, moves from B2 through the *nabo* to B1; all the young men move to B with their emblems of virility.
6. Sacrifice of the bull.
7. Sacrifice of the young male camel.
8. Sacrifice of the female cow.
9. Sacrifice of the female camel.
10. Elders move with their stools to the west (fire) side; the *dabela* and the three *affata* return to the east side.
11. The *abba dibe* closes the ceremony in the center of the *nabo* of the elders.

locations and positions in space are prescribed for particular sequences of the ritual so that it is possible to conceive of the marriage ritual as a pilgrimage, particularly when one recalls the role of the litter-palanquin in it (Turner 1974). If, as Turner suggests, the pilgrimage is a liminal phenomenon with heightened intensity, there are thus vital spatial aspects to the liminality of the marriage-cum-pilgrimage process.

Gabra marriage ritual provides a poignant illustration of what characterizes, in one way or another, all nomadic marriages. Rather than occurring as a single, ceremonial, climactic event, the marriage is enacted in slow, progressive stages over various places and spaces. No marriage tent, initially put up, remains so (fig. 3.11a). In the first stage of the marriage, the arrival of the groom's family in the bride's camp initially involved spatial displacement. The exchange of dowry components and bridewealth, which is the overture to the four-day ceremony, also involves movement between families and through the open space and camel kraals of each, as do the other obligatory exchanges in the course of the ceremony related to the creation of

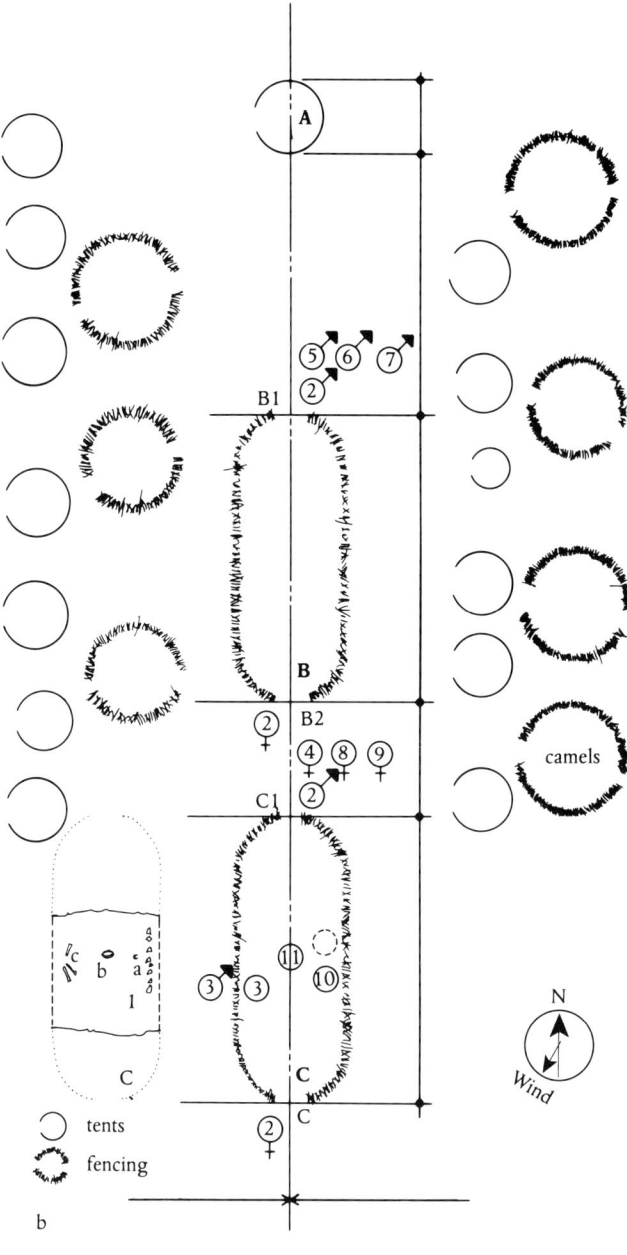

The Creative Process

the marriage tent and a new kraal. But the ritual does not end with the four-day ceremony or the consummation of the marriage; it extends over a lunar month. Every seven days the marriage tent is struck and loaded onto the camels, and the bride plus her tent-cum-palanquin are led in a circle around the campsite. Returning to the kraal, the tent is pitched again within it, but not in the same location. The location itself revolves within the circle of the kraal. The liminality of the marriage ritual, expressed in the spatial displacement of the marriage tent, ends only after a lunar month, when the newly constituted family breaks camp and returns to the groom's encampment.

The gender-discrete aspect of ritual movement in space, so evident in the marriage-cum-pilgrimage process of the Gabra wedding ceremony, is present in the environments of all Gabra ritual, those involving men *and* women, as one of their transition feasts *(kolompte)* clearly reveals (fig. 3.11b). The feast, which accompanies the transition of male generation-sets *(luba)*, is held in the camp that holds the religious and political powers of the Gabra phratry. These villages always contain a special enclosure *(nabo)* where a fire and the sacred symbols (the drum, the horn, and the fire-sticks) are always kept, and in which the solemn ceremonies are performed (Tablino 1985).

This particular, illustrated feast was celebrated in two special thornbush enclosures *(nabo)* aligned along a north-south axis. The houses and camel kraals of the two moieties that comprise this phratry were aligned parallel to the elongated enclosures, their entrances all facing west. An analysis of the complex details of the ceremony would surely yield additional insights, but what is particularly relevant to the subject of pilgrimage was the spatial, directional, and gender-discrete nature of the processionals enacted in and around these two enclosures.

The enclosure on the north was the "virile" enclosure; young men sang at the northern openings, and women sang at the southern ones. The sacrifice *(sorio)* of male animals (5, 6, 7) took place at the northern opening of the young men's enclosure (B), while the sacrifice of female animals (4, 8, 9) was performed south of it (actually north of the elders' [who are "becoming women"] enclosure). The processional movements (all involving men) occurred along the cardinal axes: that of the young men moving into a new generation set from south to north, that of the elders east to west. The north is masculine, and the south is feminine.

The participants in the ritual (all men) who occupy the space *within* the *nabo* are in a transitional state; they are "becoming," just as the bride in her marriage tent is. In spatial terms, the movement of each gender in the marriage ritual parallels their movements in this male generation-set ritual. As a consequence, if one compares the interior space of a Gabra tent, the processionals of people, tent, and wedding camels involved in the marriage ceremony, and the spatial configuration of the *kolompte* feast, movement and the occupancy of space by both genders are conjoined.

Another aspect of ritual behavior that has bearing on its architectural quality is that it persists over time in ways that other customs and behaviors do not. Which of us cannot recall the age-old retention of particular customs for ceremony, far beyond their comparable but profane day-to-day habits. This conservative dimension of ritual has particular implications for nomadic architecture created in the context of a marriage ritual. Resistance to change adds a dimension of "permanence" to what would normally be an easily disassembled structure, more responsive to altering conditions by virtue of its processual quality. The architectural permanence achieved through ritual behavior enhances and reifies the abstract process of renewal, birth, and rebirth that a woman experiences with each move.

MNEMONICS, THE ACQUISITION OF SKILLS, AND PLAY AS CHILDREN'S WORK

The enveloping polyvalence that we in the Western world have attributed to architecture takes on as much new meaning in the nomadic context as does memory itself. Of all the faculties, Rykwert wrote (1982), "memory has most to do with architecture: memory, whom the Greeks personified as Mnemosyne, mother of all the muses, is her true patron." Nomadic women use their bodies as a primary measure for the creation of its bounded, enclosed space. As individuals they

Fig. 3.12. a. A young child participating in the pitching of a Gabra tent. b. The toy reconstruction of a Rendille camel load.

come to know and appropriate their environment through sensory habit, but habit requires repetition, and rhythmic repetition is the handmaiden of a mnemonic that serves in lieu of blueprint and the written instruction or guideline for reconstruction. The marriage tent is a mnemonic par excellence because it is also a mnemonic enveloped in emotion and impregnated with emotional content. Dwellings without memory are dwellings without inhabitants.

Scientists have long known that play is widespread in the animal kingdom, but only lately have they appreciated just how profoundly important play must be to an animal's physical, mental, and social growth. Scientists believe that the intense sensory and physical stimulation that comes with playing is critical for proper motor development; some biologists have found that the vigorous movements of play help in the maturation of muscle tissue.

Through play, animals can rehearse many of the moves they will need as adults, and play serves to ease the transition into community. Play socializes an individual, and play is sexually segregated, as Erikson (1968) pointed out in his early study of gender-related spatial and architectural preferences in children's play.

From culture to culture, girls often rehearse elements of motherhood: among the nomads, playing with dolls is subsumed by playing house and how to move. The acquisition of skills related to domestic tasks is not limited to those we usually associate with domesticity, such as basketry, tending a fire, carrying firewood, sweeping, and raising children. Playing house for young nomadic girls involves the skills of tent building as well as tent transport (fig. 3.12).

Games of pretense are not pretense at all. When little girls build their miniature tents with branches and twigs, using leaves for mats, they are developing a heightened perception of their environment as well as acquiring and developing the construction skills that will be essential for their success as adult women.

Finally, when mnemonic is enveloped in emotion yet another facet of play and the transmission of knowledge is revealed. If the process of acquiring the skills of construction is enveloped in the anticipation of emotion, in the course of play during which voluntarily controlled movements are superseded by automatic, habitual ones, then the stage is set for the close accord of the imaginative and emotional faculties that underlie architectural creativity and achievement in the nomadic world and that turn the nomadic architectural styles into metaphors.

4
THE HASSANIYA-SPEAKING NOMADS: TEKNA, TRARZA, AND BRAKNA

This chapter includes a discussion of architecture of the Hassaniya-speaking Tekna by Peter A. Andrews and a paraphrased translation of excerpts from a series of movingly written articles by Odette Du Puigaudeau on the Hassaniya-speaking Trarza and Brakna nomads in Mauretania.

Architectural and artifactual comparisons among the northern Hassaniya-speaking Tekna and the southern Mauretanian Hassaniya-speakers, when viewed against the background of earlier historical accounts, provide an interesting insight into the continuities and changes in the material culture and aesthetic preferences of this westernmost part of the African nomadic continuum. Careful interpretation is both historically enriching and architecturally revealing.

The Hassaniya-speaking nomads extend from the northern banks of the Senegal River through Mauretania and Western Sahara (formerly Spanish Morocco) into southwestern Morocco. Many are bilingual, and the pronunciation, grammar, and syntax of Hassaniya, a Moorish dialect of Arabic, vary from tribe to tribe and from region to region (see location map). These Hassaniya-speakers are descendants of the Ma'qil, Hilalian Arab invaders who originated in Yemen and moved across North Africa to southern Morocco and the ocean in the early thirteenth century. They subsequently achieved political and social control over the already Islamized Berber tribes to the south in what is now Mauretania.

The Tekna are a confederation of tribes dominating the extreme southwest of Morocco. Their neighbors to the north, and in fact the northerly tribes of the Tekna themselves, are settled, but fully nomadic tribes from the south come into Tekna territory regularly to trade and, in some circumstances, to graze their animals. The Tekna resemble them in many respects of material culture and speech, and buy many of their finest artifacts from them. The Tekna are nomadic only to a limited extent: the degree varies according to the terrain and the needs of their flocks. Some rarely move more than a score of kilometers from their villages inland; others migrate up and down the coastal strip, where the pasture is richer and more reliable; still others venture far out into the more desert areas in Algeria and the Western Sahara, roaming over the great stony slope of the Hammada du Draa. Some live all the year in their tents, while others may return to a house seasonally.

All the nomadic Tekna in Morocco speak Hassaniya, but some are bilingual, speaking the local variety of Berber speech *(tašelhit)*, which predominates north of the Noun. The tribespeople are an admixture of Arab and Berber elements that can no longer be clearly distinguished. They are divided into two main sociopolitical confederations *(leff)*, the Ait Ejjmal and the more numerous Ait 'Atman. Moroccan influence has been slight in the past: most of the Tekna became independent in about 1765, and a little later they formed a separate state known

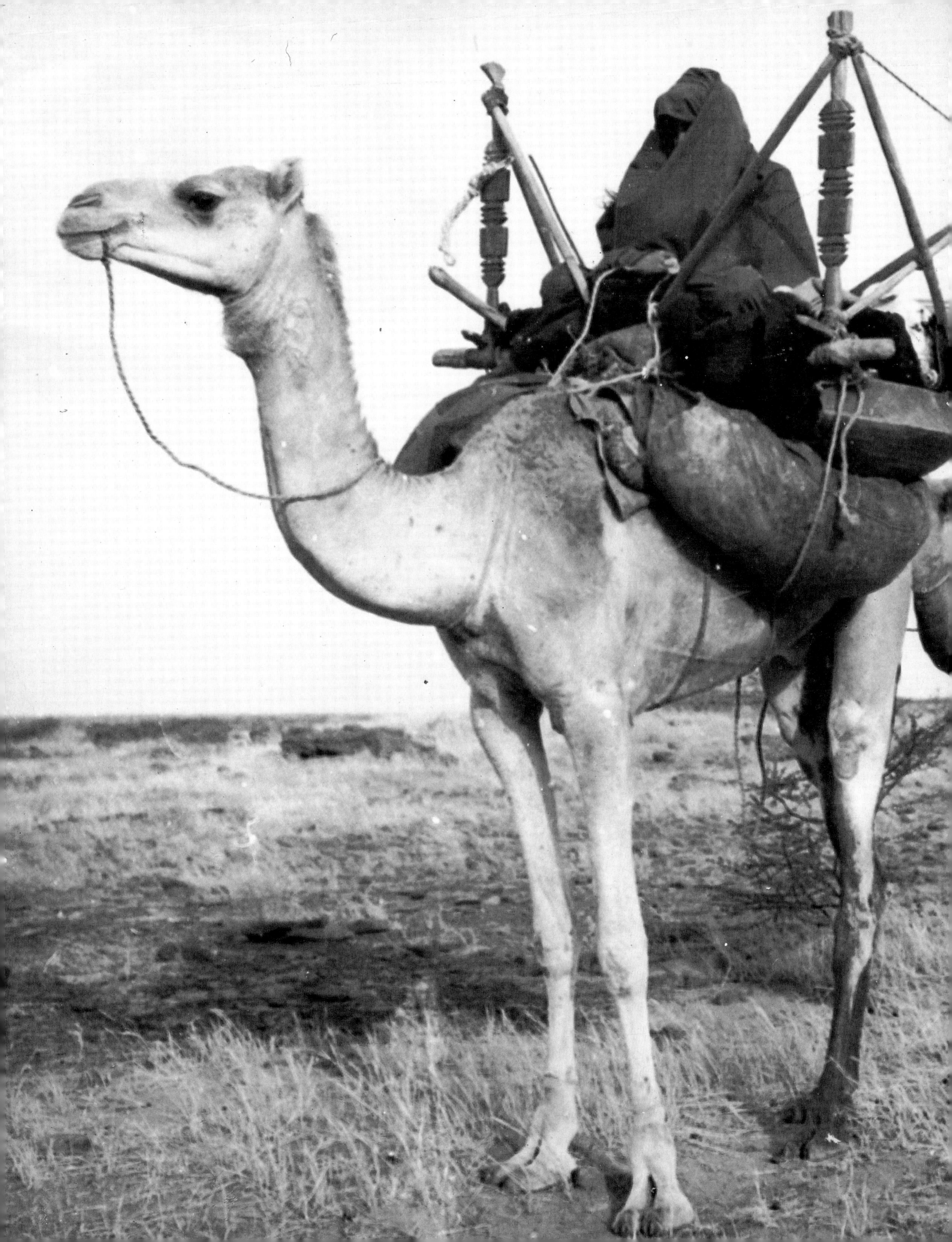

as Oued Noun. This is still the heart of their territory, and it has always been an important point of contact between Saharan and coastal peoples.

In the south, the Berber (Sanhaja and Zanata) penetration of what is now Mauretania began at least fifteen centuries ago, with nomadization that was greatly accelerated by the introduction and spread of the camel in the first centuries A.D. The eleventh century A.D. was witness to the birth of the great Almoravid proselytizing movement which expanded northwards into Morocco and southern Spain. In the following centuries the Islamized Berber societies, subject to a new impetus from the northern Arab onslaughts, forged the emirates of Trarza, Brakna, and the Hodh. The mixing of Arab and Sanhaja (Berber) societies began to take shape, resulting in the fusion which accounts for the present-day hierarchies. Another cultural consequence of the Arabization was the adaptation of the Arabic spoken by the Hassanes: Hassaniya. However, the persistence of Berber dialects is still evident among the bilingual Trarza and continues to be found in the toponymy of the country. Additionally, southern Hassaniya has also absorbed indigenous Soninke terms into its vocabulary.[1]

To this day, the population of Mauretania is often divided into "whites" and "blacks," into nomads and sedentary peoples. The sedentary cultivators are considered and consider themselves as "blacks" *(harratin)*, while the nomadic herders and traders of warrior or savant tradition proclaim themselves "white" *(beidan)*.[2] The origins of the Arab-Berber "whites," those we normally call "Moors," are almost as confusing and obscure as those of the "black" sedentarists.[3]

Mauretanian society has traditionally been organized into confederations of tribes, emirates, and clans based on the family or "tent." At the head are the nobility, the high-status warriors and the religious savants. Historically, the warriors *(hassani)* were politically preeminent vis-à-vis their religious counterparts *(murabitin* or *tolba)*, but in those parts of Mauretania where emirates existed—Adrar, Trarza, and Tagant— their position was secure only with the endorsement of the lettered, maraboutic tribes.

Below these aristocracies are first a group of client or tributary tribes, and then a network of castes. The castes of artisans, men and women *(mā'allemin)*, are of particular interest because it is they who are responsible for creating a good part of the nomadic material culture. They are particularly scorned and despised, yet at the same time feared because of the occult powers they are thought to possess.[4] Traditionally, families or groups of craftspeople have worked exclusively for a particular clan of warriors or a religious settlement *(zawiya)* and its dependencies: the men are blacksmiths and woodworkers, their wives leatherworkers.[5]

Andrews' article below is a revised abstract of an earlier extensive study which remains the most focused architectural description of the Tekna to date (Andrews 1971). In its meticulous attention to detail, it enhances the architectural focus by building on the earlier research of F. de la Chapelle (1933–34), Domenech (1946), Monteil (1948), and Caro Baroja (1955) on Hassaniya history, language, and material culture in the Western Sahara.

TENTS OF THE TEKNA
Peter A. Andrews

The country in which the Tekna move is hot, dry, and meager.[6] There are occasional oases which surprise one by their luxuriance, such as Assa. But the greatest part is semidesert, a transition from the Atlas to the Sahara. There is hardly a skyline that is not broken by one of the ranges of bare, dry hills in the distance. The pasture is very sparse, but almost continuous. . . . Trees are rare: occasionally one may be seen standing quite alone with a peculiar flat, compressed parasol of branches. There is no running water to be seen outside the villages, except when rains suddenly fill the riverbeds for a day or so. The herdsmen depend entirely on wells.

The northeast trade winds dominate the region. The sky near the coast is often overcast or hazy until noon, even in July. Nevertheless, summer temperatures are high, rising to 40–45 degrees centigrade in the afternoon. The temperature may then fall at night to 20 degrees centigrade. A hot and extremely unpleasant wind occasionally blows relentlessly from the Sahara for several days on end. Rainfall is slight, sporadic, and unreliable.

The same kind of tent *(l-ḥaima)* is used throughout the Oued Noun and the southwest, as far south as the Zemmour, by the Tekna and the Reguibat, whether they are full nomads or small herdsmen (fig. 4.1). It is very like the Mauretanian tent farther south: it is furnished in much the same way and is even subject to the same variations. Nevertheless there are enough consistent differences to mark it out as a separate type. Compared to tents in central Morocco, it is small, simple, and rather low except for the area under the peak.[7] No one can afford to carry superfluous equipment about the desert. It varies surprisingly little in size.

The Tekna always pitch their tents so as to face southwards. In doing so they not only follow the Arab tradition, but protect themselves by turning the streamlined tail of the tent into the prevailing wind. Tents are usually grouped in twos, threes, and fours, roughly in line and about twelve meters apart. Such neighbors are almost always related to one another; their camp may form part of a larger group that straggles without much order over a wide area if the pasture is good. The distance between tents is enough to keep herds apart when they are brought close to each tent at night.

The peaked silhouettes of a line of tents can be recognized from some distance, dark incidents against the dull brown of a valley floor and almost lost in scale against the cushions of mean vegetation in the foreground; or they may be discovered as a formal array on the open horizon of white sand in the south, drenched occasionally in the shadow of passing clouds, and fallible under the harshness of sunlight. Nearer, the shape emerges as an unexpected streamline. The roof is the whole form, and it tilts in each sweep of the surface. The single peak rakes backwards, away from the low, shaded mouth where the entrance side is lifted by two short props, and heaves the velum up in a gentle curve, to fall away in a much steeper slope behind. The two rear corners are pinned to the ground, and on either side the cloth sweeps down in a constantly broadening parabola spread by the guy ropes. The front is flattened and taut like an awning between the props, sloping away a little outside them to leave the sides open. The triangle of space between the edge and the ground may otherwise be filled with a tattered cotton wall, though the mouth is left empty.

Inside, the floor is clear and bright with the fresh yellow of esparto matting. Two tapered poles, the sole structure of the tent, straddle the mats and meet under the peak. The one at the front is quite clear of the roof except at the very top, and its foot rests just inside the

Fig. 4.1. Above, the front view of a Tekna Lansas tent; below, the rear view.

Hassaniya-Speaking Nomads

entrance; the rear one supports the roof for at least half its length, losing its lower end in the loose folds of cloth that form the tail skirts. The indeterminate bundles and boxes of the household are stacked on or under racks which are crowded under each of the low sides; but all the clutter of fire and kitchen pots lies outside, sheltering under the curve of the thorn hedges built out as a forecourt from either corner (fig. 4.2).

The roof is the tent: the velum (l-ḫaima) is made up from parallel strips of coffee-colored cloth (l-fliž), each with a paler stripe down the edge, all running in the direction of the length. The number of cloths, and their length, determine the size of the tent. Once they have been woven, cloths are rarely cut—trimming would be a waste of precious resources—so the loom is set up at the length decided for the tent. . . . Most tents are made up of seven or eight broader cloths (each usually 45–65 cm wide) sewn together as the middle, and a narrower (20–25 cm) cloth at either side (l-matinba; l-balla), as a lip. A tent made up from eight middle cloths is likely to measure some eight meters along the front and a meter less at the back so that the velum is trapezoidal in plan.[8]

Because the tent is peaked from the meeting of the two poles, the otherwise flat velum is marked to show where the peak is to occur. The peak is marked by a little crest, and also embroidered with parallel lines of white woolen stitching on the outside which almost certainly have a prophylactic meaning (fig. 4.3).

Surprisingly little sunlight is to be seen from the interior, for the weave is dense. It is as a shade against sun and glare, a screen against wind, dust, and unwanted glances, that it is important, and in its meager way as an insulator against winter cold. Since air does filter through the roof, an extra lining of cotton cloth (l-binya) is hung inside for the winter as a canopy, with sides that reach to the ground, and this is kept sometimes in summer too. The oiliness of the unwashed goat hair is known to prevent water from penetrating the cloth, but rain is very rare.

Where the majority of the herds consist of goats, goat hair is used alone. This is apparently the best material, but camel hair may be used, particularly if there is not enough goat hair for the whole weave. It is then

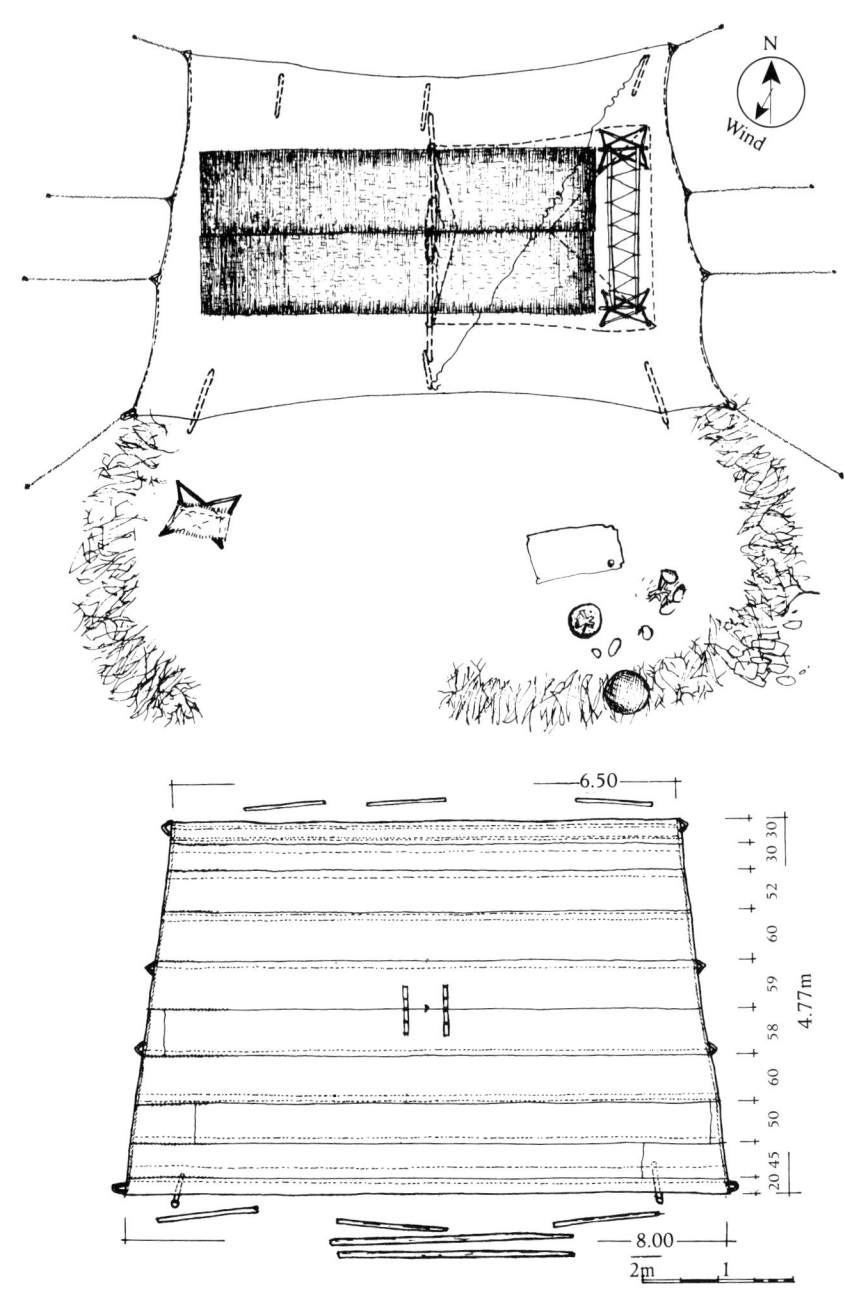

Fig. 4.2. Plan of a typical Tekna Lansas tent in the area of Taidelt. The two mats are shaded, with the women's side on the right, showing the line of a cotton canopy and the shelving. The fireplace and oven pit are in the forecourt to the right, and to the left is a waterskin on its trestle. Brushwood is shown hatched. The front of the tent is facing south. Below, a plan of the velum spread flat, with poles and props.

68　　　　African Nomadic Architecture

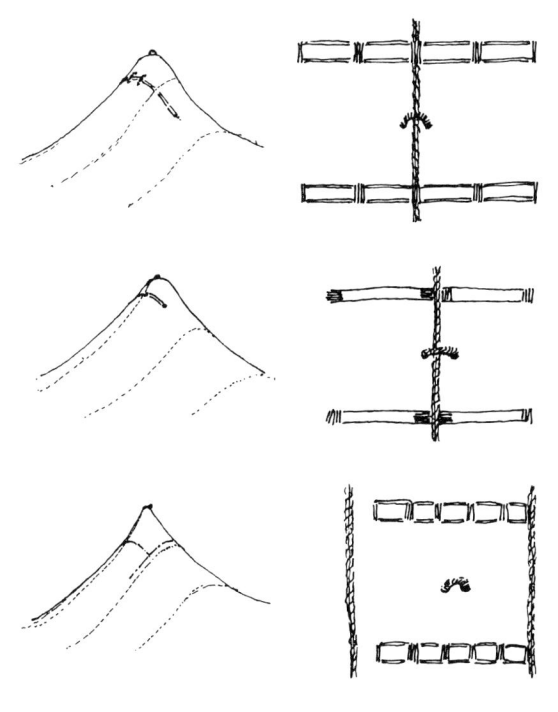

Fig. 4.3. Details of the tent crest ornament used by various Tekna subtribes.

carded with the goat hair into a mixture of which goat hair is the main element—especially so for the warp threads which must be strong enough to withstand all the tension on the velum. Camel hair can never be used by itself, for the fibers are short and weak: it is rather despised as a material, but it also has a certain spiritual power *(baraka)*. The weft threads, which are a stuffing rather than a means of strength, may contain a stronger admixture of camel hair.

The whole work of preparing and weaving the wool is done by the mistress of the tent, who works alone for much of the time. It is the women, too, who sew the cloths together, but they make a party out of the occasion, with fifteen or twenty working together. Despite all this, the tent remains the husband's property.

When a ground loom is set up for weaving tent cloth, it runs through the tent from front to rear. The tentwife weaves inside the tent, with the heddle in front of her facing the light. A cloth lasts for four to five years, and new cloths are made as needed to replace old ones. The cloths at the center will wear out most quickly because of the strain of the poles against the peak, and tents often show dark new areas in the middle as a result. A new cloth is sewn in as soon as it is ready. A woman would theoretically take twenty-four hours to weave an eight meter cloth if she worked fast and continuously. In reality, a week is needed, given interruptions and household chores.

The strips of webbing *(traiga)* used by the Tekna are vestiges of much longer girths which play a more important part in the tents of tribes elsewhere in Morocco and the Arab world (fig. 4.4). They are woven on a ground loom in the same way as the cloths. The weave is quite fine, and the tag girths, although often ragged or makeshift, can also play a decorative part in the construction of the tent. A rather similar but quite vestigial girth is used to protect the peak of the velum from the friction of the poles. It can be seen hanging down before and behind the point where the poles meet, decorated with long fringes of tassels (fig. 4.5).

However large or small the tent velum, it is always provided with fastenings for four guy ropes *(l-ḥebel)* on each of the short sides. The guy ropes at the sides and rear *(ḫwalf)* are linguistically distinguished from the corner guy rope at the front *(la-ḥagal)*. The beckets are carved out of forked or bent branches to form a broad "V" and lashed by their notched tips to the

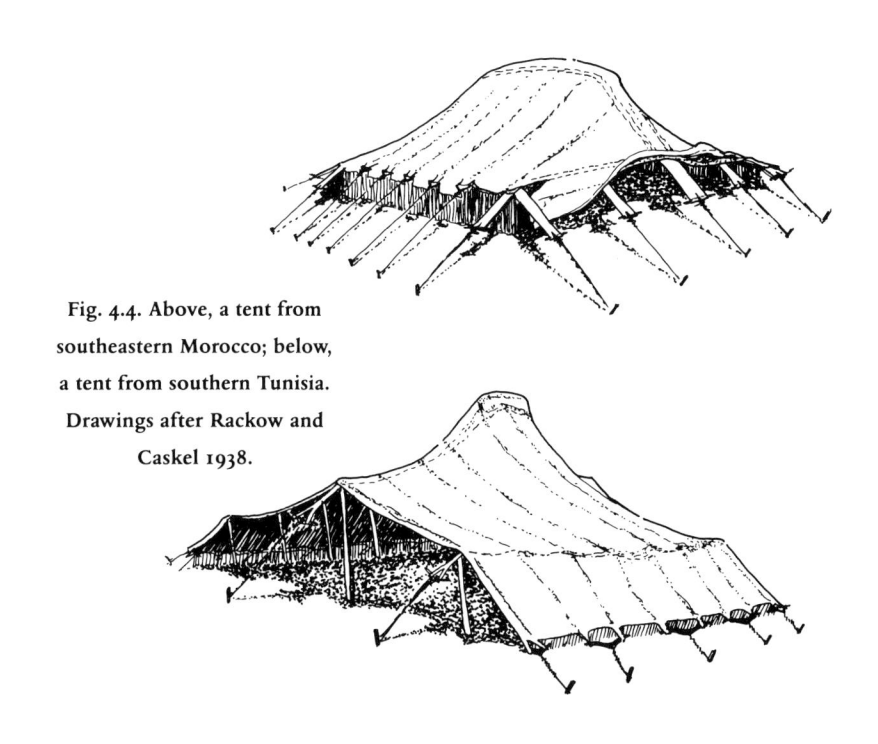

Fig. 4.4. Above, a tent from southeastern Morocco; below, a tent from southern Tunisia. Drawings after Rackow and Caskel 1938.

Hassaniya-Speaking Nomads

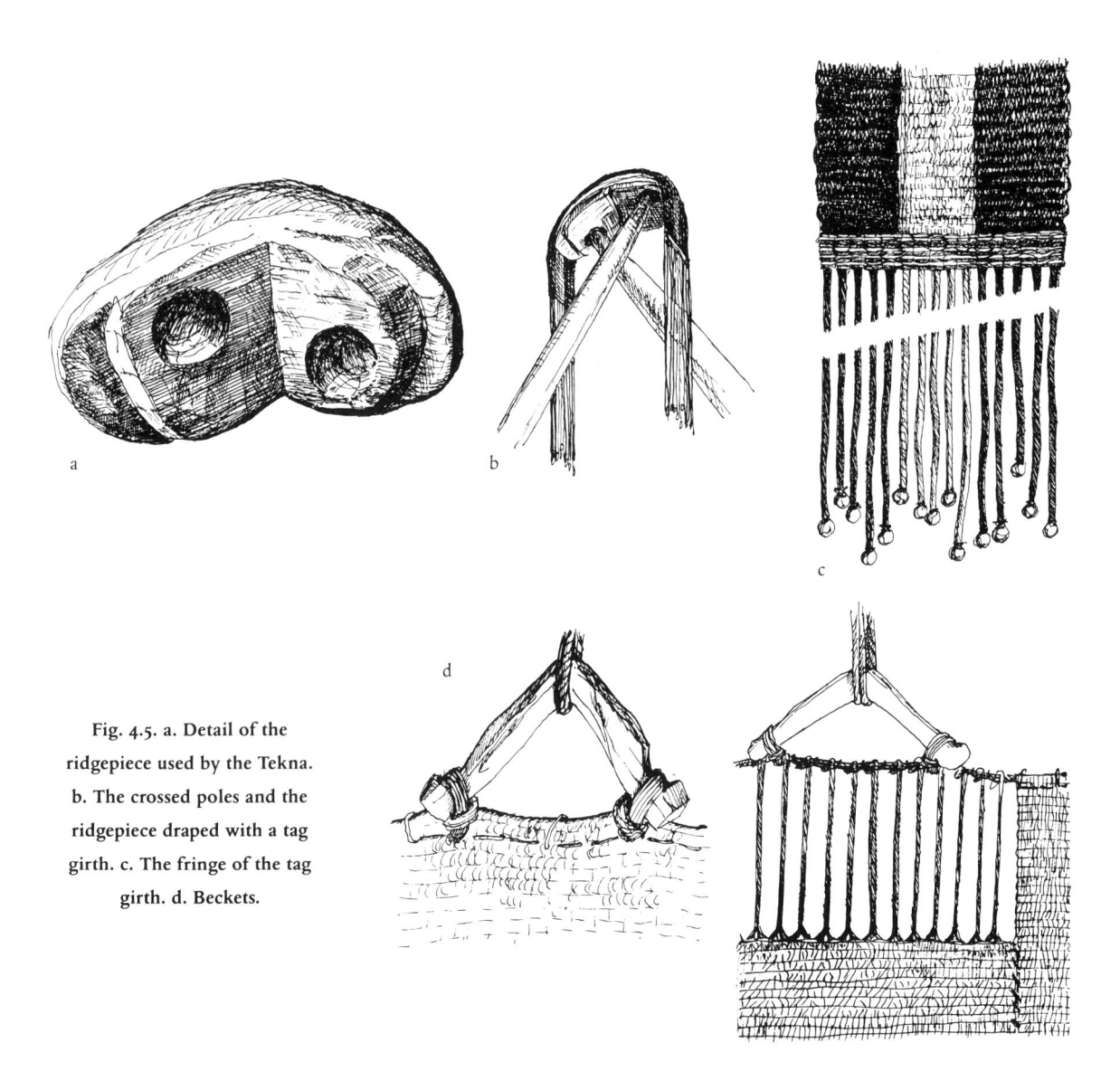

Fig. 4.5. a. Detail of the ridgepiece used by the Tekna. b. The crossed poles and the ridgepiece draped with a tag girth. c. The fringe of the tag girth. d. Beckets.

edge of the velum, one at each corner at the ends of the lip cloths, and two at intermediate points near the center of each side. The exact position of the central pair of beckets depends on the placing of the peak. The effect of the central pairs of beckets is to stretch the velum downward and outwards on either side of the peak, once the tent has been erected, so that the junction of the poles cannot slip under the cloth. Fastenings are also provided for the inner canopy which is sometimes hung inside the tent. These are simply long tails of goat hair twine stitched through the velum on the line of the peak, halfway between the peak and one or both short sides of the tent. They can sometimes be seen hanging down even when no canopy is in evidence, though it seems that they are often put in and removed as required. No girths or fastenings are found on the rear edge of the tent.

Though sisal rope is now used almost everywhere, guys plaited from the same wool and goat hair mixture used for weaving the tent velum itself are still sometimes seen, as are cords made of strips of camel leather. The traditional material for tent pegs *(l-wtid)* was Acacia raddiana *(ttalh)*, but the nomads, living on the commercial fringes of the twentieth century, have adopted its rope and pieces of its reinforcing bars and angle iron for holding up their tents.

The whole weight of the velum can be supported on the two main poles *(rkāyiz)* which meet at the peak, though they are set far enough apart on the ground to form a nearly equilateral triangle. The timber used for the main tent poles is *Argania spinosa (argan)*. A truly complete tent is provided with a ridgepiece *(ḥammar)* in which the tips of the poles lodge, holding them fast and protecting the velum from their pressure (see fig. 4.5b). When the poles are set up, they are crossed about ten centimeters from the top before they are engaged in the sockets, and this offset allows the feet to remain on the short axis of the tent floor. The whole arrangement is stable, with the ridge held in place by the weight of the velum and its slight stretching at the peak, the feet thrust hard against the ground, and the poles bearing against one another at the crossing.

The great majority of Tekna tents have no ridgepiece nowadays. Instead, the ends of the poles are wrapped together in a cloth, usually a piece of the blue cotton *(dirāʿa)* the men wear. This is enough to connect the poles and protect the velum, but since the poles, if they cross at all, cross only at the tips, they are not quite so stable as those with the ridgepiece. The disappearance of the ridgepiece is due, almost certainly, to the difficulty of obtaining pieces of hardwood that are large enough, as well as to the decline in skills, evident where these tents are concerned.[9]

Once the velum has been unpacked on a suitable site, the ground is cleared and the cloth is spread out flat over the poles, which are laid out end to end on the short axis. The cordage needs little adjustment. The women are able, from experience, to judge just the right distance from the edge of the velum for hammering in the pegs, to which the guy ropes are already fastened. Two women crouch down, then grope underneath the velum to adjust the poles. The pole tips are crossed and engaged in the ridgepiece under the peak of the tent, and as they are lifted up the feet are dragged inward and settled in position with some pulling and pushing against the increasing tension of the guy lines and the fabric. The furnishings are then brought in.

Strictly speaking, the shelving is furniture, but as by design or accident it plays a part in shaping the interior, it is worth consideration as part of the structure (fig. 4.6). Each shelf *(ar-rḥal)* consists of two trestles, two horizontal poles *(aš-šeddum)*, and a long leather cord. The trestles, which stand at either end, are each

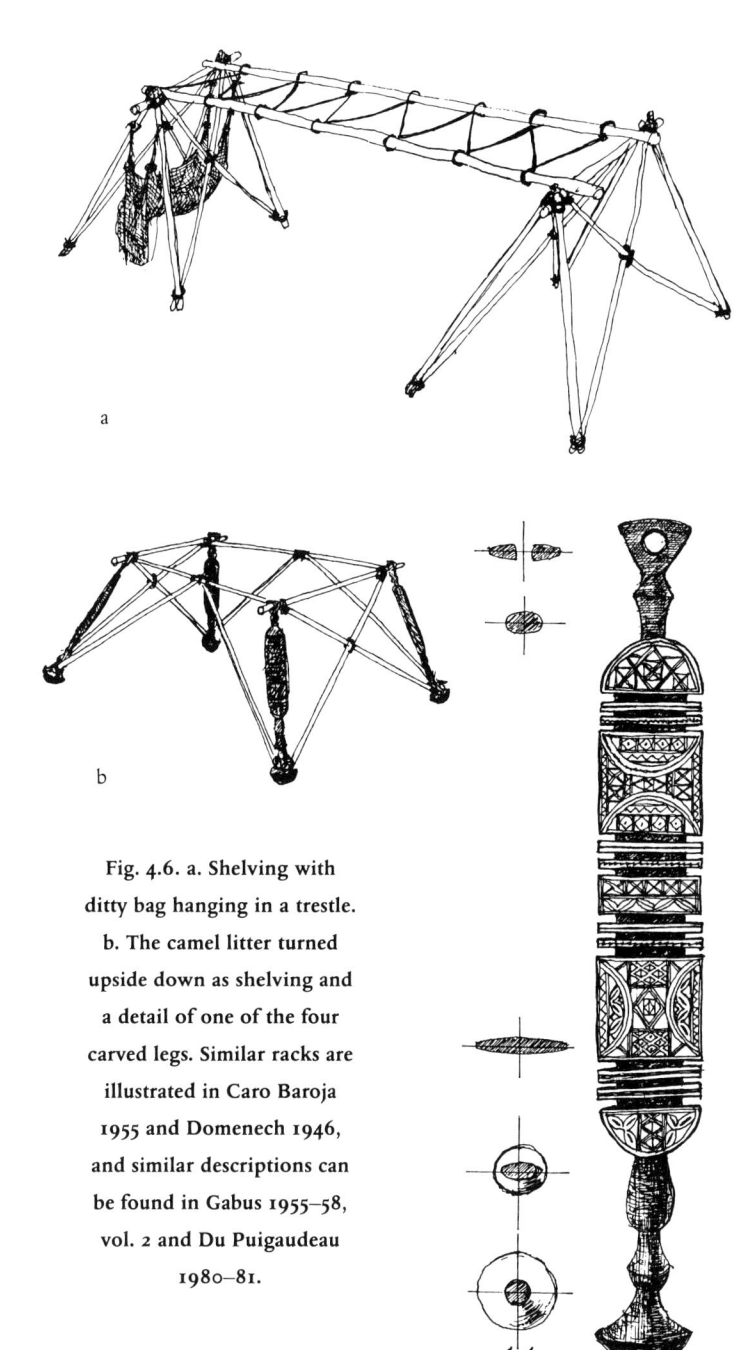

Fig. 4.6. a. Shelving with ditty bag hanging in a trestle. b. The camel litter turned upside down as shelving and a detail of one of the four carved legs. Similar racks are illustrated in Caro Baroja 1955 and Domenech 1946, and similar descriptions can be found in Gabus 1955–58, vol. 2 and Du Puigaudeau 1980–81.

made up of nine straight staves with the reddish bark left on them, notched around each end where they are lashed together with camel leather thongs. They are held firm in this position by a pair of diagonals lashed between each two legs. There are no base members. Each trestle can be folded like a pair of gates on the axle of the top staff. Two poles are placed across the trestles parallel to each other and fifty centimeters apart. The twisted leather cord is used to form the floor of the shelf running back and forth between these two

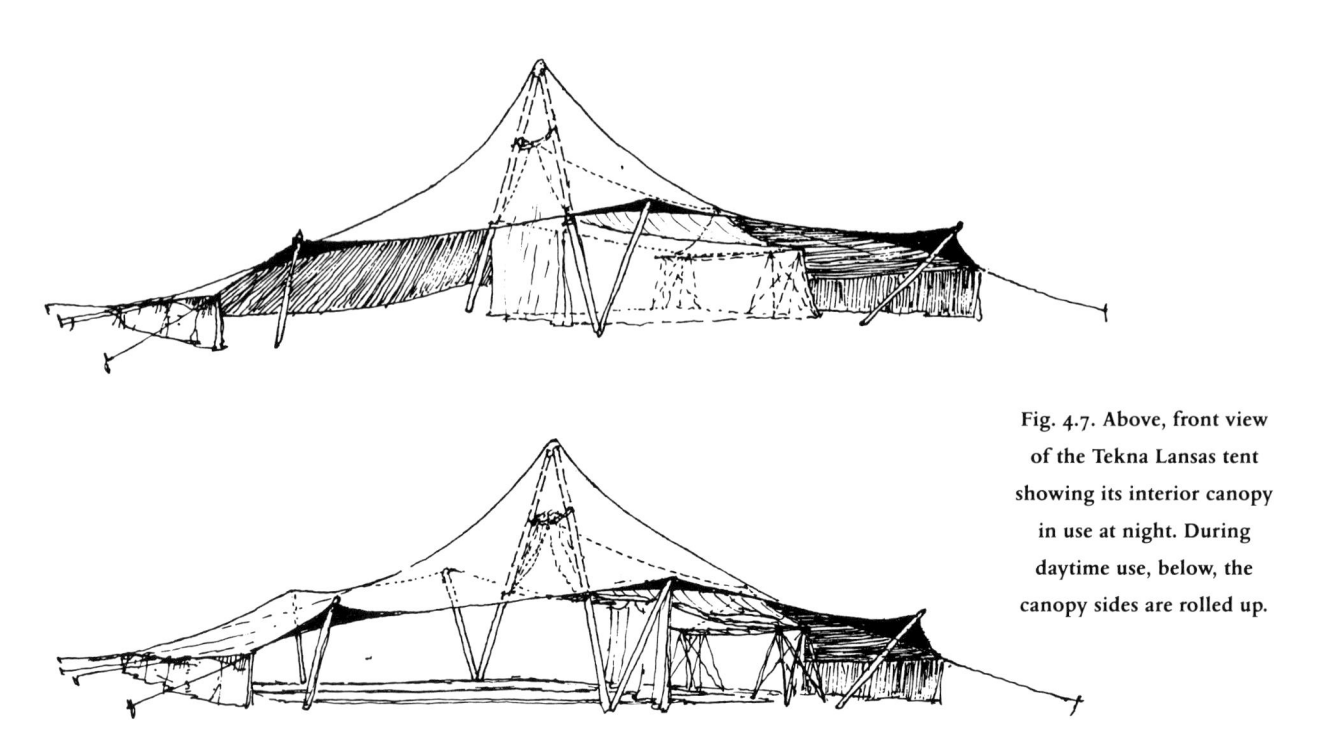

Fig. 4.7. Above, front view of the Tekna Lansas tent showing its interior canopy in use at night. During daytime use, below, the canopy sides are rolled up.

staves in a continuous zigzag. Because of its length, this cord is quite a precious piece of equipment. The wood used for the trestles is Acacia raddiana.

Another type of shelving *(ameššáqqab)*, the most elaborate furnishing within, is found in tents belonging to nomads who migrate southward. It is one of several kinds of litter used by the women on camelback for traveling long distances and should not be confused with the ordinary pack litter *(lemsama)* made of bentwood. It is turned upside down in the tent, so that its base can form a platform. It then resembles the construction of trestle gates, for there are two legs and a top bar braced by diagonals at each end, but these are held apart by top bars in the longitudinal direction instead of the poles. The legs are of blackwood in a flat section, beautifully and intricately carved in triangles, squares, and arcs, and a kind of crossribbing reminiscent of a banister. The work is Mauretanian rather than Tekna.

The shelving is often hung with a cloth *(as-suder)* that hides it completely, sometimes a patchwork of different colors, sometimes a large piece of blue hung up to screen the women at night. Traditionally it was decorated with four pieces of decorated leather each about sixty centimeters wide and ninety centimeters deep, each slit into five hanging panels of unequal width. These were mainly red, worked over very minutely with incisions forming lozenges and squares picked out in yellow and green, in Mauretanian style. Such hangings are now very rare, but the tradition of red leather is very old.

Tents may be lined in several different ways, partly for insulation, partly for privacy (fig. 4.7). Besides linings for the side cloths, which are quite common, one sometimes sees white cotton spread over the whole of the rear part of the roof *(l-iqfa; matiga)*. Linings of this kind are used in the south, near Tan Tan. The material is cotton sheeting or fine canvas, and the same white stuff is used for the more elaborate canopy that is hung from the roof for privacy and warmth, a tent within a tent. Cloth for such canopies is bought in the *souk* in one and a half meter widths, three or even five of which are sewn together into a sheet about four meters long, to cover half the tent. A married couple can retreat to this enclosure at night to obtain a little privacy, or a single woman can resort to it to preserve decorum when there are visitors about.

A tentwife works in the side of the tent next to the outdoor kitchen. This is as often on the right as on the left, and it seems to be determined by the direction of the wind. If there is one shelving element, it will be placed on this side; if there are two, this one will carry most of the household goods. The other side of the tent is the men's side, where guests are received. A second shelving element down this side may carry a carpet and a lambskin rug.

Most of the ground inside a tent is covered with matting. There are usually two long mats which are unrolled side by side between the two main poles. There is a special type of matting for tents which is distinct from another kind used in houses. This is made by poorer tent dwellers who sell it in the market. The warp is of date palm fiber rolled by hand into a yarn, twined and spaced two centimeters apart. The weft consists of pairs of twin esparto stems. Carpets are spread out on top of the mats for guests and for sleeping, and with the open mesh of the mats underneath they form an excellent insulator against the cold ground at night.

The more nomadic Tekna groups sometimes use a blanket made of dark brown lambskins sewn together, about the same size as a carpet. This is essentially a Mauretanian artifact, since the hairy sheep whose skins are used are not reared by the Tekna, but come from the Adrar, hundreds of miles to the south.

In addition to the tanned goatskin bags which are also slung from the trestles, there are one or two larger pouches dyed red, with Mauretanian ornament, a loop of leather cord at each end and a tassel at the bottom. All carefully padlocked, they hold provisions or the woman's trousseau. Other valuables are kept in a decorated leather pouch with an extravagant fringe, and the tea pot and glasses, which have an importance outweighing their value, are put in a basket with a leather neck.

Comfort is completed with leather cushions. Since the tribesmen loll as often as they sit, these are useful for tender elbows. They are generally flat and waisted in shape, with no corners and a fringe all round the edge. The ground color of beige leather may show through the design, but it is often painted over to such an extent that the main color is red, picked out in green and yellow. The leather is tooled a little to define the pattern. The style of such leatherwork may be Mauretanian, brought from the south, or based on slightly different local patterns.

Tents are struck simply by reversing the process. The furniture is taken out and loaded on the transport animals (including the upturned trestle), mats are rolled up and props removed. The dramatic tent collapse follows once the foot of the rear pole is dislodged. The velum is spread out, folded twice along its seams, and then folded backwards into the center. The poles are placed under the bundle, so that the whole can be lifted and placed on the back of the kneeling camel and fastened to the saddle.

ARTS AND CUSTOMS OF THE "MOORS"
Odette Du Puigaudeau

Du Puigaudeau's descriptions are of the tents used by the Trarza and the Brakna who move over the terrain in southwestern Mauretania. The earliest, eighteenth-century European visitors to the coast who met them left descriptions of their tents and their resources, and René Caillié's detailed, early nineteenth-century descriptions suggest that remarkably little architectural change had taken place in the course of the centuries.[10]

Numerous brief and fragmentary reports followed, but the first major study of the Mauretanian nomads —their life, material culture, and values—was written by Du Puigaudeau, who spent much of her life among them. Her pioneering work, an ethnographic and historical overview, was followed by the fieldwork of Jean Gabus (1955–58). Although architecture is only one facet of Creyaufmüller's recent documentation, his remarkably rich and detailed technological studies of material culture provide the most complete, up-to-date resource for the nomadic arts in Mauretania (1979, 1983). Despite these more recent, detailed investigations into Mauretanian nomadic material culture, the breadth and scope of Du Puigaudeau's decades of observation and experience in the desert, evoking the memory of many earlier intrepid women explorers there, remain unmatched and unsung. Hence I have chosen to include paraphrased translations from her original French descriptions in this collection.

THE CAMP
(1967:145–59, 161–62)

To the eyes of the traveler, the Mauretanian camp *(frīg)* looks like a little village with brown conical roofs gathered under a rock outcropping, in the hollow of a small valley, among a few thin trees, or from the flank of a few large dunes from which one may look out over the surrounding area—in short, in a spot that appeals to the taste of the inhabitants, depending on the circumstances and seasons. In times of difficulty, in an area of uncertainty, one keeps an eye on the distance and hides. During the season of great sandstorms, protection from blasts of wind is sought by setting up in the middle of a slope. During the rainy season, the Moor likes to see without being seen.

The primary consideration in choosing a site is its proximity to pasturage and water. Pasturage is particularly important because the animals will spend the day there and the herders will bring them back to the tents every night. Camp may be set up without inconvenience at a distance of two or three kilometers from a water source where, every three or four days, the herders will take the animals to water and will fill the goatskin water bags for the camp.

Camp is never set up in the immediate vicinity of a well, the meeting place for too many passersby whom it is wiser to avoid, even if they are friends. Hospitality is a virtue and a costly honor: though it is accorded with grace, one does not seek out occasions to offer it.

The Mauretanian camp is a village that may be taken down and transported, brought into being by pasturage and disappearing with it. When the animals have cropped the last clump of foliage, the tents are struck and loaded onto donkeys and camels, one walks for several days to another pasture guided by experience or information from a messenger or traveler, and, in two or three hours, a new village is reconstructed just like the old one.

A camp consists of the members of one family whose collective life is headed by the father, grandfather, uncle, or oldest brother. The same word *(frīg)* designates both the camp and the fraction of a tribe that inhabits it.

The tent of the chief is always planted in the center of the camp and at a distance from the others, to insure its tranquility as well as the freedom of the younger households and their children. The tents of the members of the clan are lined up in front or behind. Workers, artisans, musicians, *harratin*, and others camp on the periphery.[11]

In the region of Atar (Adrar), all the tents are lined up in a row, to the right and left of the chief's tent. In southern Mauretania, this tent is in front of the camp, with its small servants' tents behind. In the small camps *(anawal)* of less than ten tents, protocol is less strict.

Naturally, accidents of terrain, rocks, trees, small ravines, and so on may affect the disposition of the camp. But all the tents are spaced far enough apart and open in the same direction to facilitate mutual discretion by their occupants. Their raised side, the entrance *(fūm or bāb el khaīma)*, is oriented away from the wind, thus most often to the south or southwest.[12]

Among the Trarza and the Brakna, the large emiral tents are called *maḥṣar*; in the Tagant and in Adrar, *ḥella*. To the right of the emiral tents, a tent of young warriors is put up; those of the dignitaries or cadis *(khalifat, qāḍī)* are pitched to the left. These seignorial camps are less nomadic than the others. A court does not move as easily as a clan of herders. When the sheik or emir travels, the larger part of the populations are left in the fixed settlements *(zawiya)*, and usually only an escort of the favorite warriors, savants, nobles, musicians, and servants accompanies him. An experienced eye quickly recognizes a warrior camp from afar by its more boisterous liveliness, sometimes by the whinnying of a horse; a marabout camp can be recognized by the murmur of prayers, by the small isolated tents of the students, by all the shelters of rags where the domestic beggars are lodged. Both of these escape the village noises: children crying, women chattering, the complaints of kids and lambs tied in the shade of the tents, awaiting the return of their mothers taken every morning out to pasture, the dull monotonous beating of the millet pounders, the clear ringing of the hammer on the anvil of the blacksmith, and in the distance the voices of herders calling to one another and gathering their animals in the neighboring pasture. At night, in front of the tents, fires are lit round which people gather for long evenings to discuss the affairs of the community, to listen to the recitations of the old people or the improvisations of poets. On festival days, dances and chants accompanied by the drum *(tobol)* and the games of adolescents and herders animate the "town square" in front of the tent of the chief or guests.

The tent. The tent *(khaīmat)* is the most suitable dwelling for the Mauretanian nomads who have perfectly adapted it to their customs, to the climate, and to the nature of the soil (fig. 4.8). Of a thick and oily fabric of wool or hair, it is impervious to sun, rain, or sand. Its strength makes it resistant to frequent transport. It is high and spacious enough that a family may live in it comfortably. Its conical shape affords the wind a minimal hold, facilitates rapid runoff of the torrential rains, and assures sufficient ventilation for its occupants. More than any other dwelling, it is cool in the summer and warm in the winter, and we shall see, as we examine its different elements, how perfectly conceived they are for the service expected of each of them.

In Mauretania, where the short camel hair is unusable, only sheep wool and goat hair are used, and the tent is of a beautiful, even, brownish-black color. Wool and hair are carded using bundles of thorny sticks or small planks bristling with nails, then spun on a wood distaff *(meghzāl)*, into a coarse yarn with two twisted strands ("Turkish"). With her right hand, the spinner turns the distaff against her bare thigh, while her left hand, raised high, twists the yarn. This is servants' work.

But it is the mistress herself, with the assistance of women from her family, who weaves her tent on a primitive horizontal loom placed on the ground, in strips *(flīj; ifeljān)* forty-five to sixty centimeters wide and of the length allotted for the tent. The texture of the material is that of coarse rep; sometimes the regularly opposed stitches form lines of geometric designs. Weaving is the only work a woman from a noble caste may permit herself to do.

When the strips are woven, the artisan of the camp and her assistants assemble them by loose overcasting

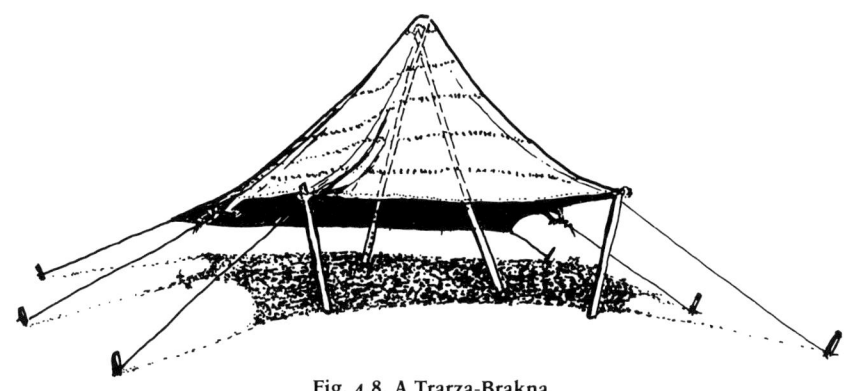

Fig. 4.8. A Trarza-Brakna tent from Boutilimit, southern Mauretania, exhibited at the International Colonial Exposition, Paris, 1931. Drawing after Rackow and Caskel 1938.

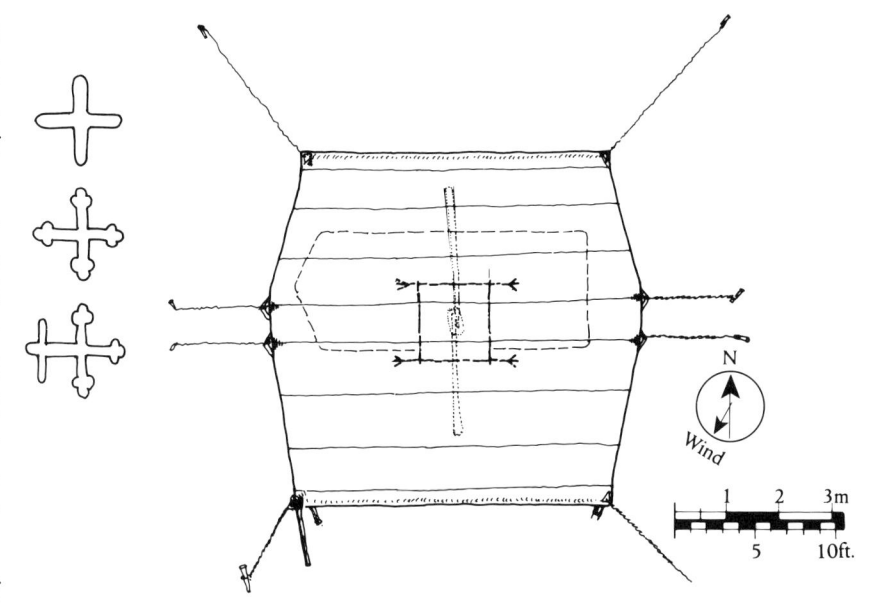

Fig. 4.9. Plan of the velum of a Trarza tent near Tagant, southwestern Mauretania. The pair of poles and the ridgepiece are dotted in and the location of the eight beckets, the guy ropes, and the two small rings that fit into the forked poles used to raise the entrance of the tent are shown. On the left are outlines drawn in the sand by travelers who must spend the night away from the camp on the open terrain. Drawings after Du Puigaudeau 1967 and Gabus 1955–58, vol. 2.

Hassaniya-Speaking Nomads

with a thread similar to that used in weaving. Around the central point, they edge, with large white wool yarn using stitches cast in different lengths, a square with sides from 50 cm to 2 m per side, which I have heard called many times the "eye of the tent" in Tagant, the "she-camel" in Trarza (fig. 4.9).

Each corner of the tent, reinforced with a piece of cotton folded back on a wooden arch or triangle *(khorb)*, is firmly stitched with wool embroidery to form a triangle. Between these corner arches or rings, the sides perpendicular to the strips have two other arches, usually larger, attached in the middle on the convex part of the border. For these arches, bent pieces of hardwood from the Acacia raddiana or the Balanites aegyptiaca (*talḥa* or *teīchot*) are used, the ends of which are pierced with a hot iron in order to sew them. In addition, the edge of the front of the tent is equipped, about 50 cm from the corners, with two iron rings which may be hooked over the forked stakes *(āwtad-el-bībān, Amūd)* to raise up the edge.

In beautiful tents, the guy ropes (*nes'a* or *khalfa*) are made of strips of sheepskin finely plaited in braids of square cross section, dyed bright red. The corner guy ropes, much longer than the others, measure six to eight meters. In Tagant, a superstition requires that the guy rope for the corner to the left of the entrance be of vegetal fibers to assure peace and order in the tent.

The dimensions of the Mauretanian tent basically very according to wealth, rank, and the degree of nomadism of its owner. A warrior chief who moves often and over long distances must be prepared for sudden departures and fast travel: his tent must be easy to put up and take down, and its weight must not exceed the load of a single camel. As rich and proud as he might be, how could he weigh himself down with a tent as large as that of a marabout, surrounded by his students, clients, and the poor, who must always remain at the center of his circle of influence? The tent of the cadi of Mederdra is so heavy that ten donkeys tied head to tail and walking with short steps are required to transport it.

An average tent measures five meters on a side. A tent of seven meters is already a beautiful tent. This is approximately the size of the tent of the emir of Tagant, which covers an area of about fifty square meters: the lateral guy ropes are more than seven meters long.[13]

The center of the tent rests on two supports *(rkāīz)* of clear, yellow Metragyne inermis wood *(agīlal)*, carefully rubbed with butter. Their length (3–4 m) varies according to the importance of the tent. The bases are rounded and swollen into club shapes to keep them from sinking into the sand: from this base, they taper up to end in points. They are often ornamented with a pious invocation or a word of welcome engraved or painted with henna. At the point of contact where the supports could tear it, the tent is protected by a short, bulging, curved ridgepole *(ḥammār)*, of which the smooth lower surface, ornamented with designs applied by a hot iron, has two diagonal holes dug out, where the pointed ends of the supports, slightly crossing, are fitted (fig. 4.10). This ridgepiece is longer in the north (Trarza) than in the south (Tagant).[14]

The four stakes *(āwtād)* that moor the tent to the ground on each side are simple branches of Acacia raddiana, rough-hewn, a little twisted, and knotty in order to grab better in the sand. Metal stakes would slide. If the sand is too loose and the thrust of the wind too strong, the stakes are buried horizontally and serve as anchors.

Mounting the tent. Raising the tent is the work of servants. Two men place the supports head to head on the sand, perpendicular to the two sides called "doors," but it is the *harratin* who stretch the covering over them, tie the cords to the poles, and plant the poles by pounding them in with a stone: it is preferable that this be a large polished neolithic stone called "sky stone" or "jackal stone" to which the Mauretanian nomads attribute beneficent powers.

The side poles are planted in the axis of the seams of the tent. The corner poles are planted farther out and lean out to provide increased resistance. This is why their cords are longer. None of these cords are equipped with stretchers, but the servants know exactly how much slack to leave them so that the raised tent is perfectly taut and balanced, without an excess tension which might pull up the poles.

When the servants have finished, two men slip under the cover, grab the poles, and slide their bases toward each other while raising the pointed ends which they fit into the holes of the ridgepiece. Sometimes a long strip of brown and white wool *(trīg)*, decorated with fringe and tassels, is inserted between the tent cover and the *ḥammār*[15] (see fig. 4.5b).

The tent goes up little by little: the massive feet of the center poles work the sand and disappear under the cover which rises, more and more pointed, swaying with the efforts of the men. The wrinkles stretch out; the red cords become taut. One last push: on the inverted "V" of its center poles, the tent has taken its beautiful conical shape; its slope slightly concave, it is clean and hard like a roof. Air circulates freely under its edge, raised a meter off the ground.

The edge of the "door" side is raised by two forked stakes or by another pole *(l-ʿAmūd)* in the middle. With the arrival of the cold, rain, or sandstorms, all one has to do is lower the height of the tent by spreading the bases of the center poles. A bank of sand may cover the edges if one wants to seal the tent completely.

On the day of departure, the two poles are slid down until they are flat on the sand, reversing the arrival procedure. Servant women pull out the poles, leaving the cords tied to the rings. They fold the tent in the direction of the seams, then roll it up crosswise around the center poles and the stakes. The men have only to tie it onto a camel in such a way that the center poles, their bases forward, protrude beyond the chest and the rump of the beast like long stretcher poles.[16]

The white cotton tent. The typical, traditional hair tent has a variation in Tagant and in Assaba: the white cotton tent of the Sudanese tribes (pl. 10). It has the same form, rigging, dimensions, and furniture as the brown tent. Raised and folded up in the same way, it is made, however, of small strips of white cotton *(jīf)*, fifteen to twenty centimeters wide, used in double or triple thickness and held together by a tight overcasting done on the right side.

These strips are the work of Sudanese weavers, brought by the caravaneers of Kiffa and Nioro in twenty meter rolls to the oases of the Tagant region where they trade them for dates and millet. The tent gable and corners are decorated with embroidered motifs in black wool.

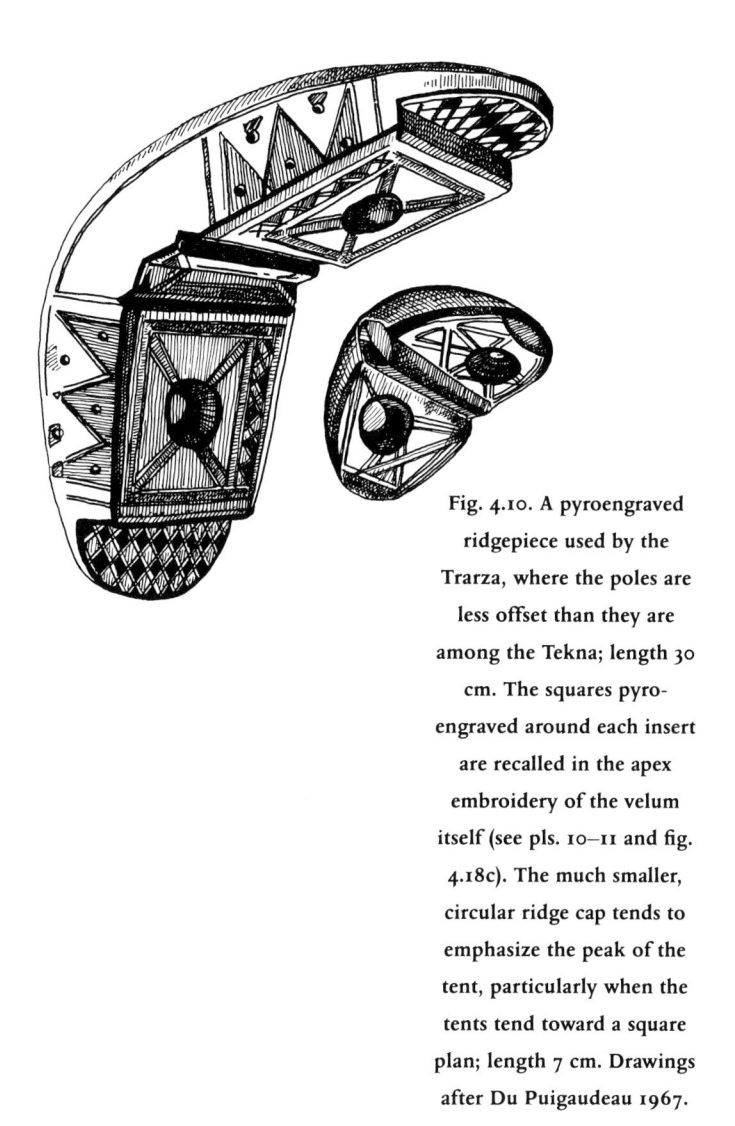

Fig. 4.10. A pyroengraved ridgepiece used by the Trarza, where the poles are less offset than they are among the Tekna; length 30 cm. The squares pyroengraved around each insert are recalled in the apex embroidery of the velum itself (see pls. 10–11 and fig. 4.18c). The much smaller, circular ridge cap tends to emphasize the peak of the tent, particularly when the tents tend toward a square plan; length 7 cm. Drawings after Du Puigaudeau 1967.

Cotton tents are less sturdy than the tents of wool or hair and have the inconvenience of absorbing water, but they are lighter in weight. By 1960 they had become as numerous as brown tents in Tagant, from where they tended to spread throughout southern Mauretania. This expansion was due to both the scarcity of skins and hair for weaving following the growing exportation of sheep and goats on foot to Senegal, and to the lack of labor for the spinning and weaving.

A good example is the tent purchased in 1960.[17] The covering is made of a double layer of strips fifteen centimeters wide, woven in Kayes. It measures six meters on the back edge, a little more at the front edge, and seven meters on the sides. The gable is marked by a ring of black wool which marks the spot for centering the small ridgepole of Balanites aegyptiaca wood. The main poles are made of wood imported from Nioro. From their top hangs a long band with a fringe *(trīg)*, woven of multicolored cotton and wool. Seven guy ropes are of plaited strips; the eighth, on the right as one exits the tent, is of twisted fibers. There are no special rings for the forked stakes; the forks are simply stuck in the corner rings, thus allowing the entrance of the cover to be raised at will.

Brown tents are often lined with a large removable piece of white percale *(benyé)* (fig. 4.11). When the tent itself is white, this second cover seems superfluous. The lining then becomes a long interior chamber lodged between the poles and independent of the tent cover. It exists only in wealthier tents, and its dimensions are variable.

The armature for it is composed of three posts of Acacia raddiana wood at each end and four arches *(ināiliyn)* made of Acacia raddiana wood in two detachable curved halves attached in the middle with ties of white percale. A double cord, tied to the second arch from the front, turns around the lining at the height of its curve, attaching the tops of the posts and the arches to maintain the spacing. It ends at the third arch from the front, so as not to block the entrance of the room.

This armature is covered with an assemblage of beautiful Sudanese blankets with woven designs on a background alternating squares of indigo wool and white cotton or white strips and plain percale. The effect is gay and charming under the whiteness of the tent, the front third of which allows room for a large shaded area in front of the tent lining.[18]

The edges of the tent are lowered all the way to the ground only in bad weather. Normally, they are raised up all the way around to insure ventilation in the tent. If the occupants wish to protect themselves from indiscreet looks or from wind or sun, poles are planted back from the edge, of which the part sticking out of the ground, decorated with designs by a hot iron, is about a meter high. A long strip of percale or of decorated leather is attached, creating a low, light wall around the tent. Ventilation is provided by the space between the strip of cloth and the tent cover.

The furnishings. Once the tent is raised, it must be provided with furnishings *(frāchāt)*. When the servant women have carefully cleaned the ground of thorns and pebbles, they smooth it and tamp it down using sticks and rolled mats. Then they cover it with mats *(ḥṣāīr)* made of stalks of grassy plants or palm laths woven with strips of leather, which make the ground as firm as a floor. On top of the mats, they lay a large piece of black lambskin fur *(fāru)*, usually three or four meters by one and a half meters, or a little smaller and more supple mat made of the skins of younger lambs *(khlef)*. Fringed cushions of worked leather, stuffed with sand, dried dung, or straw, of round or rectangular form, are arranged here and there on the mats and rugs.

The furniture is extremely simplified, and each of its pieces bears the mark of nomadic life. One finds in Mauretanian tents only those objects that are easy to fold, roll, or hang and are sturdy and supple, serving both in the dwelling and during travel. The materials used are wood and leather: there is little iron (it is too heavy), there is no breakable pottery, and no easily torn cloth.

At one end of the tent, on the left going in, are placed the wife's large saddle *(l-aḥraj)* and her personal bags *(tizigaten)* with square bottoms; on the large litter *(jahfa)* are piled the sacks *(tisūfren; ḍabāiat)* containing clothes, foodstuffs, and personal effects.

In Tagant, these sacks are piled on a rectangular structure composed of a horizontal frame resting on four uprights of carved wood *('amchchaġab)*. While traveling, the frame, turned upside down, is used as the woman's saddle, with or without the litter. On the side opposite the baggage, and in the current of air that flows under the edge of the tent and that will keep water cool by evaporation, the goatskin water bags are hung on rustic racks *(arahal-l-greb)* of Acacia raddiana wood (see fig. 4.6). To sleep, Mauretanian nomads remain in their clothes. Father and mother lie down in the middle of the tent on mats, their heads on cushions. If it is cold, one covers oneself with a lambskin mat. Babies snuggle into the warmth of their mothers' veils; older children curl up where they please in corners of the tent, among the baggage. Often they prefer to sleep outside.

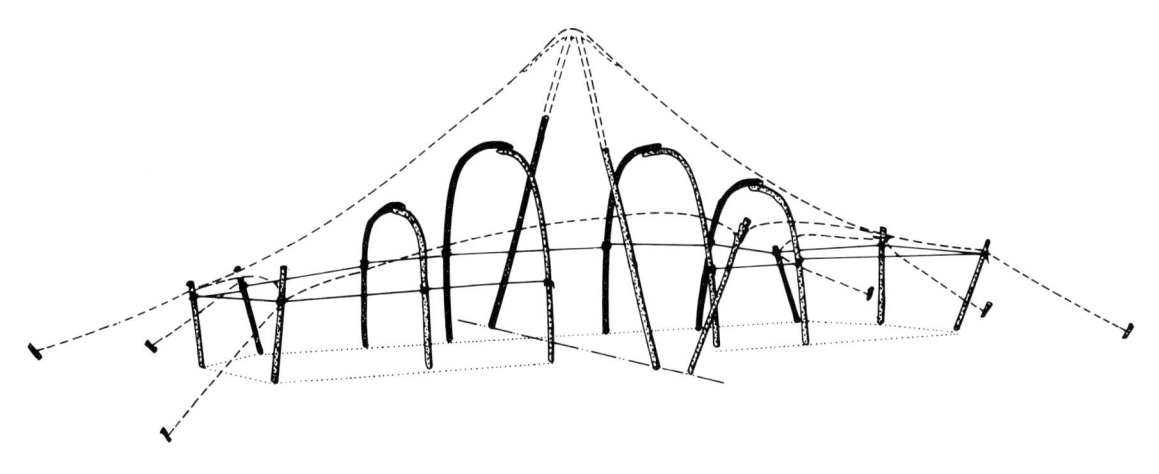

In the southeast, however, an area of Sudanese influence, there is a couch made from a wattle of straight branches or bamboo, fastened to five crosspieces by leather ties (*techgāl* or *tara*). Usually two meters long (although all sizes may be seen), it is attached to a latticework base of horizontally superimposed sticks, five or six on each side (35 cm high). The latticework base is reinforced with diagonal cross braces at the corners; uprights vertically attached by straps in the hollow of the crosses assure the spacing of the sticks. One or two other uprights on each side of the piece of furniture consolidate it. It is easy to take apart and transport (see fig. 5.8 for a mid-nineteenth-century rendering of its Tuareg version).

Sometimes the construction is simplified: the screen alone rests on four round beams supported on the ends by two other perpendicular beams, the ends of which fit into the notches of massive forked feet. This bed is much less soft than the sand, but it is useful in the south, where termites, snakes, lizards, and poisonous spiders abound. Latticework couches are especially found in the courtyards of the houses of sedentary people and in the tents of the seminomads of Tagant, Hodh, and Assaba (see fig. 10.8 for a closeup of one in a Walata courtyard).

The interior of the tent is not partitioned. There is no side reserved for men or for women. The family lives together. On certain occasions when the presence of a young woman would not be convenient—receiving a stranger, a meeting of nobles, the visit of an older relative before whom she may not appear with

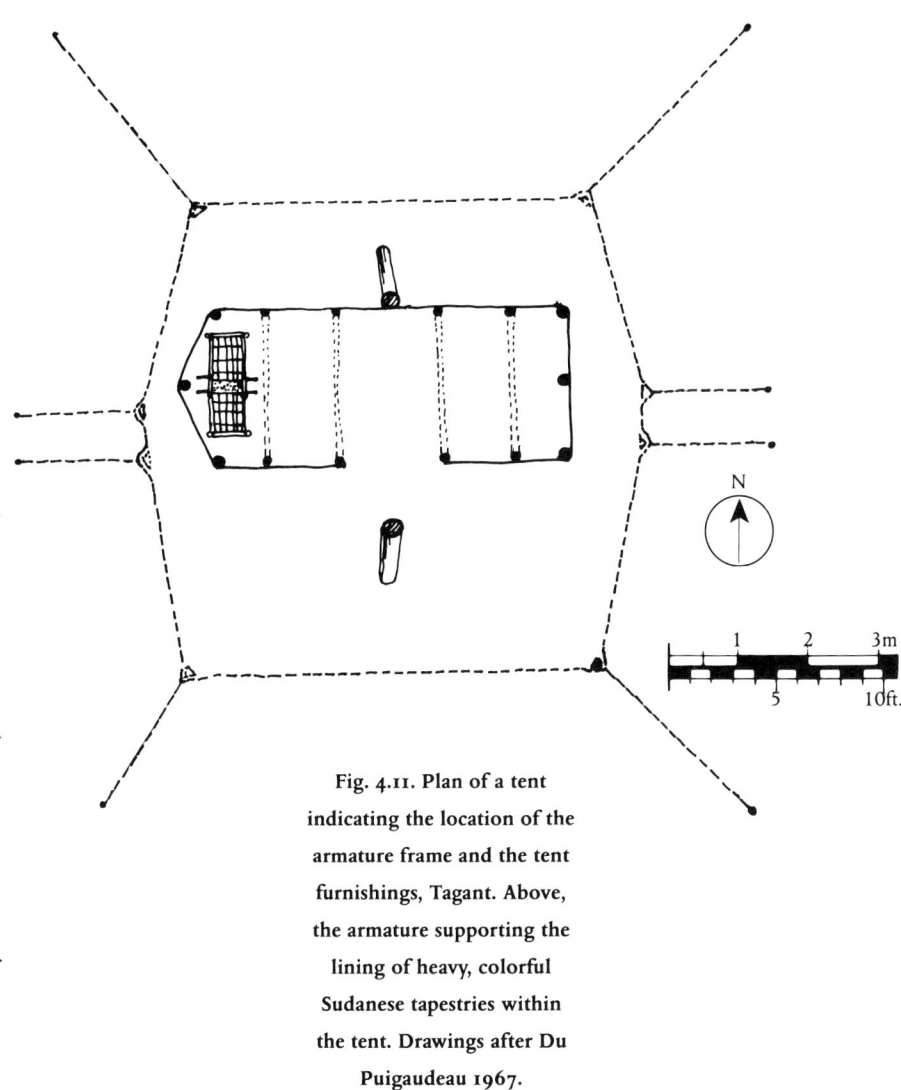

Fig. 4.11. Plan of a tent indicating the location of the armature frame and the tent furnishings, Tagant. Above, the armature supporting the lining of heavy, colorful Sudanese tapestries within the tent. Drawings after Du Puigaudeau 1967.

Hassaniya-Speaking Nomads 79

her husband—she goes to stay with a neighbor. Older women, however, are always free to stay in their homes in all circumstances.

The tent and its furnishings belong to the wife, even if it is the husband who has paid for everything. In Tijikja, Sidi u. Aleya was very fond of his white tent "as beautiful as that of the emir," all the elements of which he had purchased little by little by saving money from his salary. But his wife preferred living in a house she owned in the town. Knowing that I was looking to buy a tent, she decided to take advantage of the opportunity. "The tent belongs to the woman," poor Sidi explained to me. "If I divorce her, she will keep the tent anyway. . . . She has the right to sell it, to give it away, to burn it if she wants, with everything in it, and I can't do anything to stop her."

A bachelor never owns a tent. A man cannot live in a tent in the absence of his wife. In Boutilimit, I found one of my friends camped under a shelter of tree branches. His tent and all the household goods were stored in a straw hut. I was surprised, so he explained to me that his affairs having retained him in Boutilimit, his wife had to go off without him into the bush with her relatives. "When the wife travels, the husband cannot live in the tent: it wouldn't be proper, people would make fun of him. There are tasks to do in the tent which must be done only by women."

Until now, we have seen only the friendly face of the tent, but it can also give a signal for battle. To pull down one's tent before an undesirable stranger is a provocation. To pull it down on him after he is in it is worse, and demands revenge. Moreover, the intruder risks no greater misfortune at the time, because the tent is an inviolable place of asylum and the host could not, without dishonor, stab his worst enemy in it. This enemy, with his pursuers after him, is saved if he manages to seize the veil of the wife or place his hand on one of the two tent poles. But if he is overtaken in the bush, he is not spared.

But the true reality of a camp does not reside in the form of a tent or the size of a piece of furniture. That is only the material reality, obvious and easy to know. When everything has been measured, the essential remains to be captured: the life that brought these objects into being, the atmosphere of the camp, the courtesy, the solidarity that unite its members and thanks to which they are able to overcome the difficulties of an uncertain existence. These are the laws of a hospitality without which travel would be almost impossible in a country devoid of public refuge or natural resources.

CAMEL SADDLERY
(1980–81:181–88)

The different pieces of saddlery used by women are, naturally, more richly decorated, more comfortable, in a word lovelier than those reserved for men. They are made up of the same elements in different forms, produced with the same materials: hide, tanned or raw supple leather, silky black lambskin; a little copper and iron for the rings and buckles of the saddle-girth.

The men's saddle tends toward ease of handling, lightness, strength, and endurance. Women require elegance of form, abundance of decoration of leather, wood, or metal (sculpted, pyroengraved, chiseled, painted, or embroidered with fine strips), and stability. Their camel trappings are part of their stylishness, like the beauty of the camel. This litter is spacious enough so that one or two women, sitting in the middle on furs and cushions, can find room for their small children, a few pieces of precious baggage, or things that will be useful along the way, even a newborn kid whose legs are still too weak to follow the caravan. The mount is, most often and by preference, a female camel whose milk will feed the women and children during the trip (fig. 4.12). Thus the aristocratic Mauretanian woman *(beidāniya)* goes slowly, swaying with the regular gait of her mount, in the shade of an awning of white percale stretched on a light armature of flexible branches, curved in the form of a royal crown.

This complicated and easily adjusted apparatus does not have a name for the whole corresponding to the French word for "saddle," nor to the Berber word *(l-aḥraj)* sometimes used in the Tagant. The term *bassur*, used elsewhere, is unknown. "Palanquin" does not fit. The term used most often *(l-ḥijba)* describes woman-mount-trappings-baggage as a whole, and that only during the ride.

The trappings for women's use are basically composed of the saddle *(l-aḥraj)* which, with some variations or adaptations, is similar to the men's saddle *(raḥla)*, and a rectangular litter *(jārfa)* of knotted strips interwoven and stretched on a wooden framework or a frame *('amchchaġab)* whose four uprights of carved wood, attached to crosspieces at the corners of the litter, carry the canopy and its awning. To these essentially feminine elements must be added those that are the same for the two sets of trappings (i.e., those used by both men and women): the saddle-girth with its beautiful buckle, the tail strap, the rein and the nose ring to which it is attached, and the saddle blanket padded with wool which protects the back of the mount under the saddle.

Fig. 4.12. The saddle with its pommel and cantle; length 1.30 m; height at the cantle 80 cm. The rectangular litter is fixed to the saddle; length 1.37 m; width 77 cm. Above, the armature for the crown above the litter; length and width 1.60 m; height 3 m. Drawings after Du Puigaudeau 1980–81 and Monteil 1952.

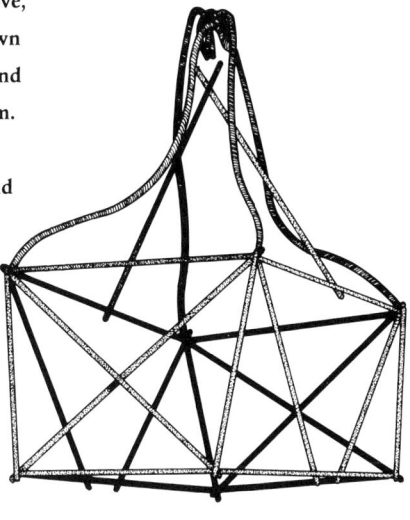

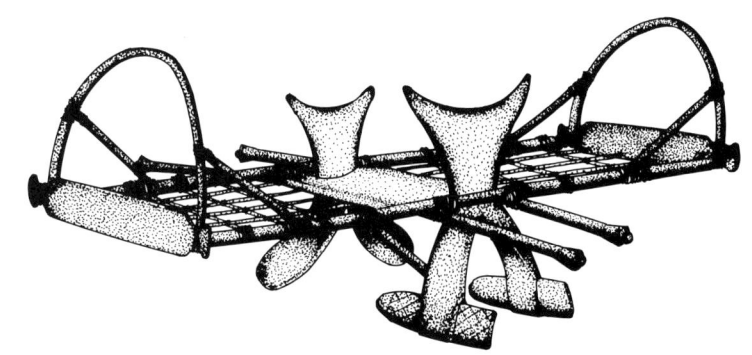

The saddle. The fundamental elements of the men's saddle are recognized in both the Trarza and the Tagant women's saddles, but the pommel *(garbūç)* and the cantle *(garbūç alūrani)* are placed far enough apart so that the litter may be placed between them. Both of them are enlarged toward the top, notched into two "horns" useful for hanging goatskins and bags or for holding onto in case of a sudden loss of balance. All these parts are covered with tanned leather dyed a bright yellow. A padded rug of red leather *(lebda)* protects the hump and back of the camel. Two wooden shafts with a slight curve in the middle connect the pommel to the cantle, to which each shaft is firmly attached by ties of rawhide, applied while wet. These are what support the litter. They also have a decorative role, and their ends, which stick out far beyond the saddle in front and behind, are carved and decorated with linear designs using a hot iron.

The litter is a strong network of small leather cords of square mesh stretched tight by solid ligatures within a rectangular wooden frame, and in the center a piece of yellow leather is attached and wrapped around two of the shafts. Along its length, the frame is edged with a strip of light, smooth, carefully polished wood. Along its width, this smooth stick is replaced by a thick, flat, deeply carved crosspiece of Acacia nilotica *(gonakie)* wood. At the corners of the two ends are attached arches of supple branches covered with black leather, like the handles of a basket. These are used for easier handling of the litter and to attach baggage and utensils to during travel. The saddle described here is the model most often seen: with a few variations in details, it is the one most often encountered, almost everywhere.

The *'amchchaġab* is the masterpiece of the Mauretanian saddlemaker (see fig. 4.6). "The Toiler," it is the frame which, during the displacements, carries the weight of the awning covered with white cotton fabric *(khteīr)* and during rest stops, under the tent, the sacks of millet, rice, and tea, the clothes and blankets, everything one wants to keep away from the ants and poisonous insects on the ground.[19]

This frame is an openwork structure whose rectan-

Fig. 4.13. The camel litter, right side up, in use.

gular base, formed by two round crossbars of light Balanites aegyptiaca wood, is placed across the shafts of the saddle. Two solid slats of hardwood made of Dalbergia molanonylon (laburnum = *sanqū*) maintain the spacing of the structure between the two bars, over the litter. Eight long sticks crossed diagonally on the rear and on the sides, and in a "V" in front so as not to hinder the woman who is driving, assure the rigidity of the apparatus. All these sticks, as well as the large round crossbars of the base, end in carved knobs and grooves which facilitate tying or their encasement with raw leather covers.

The beauty, the originality of this framework, the refined, luxurious aspect that marks Saharan production, reside in the four *sanqū* uprights attached to the corners of the structure whose flat surfaces are decorated on their outer face with very finely engraved geometric designs. The ends resting in the lower frame are carved into forks and are fitted to the round crossbars of the structure. A slender end would sink into the sand. Also, the other end is different: it ends in massive feet, rounded in the form of mushrooms, so that they cannot sink into the sand no matter what the weight of the baggage it supports when, turned over, the armature rests under the tent.

All the characteristic elements of the Mauretanian craftsman are brought together in this baggage carrier: taste for embellishing the usefulness of an object, ingenuity put at the service of decoration, the unique value of an object made for a particular person and no other, however equal in the mind of the artisan. I have never seen two identical ones, even though they are all made of the same wood and by the same workers with the same traditional tools. Thus each nomadic woman who goes off into the bush is proud of owning a work of art made especially for her, which resembles no other. This is a satisfaction of which my friends were very appreciative.

The crowning of this edifice of wood and leather so judiciously studied is a light structure *(khteīr)* of supple branches of light yellow Grewia bicolor *(imijij)* whose alternating concave and convex curves describe a sort of cage around the travelers. The base is a rectangular frame of the same dimensions as the litter to which it is attached in the four corners. Vertical branches tie it to a second parallel frame, trace the ribs of the "roof," and converge in the middle in a pointed gable. Other pieces of branch placed diagonally between the two horizontal frames echo the position of the uprights of the baggage carrier.

Sometimes the armature for the crown may be missing, and the woman simply crouches in the sun, shading her baby under her veil, on bundles of clothes and blankets folded and rolled on a mat, between the sculpted uprights of the baggage carrier-litter (fig. 4.13). Such reduced trappings might suffice for short displacements in uninhabited areas where convention does not require a woman to be hidden, or again in winter when excessive sunshine is not to be feared. But in the hot season it is both prudent and preferable to spread a piece of white cotton tied in four corners over the armature crown, thus transforming the assemblage of woman-mount-trappings-baggage *(hijba)* into a small moving tent (see fig. 5.13 for a similar canopy in use among the Tuareg).

Litter and palanquin furnishings. Saharan ingenuity has invented two great cowhide sacks *(tiziyaten)* (fig. 4.14a). The bottom is a rectangle, the edge of which, pleated in the four corners, is folded over on a shorter strip, followed by a second strip making a mouth around a final cover. Each of the two cowhide sacks is stuffed with dry straw, with sacks of millet, barley, or rice, with clothes, etc., the whole being so firmly packed that the sack becomes as hard as wood. Hung by twisted leather cords below the litter, their longest side is against the flanks of the camel. Thus they form buffers that maintain the litter on a hori-

Fig. 4.14. a. The great cowhide storage traveling sacks; base 1 m × .65 m. b. A flat, rectangular rice storage traveling sack from Mederdra; width 40 cm; length 104 cm. The profile of the rice storage sack follows the same principle that dictates the design of a waterskin. Construction diagrams after Creyaufmüller 1983 and Monteil 1952. Drawings after Du Puigaudeau 1980–81 and Gabus 1955–58, vol. 2.

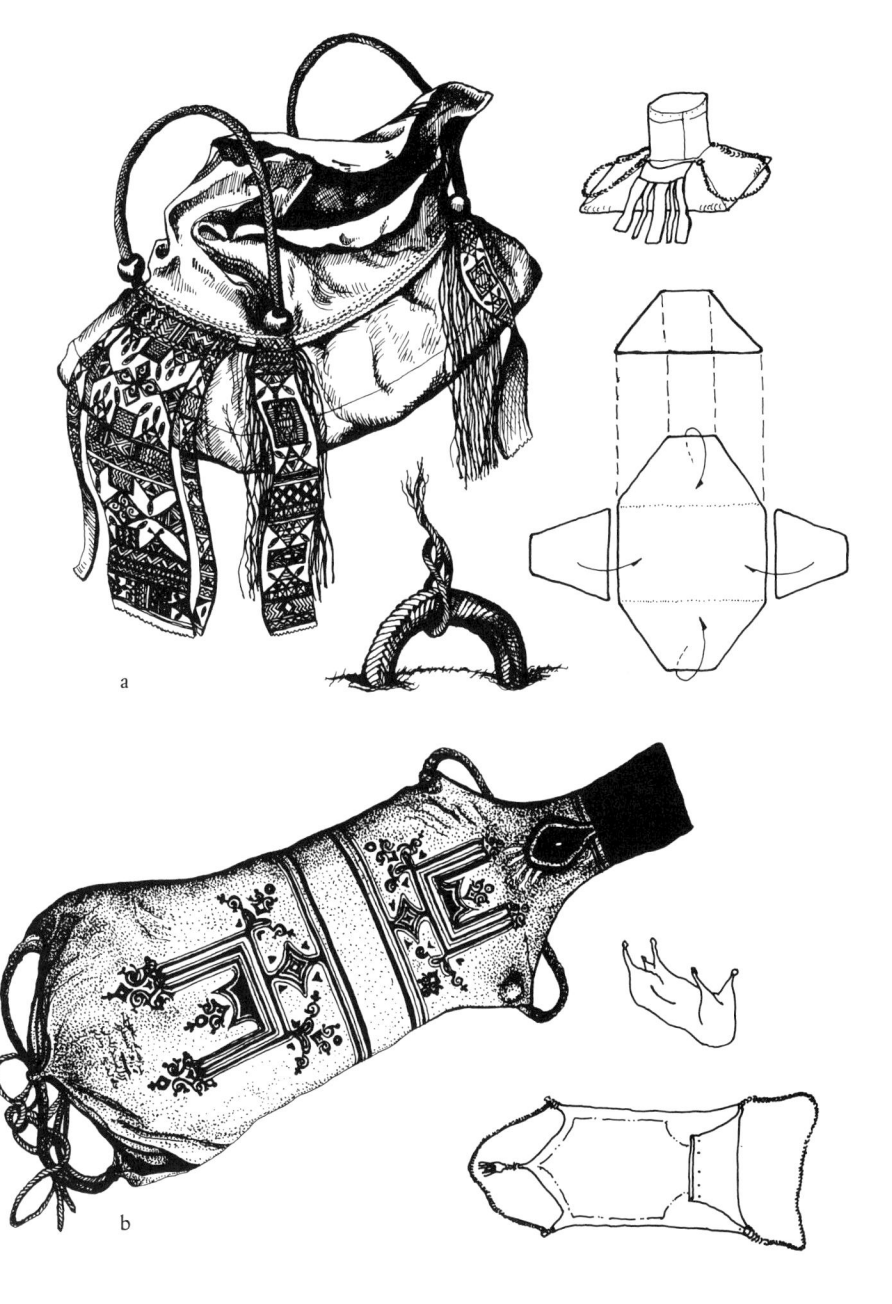

Hassaniya-Speaking Nomads 83

zontal level despite the movements of the ride or the unequal weight of the load.

All this is the armature, the pretext, the piece of equipment—meaning the prop for the minute decoration so much preferred in the Sahara. Superfluous luxury must be made of the little that one possesses. The solidity of naked leather, treated or not, plain and simple, would not be enough; there must be long supple ribbons of kidskin, falling from the neck-seams, and strips fastened together by embroidered stitches. Tassels of multicolored leather fringe burst out from the ends of twisted leather cords covered with a network of strips.

Color is worth more than the pen to render the contrast between the deep reds of the grounds and the ruddy gold yellow, or bluish green, or emerald of the designs: swastikas, Byzantine crosses, scallops and zigzags, triangles, and protective eyes cover the long fluttering ribbons of kidskin, an imagery of symbols come together to enrich the saddle, the cushions, the belt of the aristocratic woman, and the carved supports of her litter.

IMAGERY

This imagery finds its quintessence on the decorated house walls painted by women in the city of Walata (Du Puigaudeau 1957; Prussin 1986). The designs, which derive from a very gender-discrete symbolism, appear not only on all the leatherwork the women do but across the whole spectrum of surface design they have a hand in or on.

The quality and character of Mauretanian design, created by men and women alike, can also be explained in part by the religious fervor that has historically characterized nomadic society in Mauretania. The Mauretanian nomads are very religious. There are active and celebrated religious centers (*zawiya*s) in both the cities and under the tent. Religion is often transformed into superstition and takes on a magical quality. Furthermore, Hassaniya is an Arabic dialect, and Arabic script is used to write it (in contrast to the Tuareg who use the Berber-derivative *tifinar*). It is the flow of the cursive script that is transformed and stylized with great verve into the Mauretanian design so

Fig. 4.15. Above, the elongated, rectangular men's pillow; length 88 cm; width 33 cm. Below, the round women's leather cushion; diameter 45 cm. Marilyn Hoskins Collection.

characteristic of the multitude of traveling sacks *(tasūfrat)* which, like the great cowhide sacks above, are also part of the domestic furnishings and transport equipage[20] (fig. 4.14b).

Among the most intriguing design elements is one of the key Arabic letters, *waw*. Most often transformed or stylized in spirals, into a human ideogram, it is used exclusively for the ornamentation of objects of women's use and on the architectural surfaces that define women's space. The most significant of these objects is the round, fringed sheepskin pillow *(surmīye)* given to a young married woman (fig. 4.15). The woman's pillow is covered with sexual symbols stylized in the extreme, but whose sense remains evident. Triangles (associated with the pubis) sometimes end in *waw*, and the cutting out of the tongues of the fringe follows the contour of the head and womb of similar wall decorations. The same symbolic elements ornament the larger leather sacks in which the woman arranges her clothes and the patch of leather at the center of her camel saddle. The bridegroom's pillow *(usāde)* in comparison is rectangular—more closely approximating, in its profile, the *tasūfrat* above—and without fringes. Its ornamentation more often consists of a group of geometric elements: squares, lozenges, chevrons, and so on.[21]

Similarly, one finds other Arabic letters *(çad, dal,* and *mim)* in the guise of ornament, pulled from their isolated or initial form and integrated into the motifs of the skin floor mats as well as on calabashes[22] (fig. 4.16). One also finds them on the iron, copper, or silver appliqués of the woman's jewelry box, on the copper or silver appliqué of the Mauretanian harp, the playing of which is exclusively a feminine skill, as well as on wooden spoons, jewelry, and locks, all of which are made by the blacksmiths and silversmiths, husbands of the leatherworkers.

Aside from weaving and stitching the tent velum, Mauretanian women execute no manual labor. But in the region of Walata they embroider the long percale tunics worn by men. The ensemble of embroidery motifs, executed in compact white silk needle lace *(tichbok)* recalls, in its use of geometry and magic squares, the origin of another set of design motifs from the number five[23] (fig. 4.17). The number five, in its various spatial configurations, appears prominently in all the ornament. The hand of Fatima, "the most perfect instrument which God has put to the service of man," is equally a symbol of the five sacred Islamic personages, Muhammed, Ali, Fatima, Hassan, Hussein —symbol again of Providence, of the epitome, the abstraction of the Law, of Religion. The number five also translates into four points and a center, a spatial construct that implies a square, much like the Kaaba at Mecca, and the approximation of a square that the southern Mauretanian tent tends toward.

This gender-discrete symbolic imagery, which began with Du Puigaudeau's suggestion in relation to Walata house decoration, appears exclusively, and only, in house interiors—in the deeply recessed sleeping room, around its entrance from the interior courtyard, or in the women's courtyard itself—but always in what is considered women's space. Their location matches that of the similarly richly decorated furnishings in the tent interior. The same patterns, the same meanings, occupy the same spatial relationship in both nomadic and sedentary spaces.

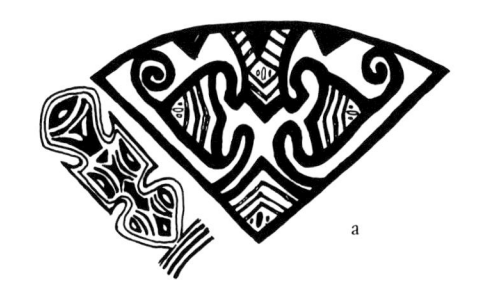

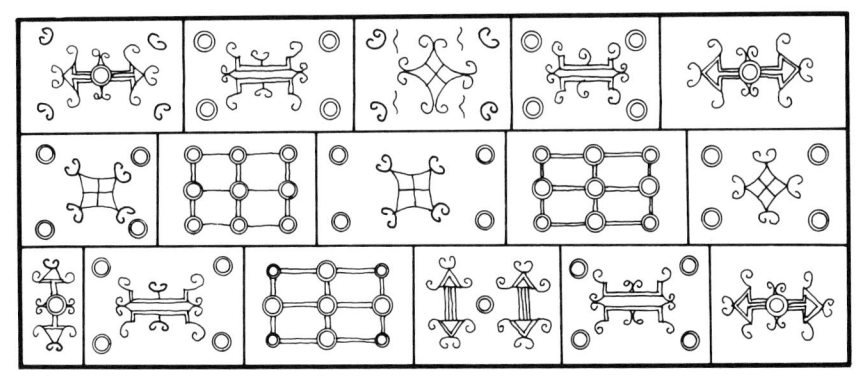

Fig. 4.16. a. Line drawing of the *waw* on leatherwork and calabashes. b. Abstracted script on the rectangular mats; width 1.52 m; length 3.70 m. Drawings after Du Puigaudeau 1957 and Gabus 1955–58, vol. 2.

Hassaniya-Speaking Nomads   85

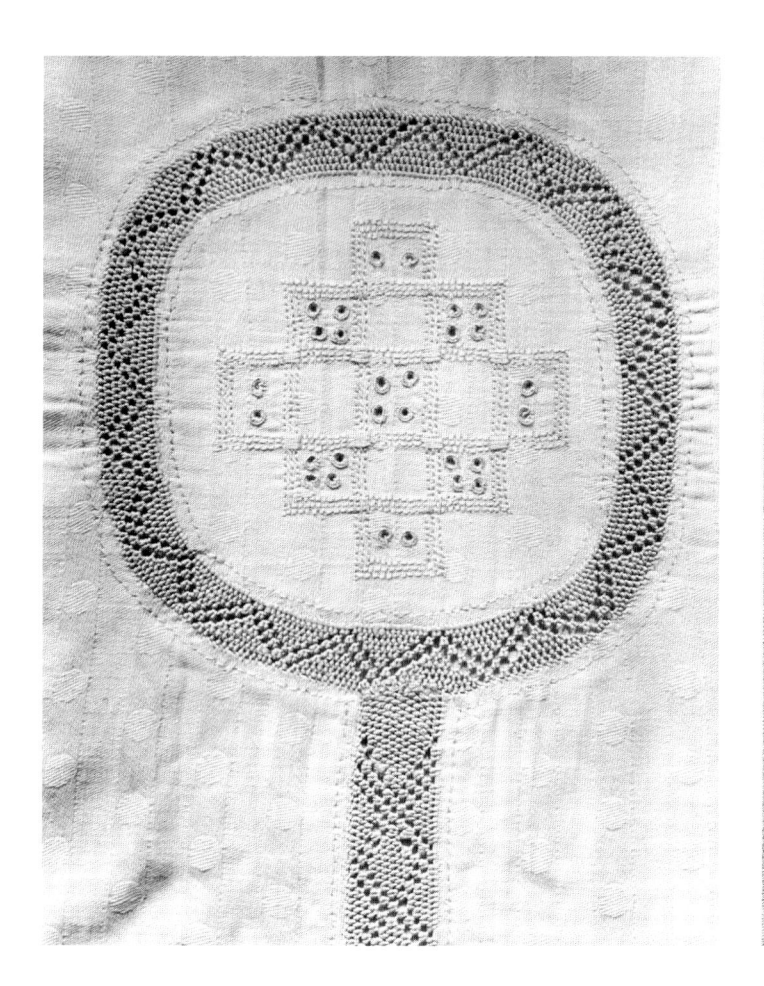

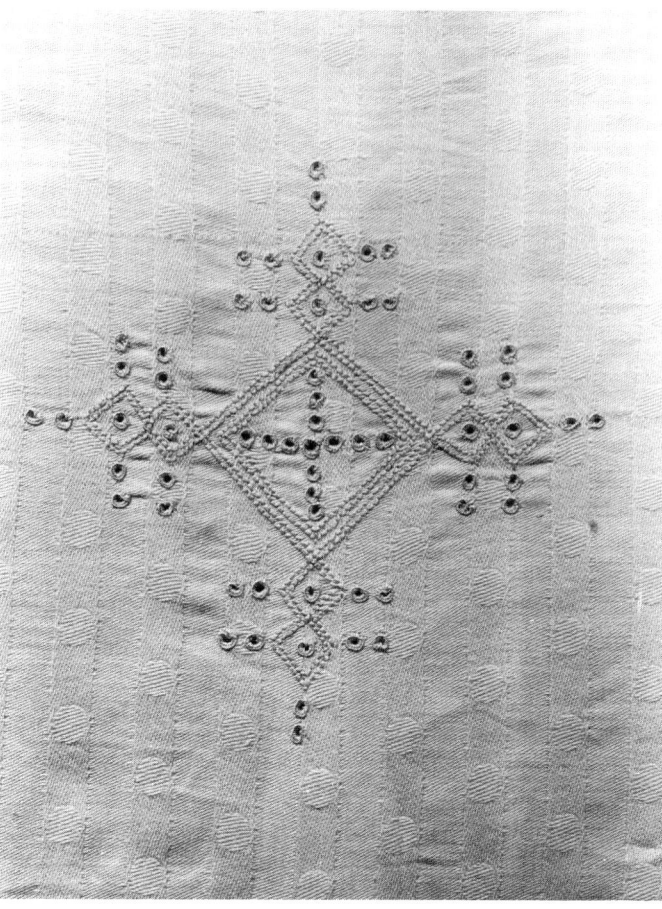

Fig. 4.17. Embroidery motifs on the long tunics worn by men and old women.

No visit to a Mauretanian camp would be complete without participation in a tea ceremony. Hospitality, particularly toward strangers, is paramount in nomadic societies. Travel would be almost impossible in a country devoid of public refuge or natural resources, and the ritual of a tea ceremony encapsulates the essence of nomadic hospitality. The recitation of greetings and well wishes ends with the classic phrase which Du Puigaudeau (1967) cites: "Now that you have arrived in this tent, you have come back to your home!" Sitting inside the tent, the brilliantly colored leather-covered tea service basket at one's feet matches the embroidered reinforcement at the apex of the tent overhead: the same embellished square patterning, first encountered on embroidery in the guise of a magic square, is both below and above, defining the volumetric cube of space (pl. 11).

BIRTHING

In her discussion of the arts and customs of the Mauretanian nomads, Du Puigaudeau devoted a few pages to the marriage ceremony (1972:191), and her description sheds a little light on the intimate relationship between the Mauretanian marriage ceremony and its panoply.[24] However, her description of birthing practices (1972:203) poignantly highlights the inseparable link, the synonymity, between birth and architecture. When her time has come, the woman giving birth stands, crouches, or kneels with her legs spread, over a hole dug into fine clean sand. Her torso thrown back, hands raised above her head, she holds onto one of the tent poles. Her mother and other women, relatives or servants, support her, while the midwife stimulates her efforts with massage, pulling, and applications of hot dressings and sand.

86   African Nomadic Architecture

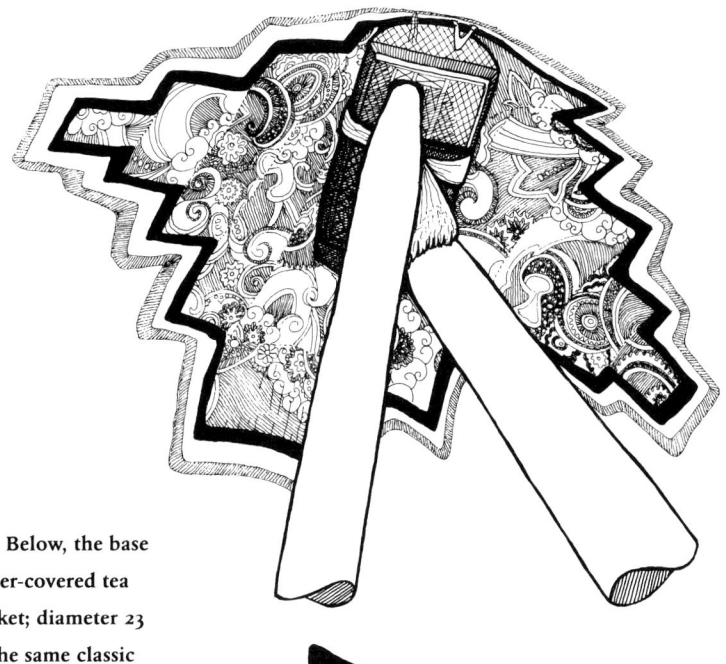

Fig. 4.18. a. Below, the base of a leather-covered tea service basket; diameter 23 cm. b. The same classic patterns are applied with henna to the hands of the bride. c. Above, the embroidered reinforcement on the underside of the tent apex. Drawings after photographs, Museum of Mankind, London, Du Puigaudeau 1970, and at Rosso, Mauretania, 1978.

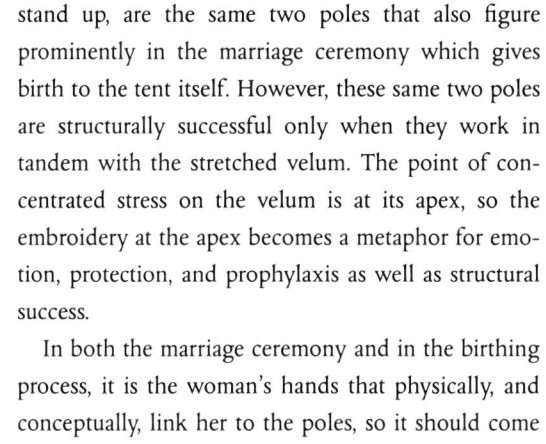

These poles that serve as an anchor for birth, the same poles without which no Mauretanian tent would stand up, are the same two poles that also figure prominently in the marriage ceremony which gives birth to the tent itself. However, these same two poles are structurally successful only when they work in tandem with the stretched velum. The point of concentrated stress on the velum is at its apex, so the embroidery at the apex becomes a metaphor for emotion, protection, and prophylaxis as well as structural success.

In both the marriage ceremony and in the birthing process, it is the woman's hands that physically, and conceptually, link her to the poles, so it should come as no surprise that the design of henna patterns painted on a bride's hands show such a close resemblance to the apex design and carry the same design configuration as the base of the tea caddy, a symbol par excellence of hospitality (fig. 4.18). A specific design in the form of an embellished square recurs in all three. The earth below, on which the tea caddy rests, is conceptually linked, via a woman's pair of henna-protected hands, to the velum apex which defines the sky above. The poles are an axis mundi, establishing a continuum in space and defining the center of life's place.

Hassaniya-Speaking Nomads   87

5
THE TUAREG: KEL AHAGGAR AND KEL FERWAN

The Tuareg (Kel Tamachek), the People of the Veil, who inhabit a vast area of the western Sahara extending north and south, are probably more familiar to the Western reader than any other nomads in Africa. The founding of cities such as Timbuktu and Agades have been attributed to them (the former in the fourteenth century by a woman; the latter as part of a consolidation under a sultanate). Caravans could succeed only under their protection, and in the course of time they were able to gain and exercise control over a vast domain. The Tuareg warrior astride his riding camel, with fiery, penetrating eyes piercing his ubiquitous blue veil, has come to symbolize the exoticism and romance of the Sahara. However, the rather remarkable renderings of the Tuareg woman astride her wedding camel in the Fezzan region of southern Libya that Lyon (1821) rendered in the early eighteenth century (see pl. 3) seem to have been forgotten, even though Tuareg myths of origin rest on a matrilineal ancestry.[1]

The vast literature on the Tuareg, which dates back to the earliest accounts by Arabic geographers and historians, encompasses all aspects of Tuareg life. Yet the Tuareg seem as elusive today as they did in the early Arabic and European accounts, although scholars have devoted their lives to documenting Tuareg culture. In addition to those whose military and political instructions took them into the heart of the desert and for whom ethnographic documentation was a *sine qua non* for negotiation and conquest, there are those—like Lyon (1821), Barth (1857), Duveyrier (1864), Benhazera (1908), Nicholas (1938, 1950), Lhote (1944, 1947), Foucauld (1951–52), Nicolaisen (1963), Gabus (1955–58), Bernus (1974, 1981a, b), and Casajus (1981)—whose interests, challenged perhaps by the exoticism of the desert and the elusiveness of its inhabitants, have enriched our knowledge of Tuareg culture with their detailed documentation.

The Tuareg trace their origin matrilineally back to the North African Berber Sanhaja. Gradually penetrating the Sahara in a still undefined time frame, they spread across vast regions, surviving by means of a range of economic activities and political suzerainties. Their diaspora involved interaction with diverse populations, and while Islamization and Arabization were minimal, political hegemony and cohesiveness were essential for survival. The eight politically distinct "drum" groups *(ettebel)*, all speaking mutually intelligible dialects of a Berber-derived language *(tamachek)*, are designated by geographic region. Two of these, the Kel Ajjer and the Kel Ahaggar, are known as the northern Tuareg. The other six—the Kel Adrar, the Kel Ayr (to whom the Kel Ferwan belong), the Kel Geres, the Iwllemmeden Kel Dennek, the Iwllemmeden Kel Ataram, and the Kel Tademaket—live on the southern outskirts of the true desert and are known as the southern Tuareg (fig. 5.1).

Their complex socioeconomic hierarchy, which is as relevant as their political structure, is divided into free nobles *(imajeren)*, the religious literates in Arabic *(ineslemen)*, vassals *(imrad)*, their intermediaries *(izeggaren* or

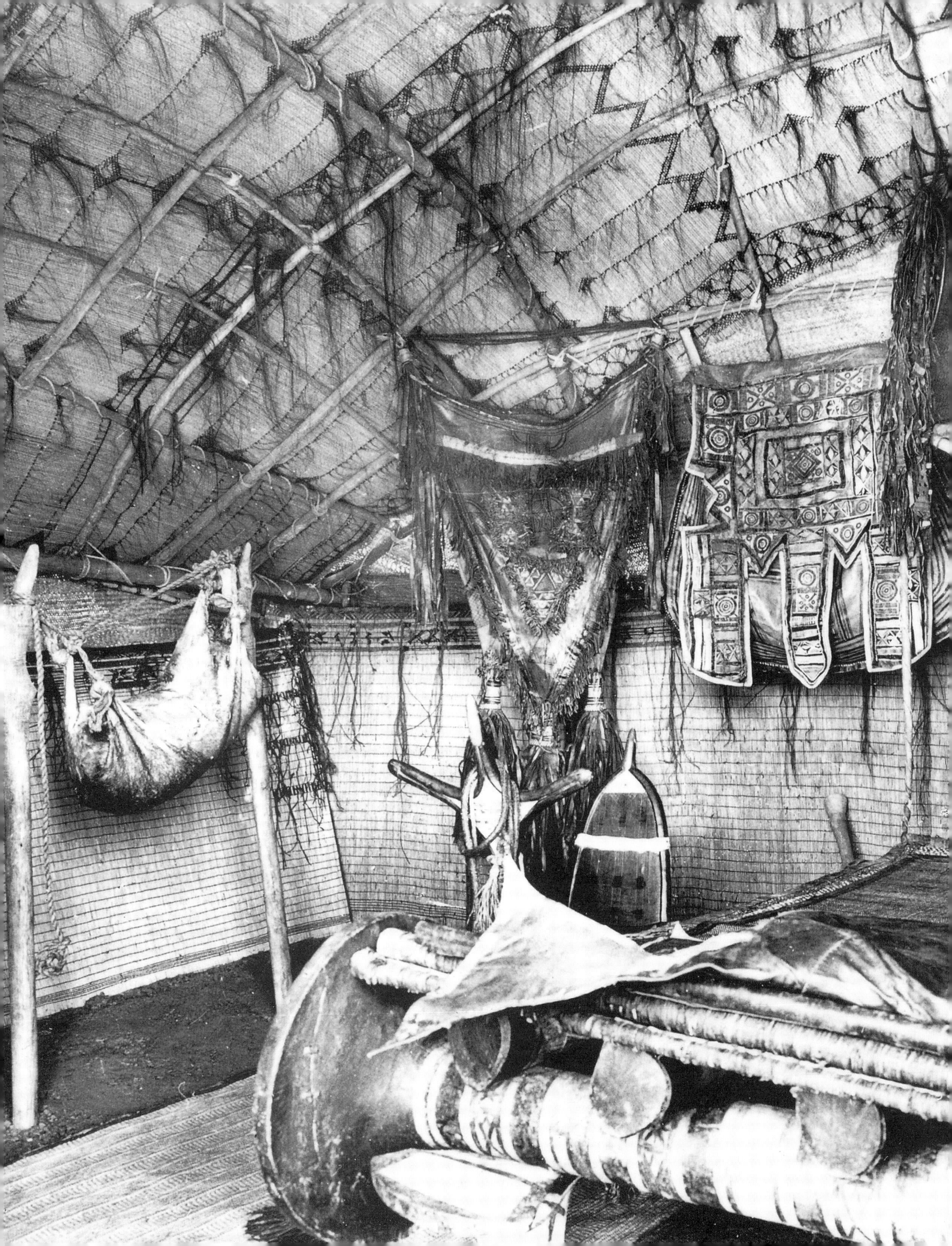

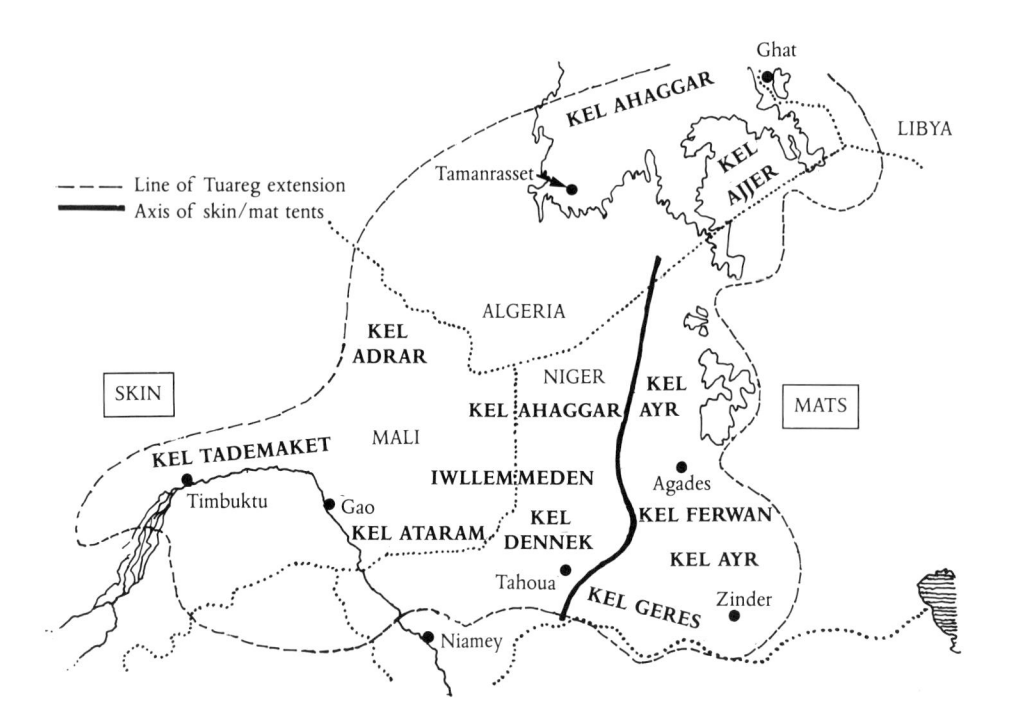

Fig. 5.1. Map showing the location of Tuareg groups and the suggested axis separating skin tents and mat-covered armature tents. Drawing after Bernus 1981a.

Fig. 5.2. *(opposite)* a. A leather tent from the Niger Bend, similar to those used in the Ahaggar.
b. A mat-covered armature Kel Ferwan tent, Niger.

harratin), slaves *(iklan)*, and endogamous artisan castes *(ineden)* who are outside the hierarchy—the blacksmiths or woodworkers and their wives *(tenaden)* who are the leatherworkers and the basketmakers. As free men and women with a position similar, in some ways, to that of the religious literates, their artisanry is distinct from the woodwork, leatherwork, and basketry practiced by men and women domestics "under the tent," that is, non-guilded artisans.[2] The intricacy that characterizes the endogamous artisan Tuareg families is further complicated by the position of those related families resident in urban centers rather than being attached to political hierarchies.

The written form of the Tuareg language *(tifinar)* derives from an early Libyco-Berber script.[3] Early accounts suggest that the script was better known by Tuareg women who taught their daughters, just as it is also the Tuareg women musicians and epic poets who have transmitted the oral traditions. Given what were historically systems of matrilineal succession and inheritance, the preservation of cultural identity was in great measure their responsibility and role.

The architectural typology of the Tuareg tent was examined in great detail by Nicolaisen (1963). Other authors who have subsequently enriched his typology all continue to honor his interpretation which divides Tuareg tent types into two major categories—skin tents and mat-covered tents—along geographical lines (see fig. 5.1). The geographical division of cultural preference along a north-south axis is not, however, a rigid division, nor is it completely accurate. If, as these various authors have suggested, the preferences are related to available natural resources (specifically the presence of the dum palm), then an east-west axis reflecting the biogeography of the region would be equally relevant. It is also not uncommon practice for the same Tuareg group to alternate between a skin-covered tent and a mat-covered tent, depending on the season and their patterns of migration. As a consequence, structural differences may be an equally important factor. The relationship between gender-discrete skills that characterize the exploitation of primary materials and resources upon which the repertoire of Tuareg architectures depend is equally important in understanding and interpreting the variations in Tuareg tent types.

The contents of this chapter were selected in order to illustrate two extremities in the spectrum of tent types preferred and used by Tuareg groups: the Kel Ahaggar and the Kel Ferwan (fig. 5.2a, b). By comparing the use of materials, resources, spatial organization, and structural systems, and how these correspond with variation in marriage ritual, what emerges is a fascinating overview of both cultural similarity and diversity in the symbolic aspects of Tuareg space. Like the Hassaniya above, comparison also evokes some interesting potentials for a historic interpretation of particular architectural features which contribute to stylistic variation.

The Kel Inteser (of the Kel Tademaket drum group), who migrated from the Ahaggar and now live in the region of Lake Faguibine, Mali, utilize a skin tent which has received little attention. Nicolaisen (1963), who discusses it in the context of the Kel Ahaggar marriage ritual and general tent history, describes it briefly but does not include it in his graphic typology. When viewed in the context of the Kel Ahaggar marriage ritual that he describes, it evokes the possibility of a particularly poignant, certainly intriguing, historical connection between the Mauretanian nomads, the Kunta, and the Kel Tademaket.[4]

The Kel Ahaggar skin tent (Foucauld 1951–52), from the region around Tamanrasset, consists of the skin velum, a single pole and its cap constituting a T-shaped mast, and a set of perimeter pickets. The skin tent used by the Iwllemmeden Kel Dennek (Nicolas 1938, 1950) also depends on a single central pole and a cap, but the cap is stabilized by four interior posts and a set of guy ropes.

The description of a Kel Ferwan tent (Casajus) is followed by a description and interpretation of the Kel Ferwan marriage ritual. The attentive reader who chooses to compare these variations in structure, material, behavior, and creativity reflected in marriage ritual may be encouraged to speculate further on the historical reasons for such variant configurations within a common cultural tradition, just as Nicolaisen (1963) and Bernus (1981a, b) have already begun to do.

TENTS AND MARRIAGE

Among all the Tuareg, northern and southern, the tent comes into being with the marriage ceremony. Despite both ceremonial and architectural distinctions, the term for marriage (*éduben* or *éhen*) is synonymous with the term for tent *(éhen)*. The term is associated with numerous expressions related to marriage: "to set

a

b

up the tent" or "to fabricate or make a tent" means to get married. To ask a woman if she is married, one says "Have you made a tent?" The woman is said to be the "tent-custodian," and sometimes she is also called "a tent" *(éhen)*. To marry, for a man, is "to enter a woman's tent." The womb is also called a tent, and women can collectively be referred to as "those-of-the-tents" (Casajus 1983).[5]

The way in which the term is used is similar to the way in which we use the term "house." We speak of housing something, that is, of enveloping, accommodating it, just as the nomads also use the term in reference to the leather casing of a knife. We also speak of the "House of Rothschild" in the genealogical sense, just as among the Tuareg one can be said to descend from a great tent, that is, a powerful, illustrious family. It has a further sense for the nomads: the tent is a metaphor for the institution of the family. Because the family is matrilineal, the tent becomes a metaphor for matriliny and an allegory for maternity.

Women are responsible for every part of the tent with one exception: the elaborate, richly ornamented ridgepoles and ridgepieces, essential for the structural success of a true skin tent, are carved by the blacksmiths. Among the northern Tuareg, however, they may be carved by the noble women who are skilled in woodworking (Nicolaisen 1963).[6] These are the same women who also carve the *tifinar* script onto the poles and their ridge caps. It is the Tuareg women who are the creators, bearers, and transmitters of the meanings and design that make up the architectural and visual imagery.[7]

The description below of the Kel Ahaggar marriage ritual, based on Nicolaisen (1963:471–72), takes on new meaning in this context not only because it is so revealing for the interface between ritual behavior and architecture, but because it highlights the critical role of the supporting tent poles which were equally the focus of the Hassaniya birthing process. A historical, cultural connection is implied, as well as an architectural link in the shadows of time, despite current differences in architectural style and practices among the Hassaniya and the Kel Ahaggar.[8]

THE KEL AHAGGAR MARRIAGE CEREMONY

According to Nicolaisen, the wedding ceremony, held close to the camp of the bride's family, is attended by relatives and guests from other tribes. On the first day of the wedding feast there is an afternoon ceremonial ride followed by an evening of music, singing, and dancing in which all except the bride and groom participate. They remain separated from each other, faces closely veiled, in tents hidden from the wedding place and pitched in opposite directions.

Preparations are made for the first ceremonial meeting of the bride and groom at this wedding place shortly before midnight. Digging with potsherds, with wooden and metal containers, or their hands, the women build a little sandhill *(adebel)* about one meter high, just big enough for two people to sit on. The wedding tent is then brought to the ceremonial place with loud cheers, shrills, and drumming. A woman lies down on the ceremonial hill with a pole in each of her hands, pressing the tops of them firmly against each other. While the woman is lying down, two men position themselves, one on each side of the hill. They then throw the tent skin between them three times over the sandhill and the woman. Once done, the skin velum is suspended over the sandhill in a very imperfect way, the sheet resting on the two poles buried in the ground in the front and upon a shorter pole at the back.

Shortly after the wedding tent has been erected, the groom arrives at the ceremonial place in a procession with a great many young men. The procession circles the tent three times, counterclockwise, and the groom is led into the tent where he sits on the sandhill. Shortly afterward, the bride is led toward the wedding tent by a procession of young women singing, drumming, and shrilling. Arriving at the tent, they circle it clockwise with the bride three times and then stop before the entrance. When the pair of sandals which they now claim has been handed over, the bride is led into the tent and placed upon the sandhill behind the groom. Shortly before sunrise, bride and groom leave, returning to the individual tents from which they came.

In mid-morning the wedding tent is taken down and re-erected in a normal way, a short distance from where it was first pitched. The sandhill is left untouched, and in time the wind obliterates it. The velum is attached to twelve poles around the structure, and mats are drawn around the lower part of the tent. However, the interior arrangement still differs from a normal tent in that a long and very flat sandhill (in contrast to the first) is built, and, covered with colored blankets, it serves as a sitting place for bride and groom.

Just before midday, the veiled groom, accompanied by young men whom he leads, returns to the tent, enters it, and sits down on the low sandhill. At darkness, the bride is led to the tent where she is placed beside the groom on the low sandhill. Wedding guests sing, drum, and dance through the night in front of the wedding tent and leave the next morning to return to their own camps.

The newly married couple remains in the tent for seven days, during which period they can leave it only after darkness. When the seven-day stay is over, the bride remains in her father's camp for about a year before joining her husband's camp.

MARRIAGE RITUAL AND ARCHITECTURAL HISTORY

It is clear from the above description by Nicolaisen that the Kel Ahaggar marriage focuses on the ritual act of erecting a pair of poles just as the Hassaniya birth does; yet it is only among the Kel Inteser (now part of the Kel Tademaket), who migrated from the north to the region of Timbuktu and Lake Faguibine, Mali, that a two-pole tent is found in daily use. Two central oblique posts carry a slightly curved crossbar whose underside is incised and into which two holes have been shaped to receive the posts (fig. 5.3a). The tent structure varies little from those in Mauretania: the singular difference appears to be the use of a leather rather than a woven velum.[9]

A number of scholars have suggested that the Kel Inteser are Arab in origin and that these double-pole tents are ultimately derivative of the North African black tents, and indeed the use of two poles by the Arab Dermchaka (who occupy the area over which the Iwllemmeden Kel Dennek move) was documented by Nicolas (1938) many decades ago. The intriguing questions that remain are how and why it became so integrated into the Tuareg ritual process and took on such symbolic significance.

The Arab Dermchaka also have close ties with (and have been identified as) Kunta families who migrated from Mauretania. Over time, there has been a slow movement of migration from Mauretania to the confines of Mali-Niger (Gallais 1975). These Arabic-speaking Mauretanian tribes found on the Niger Bend, such as the Berabich of Gourma in northern Burkina Faso, have preserved their originality and independence. As everywhere else, their advance was stimulated by commercial interests and activities as well as pastoral needs; it was facilitated by their Islamic religious fervor and Arabic-speaking reputation. Early in this century, it was noted that they occupied the entire region northwest of the Niger River: the urban center of Timbuktu marked the eastern extreme of this expansion of Mauretanian culture. Barth had already encountered the Kunta in his mid-nineteenth-century travels through the region, and in his rendering the velum appears to have been made of leather

Fig. 5.3. a. The Kel Inteser ridgepiece for a two-pole tent. b. The Kel Ahaggar ridge cap supports one pole skin and a velum without guy lines. c. A Kel Dennek ridge cap with four guy lines, used in combination over a single pole, for their skin tents. Drawings after Lhote 1947 and Nicolas 1938, 1950.

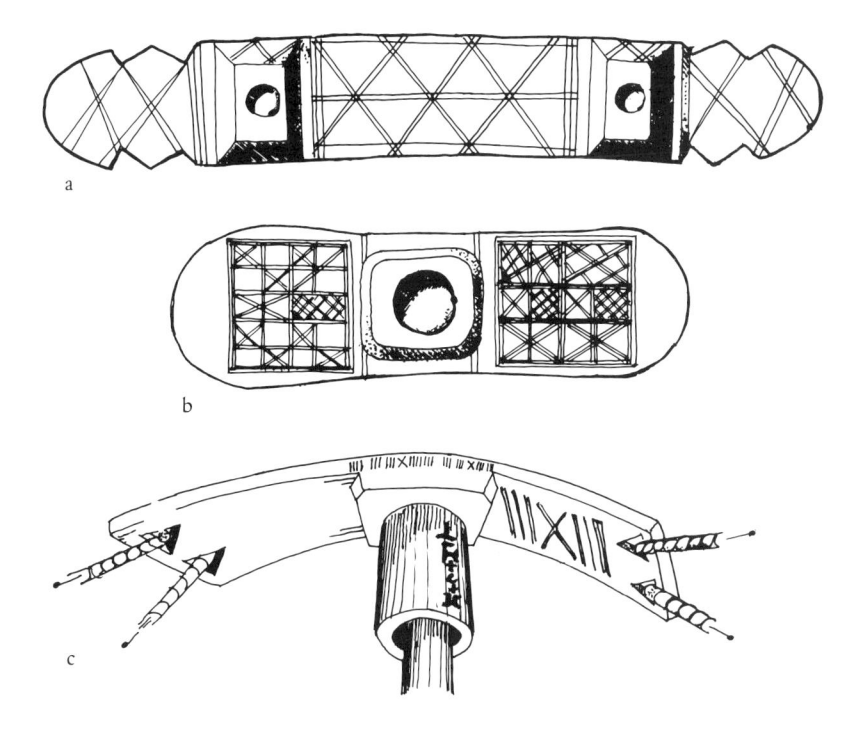

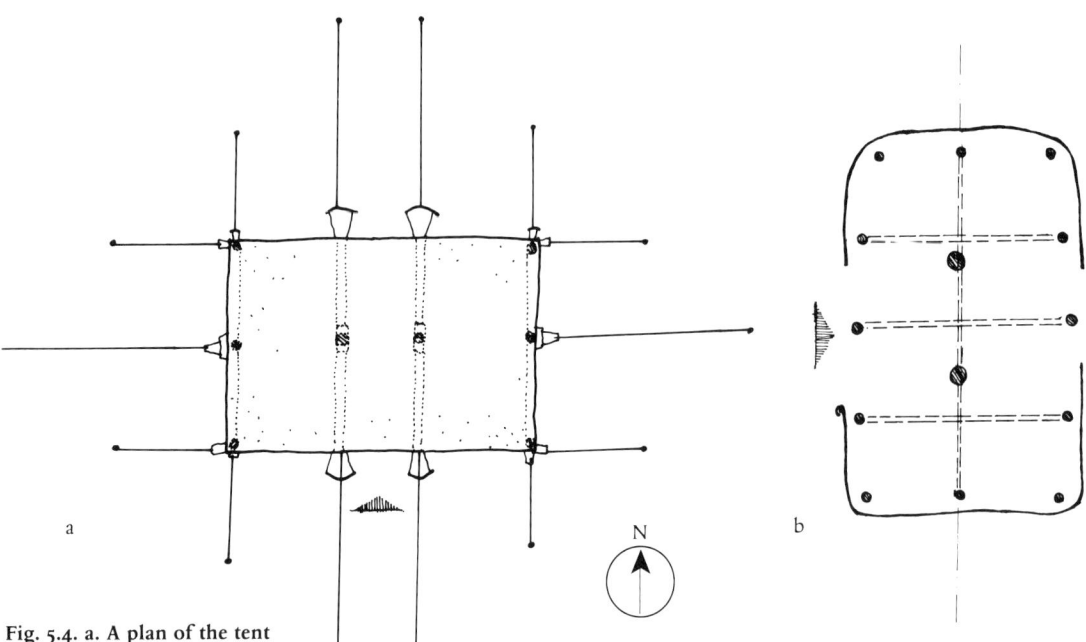

Fig. 5.4. a. A plan of the tent used by the Ulad 'Ali, Libya. b. A two-pole tent structure recorded in the Gourma region (in the Niger Bend) early in the century. Drawings after Laoust 1930 and Chudeau 1910.

rather than woven, and the central arch (made of two bent members) appears to have replaced the two poles (see fig. 5.9). The Kunta continue to use a pair of T-shaped poles in their very large tents, but have substituted a leather velum for a woven one. According to one author, they obtained their leather skins from the Tuareg (Geneviève 1950).

The structural principle recalls that involved in the tents of the Arab Ulad 'Ali of Libya (Laoust 1930) who use two separate poles, each with its own ridgepiece, and a traditional girth system to obtain tension in the velum (fig. 5.4a). Structurally, the girths act similarly to a pair of arches; in plan they are equivalent to two pairs of forked poles, similar to those used by the Kel Dennek below. Could it be that, in the course of time, one of the two poles and its ridgepiece may have gotten lost or was abandoned because it no longer carried the same import? But these large tents are associated not only with the Kunta but with northern Tuareg nobility, and a marriage ceremony described at the turn of the century reveals the process of structural change.[10] In the ceremony, it is a pair of bent arches, rather than a pair of straight poles, that figures in the ritual.

An early account of the sedentarized Tuareg at Sifanara (in the same Gourma region occupied by the Kunta above) provided yet another insight for the possible diffusion of structural change from southern Libya (fig. 5.4b). Chudeau (1910:666) wrote:

The huts are remarkable by their carpentry which is identical to that of the skin tents used by all the Tuareg. Two central forked posts and twelve smaller ones describe a rectangle with a north-south axis. A long flexible branch, spanning the two center poles over to the middle of the two short sides (the north and south sides), is the main roof element. On this carpentry (which is lacking in the skin tents) are posed some thick straw mats; much smaller, simpler mats form the vertical walls, leaving two openings, one on the east and one on the west.

In simple terms, instead of a girth, the Tuareg have substituted a thin arch spanning the long direction, and they have substituted the three secondary arches for the cross girths. Chudeau then points out, however, that for the Ahaggar nomadic tents the long axis is ordinarily east-west and the only opening is a single door, customarily on the south side. There is thus a ninety degree rotation in space when the Tuareg become sedentary or when the dwelling is inhabited by sedentary serfs. Equally relevant is that sedentarization and the hierarchy of class occupancy (by other than the noble families, i.e., the serfs) find expression not only in the substitution of bent arches for a stressed velum but in spatial rotation. It is a point to return to.

KEL AHAGGAR TENTS

Although the marriage rituals cited above involve symbolic behaviors associated with a two-pole tent, the northern Kel Ahaggar in the Tamanrasset region have traditionally used a single pole with a ridge cap, perpendicular to the ground, to hold up the velum of their tents[11] (see fig. 5.3b). In fact, the interested reader who peruses Foucauld's *Dictionnaire* (1951–52) in search of a Tuareg term or description for "tent" will be disappointed. His description of the northern Tuareg skin tent is tucked into an entry for one of the side poles of a tent to which the velum is attached *(tasdest)*. Under this heading, he describes the tent as a whole (1951–52, 1:247–49).

The skin velum of the Kel Ahaggar tent he describes is supported in the middle by a single wooden pole capped by a ridgepiece, perpendicular to the earth *(tamankayt)* (fig. 5.5). This single structural pole is the only one under the velum; all the others are outside it, a little distant from its periphery and sunk into the earth. Cords corresponding to these exterior poles are fixed to the velum: one attaches one of the cords to each of the poles in tensioning the velum. It is these poles or pickets around the tent, in combination with the central pole within, that sustain the tent and stretch the velum. No other pickets are used.

The poles around the velum, with one exception, vary little in size or profile; in an ordinary tent there are twelve, three in each cardinal direction. The northern Tuareg tent is ordinarily oriented north to south, with the door on the south. The twelve poles and the *tamankayt* together are called "poles of the tent" *(aġet)*.

The importance of cardinal directions is reflected in the discrete and differential terms used for these peripheral poles in the context of the sides of the tent on which they are located, that is, their structural positions in space. Those at the east and west sides *(tasdest)* are differentiated from those on the north *(unnus)* and those on the south *(madar)*.

The special term for the singular, highly elaborated

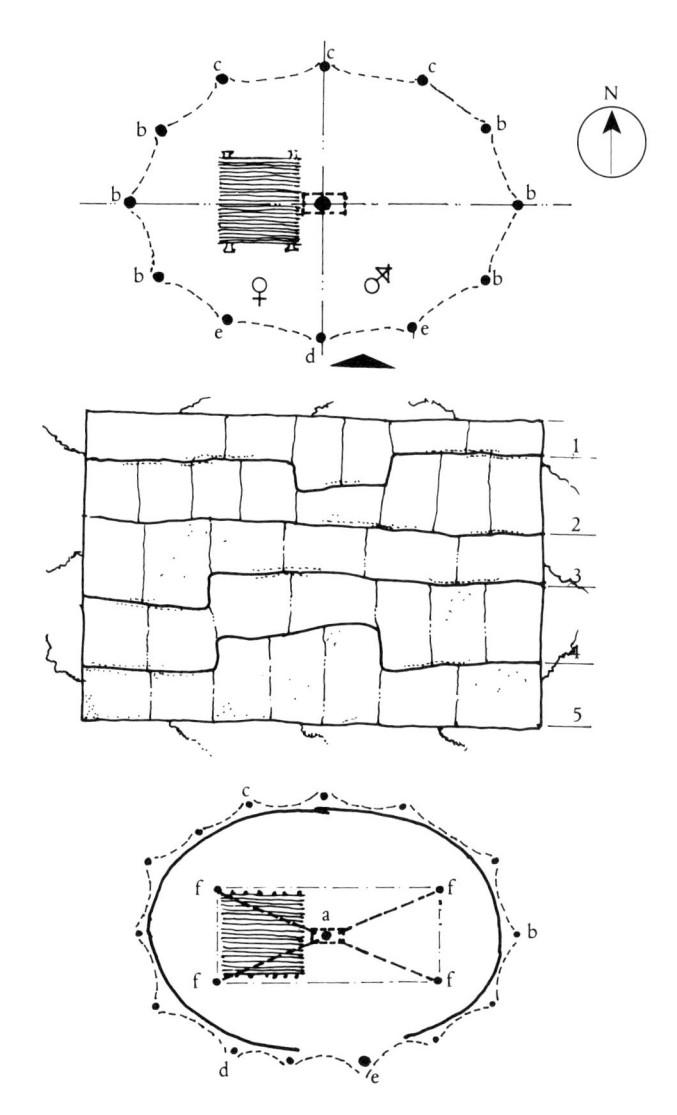

Fig. 5.5. Above, plan of a Kel Ahaggar tent. *Legend*. a: *tamankayt*. b: *tasdest*. c: *unnus*. d: *igem*. e: *madar*. In the center, plan of a skin velum *(éhakit)* consisting of five strips *(tarḍa)*. Below, plan of a Kel Dennek tent. a: *tamankayt*. b: *tasdest*. c: *unnus*. d: *igem*. e: *madar*. f: *agegu* or *tigettewin*. Drawings after Foucauld 1951–52, vol. 1, and Nicholas 1938, 1950.

The Tuareg

center entrance pole *(igem)* suggests that there is a conceptual differentiation that informs the decision to elaborate on this central exterior pole marking the entrance *side*, distinguishing it from its eleven counterparts by name and profile. True, the notched surface facilitates the graduated raising or lowering of the tent velum, but this elaboration at the entrance is an aesthetic expression of both enclosure and entrance. In defining the doorway, it is a surrogate for the architectural facades throughout history in which lintels, surrounds, and thresholds emphasize wall openings and define spatial boundaries. It is equally an architectural expression for the very elaborate ritualized handclapping that announces the visitor to the tent.

The rectangular skin velum *(éhakit)* is composed of a certain number of bands of goatskin or sheepskin sewn together. In its narrowest sense the name designates an awning.[12] Each band *(tarḍa)* is the width of a skin and the length of the velum on its long dimension. These bands are juxtaposed and sewn together, often patched, with leather thongs (see fig. 5.5). Although the bands are of equal length and width in principle, they are not precisely regular in either direction. The dimensions of a velum are given by saying that it has such and such a number of *tarḍa*, and each is composed of so many skins. These hides come from sheep and goats: cowhide is too hard and has a tendency to shrivel up in the rain.

Making a tent cover requires amassing a considerable number of hides, and the process of collecting them, like the process of constructing them, is similar in both the north and south (Bernus 1981a). The women from one family visit all the neighboring camps to collect these hides. Custom requires that the visitors be well received and well fed. They go from tent to tent, socializing, talking to one another, in the hope that each will offer to contribute.

The assembly is almost always done in a collective fashion, bringing together women from the entire camp and even neighboring camps (Bernus 1981a). All young women, married or single, are invited to attend, whereas men participate only with contributions of food. To this end, a strip of leather is sent to each tent, a signal of the collective invitation. The collective women's work ("invitation of the hides") is often accompanied by a woman violinist invited for the occasion, although the hostess herself does not participate, involved as she is in food preparation for her guests.

The sewing procedure for assembling the skins resembles the way in which the woven bands *(ifeljan)* of the velum in a North African or Mauretanian tent are assembled. First a series of long strips resembling the woven ones are created; these are then sewn together at their edges, creating a rectangle or an elongated square.

The skin velums, however, never seem to be rectangular: they appear oval. The rectangular velum is rounded out by the tension created when the velum is stretched from a central apex to its set of perimeter poles. Structurally the velum offers the best resistance to wind if the poles form a circular perimeter (comparable to a drumskin), so the oval plan is thus a kind of compromise: the central pole setting up forces that tend toward a circle.

KEL DENNEK TENTS

A structural variation in the skin tent, expressing a rectangular, rather than a round or oval configuration, appears in the constructions of the southern Iwllemmeden Kel Dennek who inhabit the plains around Tahoua, Niger (Nicolas 1938, 1950) (see figs. 5.3c and 5.5). The Tuareg in this region use a central pole and cap plus two additional sets of poles on the interior. These poles, connected to the central pole by a set of four guy ropes, demarcate a rectangular space within the tent. The spatial and conceptual expression of a rectangular space within the tent becomes clearly defined behaviorally and structurally, as the construction process reveals.

The tent cover is spread on the ground in an area cleared by the women slaves. Holes are dug to set two pairs of posts on each side of a central point at a distance of about 2 meters. The two pairs of forked poles *(tigettewin)* are planted, their tops leaning slightly to the outside. The holes are then filled with dry sand and closely packed. Then a central wooden pole *(tamankayt)* capped by a ridgepiece *(asulan)* is arranged in the middle of the quadrilateral space defined by the four posts and set perpendicular to the earth, but not buried in the ground. It is kept upright by the weight of the velum above, which is itself kept in place by external poles around the periphery. Ropes are tied to each of the four poles, and these are stretched up to and into the four holes of the small ridge cap.

The velum is extended over this support system and fixed in place. Exterior forked poles are planted, and the thongs that have been sewn to the edge of the velum are attached to them. These poles are not part of the baggage carried during moves except in the northern area where wood is scarce. They are simply stripped branches of Seyal acacia, in contrast to the more valuable Commiphora africana *(adaras)* wood used for the central pole and its cap. The four lateral poles are of Calotropis procera or a red wood from Nigeria.

The morphological meaning of the word *tamankayt* (according to the people themselves) should be sought in the verb for "support" in the moral sense, to suffer, to sustain, make an effort to support. The noun, the action of supporting, or the fact of supporting or having supported, is comparable to the word *ahennaka*, a palanquin for women comparable to a tent and composed of a structure holding up a piece of cloth (see fig. 5.13).

The four forked poles that physically define the quadrangle of "inhabited" space recall the four sides which are linguistically distinguished, just as they were by the Kel Ahaggar above. What is of equal interest is Foucauld's observation that the Kel Ahaggar sometimes replace the same single pole by two wooden arches (each called *agegu*), set parallel to each other about 1.5 meters apart. Would these two arches have been used in lieu of the two poles described by Laoust (1930) for southern Libya or Chudeau (1910) for the Tuareg in the Niger Bend? Of greater interest is the Kel Dennek use of the term *tigettewin* for the two sets of forked poles which are also used by the Kel Ferwan for the four corners of their mat-covered armature tents. The Kel Dennek tent structure seems to provide the architectural link between the Kel Ahaggar and the Kel Ferwan (see fig. 3.10).

Tifinar. The protective and supportive function of the *tamankayt* also extends into the spiritual realm. Traditionally, the women of the tent carved incantational phrases, in *tifinar*, on the central posts and ridgepiece, further enhancing its role as spiritual guardian and physical mainstay of the tent interior (see fig. 5.3a–c). Even today, amulets suspended from the ridgepiece further insure the inhabitants' well-being (Laoust 1930; Nicolas 1938). The script can be written horizontally or vertically, from right to left or from left to right, boustrophedon style, very much like Arabic (fig. 5.6). As a consequence, again like Arabic script, the letters can be graphically manipulated to create patterns that are seemingly abstract to the uninitiated but communicate meaning to those who are literate (Marcy 1937). The background to this tradition was already evident in the ancient rock engravings in the Hoggar and Tassili, where the written incantations frequently implored help or protection. It is more often used now for what could be called "amorous commerce," much like our present-day graffiti.

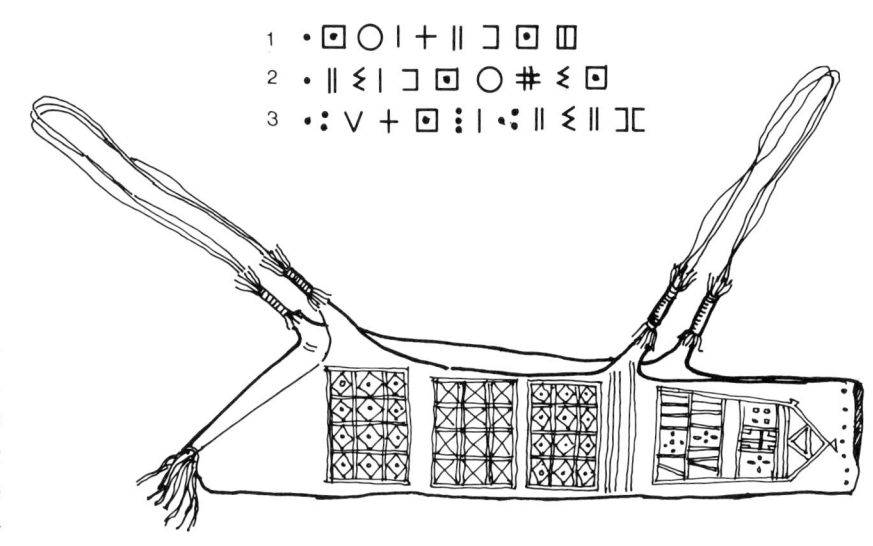

Tifinar is not a cursive script; it consists of combinations of singular lines and dots which lend themselves to a gestalt of geometric patterns, in contrast to the arabesque quality that Arabic script, particularly the kufic script used by Mauretanian nomads, evokes. The same geometry of the written word carved by women into the central poles of their leather tents can be found on the range of leather artifacts whose creation and applied decoration is also part of their repertoire of skills and that define the tent interior.

Kel Dennek interiors. The interior of the tent is surrounded by a mat wall *(éseber)* 5–6 meters long, about 1 meter high, which is unrolled vertically around the

Fig. 5.6. Above, *tifinar* transcription of a marriage chant. 1. The name of God be upon them, seven times. 2. Preceding the name of God. 3. On our daughter who has left this evening (to join her husband). Below, a saddle bag in which the script is integrated with the geometry of a magic square. Drawings after Benhazera 1908 and Lhote 1947.

bed for protection from the wind and sand that blow in under the tent cover, or to obtain family privacy (fig. 5.7a). It is a long screen, made of the fine straw of the Panicum turgidum *(afazo)* plaited with leather thongs, edged by a leather border on its upper part and often decorated with leather fringes and wool embroidery in green and red. Richly embellished, it may also be arranged at will to divide off any particular space under the tent, and it may be unrolled or moved according to the weather, the time of day, or activities within.

During a calm day, these flexible mat walls (there may be two) are rolled up to allow maximum ventilation, visibility, and social interaction. In the evening, they are extended around a series of carved poles, creating a contained interior space around the bed. The physical boundaries of living space are flexible, fluctuating to accommodate time and space.

The specially carved poles that hold up the screens may be flat, pierced and carved in a series of crosses, or cylindrical, their tops carved into a series of truncated cones. The carving of these poles is always the work of the specialized craftsmen, but it is the women of certain tribes who specialize in the making of the *éseber*.[13] The fabrication of a screen, like that of the velum, involves the cooperation of several women at a time.

The same kind of architectural interplay among spatial concept, physical structure, and symbolic meaning that envelops the *tamankayt* extends to the *éseber*. The name for the mat itself stems from the term "to obstruct" (Laoust 1930:167), and since these screens do indeed protect the tent interior from blowing sand and from prying eyes, there is nothing remarkable in the etymology. But the obstructive quality transcends the physical. The widespread practice is that a newly delivered mother must remain within the mat-enclosed courtyard for the forty- or sixty-day postpartum period because during this time she is most vulnerable to the "demons of the void" (Nicolaisen 1961:126). She may venture outside her sanctuary only if armed with a knife or a bar of iron, an element recognized to have apotropaic powers. On cold nights, or during bad weather, the mats are drawn tightly around the bed or placed behind the bed, to the east, across from the opening of the tent.

The many iconographic motifs that Gabus (1955–58) documented for the mat wall can more readily be appreciated when viewed in the light of the assemblage of furnishings it surrounds. Even if the field design is left out, the twenty to thirty centimeter border strips are always heavily reinforced. Structural reinforcement is, to be sure, one obvious reason for the heavily worked edges, but the concept of the mat as a mystical barrier, as a system of protective enclosure, as a stage setting for things within, is also crucial to the convention. The mat wall mediates between the human, interior space and the demonic "bush" beyond, like a spiritual alarm system geared to detect unearthly dangers inaudible to the human ear. The purpose of the screen is not only to surround and protect the bed, the focus of interior space, but to define an interior volume in which the wealth of color, texture, memory, and meaning that permeates and impregnates the interior of the enclosed space could constitute a closed system of imagery.

Among the Kel Dennek, the interior of the tent (literally, "the middle of the house") is divided into two distinct parts: a "men's side" and a "women's side." The noble part, reserved for the men, is the east. Here the man keeps his tools, clothes, and weapons, his riding camel saddle, his horse saddle, supplies to be distributed, and, in the case of a war chief, the drum of command *(ettebel)*. The west is reserved for the wife and her possessions: the bed *(tédabut)*, her clothes, her camel litter, the palanquin *(ahennaka)*, the camel pack saddles *(asedfer, aruki)*, the cooking implements, and sometimes the violin and its bow (the instrument reserved for women).

Bernus (1981a:131) describes the tent interior differently for the Iwllemmeden Kel Ataram who also live under a skin tent. In contrast to the Kel Ahaggar and the Iwllemmeden Kel Dennek above, the tent cover is placed over the armature lengthwise, along a north-south axis. The openings are located to the east and west on the longer dimensions *(igem)*. The shorter dimensions *(tedele)* are on the north and south.

The space inside may be divided into three major spaces: the center ("between the centerpoles"), the north, and the south. The north is the part reserved for the wife (it is between the two northern posts that she arranges her things, her clothes, her saddle). The south is the masculine part; it is there, often on a wood support made of two short strong forks, that the leather sacks are stored containing millet reserves, clothes, and a man's valuables (frequently protected by a padlock), a saddle and weapons.

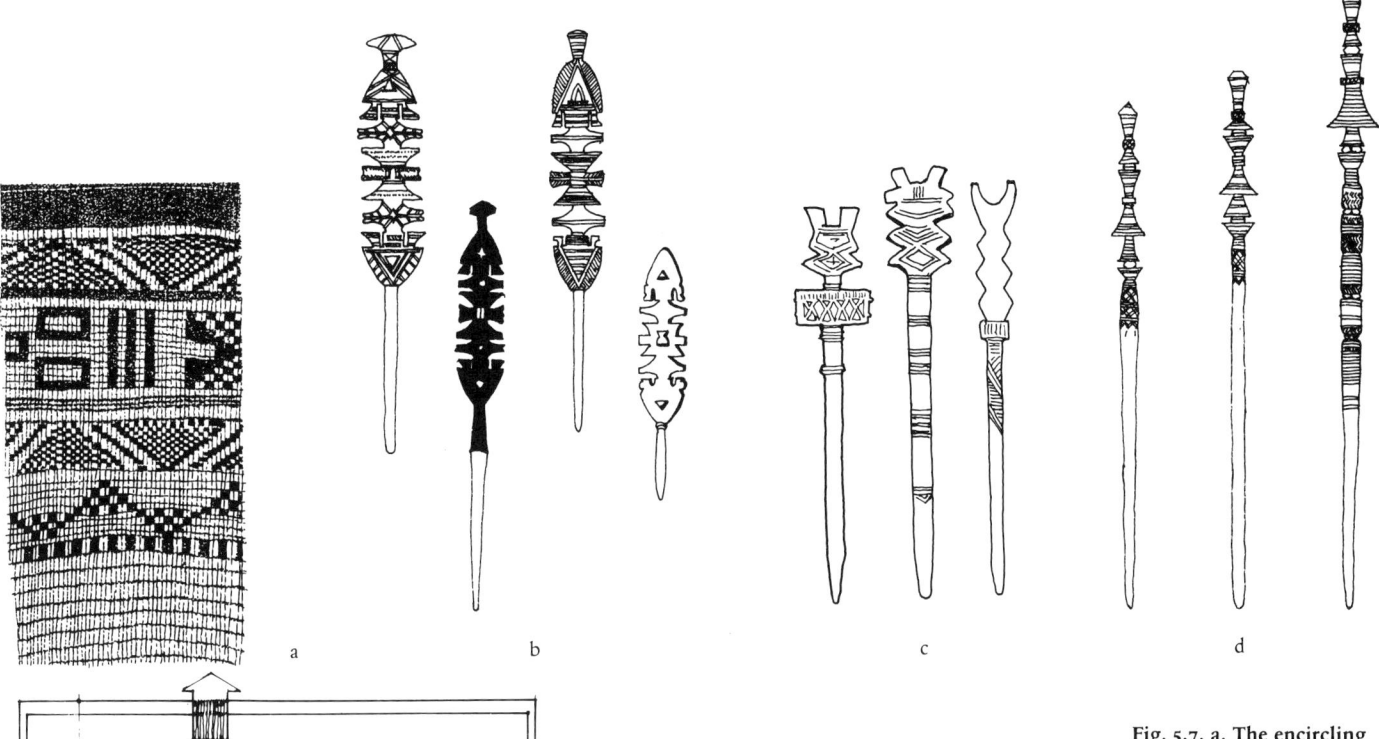

The spatial variations that occur as one moves from the northern Tuareg groups to the southern ones are matched by gradual structural and material changes, as a mid-nineteenth-century woodcut by Barth (fig. 5.8) and the interior of a Kel Ferwan tent in the Musée Ethnographique, Niamey (fig. 5.9), both illustrate. In the woodcut, the velum is of leather, but an arch appears to have been substituted for either a vertical pole or a pair of poles. The surrounding wall mats, a pair of trestles supporting leather baggage, and two reed bedframes are clearly delineated. The changing availability of particular building resources, reflected in the substitution of an arch for poles, is matched by the substitution of a pair of "Sudanese" beds for the classic Tuareg ones. The Panicum turgidum *(afazo)* stalks are bound together, so they cannot be disassembled for easy transport. They are the same kind of beds Du Puigaudeau described for the more southerly Hassaniya-speaking populations in Mauretania. At the same time, the arch now defines the gender division of space reflected in the pair of bedframes.

The northern interior of the tent in the museum at Niamey (note the men's riding saddle and its equipment) illustrates how the pairs of forked poles that had been used for the typical Kel Dennek tent have now become a pair of trestles used by the men to hang their leather waterskins, whereas the tent still retains the classic Tuareg bed that can be disassembled. The central arch and secondary laths and roof mats, including an interior woven ceiling mat, have replaced the leather velum. These transitions are best understood by following the interpretive descriptions for the Kel Ferwan who live east of the Kel Dennek, since obviously the illustrated tent is of a similar genre.

The Kel Ferwan, who form a confederation of nomadic tribes in the plains surrounding Agades and are part of the greater Kel Ayr political federation, do not live in skin tents like the Kel Ahaggar or the Iwllemmeden Kel Ataram and Kel Dennek. Both nobles and commoners live in mat-covered armature tents (Casajus 1983) (see fig. 5.2b).

There is as much order and meaning in the archi-

Fig. 5.7. a. The encircling wall mat *(éseber)* and a detail of designs on it; height .86 m; length 5.40 m. b. Carved poles used to hold up the wall mat. c. Forked poles used on the interior *(tigettewin)*. d. Entrance poles *(igem)*. Drawings after Lhote 1947 and Gabus 1955–58, vol. 2.

The Tuareg 99

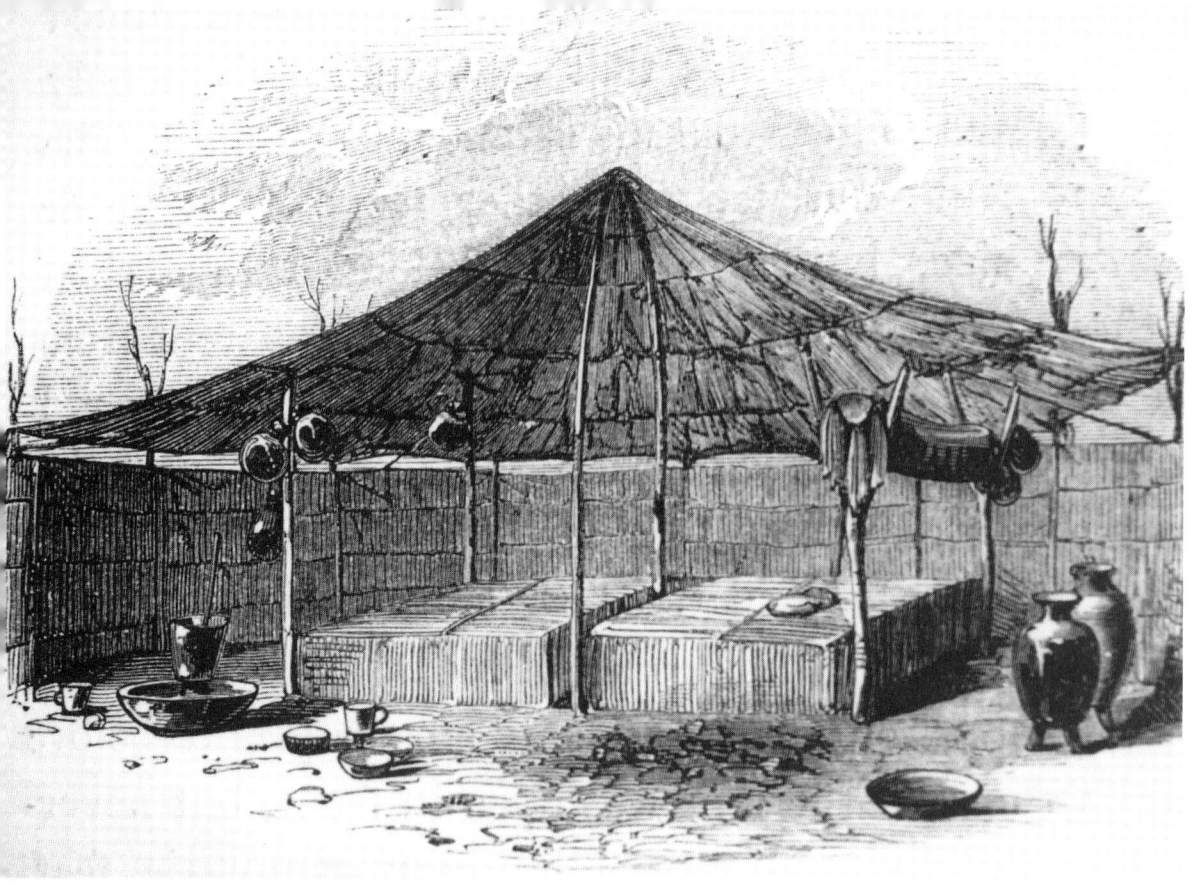

Fig. 5.8. A Tuareg tent recorded in the mid-nineteenth century. The center pole has been replaced by a single central arch, and the wall screens, the pair of trestles, and two reed bedframes are clearly visible.

Fig. 5.9. Interior of a Kel Ayr mat-covered armature tent interior at the Musée Ethnographique, Niamey, Niger.

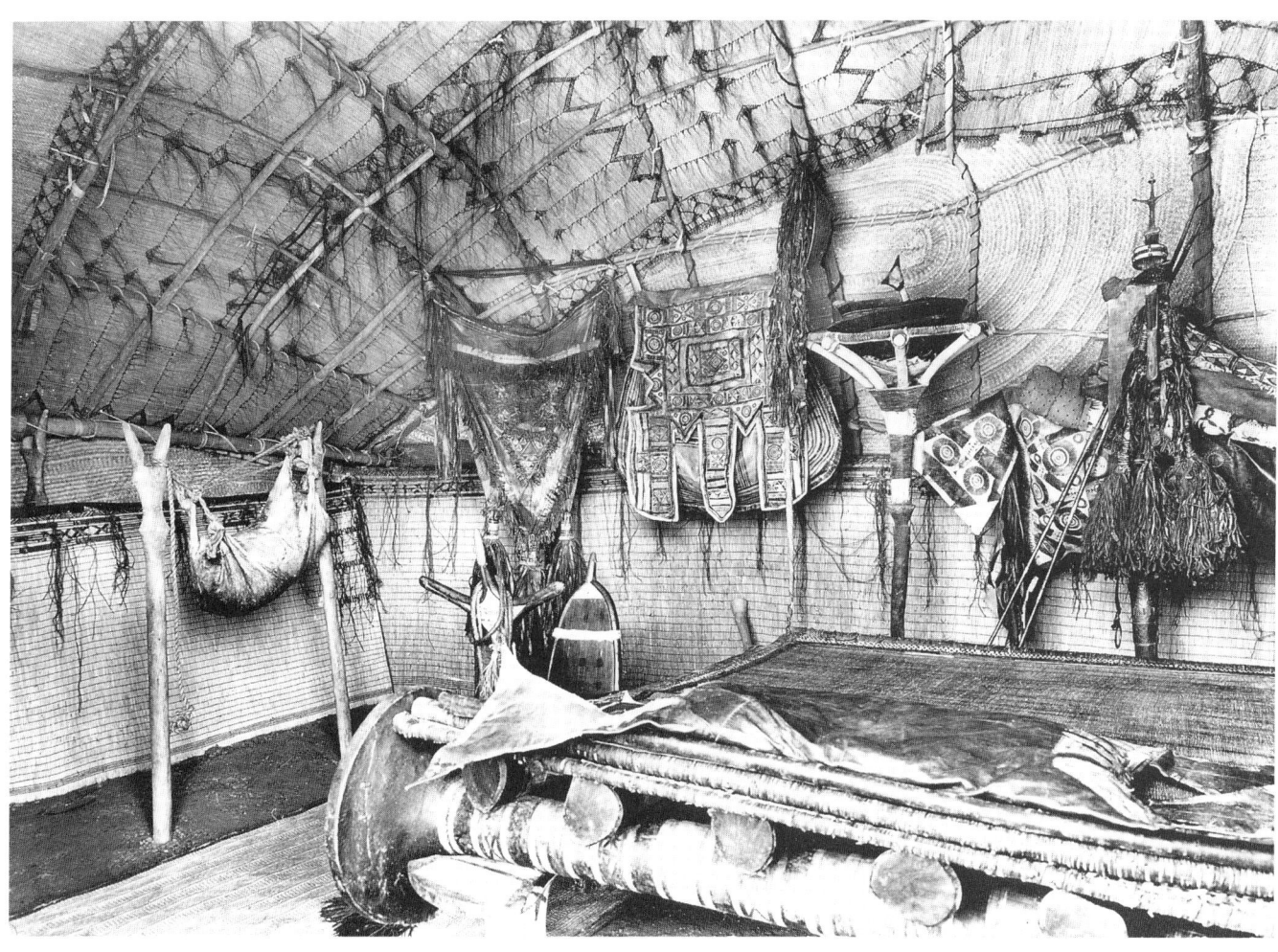

tectural elements of a mat-covered armature tent as in those of the more exotic leather tents; even more intriguing are the parallels in the ordering of interior space. Even though the structural elements used to define space may not be identical, they are equivalent, as the intriguing descriptions below by Casajus reveal.

KEL FERWAN TENTS
(1987:44ff)

Casajus writes that the Kel Ferwan tent, which belongs to the wife, was given to her by her mother when she married. More precisely, when one of her daughters marries, a woman gives her part of the components of her own tent and keeps the rest; the missing components are then made up again by slaves or blacksmiths.

The tent is made of mats attached by cords to a heavy wooden armature. The mats are made of the leaves of young dum palm trees (Hyphaene thebaica). Each leaf is cut lengthwise into two or three thin strips of the same size. The leaves, tied in bundles, are sold by slave women to free women who do not stoop to doing this sort of work. The leaves may be sold already cut and sized, but splitting and sizing the leaves, as well as plaiting the mats, are tasks performed by women of all social levels, and to which they devote a great deal of their time. Young daughters begin at a very early age to imitate their mother, rapidly acquiring great skill in this delicate activity.[14]

The tent armature is a rather complex set composed of different sorts of elements, each with its proper name (fig. 5.10). The arches *(egegu;* pl.: *igagan)* are made of roots of the Acacia raddiana *(afagag)* which have been stripped of their covering by being heated over a fire. They are bent into shape and then buried in the sand for several days. Digging up and stripping these roots can be the work of a slave or a free person, but it is the owner of the tent herself who takes charge of the bending. The different arches have specific names.

The end arches a and a' *(telisawt)* are distinguished from the central arches b and b' *(taqqeqqewät* and *anebetter).* In a very spacious tent, there may be two or more pairs of central arches, whereas in the meager tent of a poor family the central arches may be absent.

The ten pairs of transverse laths, 1, 2, 3 . . . *(alellew;* pl.: *ilellewan)* are usually also made of the roots of the Acacia raddiana. Their preparation is similar to that of the arches, and they are preformed in the same way. They are attached with cords to the arches and to the lateral bars supporting the laths. The laths located at either end are also designated by a specific term *(tesegdemt)* from the verb "to cut," because they "cut" or end the series of transverse laths.

The term for the lateral bars A and A' *(esseger;* pl. *izegar)* derives from the verb "to throw." It designates the mat that one "throws" on the ground for a visitor to sit on; transverse laths are thrown on the horizontal bars the same way. The two lateral bars have a bulge in the middle and are carved from the wood of

Fig. 5.10. a. Armature of a Kel Ferwan armature tent. *Legend.* a, b, a', b': arches; A, B: lateral bars; t: vertical stakes; t': supports; 1, 2, 3: transverse laths. b. Seen from above, the rotated orientation of the armature when first erected as a nuptial tent on the left and its conventional orientation on the right. c. The tent as an image of the cosmos. Drawings after Casajus 1987.

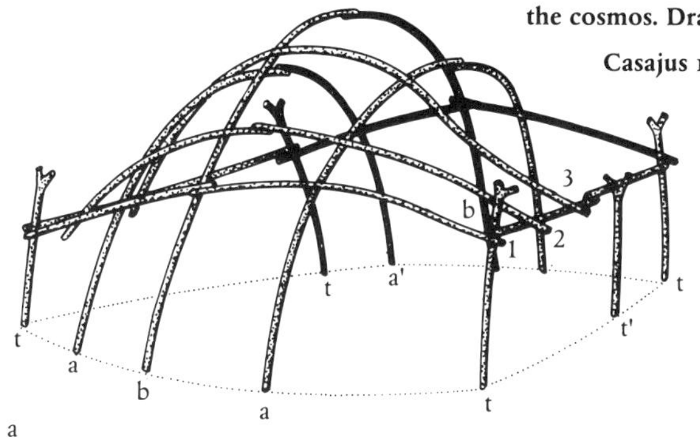

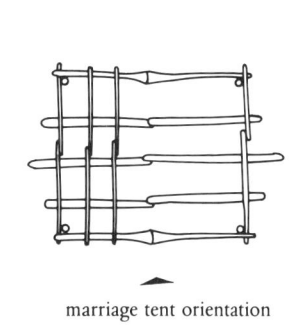

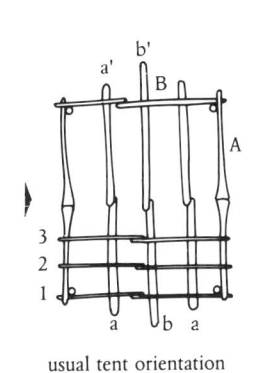

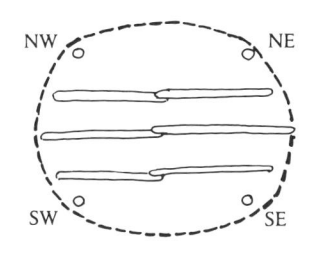

the Balanites aegyptiaca *(aboragh)*; their ends are carved in the same way as those of the transverse laths, which allows them to be tied with cords to the corner stakes. These bars, as well as the vertical stakes t *(tagettewt*; pl. *tigettawin)* and the supports t' *(tɩsɛdɛlɛwt*; pl.: *tisedelawin)*, both carved from the wood of the Acacia nilotica *(teggart)*, are made by the blacksmiths. The four corner stakes are designated by the same term used to designate a "pillar" in masonry. It may also be a pillar in the sense of a "fundamental element." The four stakes, the fundamental elements of the tent, carry important connotations.

A tent is normally always placed with the transverse laths (1, 2, 3 . . .) parallel to the north-south axis. First the lateral bars are placed on the ground, parallel to the position they will occupy when the setting up is concluded. To accomplish this, the central bulges are aligned in the north-south direction. When the two lateral bars are arranged, holes are dug next to their ends for the four corner stakes. Thus each "side" of the tent faces a cardinal direction. After the stakes are installed, holes are dug for the arches, which are placed beginning on the west. Finally, the transverse laths are attached to the horizontal bars and the arches, the laths on the ends first, then the others, starting with those to the south. One piece of cord is used to tie all the laths to each pair of arches and horizontal bars. The same term used to designate all the cords *(tɩrazɛmt)* used in the setting up of the tent armature is also used to designate a camel tether. They are made either by blacksmiths using strips cut from goat or sheepskin, or by slaves or free persons using strips of mature palm leaves.

The mats are thrown over the laths, oriented lengthwise perpendicular to them and parallel to the arches. The generic term for mat *(asala)* subsumes various types allocated for specific purposes. First, two to four oval mats are put in place, those in the middle partly overlapping those on the outside. These are covered by a larger oval or rectangular mat. The lateral oval mats are attached to the armature by the cords, the ends of which are tied to the north and south arches. The larger mat is attached in the same way by cords tied to the corner stakes and to the arches. These cords are made from mature palm leaves by slaves or free persons.

In the tent of a wealthy family, the mats are not laid the same way on the laths but are placed on one or two ceiling mats *(ɛwɛrwɛr)* made from Panicum turgidum *(afazo)*. The rush mat is rectangular in form, its longer dimension oriented north-south in the tent, and it is visible from inside the tent (see fig. 5.9). In contrast to the other mats, it is not made by the women, but obtained from itinerant Igdalan, an ancient Berber tribe settled in Niger. There is a type of tent mat *(alakakkad)* that has ornamental motifs woven from goat or horse hair and whose decorative effect is justifiably admired.

Finally, two long rectangular mats *(eghaläy*, "to go around") encircle the tent. Their weave is tight enough so that they are more or less waterproof. It is water running over the ground rather than the rain itself that must be feared during the rainy season. The combined length of the lateral mats is a little more than the perimeter of the tent, so that, if they are completely unrolled, the tent is totally closed. It is possible to arrange an opening by rolling up one of the ends on the west side. A tent is usually closed on the east, and one enters on the west.

The orientation of the tent armature follows a north-south axis (that of the transverse laths) and an east-west axis (that of the arches). On each of these two axes the two opposing poles are each charged with different values. This polarity is already obvious during the setting up of the tent, where the laths to the south are always put in place before those to the north, and the arches to the west before those to the east.

The arches are compared to a vertebral column, the transverse laths to the ribs, the lateral bars to the arms, their bulges to elbows, and the opening on the west side of the tent to a head. Thus the tent evokes the image of a person whose head faces west. This orientation is characterized by saying that the tent "looks" to the west.

The tent is normally entered from the west. In poetic language, "to enter a tent from the east side" is the euphemistic equivalent of visiting a woman whose husband is away or a divorcée with loose morals.

More than one poem evokes in this way the midnight visitors who tie up their mounts on the west side of the tent but enter on the side closest to their hostess of the night, the east. The proverbial phrase "leaning against the *igaydan*" (the storage trestle found on the east side of the tent) means "courting the wife of another." Thus, at least in proverbial and poetic language, there exists both a licit and illicit entryway to the tent.

The major part of the day is spent to the west of the tent. The east, on the other hand, is reserved for prayers. Since the tent "looks" to the west, one prays behind the tent with one's back turned to it. One is also on the east side for a lovers' conversation, of course, but when one is east on the inside of the tent, one faces west to the outside.

If the wall mats are raised during the day, great care is taken, as soon as evening falls, to lower the one to the north: a tent left open to the north would be exposed to the worst dangers. The dangerous spirits (*kel esuf* or *aljinan*) usually keep to the north side of the tent, and they appear most readily at nightfall.[15] The threat of these, ever present or at least latently so, prevents a woman who must take care of her needs at night from leaving the tent by the north side. Although a man may have less to fear from these spirits, it is better if he also avoids the north side of the tent. The south side of the tent is the least dangerous; it is even the source of divine benediction *(baraka)*.

The south and north sides of the tent, respectively charged with benediction and danger, reflect a more general opposition in the world between the auspicious south and the inauspicious north. "To the south (*agela*, the "right") stretch the fields of millet from which our food comes, while to the north (*ayr*, the "left") are found only the desert and hunger."

The bed is oriented east-west, and a couple lies with their heads to the east, the man to the north, and the woman to the south. Thus the husband protects his wife by barring the way of the dangerous spirits. But this also corresponds to the idea among the Kel Ferwan that the south is marked by a feminine character and the north by a masculine character, in contrast to general schema for leather tents.[16]

The Kel Ferwan tent as a cosmos. Another Tuareg belief establishes a correspondence between the tent and the world: the tent is an image of the cosmos. The polygon formed by the anchor points of the four stakes and the arches approximates the form of a circle (see fig. 5.10c). This circle, it is said, is similar to the circle of the world and the rounded form of the roof of the tent replicates the vault of heaven. The four corner stakes are considered analogous to the four pillars that support the vault of heaven. No one has ever seen the four pillars of the world, but, in order that men believe in their existence, God has placed in the sky four stars that duplicate them. These four stars form a set called "the roof" *(tafella)* which corresponds exactly to our constellation of Pegasus. When they are at their zenith, the position of the square they form corresponds exactly to that of the four pillars of the world.

The Tuareg claim that it was by looking at these stars that their ancestors learned to construct their tents. The claim recalls the Arab tradition that the Kaaba is a tent from the sky, sent by God to Adam. Some men add that the four corners, whether it is the four stakes of the tent or the four pillars of the world, are the material image of the Pillars of Islam which represent the fundamental duties of the believer.[17]

Kel Ferwan marriage. While this manner of seeing the tent is not unique to the Kel Ferwan and the Kel Ayr, what is unique is its particular orientation toward the four cardinal directions which reflects a rather precise ninety degree rotation in space. This alternate orientation uses a set of spatial values to establish a set of symbolic gestures which distinguish the Kel Ferwan from their western and northern relatives. The key to understanding the rotation in space that distinguishes northern Tuareg leather-covered tensile structures from southern Tuareg mat-covered armatures lies in Casajus's own description and interpretations of the Kel Ferwan wedding ritual which invokes a rotation along the major axes in space (1983:228ff).

Casajus writes that the Tuareg regard a tent as a female domain, in relation to which a man is in some sense a stranger. A woman has the same status in her sense a stranger. A woman has the same status in her own tent as she has in her mother's: she is at home in both. Conversely, a man is a guest in his wife's tent. When Tuareg say that "a woman's tent is her mother's," it does not mean that a woman's tent actually belongs to her mother, but that in her own tent she has the status she had in her mother's tent. The social phenomenon coincides with the fact that a woman's tent is partly made of elements from that of her mother.

This close identity between woman and tent is also a consequence of the fact that throughout a woman's life her status remains the same vis-à-vis the tent, first her mother's, then her own, whereas it is the lot of a man to move from one tent (his mother's) to another (his wife's) in which his status is quite different.

The wedding tent, which after the marriage will be the tent of the newly married couple, is put up near the camp of the bride's family. On the day of the ceremony the bride spends the day in a tent of her family's camp, while the bridegroom stays in his own family's camp or in a bivouac at some distance from the bride's camp. All the guests of both families will spend the day in or near the bride's family's camp.

This tent is not put up in the usual way. The two lateral mats are placed in such a way that the two entrances of the tent are not situated to the west and east, but to the north and south (see fig. 5.10b). At sunset the bridegroom is led to the wedding tent. As his friends pretend noisily to negotiate with female relatives of the bride at the western side (the normal entrance) of the tent, the bridegroom and his best man discreetly enter the tent by the northern side. Since there is a horizontal beam on the southern and northern sides of the tent, the bridegroom is obliged to enter it by crawling on his hands and knees.

Very late in the night, sometimes just before dawn, the bride arrives in a procession of women. The procession circles counterclockwise three times around the tent, and the bride is finally led into the tent on the southern side, again only after negotiation and gifts.

On the first night, the bridegroom must behave as if he were the mother of the bride; on the second night, as if he were her little sister; and on the third night, as if he were her male cross-cousin; only then, on the third night, is the marriage consummated. This means, of course, that the bridegroom must be gentle and motherly on the first night, and cheerful and willing to help on the second night; but it is remarkable that he must act as if he were a woman (a sister or mother) during these two nights.

For seven days the tent will be empty during the day and occupied by the couple only at night. Each morning, before sunrise, the couple go back to their respective camps, returning to the wedding tent at night. On the seventh day the side-mats are ceremoniously put back in the right position, and the tent is dismantled. The two spouses then move with their tent to the husband's family camp.

The bridegroom enters the tent by the northern side—the male side and the side of the dangerous spirits. By entering the tent on the northern side, the bridegroom affirms himself as a husband, the man of the tent. The bride, on the contrary, enters the tent by the southern side, the side where she was born and where she gives birth. Even if this tent is new for her, her status will remain the same as the one she had in the tent where she was born; her place of entrance marks this continuity.

On the other hand, the bridegroom is a guest in the tent he enters as a husband. This explains why he must wait for three nights before consummating the marriage. When asked about this, informants compared it with another custom: when a traveler comes to spend some days at a camp, he must first spend three days just outside it, during which all the necessary requirements of hospitality are observed. It is only after these three days that he is admitted into the camp itself, where he can then share the same plate as the other men.

The side by which the bridegroom enters the tent is also the side of the dangerous spirits. Informants compare the unusual orientation of the wedding tent to the orientation of graves, even though the bed itself has its usual west-east orientation.

The Tuareg consider that one dies in a tent and not in a camp. Except for those who die in war and are buried on the battlefield, a dead person receives the funeral rites in a tent. Of course this tent is situated in a camp, but they also say that after death men (and women) become spirits who will always haunt the tent where they died. This tent is inherited matrilineally and so moves from one camp to another. One can thus say that for the Tuareg it is the tent and not the camp that is of greatest importance.

As Casajus has described it, the marriage orientation of a Kel Ferwan mat-covered armature tent is identical to the normal orientation of the skin-covered tensile structures described above. The prescription for a northern orientation in the marriage context suggests a ritual inheritance whereby the northern ancestry is reinforced. It is a metaphor equivalent to the pitching of a Hassaniya two-pole tent which the Kel Ahaggar, who customarily use one pole, act out in their marriage ritual.

Moving the Kel Ferwan tent (1987:71ff). That men and women do not inhabit tents and camps in the same way becomes even clearer during the camp move when the set of tent furnishings, rather than the arches that envelop it above, are used to define interior spatial relationships.

Before pitching their tents, the women place the furnishings, starting with the forked stakes or trestles *(ighaydan)* carved from Acacia nilotica *(teggart)* wood (fig. 5.11). On these a woman places her clothes, linens, blankets, and bags of valuables. It was with these trestles that she finished taking down the tent when she left the previous site, [and these are the same kind of trestles the northern Tuareg use].

She then sets up the bed *(tedebut)*, made of wood crosspieces resting on two heavy rails. Each bed rail may in turn be held up by means of two lighter supports *(tisedkal,* "to raise up"). The heavier members are carved from wood of the Balanites aegyptiaca *(aboragh)* whenever possible; the lighter members from the wood of the Acacia albida *(atɛs),* the Acacia raddiana *(afagag),* or the Commiphora africana *(adaras)* tree. A wattle of stalks, its edges sometimes reinforced with leather, is thrown over the crosspieces of the bed to serve as a mattress. Like the rush wattle mats above *(ɛwɛrwɛr),* these mattresses are made only by the Igdalan. Furnishings are completed by a tall dish stand which flares out at the top into a set of three bent branches to create a circular receptacle into which a bowl of curdled milk can be placed.

SPATIAL PRECAUTIONS

Every tent must contain two pieces of furniture: the pair of trestles and the bed. Although pieces of furniture other than the wattle mats are made and decorated with pyroengraved designs by Kel Ferwan or Kel Geres blacksmiths, the pair of trestles must remain without decoration (Casajus 1983).

This particular proscription seems singularly related to its primary position in the order of establishing interior space, and it appears to be, without question, related to the way in which the forked poles under a skin-covered tent were used to symbolize the act of setting out space (see figs. 5.8–9). What the above descriptions also highlight so poignantly is that the pitching sequence begins, not with the armature, but with the bed and the forked trestle. It is these two components that establish the spatial dimensions within the contained space: the bed dictates the positioning of the four exterior corner stakes (which carry the same linguistic designation as their forebears in the Kel Dennek tent); the trestles define an axis of

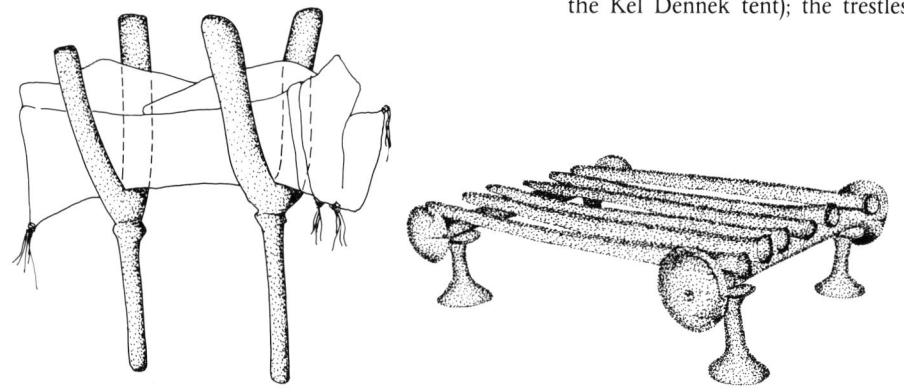

Fig. 5.11. The interior furnishings that establish the space of the tent: left, the storage rack; center, the bed; right, the bowl support or stand *(tejikant).*

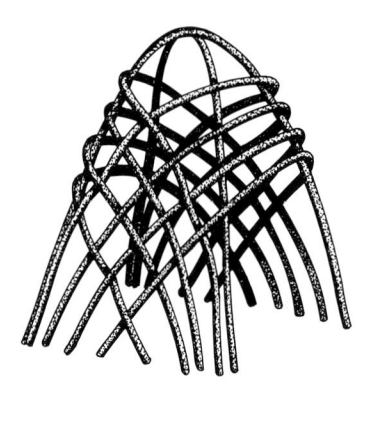

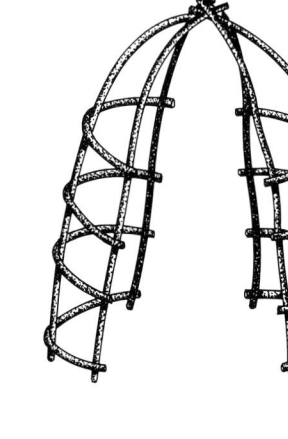

Fig. 5.12. Below, the armature of a noble Tuareg women's riding camel saddle and litter. Above, three styles of bentwood frame for the canopy *(ahennaka)* over the saddle. Drawings after a photograph, Musée de l'Homme, Paris, Nicolas 1950, and Lhote 1947.

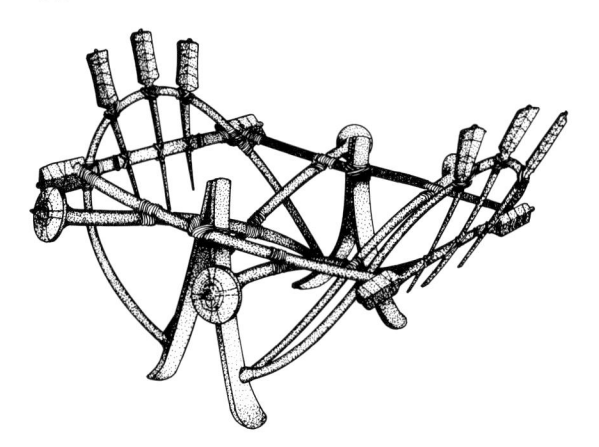

orientation that ultimately recalls and validates northern ancestry.

The particular precaution taken by women when they prepare to strike their tents further emphasizes the opposition between the security of contained, enclosed space and the dangers of open space outside: they paint around their eyes with an ochre powder *(tamazgut)*. Reputed to provide protection from the sun, there is reason to believe that its use has a deeper connotation since in their daily chores women are constantly exposed to the sun. It is only when the camp is being moved that they must protect themselves, as if they had more to suffer than men from the deprivation of their tents. So close is the proximity between women and their tents that the one occasion when they are without tents could not be without risk for them.

Casajus (1987:74) points out that the Kel Ahaggar use this same ochre powder. According to Duveyrier (1864:146), it is felt to protect them "from exterior atmospheric influences," which is approximately the property attributed to it by the Kel Ferwan. However, another observer added that Kel Ahaggar women going to visit a woman who has just given birth put "yellow ochre" around their eyes to keep away the "evil spirits" that prowl around the tent, that is, the same evil spirits referred to above. The danger to which women are exposed during moving is thus undoubtedly greater than what could happen to them from simple overexposure to the sun and seems to have something to do with the evil spirits which usually stay outside of the tent and become suddenly more menacing for women unprotected by their tents.

PALANQUINS AS PROTECTION

The precautionary measures incumbent on Tuareg women when moving through dangerous space finds quintessential poetic and material expression in their most brilliant creations, the dramatic and colorful repertoire of litters and palanquins—miniature moving tents—used by every respectable wife for every move. Initially created for the journey that is part of the marriage ritual, the palanquin has evolved into a fundamental metaphor. Logically, the most beautiful

Fig. 5.13. A noble Tuareg woman riding inside her litter with its protective white canopy. The tent armature and her slaves riding on donkeys can be seen behind.

ones were found among the aristocratic northern Tuareg, the Kel Ahaggar. Their framework is covered in leather, heavily encrusted with metal and hung with amulets carrying prophylactic value (pl. 12). Suspended, one on each side, are the large, brilliantly colored leather traveling bags *(arreġ)* (pl. 13).

The square framework of the litter recalls the structural frame of the bed, and indeed the terminating rondels on the litter match the turned knobs of the bed rails and posts (fig. 5.12). Careful scrutiny of the seeming complexity of the curved armature is particularly revealing. The meticulous reader will recognize, in the curved diagonal cross members that tie the two forks of the saddle together, an ancestral affinity with a simple pack saddle (see figs. 3.5–6). Furthermore, the bentwood arches projecting perpendicularly from the forks of the saddle signal its relationship to marriage litters elsewhere, and the three abbreviated but terminally decorated bentwood members rising from the litter on each side suggest an affinity with the enormous cagelike palanquins among the Kel Ahaggar.

Canopy armatures *(ahennaka)* for these litters, constructed separately, are nevertheless as varied as the tent structures themselves. The more modest ones, often intricate armatures fashioned from the bent roots of available acacia species, are often seen among the more southerly Tuareg (Nicolas 1950) where they may be used on oxen rather than camels. Because these armatures covered with fabric are separate entities, they can serve as a sweat chamber (or bathing enclosure); better yet, they may be used as a small room to shelter young sleeping infants (Lhote 1947).

Their multipurpose functions are, however, all related and gender-specific; all are subsumed in one or another way under the concepts of protection, containment, and enclosure. But these litters and palanquins become more than the mere counterpart to the protection afforded by a woman's tent: they concentrate and miniaturize her container of space. When viewed in the light of the emotional content and liminal quality that envelop the marriage ceremony, and in the context of the importance attached to movement in space itself, then this particular quintessential embodiment of an architectural-cum-artifactual metaphor should come as no surprise (fig. 5.13).

The Tuareg

6
THE TUBU: NOMADS IN THE EASTERN SAHARA

The Tubu nomads, the third largest nomadic culture in French-speaking Africa, inhabit the regions in and around the Tibesti mountain range. They were unknown as such to the Western world until the early nineteenth century.[1]

The Tubu do not refer to themselves this way. "Tubu," a Kanuri word, seems to signify "inhabitant of Tu" or Tibesti. More specifically, it arises from *tu* ("rocks") and *bu* ("person"). The word *tu* also designates the Tibesti mountain range, so that Tubu has become the general designation for a cultural group that had its ethnic epicenter in the Tibesti mountain range but subsequently migrated in various directions (see location map).

In the more recent literature, the Tubu have also been referred to as Téda and Toda. In reality, the Tubu include not only the Téda in the north but the Daza in the south.[2] At first glance it appears simple to divide the Tubu into those in the north speaking a Téda dialect and those of the south speaking a Daza dialect. The Téda camel herders are economically concentrated in the northern palm oases, and the Daza cattle herders are concentrated in the south, so one might say, as Le Coeur has (1950), that the Téda is the Tubu of the desert and the Daza is the Tubu of the steppe, and together they constitute the nomadic part of the Kanuri people. At the present time, the Téda are settled in the broad valleys *(enneri)* south and southwest of the Tibesti mountains, while the Daza inhabit the grazing lands south and east of Borku.

However, the situation is much more complicated: language as well as life-style and habitat distinguishes Téda from Daza and Tubu nomads from Kanuri agriculturalists. It has also been suggested that the term "Téda-Daza" more accurately reflects the complex historical and geographical condition of the ethnic groups occupying this region. In the literature as well as in the field, one frequently encounters the term "Goranes" in reference to the nomads in this region. Goranes is the name given by the Arab-speaking populations to the southern Tubu, particularly those in the Chad region, Téda as well as Daza.[3]

By extension, the Tubu habitat stretches from the Libyan desert in the north to the southern limits of the eastern Sahel. The area of dispersal is immense: it is some eighteen hundred kilometers from the northern oasis of Kufra in the heart of the Libyan desert to the mountain plateaus northeast of Zinder, Niger. Beyond their Tibesti homeland in the eastern Sahara, Tubu groups inhabit the northwest of Ennedi and the Kawar and Djado regions, as well as northern Kanem and Borku, intermingling with Kanuri peasantry. The Ennedi itself has no centers of sedentary life: all its inhabitants, Téda, Daza, and Bideyat, are either camel or cattle pastoralists.

The slow migrations that have led to the dispersal of what constitutes an agglomeration of related nomadic populations covered many centuries. In the first half of this millennium, the Tubu dispersed toward Kanem in the south and Fezzan in the north; in the second half, there were migrations from Kanem and Borku back

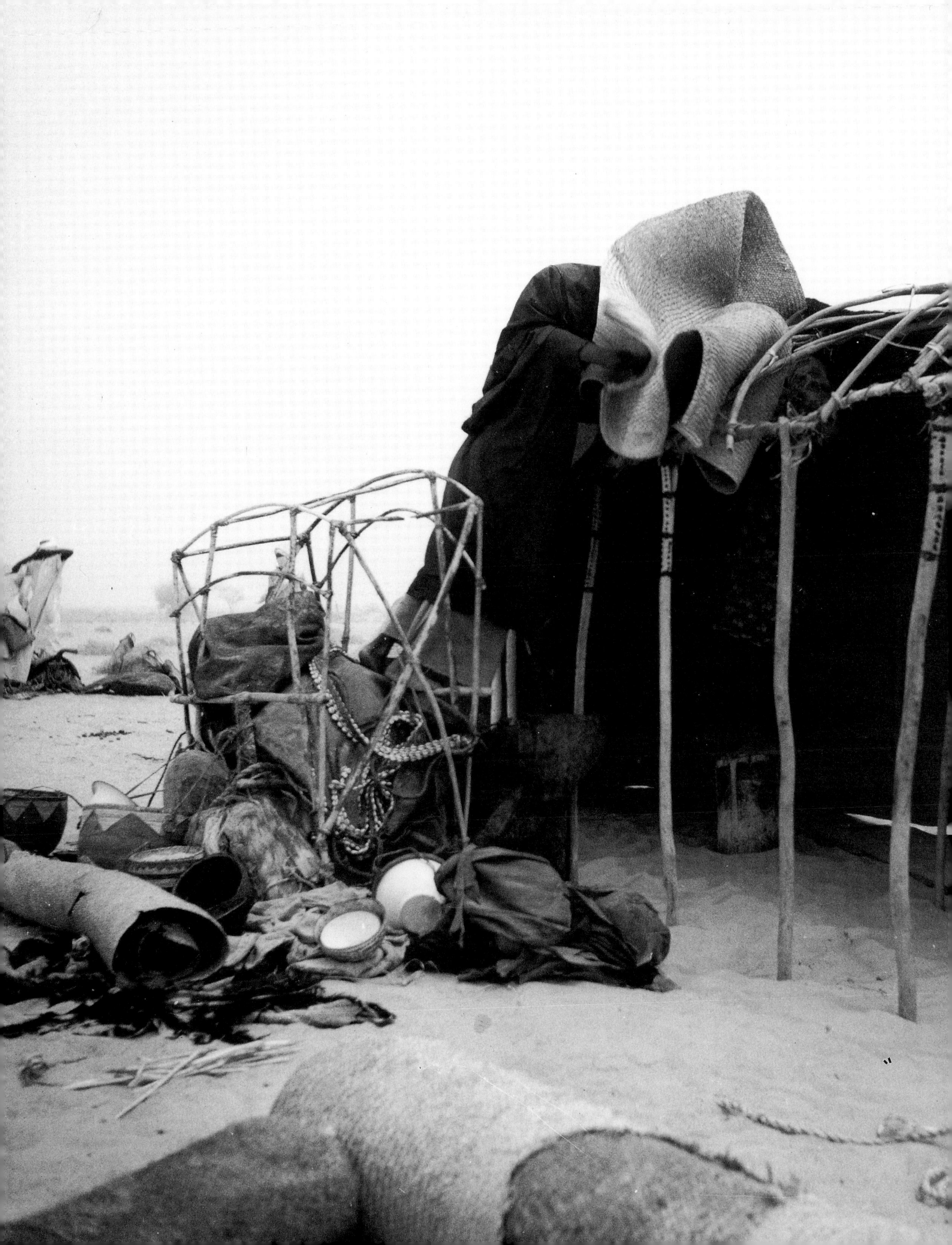

toward Tibesti. It seems certain that at one time the Kufra oasis was heavily populated by Tubu, but with the various Arab invasions, many migrated back toward Tibesti. Singular Tubu families can also still be met with in the southern Fezzan (near Gatrun in the Murzuq region), just as Lyon had (1821) in the early nineteenth century.

The Arabs, who now constitute a vast group in Chad, have also played an important cultural role in the history of the region. Migrating west from the Sudan, in the course of the centuries they infiltrated the length of the subdesert zones. Arabic was the single written language until the colonial era and continues to function as the trade language in a popular form *(tourkou)*. Camel and cattle herders as well as traders, they have left a strong material imprint on the indigenous cultures with whom they interacted. The western Téda have also been in close contact with the Tuareg Kel Ayr and the Kel Ajjer in the northwest since at least the sixteenth century, even though the Ténéré, an immense desert space, separates the two cultures. In the south, the Tédas of Tibesti were involved in the foundation of the Kanem kingdom.[4] Surely one should look to these centuries-long historic relationships for the striking similarities among the arts and architectures of the Tubu, the Arabic and Tuareg cultures in this part of the eastern Sahara. Their inclusion in this anthology is, in fact, a result of encountering so many similarities in the course of perusing the literature.

The Tibesti region is crowned by the extinct volcano Emi Kussi, the highest pinnacle in the Sahara (3,515 m). The black basalt slabs of this extraordinary, impressive, scenic mountain massif of volcanic origin rise from a pedestal of ancient sandstone slabs (see fig. 2.2). Between the steep, precipitous mountain range run broad valleys and grass-rich expanses of plateau *(tarso)*. The valleys of north and central Tibesti, particularly endowed with water sources, support oases within which stands of palm and gardens flourish. The plains on the southwest flank of the mountain mass are of particular significance since their comparatively rich vegetation continues to support camel breeding. It is perhaps this unique ecological configuration that contributes to the symbiotic relationships among sedentarists and pastoralists which characterize this particular part of the African desert and creates the difficulty in establishing cultural divisions among Téda and Daza.

Some Tubu families live the entire year in the oases where they grow barley, wheat or corn, millet, and above all date palms. Among others, one part of the family remains behind in the oases to tend the crops, while another part of the family grows up on the plains tending to their herds, returning to rejoin their families in the oases for the harvest and trade season. In general, however, the Téda camel herders live north of a diagonal axis (following the sixteenth to the eighteenth parallel) that divides the Tibesti from the Ennedi ranges, and the Daza cattle herders (and those of the Tédas who live with them) live south of it.

Nevertheless, herding is paramount everywhere in Tubu country. The herd of every Tubu is for man and woman the source of all material life. It furnishes both with milk and meat, with the skins from which waterskins, sacks, sandals, rope, coverings, belts, and tent parts are made. By selling animals one obtains millet, dates, condiments, cloth, jewelry. With pack animals one can transport the house and its furnishings from one site to another.

Alongside the Daza seignorial clans of herders and warriors live the Azza hunters and artisans. Although free, they are considered as vassals *(mellen)* of other clans and constitute a segregated group. Their inferior position derives from the two activities which others hold in either contempt or awe: hunting and artisanship.[5] They specialize in the great antelope hunts and forage, they maintain the wells, and as blacksmiths they work in wood and at the forge.

Unlike their Tuareg neighbors, the Tubu have received little written notice over the decades, perhaps because of the harsh terrain in which they move. The few detailed accounts there are vary considerably, often contradicting each other in their details and cultural interpretation. In attempting to synthesize a description of Tubu tents and tent furnishings, which I have never been witness to, I have drawn heavily and extensively on the field research of the few observers who have worked, lived, and traveled in the Tibesti region during this century. Information contained in

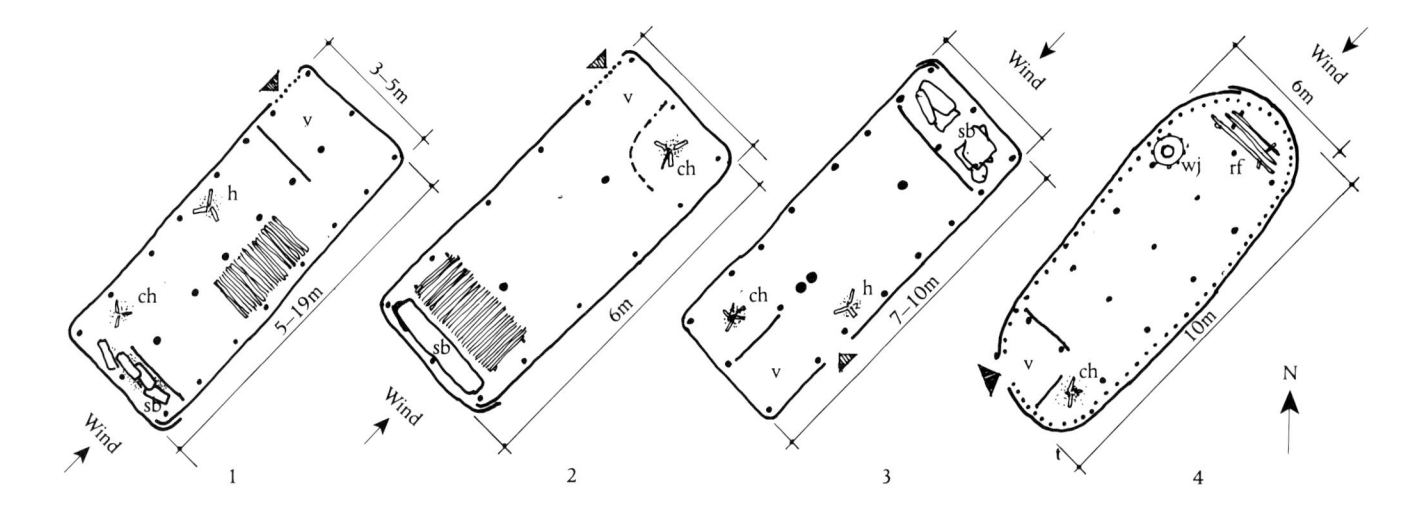

Fig. 6.1. 1. Plan of a Daza tent in the region of Zouar, southwest Ennedi. 2. Plan of a Tubu tent in the region immediately around Gouré, west of Lake Chad. 3. Plan of a Tubu (Daza) tent at Enneri Ogu, southwest Tibesti. 4. Plan of a "Goranes" (Daza) tent in the Borku region. *Legend.* ch: cooking hearth. h: hearth. rf: roost for fowl. sb: storage for saddles and baggage. v: vestibule. wj: water jar. Drawings after Le Coeur 1950, Grall 1945, Fuchs 1961, 1971a, and Schiffers 1957.

the ethnographic dictionary compiled by Le Coeur (1950) and in the monograph compiled by Chapelle (1957) has been supplemented by Fuchs' more recent research (1961, 1971a, b) and his collections in the ethnographic museums of Stuttgart and Vienna. Supplementary details were extracted from the published observations of passing military or medical visitors.

TUBU TENTS

From a distance, the nomadic Tubu camp does not offer the classic look of nomad camps. No tent peaks reaching for the sky, but rather a series of long grayish hangars, oblong or rectangular in form, with bulging backs (pl. 14). These are not tents of cloth, nor of goat or camel hair, felt or hides, but mat tents that look like the inverted hulls of river barges.[6]

The same Tubu word *(yaobi)* is used to designate not only the stone houses that characterize the Téda world on the mountain but the mat-covered tents that characterize both the Téda and Daza world in the plains neighboring on the Tibesti.[7] The general impression left by those describing the Tubu mat-covered tents is that they differ little from each other.

There are, in fact, considerable variations in structure, in form, and in the choice of building materials for various elements (fig. 6.1). Daza (Goranes) tents are more rounded, and their armatures approach a beehive form, albeit elongated, whereas the Téda tent structurally resembles a tensile structure, even though mats are used for walls and roofing. It appears to resemble more closely the tents of the Mahria and the Arabs.

The Daza tent (fig. 6.1, no. 1) that Le Coeur included in his dictionary and the "Tubu" tent (no. 2) that Grall documented are oriented the same way, and their openings are located in the same position. In the former, however, the bed occupies the center of the interior space (not unlike the way in which the Kababish locate their beds), and in the latter it is located at the far end. The organization of space in the Daza tents that Fuchs measured in southwestern Tibesti (no. 3) match Grall's, but the entire tent appears to have been rotated a half circle, as does the rounded plan of a "Goranes" tent in the Borku region which Schiffers recorded (no. 4). Built up as a thick armature of palm leaf ribs (as indeed his photographs show), the interior recess, instead of housing the baggage and bed of the nomad, is a roost for fowl, and the nonportable pottery water jar. According to Fuchs (personal communication, 1992), this kind of armature "tent" belongs either to the sedentary (or semi-nomadic) Daza oasis dwellers, serving them as a "permanent" tent, or, more accurately, as a nonmovable, mat-covered armature hut. It also serves the nomads as a second tent during the date harvest when they come to the oasis (fig. 6.2). It has also been suggested that those of the Daza are the most spacious, most comfortable, and best maintained because the raw

The Tubu   111

Fig. 6.2. A Daza encampment in the Borku region, at Tigi, southeast Tibesti.

materials required in its construction are more abundantly available to them. At the same time, among the Daza, because woods for this armature type of tent are easier to find, considerable parts of it are left behind with each move in order to lighten the transport load.

These differences, however, require additional commentary. In addition to variations in the form and structure of the mat tents used by the Tubu, they are pitched in different ways according to the season. Tents are oriented according to the prevailing direction of the wind, and entrances are accordingly always on the lee side. During the dry season, they are oriented so that the shorter end, heavily weighted down and anchored by means of bed, screens, baggage, etc., provides a bulwark against the northeastern wind. During the rainy season, the entire tent is rotated so that the entrance, still on the lee side, is now in the northwest corner and the bed and baggage in the southwest. The overturned hulls that these armature tents remind one of is not a farfetched association: they resist the winds the same way the hull of a boat resists the forces set up by its movement in the water.

A number of authors have argued that the presence of this type of tent—and its variations—may be linked to the ubiquitous presence of the dum palm (Hyphaene thebaica) throughout the entire region, at both low and high altitudes.[8] The weakness of this hypothesis, as was pointed out elsewhere, rests on the failure to consider the tent's primary *structural* elements or the building materials used for them in addition to the tent coverings. While it is true that the prevalence of the dum palm may explain the preference for the woven mat coverings, the armature members are equally a factor. Another factor to be taken into account is that there is a very distinct gender-discrete set of roles in the creation of the Tubu mat-covered armature tent: the major structural elements are fashioned by the Azza woodworkers, and it is they who may help dig the holes into which the pickets are placed (recalling their role as well diggers, perhaps). Then it is the Tubu woman who pitches the structure and covers it with mats (fig. 6.3).

The mat covering of the tent is supported by a primary set of forked poles made from acacia roots *(tefi)* very much like the ribs of a boat's hull support its

African Nomadic Architecture

Fig. 6.3. A Tubu woman putting up her tent in the northern Ennedi region.

Fig. 6.4. The armature is clearly seen in a Tubu tent under construction.

The Tubu 113

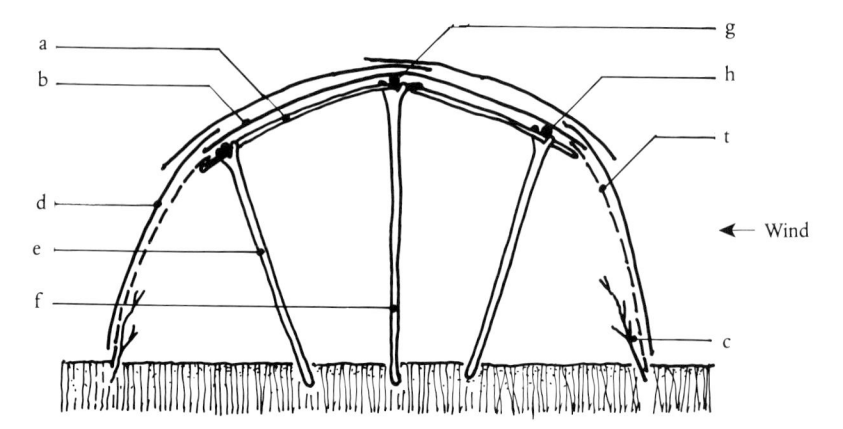

Fig. 6.5. Section through the tent illustrating structural shifts in response to seasonal wind changes. *Legend.* a: acacia root or palm frond lattices *(djerids)*. b: skin lining *(kelefu)*. c: branch reinforcing. d: mats. e: acacia poles *(tebi)*. f: center poles *(dobal)*. g: center ridge beam *(yaobi dahao)*. h: lateral beams made from bundles of acacia root or palm frond. t: secondary armature members *(tumuzeri)*. Drawing after Chapelle 1957 and Grall 1945.

sheathing (fig. 6.4). These stakes *(dobal)*, placed to create a central row and two exterior rows at a distance of approximately 1.75 meters, run the whole length of the tent, marking its longitudinal axis. The exterior rows of poles are held together by a long ridge or "eave" of light poles, made from bundles of either acacia roots or palm ribs. A larger bundle rests on the forks in the center row forming the main support rib of the ceiling *(yaobi dahao)*. The central stakes are longer than the exterior poles, so the roof ribs *(djerids)* must be curved or bent to meet the exterior ridges. Long thin laths made from the stripped ribs of date palm are then spaced several centimeters apart and attached across these ridge supports. It is in those areas where curved acacia roots are used instead of palm laths that the tent takes on a more rounded appearance.

The whole is attached with three lengths of cord that run along the main ridge supports, attaching each lath crossing with a simple knot so it is easy to untie. Two long mats, placed vertically and laced to the stakes with metal pins, encircle the tent and form the sides. Two other identical mats, placed horizontally and laced to the ribs which span from one wall to the other, form the roof.

The acacia roots used for the primary tent poles are of a very hard, close-grained wood and grow absolutely straight. The fork at the top is obtained by splitting the wood, then forcing the edges of the split over the heat of a fire. The strong leather tie that prevents the split from opening further becomes the basis for the red and black designs decorating the upper portion of the stake.

The mats *(kowe)*, made from the leaves of the dum palm, are woven in the south by the Azza women. Approximately 1.6 meters wide and 12 meters long, they limit the size of the tents. Taking into account that the mats have to overlap, tents are rarely more than 8 meters long and 3.5 meters wide.

The older the tent, the smaller it is. As portions of the mat become unusable, as the edges are eaten away, greater overlap is required. Newer mats, which can more easily be rolled up, are used for the sides, those that are more worn are used for the roof. The Téda of the north, who are poorer and who have a hard time replenishing their mats, have less spacious and beautiful tents than the Daza of the south. Lacking the longer or more numerous stakes available to the Daza, Téda tents are often shorter and lower.

The mat house is pleasant to live in. Its semidarkness, pierced by a few gleams of light sliding through the holes of the mats, is a respite from the harsh daylight. Its relative coolness is maintained by constant air circulation through the mats and especially at ground level due to the possibility of raising and rolling up the mat either on one side of the house or the other according to the play of sunlight and shadow.

During winter, the sides of the tent are carefully lowered right to the ground. On the windward side, all the skins one possesses are stretched between the mats and the stakes. The door is narrower, and a lower partition of mats, with a very low opening, separates the entrance from the rest of the tent.

In the tornado season, not only is the tent rotated (as noted above) but instead of being put up with vertical sides, it is put up as a half cylinder or tunnel for further protection from the violent winds and to facilitate water drainage (fig. 6.5). For this, the two rows of side stakes are inclined outward, and are planted inwards toward the center of the tent width instead of at the edge. In addition, numerous very short stakes, made of any kind of branches, are implanted at the baseline around the bottom of the mats, holding the mats laced to them firmly on the ground.

The structural problem, however, is that a secondary armature of bent wall members is needed to obtain the tunnel-like form. By including a reference to this secondary armature in describing the mat-covered armature tent, Le Coeur (1950) provides, in a single remark, a more satisfactory structural description (and explanation) for these armature tents. He notes that "on this armature [i.e., of primary poles and lintels or beams] are placed the regularly spaced vertical canes *(tumuzeri)*, their tops bent over in the form of a half cradle to tie into the central rib. It is on this sort of a cage that the mats are placed." Logic suggests that when these secondary stakes are extended, they turn into the secondary armature of the Daza (or Goranes) tent.

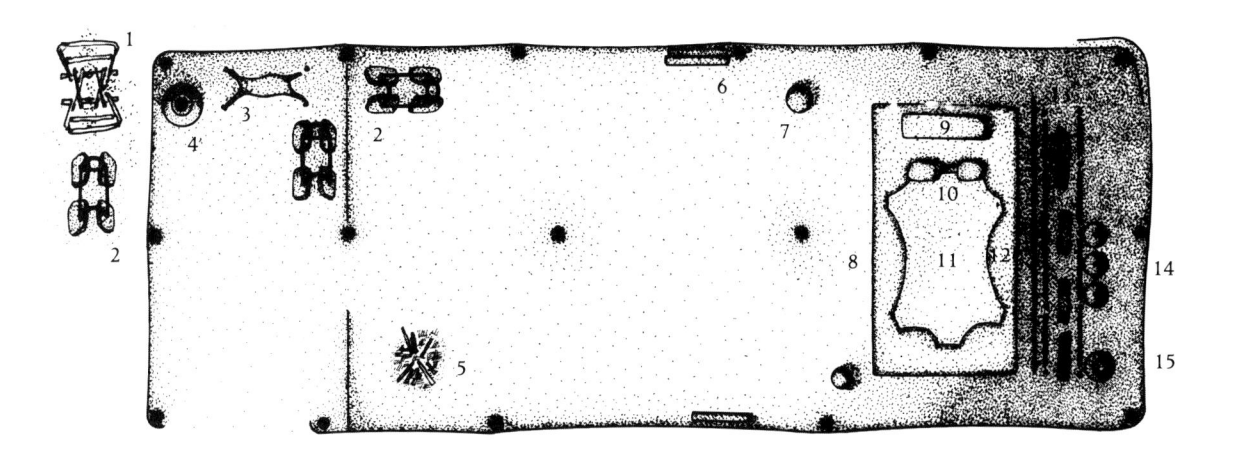

The secondary armature of the Goranes tent, which results in a half shell with similarly rounded ends, provides perhaps the most satisfactory structural solution to wind resistance. The resultant rounded form of the tent plan, in conjunction with its curved mat wall surfaces and roof, offers the least resistance to the fierce tornado winds since they flow easily around and over its mass. Ultimately they become more important structurally than the primary framework of poles and roof ribs on which the more northerly tents depend.

The entrance to the tent *(koe)*, always in the corner opposite the sleeping space, leads into a vestibule created by a separation screen (fig. 6.6). The term for the tent opening *(kachimbet)*, the "mouth of the tent" or the "mouth of the house," refers equally to the family based on the patrilineage of a single ancestor and to the group of tents, fictive or real, that make up a camp.

The kitchen, located near the door, is often separated by a small partition of mats. The cooking area is to the side, about one meter from the partition, and

Fig. 6.6. Plan of a Tubu (Daza) tent and its furnishings. *Legend.* 1: women's saddle. 2: men's saddle. 3: waterskin on supporting poles. 4: water jar. 5: hearth. 6: hanging sacks. 7: bowl support. 8: bed on pickets. 9: clothes and jewelry coffer. 10: hourglass-shaped leather pillow. 11: sheepskin cover. 12: leather backdrop. 13: baggage support with provisions sacks and a cover. 14: storage containers. 15: butter churn. Drawing after Chapelle 1957.

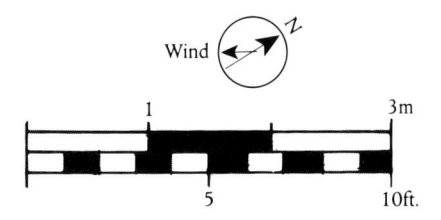

always placed in the same spot to avoid burning the feet by walking over the coals. The waterskins, suspended from two stakes, are placed near the door.

The interior of the tent is very clean; the sand is fine, carefully swept and frequently replaced. Daylight filters through the side mats, and sunshine is sifted through the roof mats. However, at the end of the tent opposite the entrance, where the bed and baggage are found, between the roof ribs and the mats that form the roof, the section is reinforced with a hide tarpaulin (*kelefo* or *kulufu*). The smooth sides are turned in during the dry winter season and turned out during the rainy season in order to allow water to run off. The large bed with its goatskin covering, on which the family sleeps, is located under this cover.

This tarpaulin, assembled from eight to ten antelope skins sewn together, is fabricated by the Azza.[9] The magical character ascribed to the Azza hunters apparently extends to the selective use of antelope skins (always associated with and tanned by the Azza hunters who have killed them) for this particular tarpaulin, imbuing it with a particularly potent spiritual power. A similar quality is ascribed to the leather clothing *(farto)* which is also made of antelope skin. Several Téda clans have a taboo that forbids the wearing of leather clothing, but the Azza always wear them, and nothing else, when engaged in hunting or in ceremonial dances (Briggs 1960).

The bed *(cage)* consists of forked sticks planted in the sand onto which wooden crosspieces are placed. The whole is covered with slender branches and a solid mat of interwoven straw and leather. The bed itself is not a movable piece of furniture to be taken along when one moves, but a framework rebuilt with each installation.

At the back of the tent, several centimeters behind the bed and directly below the antelope skin tarpaulin above, hangs the camel palanquin cover (*dela* or *odri*). It forms a decorative panel in the shape of a butterfly or rectangle (fig. 6.7).[10] Decorated with cowries arranged in bands, chevrons, triangles, or circles, it is the jewel of the bride's trousseau: made for her by her mother with the assistance of relatives and neighbors, it is the single, but critical, exception to the Azza monopoly on the fabrication of leather goods.

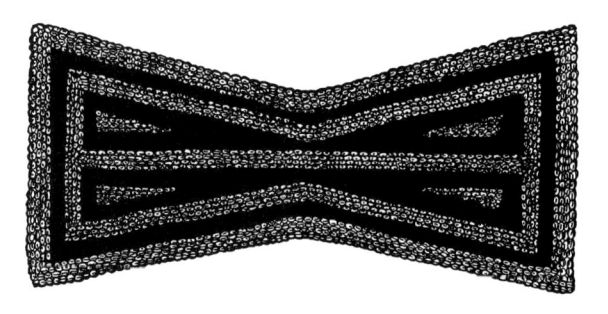

Fig. 6.7 Two styles of the cowrie-decorated leather panel which is hung as a backdrop behind the bed and used on the palanquin. Above, a *kubu* or *odri*; below, a *dela*; height 1 m; length 2.5 m. Drawing after Chapelle 1957.

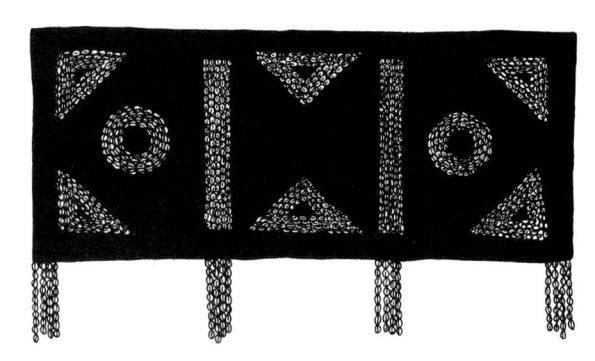

As the indispensable ornament of any Tubu tent, the most beautiful panels are the pride of the women who own them. Two or three meters wide and up to one meter high, the *dela* may be made of plaited or solid leather. It is decorated with leather braids or bunches of cowries hanging down. The simple designs of old panels tend to be more complicated today, as motifs found on blankets or rugs from North Africa, or on copies of these coming from Europe, are imitated. Rosettes, stars, and Solomon's seals are appearing. But cowrie shells are becoming more rare and costly, and appear less frequently on the panel.

At the top of the panel are hung the false rein and the breast strap decorated with cowries and copper bells worn by the woman's camel mount. Plates of plaited straw, their edges decorated with strips of leather, are added along the upper edge (fig. 6.8).

Behind the decorated leather backdrop, in the narrow space that separates it from the back of the tent, can be found the large antelope hide double bags which contain the grain reserves and most of the family's personal effects. They are hung from tall stakes or rest on the women's palanquins. Over the stakes the folded rugs and blankets are placed horizontally on crosspieces, the pile rising more or less according to the wealth of the tent, their multicolored edges showing over the decorated leather panel. Among the Azza, baggage is enveloped in an enormous tanned leather sack whose dimension matches the width of the tent. Milk and butter pots of plaited straw, the large butter churn, the harness trappings (leather saddlebags, nose ring, etc.) join the assemblage.

While the wife's belongings are carefully arranged behind the bed, everything belonging to her husband is haphazardly strewn along the sides of the tent. His saddle and arms are near the entry or are placed on the roof when he sleeps outside.

The middle of the tent, from the entrance to the bed, is always kept clear. The winnowing basket, knives, awls, spear blades, all flat objects, are inserted in the ceiling between the laths and the roof. The coffer *(kisimunto)*, containing silver, jewelry, festive clothes, sugar, and tea, is placed at the head of the bed, on the side from which the wind comes. The double cushion that serves as a pillow for the couple *(odru)* is at the foot of the coffer. Thus the Tubu woman sleeps in direct physical contact with, or in the shadow of, her treasure.

THE AZZA

All that touches on the processing of wild animal skins is reserved to the Azza: using the bark of the *tefi* (Acacia raddiana), they tan, dye, and manufacture leather sacks both large and small. Innumerable herds of gazelles, troops of antelope and ostriches, more rarely giraffes, inhabit the entire region between Lake Chad and the desert proper, and these are hunted, professionally, by the Azzas. After the hunt, the spoils are divided: the meat is dried and resold to the nomads, the doeskins, solid and supple, are tanned on the return to the camp and assembled into large panels that serve to cover the side of the tents exposed to the wind and to fabricate sacks of different sizes and leather cord.[11] Azza hunters (or herders) also manufacture all the tent poles, the mortars and pestles, the saddles, the wooden plates and spoons. It is also with these skins that the Azzas pay their tribute to the Dazas.

In addition to the Azza hunters and tanners, there

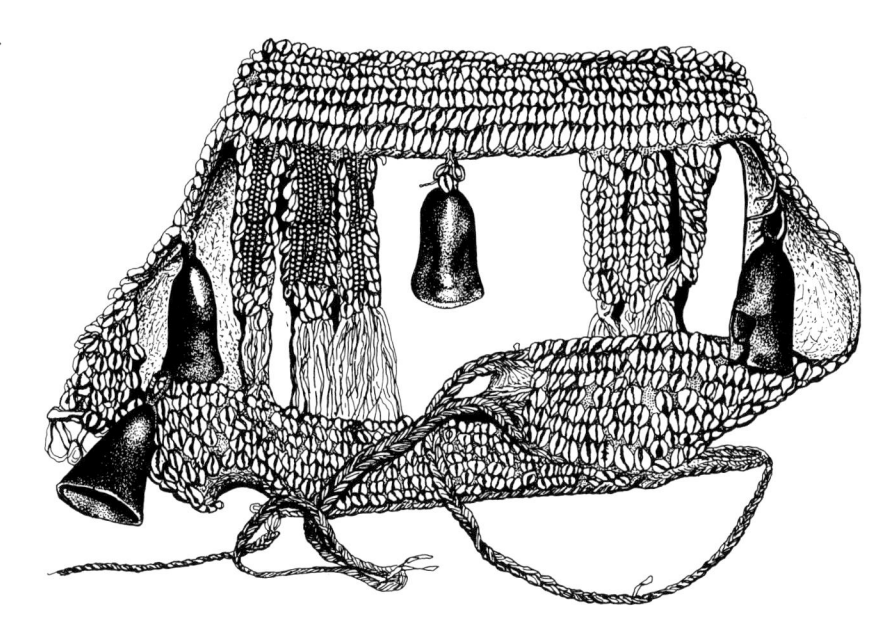

Fig. 6.8. The cowrie shell breast dress used on oxen by the Arab Wadai women is similar to those used by Tubu women for their camels. Museum für Völkerkunde, Vienna, Fuchs Collection. Drawing after a photograph.

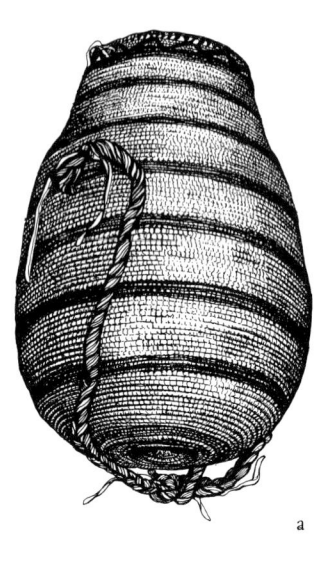

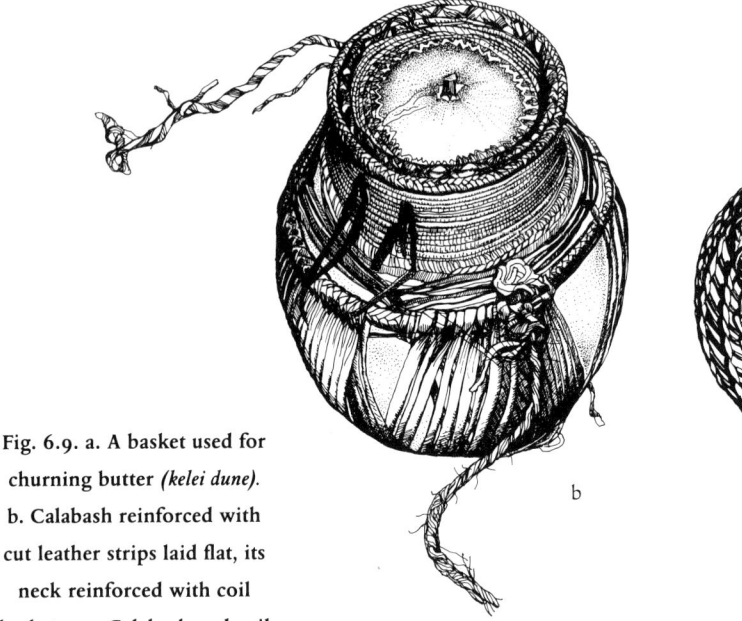

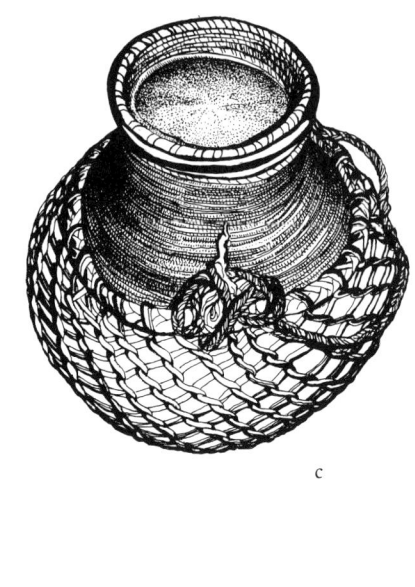

Fig. 6.9. a. A basket used for churning butter *(kelei dune)*. b. Calabash reinforced with cut leather strips laid flat, its neck reinforced with coil basketry. c. Calabash and coil technique basket using dum palm leaf fibers, with a looped thong carrier.

are the Azza blacksmiths who can be found at Manga, Kanem, and Bahr-el-Ghazal, in Borku, Tibesti, and Ennedi. They have other talents: they are the musicians and entertainers, traveling from camp to camp, either on their own initiative or on command. Their wives are the potters; no others know how to fabricate the clay pots. They claim, most of the time, that they came from Ennedi, and, as in many other African societies, the Azza blacksmiths occupy a place apart in Tubu societies.

All basketry manufacture, in a coil technique using the dum palm leaves, is in the hands of the Azza women (fig. 6.9). They make the basket containers ornamented with leather and cowries, the basket covers, the tent mats, and the bed mats (Chapelle 1957). In the course of his travels south of Murzuq, Lyon (1821:227) was equally struck by the quality of the Tubu women's basketry: "Their chief occupation seems to be basketmaking; and they also form drinking bowls out of palm leaves, which they ornament with strips of colored leather, and execute with much taste and neatness. All the Fezzaners who come here to trade return loaded with these baskets, as presents for their families."

The kind of basketwork Lyon referred to can still be found: the enormous coil basket *(kelei dune)* used for churning butter; the calabash container *(aforay)*, its neck richly reinforced with coil basketry and its body reinforced with cut leather strips laid flat; the calabash with an applied coil technique protected by a looped thong carrier *(kelemi* or *kelei sene)*; a large, round coiled basket made from dum palm leaves and reinforced with a red leather base *(balkaye)*; and a rectangular coffer *(kisimunto)*, again of dum palm leaves, with base and sides enveloped in red leather edged with decorative triangles, that serves as a small chest in which tea, money, and a woman's valuables are stored.

However, while almost all the objects used in the Tubu tent are fabricated by the Azzas and their wives, any Téda or Daza, whether a notable or a commoner, can make a sack for his personal use and any woman can make a basket for her personal use (Chapelle 1957). As elsewhere, the work is divided among the sexes, but this division is apparently not as rigorous: each person fabricates or repairs that for which he or she has a personal need. The distinction is that the Azzas work for others, for sale and to pay tribute.

The division of labor conveyed by the above descriptions is neither as rigidly observed nor as simply

Fig. 6.9. d. Round coiled basket made from dum palm leaves, reinforced with red leather. e. The rectangular basket woven from dum palm leaves used by women to store their valuables. Museum für Völkerkunde, Vienna, Fuchs Collection. Drawings after photographs.

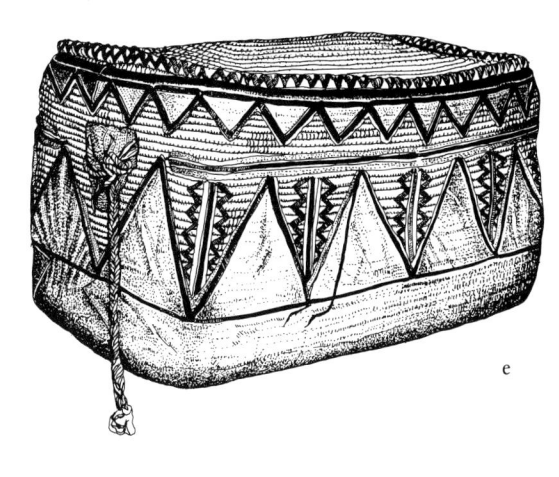

defined as it may appear, because although there is women's work and men's work, there is also the work of the noble clans and the work reserved for the Azza. Le Coeur, in a rather fascinating early attempt to elicit a Tubu aesthetic (1953), documented the particular tasks permitted to and considered respectable by social class as well as gender.

For him, the noble work of men included rope making, whether it be braided from the ribs of the dum palm or the bark of the Acacia raddiana, or cut finely into thongs from the neck of the cattle or large antelope. Men's "noble" work also included the manufacture of goatskin or antelope skin water containers and the fire-sticks, one of hardwood, one of softwood. On the other hand, although it was considered a disgrace for Daza noble men to tan leather, their wives could specifically tan the leather for the *dela*.

The menial work of men, primarily tanning and leatherworking, rested primarily in Azza hands. It is only they who could tan and dye the skins, fashioning the men's traveling sacks *(malamala)* and the women's haversacks *(mogala)*. They also fashioned the personal sack *(oru* or *olu)* made of calfskin dyed red, which is given by mothers to their daughters as a marriage gift. Azza men also made the conjugal pillow (consisting of two cushions of calfskin or male goatskin joined with a central band and similar to those used by the Mahria), as well as the special tent lining *(kulufu)* of antelope skin. Even though both are part of a Tubu bride's trousseau, they were not made by the Azza wives.

Apparently, the attribution of "nobility" to some aspects of leatherworking and not others may well be a reflection of the particular sociocultural attitudes within Tubu society. An even clearer reflection of value judgments placed on various artifacts by virtue of their creators is the fact that the broad range of baskets and tent mats made by the Azza women were, according to Le Coeur, also considered as menial work.

THE TUBU MARRIAGE CEREMONY

The creation of a new Tubu domicile, its tent and furnishings, all unfolds in the course of the marriage ceremony (Noel 1920:119–23; Le Coeur 1950:68–72; Chapelle 1957:278ff).

Most often a marriage *(azuner)* is held during the period of the date harvest, when long stays in the palm oases facilitate social interaction and social obligation, as well as the acquisition of necessary bride prices and bridewealth. On the given day, the groom sends millet and goats, sometimes a cow, to the camp of his fiancée. The bride's mother prepares many plates of food. When the two families live near each other, the mother of the groom sends some from her side. All the women from both camps contribute.

A mat tent is erected, its construction and furnishing supervised and supplied by the mother of the bride. The marriage tent is erected in the course of afternoon negotiations among the two families. It is divided into two compartments, sometimes separated by a room in the middle. At the center, a man faithful to his wife symbolically pushes in a "stick from which to hang a goatskin" *(sine yedi)* at the foot of the central pole. A libation of a porridge made of grain (millet, wheat, or barley), milk, butter, and water *(sadaka)* is buried at its base as a ritual and a propitiatory offering. The small stick that was planted at the foot of the central pole is decorated with three red circles. The extra butter is used by the women who are present to anoint their hands and arms.

An earlier account enriches the picture with additional details (Noel 1920:121):

In the center of the house two forked pickets, attached together, are planted, one long like those which serve for the construction of the house, the other short, stripped of its bark, on which three red rings have been painted. It seems that in the absence of these pickets, no woman desiring a husband will enter in this house, or at least, she will not remain there. The seventh day (of the marriage), these pickets will be buried outside, well shaded, and the earth that will cover them will be moistened with water.

Le Coeur (1969:152) referred to the presence of this same sacrifice *(sadaka)* in a Téda marriage he witnessed. It is tempting to call attention to the three rings that appear on the forked poles of Tubu (Arna) tents north of the Ennedi mountains in figure 6.3. While Peter Fuchs has suggested (personal communication, 1992) that the pair of center poles that he recorded were only a matter of structural stability, one cannot help but wonder whether there is an unspoken relationship between physical and conceptual stability.

While waiting for the groom, dancing takes place around a drum suspended from a post, which is being struck with great frenzy: young men dance with daggers drawn; women dance with short lateral steps. The older men, seated in a circle, animatedly discuss the final touches to the marriage contract amongst themselves. The exchange of gifts is reviewed, last-minute demands are countered, the wise conciliate differences, compromise is reached, and, to seal the agreement, if there is a man present who can do it, he is asked to recite the opening verse from the Koran.

Finally, as the climax to this heated activity, the groom appears, mounted on camel or on horseback and accompanied by his mounted friends. The groom remains impassive and still on his camel, while the women who have come out to meet him ululate and his mounted friends prance about. Several stops are made like this, marked by dances and exploits. Then, toward evening, the group arrives at the nuptial tent. The groom and his troop circle it three times while the roof is struck with a spear and, if possible, gunshots are fired. The groom is seated on a mat in front of the tent.

During this time the bride is hidden at the home of one of her friends: she has buried herself under some baggage or under a sheepskin. The friends of the groom approach with a camel, but the women, young people, relatives of the bride, the blacksmiths, and the armed Azza have gathered in front of the tent where she is hiding. A mock combat takes place with shouts and gunfire.

Even when the combat is just a sham, it is considered good form for the bride to resist. She arrives sobbing at the nuptial tent, she is taken around the tent three times, then taken off the camel, carried over the threshold, and put in the room reserved for her.

The next morning a goat is sacrificed and cooked. In the afternoon, the maid of honor unties the three medial braids which ran from the bride's forehead to the nape of her neck and plaits the hair into the two braids of a married woman. Between them, she pours a little milk, making sure that it runs down the middle of her forehead and onto her nose. As a virgin, she wore three medial braids; as a married woman, she will wear only two.

Then a piece of scented wood is placed on the fire. When it is just an ember, it is placed on a flat grindstone. The bride, passing her hand under the mat that separates her compartment from that of the groom, grasps the small stone that serves as a pestle, the groom puts his hand over hers, the woman who dressed the bride puts her hand over that of the groom, the man who has been assisting the groom seizes the hand of the woman, and the four hands together crush the scented ember. It is on the evening of this day that the marriage is finally consummated.

The newlyweds remain for seven days in the nuptial tent. During this seven-day confinement, food is prepared by the bride's mother. On the last day the newlyweds come out of the tent and seat themselves at opposite ends of a mat. A sack of flour or a mortar full of dates is placed between them. They fight over it, and it is claimed by whoever is able to grab hold of it.[12] Presumably, as elsewhere, possession establishes household authority!

On this same last day, the groom begins to circulate, paying visits within the camp, soliciting gifts. It is also on the seventh day that the husband visits his father-in-law, and, if he has not yet done so, obtains gifts to compensate for those he received during the engagement.

The bride's mother brings silver jewelry. As a girl, the bride wore only copper rings on her ankles; she wore only bracelets or necklaces of no value and in her nostril only a piece of wood or a few strands of straw. Today a small silver ring is put in her nostril, a silver spiral as a frontal, and a silver plate in the form of a trident knots and holds her braids at the back of her neck. Silver cylinders are placed on her ankles.

It is also on this last day that the mother of the bride presents her daughter with the leather hanging *(dela)* described above, which will be the indispensable ornament of both the bride's tent and palanquin. An essential part of her trousseau, it is the pride of every married woman. It is never replaced, even when old and worn, and remains a continuing, renewable reminder of her wedding day.

The newlyweds remain another three days in this special tent. Then it is taken down, and the bride goes to live near her parents in her own tent. The husband goes back to his occupations, paying his wife more or less frequent visits. She cooks for him each time he comes, and sleeps with him, but otherwise treats him

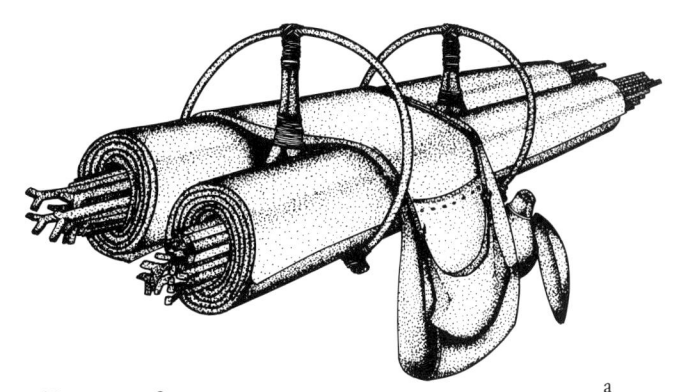

Fig. 6.10. a. Transport of the tent on a pack saddle. b. A Tubu women's pack litter. c. A Téda women's palanquin. Drawings after Chapelle 1957, a photograph taken at the Museum für Völkerkunde, Vienna, Fuchs Collection, and Le Coeur 1950.

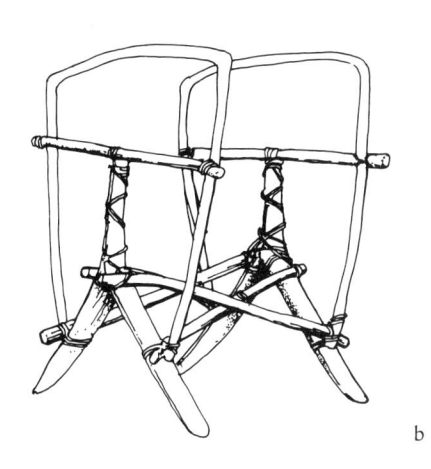

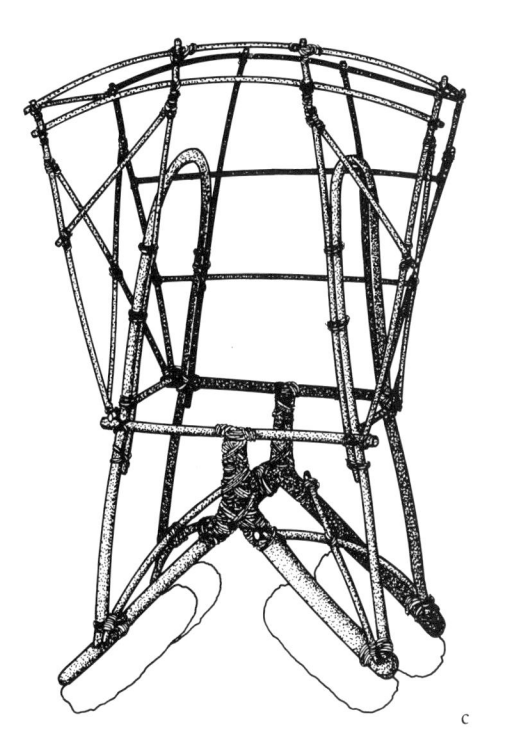

The Tubu

as a stranger. After the birth of the first child, or at the end of two or three years, the man gives his mother-in-law two or three beautiful male camels, after which he may then take his wife back to his own camp, in his own country. Family life as we know it does not begin until this time.

Parenthetically, it was of interest to me to learn that among Tibesti oasis dwellers who customarily live in stone houses, bride and groom spend their first seven nights together in the same kind of mat-covered tent that has been described above. It is built especially for the occasion by the women. The marriage ceremony, which provides the behavioral framework for, and places Tubu arts and architectures in, cultural context provides, at the same time, the mechanisms for the continuing attachment to a nomadic ideal.

SADDLES AND PALANQUINS

In contrast to the Saharan riding saddle used by her husband (see Chapter 3 above), the Tubu woman uses a simple pack saddle *(gommo)* to transport a tent, herself, or both (fig. 6.10a). It is essentially an armature built up onto the smaller saddle *(buroro)* used to load household baggage. The two bentwood arches are fastened, one parallel with each fork and perpendicular to the axis of the camel's back, to a common pack saddle with diagonal rather than parallel traverses. They rise waist-high, front and rear, serving as a sort of guard rail for the two or three young children that the wife settles around her. If a woman is traveling without her tent, she sits in front of the camel's hump; she may steer her mount or make it trot as a man would do. When this pack saddle holds a tent, the large mats, rolled up, pass through the arches. Usually these arches are no higher than the pommel, but when they are (as in fig. 6.10b), crosspieces are added to reinforce the two bentwood arches.

The Tubu woman's palanquin *(kobode)* uses a more elaborate geometry for its canopy construction (pl. 15). In contrast to the *gommo* (and to the Tubu *adofa* illustrated in Chapter 3), the large bentwood curves, seemingly an elaboration on those used for the pack saddle, not only extend much higher, but are placed perpendicular to the primary forks of the saddle itself rather than parallel with them (fig. 6.10c). Built up onto the same basic pack saddle, the bentwood arches are structurally tied to the pommel and the cantle with four struts forming a parallelogram. This parallelogram serves as a base (or litter) for the lightweight, extended superstructure above. The roof of the extended superstructure is composed of thin acacia branches or tamarind roots, recalling the roof members (*djerid*s) on a Tubu tent armature (see also fig. 6.4).

The position of the two bentwood arches is critical in the context of spatial orientation and function: they have been rotated ninety degrees so that, instead of being parallel with the forks of the basic pack saddle, they are perpendicular to it. When seen in the light of the articulated rectangle of the litter below it, not only is an interior volume defined; as a marriage palanquin, the rotation establishes a different conceptual—and spatial—relationship, a liminal state vis-à-vis the outside world, during the wedding journey.

Like the pack saddle *(gommo)* above, the palanquin *(kobode)* is loaded with a large leather double bag containing flour and other food provisions. The cooking utensils are piled to the right, to the left, and behind, the pottery is held in nets, and the coffer for precious objects is wedged in with the rugs and cushions. The rolled mats are hung to the right and left. Around the outside, at the back of the palanquin, a leather curtain is hung, decorated with cowries, geometric figures, circles, and chevrons: it is the *dela*, the main decoration of the tent interior. Cushions, brightly colored striped blankets, and Tripolitanian rugs make up the seat onto which the wife and her youngest children will hoist themselves for the journey. Copper bells are hung right and left, plates of plaited straw, plates of wood, and imported, brightly colored enamel bowls are hung from the armature. A belly strap and a breast strap, the latter decorated with cowries, anchor the entire framework in place. Sometimes the copper or iron nose ring is decorated with a spray of ostrich feathers. A large false rein, made of cowrie-decorated leather, goes over the nose of the camel and is hung from both sides of the pack. Sometimes it is made even more pretentious by a large wooden pole added at the top, from which ostrich plumes sway and from which bundles of white cloth flutter.

The pivot around which Tubu material culture and its sociocultural patterns turn—the tent, the palanquin, and the marriage ceremony—is the *dela*. The *dela*, the primary material symbol of the marriage ritual, encapsulates Tubu material life in its entirety when it serves as a stage setting for the unfolding of the marriage drama; it establishes the focal point of interior space. In transit it fulfills a similar role but in reverse: it has been turned inside out, so it is in full display at the back of the camel's palanquin. Linking together all aspects of Tubu nomadic life, it becomes the most dramatic display of the Tubu nomadic ideal and a wall of protection from the unseen, invisible dangers ever present behind one's line of vision.

7
MAHRIA TENTS: THE WOMAN'S DOMAIN

Uta Holter

The shelter people choose to live in is influenced not only by climate, geographic location, and available materials but also by their life-style. In the case of the Mahria, it is a life of mobility: material culture is adapted to life with camels in the desert and the thornbush savannah. Their "house" is a tent. Their "cupboards" are containers—baskets and leather bags—suited for storage and transport.[1]

The Mahria are Muslim, Arabic-speaking nomads. They belong to the tribal federation of the northern Rizeigat living in northern Darfur, Sudan (see location map). Their tribal center is about fifty kilometers north of Kutum, and many of them spend the summer in this area. Their migrations are dictated primarily by the needs of their animals. At the beginning of the rainy season, in July and August, they migrate northwards with their camel herds in order to exploit good pastures. If the rains have been sufficient during the winter months, they will move as far north as the Wadi Howar, in order to take advantage of the *jizzu* pastures (i.e., ephemeral plants). In February they return to the south in order to spend the summer close to the permanent wells.

In Mahria society, the men's domain is the public life of the camp and the tribe and the management of the camel herds. The women's world is the tent: the private, domestic sphere of the family. The Mahria nomads call their tent *beet,* a term that means both "house" and "household." The tent belongs to the man, but the woman is its mistress: it is the place where she performs many of her daily tasks and receives guests. Within it, she begins her married life, gives birth to her children, raises them, and spends her declining years.

THE CAMP

A tent is a sheltered place in a desert-like surrounding which guarantees some privacy and intimacy, whereas the camp extends and makes possible an everyday social life beyond the limits of a single tent unit. A camp is named after the most respected male person, for example, "Ali's camp" or "the people of Ali" (*fariig Ali* or *naas Ali*).[2]

The Mahria have two kinds of camps: mobile and stationary (close to a permanent well). Mobile camps differ from stationary camps in tent size, location, style, and decor as well as in the way they influence social life and women's daily tasks. In the former *(bi buyuut),* camel herds and households migrate together. In the latter (those close to a permanent well), camel herds accompanied only by herdsmen *(bi azaba)* migrate separately from their families.

The general term for a camp *(fariig)* refers to a collection of tents as well as a winter camp. The term used to designate a summer, stationary camp *(damra)* can also mean a camp of nomads who have decided to become sedentary. The campsite is called *daa'ira el beet.*[3]

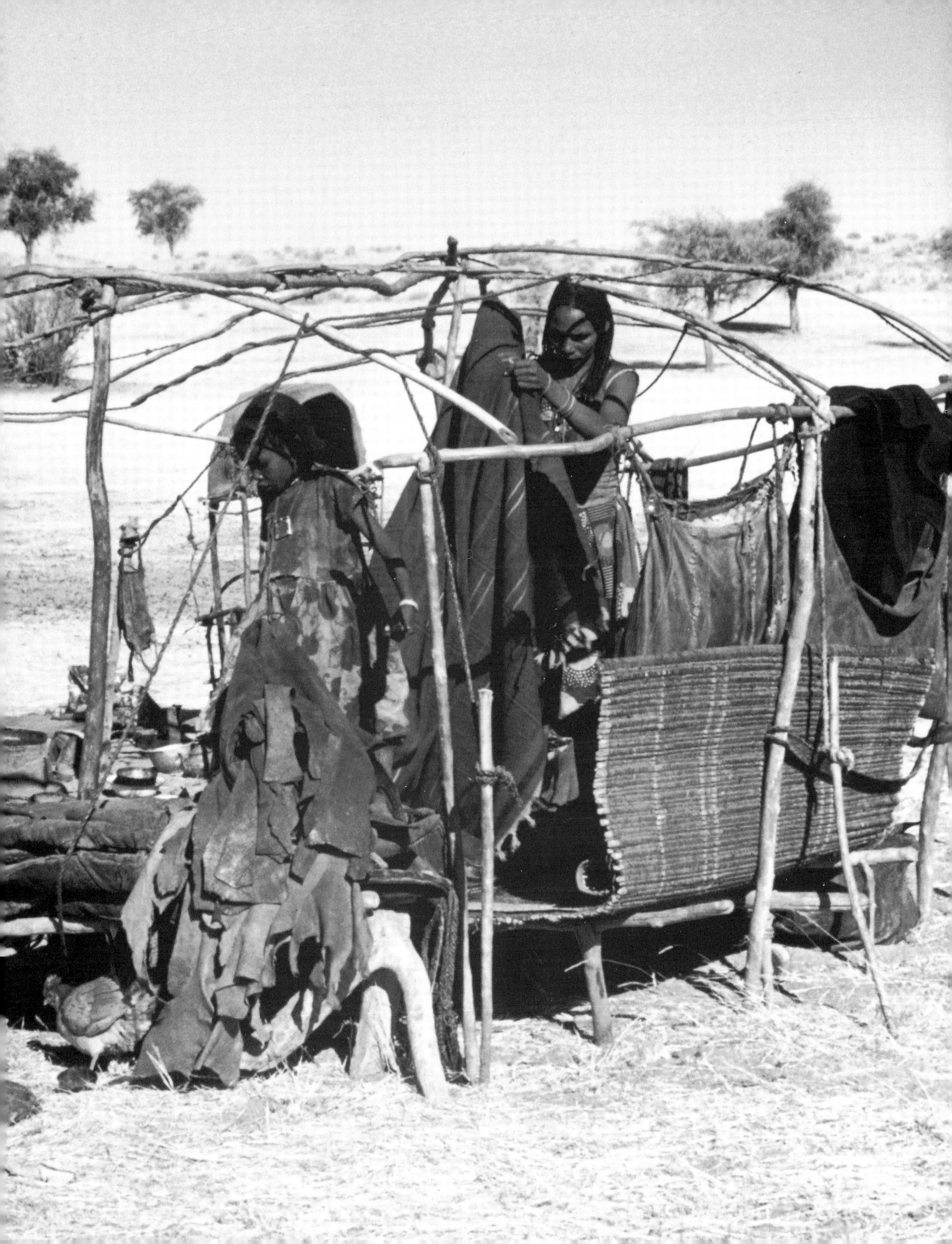

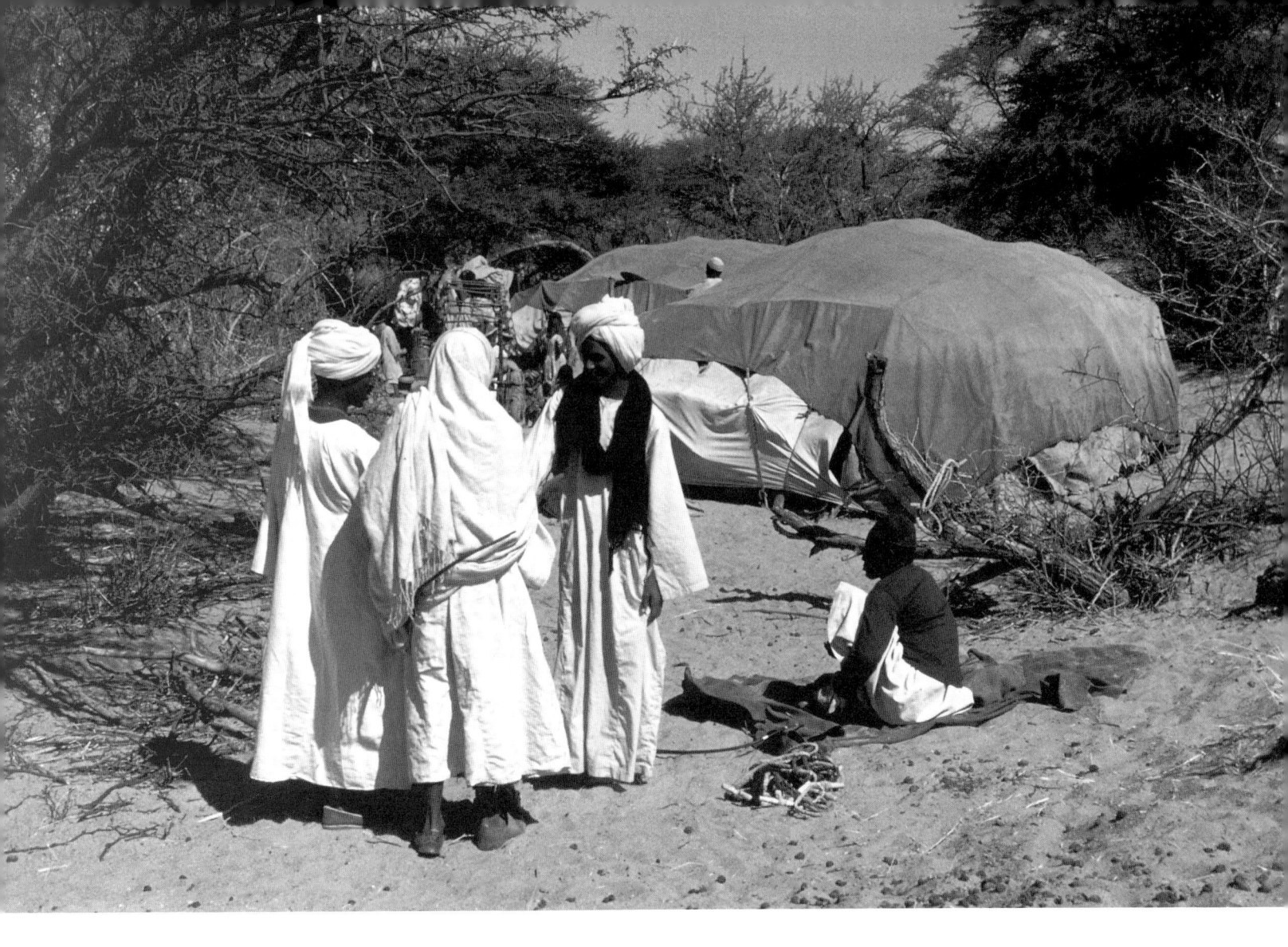

Fig. 7.1. Mahria winter mobile camp in a sandy riverbed or wadi. The man in the forefront is holding a camel whip, the man seated is repairing a *jiraab* (Arabic), made of gazelle or antelope hide (1.0 m × 50 cm). The bag is used by men to keep and transport their clothes and objects of value. On the ground, at his left, is a goatskin bucket used to draw water from the wells. The camp consists of five tents standing close together since the people are all closely related, but also because the riverbed is narrow. The sandy ground and the trees which give shade and shelter from the wind are preferred.

The nomads pay close attention to the choice of a campsite. During the winter, when the animals do not need much water or no water at all (as is the case when they graze in ephemeral plant pastures), the households accompanying the camel herds form small camps in the isolation of the semidesert or thornbush savannah. They may be far from permanent wells and villages. The nomads will choose a clean place, an area with good pastures and trees for animal fodder and for shade. During the dry season, tents might also be pitched in the sand of a dry riverbed or wadi, as the sand is clean and large trees are close by (fig. 7.1). An area with bushes is also desirable in order to hang containers or store objects. Stationary camps are close to permanent wells and preferably to a school and market.

The number of tents in a camp is not stable; it may even vary from one season to the next. The size of a

Fig. 7.2. A mobile winter camp consisting of six tents, three bivouacs, the resting places for camels at night, and the folds for goats and sheep on the west, inside the camp, close to their owner's tent. Male and female camels are kept separately. All the members of the camp are related either by blood or marriage.

The owner of Tent 4 is the oldest man. He has three wives, who all live in the same camp (Tents 2, 4, and 5). He shares his tent with the youngest, that is, the third wife and two small children (four persons).

His first wife, who is already old, lives in Tent 2 and belongs to her son's household. This man is in his best years and is very respected. The camp is named after him, although he is not the oldest man. He has two young wives: his first wife and their six small children live in Tent 1, his second wife and her two small children live in Tent 3. Since his children cannot yet help in herding the camels, he needs three herdsmen, who sleep in the bivouac next to the three tents (Tents 1, 2, 3) forming his household. He supports all these persons.

The woman in Tent 5 (the second wife of Tent 4's owner) is also old. She shares her tent with her marriageable daughter. She is supported by her eldest son who, because he was divorced at the time, did not have a tent of his own. Together with two brothers and a herdsman, he sleeps in a bivouac about fourteen meters west of the front of his mother's tent. Mother and daughter cook for all these men and boys. Recently provided stores of animal salt serve as a kind of windbreak for the men sleeping in the open on the east side of the bivouac.

Tent 6 is inhabited by the mother-in-law of the head of household of Tents 1, 2, and 3. She shares the tent with two small sons, two marriageable daughters, and one recently married daughter. This young woman should already be living in a separate tent, pitched next to her mother's, but the family is poor and the young husband has not yet returned from Libya. He had gone there as a labor migrant to earn the money for buying the tent and those household items not manufactured by the nomadic women in situ.

The head of household and one adolescent son sleep in a bivouac south of the tent, taking advantage of a big tree. This family is of a different subtribe, which may explain the greater distance from the other tents.

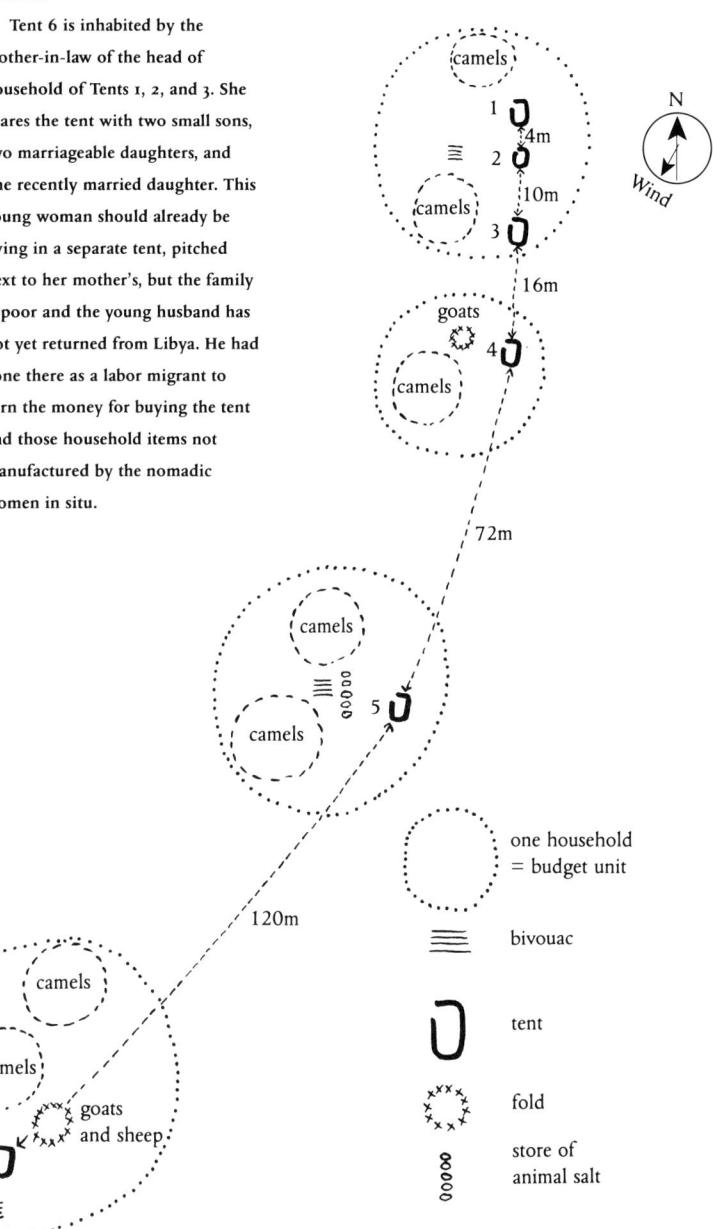

camp (i.e., the number of tents and their arrangement) is influenced by its degree of mobility and varies according to changes in the domestic cycle of the households. As a rule, mobile camps are small, usually consisting of five to six tents, never more than ten. Stationary camps may consist of as many as thirty tents, especially when they tend to remain permanent over a long period of time, an indication of the transition from a nomadic life-style to a sedentary one.[4] Large camps split into small units when they intend to migrate. These units sometimes pitch their tents about six to ten minutes' walking distance from each other.

Not all the nomads fancy life in a small camp. The women clearly said that they preferred large camps, because they were livelier; there were more people and guests. The men said they preferred small camps because there was less arguing and quarreling.

Traditionally, tents belonging together are aligned north to south, and most nomadic Arabic-speaking tribes in the area still follow this rule. The Mahria, however, do not always adhere to this pattern, often varying it in order to take advantage of the natural landscape (fig. 7.2).

Mahria Tents

The arrangement of the tents expresses Mahria rules of residence which dictate that married brothers should live in the same camp as their father. Sons pitch their tents immediately north of their father's tent. Other relatives follow southwards. An old woman's tent will be pitched south of the tent of the son who takes over responsibility and care for her in her old age. During the first one to two years of marriage, a young couple will locate their tent next to the wife's mother. A childless old woman should be cared for by her brother or her brother's son, and accordingly pitches her tent next to his. A widowed or divorced woman returns with her children to her mother, and she either places her tent next to her mother's or, if her husband did not leave her a tent, moves in with her.

Tent arrangement also follows individual social preferences, dislikes, or dependencies. In a polygynous household, a man may keep his wives in the same camp with the tents close by, or he might locate them in separate camps if they do not get along well together. He then has to travel between those camps, spending several days with each of his wives. Having wives in different camps is a way of avoiding conflicts, but it is also practical: one wife may live in a stationary camp and care for her husband's old mother, while the other will accompany him on migration with the camel herd. Sons often prefer not to live in their father's camp in order to avoid his authority. A woman whose sons avoid taking over responsibility for her in old age may live with a daughter and have her tent next to her daughter's, but this is not the norm. The configuration remains constant when a mobile camp moves to a new site.

The distances between individual tents and groups of tents vary from only a few to over a hundred meters. Tents belonging to one household (i.e., one budget unit) generally become a cluster, and the distance between clusters will also vary. In one case, for instance, an old woman's tent was only three meters from her son's because she got along well with his wife. Another old woman had her tent sixteen meters away; she complained about the lack of harmony with her son's family.

A camp consists of tents, bivouacs, and the animals' resting places. Some of the adult men and adolescent boys have to sleep outside in the open, even in winter. These are the herdsmen who are employed by those households that do not have enough men to herd the camels. They are also the male members of the households with marriageable girls. By the time the daughters reach puberty, the father and adolescent brothers should no longer sleep inside the tent. These men and boys form bivouacs *(zara)* on the western side of the household's tent to which they belong, at a distance of four to fourteen meters. The animals spend the night next to the tents of their owners. The fold for goats and sheep *(zariiba)* is fenced, but the resting place *(door)* for the camel herd *(muraah)* is not. Male and female camels are kept separately.

Occasionally, during the rainy season, the nomads place salt *('aṭruun)* for the camels at the threshold *(baaṭiiya)* in the middle of the doorway. The salt is either bought at the market or dug and transported on camelback from Bir-el-Atrun (ca. 500 km N–NE) by the nomadic men themselves. The journey *(malḥalla)* is preferably made during the dry season, that is, winter, when salt can also be stored outside the tent. It is then placed next to the bivouacs where it can be protected from the camels who are very fond of salt. Branches are placed on the ground under leather sacks and stores of food to protect the contents against termites.

The nomads clearly do not like the odors that occur when skins and hides are cleaned, when tar is produced for the tanning process, and when wood that produces smoke is used as firewood, for example, Balanites aegyptiaca *(hejliij)*, Boscia senegalensis *(mukheet)*, Capparis decidua *(tundub)*, or Commiphora sp. *(gafal)*. Therefore these activities are performed outside the living area of the camp. These areas also serve for the disposal of cooking ashes and as latrines.

An increasing number of households have recently become sedentary in response to the deteriorating situation in the drought-stricken area. In these stationary camps the tents are larger and covered with mats. The nomads are expert at improvising and re-using old material; the women construct shelters *(rakuuba)* from wood and remnants of wornout mats and canvas for use as sunshades and as protection over the cooking place. They build wooden fences around the tent area and prepare special spots on the ground for drying fermented millet *(madagg)*. The soil is hardened by sprinkling it with the water of leavened millet. If the situation presents itself, the nomads will not hesitate to break camp in order to migrate again.

In mobile camps, it is only during the day, while the camels are being herded by the men and boys, that women, children, and old people remain alone. Stationary camps, on the other hand, consist mainly of women, children, and old people, since the men and boys accompanying the herds visit their families only when they come to water the animals (every eleven days in winter and five to seven days in summer). Consequently women in stationary camps neither milk the camels nor churn butter, and camel milk is largely absent from the daily diet. Children normally herd goats, but as more and more children attend school, women also have to assume the responsibility of caring for the goats.

During those periods when the men are away herding camels, fewer guests arrive. Since it is mainly the men who attract guests, and the presence of men and guests demands proper meal preparation, there is less work for women during these periods of absence. This situation, however, changes remarkably on those days when the camel herds are watered.

Decisions related to the grouping of tents and to breaking camp and relocating it are made by the men. The decision to move the camp is primarily dictated by the animals' needs, for example, when a new grazing area for the camels is necessary or when a campsite has become too heavily laden with excrement. However, personal reasons, such as a wife's illness, may also influence the decision.

THE WOMAN'S DAILY TASKS IN A MOBILE CAMP

Although the man is the head of household and the main decision maker, the woman is the almost exclusive user of the tent. During the day, when men and boys are herding the camels, women, children, and old people are often the only inhabitants of the camp. Men will also leave the camp and their families for days or even weeks, in order to buy provisions, sell animals, or visit the local authorities or relatives in another camp.

The woman's daily round in a mobile camp starts shortly before sunrise when she rises, washes, prays, and lights the hearth fire. The fireplace *(ladaaiya)*, consisting of three stones, is outside the tent, a few yards from the entrance. She then milks the camels and prepares the tea, using camel's milk in lieu of water. A family often drinks tea together in the morning, but because of the segregation of the sexes, men and women do not share their meals. Women are supposed to eat out of the sight of men.

After tea the woman prepares a meal for the herdsmen or gives them some leftovers from the previous day. Then the camels are taken out to pasture, returning to the camp only at sunset. The animals spend the night close to the tents of their owners, often hobbled to prevent them from going astray or being stolen. In winter, before the day gets hot, the women sit next to the fire and churn butter from soured camel's milk.[5]

The staple food is bulrush millet (Pennisetum sp.: *dukhn*). Most of the time the millet is fermented by letting it sit in the sun in a basket, outside the tent, for several days. The fermented millet is spread on an old piece of canvas or a mat of palm leaves and left on the ground to dry, not far from the tent, where it can be protected from birds and goats. Millet is ground on a grinding stone, cooked to the consistency of a porridge *('aṣiida)*, and eaten with a sauce *(mulaaḥ)* of dried ingredients such as okra, tomatoes, red pepper, meat, and onions.

The nomads eat two or three times a day. Breakfast *(faṭuur)* is taken in the morning at ten A.M., lunch *(ghada)* between two and three P.M., and supper *('asha)* around six P.M., after the men have returned to the camp with their camel herds. Meals are eaten outside the tent, the women sitting close to the tent wall and out of view of the men who sit at a distance from them. It is only during the winter, when the temperature is low and the cold winds are blowing, or during the rainy season, when it is raining heavily, that the women pray, grind millet, prepare tea, or even cook a meal on a fire inside the tent. They may also sit next to the fire for warmth and a chat during the cold winter evenings.

The Mahria are very fond of children, and child care, a woman's major responsibility, parallels her daily tasks rather than occurring separately from them. No area in and around the tent is prohibited to children, but they are carefully looked after in order to prevent them from getting too close to the open fire or from helping themselves to provisions, especially sugar, stored in the tent.

The primary tasks that take the nomad woman away from her tent are the collection of firewood and the fetching of water. When the wells are at a walking distance of more than an hour (in mobile camps the wells might be several hours away), the water is fetched by men. Other occasions that take the woman away from her tent are the ride to a market, attendance at a life cycle festival, the gathering of wild rice (Echinochloa colonum: *kereeb*), wild fruit and resins *(ṣamugh)*, or bast fiber *(liha)* and grasses for the manufacture of baskets and mats.

Mahria women are responsible for the production and maintenance of most of the furnishings of the tent, tasks that occasionally keep them quite busy. Some tasks are carried out in company with other women, chatting and drinking tea. Women are experts in leatherwork, basketry, and mat weaving, and it is they who strike and pitch the tent when the camp moves.

THE TENT AS SHELTER: CONSTRUCTION IS WOMEN'S WORK

In former times the Mahria had mat tents. Therefore, the women still know how to weave mats and still make them for use when they are stationary. Today they use canvas, although some of their eastern neighbors still use the old variety. Canvas is easier to transport than mats: it is lighter and takes less space on the camel's back. Mats become very heavy when it rains because the plant material soaks up the water. On the other hand, mat tents provide better insulation and more air circulation within the tent, keeping the tent interior cooler in the summer and warmer during the winter. The nomadic women still know how to manufacture the mats, but they use them only in stationary camps as roof and side walls over the canvas. Mats are no longer used in the mobile camps. The nomads said, however, that if they did not have a canvas tent when they migrated, they preferred to take mats (*shukkaaba*; pl.: *shakaakiib*). The size and construction of a tent differ according to the household's mobility and the phases of the domestic cycle.

Tents in a mobile camp. When nomads migrate they carry a smaller number of wooden frame tent parts in order to reduce the weight the camels must transport. Accordingly, tents are smaller than when they become stationary for longer periods of time. In the beginning of the rainy season, the nomads move north with their camel herds to take advantage of good pastures until the end of the winter. The camp is moved periodically, sometimes after only two to three weeks, sometimes less than a mile away. Tents for a family with several children may be similar in size to the small tents in a stationary camp (length 4.00–4.40 m; width 2.40–3.00 m; height ca. 2 m).

The construction of the tent is completely the woman's responsibility (fig. 7.3). As a rule, she strikes and pitches the tent by herself, while other family members may be busy looking after the children, processing food, collecting firewood, or tanning. Men lend a hand only with the loading and unloading of camels and with carrying heavy objects. Old women are helped by their sons and daughters-in law.

Tents are erected lengthwise, north to south, with their entrances on the northwest corner (fig. 7.4). The entrance, or "mouth" of the tent *(chashm el beet)*, is synonymous with "exit of the house," "lineage," or "clan." The shorter north and south walls *(lafaafa)* are distinguished from the back, east wall *(hauwaaga)* and the front, west wall *(giddaamiiya)*. The interior (*boṭn el beet* = "inside the house") derives from the word for "belly" or "womb" *(boṭn)*.

The wooden wall frame of the Mahria vaulted tent consists of a number of posts, pegs, arches and stringers made from Balanites aegyptiaca *(hejliij)* and Zizyphus sp. *(nabag)* (fig. 7.5; see also fig. 7.3). All the elements can be bought in the market, but most often they are collected by, cut, and if necessary bent by the women. Forked posts and pegs are stuck about thirty to thirty-five centimeters deep into the ground, while

Fig. 7.3. Above, pitching a tent at the new campsite. In front (on the south side), the rack with folded empty sacks for storing millet and animal salt; on top of them, a camel or cowskin bag used by men to keep and transport their clothes, utensils, and sometimes also sugar and tea. Next to it, three baskets (two '*umra* and a *hanga*) and, hanging from the armature, a red double pillow. The fat container made from the neck skin of a camel can be seen next to the woman adjusting the tent frame, immediately above the pack saddles on the ground below. Below, the tent armature, the bed framework, and its backdrop are clearly visible.

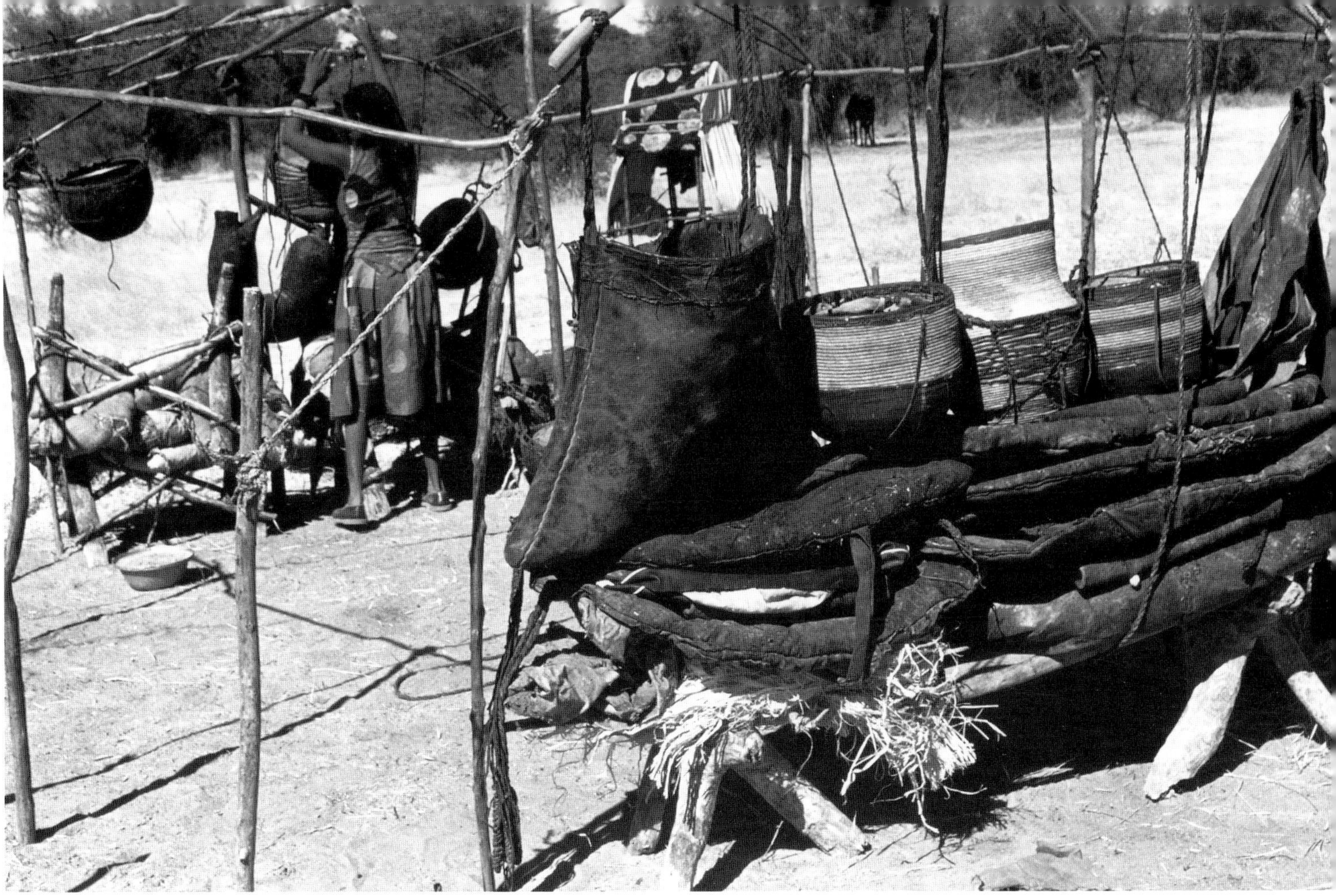

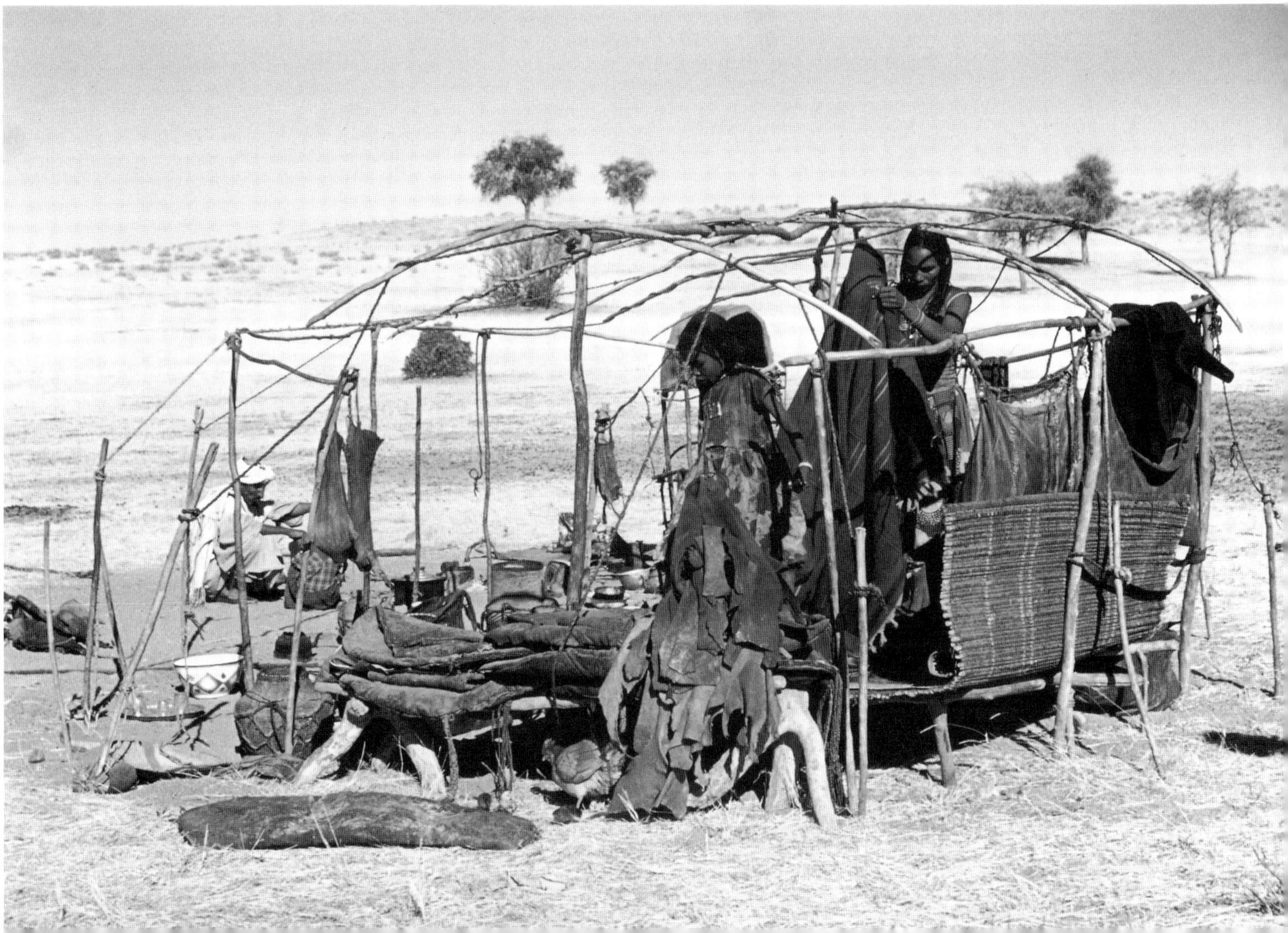

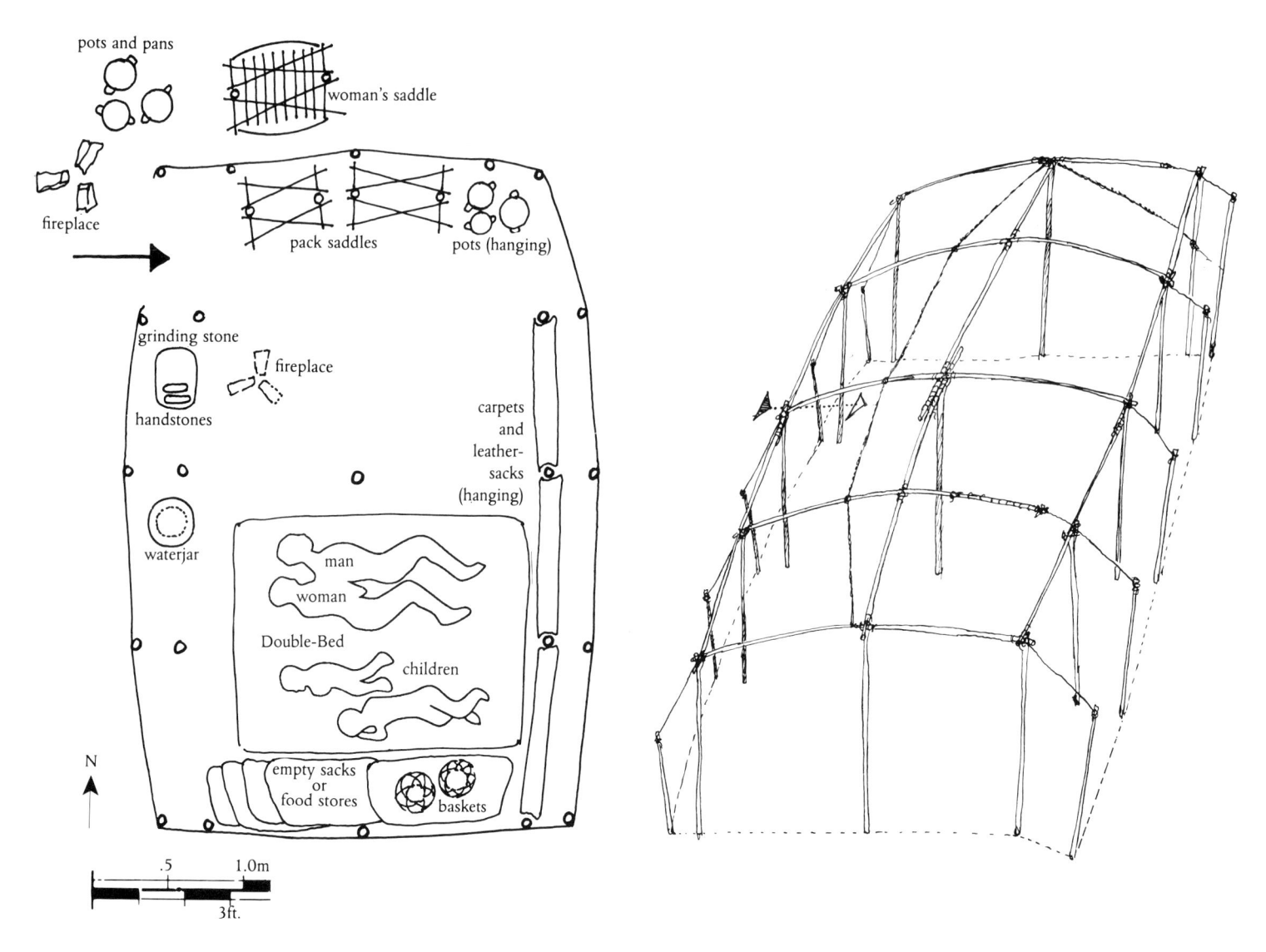

Fig. 7.4. The ground plan of a
tent in a mobile camp.

Fig. 7.5. The framework of a
tent in a mobile camp.

stringers and bent arches are fastened to the forked posts above to form the roof members. The armature is then covered with one or several sheets of canvas.

The tasks involved in pitching the tent, which take from two to two and a half hours, follow a very precise order (see table 7.1). First the camels are unloaded, and the new site for the tent is swept clean of thorns and stones. Then the exact place and perimeter of the tent are marked out: the pack saddles are placed to the north, the rack and the sacks containing the food stores are placed to the south, and the four bent stringers of the tent roof mark the side walls. The woman then digs the postholes (about thirteen) with a short-handled, iron-shod digging stick and hammers the posts into the ground with the handstone of the millet grinder. Three parallel rows of posts run north to south. They consist of a middle row made up of one main post in the center *(jahuuba)* and two supporting posts at each end *(khaasra)*, and two additional rows thirty to thirty-five centimeters adjacent, consisting of four to five forked posts *(ash shi'ab el giddaamiiya)* for the front row on the west) and five on

132   African Nomadic Architecture

Table 7.1. Labor time involved in pitching a Mahria mobile camp tent

Unloading the camels	5 min.
Cleaning the site	20 min.
Marking the tent perimeter	30 min.
Digging the postholes and placing them	28 min.
Setting in the tent pegs	12 min.
Constructing the roof framework with ropes and lashings	20 min.
Furnishing the tent	20 min.
Spreading and tying the canvas over the framework	ca. 20 min.
Total	2 hrs. 35 min.

the back east row *(ash shi'ab el waraaniiya)*. The general term for a forked stick is *shi'ba*.

To form the tent wall, about twelve pegs *(witid)* are set into the ground at a distance from the two outer rows (35 cm on the back side and 80 cm on the front side). Shorter pegs (70–80 cm above ground) are used on the back side and longer ones for the front, the longest located at the entrance. If the pegs are slender, two are sometimes tied together.

Tent roof construction usually consists of a straight ridgepole *(el 'amuud el jahuuba)*, but sometimes two poles are tied together or only a rope is used. Parallel to the ridgepole and fixed atop the forked posts, one on each side, is a longer stringer at the front side *('amuud el giddaami)* and on the back side *(el 'amuud el waraani)*. Their length varies according to the tent size, and sometimes two stringers are tied together for greater span. Then five (or fewer) bentwood arches *(muṭrag; pl.: maṭaarig)*, approximately three meters or longer, accompanied by long ropes *(habl wojegh)*, are tied to the posts and pegs, stabilizing the entire structure. When these bentwood arches are too short to rest directly on the forked posts, the ropes are stretched to join the arch to the post. Cloth or bast fiber lashing *(rubaaṭ)* is used to tie all the members to each other at their intersections. The bast fiber is made from Acacia mellifera *(kitir)*, Acacia tortilis *(seyaal)*, or Bauhinia rufescens *(kulkul)*. When the tent is struck, these lashings are carefully opened so they may be reused. Nothing is thrown away that cannot be easily replaced.

As soon as the tent armature has been assembled, it is completely furnished. Only after it is furnished is the canvas *(mushamma* or *kheema)* thrown over the framework and fixed by shorter or longer lashings to tent posts or to pegs close to the ground. Depending on the size of the tent, the canvas may be in one or more pieces. The pegs also provide an additional support to those parts of the canvas that form the tent wall. There are no long ropes over the canvas. The tent entrance is covered by a smaller piece of canvas.

When migrations are long and take several days or weeks (as happens after the winter when the nomads return south), or during periods of drought (when the nomads move to southern Darfur), then a camp is pitched for one or possibly two nights, and tents are only provisionally put up. As a rule, the least possible number of posts (six) and poles (three) are used. The tent entrance is *lower* than two meters (its normal height), and the canvas is loosely laid over the armature. The front (north side) is left quite open.

Breaking camp. The day on which the nomads break camp is called *joom el maṣṣaar* (fig. 7.6). Breaking camp—striking the tent *(taftiish el beet)*, moving to a new campsite *(malhalla)*, and pitching the tent *(bunaa el beet)*—may also require a whole day. Although it involves much work, it can have an entertaining component. For example, the women at one camp had especially brewed millet beer. Food, however, is not prepared during the day: instead, leftovers are consumed. A decision to break camp may also be postponed for a day. For example, in one camp a camel had to be slaughtered in an emergency, and a herd of goats had disappeared during the night and had to be found. Another camp passed a market on market day and decided to spend a day at the market to stock up on provisions.

The same precision of activities that characterizes the pitching of a tent is evident in striking it (see table 7.2). No visible preparations are apparent to an outsider on the morning of the day in which the camp

Fig. 7.6. A mobile camp is ready to move. The tent canvases have been taken down, the armatures have been dismantled, and the furnishings are waiting to be loaded. Some of the camels are already loaded: the camel on the far right with tent ribs, the center camel with its *jungula,* the left camel with its *johfa,* a sign that a recently married woman lives in the camp. The wooden box pierced with holes serves as a chicken coop.

will be broken. Tea is drunk in a leisurely manner, and a woman may even start fermenting millet or processing tar for tanning. Suddenly, as if by an invisible signal, at about 8:30 A.M., the women get up and begin striking the tents. The men help by saddling the camels and loading the heavy objects. Breaking camp takes about two hours. The process is rather leisurely, and if guests arrive they are served tea in the midst of it.

The loading and transport of an eight-person household, for example, requires four camels. An old woman, by contrast, needs only one camel to transport her few belongings. First, all the lighter objects, such as baskets and leather bags which are standing

Table 7.2. Labor time involved in striking a tent and loading the camels

Taking light objects out of the tent	10 min.
Opening tent lashings	5 min.
Striking the tent frame	20 min.
Tying parts of the tent frame, folding canvas	35 min.
Loading camels	45 min.
Total	1 hr. 55 min.

and hanging in the tent, are carried outside and spread on mats. Remaining furnishings will be left to the end. The lashings close to the ground are opened, the canvas is removed, the ridgepole, arches, and stringers are placed on the ground, and the posts and pegs are pulled up. Then the ridgepole, arches, and stringers are tied together, the posts and pegs are tied together, the canvas is folded (*taṭbiig el mushamma*), and food as well as craft material leftovers are stowed away. In the meantime, the two adult men in the household have folded and removed their bedding from the bivouac. Finally, the four camels are loaded (*shadd el jumaal*) with the help of the two adult men.

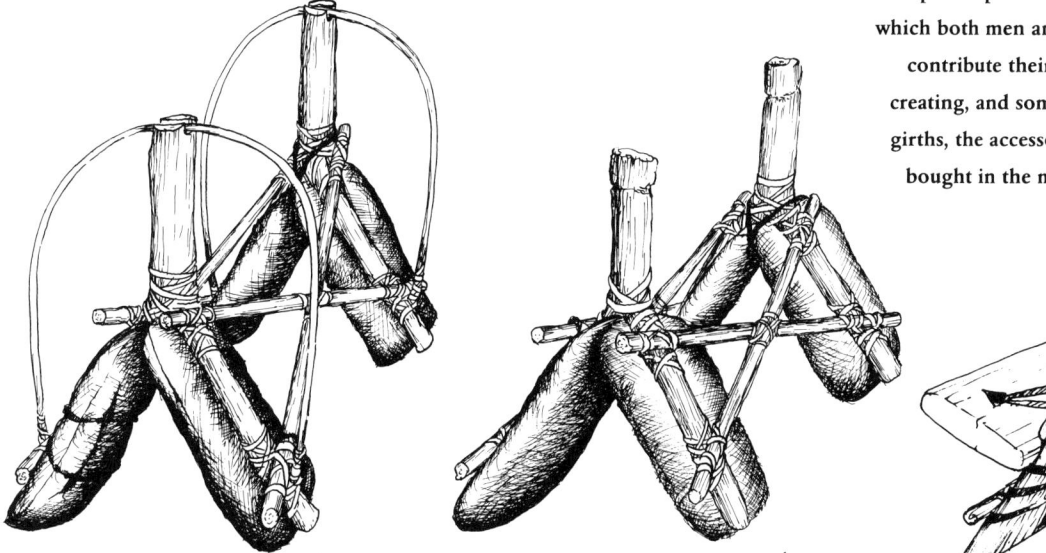

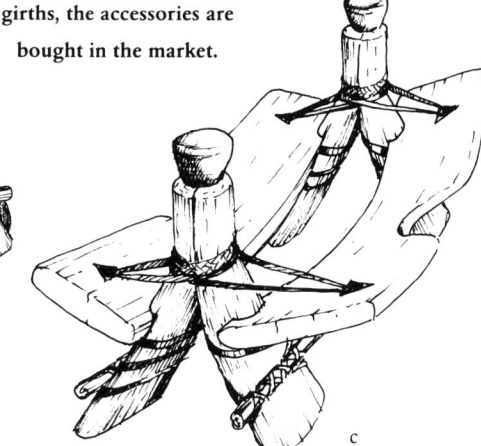

Fig. 7.7. The pack saddles are manufactured by the women. They buy the wooden parts (*hejliij*) at the market, but they bend the bows (*shiheet*) and tie the different parts together with leather strips. The braces for the *hauwiiya* saddle are made of Zizyphus sp. (*nabag*). The Mahria nomads use four different kinds of bolsters for pack saddles: different round and rectangular sizes. They are made by the men of dry grasses (*beiad*) which they plait, stabilize with a net of cords of bast fiber, or cover with pieces of old cloth. Saddles are fixed to the camel's back with different leather girths. a. *jungula*: used to carry the long wooden parts of the tent frame; height 75 cm in front, 70 cm at back; width at base 66 cm in front, 65 cm at the back. b. *hauwiiya*: height 66 cm in front, 63 cm at the back; width at base 71 cm in front, 74 cm at the back. The bolsters shown in the sketch are made of jute sacks and filled with crushed millet cobs. They may be in one piece (back) or in two pieces (front); length 86 cm; width 25 cm; thickness 14 cm. c. *serij*: height 43 cm; width 44–48 cm; length 50–60 cm. This wooden riding saddle, whose parts are lashed together using leather thongs, is bought in the market. The pommel and the cantle may be covered with leather. Two bolsters are needed for one saddle and are put astride the camel's back, keeping the hump in their middle. Other accessories are one lined leather cover placed on the wooden saddle seat and another for the camel's neck (both to protect the rider), leather girths, a bridle, and a whip. Except for the whip, which both men and women contribute their labor creating, and some of the girths, the accessories are bought in the market.

a b c

Mahria Tents

Loading one camel takes about fifteen minutes, and the first two camels are loaded simultaneously. They are loaded differently. The first camel (with a special saddle, *jungula*, for the long wooden parts of the tent frame) is loaded with all the tent components (i.e., the arches, stringers, posts, pegs, and canvas, plus the stand for hanging water bags and the bed) by the father and his adolescent son (fig. 7.7a). The second camel (with the pack saddle, *hauwiiya*) is loaded by a woman with a mat made from palm leaves and bought at the market *(bursh)*, earthen water jars, baskets, leather bags, pots, and bowls (fig. 7.7b). The third camel (with pack saddle) is loaded by the two men with heavy sacks of millet and animal salt plus grinding implements, mortar and pestle. When loaded, these three camels will leave the camp with the father and one daughter of the family. The fourth camel (with the riding saddle, *serij*) (fig. 7.7c) is loaded by a woman with leather bags containing kitchen tools, the father's and son's blankets and clothes, plus the father's sword and a horse's ridding saddle.

A camp does not always move as a complete group or in a single row. In the above case, single family members moved off as soon as one or several of their camels had been loaded, and the last person had left the campsite by 11:30 A.M. The site that for nineteen days had been "home" for six "tents" (i.e., four households and thirty-three persons) was now empty, free to rejoin the isolation of the semidesert.

Tents in a stationary camp. When nomads intend to remain stationary over a longer period of time, they may decide, if they have the means, to build larger and stronger tents in order to enhance their living comfort. These larger tents may reflect a family's improved economic status, but at the same time they may also reach a size and weight that militates against camel transport. Tents of a household with several children are about 4.40–5.60 m long, 3.20 m wide, and over 2 m high. A poor household's tent may measure only 4.0 × 2.40 m, the tent of a young family without children or only one or two infants 4–4.40 × 2.40 m, and an old woman's or an old couple's tent usually measures about 3.20 × 2.40 m.

Pitching a tent in a fixed camp takes more time than in a mobile camp. When a larger tent is constructed, more posts and pegs, stringers and arches are required. There are two main posts on the central line instead of one, with a diameter up to fifteen centimeters. The two rows of posts *(shi'ab)* consist of seven posts in each row, and there are ten pegs on each side. Occasionally wooden tent posts and pegs are taken out of the ground in order to remove a lower section that may have been eaten by termites.

The armature of a tent roof in a fixed camp always consists of a straight ridgepole flanked on each side by two long bent stringers *(gugaai shaiyaal)*. These stringers are wrapped with long ropes for additional stability to support as many as twelve arches (depending on the size of the tent) laid over them. Sometimes shorter stringers are tied together. There is also a stringer along each side wall, without the accompanying rope, at a height of about 1.70 m. The stingers are more or less straight. The arches (ca. 3.60 m long and 3 cm thick) are also accompanied by supporting ropes. All the ropes are tied to the tops of the forked posts, and shorter ropes connect posts and pegs at the top.

When the canvas is thrown over the frame, long ropes are stretched lengthwise over the middle *(rubaat)* and crosswise *(jagaai)* over the wide side of the canvas. They are also tied to some of the pegs close to the ground. When households decide to start moving once again, they store parts of the tent frame, as well as the heavy posts, with households that remain behind. There are two different types of mats, one to cover the tent roof *(shukkaaba)* and another to cover the side walls *(sherkaaniiya)* (fig. 7.8).

Mats are not (with the single exception above) used in mobile camps. For the tent roof, the women plain weave together a species of grass, Cymbopogan proximus *(mahareeb)*, and a bast fiber from the Bauhania rufescens *(kulkul)* in a two-strand twining technique. To manufacture the mat, the grasses are spread on the ground in parallel rows and then tied in "seams," starting from the center. The first seam is made with two-strand twining *(habl el badad)*; for the subsequent simpler plain weave seams *(toof;* pl.: *tiifaan)*, the weaker bast fiber of the Acacia tortilis and the Acacia melli-

Plate 1 (above). The *mapalia* tent represented on a mosaic from a Roman villa at El Alia, near Mahdia, Tunisia, second century A.D.

Plate 2 (below). Parasol tents replace castles as symbols of kingship on a portolan sailing chart, A.D. 1559.

Plate 3. An early nineteenth-century rendering of a Kel Ajjer bride from the Fezzan region, southern Libya, en route to her husband's camp.

Plate 4. Part of the geological formation north of Isiolo, northern Kenya, which provides a topographic locus for spatial orientation.

Plate 5. Light is reflected off the crystalline surface at the site of a recently departed Gabra camp in the Chalbi desert, northern Kenya.

Plate 6. An acacia and a dum palm frame the grasses south of the Chalbi desert.

Plate 7. Gabra women loading their camels, preparatory to shifting camp in the Chalbi desert, northern Kenya.

Plate 8. Tuareg women leatherworkers.

Plate 9. Mahria women putting up a marriage tent.

Plate 10. A Mauretanian camp of white tents. The crest embroidery at the apexes is faintly visible.

Plate 11. Apex reinforcement on the interior of a white tent, Rosso, Mauretania, 1978.

Plate 12. The large leather Tuareg traveling sack used only by women, primarily from the Kel Ahaggar tribe. A cooperative work, the sack sometimes takes more than a year to complete.

Plate 13. The decorated Tuareg women's camel saddle.

Plate 14. A Tubu (Daza) tent in the Enneri Ogu, southwestern Tibesti.

Plate 15. A Tubu woman in transit, riding inside her litter-palanquin.

Plate 16. The southeast interior corner of a Mahria tent where the bed is located. Five goatskin bags are hanging from the ceiling. The light-colored bag has been tanned with lye (a mixture of water and the ashes of Acacia albida and Acacia seyal). A double pillow, dyed red, hangs on the right. A carpet and mats used for the side wall of the tent (in a stationary camp) lie under the leather bags, and a bed blanket is visible in the foreground.

Plate 17. The Mahria wedding camel itself is elaborately coifed with a headgear decorated with cowries and black ostrich feathers.

Plate 18. A typical Rendille tent.

Plate 19. The interior, back wall of the Rendille tent.

Plate 20. A northern Somali tent in the environs of Beled Weyn.

Plate 21. The interior of the Somali tent. The main structural members, the secondary bent frames, the corner of the hung mat, and the location of the two woven water containers in their carriers can be clearly seen. Note the difference in construction between them.

Plate 22. A Fellata-Baggare marriage tent, in Sudan.

Plate 23. Even before the bentwood frames that articulate the container of architectural space have been set in place, the furnishings, by their relationship to each other, define the scale, volume, and spatial organization of a Tuareg Kel Ferwan tent.

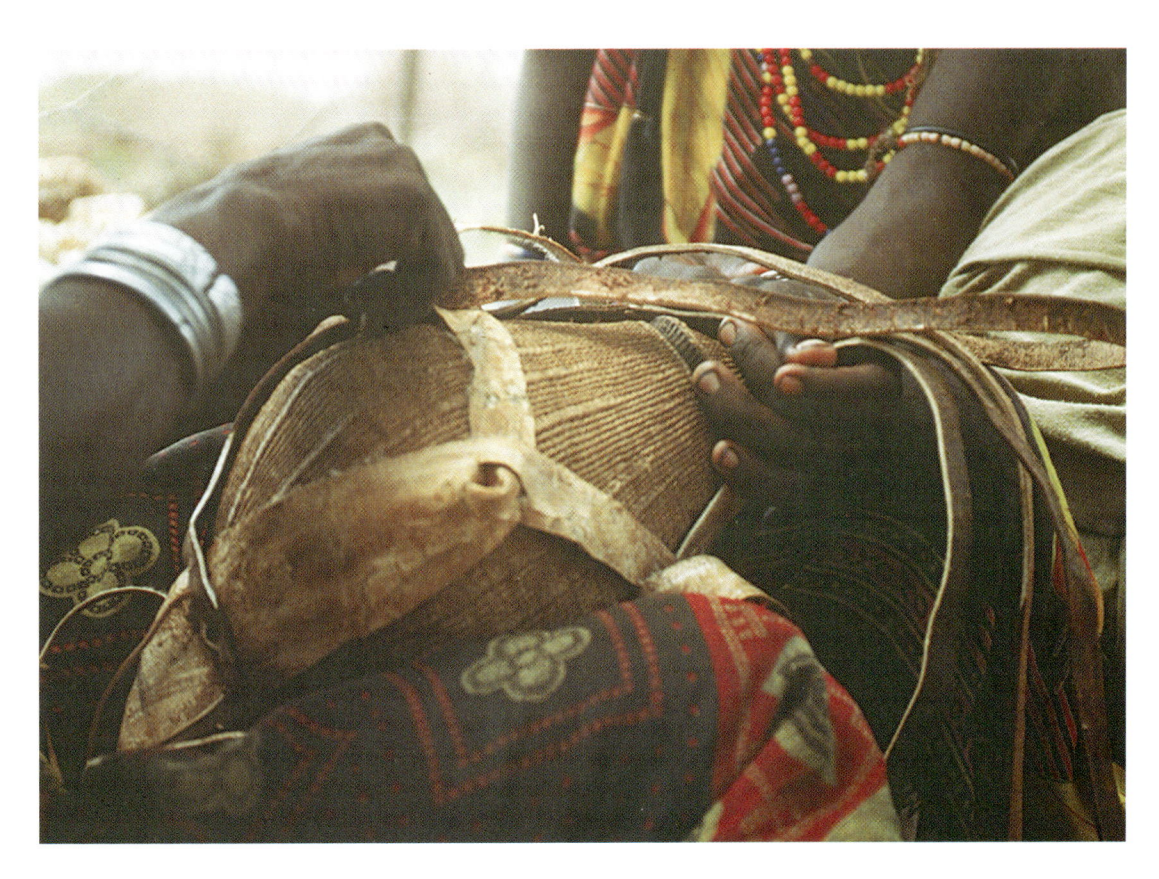

Plate 24. Putting the finishing touches on a Gabra woven milk container.

fera is used. It took a woman about four days to complete a mat, aided by eight women of the camp, each of whom plaited one row most of the time. The total working time was twenty-eight to twenty-nine hours, excluding the several days needed to collect and prepare the material. The finished oval mat, whose size conforms to the tent roof (ca. 4.50 m long, ca. 2.0 m wide at the ends, and 2.50 m wide in the center), is also waterproof.

The two mats surrounding the side walls are made using a diagonal braiding, twill technique. The women use the Panicum turgidum grass *(sumaam)* and bast fiber primarily from the acacia trees. The grasses are spread on the ground in two parallel rows, their heads meeting in the center. They are first fastened in strands and then, starting from one end, 4 cm-wide bundles are tied together and the plaiting begins. New grass may be added during the process. Finally, the grass is again tied in bundles. The acacia bast fiber is used at both ends to prevent the mat from unraveling. These mats are about 3.50–4.50 m long and about 1.20 m wide. One woman, helped by another, will work five hours and ten minutes over two days, excluding preparation of the materials.

Mats, especially those made for tent roofs, more or less fit the size of the tent. Even though mats used as side walls are protected from goats with thornbushes, they must be replaced every two to three years. The material used for both types of mats is collected by women. The grasses start growing during the rainy season (July–August), and the mats are manufactured during the winter (November–January). Obviously, if there has been a drought, no grasses will have grown.

THE TENT AS HOME: FURNISHINGS AS PRODUCTS OF THE WOMEN'S CRAFTS

The arrangement of tent furnishings is similar in all tents, although these furnishings may differ according to size, age, and the wealth of a household (pl. 16). The interior is sometimes decoratively hung with large cloths *(juwaani)*. When synthetic cloth is used, although it may look attractive in the nomad's view, one almost cannot breathe in the tents because the air

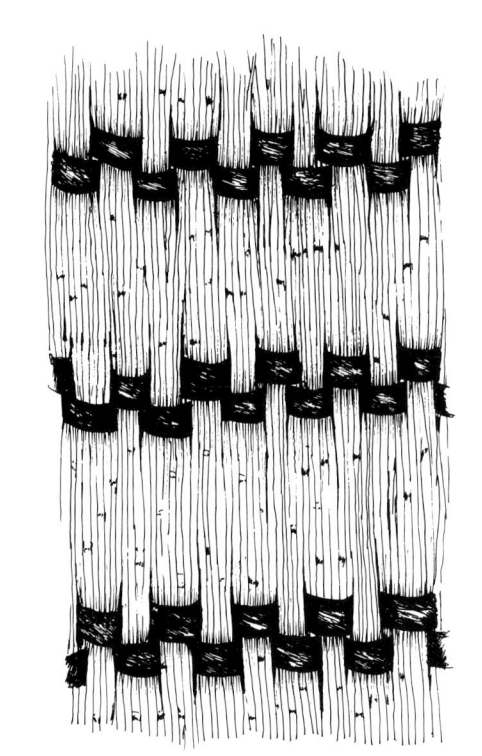

Fig. 7.8. Above, detail of mat for the tent roof *(shukkaaba)*; length 4.50 m; width at ends 2.0 m; width at center 2.50 m. Below, detail of mat for the tent side wall *(sherkaaniiya)*; length 3.50–4.50 m; width 1.20 m.

cannot circulate. Most often, the exposed armature of the tent is used to hang baskets, calabashes, leather bags, and occasionally a carpet. The ground is usually bare. A mat bought at the market (*bursh*) or a carpet is spread only when visitors arrive.

Like other Muslim societies, the Mahria segregate the sexes, but unlike other nomadic tribes, their tents are divided by neither a curtain nor a rug. When unrelated visitors arrive at the camp and are invited inside a tent, either men or women may remain outside. When festivities that accompany the life cycle are observed, men normally gather in the open, while women sit together inside the tent.

Most of the furnishings inside the tent are manufactured by the women. For her daughter's marriage, a mother will spend from one to two years producing the necessary artifacts for furnishing the tent (*'idda*). As the household grows, or when wornout objects need replacement, the woman will make them. The two predominant techniques are leatherwork and basketry. Transportation, a key function in nomadic life, is based on leather and basketry equipment, that is, on objects and containers that can conveniently, easily, and suitably be transported by camel. In the desert environs, the easily available raw materials are animal skins and grasses. Weaving is not known.[6]

Leatherwork. Mahria women are expert at tanning hides and skins (*jilid*; pl.: *jiluud*) and at manufacturing objects of leather. Except for kitchen utensils and the tent itself, there are few objects that are not made of leather or where leather is not used in conjunction with other materials. Leather is used primarily to manufacture sacks and bags, but it is also used on baskets, saddles, and riding equipment as well as for the special decoration found on women's riding camels. Thongs are used for repairs, to connect tent poles, to fasten the roof canvas to its armature, and to hang containers. In the main, women tan goatskins and camel skins, but cowhides are also tanned. The men slaughter the animals and remove the skin from the carcass. All subsequent tanning processes are in the hands of women alone. They cleanse the hides and skins of the remaining blood and flesh, and macerate them. Most of the time the water in which millet has been leavened is used in the fermentation process, and the dry pods of the Acacia nilotica (*garad*) are most often used as a vegetable tanning agent. Tanning involves several processes: (1) the preparatory process of fermentation and maceration; (2) cleansing the hides and skins; and (3) tanning and finally currying the hides and skins.

Although men engage in certain aspects of leather production, the majority of leather artifacts are produced by women. Labor is divided among men and women for processes such as the production of rope (*habl*; *habl wojegh*), of reins (*rasan*), and of water bags (*girba* and *suuga*): the men plait and twist the rope after the women have cut the leather into strips, and they sew the leather for the water bags together. In addition, the goatskin bolsters (*taafa*) for the riding saddle (38 × 70 cm), which are used in pairs, are tanned by the women, but the men sew the bolsters and fill them with camel's wool.

The manufacture of a large sack (*garfa*), for storing and transporting millet and animal salt, requires one camel or cowskin (fig. 7.9a). This type of sack is relatively a rough-finished product, but it is very strong and will hold fifty to eighty kilograms. It has a narrow bottleneck opening, handles, and braided straps made from eight to ten thongs of leather in a "Chinese braid." A single household may have ten to twenty such sacks. After the tanning process, which takes about a month, the women treat the leather with tar (*gutraan*) distilled dry from the seeds of a species of watermelon, Collocynthis citrullus (*battiikh*).

Bags used for carrying water, and the goatskin bucket (*deluu*) used to bring water up from the well, are treated similarly after the tanning process in order to render the skin dense and watertight. The tanning process takes about seven days, and the tar treatment dyes the leather a dark brown color. Water bags are created out of whole goatskins (when the animal is slaughtered, only the neck is slit). They contain sixteen to forty liters and last little more than a year.[7]

When a softer leather or a lighter brown color is desired, for example, for the small, light, goatskin leather bags (*dabiya*) used by every household to store

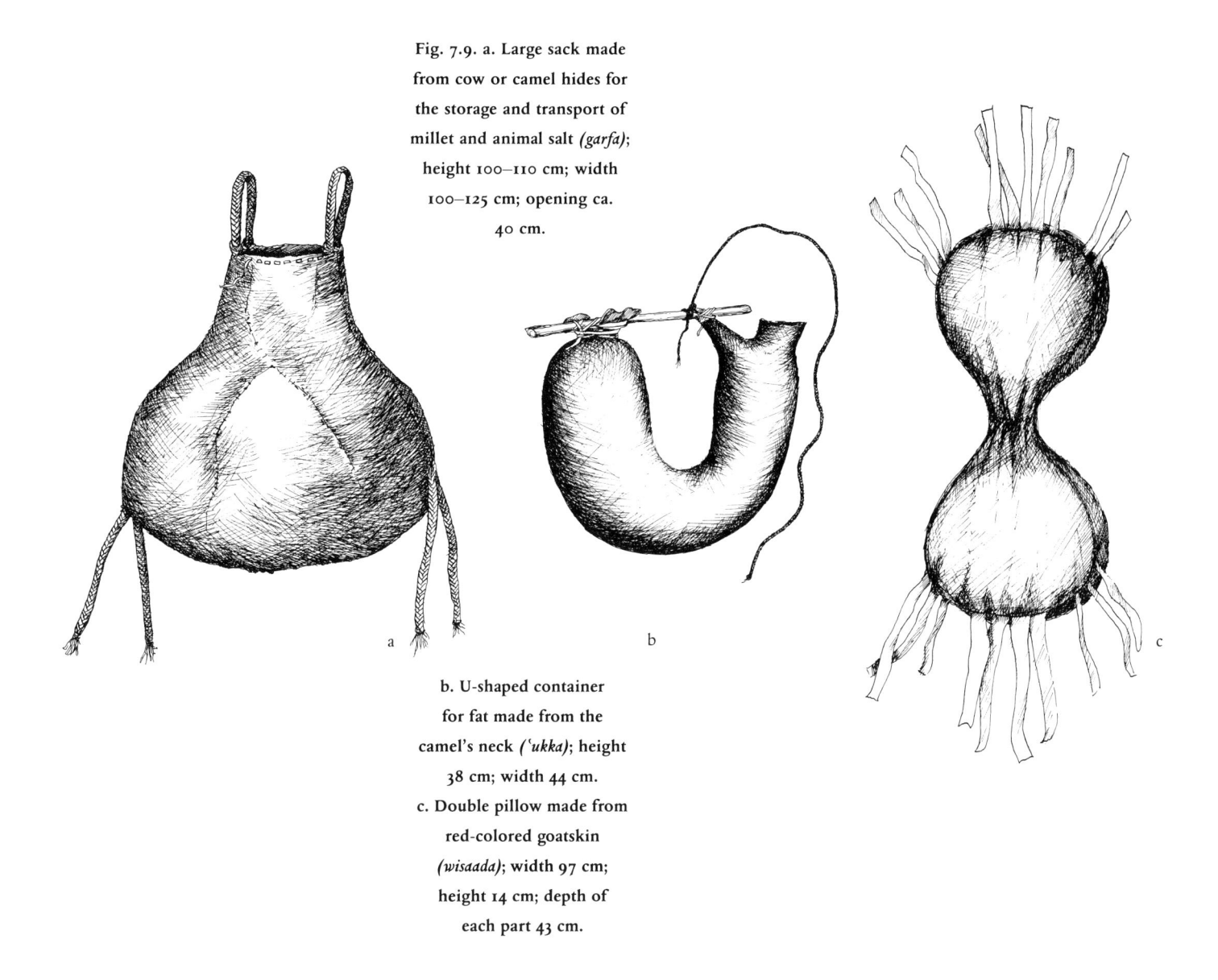

Fig. 7.9. a. Large sack made from cow or camel hides for the storage and transport of millet and animal salt *(garfa)*; height 100–110 cm; width 100–125 cm; opening ca. 40 cm.

b. U-shaped container for fat made from the camel's neck *(ʿukka)*; height 38 cm; width 44 cm.

c. Double pillow made from red-colored goatskin *(wisaada)*; width 97 cm; height 14 cm; depth of each part 43 cm.

objects of value and rice and sugar, the skins are treated with a lye created by mixing water with the ashes of Acacia faidheriba albida *(haraaz)* or Acacia seyal *(talha)*. The skins are removed in one piece, and the leather from the legs of the animal is sometimes plaited and knotted together to form a handle or strap.

The Mahria also manufacture a uniquely shaped, fat container *(ʿukka)* from the throatskin of the camel (fig. 7.9b). For its preparation, a rare form of bating with goat dung, reputed to facilitate the impregnation of the tanning agents, is employed. The help of two men, pulling the leather with all their strength, is needed for the currying process. This container is gradually disappearing from nomadic households as bottles replace it, and many women have lost the skills and knowledge related to its manufacture.

The traditional double bed *(seriir)* and the large double pillow *(wisaada)* are most important for the new nomadic household. Both must be readied in time for a wedding. The bed consists of a mat (2.25 m × 1.50 m) made from palm ribs and tanned camel or cowskin strips which are plaited by the women. The

Mahria Tents

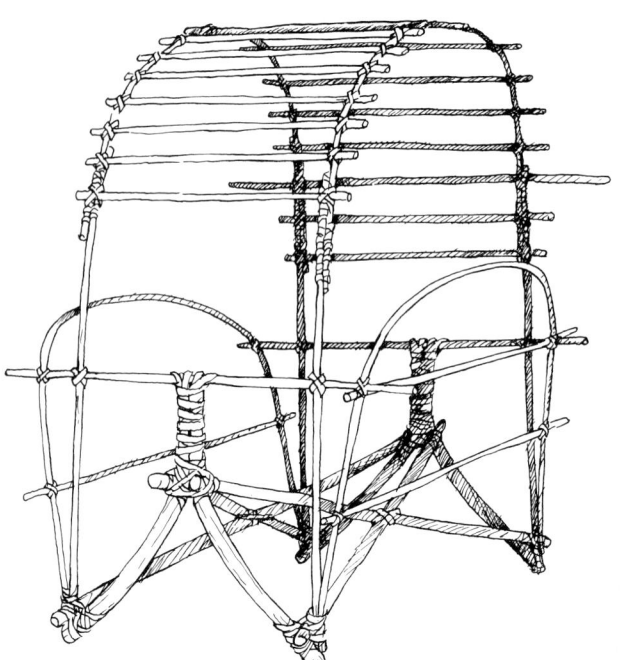

Fig. 7.10. Woman's riding saddle *(johfa)*. On the left, the armature of a young woman's ridding saddle *(johfa)* with a special armature above *(basuur)*; height 155 cm; width and length 75 cm. The saddle is made of Balanites aegyptiaca; the bows and bowtops, made of the branches of Combretum aculeatum, are bent by the women; the bow cross ties are made of *besham,* a tree that is also used to make spear shafts. On the right, the *rahuula* is elaborately decorated with carpets woven of goats' hair *(shamla)* and a cover of red goatskin decorated with cowries *(hamr ash shuuf)*. The basket frame on the left (normally used to carry the large earthen water jar) is filled with household utensils.

African Nomadic Architecture

mat lies on a knee-deep "rack of gabled posts" *(dakaaka)*, which are sunk into the ground. It is rolled up for transportation. The seven goatskins from which the pillow is made are treated with lye. After the tanning process, the leather is dyed a bright red on the smooth side with a synthetic powder *(tifta)*. Then the leather is cut and sewn into an hourglass-shaped pillow with long, wide fringes and filled with cotton (fig. 7.9c). The pillow lasts about four years.

The masterpiece of a woman's leatherwork is her camel-riding saddle *(johfa)* with decorative camel trappings and a special litter *(basuur)* that protects her from the sun and from the stranger's gaze when she is seated in it (fig. 7.10; pl. 17). This saddle is a major part of the young woman's dowry, and when she dies her daughter will inherit it. This saddle is first used when a young husband takes his wife to his own camp, after the first phase of post-marital residence with the bride's mother. Later on, a woman uses it only during migrations or when she has a little baby.

Its creation will occupy a woman's time for weeks or months. The most spectacular component of the entire assemblage is the leather mat *(hamr ash shuuf)* that covers the back and front of the litter. After the fifteen required goat (or gazelle) skins have been tanned, they are dyed red and decorated with cowries in an intricate pattern. The sewing alone takes her about ten days. In addition, a number of leather girdles of varying length and width, which will hang almost to the ground as decoration, must be plaited.

Basketry. Using coiled basketry, split stitch, and plain wrapping techniques, women manufacture two different kinds of baskets (*'umra* and *hanga*) from the leaves of the Hyphaene thebaica dum palm *(doom)* or the Phoenix dactylifera date palm *(tamur)* (fig. 7.11). The

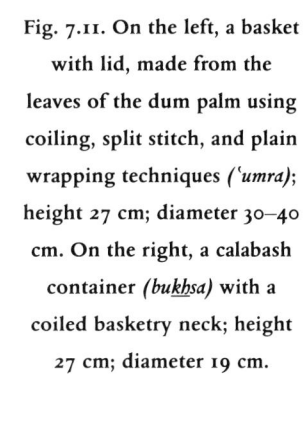

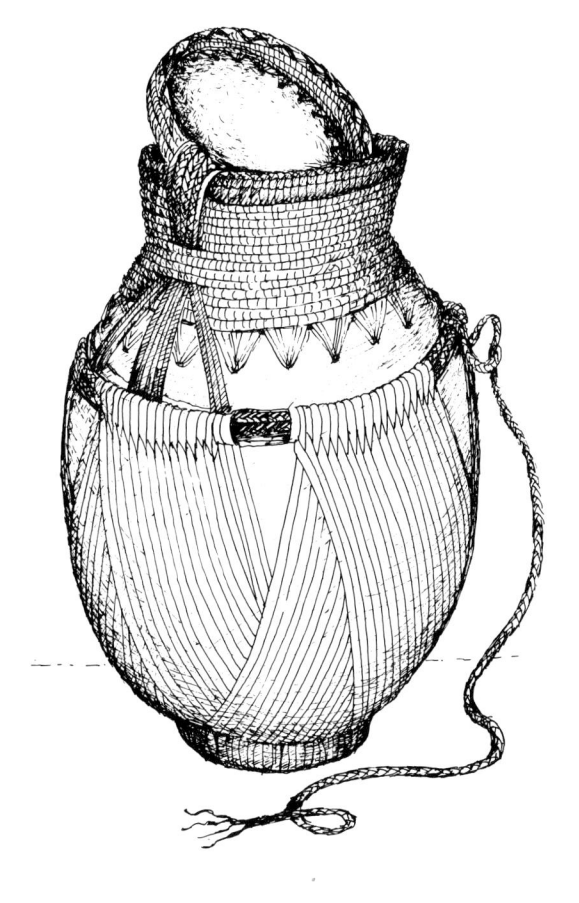

Fig. 7.11. On the left, a basket with lid, made from the leaves of the dum palm using coiling, split stitch, and plain wrapping techniques (*'umra*); height 27 cm; diameter 30–40 cm. On the right, a calabash container *(bukhsa)* with a coiled basketry neck; height 27 cm; diameter 19 cm.

finer parts of the palm leaves are used as braiding material, and the veins are used for the cores. The baskets are decorated in various ways, by alternating black and white material, into striped or checkerboard patterns. All the baskets have a lid fixed to one side of the basket with several short leather braided ropes and leather straps used to suspend them from the camel's back during transport. The 'umra has a wide opening, and its bottom is covered with red goatskin. It is used as a clothes container and to store objects of value and other possessions not carried in large quantities. The hanga is made the same way, but its shape differs and the leather covering the bottom is rather coarse.

Bottle-shaped calabashes are also transformed into containers (bukhsa; pl.: bukhas) by adding a neck of coiled basketry and finishing the basketry edge with a braided leather edge and a lid. Although some are made smaller, those most frequently made and used vary in height and diameter (30–40 cm and 20–30 cm). Larger calabash containers are sometimes embellished around the bottom with red goatskin in an "hourglass looping" pattern. These containers serve various purposes: they are "cupboards" for clothes, jewelry, soap, perfumes, and a number of other small items such as flashlights or small amounts of food.

Every household has one basket for churning butter (kambuut) and another to ferment millet. Because of the material and the technique used in manufacturing them, they absorb liquid and thus become impermeable. Baskets may last as long as ten years, and even then, wornout baskets are sometimes used to hold cooking pots in transit and in the tent (pots are dirty).

Women also plait covers (burṭaal) and shallow bowls (ṭabag; pl.: ṭubaaga) to protect food from dust and insects, as well as to winnow millet and dried vegetables once they have been pounded in a mortar. The same basketry techniques are used in their manufacture, but the braiding materials also include (in addition to palm leaves) grasses such as a species of Eragrostis (banu) and sometimes the roots ('irig) of the Acacia senegal tree (hashab). The softer parts of the leaves are used as braiding material, the veins to fill the rolls. They sometimes also use the grass or the roots as

Table 7.3. Basket making

Nature of work	Time in days/ unit of work	Total amount of work in days
Basket		
1. Basketry: 2–3 rolls	1	
72 rolls total		25–28
2. Work with cowskin	1	1
3. Work with goatskin	1	1
Lid		
Basketry and leatherwork	2	2
Preparations		
1. Buying palm leaves (trip to market)		6 hours
2. Splitting palm leaves		several hours
3. Dying palm leaves black or		one month
4. Bleaching palm leaves		several hours

filling material for the rolls.[8] When wornout, they serve to fan the fire or as sieves for leavened millet.

When asked how long it takes to make a mat or basket, nomadic women have a definite idea of the time they will need. However, the information sometimes varies from one woman to another as well as with recorded field measurements. For a basket (hanga), one woman said she needed ten days; another said a month was required (see table 7.3).

In measuring the time actually needed for one such basket (height 42 cm, diameter 42 cm at mid-height), I discovered that it took 86.5 hours for the basketwork alone (the time expended for leatherwork and leather decorations could not be measured). The woman who had told me she needed only ten days to make a basket would in fact have had to work more than eight hours per day to make it—an improbable accomplishment, given the demands of other daily tasks.

To measure work in terms of "minutes," "hours," or an eight-hour day is a concept that means nothing to nomadic women. They measure their work in terms of "days" or "mornings." As a measurement of time, a "morning" begins after the first meal of the day and ends with the second meal. But meals are often eaten earlier or later. A "working day" always ends before the last meal.

Even if a woman measures her working time in "days," she will not work the whole day without interruption on a mat or basket. A number of other daily tasks occupy her time. The number of people in a household and the number of able-bodied women and girls who can share in the necessary housework will strongly influence the amount of time a particular woman can spend on the manufacture of a particular artifact.

The objective measurement of time allows one to assess the validity of the time responses given by the women and to distinguish between their response and reality. The comparison shows, for example, how and on how many days the individual jobs are distributed and how reliable the data are. The estimated times given by the women are not always correct: there may be different reasons for the varying times given by them. First, women do not always take into account the tasks involved in the preparation and preprocessing of materials. These consist of: first, those processes that extend over longer periods of time even though little actual work is involved; second, work-intensive activities such as the gathering and cutting of grass, roots, and bast fiber; third, work such as excursions to gather firewood, to fetch water, or to go to market, where obtaining the raw materials needed to manufacture the artifact constitutes only part of the specific work objective. Furthermore, the pace of work varies among women.

A comparison between the *necessary* working time and the *actual* time spent on the work also reveals why nomadic women sometimes work more slowly or interrupt their work. The manufacture of mats or beds, the repair of a tent, or the erection of a wedding tent are always small social events. The women are not only eager to offer assistance, but to take the opportunity to exchange news or to engage in a long chat without disturbance. Tea is served during the work; the women can bring their small children and tend them at the same time. They may stop to pray, to drink tea, or work more slowly in company. Sometimes the arrival of female visitors in the camp provides a reason for the women to visit the tent of their hostess, to honor the guests and to enjoy their company. But at the same time, they may also bring lighter leatherwork or basketwork with them, and thus continue with their own work while profiting from the social exchange.

The tent's furnishings. The tent typical of a newly-wed couple will start with a double bed and one large pillow, about eight baskets, one container made from a calabash, two to three covers or bowls, four light leather bags, ten to fifteen large sacks for millet and animal salt storage, two to four water bags, and the woman's riding saddle with its decoration. Over time and the domestic cycle, artifacts and material goods will be added to it, but most of the furnishings inside the tent will continue to occupy a more or less fixed space. The north and south end spaces are reserved for the stores of food (mainly millet) and smaller quantities of animal salt. They are kept in large leather sacks standing on the ground or lying on a wooden rack *(shi'ab er rahal)* near the southern tent wall. Here too the empty sacks are stored, and above them, the baskets—the nomads' cupboards.

The pack saddles are kept at the northern end of the tent, and all kinds of objects and containers for cooking material or foodstuffs are placed on them. Objects that are not used daily, such as carpets, rugs, and the large, decorated leather bags (*mufrah* and *mukhlaaya* which the men use on long trips), are hung from the lower stringers on the east side. When the nomads migrate, the valuable woman's riding saddle decorations are often left behind with a sedentary relative. Unless the woman has a baby and needs special protection during the migration, the riding saddle with its litter will also be left behind.

The traditional double bed is always located in the southeast corner of the tent. At first it is used by the parents and their smaller children; later on, by the mother and her daughters. The bed is positioned east to west, with all heads facing east. The father always sleeps on the north side of the bed, closest to the tent entrance. Nowadays some of the wealthier nomads, who may have become sedentary, own metal beds. These, used by the men, are placed inside the tent, along the eastern wall and/or on the northern side.

The grinding implements are located a few steps from the right side of the tent entrance, adjacent to the tent wall. The implements consist of a milling stone *(murhaaka)* and two handstones (*darraasha* and *raddaada*). Adjoining them are an earthenware water jar *(duwaane)* and sometimes a hollow for chickens. Further to the right of the entrance, women will light a fire on cold, windy, or rainy days. If guests sit inside the tent, it is mostly in the northern part, on a mat or carpet spread on the ground. Only occasionally will nomads sit on the bed.

Other things kept outside, not far from the tent entrance, are the cooking utensils such as pots and pans. These can be stored in bushes or trees or simply left on the ground. Mortar *(fundug)* and pestle *('amuud)*, as well as the wooden framework of the woman's riding saddle, can also be placed in that area.

THE TENT: WOMAN'S DOMAIN IN THE DIFFERENT PHASES OF HER LIFE CYCLE

Marriage. The domestic cycle begins with marriage *('iris)*, and the tent is the first home for a young married couple. The choice of a marriage partner is a family decision. By the time a young girl reaches marriageable age (i.e., about fifteen), her marriage partner has already been chosen. Negotiations between the bridegroom's father and the father or brother of the girl he has chosen for his son have already been completed. The bride *('aruus)* is usually from the same tribe, preferably from a closely related family, for example, the daughter of one of the bridegroom's father's brothers. Patrilineal kinship plays an important role. In some cases, a young man may be asked for his consent to the choice of a marriage partner, but a girl is never consulted. There are, however, ways through which a girl can find out who has been chosen as her marriage partner. Sometimes she is even able to influence her parents' choice, but normally it is only on the night of the wedding that the bride can refuse the bridegroom *('ariis)*. If her parents agree to her wishes, they must return the brideprice, but they can also force her to honor the marriage contract.

The brideprice *(mahr)* is agreed upon by the two families, and although it is paid by the bridegroom's father or brother, the bride's mother takes an active part in the negotiations. The brideprice may consist of two camels, the money for the materials needed by the bride's mother to manufacture the tent furnishings, the food for meals during the three wedding days, and presents and clothing for both the bride and her mother. Nowadays, many young men go on labor migration in an attempt to earn the money they need for their wedding. When successful, they will bring the canvas for the tent, cooking pots and pans, bed, blankets, and other necessities, in addition to money.

Beginning in the camp of the bridegroom's father, a marriage celebration extends over three days. On the morning of the first day *(sihaar)*, the young couple's fathers or adult brothers execute the wedding contract *(sufaah)* in the presence of the men of the camp. A *faki* (a man well-versed in Islamic scripture, a healer) starts with the reading of the opening sura of the Koran. Then, in front of witnesses, the two fathers agree to the marriage of their children. Usually the men sit in the open, at a distance from the tents. Neither women nor the young couple are present. Bride and groom wait separately in their respective parents' tents. The bride, in her father's camp, might be several hours or even a day's ride away from the camp of her suitor.

Once the guests have arrived in the bridegroom's camp, the young men race into it on their camels, passing dangerously close to the young women who stand observing and applauding them adjacent to and close by the tents.

The women of the camp share the major responsibility for the wedding preparations. Animals are slaughtered and food is plentiful. The meals served on these festive occasions *('azuuma)* are prepared by the women outside, close to the parents' tent. The women eat inside the tent, shielded from the view of the men who eat at a distance, in the shade of a tree. The old women sit in another tent, separated from the young women and marriageable girls. Everyone squats on the carpet- and mat-covered ground amid the continuous flow of conversation.

In the afternoon, the young people dance and everyone drinks millet beer *(mariisa)*. The men, the bridegroom in their midst, sporadically shoot into the air with their machine guns. The women spend the night in the tent lying next to each other on the ground, their small children crouching next to them. Festivities provide important occasions for meeting and for the exchange of news.

On the second day *(gayoola)*, the dancing, drinking, and good food continue in the bridegroom's camp. The bride, however, remains in the southern part of her mother's tent, seated on a mat and hidden by a cloth partition. Her mother and other women of the family spend hours preparing her for the wedding. Her hair is plaited, she is bathed, perfumed with various scents, decorated with henna, and dressed in colorful new clothes and gold jewelry. She is forbidden to leave the tent and, except for some tea and milk, to eat.

Meanwhile, the other women of the camp erect the wedding tent near the bride's mother's tent (see pl. 9). The tent poles are especially prepared with a lotion made by boiling the dried and pulverized pods of Acacia nilotica in water for fifteen minutes. This gives the poles a red color which is said "to be beautiful" and "to make the wood strong," qualities expected from the bridegroom. The tent is erected with the entrance facing east or southeast. After the canvas is laid over the top, the women sprinkle it with the water of fermented millet. They say millet is a symbol for many children, because the heads of millet contain many seeds. Water also symbolizes "coolness," which the nomads want the tent to be. The term "cool" or "cold" *(baarid)* is also used for a riding camel, meaning "good" and "fast." Pitching the wedding tent takes about fifty minutes, after which the middle-aged and older women celebrate by singing and dancing within it.

The only furnishing within the tent is a leather mat (from the traditional nomadic bed) laid on the ground on the northern side. A space is left between the tent wall and the bed, for the bride. There she will sit and eat, unless she is alone with the bridegroom. A dividing curtain *(khuujaliiya)* separates the whole northern section from the southern section of the tent where the bridegroom will sit and accept the congratulations of his brothers and friends.

In the evening, shortly after sunset, the bridegroom and his wedding party arrive in the bride's camp, where they are received with excitement and joy. After dismounting from their camels, four young men attempt to force their way into the tent of the bride's mother, in which the bride is waiting, but they are prevented from entering by three young, close, women relatives of the bride. The bride's mother must first give her consent, and the young men must pay a sum of money equal to the value of a goat. This payment, kept by the three young women, is for having plaited the bride's hair. Only then are the four young men allowed to enter and fetch the bride, covered by her white or colored veil. She crouches on a bolster of the camel's saddle, and the young men, in a matter of seconds, carry her to the wedding tent. Then they lift up the bridegroom from his camel, still seated in his riding saddle. Carrying him high above their heads, they circle around the wedding tent before allowing him to enter. The marriage is finally consummated under cover of darkness amidst the noise of the young people dancing around the tent. Singing and drinking continue through the night.

Early the next morning, young men come to visit the bridegroom. The bride must turn her face away to the wall. While he is allowed to eat everything, only special food, such as rice, is prepared for and permitted her. Food and drink are brought to her only by unmarried girls or sisters who must enter the tent from beneath its northern rim, instead of the regular entrance.

On the third day of the marriage *(el 'aab)*, the presents for the bride are displayed for all to see and to laud the generosity of the bridegroom's family. Dancing continues, but after a good meal the guests leave for the ride home.

The young family. The young couple spends seven days in the wedding tent. The bride is supposed to stay inside all the time, beautifully dressed and available for her husband. She washes every day.

After this week, the tent is pitched next to the bride's mother's tent, its entrance now westwards and the bed properly installed in the ground even though the tent is not yet fully furnished. The couple will start to furnish the tent properly only after a month or so when the young husband must begin to tend his camels again. The young wife has considerable free time which her mother expects her to spend helping with the daily work. Only when her husband returns to the tent will the young wife cook for him and spend time with him inside their tent.

Even though tents may be standing close to each other, the tent is a sheltered place in a desert-like surrounding where privacy and intimacy are possible to a certain extent, even though noises and conversations can be overheard through the thin walls. The affectionate gesture by a wife *(dilka)* is extended to, and much appreciated by, a man returning home from a long exhausting camel trip. Actually, *dilka* is a special skin care preparation made with a scented and refreshing paste which only married women are allowed to use, but in special circumstances they will apply the lotion to their husbands, inside the tent.

When the young husband is away from the camp, his wife will cook and eat with her mother and sisters. The mother will make use of this time to complete the young wife's riding saddle with its litter and camel trappings. These must be ready on the day the young husband wants to move his wife to his own camp. If the relationship between mother and daughter has been a good one, the daughter's move brings sadness. The mother has helped and advised her daughter during her first pregnancy and birth. She has appreciated her daughter's company and help. Close mother-daughter relationships are a Mahria ideal; a parallel ideal is that Mahria women should not have to work too much when they grow older.

The day of the young couple's move *(rahuula)* is celebrated with plentiful food and dancing. The women of the camp decorate the young woman's riding camel and present her with small gifts (pl. 17). She, and possibly her first child, are placed in the beautiful litter for the first time. Her mother accompanies the party, and the entire household departs for the new camp, often the bridegroom's father's camp. The arrival is equally celebrated and the tent is pitched either immediately north of the young man's father's tent or adjacent to that of one of his brothers, according to the residence rules above. At this point, the tent should be fully furnished.

The phase of the life cycle during which a young woman gives birth to children and is responsible for her growing household (when she is called *mara' ṣeghiira*) is the most work-intensive period of her life. Many people must be cared for as the household grows, yet there are still few daughters old enough to lend a hand with the mother's daily work. Babies are breastfed for twenty to twenty-four months and are carried on the mother's back until the age of three. However, when the baby sleeps, the mother will lay it on the huge bed inside the tent, covered with a cloth to protect it from the insects.

A young daughter begins to learn the duties and acquire the skills of being a nomadic woman at the tender age between three and five. First playing, she is called *ṭifla*, and as she gradually takes over tasks from her mother she is called *bitt*. Only at the age of fourteen to fifteen, when a girl is capable of performing all the tasks in a nomadic household, is she an eligible marriage partner *(ṣabia* or *shaaba)*.

The festivals of childhood. The tent is a central place for the three important events in childhood: birth, name-giving, and circumcision.

When a woman is about to give birth to a child, women of the camp lend a hand and a midwife *(usta)* is informed. Men are forbidden to assist. The birth *(wilaada el ḥabl)* takes place in the northern part of the tent on the ground. A rope is fixed at the ridgepole of the tent roof, serving as support for the woman who keeps it in her hands while she is giving birth. Crying is frowned upon. The mother-to-be kneels on the ground while one woman supports her back with her knee and another fetches the baby from the front. The blood and placenta *(tabʿa)* fall into a hole in the ground, but afterwards the placenta of a girl baby is buried in a hole (the depth of an ell, ca. 1.15 m) about a meter beyond the southern side of the tent, whereas that of a boy baby is buried on the northern side.[9] A handful of millet grain is thrown on the placenta, and the water from the baby's first bath is poured over it so the millet will grow. A branch of the dum palm is planted in the ground to mark the spot.

The mother spends the next few hours lying on the bare ground north of the bed, after which she is washed with warm water, her clothes are changed, and she moves onto the bed which has now been screened off by a curtain as in the wedding tent. A mosquito net *(naamuusiiya)* might be used to cover the bed during the rainy season. The newborn is bathed with warm water and fed a mixture of warm water, camel urine, salt, and sugar.

There will be little rest for the new mother after birthing: her other small children will share her bed, and guests will arrive shortly to congratulate the parents. Women guests bringing small gifts for the mother and child will sit in the tent drinking tea, chatting, and noisily expressing their happiness, while the men remain outside with the new father. A goat is slaughtered and a meal prepared.

The new mother will leave the tent after seven days. Allowed about a month to rest, she will spend it inside or close to the tent. The postpartum sex taboo lasts forty days, and only after this time will she have her hair replaited. As a rule, a female camel is given to the newborn child.

The name-giving *(simaaya)* takes place seven days after birth, occasionally one or two months later. Many visitors attend, and it is celebrated with a meal for which goats or sheep have been slaughtered.

Circumcision between the ages of ten and twelve is the norm for both boys and girls. For the girl, it is performed before puberty by a midwife, inside the girl's mother's tent. It is accompanied by a large festival and is an important event in a girl's life. She is dressed in new clothes like a small bride and is given presents.

Mature motherhood and old age. A woman is fully recognized as woman and mother *(maraʾ kabiira)* when her older children have reached an age at which they can be of help and her daughters can take over her duties. There might still be small children in the household and new ones yet to be born, but the mother is pleased, particularly if she has a marriageable daughter. Now that part of the workload has been removed from her shoulders, she is free to spend part of her time with crafts.[10]

Menopause marks the onset of old age, and normally a woman's husband will no longer sleep with her. If he is polygynous, he will stay with a younger wife. The old woman *(ʿajuuz)* now pitches her tent next to that of her son, to whose household she will now belong. Sons are financially responsible, and daughters-in-law are responsible for the day-to-day care of aged parents.

Once all her children are married, an old woman lives alone or with her husband in her tent. In many cases, she may be given a granddaughter "on loan" to keep her company and carry out minor household duties such as collecting firewood or water, washing clothes, or sweeping out the tent. The grandmother will share her bed and tent and teach her granddaughter the daily tasks, thus playing a key role in the child's early socialization.[11]

An old woman's tent is smaller than it had previously been by as much as half (ca. 3 × 2 m). The distance from her tent to that of her son's, which might vary from three to twenty-four meters, is also a reflection of the nature of the relationship between mother and son. The tent furnishings have been reduced to a minimum. Wornout baskets and bags are no longer replaced. Except for a bit of tea and sugar which she can use to serve her guests, stores of food are no longer needed. Traditionally, an old woman shares her meals with her daughter-in-law and grandchildren. In contrast to its normal direction, her bed is placed south-north, her head pointing to the north.

An old woman spends most of her time close to her tent. She may take long naps inside during the day, or she may pray. Generally, however, she has more free time than the younger women, and as long as she is strong enough, she can ride to other camps to participate in their festivities. On her return, the women of her camp will visit her in her tent and listen attentively and at length to her detailed account.

Death and its memorial days *(karaama)* are the last occasions for family and relatives to meet and share a meal in memory of the deceased. The Mahria have no graveyards: corpses, wrapped in cloth, are buried the same day, not far from the campsite (e.g., 100–200 m). The corpse is placed in a shallow grave and covered with stones, moistened soil (for which the old women bring the water), and thornbushes to protect it from wild animals. Prayers are recited. Graves for men, women, and children vary only according to the length of the body. The direction of the grave is north-south, so that the head of the deceased, on the south, can face east, toward Mecca. Head and feet are both marked by a stone.

As soon as they receive the message of a death, relatives and friends, even from distant camps, gather on the site to express their sympathy and to mourn. Animals are slaughtered, meals are prepared, and tea is served. Women's cries fill the air. Women mourners huddle inside and close by the dead person's tent, while the men remain at a distance outside it. Only a few men and some of the elder women are permitted to participate in the burial itself.

FUTURE PROSPECTS

This chapter has attempted to describe the life of nomadic Mahria women—a domestic cycle punctuated by daily chores, sadnesses, and joys. The tent is central to this cycle. It is the women's domain. In general, their influence is confined to the domestic sphere. They play an important role in maintaining the well-being of their families, although important decisions concerning family affairs remain with the men. When men's herding responsibilities dictate an absence from camp, women become, in effect, heads of household.

A tent is more than a simple shelter and place to sleep. The woman's creative talent and a household's wealth are reflected in a Mahria tent and its furnishings. Not all tents look exactly alike. The interior of one tent may be cleaner and "nicer" than that of another, depending on a woman's taste, industry, and skills. Some women are better artists than others in manufacturing baskets and make a greater effort to renew wornout objects and to decorate the inside with carpets or curtains. Some are also prouder of the way it is arranged. I have come across tents that were in extreme disorder and others that were beautifully arranged and kept.

A tent also mirrors the sequential phases of every woman's life cycle; it is the place where nomads are born, grow up, and die. It is "home" to them. As a rule, women are proud to invite a female visitor into their tents.

When a young woman marries, her tent furnishings are few and new. They have been created by her mother, who at the same time has also transmitted the skills and knowledge of creating them to her. As the growing household imposes new requirements, a young married woman will see to the furnishings herself. It is only after her daughters have reached a marriageable age, have married and left her tent, that the labor time invested in craft production will diminish. As she grows older and becomes increasingly dependent on her son and her daughter-in-law, the need to produce new items for her tent decreases. Tent size, space, and furnishings are gradually reduced, reflecting the approaching end of her productive life.

Nomadic women enjoy greater freedom than women in sedentary Muslim societies, also evident perhaps in the missing tent divider curtain. Mahria women do not wear a veil inside the camp (unless a foreigner arrives) or when they collect firewood or water. In recent years, with the transition to a more sedentary life-style in permanent, stationary camps, the nomadic women have lost part of their freedom. Their lives become more restricted as they begin to adhere to the rules for women in sedentary Muslim society. Children are encouraged to attend school, and migrating camel herds are no longer accompanied by households but only by the herdsmen. As a consequence, camel milk and butter, even meat, are absent from the diet, particularly that of women and children. Women's daily chores no longer include all the tasks related to the presence of herds in a camp, such as milking, churning, hobbling them in the evening, or to the striking, pitching, loading, and transporting of the tent. Part of the repertoire of containers essential for transport and furnishing, traditionally their handiwork, is obsolete. In the process, the women become market-oriented, but their craft skills and products are less and less in demand. The essential setting for their creativity evaporates, and this special, albeit major, part of nomadic material culture slowly disintegrates and disappears.

8
RENDILLE HABITATION

Anders Grum

The Rendille in northern Kenya are Eastern Cushitic camel pastoralists who for many centuries have lived and moved with camels in the low-rainfall, semidesert lowland between Lake Turkana and Mount Marsabit[1] (see location map). Today they number just over ten thousand persons. To the south, between the Milgis and Merille rivers, they share the land with an additional nine thousand Ariaal and Ilturia who have become culturally integrated with the neighboring highland Samburu cattle herders. Besides camels, the Rendille herd goats and sheep. Earlier in this century a small number of cattle were introduced into their herding stock. They live and move in about one hundred extended family units, varying in size from twenty-five to six hundred people. The largest settlement observed consisted of one hundred and thirty-five houses. Such settlement units *(goob)* define both home and clan or lineage.[2] On average, family units move six times a year, at times only a few hundred meters, at other times hundreds of kilometers (see Chapter 2 above). They move mostly in search of pastures, though sometimes also for water or for reasons of security (fig. 8.1).

SETTLEMENT PATTERNS

Most commonly, a settlement has thirty to fifty houses. Each married woman or widow owns a house which was built for her on the day of her marriage. There are ten Rendille clans, and with few exceptions they are exogamous. All the men and children of a settlement belong to the same clan, whereas all the wives are daughters of other clans and other settlements. The light and portable structures are erected in a circle surrounding the thornbush-fenced camel pens *(sum-ki-gaal)* (fig. 8.2). The settlement is demarcated by a perimeter fence *(tikhorat)*, and in a central stone enclosure *(naabo)* a fire is kept burning day and night. This is the elders' meeting place, the religious center and the "management" center of the settlement.

The spatial arrangement of a settlement approximates a circle oriented toward the west, that is, all houses are placed with their doors facing a point to the west just outside the circle (fig. 8.3a). The houses are positioned clockwise in order of lineage seniority: the most senior house can be found immediately north of the west point with its door facing southwest toward the principal entrance. The last house of the circle then forms the other side of the entrance and faces northwest. Smaller gates in the perimeter fence lead to each individual house.

The number of houses in the circle seldom exceeds thirty, so when a settlement is large, one or more semicircles are added on the eastern side. Each semicircle is a family or subunit of the same clan, and this overall configuration is maintained whenever the community moves to a new site. When other members of the clan, or occasionally in-laws, want to join, there is never any doubt about their correct place in the spatial system. A

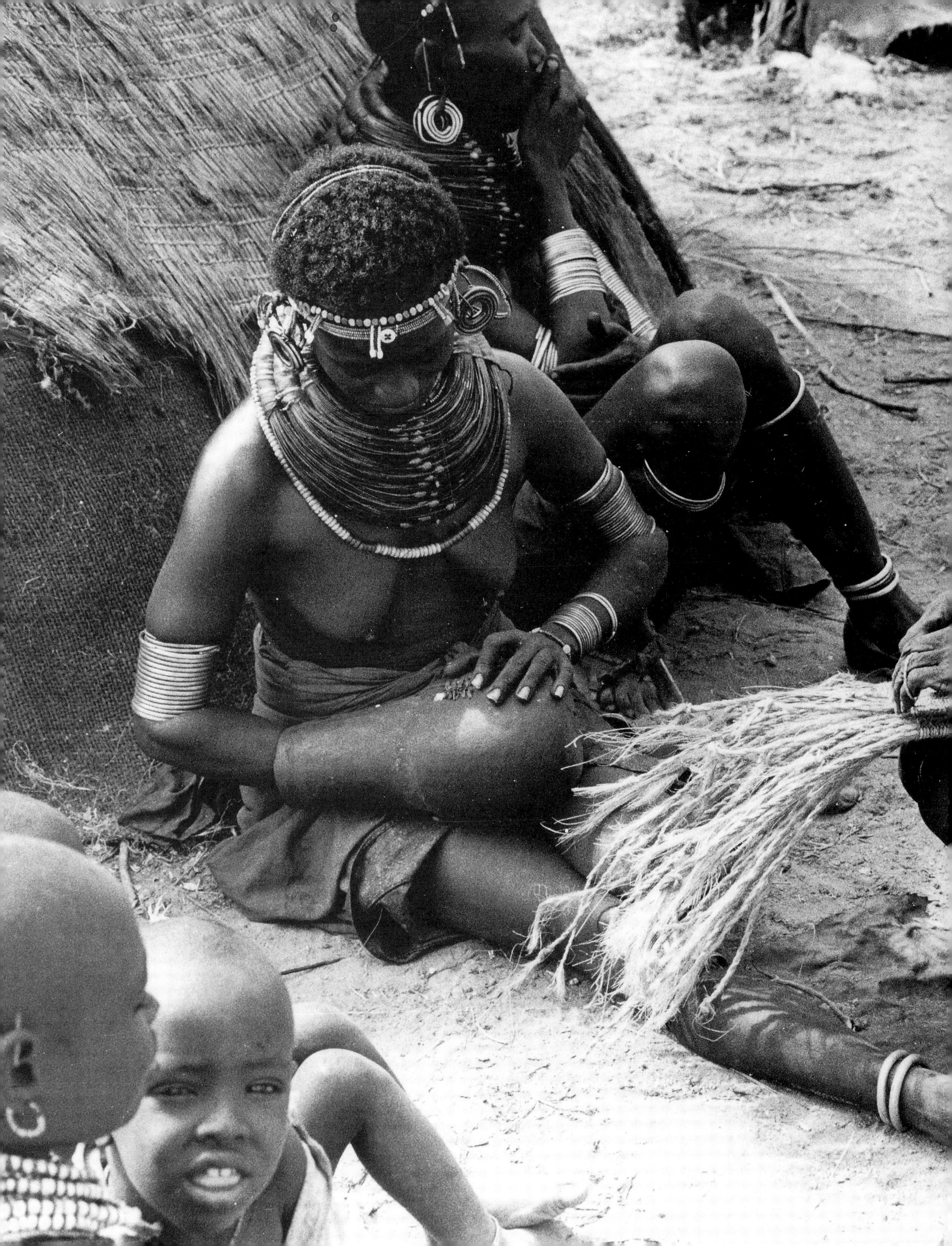

Fig. 8.1. Pack camels have been loaded, and people are ready to move.

Fig. 8.3. a. Settlement layout *(goob)* of Goob Wambile. *Legend.* 1, 2, 3, 4...: the order of tents by seniority and familial group; c: camels; cf: camel foals; yc: young camels; N: *naabo*; m: *muruub*s with milk.
b. Diagram of the *manti* or *lagoraba* settlement.
c. Diagram of the *naabo* settlement.

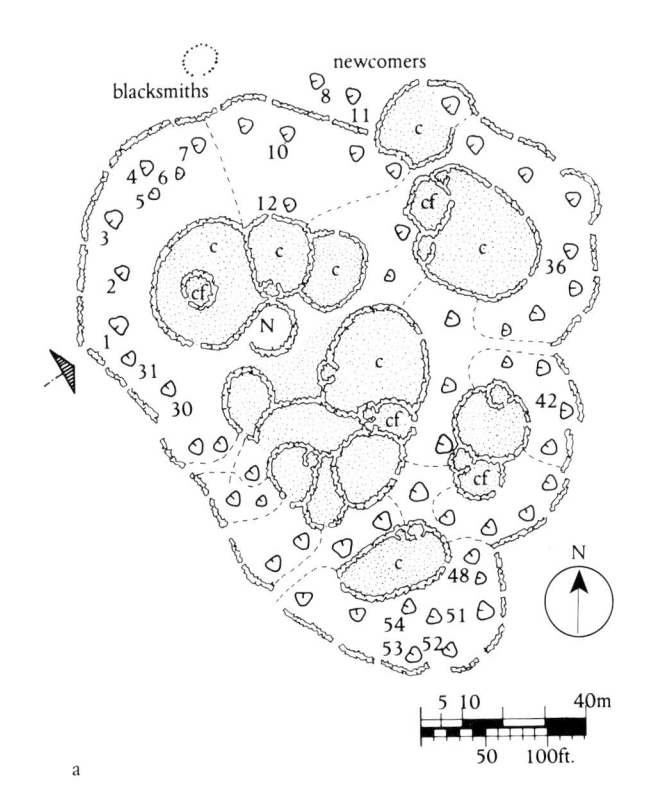

a

Fig. 8.2. The camp in the early morning before the camels are taken out. The typical Rendille lowland semidesert with small volcanic hills can be seen in the background.

- cf camel foals
- ◯ symbolic stone houses
- Ⓝ *naabo* of stones

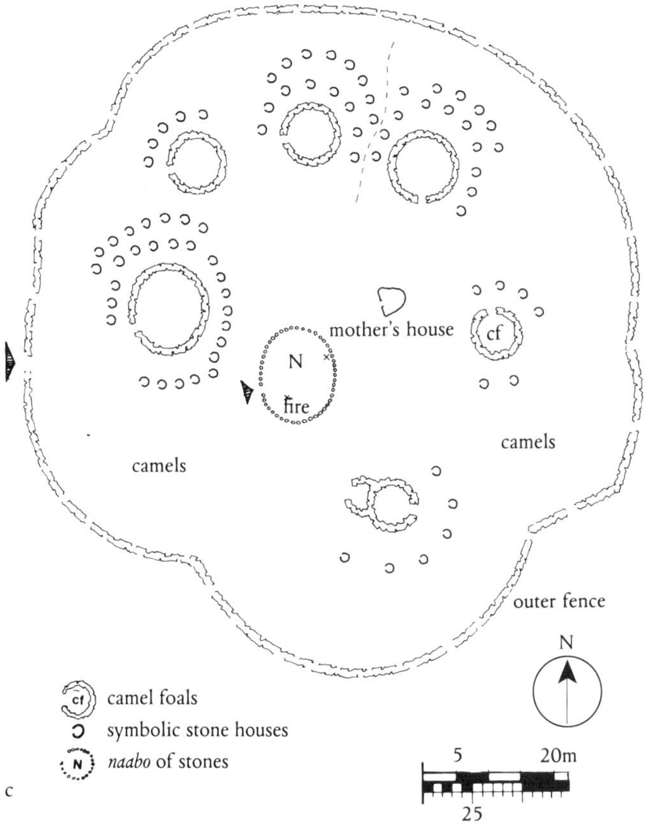

house can leave only when the entire settlement breaks up to move to a new location. Newcomers are left to build their houses outside the perimeter fence until the next move of the settlement, when they can fit into the line.

Rarely will all animals be present in the encampment at the same time. Nowadays most camels are herded by unmarried warrior herdsmen far away from the settlement, and at night they are kept in highly mobile satellite camps *(gal-i-foor)*. Similarly, goats and sheep are herded by girls and unmarried young women and kept in less mobile, small stock satellite camps *(adi-foor)*. Hence the space taken up by a camp varies, depending on which animals are accommodated at a given time. However, the overall configuration always remains the same. Within it, camels are corralled in family herds, and each woman keeps an enclosure for her goats and sheep. The camel camps have neither houses nor structures, other than minimal fences for the youngest animals and small central enclosures *(kull)* in which the herdsmen and boys sleep at night and take their two daily meals of milk mixed with a little blood. The girls' small stock camps are the same except that they may have a few more enclosures.

OTHER SETTLEMENT TYPES

The *goob* is a physical expression of Rendille family life and clan lineage. Similarly, there are various special forms of camps or settlements which are integrally linked with the Rendille age-set system and its associated rituals.

Seen superficially, there are just three stages in the life of a Rendille man: boy, warrior, and married elder. Yet there are six age-set rituals in his progression through life which, over a period of fourteen years, strengthen the group's solidarity and lead the age set in and out of the three main stages. The six rituals manifest a progression in social responsibility and status, and each one has, in a sense, its own progression in architectural form.

The first three group rituals of an age set, which relate to circumcision and preparation for warriorhood, involve no special settlement arrangements.[3] However, one year after the circumcision, the most spectacular of all Rendille ceremonies, the "camel stampede" or "chasing of the camels" *(galgulame)*, takes place. Ideally, for this ceremony, all members of the tribe, with all their camels, or at least all those houses that have warrior sons, should gather at the shores of Lake Turkana and live, for one week, in a single, enormous circular encampment. The houses of nine of the ten clans follow one another in order of lineage seniority as in camps, the two moieties forming a northern and southern semicircle. The tenth, the Odoola clan, forms its own smaller circle nearby. The diameter of this large encampment is reported to be so great that wild animals do not realize they are surrounded by one single human settlement. At this ceremony the new age set receives its name, and the warriors all take part in a ritual bath in the lake. The "chasing of the camels," which has given its name to the ceremony, could be interpreted as a ritualized test in camel herding.

The last and most important group sacrifice of warriorhood, "the day the camel bull is sacrificed" *(manti or lagoraha)*, occurs in a sacrifice *(sorriyo)* month of the year before warriorhood ends and is performed by warriors of all clans gathered together for a few days in an oversized camel camp *(foor)* (fig. 8.3b). Surrounded by an outer fence, each participating clan or subclan constructs a thornbush enclosure for the young camels and a smaller one for the calves in a circle in order of lineage succession. In the center of the camel camp, a circle of stones is constructed in which, at full moon, a white camel bull is sacrificed and burned to ashes.

Eleven years after circumcision, the age set performs the sixth and last ceremony *(naabo)*, which effectively ends warriorhood and makes the age set eligible for marriage. This ceremony, with steps leading up to it, is quite complex, and a description goes beyond the scope of this chapter. During recent years it has brought tension between the two moieties of the Rendille to such an extent that the two now hardly communicate, and in 1989 there were no intermarriages between the two moieties. However, again it takes place at full moon on an inaccessible lava plateau, and again it is basically a large camel camp (fig. 8.3c). On this occasion the warriors jointly build a circle of boulders to symbolize their ascent to elderhood and future access to the stone enclosure in their own settlement. Each man also builds a smaller ring of stones to symbolize his future house. Within the ring, he places six stones to represent the hearth and next to it a bigger and a smaller stone (to represent his future wife and child) and a few sprigs of cactus whose milky sap represents the wish that women and animals may produce enough milk to sustain life in the future. In front of these symbolic, future houses, the men sacrifice a small goat, a ritual each head of household performs four times a year in his own community camp. Four members of the age set are selected for particular symbolic roles, and the mother of the most propitious of the four, Gudur, participates in the ceremony by building her real house next to the circle of stones.

The progression in sacrifice as well as in built form which the six rituals of the male age sets express can be summed up as follows:

1. Boys of all clans, wilderness, and sacrificed goat
2. Boys of all clans, wilderness, and sacrificed bovine ox
3. Circumcision, parents' camp, and communal "white house" *(min-ki-dakhan)*
4. Warriors, camels, parents' houses in an all-clan settlement
5. Warriors of all clans (except Odoola) in a camel camp, with no houses and a white camel bull sacrificed in a circle of stones
6. Warriors, camels, symbolic circle of stones, and symbolic houses and individual sacrifices of a small goat.

THE HOUSE

The Rendille house (*min*; pl.: *minan*) is a portable, demountable structure (pl. 18). Although the size will vary according to need, the structural principle is exactly the same for all houses. Two of the Rendille clans, however, each have a traditional variant: all of the Odoola clan with affiliations to the Gabra, and the Gaaloora (also called Amomisa) subclan of the Galdeilan, who are said to have historic ties with the Geleba (Dasanech) living at the northern end of Lake Turkana.

The "standard" house, as it is used by 95 percent of the Rendille, a majority of the Ariaal clans, and the Ilturia with Samburu affiliations, is almost circular, but widened on each side of the entrance, forming two

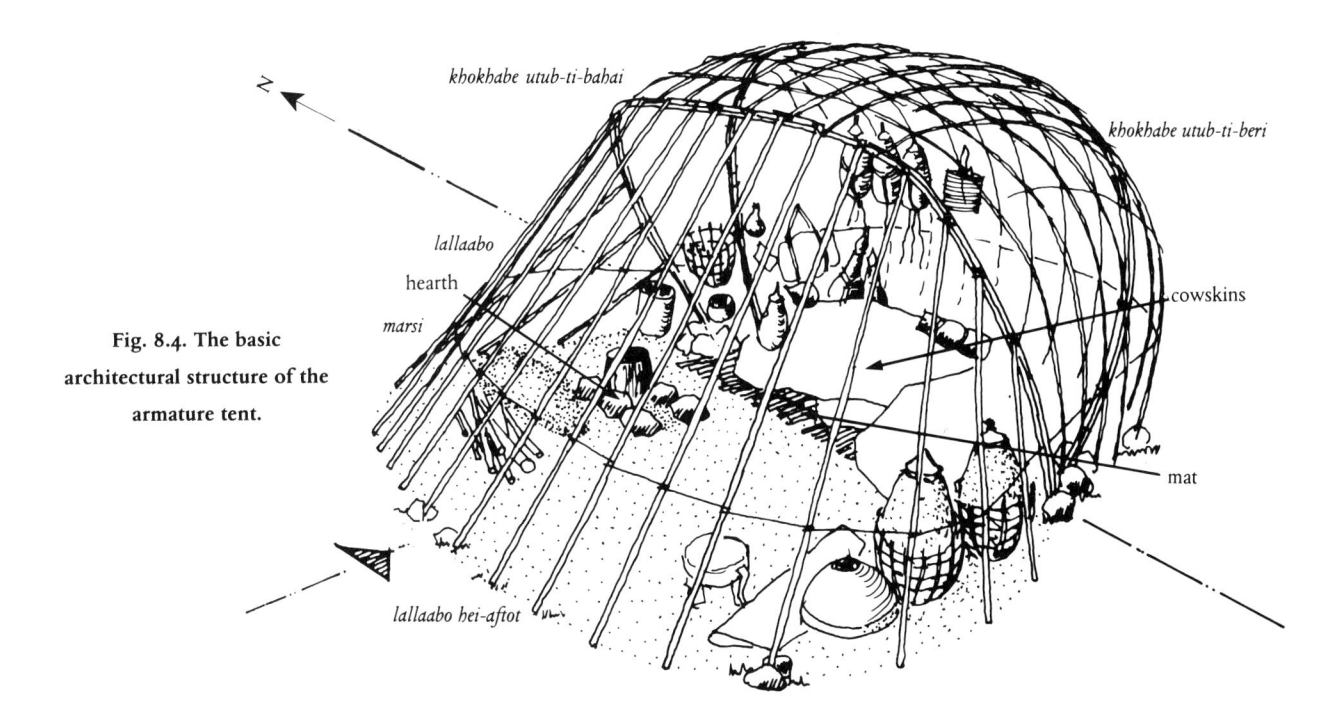

Fig. 8.4. The basic architectural structure of the armature tent.

Rendille Habitation

pockets. House sizes vary: the mean diameter is three meters and the mean height is just under two meters, just enough for a tall person to stand upright. The floor area varies from seven to twelve square meters. In a larger house an average person can stand upright over half the floor area. The volume is differentiated: low spaces are used for storage and higher spaces for human activity and movement.

The structure of a typical Rendille house consists of two arched frames *(khokhabe)*, set in a basically north-south direction (figs. 8.4, 8.5). Both the front arch *(utub-ti-bahai)* and the back frame *(utub-ti-beri)* are made of two or four thick, pre-bent sticks (30–35 mm in diameter). The sticks, overlapping 70–90 cms, are tied together with ropes *(yabar, girfo,* and *sah)*. The women plait these ropes from fibers of Sansevieria robusta N.E. Br. Agavacea, a wild sisal *(eyma)*. The only type of wood used for the house structure is Cordia sinensis Lam. Boraginaceae *(gaer)*, which grows along the banks of the Milgis and Merille rivers. Occasionally a stick of another kind of wood might be seen in between.[4]

If the ground is suitable, the ends of these two arched frames are buried .50–1.0 m below the surface, but often the ground is too hard and a few stones are placed around each base. When the front arch is raised, it is kept in position by one or two of the straight sticks *(lallaabo)* forming the front, usually the two framing the doorway *(lallaabo-hei-aftot)*. Similarly, the back frame is raised and supported by the pre-bent ribs forming the back wall *(lallaabo-hei-beri)*. Their curved shape is continued by the roof ribs *(utub-ti-saraat)*. Both types are of a thickness of 15–20 mm and are spaced 25–30 cms apart. The last part of the structure to be fixed would be the four or five bent sticks *(ogoseyneey)*, each 15–20 mm thick, arranged fan-like between the main frames across the top of the curved roof ribs. The straight sticks in front are connected by means of a tie-rope *(marsi)*.

All joints are made with rope. The straight front sticks and the roof sticks are tied to the two arched frames with short, thin sisal ropes, each with a noose *(yabar* and *girfo)*, and the curved ribs of the back wall and the roof are tied to the back arched frame with four or five thinner ropes joined in one loop *(sah)*. A long rope *(marsi)* joins the back ribs to each other above the wall skins and at both ends to the main frames. Often a middle portion of it is wound up in a bundle which is said to symbolize the woman of the house.

The structure is elastic and will constantly sway a little in the wind, but it will resist the very strong storms and whirlwinds so common on the plains and most feared along Lake Turkana, part of the Rendille territory.

Once the structural parts of the house have been erected, the roof mats *(dhulbenye)* are attached. Usually around a half meter square in area, these mats are knotted by the women out of the wild sisal they collect on the mountains surrounding the Rendille lowland. The mats provide shade from the sun, while the outside long pile leads the rainwater off, and yet the porosity of the cover allows for evaporative cooling. Each mat has two ropes, one in each upper corner, used to fix the mat to the structural armature. The covering begins around the lower walling with the oldest mats; these are the most worn and therefore most porous. The best and newest mats cover the roof area. A larger house will require forty-five to fifty mats. At the front of the house and at the sides, the mats reach almost to the ground, while at the back they are lifted 40–50 cms above ground, allowing for the possibility of controlled through-ventilation. To prevent the mats from blowing off in the wind, they are tied down with a long sisal rope *(yaraf)* around the sides and in the back. A kind of creeper plant *(sarkhudum)* is spread over the roof to hold the mats down in the wind.

All the parts of a Rendille house are made of materials naturally available in their environment. Collected by the women and partly by the men, they are processed by the women and gradually replaced as they wear out. The only exceptions are the five or six cow skins which are obtained from cattle herders or from a slaughterhouse in town. Two half skins *(afaf)* are hung inwards from the sloping door posts *(lallaabo-hei-afaf)*. These mark the doorway and block the western afternoon sun. Two or three cow skins *(khod*; pl.: *khodad)*, specially cut and stitched, are hung against the back wall inside the house. These skins effectively block the wind at night and at the

Fig. 8.5. Above, the women remove the bark from the fresh *gaer* sticks and bend them in the shape required for houses. Below, the women build a new house.

Rendille Habitation

same time provide a heavy backdrop to the most private area of the house. At least one of these cow skins is made to fold up when through-ventilation is required. Camel skins are not used in houses, neither as walls, doors, nor floor coverings. I have seen camel skin used only for rope or thongs, or as a protective covering for gourds or for a small, wooden milking container *(soror)* herdsmen use for drinking water or women use when milking goats and sheep.

The interior of a Rendille house is divided into a front, western half which is more public and utilitarian, and a back, eastern half which is more private (fig. 8.6). Similarly, in the other direction, it is divided into a northern half which is essentially female and a southern half which is essentially male. The house is one space in the sense that it is never partitioned. At the same time, it is clearly divided into several symbolic and functional spaces. The domed eastern half is the actual private living area. It has the best rain protection, it is higher, and the floor is covered. The lower front part is more for storage and for visitors.

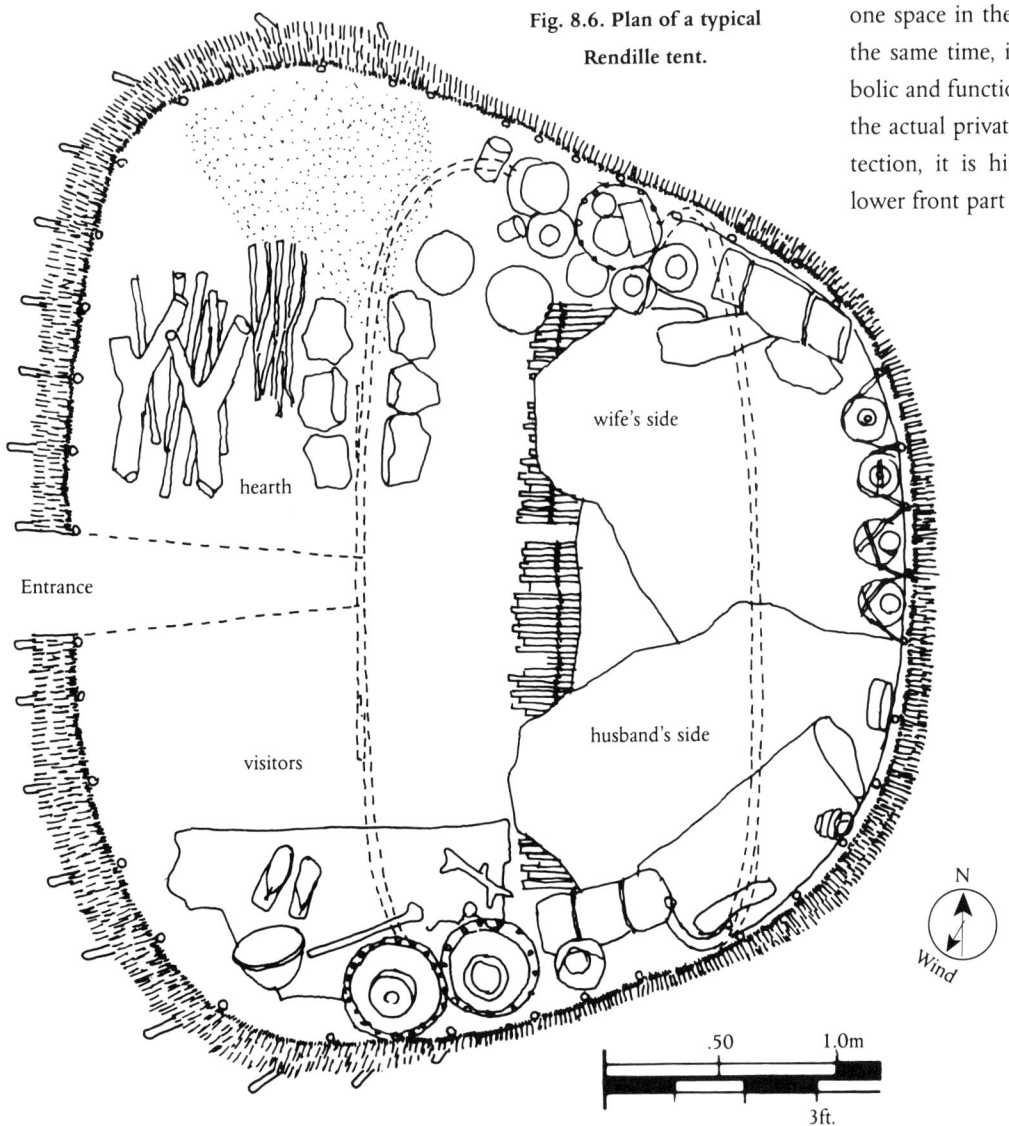

Fig. 8.6. Plan of a typical Rendille tent.

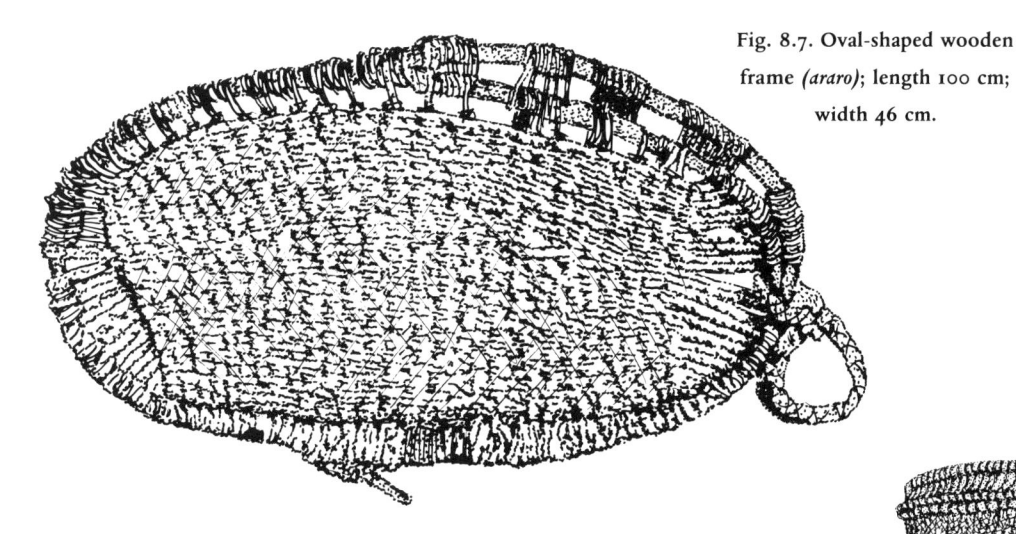

Fig. 8.7. Oval-shaped wooden frame *(araro)*; length 100 cm; width 46 cm.

Fig. 8.8. a. *muruub*; height 25 cm. b. *bangkhech*; height 22.5 cm. c. *haan*; height 60 cm.

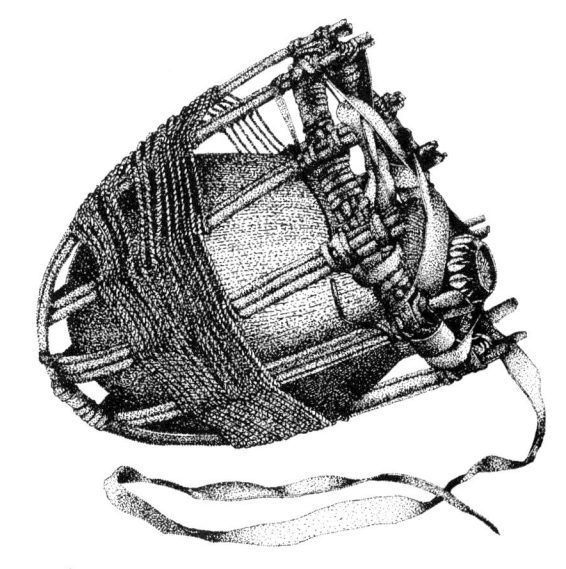

FURNISHINGS

The first belongings to be brought into the house, often before it is complete, are the two pairs of oval-shaped wooden frames *(araro)* filled by interwoven camelskin thongs (fig. 8.7). They serve as packing frames on the camels when the women transport water containers. The four frames are placed along the back wall and tied to the curved sticks before the wall skins are fixed.

The next to be placed in the house are two roller mats *(ilaal)* over which two cow skins *(niib)* are unrolled. These are used for sleeping or sitting on at the back, eastern half of the house. The roller mat is made of the stems of the leaves of the dum palm *(baar)*, cut to length, dried, and tied together in two lines with camelskin thongs to form a flat "floor" which can be rolled up for easy transport. These mats are extremely strong and will last a lifetime despite the rough treatment they receive during transport. The only part of the house that is not transported from one site to the next are the hearthstones and the roof creepers.

Generally, the hearth is considered the center of family life and the symbol of motherhood. In most African cultures, the hearth is built of three stones. Among the Rendille, three is also a female number, but the hearth always consists of six stones, two rows of three.[5] In all houses (except those of the Odoola clan) the hearth is in the northwestern quadrant, to the left of the entrance looking in. The houses of the

Rendille Habitation 159

Odoola clan always have their hearths to the right when looking in, similar to the Gabra.

The house has no smoke outlet. The Rendille do not need fires for heating, and they do not cook very much. The little smoke there is escapes through the tiny crevices in and between the roof mats. The advantage here, as among all straw or mat-roofed housing, is that the smoke keeps termites and other insects away and protects the wood and the sisal roof mats.

The hearth will always be on the north, to the west side of the house, because of the way the settlement is arranged and the houses placed. The prevailing wind is from the southeast, and most of the smoke leaves the house easily through the entrance or through gaps in the mats without passing through the entire house.

There are normally no outdoor cooking fires. They would be impractical and hazardous in the strong wind. However, on the evening of the new moon, every housewife of the *iberre* families (those who have the power to curse) will light a very small fire in front of the house and perform a symbolic cleansing of the camel milking vessel *(muruub)* (fig. 8.8a). To the left of the entrance on entering, firewood and a heap of ash are stored adjacent to the hearth. On the northern, kitchen wall, various household items are hung. The black clay cooking pot *(dhiri)* made by the Ndorobo in the Ndoto mountains, sits in a protective wickerwork basket *(enjel)*. Below it hangs a ritual milk container *(dubhisso)* associated with childbirth and marriage, made of the root of the wild asparagus *(ergek)*.

Beside the cooking pot hang other containers: one for storing camel's fat *(udham)* is made of folded camel skin, closed with a wooden stopper and placed in another wickerwork basket; the large, drum-shaped *mbarambara* and the small *bangkhech* in which dried meat, fat, or milk is kept; the slightly different shaped *nyabur* for similar purposes; and gourds *(oror)* for cooking oil and for cosmetic body oil *(ororo)*. Nowadays most houses would also have an aluminum cooking pot, two or three enameled cups, and a kettle.

In the southwestern quadrant, to the right of the entrance, are the belongings used mainly outside the house: the large water containers *(haan)*, the camel-milking vessels *(muruub)*, the water bucket *(okole)* made of giraffe skin and used when watering the camels form the deep wells, the man's carved stool *(kombor)*, his headrest *(kombor-ti-matah)*, his knobkerrie *(khokhoom)*, and sometimes his bow and a quiver of arrows (fig. 8.9). Normally, animals are not kept in the house, but occasionally an ailing kid or lamb will be kept indoors for a short period in the corner near the water containers. Next to the fire is the wife's place, where she sits on the floor skin and does all her housework. All utensils are within arm's reach. Only firewood and water are out of reach, and these are usually handed to her by a child.

All belongings used in the house, as well as clothing and personal ornaments, have their fixed places on the end and back walls or on the floor along the wall (pl. 19). Hanging in leather slings in a specific order against the cow skins of the back wall are, from left to right, the ritually important woven containers: the *gigo* for fresh milk and the *madhaal* for fresh and sour milk (fig. 8.10). Both, like the ritual milk container associated with marriage and childbirth, are made of the wild asparagus root and decorated with brass wire, long decorative leather straps, and cowrie shells. Below them, the more utilitarian carved wooden containers *(kuul)*, with a drinking cup as a stopper, are

Fig. 8.9. The interior southwest section of the tent with its large water containers.

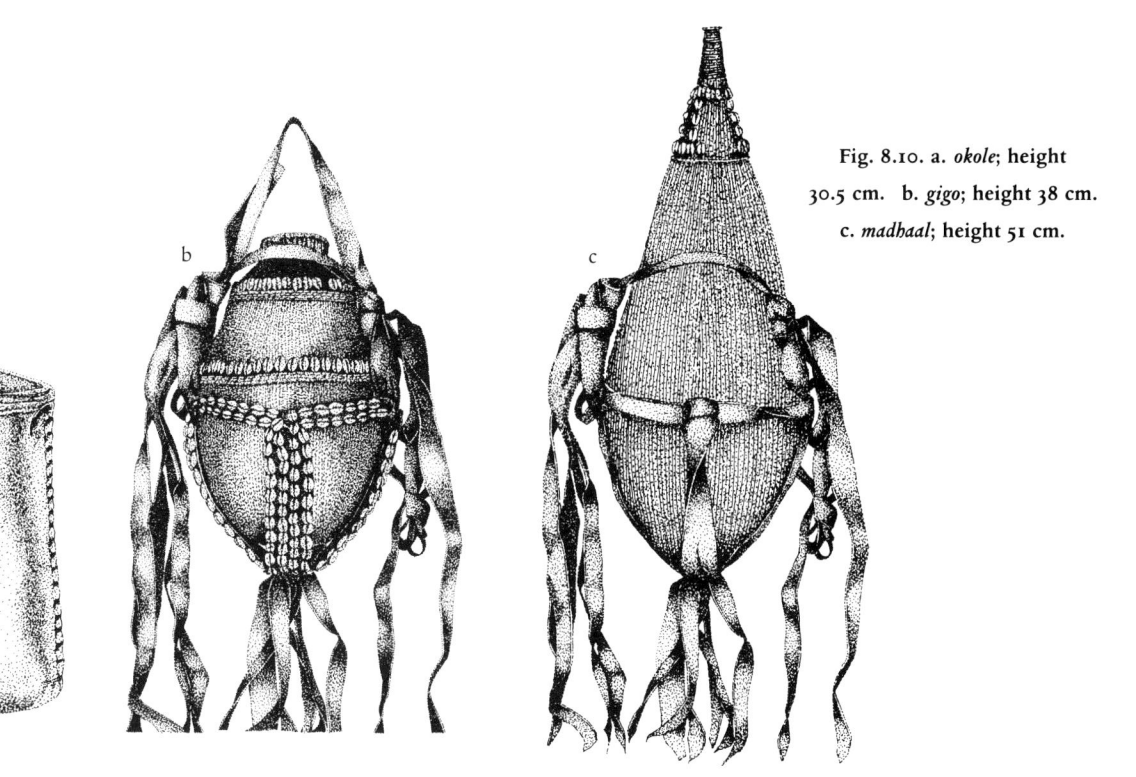

Fig. 8.10. a. *okole*; height 30.5 cm. b. *gigo*; height 38 cm. c. *madhaal*; height 51 cm.

Fig. 8.11. In the afternoon, one woman repairing a container and another weaving the *ugar-ti-haru*.

propped up between the skins of the wall and those of the floor.

The milk containers are joined by other ceremonial possessions such as the wife's ceremonial cape *(okko)* made from the skin of the goat sacrificed on the last day of her wedding ceremonies and decorated with cowrie shells and small iron bells. Then (in those Rendille houses occupied by lineages who possess the power of the curse) a small sisal bag *(ugar-ti-haru)* containing dried cedar leaves *(haru)* and two pieces of ivory *(irr)* is stored (fig. 8.11). These are used during a small house ritual observed in the evening of every new moon to maintain the power. Next, various ropes are hung: the long and strong plaited thongs of camel skin used when tying the camel loads and also for leading camels, and the heavy plaited sisal rope also used when tying camel loads. Sometimes a two-color twisted rope *(herar)* used to decorate the neck of the breeding camel bull is also hung at the back wall.

In those houses in which heads of lineages reside, one can also find, at the top of the back wall, a large spiral horn (*mahalole* = "greater kudu") blown to summon herds home for the *sorriyo* and *almodo* ceremonies and similar events. In the leading house of Wambile of the Dibsahai clan and a few others, one would find a more important ritual horn made of elephant tusk *(arab)*. Behind the cowskin lining at the back wall and invisible to the visitor, a few other ritual items are stored, notably the long, straight, smooth stick of dark hardwood *(gumo)* carved at the upper end into a phallic-shaped knob and used by males at ritual sacrifices. Also kept behind the cowskin lining, but only in the *iberre* houses, is a bundle of insignificant-looking thin, light sticks with a short fork at one end. These sticks are to the best of my knowledge not used in any ritual; they are just kept in the house to maintain the power of the curse in the family.

The left, northern side of the house is the wife's. Her sleeping place is the same as where she works during the day. The sleeping place for small children is next to her on the middle of the two roller mats and the cow hides. At the opposite end is the husband's "corner." They all sleep with their heads toward the skin wall and their feet toward the door. For the first week after childbirth, a woman will sleep in her husband's place and he in hers. Children sleep with their parents until they are seven or eight years old. Older children will sleep with a grandmother or another widowed relative. They can sleep in their mother's house until puberty, but only when the father is not there. Older men tend to sleep in the *naabo*, close to the camels.

The wife's sitting place in the house is to the left on entering, next to the fire and the cooking utensils. The husband and male guests will sit to the right on skins or on stools outside the skins. A woman would not sit on a man's stool. Female guests will sit on the floor skin near the wife's side. Women and girls will mostly sit in the house only when the man is not there, and the wife's mother will enter her daughter's house only if her son-in-law is not there, while a father of either husband or wife will sit on or next to the firewood. If there are warriors (other than their real brothers) present in the house, girls will leave the house.

When a woman gives birth, the situation is dramatically altered. Anne Beaman (1981:170–71) writes:

During the latter stages of labor, a woman moves over to her husband's side and the husband leaves. The woman gives birth on that side, toward the front of the house so as not to bloody the cowskins, and other women take charge of running the household from the wife's normal place by the fire. During a lying-in period of nine or ten days (depending on the moiety of the husband) the woman remains on the husband's side and the husband must find other sleeping quarters elsewhere. After that time, when a woman would have recovered enough from a normal birth to resume at least minimal household command, the debris of the birth and early infant care is burned, the brush under the *ilaal* is renewed, a general housecleaning is conducted, and the wife returns to her normal position in the house.

The reversal of functions of the spaces in the house is both practical and symbolic. Practically, while recovering from childbirth, a woman cannot effectively maintain full control of her household. By moving away from the fire, she leaves room for other women to cook, fumigate the milk containers, and perform other necessary household chores. Symbolically, by usurping her husband's space, she transforms the whole interior of the house into a female sphere, separating the practical female functions in childbearing from the ritual male functions that take place outside the house in conjunction with the same event.

Although the husband is considered head of household and has a real claim in the house as his residence, the interior of a Rendille house is essentially female territory. If a marriage breaks up before children are born, the husband takes back his bridewealth but the wife keeps the house. A husband cannot rightly send his wife out in order to have privacy to talk with men. Men who want to talk where there are no women must go somewhere else where there are no houses.

The differentiation between the feminine, domestic interior of the house and the exterior space is expressed through the seating arrangement of men and women outside their houses. Inside the house, females sit to the north and males to the south, but outside the order is reversed: a man and his male friends sit to the north of the door. The distinction between a domestic fire and a ritual fire is made the same way: inside, the fire is to the north of the door, but in the community circle of stones the fire is to the south of the entrance.

A NEW HOUSE

Among the Rendille, only a married woman can have a house.[6] A new house is therefore established as an essential part of the wedding ceremony. Indeed, the Rendille term for wedding or marriage is *min discho*, or "house building."

Although there are rare circumstances in which a woman may acquire a house without acquiring a husband, they are indeed rare, and a man cannot have a house without a wife. A widower, unless he is very old and helpless, can only maintain a home by remarrying. Similarly, I have seen one case where two grown-up daughters maintained their mother's house after both parents had died and until the time when they themselves could marry.

The verb "to marry" is synonymous with the verb "to build." The wedding ceremony takes place in the bride's camp over the span of a week. The preceding negotiations can sometimes be protracted and, in principle, involve the agreement of all the men of the two clans directly and quite often the women, but indirectly. Eventually a day will be agreed upon, and when the girl's mother has been notified, she will begin to prepare new milk containers, house components, and other artifacts required for the marriage. The bride-to-be may be away herding goats and sheep and may not know about her forthcoming marriage until the last moment.

The first stage of the ceremony is the journey *(gurro)* of the groom and his party to the bride's camp: the women drive a camel loaded with house parts and containers of milk for their own needs, while the men bring some of the camels of the bridewealth *(guno)*. All should arrive at the main approach on the western side of the bride-to-be's encampment on a Friday after sunset. *Gurro* is also the name of a clan-specific song with words composed for the occasion, mainly in praise of the groom, which is sung by the women en route and at the ceremony. A symbolic procession from the groom's camp to the house of the bride's mother is repeated three times: late on Friday night, again on Saturday night, and finally on Sunday morning after the circumcision of the bride *(khandi)*. This clitoridectomy, which transforms the bride from a girl into a woman, takes place, just like giving birth, on the husband's side in her mother's house. After the clitoridectomy, the groom presents the bride's mother with the "ewe of the back of the house" *(suben-ti-min-dubis)*. This ewe is tied to the back framework of the house, while another ewe is sacrificed by the bride's father.

After the third procession, a site is chosen for the bride's new house (just like any other newcomer to the community) immediately outside the mother's house, where the daughter will later fit into the line behind her mother. A small goat *(galmorsi)* is sacrificed on the spot. The men gather in front of the bride's mother's house to pray for the bride and the marriage, to drink tea, to receive tobacco, and to oil their heads and their herding sticks. Inside the house, friends congratulate the bride, the women begin to undo the beads she has worn as a girl, and construct the fiber necklace signifying her married status *(bukhurcha)* (see fig. 8.5).

Then the mother's house is dismantled and the bride is left sitting there, covered only by a few sticks, skins, and mats, until the house is rebuilt around her on a smaller scale after her own new house has been completed. The large group of women, working to-

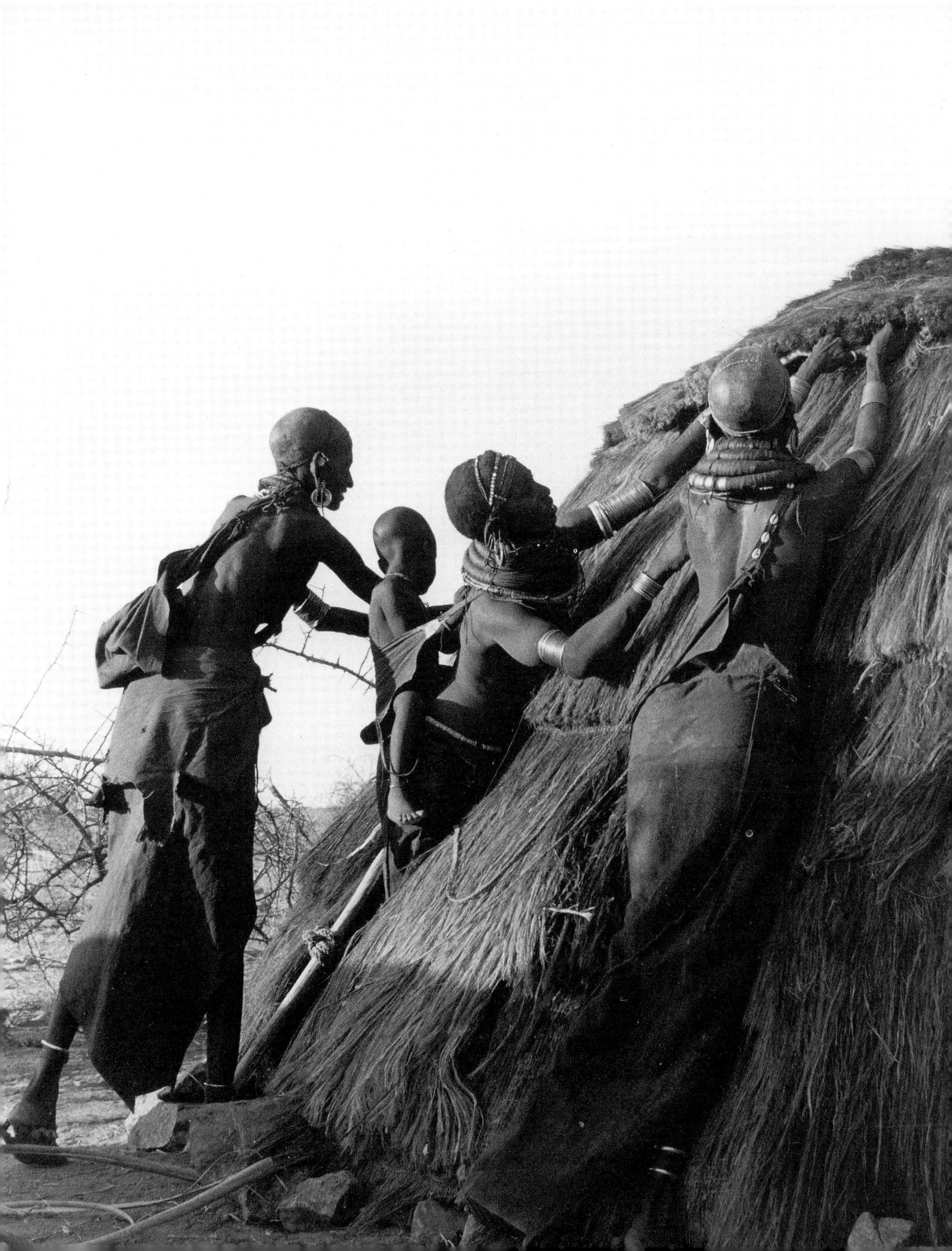

gether in high spirits and with much discussion, carry the available sticks to the new site, sort them according to category and quality, and begin to construct the bride's new "white house" *(min-ki-dakhan)* as carefully and perfectly as they can (fig. 8.12). Meanwhile the men build a thorn fence around it, setting it apart from the other houses.

At the same time, elders representing the two clans gather in two groups a little apart from each other, on the ground outside the fenced camp, to reach agreement on the details of the bridewealth. Although four female and four male camels are the prescribed number for all Rendille marriages, the quality, age, and condition of each animal has yet to be agreed upon. A message-bearer, his head covered and with a green twig from one of the trees used for blessings (*gaer* or *gey kuku*) in hand, walks between the two groups and reports the offer of the groom's family to the bride's group: "As God has heard and the earth has heard, they offer you a gray six-year-old." One offer may be accepted, then one or two may be refused. When the negotiators speaking for the bride's camp feel that acceptable offers are not forthcoming promptly enough, they will signal the women who are working on the new house to pull it all down again. "Forget that marriage!" With great excitement, the house can go up and down several times before agreement on the bridewealth is reached and the house is completed.

That night the bride and groom enter the house for the first time. From the bride's mother's house they walk slowly in single file, accompanied by a woman friend and the groom's "best man." The bride wears her mother's leather ceremonial cape *(okko)*, carries her ritual milk container *(dubbisso)* on her back like she would carry a baby, and has a small stone mortar *(gindot)* under her arm. In the house she will sit down on the skin in the southeastern quadrant, the spot that will later be her husband's sleeping place. The groom gives her a string of red and white beads, the "beads of the camel bull" *(irti-ti-or)*, and as a sign of acceptance she wears the necklace until the birth of her first child, after which it is cut up and used in necklaces for children.

The groom and his best man kindle two fires in a sandal with fire-sticks: one for the inside hearth and the other for a fire outside, northwest of the door *(dab-i-birnan)*. Here a male camel calf *(nyirakh-i-birnam)* is sacrificed after it has been driven around the new house four times. The cooked meat is given to other people, while the skin, bones, and other remains are completely burned. But the groom still cannot sleep in the house. Only the bride and her unmarried girl friends will sleep there.

Two days after the building of the new house (on a Tuesday), a goat *(wahar okko)* is sacrificed in front of the new house and the groom offers cooked meat to his in-laws in a small ceremony formally establishing affinal relations. The bride's new ceremonial leather cape is prepared from the skin of the goat. This sacrifice also occasions the completion of the house: the milk containers (*madhal* and *gigo*) may now be hung along the back wall, and the water containers may be brought in.

Afterwards, the groom's wedding party breaks camp, packs up, and heads for home. At that point, the bride moves from her husband's sleeping place to her own and the groom may now sleep inside the house. However, the marriage still cannot be consummated, and the "best man" will sleep there with him. Only when the women of the bride's family are satisfied that she has recovered from her wounds (ideally, seven days after the circumcision) will the consummation of the marriage be sanctioned by the sacrifice of "the ram of the cloth" *(helim-ki-dafaret)*.

The newlyweds and their house usually remain in the wife's *goob* for some time. Some couples may stay for years, a few may remain there for life, but most will move to the husband's camp and settle with his family either when the wife is pregnant or just after the birth of her first child. The husband must offer a large, fattened ox-camel *(dufaan)* for sacrifice. The fat is rendered into an oil which is then daubed onto the roof mats. On this special move, one pack camel will be especially loaded so that the wife may ride it. It is one of the rare occasions when a Rendille would ride a camel.

Fig. 8.12. The final touches being put on the bride's new house.

GAALORA AND ODOOLA HOUSES

The overall appearance of the Gaalora and Odoola houses does not differ much from the houses of other Rendille clans. These two variant types of houses are just as portable and, when covered with the same roof mats, appear almost the same. Only few differences can be observed, but the structural principles are quite different in some essential respects (fig. 8.13a–c). There is quite strong evidence that the Odoola and the Gaalora were adopted into Rendille society toward the end of the sixteenth century and the middle of the eighteenth century respectively.[7]

Whereas the standard house has two arched frames *(khokhabe)*, the Gaalora house has only a front frame; whereas all the front poles *(lallaabo)* of the typical Rendille house are straight and slant forward, only the two door posts of a Gaalora house are straight. The others are curved like the back poles. In the Gaalora house, the roof ribs curve down as a back wall and at the bottom are lashed to small stakes driven into the ground.

The Gaalora subclan is often called Amomisa, a term that may derive from the small piece of woven sisal their women place above the door *(amomisa)*. This woven piece, serving neither ritual nor decorative purpose, is merely a sign that no man may enter the house.

Although the exterior of the Odoola house is not easily distinguished from the other Rendille houses, it differs considerably in both plan and structure. The plan is more like a rectangle with rounded corners. Instead of being arched, the front frame consists of two long sticks that rest on the ground at the corners and meet above the doorway. Together with four straight poles, the front frame supports a crossbar. Two of the poles form the doorway, which is narrow at the bottom and widest just above shoulder height. While very convenient for a person passing through it, this profile does not accommodate the door skins so well as the standard house does. The rest of the structure is then made up of thinner bent sticks *(utub* and *ogosyneey)*.

The most surprising difference between the Odoola house and the typical Rendille house is that the inter-

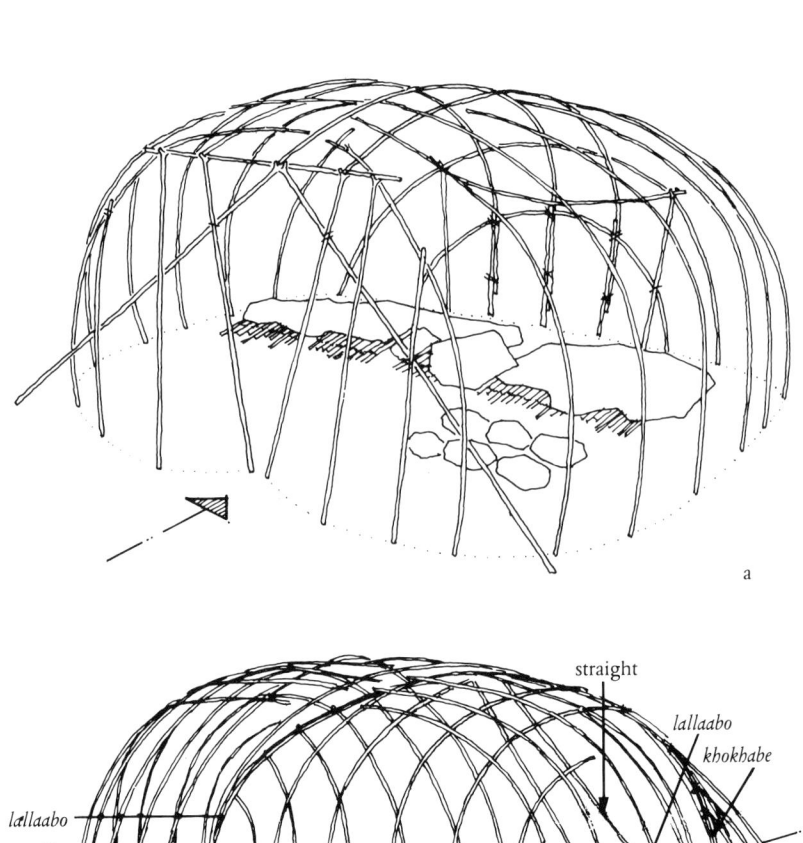

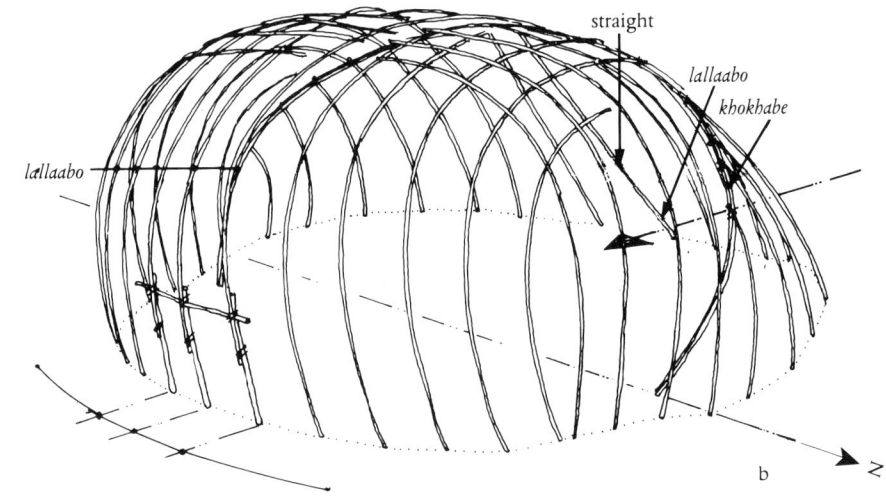

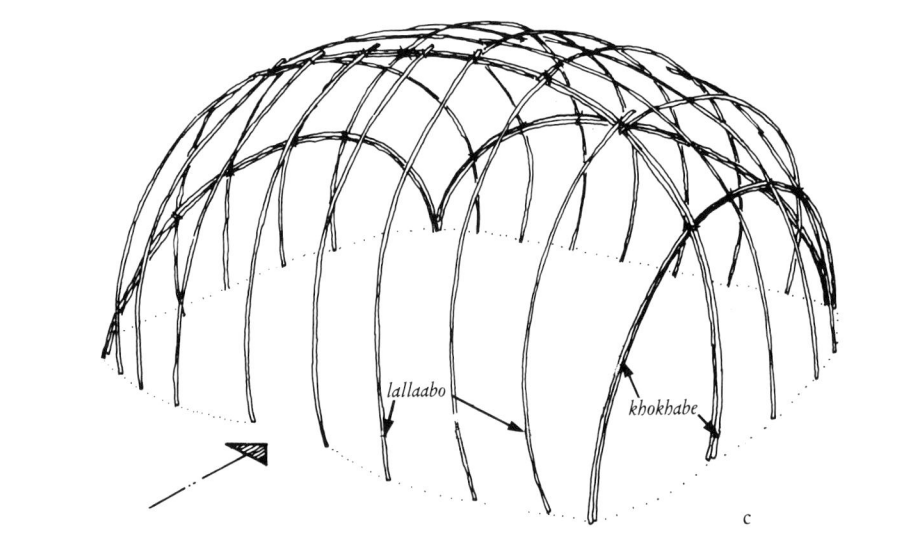

166 African Nomadic Architecture

d

Fig. 8.13. a. An Odoola house with the curved front and the two slanting supports sticking out. b. A Gaalora house seen from the back. c. Framework of a mourning house. d. The *min-ki-meerat*, a temporary shelter for a warrior who has killed an enemy.

nal plan of the former is a mirror image of the latter. The arrangement of outside spaces and the place of the sacrifice in front of the Odoola house is also reversed so that it is identical to the organization of Gabra space (see fig. 2.15).

OTHER HOUSE VARIATIONS

The large, beautifully constructed house of a newly-wed woman may deteriorate and shrink in size over the years, and some of the roof mats may be replaced with cardboard, metal sheeting, and plastic materials. However, many women maintain their full-size houses with pride and regularly replace deteriorating sticks, mats, and other components until their husbands die and their youngest daughters have married. Thereafter, the house is gradually reduced to a very small structure, a widow's house *(rekkey)* which no longer has to conform to standard shape and construction.

If a woman dies before her husband, he will soon remarry and the deceased wife's house is maintained by the new wife. However, when a husband dies before his wife, her house is dismantled and it is reassembled somewhat differently for the month of mourning. The main arches are used as three low back and side arches, crossing at a low level. It resembles a traditional Oromo house, although much lower. With curved sticks forming the entrance, it becomes, however, a tatty, spineless, low, oblong structure, about the same area as a normal house and equally covered with roof sticks and roof mats. After the purification ceremonies and the headshaving of mourners, it is reassembled into its standard structural form.

Occasionally, an even more miserable widow's house may be seen, maintained by a warrior with no living parents. It stands as a symbolic representation of his mother's house, only to provide him with a site for the sacrifice that is so important for the well-being of a family's camels.

Every fourteen years, guided by an unwritten but well-functioning calendar, a new age set of young men is initiated into manhood and warriorhood by

Fig. 8.14. Breaking camp and loading of a pack camel.

circumcision. Each clan and settlement performs the ceremony for its group of initiates. At dawn, they gather in a shade structure *(gaim)* made of branches and leaves, some sixty meters west of the encampment. The young men, stripped of all their ornaments, wear only a blackened goatskin around their loins. Each initiate, in order of lineage seniority, sits on a large boulder in front of the shade structure and is firmly held from behind and by each leg. After a successful operation, the initiate is offered gifts of camels. Only when satisfied with the gifts will the initiate leave the stone and return to rest in the shade of the structure.

Later in the day, the women will construct a "white house" *(min-ki-dakhan)* in which the initiates will recover and spend a month. In 1979 the circumcisions at Goob Wambile were postponed for some days, and although all the preparations were witnessed, I had to leave two days prior to the scheduled circumcision and therefore was unable to witness the ceremony or the building of the "white house."

However, Anne Beaman (1981:455), who was able to witness that of Goob Kimogol of the Sahle clan, noted that "the form of the *min-ki-dakhan* is essentially like that of an ordinary Rendille house, except that, as it must be big enough to provide sleeping space for all the initiates, it is somewhat taller, and perhaps quite a bit broader than an ordinary house." She notes further that "the broader the *min-ki-dakhan*, the more likely it will require vertical poles to support the span." The structure described to me by Kawab Bulyar from his own circumcision in 1965 was probably made to accommodate a larger number of initiates. Consequently it had more vertical supports, and it must, as a structure, have been further removed from the ordinary Rendille house.[8]

Over time, the Rendille have had to defend their territory and their livestock against human predators, and occasionally a Rendille warrior will kill an enemy. The killer *(meerat)* will be celebrated as a hero, but at the same time he is ritually impure, cannot touch the camels or his lover, and cannot enter a family house. Until the purification ritual (which occurs a month later), he will spend his time wandering in the bush, composing and singing the epic "song of the killer" *(gei-meerat)*. At night he will visit one camp after another, a goat will be slaughtered in his honor, and a small wigwam-shaped structure *(min-ki-meerat)* will be erected for him by the women at nightfall (fig. 8.13d). Constructed of the same poles normally used in loading camels *(lallaabo)* and covered with a few mats, it is very rarely seen because it is dismantled early the next morning.

With the camel as a large pack animal, the Rendille are highly mobile. When the pastures are about to be exhausted, the elders will begin talks about the next move and scouts will be sent to investigate potential new grazings. After days of discussion, a day and a place are finally agreed upon and the elders hurry back to tell their wives.

The next morning the women are up before dawn and, assisted by their daughters, dismantle the houses and load them on the camels (fig. 8.14). The components that make up a house and its contents also make up two camel loads. The *khokhabe* are again the main frames of the camel load. Tied to the sides of the camel, they curve up and meet high in the air. In the space between them are packed the *utube,* the *lallaabo,* the rolls of *dhulbenye* and *ilaal,* topped by the high cone of the *khodad.* In front are hung various milk containers, the large *haan*s, and the *dhiri* cooking pot in its *enjel.* At times a space is made in front of the load for a child to ride should it be too young to walk, or a very old or sick person to be transported. Otherwise the Rendille would only ride a camel on the special occasion when a bride is moving with her husband to his *goob* for the first time.

In just over two hours an entire camp is on the move, and by mid-afternoon camels and people will be resting forty kilometers from where they woke up the same morning. If the move is longer, camels will be unloaded and given some hours to feed, people will sleep in the open, and the move will continue the following morning. Before sunset a "village" of two to three hundred people will be reestablished, the women will have built their houses, and the men will have fenced the animals.

9
HANDICRAFTS OF THE SOMALI NOMADIC WOMEN

Arlene Fullerton and Amina Adan

The Somali Democratic Republic, Africa's easternmost country, juts out into the Gulf of Aden and the Indian Ocean, producing the sharp angle of the Horn of Africa.[1] The climate of hot temperature throughout the year, strong winds, and sparse rainfall is reflected in the terrain, particularly in the large stretches of northern and central rangelands, which consist primarily of semi-arid and arid plateaus and plains.[2] It is a terrain for nomadic pastoralists, who make up about half of the population (see location map).

In this semidesert, the Somalis have developed a portable house *(aqal)* that is in complete harmony with its environment.[3] The land may look barren and hostile, but it contains all the necessary material for the portable house and its contents. It is a brilliant illustration of the economic use of limited resources—an invention forced by the conditions of life and totally Somali in character. Yet the ingenious skill that produces these crafts has been rather neglected by foreign scholars and taken for granted at home.[4]

The reasons for this neglect are built into the very nature of Somali society. In this nomadic society, there is a particularly sharp division of labor by gender.[5] The women are responsible for the house and nearly everything in it, from the covering of the house to the smallest milk pot within. They have little time to think of their work as "art," as they are too busy supplying the necessities of shelter. Their craft is all part of their housework, and (as women the world over know) housework is never admired or appreciated on its own but only negatively noticed when it ceases to be done.

It was poetry, recitation, and rhetoric, rather than handicrafts, that had long been recognized as the main art forms in Somali nomadic life. I. M. Lewis (1981:38–39) wrote that "Somalis attach great importance to oratory and poetry. It is in these fields rather than in the plastic arts, which are little developed, that Somali culture's most impressive achievements are to be found. This corresponds to the nomadic bias of a people used to travelling light with few material encumbrances—but a richly compensating gift of language." Oral poetry was committed to memory by poetry reciters and listeners in general and passed on faithfully word for word, with credit given to the poet, so that even today the poems of the past can be collected, collated, and translated into other languages. It must be remembered that poetry was largely the domain of men, though women were not entirely excluded from certain genres such as the *buraambur*.[6]

A decidedly male bias comes through in the above reference to a 1978 UNESCO and UNICEF report. Arte (1978:16) writes that "to the nomad, poetry is the most important art and much time is spent composing new poems and reciting the age-old ones that have been passed on. . . . Arts and Crafts among the Somali nomads centre on woodcarving: camel bells, wooden spoons, forks, dishes, walking sticks, etc." It is interesting that the arts and crafts of which the author speaks is woodcarving, the one and only craft executed by men. There is no

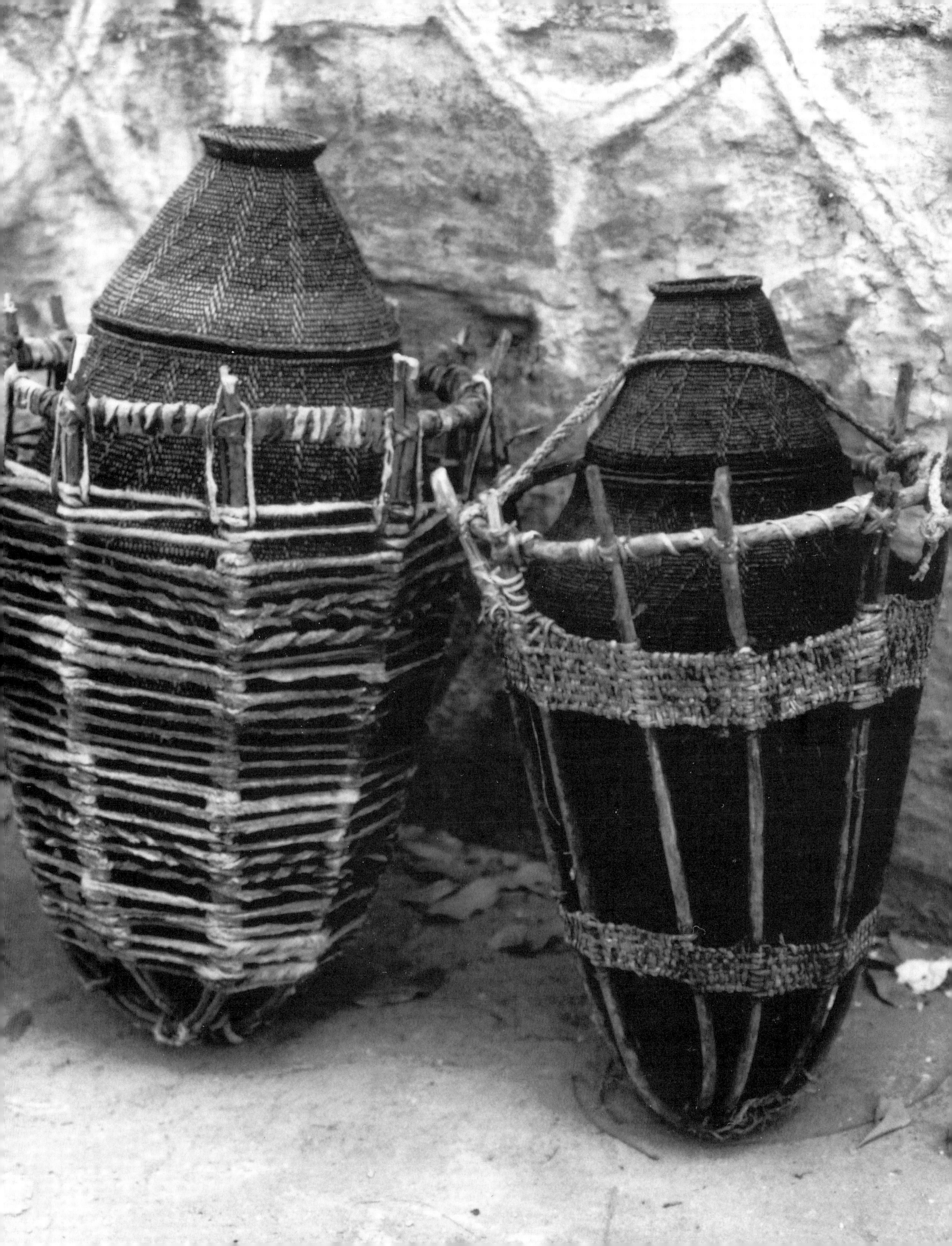

mention of the house and all the woven items created by the women.

Lastly, when examining the reasons why Somali crafts have been generally overlooked in the West, we must remember the extraordinary popularity and interest in dramatic carvings, such as ceremonial, celebratory, and ritual masks found in other parts of Africa. These objects are alien to a nomadic Muslim society and play no role in Somali life. Therefore there exists a general assumption made by visitors that there is little of visual interest in Somalia. As a result, there has been virtually no real foreign excitement over the traditional Somali handicrafts created by women nor among an indigenous population that sees these as merely an extension of housework.

Once ubiquitous, these crafts are now fast disappearing. As one tours the country, one finds portable houses covered with canvas or plastic sheeting instead of traditional woven grasses. In the Hargeisa market, it is possible to find rows of brightly painted large water containers for sale in their traditional shape, but made out of metal instead of woven fiber. Also, the familiar yellow plastic quart oil containers can be found sitting in the baskets (*saabs*), instead of the woven milk pots (*aagaans*) for which the baskets were originally made.[7] This evidence points to an accessibility and availability of new materials which are easy to obtain. Also, a certain amount of urban expansion and correlated urbanization and resettlement are taking place, hence these heavy metal water containers which could only be used in more permanent dwellings, situated close to a reliable water supply. Somalia is undergoing many changes very quickly, and this is also reflected in the life-style of its nomadic population.

This chapter will highlight the nomadic handicrafts created by women in Somali society and focus attention on their merits. We will examine the *aqal*, its construction, coverings *(saari)*, and decoration *(qurxin)*, and then look at some of the smaller household items *(gurgur)*, the things that can be picked up, and some of the ceremonies that are connected with a few of these items. These handicrafts are all part of the work women have been doing for generations along with their daily chores of child rearing, cooking, herding the smaller animals, retrieving firewood, washing, and cleaning, to name but a few.

THE *AQAL*

The portable nomadic house, which in Somali is known as an *aqal*, is a hemispherical dome 1.5–2.13 m in height, and constructed of three component parts: semicircular shaped poles that give it its strength and form, vertical poles used for reinforcement, and layers of woven mats made of grass and acacia fibers used for covering and decoration. All three are tied together as an intricate web to form a strong impermeable package (pl. 20). This portable house is of female construction and execution. It is the gift of the mother and female side of the bride's family, and each female has the responsibility of mounting and dismounting her house for each move, maintaining and repairing its component parts, and eventually providing additional portable houses for her own daughters or womenfolk.[8]

The *aqal* takes its shape from the curved poles generically known as *dhigo*, which can be divided into two types depending on the thickness and function required. *Qabax*, the thicker curved poles, are the main structural supports of the house; *lool* are the thinner curved poles that have no structural function on their own, but rather help to implement the shape and help hold the coverings tightly in place.

The *qabax* are obtained from the roots of the acacia tree. There are many known species of acacia growing in Somalia, but the ones most used for this purpose are the Acacia nilotica *(maraar)*, Acacia bussei *(galool)*, Acacia mellifera *(bilcil)*, and Acacia spirocarpa *(qudhac)*.[9] To get the root, the women dig as far as their elbow in depth, to the point where they can locate several roots of the tree. They never touch the main foundation root, as it is far too deep and its removal would destroy the tree itself, but they use instead the lesser roots of, say twelve meters, which are cut, removed, and straightened out. To give these roots the curved shape of the *qabax,* they are warmed, without being burned, by warm ash and bent to the desired shape. This is done by attaching the roots between

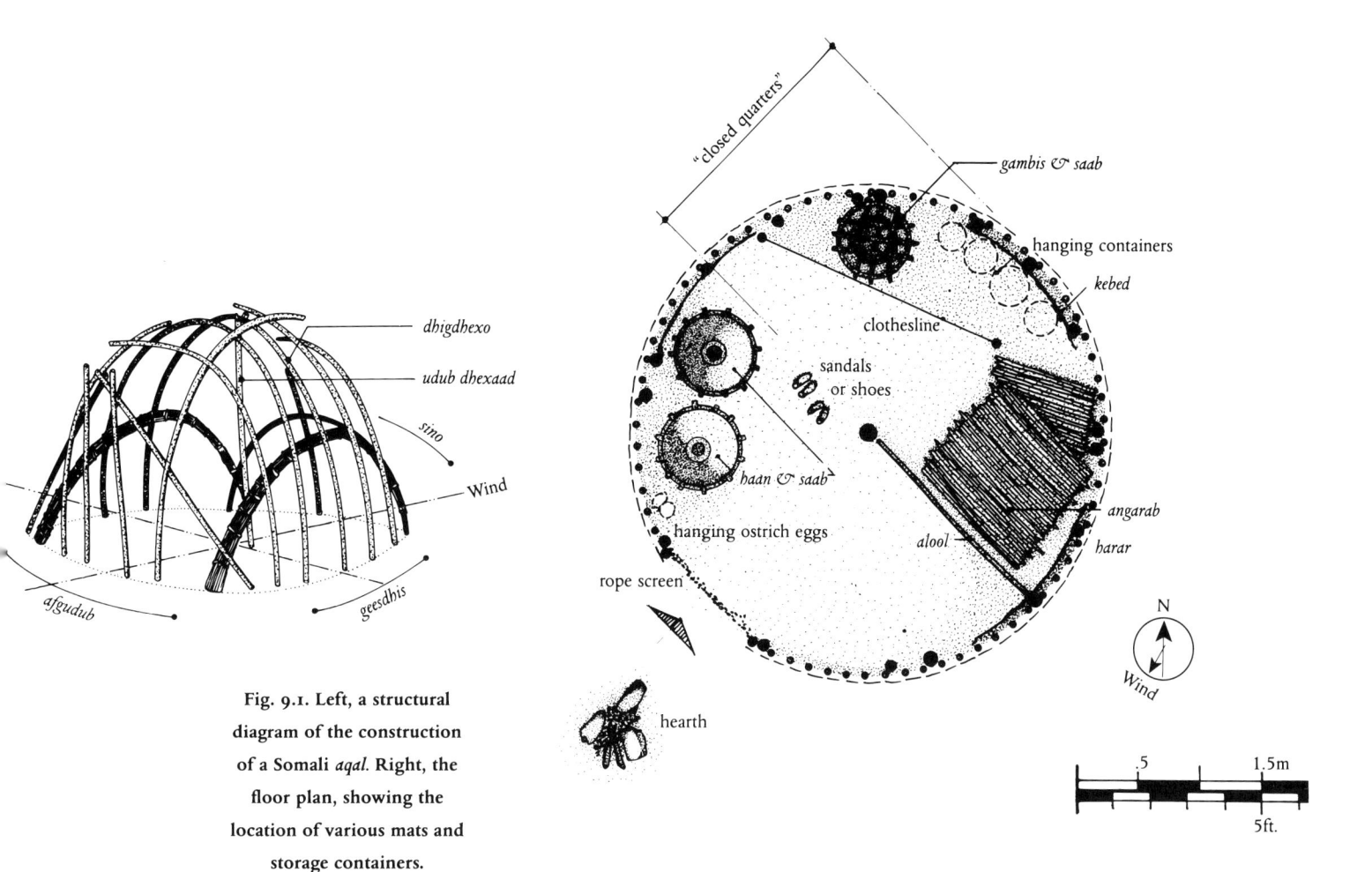

Fig. 9.1. Left, a structural diagram of the construction of a Somali *aqal*. Right, the floor plan, showing the location of various mats and storage containers.

two poles firmly anchored to the ground. Using hot metal and ash, the roots are kept warm in this curved position for one week. After the week, these newly arched roots are treated with a solution of the bark of the acacia tree *(asal)*, which protects them against termites, and they are then bound with the twine of goat or camel leather *(jill)*, and ready for use. The thicker bent poles should last from ten to twenty years, depending on the type of tree and the maintenance.

The use of specific names for each *qabax* reiterates the importance they have for the nomad (fig. 9.1). The rear of the house is known as *sino*; the entrance or mouth is called *afgudub*; the sides, *geesdhis*; and over the top of the house, in the center between the sides, are *dhigdhexo*, which have to be very, very strong. The house is constructed in the above order. When erecting it, the women start with the rear poles, that is, the *sino*. The holes for this must be dug as deep as one's mid-arm, about 45 cm, and salt or myrrh are put in the holes to keep away the termites. Then lots of pebbles are packed in around the pole to give it added strength, and the poles are pounded with a hammer or large stone before the sand is returned to fill the hole. The *qabax* must be strong enough to stand on its own and not fall; it must withstand the vigorous shaking of the women who try to test its strength. After the rear section is in place, the process is repeated with the entrance and the sides.

Handicrafts of the Somali Nomadic Women

There are no exact number of key, heavier poles required. One source said seven were needed for a basic house; another said eight; others said twelve were required for a good, respectable size.[10] The remaining poles are then used to form a network and strengthen the structure.

In addition to the heavier bent poles, tall vertical poles (*udub*s) are used to support the framework of the house. The number of vertical poles may vary between seven and twelve, and they too are planted firmly into the ground. The most important is the center pole *(udub dhexaad)*. The others are placed near the end of the primary bentwood armature to shore up each side, and again, against any particular weak point of the house. The *udub* is also used to partition the house.

Lastly, to complete the house skeleton, the thinner *dhigo*s or the curved poles *(lool)* are used to fill out the hemispherical shape and keep the covering mats taut. *Lool* is made from a thin reed-like rod *(duur)* which is quite flexible when newly cut. The pieces of reed are tied together with leather string in bundles of three to a *lool* and easily shaped when moistened and bent between the rocks into the required arc. These thinner curved members do not go into the ground; their whole purpose is to close the gaps between the poles so that the woven mats do not cave into the dome. They go over or under the heavier poles in both directions so that, as one looks through the armature within the house, one sees small square holes between the lines of poles; the smaller the separations between the curves, the better. There are usually not less than twenty *lool*s. They are then securely tied to the heavier bent members and the tall, vertical poles, and care must be taken that each component is tied firmly to the other.

All the work described could be done by two or three women, or a maximum of four; but to do it alone is extremely hard work. When the frame of the house is thus completed, it is ready to be covered.

COVERINGS *(SAARI)*

It is from the coverings *(saari)* of the house that the talents of the womenfolk are clearly visible. The coverings have a double function: utilitarian and decorative. The several kinds of weaving used will be described below.

Caws, the generic name for all grasses, has also come to refer to the large woven mats used as covering for the house, particularly in the north; it is also known as *harrar* or *raar*, depending on the region of the country. The best grass used for this purpose is *maadh*. The grass is woven in packets 6–7 cm thick and 25–30 cm long. These packets of grass form the vertical or "warp" line of traditional weaving and are reinforced every 10 cm of length with a new row of grass packets, inserted from the back so skillfully that from the front it gives the illusion that the mat is woven from lengths of very long grass. As each new row is introduced, a fringe or overhang of about 10 cm is allowed in the back, giving the reverse an appearance of layer upon layer of thatch. This endows the mat with its ingenious quality and dual function: within, it enriches the wall and ceiling with decorative surfaces, and on the exterior, its thatched texture is a protective covering, impervious to wind, sand, and rain.

The weft or crosswise thread woven under and over the grass packets is made of sisal or acacia fiber. These fibers were often dyed with natural dyes and abstract designs thus produced. More recently, imported wools are replacing the naturally dyed fibers.

There are several well-known names for *caws* design, but these tend to refer to the amount of decoration rather than to the specific pattern. For example, an all-over pattern that covers the *harrar* from corner to corner is known as *iskujoog*, and is usually the most intricate and highly valued *caws* (fig. 9.2a). *Goo* means to divide, and the name *googoos* refers to an overall pattern that is divided at regular intervals by bands of plain or undecorated *caws*. A mat with narrow horizontal strips of design is known by the number of these strips. Thus *saddexle* is one with three bands, *lixle* is one with six bands of design, and *toddobaale* one with seven bands. There are never more than seven bands in this type of design. The white one *(caasha cad)* is the *caws* left plain with no design.

In an attempt to further isolate and identify specific patterns used in weaving, the authors showed a series of slides to several women from different regions. There was general agreement on the most common

Fig. 9.2. a. Section of a *harrar* with an *iskujoog* pattern. Drawing after a photograph. b. *Harrar* with a *sinjab* pattern. c. *Kebed* with a *jeedalley* pattern.

patterns (fig. 9.2b). For example, *qardhaas* referred to designs of square or diamond shapes; *sinjab*, which means leaning from one side to the other, referred to patterns of zigzag lines or chevron shapes; *ganuun* refers to depth, as may be felt when looking down a well, and is translated into design as a vertical series of diamond shapes placed one on top of the next; and *indho daalis*, which literally means "tiring eyes," referred to the dazzling effect of alternating bars of black and white. The whole area of design would certainly make a fascinating future study, but one would need to collect systematically many more examples of design from all the regions of Somalia and interview many more women.

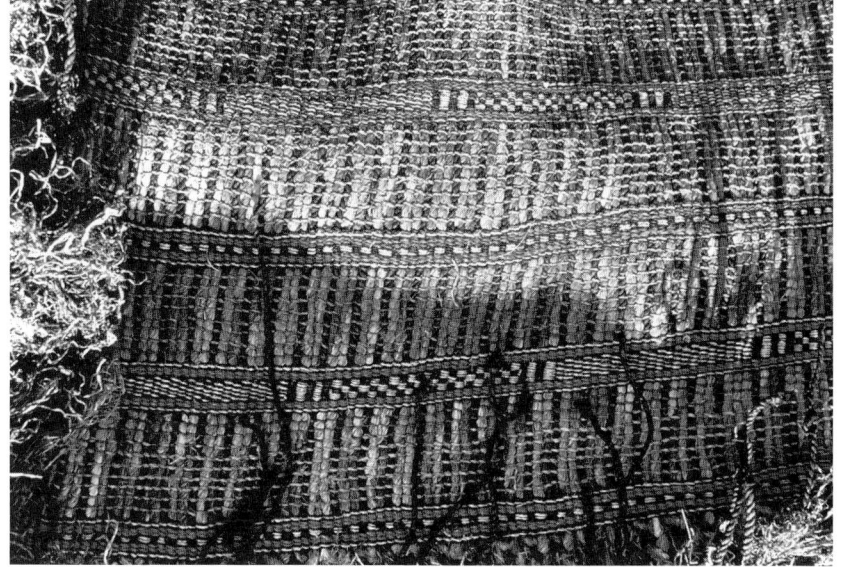

Harrar vary in size. A typical measurement might be about 4.5 m wide and 1.75 m long, but they could be considerably larger or smaller. The work is done by a mother for her daughter, or a woman for herself, perhaps with the help of another family member. It takes at least a month to complete, sometimes much longer.

The mat is finished off by braiding the top fringe of grass and is an occasion for celebration. This ceremony of plaiting is called *tidic*. The young unmarried girls are invited in the evening to finish off the *harrar*, which is not a very arduous task, but rather a social event. The girls sing and show off their skills and cleverness at reciting or inventing additional verses. Often one of the boys might try to disguise himself as a girl, perhaps with the aid of a female relative, and to attempt to break into the female ranks and "crash" the ceremony by joining the girls in song. If they discover him, he is ridiculed and thrown out. But if he is not discovered until the ceremony is over, there is shame on these girls for their lack of feminine intuition. In several of the nomadic ceremonies, cunning, intuitiveness, and quickness of mind are attributes that are rewarded with favor. It is these very qualities that may mean survival for the nomads during hard times.

A lot of work, as well as dreams, go into the making of the *harrar* mats. This is hinted at in one of the most famous *caws* songs. As in many work songs, the chorus alternates with the stanzas, and the girls take it in turn to invent new verses.[11]

Chorus: *Aay hooyalaayow hooyal*

Cawdibele belloy baydhay
Cawra daran ka Yaasiin
In sharle ba sharkood moog

Chorus

Cawskanow sabool diidow
Waqan suuqa lagu dhigin
Yaa sameeyey lagu odhan

Chorus

Geesi geel keenaa
Gaari samaysaa
Googoos loogu daahaa

(The chorus is made up of sounds rather like "ee aye ee aye oh," as found in "Old MacDonald's Farm.")

Let evil abandon us
Let us be protected by the *Yaasiin* (a Koranic verse invoking protection)
Let our hearts ignore evil
My lovely *caws* rejects the poor man
It will never be sold
It is for a brave lad who brings camels
It is for an elegant lady.

In the first verse, evil can be avoided by the recitation of the Koranic verse and by emptying one's mind of all evil or bad thoughts. In the second verse, the mat is personified and given the power to reject a poor man, which is in keeping with the wishes of the young girl herself. She also makes a promise to the mat, never to sell it, as that would be a desperate act and would signify extreme poverty. The last verse reserves the mat, and by implication the girl herself, for a brave man with lots of camels for the brideprice, which would reflect well on both the girl and her gallant suitor.

Like the *harrar*, the *kebed* is also a covering for the house. More than just having a decorative and protective function, it is the most celebrated item made by Somali women, occasioned by a forthcoming wedding. *Kebed* making is the most solemn and important preparation of the betrothal.[12] This interior mat is one of the "fine" things in a nomadic household. Placed at either the side or the back of the house, it is looked upon as a painting or as a piece of art.

The *kebed*, similar in size to other mats, is made of fibers from the Acacia bussei tree, a tree of great importance and poetic significance to the nomad.[13] To remove the fibers, a branch is cut and stripped of its thorns and thick bark, and the white fibrous tissue inside is chewed until softened and broken down into strands of individual fiber. It is known that while chewing the women will not have dysentery. As one can imagine, it is a slow, laborious procedure to get enough acacia fiber to complete the *kebed*.

As with the other mats, the new rows of acacia fiber are introduced from the back, and an overhang of layers of fiber serves the same protective purpose. Because the material is fiber, rather than grass, the reverse is more shaggy and springy in appearance, instead of the strawlike thatch found on the back of the *caws*.

Kebed designs generally follow the patterns used in the manufacture of *caws,* but there are two patterns of design reserved exclusively for it: *baraley* and *jeedalley*. *Baraley* ("the one with dots") traditionally alternates large distinct leopard dots *(barshabeel)* with narrower, insignificant "disordered" ones *(quban)*. Between them are vertical line dividers *(kabaal),* which are like the wooden poles. The *jeedalley* ("one with the whip design") refers to very narrow horizontal strips of design alternating with plain bands (fig. 9.2c). Formerly, only naturally dyed fibers were used for the weft, but in recent years there has been an introduction of colored wools here too.

The *kebed* is not made by one or two women alone; it is a communal effort marked by a festive ceremony. The owner of the *kebed* will start it and will invite others to join her only after she has completed the width she needs (perhaps 3–4 m) and about a handspan of the length. She must have all her materials ready, the fiber in bundles, the dye colors already prepared, and enough food and drink to feed her "army" of workers. The mat is tied between two poles, and the weaving continues on consecutive days until it is completed. It might take eight to ten women three to five days to complete. But it is a planned and organized event, one that they need to get consent for. For example, it must be arranged so that it will not interfere with the packing and migration of the family. If the other women accept, they are committed to see the project through. They usually work a large part of the day, certainly afternoons, and leave their own family chores to others. The women think of *kebed* making as cementing the bonds of sisterhood, as perhaps men might think of war as uniting them in a brotherhood. There is much singing and laughter, which makes the work lighter.

Below are two *kebed* songs, recorded by the authors. The first illustrates the mat's dual function of beauty and protection from the elements.

Baranbarshaalley, buul shareeraay
Ma maataan bah kuu helay
   (and repeat)
Geedba, Geedka u dheer laga garaacyeey

Galool mudhay mullax looga diiryeey
   (and repeat)
Naagaan daahaaga ridan docodalooleey
Wan loo dilay dugaag gurayeey
   (and repeat)
Aqalaan jirin jiiddooy
Jabtooy jawdu waaroob.
   (and repeat these two lines, then the first two).

You with your delighted designs, enhance my house
   as a cover
Today I have sisters to aid me
From the tallest tree your fiber comes
You are the fiber of the highest *galool*
The woman without you in her house
Her slaughtered animals will be eaten by the beasts
She tries to pull a nonexistent curtain
Hark, certainly the thunder is the sound of rain.

The first four lines, spoken to the *kebed* itself, are praising its beauty, its use as a cover, and even its origins from the very highest acacia. But we are reminded that it is accomplished with the help of a sisterhood. The last four lines tell of the dire straits a woman without such a mat could find herself in. Without it, a woman has little protection from the wild animals that would devour the family food or from the harsh weather such as thunder and rain.

The second song is from the point of view of the women helpers:

Saaxil laga keenyayeey
Wada susuureey
Siyaab aqalka loo saaryeey
Korankor cunimaynoo karibamaynee
Karuur geel ma la hayaa

It is from Saaxil
It is a beauty all round
With astonishment, a delight, we put it up on the
   side of the house
We can't eat grains, they are tough
Provide us with the sour milk of camels.

In the first three lines, the women are admiring their exquisite handiwork, which astonishes the whole community with its beauty, once it is placed on the side of the house. *Saaxil* was the old name for Berbera, and its implication for the nomad was that of an important place where exotic imports could be found. It would be like saying something came from London or Paris. In the last two lines, the women tease the owner of the mat and complain about the food she has provided for them.

Each house requires a number of both types of mats. The smallest house *(buul)* may have six or fewer *harrar*s, but the largest house with two domes, formerly used especially for weddings *(labo daryaal)*, had at least twelve.[14] The *harrar* and the *kebed* are the only types of coverings used for the exterior and interior of the *aqal* respectively. The other coverings are for interior use only.

Considerable skill is also needed once the armature of the house has been erected, starting with the smallest and most decorative pieces, the *lammo* and *hohob*, then the decorative *kebed*s and *harrar*s, and finally working outward to the purely utilitarian coverings *(dulsaar)*, those old mats which have lost their beauty but are functional against the elements.[15] A woman must use her discretion and not overload her house. Lastly, she must secure her packaged container by tying these coverings to the bentwood arches and vertical poles at one end and go round the house, over the top and then to the other side of the entrance.

Some of the interior coverings are the *alool,* the *dermo,* the *gogol,* and the *hohob.* The *alool* (typically 4 m wide and 2 m high) serves primarily as a room partition and is sometimes hung in the doorway. It keeps out the wind and keeps the interior warm. Yet, because the weaving starts 8–10 cm from the ground, it allows for some ventilation. The only woven item used upright within the house, it is made of thin vertical reeds *(duur)* woven together with shreds of old clothes knotted together to form the crosswise weft string. There is no design to the screen, but it could be very colorful, depending on the shreds used.

Dermo are floor mats used for prayer, sleeping, or sitting. They are easily damaged and therefore not walked on with shoes. They are made by weaving palm leaves *(caw)* into long strips 7–8 cm wide and sewing the strips together one by one, depending on the required length. They have a short life, but are made rather quickly. There are some very beautiful ones of intricate design which are used exclusively for guests to sit on, but in towns they are of modest design, often left undecorated or with one or two colored strands woven through.

Gogol are primarily sleeping mats used either under the *dermo* if the ground is hard, or taken off and used by the men. They are woven of grass in a manner similar to the *harrar,* but are small enough to be used as a portable bed.

The *hohob,* also known as *xig,* is the only purely decorative item in the house and the most finely woven. It is one of the few luxuries and takes a lot of time to make. Because it is finely woven, it is the same on the reverse side, and there is no rough side. Made of sisal fibers, it is about the size of a *kebed* and is hung inside from the ceiling framework. Sometimes fabric is used instead.

To obtain the sisal fiber, the sisal leaves are cut and pounded with the addition of a little water. They are then buried in a deep hole for seven days, after which they are removed and washed in a river or stream. The green will have rotted and will wash away, leaving the white sisal fibers, which must be dried before using.

The natural dyes were beautiful and stark, if somewhat limited. There were no yellows or blues. The Somalis have no word for blue and speak of a black sea or black sky. The most frequently used colors are red, white, and black. The white was the color of the undyed sisal, the red dye comes from the bark of the acacia, and the black from a poisonous plant called *dacar.* To get the dye of the latter, a pile of leaves is cooked in water for twenty-four hours and allowed to steep further in this solution for six hours before the water is drained for use. It is now more common to find *hohob*s made with brightly imported dyes.

STORAGE THINGS

Like the *aqal* and its woven mats, storage vessels that hold the family's supply of water and milk are also made by women from local plants. The "storage things" *(kayd gurgur)* are probably the most important material possessions of a nomadic family in a parched, dry environment, and yet, incredibly, they too are made of woven fiber (pl. 21).

Most of these storage vessels are made from the stem of the *qabo* plant, a cactuslike euphorbia bush with dangerously sharp thorns 5 cm long, found primarily in the Haud. The fibers lie in the center of the stem, surrounded by the sticky white toxic substance found in all euphorbia. To obtain the fiber, the bush is burned quickly all over with a blazing stick until it changes color from green to brown. This destroys the thorns. It is then left for a day while the noxious sap drops to the ground. The stems are hacked open and the fibers drawn out and arranged in bundles of about fifteen strands of fiber to a bundle. These bundles are then plaited for easier storage and transportation. The euphorbia can thus be kept for at least a year or two, if protected from insects and pests. When using it, the fibers are immersed in water to make them flexible. Although Drysdale (1954:3) wrote that the labor of collecting the fibers usually falls on the young men, but the task of weaving the fibers into milk or water vessels is left to their dextrous womenfolk, some of the women interviewed more recently said they themselves were responsible for obtaining, as well as plaiting, the fibers.

The largest container *(haan)* made from this euphorbia bush is used for fetching and storing water (fig. 9.3). An average water container holds between thirty and thirty-four liters of water, and usually four such *haan*s make up a full camel load, with two balanced on each side. The container is an elongated oval shape, its widest girth slightly above the middle of the vessel, narrowing gently to the bottom and the top. On the top of it sits an inverted bowl-shaped lid *(aagaan "ka")* which, when properly tied on with a special leather string *(lingax)*, makes the container spillproof.

The *haan* rests in a conical basket *(saab)* made especially to protect it. The conical basket is made of bent twigs tied together with leather or string made from old clothes. The armature cushions the container within and also allows for easier handling. It is a means of attaching the water container securely onto the camel and also for keeping it upright in the house. The *saab* is a very useful invention; besides holding the storage container, it is sometimes hung in the

Fig. 9.3. Above, various sizes of *saab*s involving a more intricate construction. Below, *haan*s in their *saab*s. A *kalax* hangs from the *haan* on the left.

Handicrafts of the Somali Nomadic Women

Fig. 9.4. Various kinds of fiber *dhiil* and their range of decoration.

house on its own to keep things out of the reach of children, and sometimes, to give clothes a good smell, the clothes are draped over the armature which has been inverted over a burning incense burner. When used this way, the *saab* is known as a *gambis*.

The *aagaan* is a similar but smaller container. *Aagaan* in this case is a feminine noun which takes the article *ta*; it should not be confused with the lid of the *haan* above, also called *aagaan,* but which is a masculine noun and takes the article *ka*. The *aagaan ta* is a milk vessel, used to store milk during the night, when the camels are a few kilometers from the camp. It is very similar to the water container in shape and construction, and, for convenience in loading and unloading pack camels, it too comes with its own armature. The main difference is one of size.

When the camels are in the camp, it is easier to use an even smaller milk container *(dhiil)*. On average, it holds four to seven liters of milk, but can be considerably larger or smaller, depending on the family's needs (fig. 9.4). For example, a mother carrying an infant under two years old may also bring a very small milk container for the child with her while grazing her animals. The small container does not need a supporting basket, as it is not for loading on a camel. It is freestanding, with a small hemispherical base that narrows into the body of the basket, and this base is symmetrically matched on the top by the base of the inverted cuplike cover *(buqul)*. The actual body widens gradually to the middle where there is a ridge called *kelli* and thereafter diminishes upward until the base of the *buqul*. *Dhiil*s are often decorated with leather and have leather straps by which they can be carried.

Hadhuub is the generic term for all uncovered milking vessels or drinking containers, although the difference in their function is reflected in the difference in their shape. All uncovered milking vessels are freestanding, wide-rimmed to catch as much milk as possible, and diminishing to a narrow flat base.[16]

The *qarog* or *doobi* is a communal drinking bowl for camel's milk and is used exclusively by the men (fig. 9.5). These drinking vessels resemble a sawn-off *dhiil* or drinking cup with a base. They sit on a hollow, woven, semicircular stand *(sariir)* and, like the milking

Fig. 9.5. Left, a milking basket *(qarog)*; height 28 cm. Right, construction of the fiber walls of a *xeedho*; height 42 cm. Drawing after a photograph in Loughran et al. 1986.

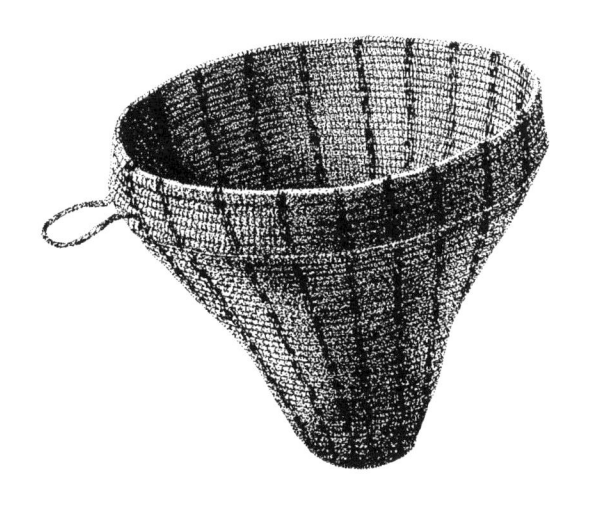

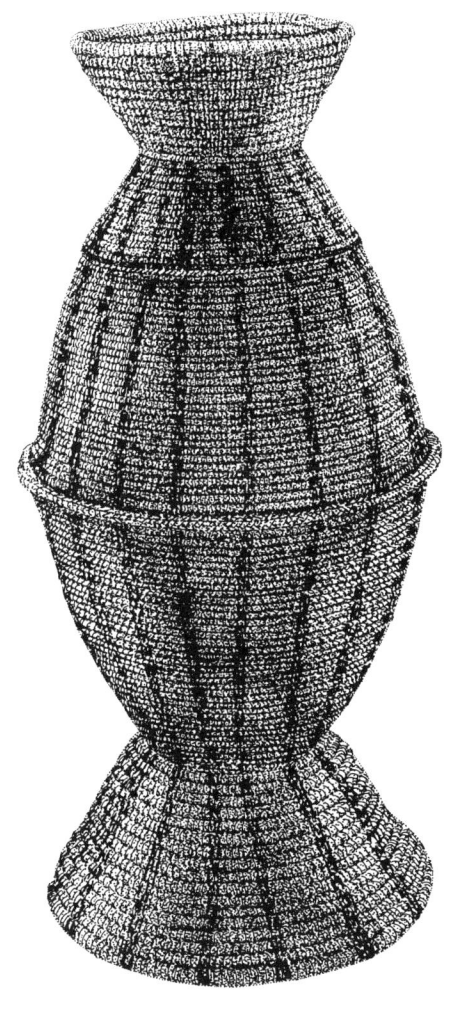

Handicrafts of the Somali Nomadic Women

vessels, widen out, but then narrow inward slightly to accommodate the lip. The smallest size mug for individual use is called a *dhiil*, but it is of the masculine gender and takes the article *ka,* distinguishing it from the milk container of the same name, which takes the article *sha*.

These various *hadhuub*s, like all the container baskets above, are woven from the euphorbia in much the same way. The fibers are first soaked in water to make them pliable and then stripped to the required thickness. The actual plaiting process has been described by Drysdale (1954:4):

Eight to ten slender strips are held together (known as *idhan*) and coiled in concentric circles starting at the base of the vessel. These coils are secured by one slender strip of fiber *(gu'un)*. This single strip is woven round the *idhan* in two degrees of density. The base of the *dhiil,* for example, is loosely woven because it merely acts as a stand and is not expected to hold milk. But the body of the *dhiil* is very closely woven. It is also strengthened by additional stitches which run interlaced patterns down the side of the vessel. The only instrument the women use is a ten cm. prodding needle *(muda)*.

Although the actual weaving is not very intricate or difficult, the real skill is in creating a symmetrical shape and one so tightly woven that it will, when treated, hold the precious liquid it was intended for.

When completed, each container is sealed and sterilized by treating it with a solution of *asal*. The solution is made by boiling pounded bits of bark from the Acacia bussei in water until it is deep red in color. This solution is then poured into the container and tightly covered. The solution is swilled around the entire container and so shaken each morning and evening until the solution is completely absorbed. The solution gives the container a thin waterproof coating, protects it from termites, and also dyes it a deep red. This curious phenomenon as to why the *asal* solution should help make the vessel watertight was explained by women who well knew the characteristics of the plants they were working with: "*Qabo* is a living thing, and *qabo* keeps its life. When it is burnt, its water is drawn out. It is necessary to try to get back to its first nature (original state), which is that of a holder of water. By putting a thick solution of *asal* in the *qabo*

every few months, one is putting back its water."[17] The *asal* coats the fibers, leaving some red residue which fills the spaces in the weaving, and the water makes the fiber expand and so tighten the weave.

Although this solution is used for all containers, thereafter the process of sealing those used for water is different from those used for milk. The insides of water containers are rubbed thoroughly with the fat from the cooked meat of camel or goat *(xayr)* to make them completely watertight. Milk containers are first swilled with curdled milk and then scrubbed with smouldering sticks of the Terminalia parvula *(meygaag)*, Cadaba heterotricha/mirabilis *(higlo)*, or Balanites glabra *(kidi)* tree. The branches of these trees, when burned to a white ember, have a sterilizing effect, cleansing and sealing the milk containers at the same time. The milk, while extinguishing the charcoals, causes much smoke and is itself evaporated. Eventually, through the repetition of this process at regular intervals, the container acquires a black shiny crust *(cul)*, which imparts a decidedly smoky taste to the milk kept in it and keeps the vessel sealed and clean.

Mention should be made of the *qarbed* and the *sibraar*, which are also containers for liquid, but are made from the whole skins of goats or sheep, which have been removed from the animals as one might remove a shirt. The legs and openings are tied and sometimes decorated with glass beads or tassels. The *qarbed*, also known as *xab*, is used by women to carry water from the well to the house, in places where the euphorbia plant is not readily available. It was particularly used by people who had settled near a town or regular water supply, but has largely been replaced in recent years by plastic containers that can do the same job. Water kept in the *qarbed* was pleasantly cool, and the combination of *asal* dye and the leather was credited with this phenomenon. The *sibraar* is much smaller and is made by and used exclusively by men.[18]

Ghee, or clarified butter, is usually stored in containers of leather made from camel skin *(qumbe)*. The leather container is circular in shape and found in two sizes: the larger one holds about twenty liters, the smaller one about ten. Because it is such strenuous work, *qumbe* making is a job for the men, except for the lid, which is woven by the women. To make a *qumbe,* the camel skin is cleaned, dyed with *asal,* and tanned. The ends are gathered up and stitched around three strong sticks that form the neck of the vessel. The sticks overlap and cross at each of the three angles, forming horns. These horns are tied to three poles in the ground, and the container is thus suspended while sand is poured into it and pounded into a tightly packed circular form. After several days, the sand is poured out and the container is cleansed in *asal* solution before the *ghee* is stored within. It is the women's job to weave a lid of *qabo* and make the *saab* for the *qumbe,* so that it can be transported by camel.

The *teped* is a smaller container of leather and more elongated, rather than circular in shape. The skin is gathered to the neck. Twigs about 8 cm long are placed vertically into the opening of the neck and then tied. Here, too, sand is used to give the container its shape. Another type of *teped* is made from calabash or the dried, brittle shell of a gourd and is also used for the storage of clarified butter. As gourds are easily broken and only found in the Jigjiga area or imported, they are less generally used. The *teped* is also fitted with a woven lid of *qabo,* which is sometimes covered in leather, and a *saab* for carrying it.

There exist a number of other storage containers, not used to hold liquid and therefore made from other materials and treated differently from those already discussed. These items are something of a nonessential refinement to nomadic life, rather than a basic necessity. The *abaxad,* for example, is a rectangular-shaped footlocker for the storage of bedding (fig. 9.6a). It consists of two sections: an upper box that fits snugly over a lower one, often with built-in pockets for jewelry. It is woven of dried fronds of palm and often covered with tanned leather decorated with designs of shells and beads, and is something a woman might make for her daughter's marriage.

A similar, though smaller box, rectangular in shape *(gandi),* is used for tools. It may be leather-covered, but it is usually less elaborate. A small woven bag with

Fig. 9.6. a. An *abaxad* with its cowrie decorations.
b. A *xeedho;* height 45 cm.

a

b

Handicrafts of the Somali Nomadic Women

long straps *(weynbaa)* is used by women to carry the work they wish to do, such as fibers, or their plaiting, while they are out grazing their animals. It is often covered in leather and decorated with fringes or shells. A small covered basket made of palm frond fiber *(qufad)* is for the storage of needles and small things.

THE *XEEDHO*

Because of its symbolic and ceremonial function, the most interesting and valued storage container created by Somali women is the *xeedho*, an hourglass-shaped container for food that has come to symbolize the female: both her virginity and fecundity (fig. 9.6b).

It has been suggested that the *xeedho* takes its name from the wooden bowl in which the food (meat, *ghee*, and dates) that came originally from Arabia was packed.[19] In modern usage, the term *xeedho* refers not only to the bowl itself, which has been replaced almost entirely by imported enamel bowls *(fujaan)*, but also to the whole curvaceous woven container.

This container is woven from the dried fronds of the palm and is made in two sections, the base and the cover, both called *sati* (see fig. 9.5). These join in the center to form the belly of the container, in which the enamel food bowl sits. The two sections may mirror each other exactly, or the lower section may be more circular and the upper section more elongated: each part is joined on top and bottom to a hollow, bowl-like extension or stand *(sariir)*. Traditionally, the container is covered in fine sheepskin *(saan)*, and decorated with cowrie shells *(aleel)* and beads. This decoration follows certain rules. For example, the hemispheres at the top and bottom of the container are entirely covered with cowrie shells, as are the straps that fasten the two sections together. Also, there is always a band of shells about 2.5 cm around the edges of both the base and the cover, where they join. The cowrie shells are stitched in a formal pattern in neat rows running horizontally or vertically, occasionally interrupted by a line of small red glass beads. The shells are not pierced but threaded through the lip of the cowrie and pulled tight, and each shell is stitched on separately.

The care taken in the design of the *xeedho* is matched by the care and presentation of the food offered within. The dish *(muqmud)* is a preparation of meat and *ghee* with dates and spices added for ceremonial occasions. It is very nourishing and can be kept for long periods.[20]

The *xeedho* thus filled by the bride's mother or aunt is an important feature of the seven-day Somali wedding celebrations. The *xeedho* ceremony takes place on the evening of the sixth day, and it is a clear reference to the virginity of the bride. The hourglass container is dressed in white cloth like the bride and then tied and knotted very carefully with a specially decorative string *(lugcarre)*, a three-strand braid of sisal string with one of the strands of a different color. This special knot tying alludes to the Somali practice of infibulation of girls ten years and younger, which ensured their virginity. It is the female relatives of the bride who are responsible for dressing and knotting the container for this ceremony. The tying pattern is often the same, but each family has its own special secret knot. The decorative three-strand braid encircles the cover extension several times and then drops down to the lower strand, forming vertical lines over the bowl of the central section each time this is repeated. Each line preserves the sisal string braid, and no line seems to overlap another. Eventually, a knot is made so indistinguishable, and so much a part of the overall pattern, that even for those watching it being tied, it is impossible to find the knot. The knot may even be sewn into a tuck of the white cloth. The undoing of the braiding and knot, primarily a northern tradition, is a task that is set for the groom's male relatives, for it is they who will be called up that evening, one by one, to exhibit the tact, agility, grace, and subtlety needed. After the *xeedho* is tied, it will be further dressed with earrings and necklaces and finally veiled with a striped silk shawl *(subeycad)*, like the bride herself. Thus cord and knot play a critical symbolic role: the knot and tying ritual is a reference to infibulation, whereas the ceremony of undoing the container is a reference to the groom's access to his bride.

At this ceremony, the bride and groom are spectators, there to enjoy the evening's festivities. They do not participate because nothing must be allowed to disturb the harmony of their relationship, even in jest.

The ceremony is really a contest between men and women and, on a second level, between the bride's side and the groom's. The female relatives of the bride have dressed the *xeedho* and tied it with a secret knot, and it is the task of the unmarried male relatives of the groom to try and undress it by undoing the knot and thus get to distribute the delicacies within. Usually a maiden aunt of the bride acts as the protector of the ritual container and is given a long reed to beat any male who may abuse it or treat it too roughly. There is a panel of three judges: elders chosen from both families who assign the "punishment" for each individual young man who tries and fails to undo the knot. The young man may be asked a serious riddle, or more frivolously to sing a song in the manner of Michael Jackson. He may be asked to create a poem for the occasion, answer a question of history, or even hop on one foot. If the knot is undone too quickly, for example, in less than ten tries, it reflects badly on the females of the bride's family. On the other hand, if the knot is not undone after the whole evening, the ceremony could continue the next night, but eventually the men may have to admit defeat and bear the disgrace and humiliation of such an admission. So symbolically tied is the *xeedho* to the bride, that if a young man should in desperation try to use a knife to cut the knot, his family may even have to pay some pardon money *(xaal)* in the form of livestock or cash to the bride's family for this unacceptable use of force.

But usually it is all done in a playful and teasing way, and eventually the container is "undressed" and the knot undone with skill and tact, and the families enjoy the evening and all the good fun attached to it. When the container is unwrapped, it is the duty of the man who was successful to remove the domed cover of date paste cleanly and in one piece with a special knife for this occasion. Afterwards, the dates and *muqmad* are distributed to all present, including the bride and groom.

This marriage container is used on two other occasions, less ceremonially. It is used as a gift to a female relative who returns to visit her own family. If, for example, a married sister returns to visit her brother, she will be given a *xeedho* filled with *muqmad (dhibaad)*, which reflects well on her sister-in-law's abilities as a good housewife. She will bring the filled container to her husband's family, where a male relative of her husband will slice off the date cover in one clean swipe. The dates are usually given to the women and children, and the meat with butter is reserved for the men. It is Somali etiquette that the container is eventually returned to its owner, in this instance to the sister-in-law; for the wedding ceremony, the bride's mother or aunt, with a gift within. This gift should be something of value, such as a piece of jewelry or silk, rather than food. The *xeedho* is also used in the house to store *muqmad* during the dry season so that the men have additional nourishing protein during this lean time.

Those who know Somalia well will notice that the authors have been selective about the handicrafts chosen for inclusion. A full study of the crafts of Somalia would be a much larger undertaking. Many of the beautifully carved artifacts, such as wooden spoons *(fandhaal)*, headrests *(barkin)*, water or salt troughs for animals *(qabaal)*, and camel bells *(koor)*, are but a few of the items crafted by men. Exquisite jewelry and fine woven cottons are among the crafts found in the coastal towns, and there are many others, such as clay pottery, belonging to the settled agricultural areas, which have also been purposely excluded. Their exclusion naturally does not imply any criticism, but only a desire by the authors to focus attention on an area of study that has previously been ignored—the work of the nomadic women.

The crafts discussed in this chapter were created by Somali women to suit the nomadic way of life and the limited resources of their surroundings. Their work exhibits not only masterly control of their environment but certainly an imaginative and practical ingenuity. These works can stand aesthetically on their own and yet are intricately tied to the land and lifestyle of the people who produce them. The pattern of life is changing for Somalis, and it would be an enormous sadness if, in years to come, these crafts were forgotten and relegated to an obscure past. It is the modest aim of this study to help prevent this from happening.

10
THE NOMADIC AESTHETIC

Having begun the Introduction to this book with Le Corbusier, it seems fitting to end with a long-forgotten remark credited to him, for which I can no longer even find a proper citation. "Every product of the spirit or of the hands," he once wrote, "carries the imprint, the mark, the stamp of a concept of beauty." Implied in his remark is the close fit between hand and spirit. One has only to observe the maternal caressing manifest every time a woman fondles the curved surfaces of a woven container she has made, every time she lovingly tightens the thongs and wrappings that hold her house together, to sense the deep feeling of association and intimacy with the object. Therein lies the basis of the nomadic architectural aesthetic.

This same close fit comes to mind in a photograph, published early in this century, of a group of Somali women (fig. 10.1). The photograph recalls similarly dated ones from my own family album in which relatives continue to be identified or recognized only by the tools of their trade or the creative products of their labors. Undoubtedly, the photograph may have been staged, but if my own experience with photography in Africa is any guide, photographic poses called for the exhibition of one's prized possessions and very best attire. The proud stance in which the *qabax,* the key structural building element of her *aqal,* is so prominently displayed, conveys the Somali woman's prized possession; it speaks to her pride of place and her sense of space. Therein, too, lies the architectural aesthetic of nomadism.

ENVIRONMENT AND SPACE

The three basic elements that distinguish nomadic architecture from its sedentary relatives—mobility, gender, and ritual—unfold in a unique environment. In contrast to the woodland savannahs and the rain forest, desert light enhances and intensifies visibility. There are few interruptions to the infinite line of the horizon, in contrast with the limited perspective the rain forest imposes on the viewer, in which the undergrowth and overgrowth of dense vegetation create a solid volume that must be carved out. In the desert, the sky above is a dome; in the rain forest, the vegetal cover forms the sky of the dome. Light and shadow, agencies that reveal architectural form, not only behave differently in the desert than they do in a forested environment, but evoke different architectural, behavioral, and conceptual responses. The affective presence in turn creates a singular sense of place and space. These unique environmental qualities are instrumental in structuring another architectural dictate: movement in space.

Constant movement in space hones the senses differently. The unique sensibility is also the end product of a life of constant and complete integration with the landscape: the nomadic tradition embraces a different sensi-

Fig. 10.1. A Somali woman, posed for the European camera against a painted backdrop, displays the most important architectural component for her house.

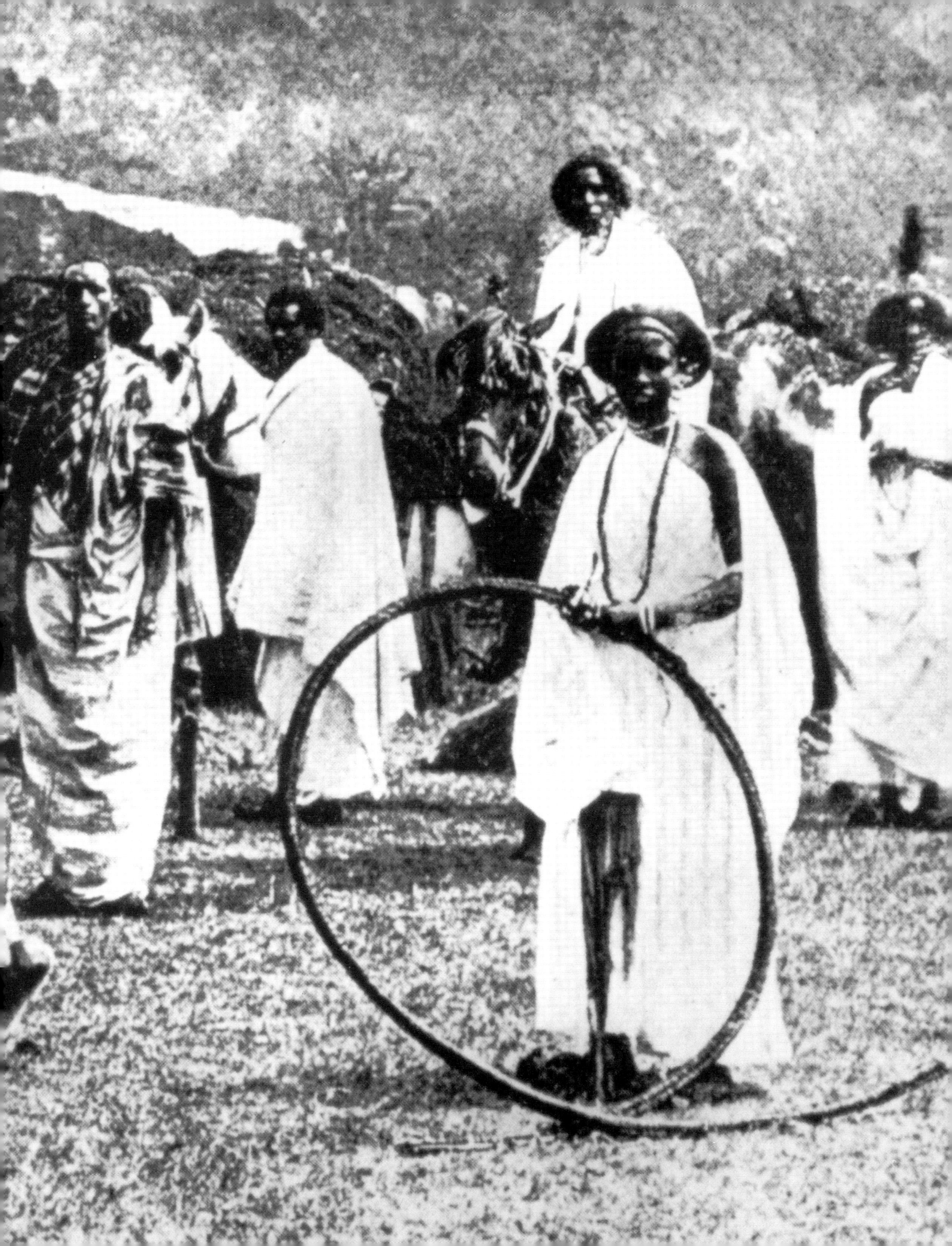

bility about the natural environment than that found in the Western sedentary tradition. The intent of human life is not to oppose and endeavor to control nature, but rather to maintain a dialogue with the natural environment in order to find union with it; only by doing so can the nomad survive.

The essence of the nomadic philosophy of nature lies in what could be characterized as a cultural ecology. There is a feeling that something must be continuously returned to the natural cycle in the process of exchange in such a way as to preserve the balance of life. Implicit in the nomadic architectural pursuit is a responsibility to elicit from a site those formal characteristics that will both accommodate the ongoing lifestyle and be receptive to the traditions people strive to carry into the future. The architectural medium transforms sensibility of place into sense of place.

The way in which people organize space is a subject central to aesthetics. In all nomadic societies, the manipulation of space is paramount. Space not only structures behavior, but is used as a type of nonverbal system for the communication of aesthetic concepts and appropriate behaviors, as does any iconography, or systematically elaborated two-dimensional (i.e., surface) representational tradition. Space itself is used as a visual metaphor.

Space for the nomad exists only by virtue of human occupancy. Architecture (and the built environment in general) also exists for people only when they occupy a space. Practices in African land tenure provide a clear analogy from which a parallel could be drawn: grazing land is distinguished from "bush" land; it "belongs" to people only when it is being used. When not in use, it reverts back to the community or to the bush. Similarly for the built form: it exists only when occupied, only when people's voices fill it with resonance. The marriage, which brings a new tent into being, brings with it the expectation of new occupancy. When the proprietor or owner of a building dies, the building returns in one way or another to its original, natural condition, or its remaining parts are distributed to offspring and integrated into a new occupancy. This gradual process of disintegration and reintegration is most clearly visible in the gradually decreasing size of a nomadic widow's tent.

Space is itself also used as a surrogate for the architecture or the artifact, in the communication of appropriate or prescribed behaviors. Whether on the open terrain or at the entrance to a tent, the exchange of salutations, the formalities that accompany the arrival of a stranger in the camp, follow a similar solemn pattern. In travel, the humblest of caravaneers will observe a veritable ceremonial at the approaches to a water point, to a camp, or to a tent: a distance is maintained. At this distance, a change of clothing, a meticulous and deliberately long adjustment of the veil, of the hair, the verification of one's demeanor in a mirror, the placement of the amulets, is pro forma. It is the ceremonial ritual, the behavior itself that defines space and plays the most important role in interpersonal relationships. Boundaries invisible to the Western eye are clearly recognized; there are no fences, no doors, no marked thresholds in the physical sense, but only in the behavioral sense. Behavioral boundaries provide a substitute or act as a surrogate for the fixed features of both the natural and the built environment. This spatial awareness itself also lies at the basis of the nomadic aesthetic.

Mobility in space necessitates a set of architectural transformations that enhance and hone spatial awareness. When a nomadic family arrives at a new site with loaded camels, there is no human imprint on the bare landscape. The house that arrives in one form, folded flat and fanlike on a camel's back, is transformed into another, a volumetric form. Space is transformed and retransformed with each move. This unique quality should become quite clear to the reader when comparison is made with another well-known "nomadic" system of transport, the Western recreational vehicle in which the house on wheels moves in its entirety so that its interior remains intact, fixed in place. In the case of a nomad's tent, the mounting, the striking, the loading and unloading involve a periodic deconstruction and reconstruction of space which in turn are conceptually linked via the loading and unloading process. The way in which an armature or tensile structure is transformed into a pack saddle and then back into a volumetric structure involves an inversion of space, turning space inside out.

The use of space itself as a surrogate for the built

form is highlighted in the spatial inversions and reversals that characterize nomadic ritual. The Tuareg marriage ritual described by Casajus is only one example among many. Among the Beni Amer, the main ridgepole *(kasla)* of the marriage tent is planted upside down for the interval of the ritual (Paul 1950). Among the Gabra, the marriage ceremony involves a sequential rotation of the wedding tent. Among the Rendille, the two front quadrants of the tent are reversed in order to communicate ethnic identity as well as clan affiliation. Among the Fellata-Baggare in the Sudan, the colorful red mats displayed on the exterior surface of the marriage tent are turned inside out and moved to the interior to mark the end of the ceremony (pl. 22).

Spatial arrays and patterns, serving as metaphors for the cosmic order and the anthropometry of the human body, are projected onto the built environment. The symmetries (and asymmetries) of the human body are imposed on topographic space as well as on the architecture of the built environment. For example, all nomadic peoples linguistically distinguish *structural elements* used for the front from those used for the back of their domiciles, those used on the left from those used on the right, those used on the north from those used on the south, those used above from those used below. The same term is often used to designate both the architectural component itself and its position in a spatial schema. The vocabulary of building terminology is remarkably rich in comparison with the language of Western architecture where there are no longer locational terms, either single or multiple, which linguistically designate the location of particular building components. Common structural terms such as joists, studs, rafters, beams, and posts have become generalized. There once were "kingpins" and "keystones" to distinguish particular structural elements, and hewn posts and beams were once designated as right or left depending on their appropriate position, but in current Western architectural terminology a beam is a beam and a post is a post, regardless of its position.

Because of frequent moves, the constancy and security inherent in a sense of place, normally accrued from a physically fixed space, are achieved by means of a tightly knit cognitive spatial structure. This cognitive structure is related to what have been termed "pseudo-fixed features" in space. These are physical features that can be moved, and are relatively simple to move or change, but that are perceived to be fixed and are treated as if they were. The transportable components of a tent can be considered as pseudo-fixed, and they define a pseudo-fixed space.

The concept of a pseudo-fixed structure and its interior space is analogous to the "container" memories that function when there are no actual physical dividers to define appropriate spatial uses. A refrigerator provides a good illustration: some compartments (e.g., vegetable bins or meat drawers) are fixed, but there is also space that comes with no particular use assigned to it. In due course, we assign a use to it and then we continue to use the same space for these items, even though there are no physically determined reasons to do so. When we assign a particular place to the storage of selected items for which there is no divider or drawer, no vegetable bin or butter compartment, we bring to bear the cognitive structure necessary to maintenance behavior. Where no fixed feature exists, we create a "pseudo-fixed feature" by assigning it a space. That space takes on a fixed quality by virtue of repetitive use or habit. The location of milk cartons may have little emotional meaning for us, but there is great emotional meaning attached to the "pseudo-fixed features" of their environment when nomadic women locate them in space.

Phrased another way, nomadic architecture consists of sets and assemblages of pseudo-fixed features, not only of building components but a multitude of "things" normally not associated with "architecture" such as furnishings, and these are selectively located in a conceptually, not a physically, defined container of space. It is the elements themselves—such as the bed, the bedding and its support, the containers and the baggage—that define the architectural space and its setting (pl. 23).

By way of further analogy, one could consider the architecture of nomadism like the quilts that emerge from "the intimate world of female kinships, friendships and rituals" (Showalter 1986:222). Nomadic house building is also a "collage aesthetic." In essence a social institution, its formal design emerges from an organization only achievable through collective labor. The nomadic house—whether it be a tensile structure or an armature frame—becomes, like the quilt, a visual metaphor for gender-discrete, collective creativity (fig. 10.2).

Collective architectural creativity is critical in the nomadic context of architecture because it also provides the medium through which women's skills are transmitted and inherited. At the same time it raises once again the underlying question of individual creativity, on which the Western architectural world continues to place such a premium: is collective creativity possible, and if so, how does it take form in the nomadic context? How far can one stretch the constraints of the material or the technology to achieve variation or innovation? Quilting technology itself provides part of the answer. The design unit of quilting, the block or patch, is assembled into an overall design, and the assemblage is then attached to a heavy backing using a variety of stitches. The block or patch is analogous to the architectural or artifactual components, and the heavy quilt backing (which is created by women working together) can be equated with the building and spatial structure of the product as a whole. The stitchery can be compared to the images, motifs, or symbols nomadic women use to unify the total configuration. So, like the example of "crazy quilts," it is perhaps primarily in the "stitchery" and in the variation of the block unit that innovation occurs, just as architectural innovation, in great measure limited by the available (or fictive choice of) materials and technology, occurs far more often on the surface than on the basic engineering structure. But surely, just as the collectively created quilt was a major form of creative and emotional expression for women in the United States, so is the African nomadic tent.

INNER SPACE

Critical to our sense of emotional well-being is the sense of space. For the nomad, the sense of space consists of a hierarchy of spaces from the infinite, unknown expanse beyond to the known grazing lands, to the men's kraals enclosed and surrounded by their thornbush fencing, to the intimate container of space within a woman's tent, and ultimately to the litter or palanquin which in one form or another sits within her tent. With each new move, it is men who rebuild the kraal, it is women who rebuild the tent. With each new move, the litter/palanquin is either reconstructed (e.g., among the Rendille, the Gabra, and the Somali) or relocated (e.g., among the Hassaniya, the Tuareg, the Tubu, and the Mahria) in the most meaningful, critical interior section of the tent. The litter-palanquin is a tent within a tent, a container within a container. If self-identity is expressed spatially and anthropometrically, then logic suggests that the sense of space and pride of place are equally engendered.

Erikson (1968:269), in his experimental studies and observations of children at play, first observed that the most dominant property of the tasks he set them was that of space. Subsequently, in evaluating the play constructions of the boys and girls who constituted his data base, he soon realized that the spatial configurations the boys created differed markedly from those created by the girls. They used space differently: "girls emphasized *inner* space and the boys *outer* space."

Parenthetically, or perhaps relevantly, my own teaching and professional experience suggest similar parallels. Women students tended to design from the inside out, rather than working from the outside inward; and, in contrast to male colleagues, I stressed a design process that began with the accommodation of interior behavior patterns. Assigned a project involving the organization and hierarchy of functional spaces, women students responded far more easily and readily than men students. My own design experience also suggests ready parallels in the preferences for concave, "welcoming" surfaces in contrast to a preference for convex or projecting surfaces on the facades of buildings which men colleagues voiced. A not unrelated illustration is the Vietnam War Memorial in Washington, D.C., designed by Maya Lin, whose successful design derives in part from the use of the internal space of the "V" of the retaining wall to draw viewers into the intimacy of the earth's inner space.

All nomadic cultures have in common a great elaboration and emphasis on interior space and a highly structured organization of it, which Leach (1976) sug-

Fig. 10.2. Gabra women putting up an armature tent in tandem.

gested might reflect a psychological need in response to the vast desert infinity beyond them, to the ultimate isolation imposed on a tent. The richness of color, the intricacy of detail, the articulation of geometries, and the tightly prescribed patterns of spatial behavior within are unmatched outside the nomadic milieu. To be sure, some of this derives from the fact that interior surfaces and artifacts are better protected from searing sun, dust storms, and rapid deterioration than their fragile exterior surfaces. In the desert environment where encampments sit precariously in profile against the sky on the uninterrupted boundless infinity of the horizon line, the continuous, often curved, building surface strengthens the sense of concentration and further intensifies the sense of isolation (Norberg-Schulz 1971:40). Beauty lies in the opposition, the polarity, between the intensity and concentration of interior space and the boundless infinity of exterior space.

With each move, the internal organization remains fixed within; hearth, backdrop, bed, entrances are maintained in the same relationship to each other *within* the enclosed or bounded space, even when the tent is rotated in space in response to the monsoons and the seasonal winds. It moves as a complete volumetric unit: interior spaces remain in exactly the same relationship to each other regardless of external orientation. In structural terms, this volume of space is maintained by the continuity of surface, much like a sphere, which is the most difficult thing to break under normal loading conditions. Try breaking one.

The container of solid roundness and images of roundness have also been the subject of psychoanalytical explanation and more recently the focus of phenomenological explanation. Bachelard (1969:239), in discussing the poetics of space, once wrote that "when a thing becomes isolated, it becomes round, it assumes a figure of being that is concentrated upon itself." Furthermore, the concentration within creates "a concentration of intimacy."

From Mauretania in the west to Somalia in the east, the seemingly pan-nomadic architectural feature of hanging ostrich eggs within the tent is in direct contrast to their exterior display on sedentary architecture, particularly the earthen mosques that serve as beacons for the oases in which they are found (fig.

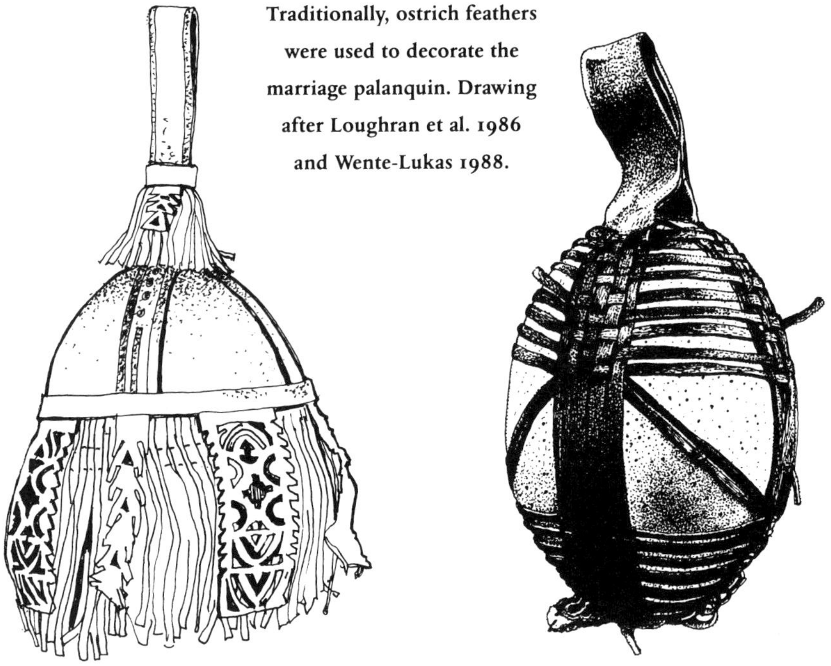

Fig. 10.3. Ornamented and decorated ostrich eggs, used by Tuareg women (left) and Somali women (right) as interior furnishings; height 30 cm. Ostrich eggs are traditionally presented to brides on their wedding day. Traditionally, ostrich feathers were used to decorate the marriage palanquin. Drawing after Loughran et al. 1986 and Wente-Lukas 1988.

10.3). Often bound in leather and decorated, they are hung above the bed to ensure many children, at the four corners of the tent, or at the entrance to the "private," sleeping space within it. Ostrich feathers are a particularly favored decorative component on the headdress of camels as well as on the palanquins used in marriage ceremonies. In all societies, they are generally referred to as "fertility symbols."

The egg has always been a universal symbol for human creation. In African nomadic thought, the ostrich egg is the most potent metaphor for human creation and fertility. Containers such as calabashes, baskets, and granaries, frequently taking on the obvious form of an egg, an *omphalos,* are the receptacles for life's sustenance (pl. 24). If one were to seek the smallest unit of a ritual that retains the specific properties of ritual behavior, then the form of the ostrich egg, and by extension its variant formal copies, is the explicit, categorical symbol for the marriage ritual. Fertility and femininity are valid only in the context of marriage and the marriage ritual. All these egg forms evoke a formal association with human creation, but all are likewise a visual metaphor for "inner" space.

In a rather remarkable (but certainly controversial and to some abhorrent) study carried out in a northern Sudanese village on the Nile, some two hundred kilometers downstream from Khartoum, Janice Boddy (1982) examined the rich symbolic context of the custom of Pharaonic circumcision. A wide variety of local customs and beliefs emerged, all of which appear to be informed by several related idioms stressing the relative value of "enclosedness" and the qualities that define it: "purity, cleanliness and smoothness."

These qualities are formally expressed by the ostrich eggs hung inside. The eggs are prized for their shape, their smooth rounded surfaces, and their creamy white color—qualities in turn associated with cleanliness and purity. Boddy (1982:689) suggests further that it is on the day of her wedding that a young woman reaches a peak of potential and appropriate fertility, defined in terms of the qualities "whiteness, smoothness, cleanliness, purity, enclosedness and imperviousness."

The egg, which so obviously symbolizes fertility, is a closed, curved, contained form; it translates into the ideal of containment. If the tent and its furnishings, from the square white Mauretanian tents to the domical Somali armature tents, come into being in the course of the marriage ritual, then logic implies that the architecture would indeed echo the same set of aesthetic qualities that coalesce in the symbolism of fertility: containment.

For the nomad, the tent is a spherical container, conceptually and in reality, an irreducible unit of space: a portable, moving indicator, a moving center, a container of intimate territoriality which personalizes the anonymity of the landscape for the peripatetic nomadic woman (fig. 10.4). Its very size communicates the nature of the feminine self and her changing status in nomadic society. Its very shape invites caress. The gradual diminution in form and contents that parallels the developmental cycle of her own life is an architectural metaphor not only for fertility and continuity, but for life itself. The act of spatial reversal and inversion, as exemplified by the Fellata-Baggare tent, is a reification of the abstract concept of containment. The web of symbolic relations thus stretches out from infibulation to ostrich egg to gourd to woven container to ritual bathing container to the enclosed space of the palanquin, and the house turns the container into an engendered culture container.

SURFACES

Profiles and forms of the concentrated enclosures are delineated by surfaces: their textures and their colors, the gradations of light and shade, the contrasts between light and shadow. By manipulating architectural space one can completely alter not only an architectural form but emotional response to it. The point is perhaps best illustrated by recalling what the Pont Neuf in Paris looked like when it was draped in fabric. The same curved form whose convex profile establishes the polarity with boundless space also creates the concave surface that evokes containment and cradling. Bachelard (1969:146) wrote of "living in the loop of a scroll," of the warmth found in the arms of a curve, of being greeted by the clasped hands of a spiral: these are poetic metaphors for space defined by surface. The Western world of high technology strives hard to achieve intimacy by means of curtains, bedspreads, carpets, and upholstered walls. The same warm woods, woven surfaces, warm colors, and soft light that we manipulate in order to achieve psychological comfort are inherent in the tent structure.

Textures also define surfaces. Surface design is both abstract and representational. Abstraction can also take different forms. The furry texture of roof mats on a Somali tent invites the same tactile sense and emotional comfort as the wool side of a sheepskin or the giving softness of a down quilt, both of which, parenthetically, are associated with babies in the Western world. The abstraction of representational decoration is particularly interesting when one compares Tuareg

Fig. 10.4. Above, a Somali tent north of Isiolo, northern Kenya. Below, a Danakil encampment, Djibouti, 1938.

and Mauretanian surface design. The neighboring Mauretanian and Tuareg populations both have a written language, Arabic kufic script in one instance, Berber *tifinar* in the other. In one instance, the pattern is far more "arabesque"; in the other it is geometric, the result of letters represented by straight lines.

In both instances, there are enough references in the literature to suggest the pervasiveness of a tradition of literacy among women over the course of time. Beginning with the script of the written language to generate a design patternwork, the system of communication on the surfaces is, in both cases, ultimately abstracted into a different gestalt. The selective application of the abstracted design onto particular architectural elements is an equivalent process of defining and articulating the role of surface in defining space, particularly contained space.

Surfaces are also defined by color, and the color white has already been referred to in the context of purity. The preference for the color red is richly documented in African history and ethnology, where the very earliest accounts of nomadic material culture make reference to it as a distinguishing feature in tent architecture. Used inside and on the outside of tents to distinguish position and power in history, it continues to be used throughout the African nomadic world, but apparently in a gender-related context.

In East Africa, red is a woman's preferred color, in both ritual and daily life; blue or black is a preferred color for men in both east and west Africa. One among many errors I committed, in the course of fieldwork among the Gabra, was in the purchase of cloth for gifts which would normally have been worn for a Gabra marriage. It was exceptionally good cloth (the most expensive in the market), but the color was deemed far too muted. Begrudgingly accepted with unhappy faces, the cloths were never worn in the course of the marriage and, to the best of my knowledge, were never worn subsequently.

The preference for red is even more evident in the ceremonial settings and ultimately accrues to the architecture of ritual. The red beads selectively used for marriage necklaces are matched by the red cloth that finds its way onto tent backdrops, leather tent linings, and the panoply of marriage palanquin appurtenances, as well as onto the interlacing of woven mats that are first displayed on the outside of marriage tents and then brought inside to grace the walls and ceilings.

The preference for red may well have had its origin in the red dyes that traditionally came from the same tannin used to make leather pliable. The tannin is a byproduct of the same acacia bark women obtain by stripping the roots dug up in the course of their gathering expeditions. When intensely saturated in highly illuminated environments, red is particularly visible from a distance. But in psychological studies of color response, it was also found that red is perceived to be the color of excitement, power, eroticism, and stimulation—the color of passion and emotion. One has only to recall the natural world of flora and fauna, where red is used for courtship, enticement, and attraction, to understand the pervasiveness of the color red in the vortex of the tent's inner space.

ALTARS

The concentration on inner space is strengthened by a tightly prescribed geometry that contrasts so strongly with the linear, hodological, topographic quality of outer space. The organization and use of the interior space of a nomadic container appears to be similar in all African nomadic societies, whether these containers are circular, square, or rectangular. Four quadrants—public and private, sacred and profane, male and female—define a balance and a dynamic equilibrium within the contained space. But the geometry also revolves around a key focal point, a conceptual epicenter, what I would like to define as an altar.

All tents have, within them, a focal point of key action, just as all rituals have a physically defined altar. An altar is essentially a stage, a theater setting, for ritual behavior; the meaning embodied in the ritual behavior focuses on it. Every nomadic society sets up one of its interior faces as just such an apse—a backdrop for the action setting—for its primary ritual, the marriage ceremony.

The trappings of the altar may vary in form but never in symbolic content. It is always the most intensely embellished, most richly colored place within the contained space. Among those nomads who have a tradition of palanquins in the marriage ritual, the altar is a combination of bed and palanquin. Among others, the altar is composed of the skins and containers, the embroidered or woven hangings that took part in the ritual and that hang above or behind the bed. The focal point of the altar space is also tied directly to the structurally critical tent face which resists the fierce winds.

CONTAINER SURROGATES: PALANQUINS

It is no coincidence that the color red, which figures so strongly in the design of the altar's backdrop, frames the most intimate space of all, the setting for the consummation of a marriage—the bed or its symbolic equivalent, the marriage palanquin or litter. The *kalau* of the Beni Amer nomads in the Sudan (Paul 1950), the *te saqwit* of the Hadendowa (Ausenda 1987), the Téda *dela*, the tannin-dyed red cow skins of the Rendille and the Gabra, the Somali *kebed*, all of which frame the bed, are either used in combination with or equivalent to the richly wrapped and hung red trappings of a Hassaniya *ameššáqqab*, a Tuareg *jarfa*, a Tubu *kobode*, or a Mahria *johfa*. Each composite of artifacts is, in its own cultural setting, an architectural setting for the ritual.

Among the Hassaniya, the Tuareg, the Tubu, and the Mahria, the tent does not offer the same sense of physical enclosure that the Rendille and the Somali tents do. Where the tent itself does not physically provide the sense of containment, it is the palanquin that serves as the focal point for concentrated space. The palanquin itself, which remains intact from move to move and defines the interior altar, becomes the primary container of space. Often the major furnishing within a tent, it is transferred from the back of the camel to the tent interior each time the tent is pitched. The bed itself, which had either been slung across the camel's back to form a litter or had been dismantled to form part of the palanquin structure, is thus located within this concentrated, miniature container of space. The artifacts that decorate the camel on which the nomadic woman rides are transferred from the litter and hung in the interior in close proximity, and they create, by means of their elaborate and embellished detail, their color and texture, the focal point, the altar within the enclosed space. The litter or palanquin, a surrogate for enclosed, concentrated space in the expanse of infinity beyond, is transformed into the focus for concentrated space within the architectural domain.

Containment thus finds architectural expression in the woman's litter or palanquin itself. Like a much enlarged ostrich egg, the palanquin is a closed container within which the protected bride can move through the dangerous, unknown, infinite space to her new domicile. It is a surrogate for protection from the unknown exterior, providing the woman with the same sense of physical enclosure and psychological security her tent cannot always provide. Moving the palanquin into the tent interior is analogous to spatially inverting the richly decorated mats in the course of the marriage ritual from outside to inside. The elaborately decorated trappings of the palanquin, highly visible on the outside in transit, are transformed into a richly decorated interior altar space. The same symbolic import extends to the vast storage sacks and their locks which hang from the litters and palanquins. And it is on the surface of the leather sacks that the pregnant symbolism Du Puigaudeau has so movingly described can be found.

A gourd that has not been pierced is not accessible. To extract its seeds, to use the gourd as a container, it must have an opening. It cannot be entered without an orifice. The metaphor or idiom of enclosure requires a counterbalance: the idiom of an opening into the enclosure, the signature of a door. The stronger the physical definition of container, the greater the emphasis on its signature, that is, the opening into the contained space. Where tents do not have "doors," it is the micro unit of contained space that accrues to itself the signature of closure. Thus decorative ideograms on the surface of the container are balanced by the locks whose keys Tuareg women display with such pride around their necks as jewelry. The finely worked locks used to close the leather sacks among the western nomads fulfill the same aesthetic and symbolic function as the covers and leather straps of coiled baskets do among the East African nomads.

a   b   c

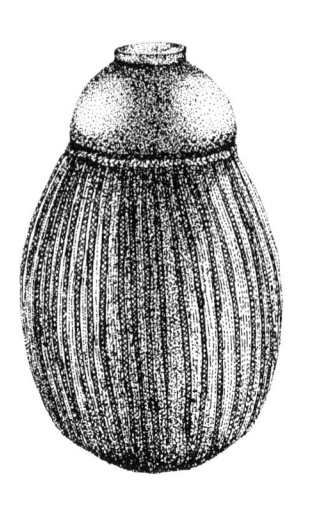

GENDER POLARITIES

Much of the content of this anthology has focused on gender discreteness in order to highlight women's creativity. The focus has given prominence to some areas of inquiry at the expense of others, and as a consequence the interpretation, which may be construed as both distorted and skewed, needs redress. African architecture, like life, is also about male and female polarities: the creation and use of the meanings attached to the inside and the outside, the infinite and the contained, also inherently involve the quality of gender-relatedness. If, as elsewhere, the poetics of space is synonymous with the poetics of gender, then we would be totally remiss if we did not consider gender-relatedness in its creation and expression.

Contained space is a binary opposite of infinite space. Contained space is women's space. Extended space, space beyond, is men's space. If one considers the nomadic domicile as a cultural unit embodying economy, politics, social structure, and so on, then domestic affairs carried out within and close to the

Fig. 10.5. a. The basketry base of an unfinished wooden Gabra container. b. A Gabra coiled basketry container with a wooden lid; height 38 cm. c. A Somali wooden milk container with leather straps and basketry rim and lid; height 31 cm. Drawings after the Katherine C. White Collection, Seattle, and the Lee Cassanelli Collection, in Loughran et al. 1986.

domicile (e.g., goat herding) are the province and under the control of women, while external and long-distance affairs (e.g., camel herding) are the province and under the control of men.

The same gender polarities that take form in architectural space find expression in the realm of artifactual technology. Among nomadic societies, wood carving, in general, is men's work. To make a wooden container, the core of a section of trunk or branch is hollowed out; an opening top and bottom is required to extract the core. The closure, top and bottom, achieved by braiding or plaiting a base and a cover or by enveloping it in leather, is always carried out by the woman of the house. The process of first opening and then closing a container is conceptually analogous to the Somali marriage tradition in which the untying of the wedding basket is a symbolic act of infibulation by her new husband (fig. 10.5a).

This gender-discrete and gender-related technological interface sheds light on the design of the artifactual end product itself, as a comparison between two kinds of Somali containers, one woven and one wooden, clearly illustrates (fig. 10.5b, c). In the first instance, the container is made by women using a traditional coil basketry technique, but its wooden cover is carved by men woodcarvers, often the woman's husband. While the purpose of the protruding lines that dominate the egg-shaped design is primarily structural (they reinforce the walls of coiling, much like integral tie-beams and pilasters buttress the walls of a building), it also is the design feature that distinguishes the particular style of a basket using strips of acacia or tamarind bark.

In the second instance, the container is carved of wood and, like its Gabra relatives, has a woven bottom, a woven lip reinforcement, and a woven cover. The wood surface, however, has been carved to replicate the structural reinforcing of the woven basket. Though there may be some minimal structural (and wearable) purpose to the carved ridging, it serves little purpose as structural reinforcement (the heavier ribs would be better placed horizontally around the wooden container). Although one cannot help but speculate about the technological, formal, and aesthetic rationale for this second wooden container which encapsulates a primordial woman's symbol, this combination of basketry and wood carving speaks to the integration of gender polarity—gender-relatedness.

Of course, the same symbiotic relationship operating in the organization of caste systems and their related, prescribed marriage patterns (blacksmiths or woodworkers and potters or leatherworkers) also

Fig. 10.6. The rear (actually front) wall of a Gabra house. a. The marriage containers have been hung on the interior. b. The ropes Gabra men use for camel herding are hung like a mirror image on the exterior.

a

b

The Nomadic Aesthetic

197

explains the parallel appearance of the same pattern on seemingly diverse technologies. Thus, for example, the same patterns (and their accompanying meanings) that are found on leather artifacts created by the Mauretanian and Tuareg women leatherworkers are found on the metalwork patterns that their husbands, the blacksmiths, fashion.

The architectural expression of this same gender polarity—and integration—is poignantly reflected in the balance between interior and exterior spaces which the architectural surfaces define (fig. 10.6a and b). On a newly created Gabra marriage house, the interior surface of the critical structural wall, the altar wall, is used to hang the ritual containers that symbolize the marriage ceremony. Directly outside, on its exterior surface, the hanks of newly made rope used by the men in herding camels are hung over a new, multicolored cloth wainscoting, but the rope itself is made by the women.

Perhaps the most striking illustration can be found in the creation of the host of saddles and palanquins used by nomadic women. All involve a combination of woodworking, metalworking, and leatherwork. Their design in each case reflects the gender-discrete yet gender-related technological process: the use of bentwood and the use of straight poles entail different technologies, as do the use of leather ties and metal fastenings. But the success of each design entails the integration of two, gender-discrete technologies.

The structural realm of tent technology itself provides an even more revealing illustration. Among the nomads who continue to use a tensile structure (i.e., the Hassaniya and the Tuareg), the women weave the *flij*s, or tan the leather for the tent velum, the men initially obtain and shape the various structural poles, ridgepieces, and beckets for it even though the women then, in an act of "taking over," carve the decoration on these wooden elements. Like all tensile structures, the performance of a velum is integral with that of its poles and beckets, but at the same time the poles will not stand up without the tension of the velum.

Ultimately, the very conditions of the Saharan environment set up a pair of polarities which find equilibrium in time and space. Half the year, the strongest winds blow from the northeast, but then the other part of the year, they reverse themselves and blow from the southwest. The nomads respond by rotating their tents and/or tent openings a half circle. Proximity to the equator imposes the same hours of darkness and light in the diurnal rhythm and a balance between morning and afternoon shadows.

NUMBER SYMBOLISM, BALANCE, AND HARMONY

The integration of gender polarities implies a sense of balance or harmony for a kind of moving equilibrium. It is an aesthetic principle which lies at the heart of things in nomadic life because it derives from the mobile life-style itself, from the environment, from orientation, from technology. The ideal, perhaps utopian, is to find an equilibrium between extremes, a sense of balance around the fragile interface between the extremes of the opposition, a harmony between person and nature, between men and women, between contained and infinite.

It is in the abstract that the ideal is voiced, and symbolic number systems articulate both the reality and that ideal. One of the most provocative attempts to integrate the reality and the ideal comes from an essay on the fundamental structures of space in Hausa cosmology and the pervasiveness of a particular number symbolism (three, four, and seven) in all aspects of Hausa life (Nicolas 1968).

A rapid perusal of all the *nomadic* societies reveals that symbolic number systems are prevalent, ubiquitously present in all aspects of their lives. All domains —social life, economic life, ritual life, and thought— manifest their systematic use and in fact the use of similar criteria. The most obvious usage unfolds in the realm of ritual.

The systematic schema of number, so often embedded in cosmologies is, in fact, no more than an expression of a *spatial* symbolism, so it should come as no surprise that the nomadic schema of number symbolism rests so often on even digits, in even multiples.

The East African generational age-set system *(luba)* is one of twos, fours, and eights. For the Rendille, the core of the marriage ceremony is a four-day affair.

Pack saddles, litters, and palanquins are based on the four sides of things, on four bedpoles and two pairs of poles, on four quadrants of space, and four sectors of orientation. Equally characteristic are four beads in alternating sequences on a necklace and mirror imagery on surface design. In ritual behavior, everything is done in pairs.

To illustrate further, I can think of no better than a pair of illustrations from the technological processes of loading a camel and building an armature tent. In building technology, there is always an "inside" performer and an "outside" performer. In transport technology, one woman must be on each side of a camel for a balanced loading process. These behaviors are dictated in great part by the underlying requirements of the technological process itself.

The element of stability completely dominates the loading process. In an engineering sense, stability is achieved by a balance of forces in tension and compression (fig. 10.7). But stability is the challenge in any construction, in anything on this earth, from the laws of gravity to the resolution of stresses in the growth of a tree. In the case of the two women loading a camel, the forces are carried down to the earth through their bodies. By pulling on the ropes in opposite directions, they create tension in the structure, and they themselves set up the lines of compression which, in balance, achieve the equilibrium of forces essential for loading success. If one's survival, even existence, depends on a technology of transport by means of a pack animal, a camel more particularly because of its hump, height, and gait, then the loads (i.e., the artifactual baggage) must by extension be equally distributed on each side. The equipoise between contrasting, opposing, or interacting elements provides the stability produced by even distribution of weight on each side of a vertical axis. In building technology, the basic assumption upon which a building is predicated rests on the same principle of forces in physical equilibrium or balance.

Balance coalesces into symmetry, but symmetry, in which there is a correspondence in size, shape, and the relative position of parts on opposite sides of a dividing line or median plane, is already present in the original state of the raw materials that constitute the

Fig. 10.7. Gabra women tightening the ropes that will secure the tent poles cum litter armature.

The Nomadic Aesthetic

repertoire of the built environment. The symmetry of the pack animal in motion along a linear axis itself sets up the structural response and reinforces the balanced proportions that give rise to the beauty of the form. The resultant skins, which are converted into sacks and bags, will influence, if not dictate, the shape and form of the end product.

Balance and symmetry are expressed in the even numbers that underlie the nomadic number symbolism. If indeed symbolic numbers are no more than an idealization of space, then the nomadic aesthetic is a quintessential expression of balance and symmetry in space.

Balance and symmetry translate into harmony. Harmony has been defined as both a pleasing or congruent arrangement of parts and a state of being marked by accord in sentiment or action. The internal calm and tranquillity that is implied also translates into the highest moral value for many nomads: it translates into Peace.

Nomadic poetry has always received far more attention than its material and visual arts, and the expression of a nomadic ethos has often been sought in its verses rather than in an examination of its material culture. Since harmony can also be defined as an interweaving of different accounts into a single, perhaps poetic, narrative, it seems particularly appropriate to summarize and conclude this exploratory search for the nomadic aesthetic and the poetics of gender by quoting a selection of Tuareg Kel Ahaggar poetry in which images of harmony are poetically expressed in concepts such as balance and contrast, while color, light, topography, poise, and grace are voiced in the visual metaphors of a feminine ideal:

> Harmony of the vase supported on the shoulder,
> Harmony of Amenna made up with kohl.
>
> Harmony of the hills of stony white
> Harmony, Amenna, of your clear voice.
>
> Harmony of the valley and of sweet grasses,
> Harmony of Amenna and of her ivory tinted skin.
>
> Harmony of the dunes back to back,
> Harmony of a glistening back,

> On the animated maiden, plump decorated neck,
> Harmony of Amenna in her entire body.
>
> Harmony of the antelope gazelle's slender grace,
> Harmony of Amenna in her haughty poise,
> Dressed in indigo blue, draped with white veils,
> White camel and ornately decorated saddle.
>   (GALAND-PERNET 1978:48)

In the tradition of her women forebears of Mauretanian poetry, Marie-Françoise Delarozière (1969:52–53) also continues to evoke the sounds, the rhythm, and the music of the desert when she writes:

> The winds bring the tents to life.
> And tranquilly, towards other camps,
>   the caravan advances.
> Donkeys and camels go,
>   carrying tents, coffers and the rubs.
> The shelters of blue cloth,
>   little round tents swollen like balloons,
>   protect the secrets of the women and the children
>   from the too torrid sun.
> The caravan advances slowly towards peaceful infinity
>   towards living infinity.

SEDENTARIZATION

Nomadic dwellings and their furnishings are, for the most part, indisputably women's architecture, so the elements of the nomadic aesthetic that have been addressed in the pages of this anthology are essentially a woman's aesthetic. But it would be amiss to consider it in isolation, because it cannot exist without the interactive, integrative role of men and *their* gender discrete value systems. It would also be amiss not to acknowledge the ongoing process of sedentarization, which nomadism has always faced, because inherent in the process is a key ingredient: gender shift in the creative process.

Nomadic architecture (in the broader definition I have chosen to give it) plays a far greater role in the transmission of culture and in the maintenance of well-being than much of our sedentary architecture because it is so integrated with rituals endowed with meaning and emotional content. This architecture, so responsive to the underlying needs of the human psyche, entails a hands-on process of creativity. The inherent involvement over time is what allows it to serve as a cultural mnemonic, reinforcing the existing value system, yet responding to inevitable change.

Every single manufactured artifact in the nomadic world was and is a design problem: it was and is consciously designed. Many of the issues designers and users are attempting to address—questions of architectural sensibility, originality and tradition, individuality and collectivity, value, content, and meaning—can be illustrated, illuminated, and it is hoped inspired by a study of the unique nomadic architectural repertoire.

But if the questions raised by the nature of creativity in the built nomadic environment are complex, those introduced by the process of sedentarization are even more so. What kinds of skills atrophy, and what new skills must be developed and acquired? How is the creative process affected by reduced labor time? How are the relationships between ritual and its material culture affected? What changes occur in human perception and spatial orientation when house transport is no longer part of the life-style? How do aesthetic values inherent in nomadic architecture change during the sedentarization process? What styles persist and what new metaphors are born? To address questions such as these in detail requires yet another volume, but some aspects can serve as an introduction to it.

The availability of raw materials. The raw materials used in the creation of tents and their furnishings, which had been collected in the desert milieu, are no longer accessible to women. Annual women's work parties, organized to collect and process raw desert materials in situ, can no longer be carried out, and substitute materials enter the building process. Architectural form is immediately affected when acacia roots (a desert resource) are replaced by cash purchased split palm timbers, cut, split, and assembled by trained, if not skilled, carpenters. Although women may continue to act as "clients," control over the production and processing of building materials shifts to those who have access to other means by which materials can be purchased and services hired. Concomitantly, the labor required in processing and producing the material components moves to other spatial and behavioral realms. The situations that contributed to and reinforced individual and social meaning in the built environment atrophy, and the symbolic values inherent in the architecture shift to other physical domains.

These incremental changes were immediately clear when the settling in of a family of Somali nomads, who had recently migrated to the outskirts of Isiolo, Kenya, was recorded (Prussin field notes, June 1986). The head of the family already had his own square "town house" in place, but his two wives had brought their houses with them and were reassembling them with the building skills and technology they had acquired from childhood. The husband's mother, whose house components had already been distributed to her married daughters, had commissioned her house from a Somali carpenter but kept a hand in the construction sequence. First she set in the center post, then the carpenter set up the vertical wattles for the circular wall. She in turn applied the daub to the wattles. Another carpenter laid up the straight, radiating rafters for the roof, but it was she who put on the circular ties to stabilize the rafters and the roof thatching. Structurally, all that remained of the "traditional" building process was the center post and a pair of knee braces (*lolota*, from *lool*) opposite the entrance. The carpenter had put these up, but it was the mother who had directed his work.

Building-transport technology. The interface between building and transport technology erodes. Although men continue to herd, wives and children remain in a fixed locale, and those architectural features that the moving process had necessitated were no longer viable. For example, the length, strength, thickness, and number of supporting house poles, previously dictated by *both* litter and house structure, were reduced in size and quantity because transport no longer imposed a structural requisite.

The continuity and maintenance imposed by the integral relationship between building and transport weaken. When houses no longer move, the repetitive experience over time disintegrates. As a consequence, the learning process acquires a new kind of cognitive structure, and the "art of memory" requires another system of mnemonics.

The marriage ritual loses its efficacy. The creation of a new domicile continues to be associated with marriage, but once the cycles of reconstruction and reassembly that reinforced the symbolic and meaningful aspects of the ritual no longer exist, the ritual loses its efficacy. Marriage ceremonies continue, but the simultaneity of marriage ritual and architectural creativity is weakened. When part of the architectural repertoire is no longer available as a contribution to the new house, as it was in the nomadic marriage ritual, then the maintenance process that provided continuity, perpetuated the memory of the ritual, and reinforced the transfer of knowledge no longer exists.

When the building sequences of the marriage ritual disintegrate, the symbolic furnishings associated with it assume greater importance. The aggregate set of furnishings persists, even though many of the items in the "set" or repertoire are no longer created by the bride or her family. Manufactured and imported cloth or polyethylene sheets replace handwoven roof mats and tanned skins; locally manufactured or imported plastic and metal containers replace hand-plaited baskets.

The organization of nomadic space changes. Once the physical demands of the desert landscape are no longer accessible, then the physical attributes of the built environment, which enable nomads to manipulate and carve out the categories they use to deal with the world, are no longer valid for them. The environmental stage on which they had lived no longer exists for them. If movement in space is as important as we have suggested it is for understanding the aesthetic of nomadic architecture, then settling will directly affect not only the technology but the perception and social organization of space as well. For example, if the marriage ritual, which creates a new house, is staged inside the cattle kraals, then what happens when there are no kraals? If the orientation of a house and its framing technology are particular solutions to wind resistance, then these elements, structures, or furnishings, which had been structural necessities, become obsolete when building systems are anchored permanently to the ground. House location, far less influenced by natural constraints, responds more directly to social and political hierarchies.

If, as is so very clear from the nomadic context, journey and inner-outer space relationships are integral, then sedentarization will affect the integrity of the inner-outer spatial relationship itself. The architectural expression of inner-outer space which underlies much of the aesthetic quality of the nomadic world assumes new meaning in the permutational process. Features such as the appearance of doors and windows which break through wall boundaries, the erosion of the tight geometry of inner space, and the substitution of physical entrance markers for behavioral definitions of space appear, articulating these new spatial relationships.

The symbolic focus of the marriage ceremony remains. The aggregate set of furnishings that make up the marriage altar continues to structure the traditional nomadic organization of space inside the sedentary domicile because they are still owned and controlled by the wife. The interior spatial arrangement of these furnishings, initially structured by the nomadic culture, continues to remain constant (see pl. 23). A case in point is the Tuareg Kel Ferwan domicile where the establishment of the key symbolic elements of marriage—the bed, the storage trestles, and the raised support for a milk container—preceded the setting up of the armature tent; even when the armature was not put up, these artifacts always were.

The tradition of locating women's furnishings in spaces traditionally ordained by marriage can be found wherever nomadic cultures begin to settle down. Among the Hassaniya in Walata, Mauretania, the artifactual elements that constituted the interior of the tent (i.e., the furnishings of marriage) are retained and integrated into the fixed architecture of the interior courtyard (fig. 10.8). The palanquin armature, which served the Hassaniya wife in her wedding journey, is perched atop bed rails supported now by ren-

Fig. 10.8. The interior courtyard of a house in Walata, Mauretania. Above the nuptial bed rests the armature of a palanquin canopy; beside it, the *asanad* for a bowl of milk.

dered stone parapet walls. Adjacent to it is the finely carved milk container support, and immediately behind is the sedentary bedframe made of permanently fixed wattles used by the long-settled agricultural Sudanese black oasis community. And the same basic design gestalt that was woven and embroidered under and over the tent is transposed and projected, albeit more freely, onto the interior courtyard walls beyond.

A similar process was recorded in the city of Agades, Niger, once the seat of a Tuareg sultanate, and now inhabited by nomadic Tuareg and sedentary Hausa populations (Dudot 1969). In the nuptial chamber, the women built a sort of dais made of four wooden pickets solidly planted in the floor and from which a cotton awning is extended. The bride sat under it for three days, receiving the visits and compliments of her friends and acquaintances, while the groom sat adjacent, on the bed. Around the room were planted a ring of posts called *sigittawen*, carved precisely like those discussed in Chapter 5 above (fig. 5.7c): two, different from the others, were located at the head of the conjugal bed, another was located adjacent to the woman's place, and a fourth close to the man's place. The others were placed adjacent to the long walls of the room. When families could not afford to purchase or borrow these carved posts, they replicated them in earthen bas relief on the walls of the marriage chamber.

A similar transposition is evident in the main room of a house in Fachi, Niger (fig. 10.9). The iron bedstead is located in the farthest corner from the entrance, and the wall behind is draped with rectangular and elliptical multicolored dum palm and hair woven mats traditionally used under the roof of the tent. Above the mats, the white enamel plates and bowls, now joined by family photographs, have been hung. The wife of the house sits proudly in the foreground of the same material symbols of marriage, artifactual and architectural, that her nomadic sisters have used for generations.

The parallel could be extended further to Nubian house decoration (Wenzel 1972), so much of which was destroyed by the Aswan Dam flood in 1964. Prior to the spectacular mud relief ornament, house decoration consisted mainly of actual objects hung on the

Fig. 10.9. A living room in the city of Fachi, Niger.

walls in ornamental patterns. These hanging objects were often those that had been used in the wedding ceremony and had been arranged afterwards on the inner walls, usually the bed chamber, or those hung up to keep out dangerous spirits or deflect the evil eye. Included among these wedding objects were the mats on which the bride and groom had sat, baskets and gourds hung in nets or hangars, the circular, shallow basket lids that covered the food consumed during the marriage ritual, and the jewelry of the bride. While the custom of hanging baskets may have served to keep termites and ants away, it is also clearly a nomadic tradition, and even when cupboards and storage closets have replaced it, the Nubian artist (who learned the painting technique from women) continues to create wall patterns that feature designs based on the same hanging baskets that symbolize her womanhood, in the antechamber of a house entrance.

At Marsabit, I found that although the "new" houses of recently settled Gabra nomads were commissioned from and built by school-trained carpenters using "urban" building materials and technologies, the interior arrangement of the dowry clearly reflected the spatial order of their nomadic relatives. Square and rectangular house units had replaced the circular armature tent, but the space within it continued to be divided into the same four quadrants. The two beds occupied the same position in relation to each other and to the "altar wall" behind, even though a fixed shelf, trade cloth, plastic jerry cans, and photographs had replaced the classic, plaited marriage containers (see pl. 24).

Ultimately, when the domicile becomes a fixed entity, the same dowry is embedded in the earthen walls of the wife's sleeping, that is, personal space, in precisely the same order, even though the objects now carry new meanings of status and social exchange. They have become elements of the fixed environment, but their position in space retains its traditional pattern.

Sedentarization ushers in a gender shift in architectural creativity. Perhaps most significantly, the sedentarization process effects a gender shift in the creation, ownership, and maintenance of, as well as the control over building, hence over architectural technology. The collective process, which marked architectural creativity, becomes dissipated. Although she continues to exercise control over its furnishings, the woman is no longer in control over the creation of her domicile, and she gradually loses legal rights over it. Consequently, the architectural value system her gender gave rise to is superseded by that of her male counterpart.

It is a well-established fact that control over one's environment, whether perceived or real, is an essential component of environmental satisfaction. Control over one's self-created architecturally defined space, particularly when it is so imbued with meaning and emotion, is essential for self-identity and mental health. If a woman's reproductive potential, with its guarantee of social continuity, is embedded in the material components of nomadic life, then sedentarization has far more dire emotional and cognitive consequences than we have yet to realize.

NOTES

1. THE TENT IN AFRICAN HISTORY

1. The author's proposed design, which was inspired by and modeled after a South African mat-covered armature tent, looked very much like our contemporary, fashionable lightweight Dome tents designed for use by serious campers and mountain climbers.

2. In his effort to unravel biblical history, the early anthropologist-cum-biblical scholar W. Robertson Smith (1903) outlined an approach in which social acts and their physical coordinates were linked. For him, cultural concepts were wrapped in the husk of a material embodiment.

3. Exodus 25–27. The Tent of Meeting was composed of ten sheets of fine twined linen (plus an eleventh for end reinforcement) of purple, violet, and crimson stuffs, finely brocaded with cherubs, sewn together into two vast sections. Each "hanging" or woven strip of goat hair was thirty cubits long and four cubits wide. The cubit, an ancient unit of length based on the distance from the elbow to the tip of the third finger, is usually about half a meter. Thus each strip was about two meters wide and fifteen meters long.

Over the first layer of linen, a second layer of woven goats' hair, a third layer of rams' skins dyed red, and a fourth layer of badger(?) skins were laid. The supporting framework for the velum, sheathed in rare metals, was made of acacia uprights and cross members.

4. These *mapalia* have also been used by Africanist scholars involved in documenting various nomadic cultures as a historical baseline. See Casajus 1987:341–43, Le Coeur 1937, Marcy 1942, Martinie 1949, and Laoust 1930 for various etymological comparisons with Latin terms, present-day Berber terms, and contemporary building practices.

5. The latticework roof frame above, resting on a circular wattle wall below, suggests that the wall was built independently of the roof and that two different technologies, wattles and latticework, were used. Contemporary nomadic armature tents are built using a framework in which roof and walls are integral with each other, whereas sedentary building technologies more often derive from a conical roof framework built independently atop a wall whose palings (or wattlings) are driven into the ground.

6. In the light of Barth's Classical education, it is tempting to cite the suspiciously close resemblance between his representation of sedentary Kanembu hamlets and the *mapalia* on the Roman mosaics (1857, 5:411). His woodcut is in sharp contrast to the illustrated lithographs (fig. 1.11), so sensitively rendered by J. M. Bernatz from his own African experience.

7. Subsequent Roman texts use words such as *canna, calamus, culmus* (reeds, canes, hollow rods, stalks, and stems, especially of wheat) to describe the building materials and the forms of rural housing in the region they designated as Numidia. These forms varied: authors evoked a resemblance to furnaces, others to round chicken coops, and still others to the overturned hulls of ships. Le Coeur, the first European ethnographer to document nomadic Tubu culture, argued that the *mapalia*, because of the Classical interpretation of overturned hull shapes, were the progenitors of the Tubu armature frame tents (1937).

8. See Frank M. Snowden, Jr., "Iconographical Evidence on the Black Populations in Graeco-Roman Antiquity," in *The Image of the Black in Western Art*, ed. Hugh Honour (New York: William Morrow, 1976), vol. 1., fig. 325.

9. In a similar vein, Marcy (1942) suggested that the

term was used in reference to the Roman suburbs (rather than the *urbs*), where the rural housing of pastoralist and agriculturalist alike was located, and with whose residents the Romans had much occasion to interact in the course of their North African expansion.

10. In fact, the mosaic scenes in which these *mapalia* occur are all rural, albeit often bucolic, scenes. Fradier (1976), in discussing a Roman mosaic from Oudna, called attention to a "tent" which probably belonged to nomads from the south who had come to seek seasonal labor. The tent in the mosaic closely resembles the *mapalia* described in Classical literature.

11. Strabo wrote: "The Ethiopians (i.e., the Bejas) at present lead for the most part a wandering life . . . (they) wander from place to place with their flocks . . . whether sheep, goats or oxen. . . . Their largest royal seat is the city of Meroe. . . . The inhabitants are nomads, partly hunters, partly husbandmen. . . . The houses in the cities are formed by interweaving split pieces of palm wood or of bricks" (Budge 1928, 2:158).

12. "The village," Burckhardt wrote, "consisted of several long irregular rows of tents formed of mats made of the leaves of the Doum tree, and containing about two hundred families of Bisharin. This is the general mode of dwelling throughout the tract of desert country lying between Egypt and Abyssinia. Two rows of poles, opposite each other, converge at the top; over these they fasten others horizontally. . . . Whenever the Bedouins remove, the tents are struck and the poles, mats, etc. are loaded upon camels" (1819:368).

13. In his discussion of the tent as an emblem of royal authority and luxury, Ibn Khaldun, the fourteenth-century Arab historian-philosopher, wrote (1958, 2:67–69):

It should be known that one of the emblems of royal authority and luxury is small and large tents and canopies of linen, wool and cotton, with linen and cotton ropes. They are used for display on journeys. They are of different kinds, large or small, according to the wealth and affluence of the dynasty. . . .

At the beginning of the dynasty, the same type of housing used by the people of the dynasty before they have achieved royal authority, continues to be used. At the time of the first Umayyad caliphs, the Arabs continued to use the dwellings they had, tents of leather and wool. . . . When they went on raids or went to war, they travelled with all their camels, their nomad households and their dependent women and children. . . . Their armies, therefore, consisted of many nomad households. . . .

The Arab dynasty then adopted diverse ways of sedentary culture and ostentation. . . . They were transformed from tent dwellers into palace dwellers. . . . Now, they used linen fabrics for their dwellings on their journeys, fashioning them into houses [tents] of various shapes and sizes . . . displaying the greatest pomp and art.

This remained the way dynasties displayed their luxury.

14. Feilberg concluded that the light structure was covered with an animal skin because the term *khen,* which signifies a temporary, provisional, light dwelling, is followed by the modifier "animal skin."

15. I am much indebted to Julie Hudson from the Museum of Mankind for calling my attention to the initial publication on this tent (Brugsch 1889).

16. A much earlier, XIth Dynasty date was initially ascribed to the funerary enclosure because of confusion in dating the archaeological remains in early excavations. However, because the inscriptions on the tent refer to other priestly representations from the XXIst Dynasty (and, parenthetically, invoke the XVIIIth Dynasty Queen Hatshepsut, also known as the "woman-king"), a tenth- or eleventh-century B.C. attribution has been suggested for it (Lucas 1926). The tent is now housed in the Cairo Museum.

17. What is equally intriguing is that cattle worship was apparently a traditional aspect of the Egyptian belief system in this region at that time.

18. The spoils of war from the Syrians at Megiddo included seven poles of (myr) wood wrought with silver. A further six tent poles wrought with bronze and set with costly stones were taken a decade later (Drew 1979).

19. Agricultural expansion into the southern Djebel, defended by a series of fortified farms in areas of greatest settlement and major forts on the desert edge, took place on an enormous scale. Not so parenthetically, these Roman forts were organizationally and architecturally laid out by using tent space as a measure.

20. Pliny's account of Cornelius Balbus' campaigns against the Garamantes (20 B.C.) and those of Valerius Festus (A.D. 69) were only two of a series of Augustan campaigns carried out along the African borders of the Roman Empire.

When Julius Maternus marched to Garama and joined the Garamante king in a four-month expedition to the lands of the Ethiopians, one can only wonder whose military style and whose accoutrements were used when they joined forces. Perhaps the answer lies in Tacitus' account of a serious war in Africa started by Tacfarinas, a Numidian who had been a Roman auxiliary in the first decades A.D. After deserting the Roman legions, he equipped and organized his native forces into units on the Roman model. Consequently, to keep Tacfarinas engaged, it became necessary to train mobile Roman columns especially for desert conditions.

21. Although Polybius provided the most readily available source for information on Roman military strategy and tactics, there are handbooks used by Roman military surveyors which contain detailed descriptions of marching camps, including a camel corps.

22. Calfskin was preferred because it is more pliable and has a consistent thickness. The direction in which the skins were laid and sewn was also important because skins are stronger along their axial dimension.

Trajan's column illustrates these tents and how they were transported on pack mules (Frank Lepper and Sheppard Frere, *Trajan's Column* [Wolfboro, N.H.: Alan Sutton, 1988]). Also on the column is the representation of a cavalry of North African "irregulars," part of Hadrian's fighting force.

23. Lawrence J. F. Keppie (*The Making of the Roman Army* [London: B. T. Batsford, 1984], p. 180) notes that when the empire's legions were first formed they consisted primarily of recruits from Italy, but by the early second century only one-fifth of the legionnaires were Italian, and after A.D. 117 "the contribution of Italians to the manpower of the Legions was negligible. Most were from the Provinces."

24. The etymology of some of the Latin terms relating to tents and nomads merits mention. The word "tent," according to Webster's Dictionary, derives from *tenta*, the feminine of the Latin *tentus*, the past participle of the Latin verb *tendere*, "to stretch." A fabric or leather velum must be stretched to be stable, and *tentorius* became synonymous with *pelles* ("tent-skins"). The term *pellis* ("skin, hide") referred not only to the material itself but to articles of clothing made of skin as well as a tent for soldiers (C. T. Lewis and C. Short, *A Latin Dictionary* [Oxford: Clarendon Press, 1962]).

Papilio was not the only Latin term used in reference to the Roman military leather tents; *tentorium, tugurium, tabernaculum, contuberium,* and *praetorium,* presumably designating different tent types in different contexts, were also commonly used. *Tentorium* referred to a tent stretched upon cords as distinct from a *tabernaculum* which was formed on a framework of wood. Both were military tents, and both these latter seem to be characterized by a goatskin leather or a woven velum. When it was a matter of long sojourns in one place, the fortified camp was set up with *tabernacula*; when the stopover was short, tents were pitched. *Tugurium,* as used by Cicero, referred to a peasant's hut or cottage. Writing about the wars between the Byzantine Empire and the North African populations, Corippus made reference to both their *cannae* (i.e., huts made of reeds, *canna*) and to the *tentoria* which were in use among the nomadic Numidians.

Pliny used the terms *nomades* and *vagae gentes* synonymously in reference to the Numidians. The Latin term *nomas, nomadis,* refers to pasturing flocks, and *nomades* refers to pastoral people that wander about with their flocks. The term *Numidian* itself seems to be etymologically derived from *nomades* and came in time to be used in reference to them, for example, the (wandering) Numidians.

25. El Bekri (1965:330) wrote of the people of Ghana that: "On the death of the king they build with raised and extended branches of wood a large dome on the site which ought to serve as tomb. . . . After placing the body on a couch covered with rugs and cushions, they place it in the interior of the dome. Eventually, the edifice is covered with mats and cloths, on top of which earth is thrown by the multitude until it forms a large hillock." See Reygasse 1950 for a survey and discussion of this type of tomb; see also the discussion in Prussin 1986.

26. In the sources that address the Almoravid *ribat,* there is no reference to a citadel as such (Moraes 'Farias 1967). It is, however, noted that when the Gudala rebelled against Ibn Yasin, the Almoravid founder, this religious reformer simply moved to the *tents* of the Lemtuna tribe (p. 803). It is reported that when his austere Malekite doctrines were rejected, his *tent* was burned and his followers were looted and driven out.

27. In 1248 Louis IX received a parasol tent, that is, a sultan's pavilion, from the king of Armenia. In turn, Louis IX presented "a handsome linen tent, made like a chapel, very costly for it was all of a fair, fine scarlet cloth," to the khan of the Tartars.

Accounts of the Holy Grail, tales of the Crusades, marriages, tournaments, and royal ceremonies all bear witness to the pervasiveness of this tent imagery. By the end of the thirteenth century, the fabric pavilion was an essential part of every knight's equipment, and the silken, embroidered, gold-pinnacled tents continued to be part of French chivalry through the fifteenth century. The most splendid military display of political authority familiar to the Western world unfolded at the great festival held in 1520 on the Field of the Cloth of Gold, at a summit meeting between King Francis I of France and Henry VIII of England. Vying with each other for power and prestige, their entire courts were housed in hundreds of pavilions constructed of timber masts and canvas velums over which great quantities of rich textiles, velvets, and satins were sewn.

28. Nordman, in his study of the nineteenth-century movements of Moulay Hassan, calls the phenomenon a "fait du voyage monarchique" (1980–81:127). As a parallel, he cites the celebrated discourse pronounced by Emperor

Charles V at Brussels in 1555, in which he recalled the number of voyages he made in the course of his reign: nine trips to Germany, six trips to Spain, seven to Italy, ten to Flanders, four to France, two to Great Britain, and two to Africa, in addition to which he navigated the Mediterranean eight times and made four ocean voyages. The time spent in travel amounted to almost a quarter of his reign, and if he had not carried his own bed, he would have had to pass the night in 3,200 different beds.

When the young Charles IX was proclaimed king, he and his mother (Catherine de Médicis) undertook extended travel in France (1564–66), accompanied by a court of both household and military attendants, which entailed twenty-seven months of displacement made in more than two hundred stages.

29. Barth's mid-nineteenth-century account of the governor's encampment (the Caid) at Tarhona (1857, 1:66), in which he found a *Turkish officer's green tent* (my italics) surrounded by smaller ones and a dozen Bedouin tents, is another illustration.

Douls's description of the encampment of his captors on the coast of Mauretania (1888:202) also vividly evokes the architectural symbolism in the service of political power: "At evening, we arrived in view of the camp of the Grand Sherif. In the middle of a plain, a multitude of tents close one against the others surrounded a more elevated tent, whose color and form revealed a European fabrication. It was octagonal, in the form of a cupola, and in raw white linen. The audience tent of the Sheik, equally in linen, had neither the form nor the dimensions of the first and was almost lost in the corner of the camp."

30. The two tents that Pankhurst (1983) illustrates are now in the Museum of Mankind, London. These tents were manufactured locally, but because they were fabricated by resident Armenians, it is tempting to speculate about the prototype on which they were modeled.

31. A fourteenth-century Arabic chronicle documented the earliest evidence in medieval Ethiopia for the extensive use of tents by the then-emperor and his army. "Prester John's white tents," according to the first European eyewitness account by Alvares in the sixteenth century, "were in contrast to the one very large red tent pitched, which they say is set up for great festivals or receptions" (Pankhurst 1983:162).

32. Early descriptions distinguish between the tents of rulers and those of the army by both terminology and color. They distinguish between tents used for royal residences, both those of the king and his consort, and tents used for assembly, for churches and storing church vestments, even those used for baking the sacred host. There were also tents used for the treasury and for the judges' court and others for the kitchens and cooks, as well as those specially designed as wardrobe tents.

33. At the beginning of the nineteenth century, the population of the Muslim town just southwest of Gondar included many "tent-men" who were responsible for pitching and striking tents and who also cared for the baggage and field equipment of the nobility and the king.

In addition, there was another major tent center, inhabited by "Mahometan" tent makers who followed the army and pitched the emperor's tents, at Emfraz, a town east of Lake Tana (Bruce 1812).

34. Among those he encountered at the king's court were a group of "Malays," traders from an interior nation "bordering on the Moors" who "buy hides, and skins, which they tan and work into horse furniture, tobacco pouches, and other useful articles; and carry some bales of skins back with them" (Dalzel 1793:132–34).

35. Unfortunately these tents were often totally inadequate for their purpose. Barth (1857, 1:85–86) complained that the tents they received (imported) "were quite unfit for the country whither we were going. They were so light they could hardly withstand a strong blast of wind, they scarcely excluded the sun."

36. See Cauvet 1925–26 for an early detailed and broadly based survey, Monod 1967 and Monteil 1952 for camel-riding technologies in Africa, and Bulliet 1975 and Gauthier-Pilters and Dagg 1981 for a historic analysis and other considerations. Epstein (1971) discusses camel domestication in the context of other domesticated African fauna.

37. The recent finds of camel bones and the representation of a camel plus its rider engraved on top of an altar in a tented sanctuary suggest that a revised date for the first documented use of domesticated camels on a large scale was in the context of the eleventh-century B.C. invasion of Syria and Palestine by the Midianites (B. Rothenberg, *Timna, Valley of the Biblical Copper Mines* [London: Thames and Hudson, 1972]). The association of camels, camel riders, and a tented sanctuary seems particularly relevant to the interface between tents and camels in reconstructing their joint history.

38. In another example from the same city, a floor mosaic of vines in the House of Silenus (A.D. 260–280) is bounded by a frieze in which a one-humped camel is represented in the company of a host of wild animals (elephants, lions, etc.). A third example from the House of

Silenus illustrates a young African behind a dromedary, surrounded by a frieze of grapes and grapevines (Jehan Desanges, "The Iconography of the Black in Ancient North Africa," in *The Image of the Black in Western Art,* vol. 1, fig. 350).

39. A requisition of four thousand camels was imposed on the city of Leptis Magna in A.D. 363, suggesting both its agricultural and military value (Leschi 1942).

40. Desanges, "Iconography," fig. 340.

41. According to the historians of the time, Procopius and Corippus, the Vandals themselves used fighting tactics that depended on camel line formation (Epstein 1971, 2:567). But again, the military accounts suggest that these were pack animals, not riding mounts.

42. A mid-nineteenth-century account of a Beni Mzab family migration in Morocco provides a vivid portrayal (Tristam 1860:68–69): "First came the Sheik on horseback, with his long-barreled flint and steel gun slung across his shoulders. . . . Next followed scores of camels, laden with tents, firewood, waterskins, and all sorts of household utensils."

43. When Jackson visited Fez, Morocco, at the beginning of the nineteenth century (1809:71), he counted nearly two hundred caravans there, many of which were traveling between Fez and Timbuktu. Each consisted of as many as a thousand pack camels.

44. In a rather remarkable subsequent study, Morgenstern (1942–43) developed the analogies in great detail by considering the various functions that the Ark, the *kubba,* the *otfa,* and the *mahlmal* held in common, among which were going into battle, selecting the road to be followed through the desert, and imparting oracular decisions. He concluded that all three sacred objects must originally have been regarded as the abode or container of the tribal deity or deities and that the *mahlmal* as well as the *otfa* are but a survival of the ancient *kubba* or tent which housed the sacred images *(betyls)* embodying female deities. The Ark was originally not a boxlike structure but rather a small tent-shrine, regularly mounted upon a woman's camel saddle, synonymous with a marriage tent.

45. Ayoun and Cohen 1981, Camps 1987, Hirschberg 1974, Ibn Khaldun 1927, and Jacques-Meunié 1982 contain various accounts of her resistance efforts and her Judeo-Berber lineage.

46. See Barth's woodcut (1857, 5:121) showing "the noble ladies of the Kel-hekikan Tuareg tribe on camels, in an open cage or *jakhfa.* On the head of the camel, a rich ornament."

47. Lyon (1821:299) adds a description to his drawing:

A frame being fixed on the back of the animal, the bride is placed in it, and while thus sitting, is housed over with carpets, shawls and ostrich feathers. In travelling from place to place, or in searching for pasture ground, the people make use of these frames; but they are in such cases generally uncovered, and have baskets, or other framework, attached to their side, in which the young children are placed. An Arab [sic] family on its march presents a very extraordinary appearance, the camels being laden with tents, cooking utensils, women and children. The men walk, driving their flocks before them, or ride their horses, frequently without bridle or saddle.

The late nineteenth-century palanquin that Nachtigal (1971–87, 2:345) recorded for the more distinguished Ulad-Suleyman families appears to be a copy of Lyon's earlier drawing and raises some interesting questions of cultural identity which need both investigation and further explanation.

2. ENVIRONMENT AND SPACE

1. The best, most recent, and most explicit overviews on the Saharan environments are found in Göttler 1984 and Fuchs 1991.

2. Ferree then continued (1890:151): "In a treeless country, for the dwellings of nomadic tribes, the first resort is to skins . . . skins are the most serviceable material." We know today that while the American Indian or the Inuit practices of softening skins are common in a treeless country, trees are essential for the tanning processes common in other parts of the world. And, of course, nomadic dwellings make use not only of skins, but of woven and pounded materials as well.

3. A moving poetic illustration, one among many, comes from the oral poetry of the Hadendowa nomads in the Sudan (E. M. Roper, "Poetry of the Haḍenḍiwa," *SNR* 10 [1927], 155): Osman Digna compelled his nomads to keep on the move for the good of their souls, and he himself never stayed more than a day or two in any one spot. If he found even an old woman squatting in one place instead of roving as a true nomad should, he had her moved on forcibly. In a four-line verse, such a woman complains that the hill she loves cannot be tied in her baggage and be put on a camel; it must remain behind. The story goes that, on hearing her words, Osman Digna allowed her to return and stay by her hill.

4. During fieldwork among the Gabra in northern Kenya, my Dome tent was bent precariously out of shape and nearly collapsed from wind velocity, despite the manu-

facturer's assurance that it would withstand Himalayan snowstorm winds. However, Gabra tents barely moved. More recently, in the course of making a film, these same unexpectedly strong winds contributed a totally unplanned, but welcome, continuous sound accompaniment.

5. The truly indescribable impression that a sandstorm leaves on those who have never been in one before was vividly conveyed by graphic portrayals in the earliest European accounts (Lyon 1821:70; pl. 1).

6. The importance of light and shade in organizing people's behavior in and around their dwellings is abundantly familiar to every fledgling photographer who brings back rolls and rolls of overexposed film or, even more frustrating, exposures in which subject matter is in too much light and too much shadow at the same time.

7. The climatic changes in the desert and on both its margins, which resulted in the present pattern of flora, have been well documented and established. It is now known from pollen deposits that the desert was sufficiently moist to have harbored Mediterranean scrub and dry woodlands as recently as five thousand years ago. The cycle of desertification began three to four thousand years ago and, probably aided by humans and livestock, the course of development of its woody plants changed. Much of the Mediterranean flora had almost disappeared by about 2800 B.C., replaced by an invasion of Acacia species from the south. It was only in the upper contours of the Saharan mountain ranges that isolated Mediterranean flora such as the olive and the cypress persisted.

The fourth-century B.C. Greek philosopher-botanist Theophrastus referred to and discussed a remarkable number of trees that are still part of the vegetal repertoire in Africa's nomadic belts: Acacia arabica, Acacia tortilis ("the only tree which grows on part of the Red Sea coast"), Acacia albida, Asparagus acutifolius, Balanites aegyptiaca, Panicum milliaceum, Tamarindus indica, Tamarix articulata, Zizyphus jujuba, Zizyphus lotus, Zizyphus spina christi, Hyphaene thebaica, and Phoenix dactylifera ("the date palm in Libya").

Even earlier, acacia *(shittim)* was the appropriate wood used by the Hebrews in the Sinai desert for their Ark, Tabernacle, table, and altar—the furniture, altar, palanquin, and tent structure of a nomadic people. As early as the VIth Dynasty, acacia, obtained from Middle Egypt and Nubia, was being used by the Egyptians for furniture, coffins, chests, boxes, and bows. Theophrastus mentioned that roof timbers of twelve cubits could be cut from the acacia.

Native acacia was also used extensively by boat builders. One of the commonest types of cargo boats on the Nile *(baris)* was made of pieces of acacia two feet long, fitted together like bricks. Owing to its strength, the wood was used for the ribs of ships. Particularly prized for its bending ability, it could also be used for the main timbers of the hull. In the sixth century B.C., Amasis could boast that he had found the sacred barge of Osiris at Thebes, made of acacia, and rebuilt it with cedar. In the summary of the revenues of the gods in the reign of Rameses III (1182–51 B.C.), the seventy-eight itemized tow boats, canal boats, and boats for cattle transport were made of acacia; it was particularly prized for its bending ability (Meiggs 1982).

In addition to acacia, the tamarix and the zizyphus (identified at the Ashmolean Museum) were also used in Egypt during the Middle and New Kingdoms. The date palm (Phoenix dactylifera) was often represented on Egyptian tomb walls. The dum palm (Hyphaene thebaica) is also represented in an unmistakable manner in several XVIIIth Dynasty tombs in the Theban necropolis. The characteristic bifurcation of the trunk, exceptional in the palm family, was commented on by Theophrastus. He also described the wood as being very hard and compact and therefore very different from the date palm. At the time he wrote, the dum palm grew only in Upper Egypt, not in Lower Egypt.

Acacia raddiana appears to have already migrated into North Africa by the time of the Roman conquest, since it has been identified in Roman buildings.

In the middle of the last century, the cypress was still being used by the Tuareg for utensils and light construction (Tristam 1860). Four years later, Duveyrier (1864) noted that the villagers of Ghat and Djanet used the timber of this cypress *(tarout)* for construction purposes. The cypress would have been extensive in the Tassili n' Ajjer and even in the Hoggar until quite recently, but few specimens remain today (Ozenda 1958:91).

8. Quezel (1965:160) refers to this ecosystem as the "Savane désertique à Acacia-Panicum."

9. Despite their predominance, little work has been done on acacia ecology in other than applied contexts, and much of the published information relates directly to their use in economic roles other than construction. For the most recent discussion, see New 1984.

10. Botanically speaking, roots develop as naked axes without superficial appendages: their chief functions are water absorption and anchorage. In contrast, the chief functions of shoots are photosynthesis, storage, and reproduction. They develop branch systems, leaves and/or spines, and reproductive organs.

11. More than a century and a half ago, Pallme (1844:132–33) marveled at the acuity of the Kababish nomads in the Sudan:

> Their accurate acquaintance with the roads in every direction across the desert is truly wonderful. They readily shape their course by the heavens by day or night, know exactly where they are, and can tell to a nicety the exact distance from the position in which they may happen to be to any other place. Their senses of both sight and hearing are so acute and quick, that they can distinguish, at the greatest distance, objects which a European could only see with the aid of a telescope; they can even at night-time perceive camels at long distances, seldom deceiving themselves in the estimation of their numbers.

12. Given a desert environment, the nomadic preference for intense hues and high contrast, which the reds, indigos, and whites provide, is easy to understand: perceptually, the color red has the longest wavelength of visible light and it seems to advance, so red objects appear larger and closer than those of other colors.

Furthermore, my guide in the Chalbi desert was always dismayed when, unlike him, I could perceive neither the change in the texture of the sand (which the pressure of the vehicle's tires had made) nor the subtle leaf configuration on acacia trees which distinguished them from one another. As a consequence, I could never retrace my route without his help, but after all, I had been raised in quite a different milieu!

13. Cognitive style has been defined as the characteristic self-consistent modes of functioning that pervade an individual's perceptual and intellectual activities.

14. See, for example, historic usages listed in the entries for "space" and "boundary" in any English etymological dictionary.

15. The difficulties that have plagued scholarly efforts to locate Niani, the ancient capital of the kingdom of Mali, result from this same phenomenon, at least in part, because Ibn Battuta described its location only in terms of the days of travel needed to reach it and its vague topography.

16. Among the conceptual skills related to spatial perception that we Westerners acquire as we grow up is our understanding of the pictorial representation of three-dimensionality and the perspective rendering of receding space. This understanding of the current conventions for representing space and distance in two dimensions is acquired in the course of our education and experience and in the transmission of knowledge about the space and its boundaries. These conventions evolved in the course of the development of Renaissance science and thought about the universe from a geocentric to a heliocentric interpretation of space, a shift that in turn affected how people thought about themselves in space. The new relationship between person (observer) and environment (what is being observed) set the basis for the laws of "scientific" perspective.

The medieval painter did not conceive of his subject in terms of spatial homogeneity; rather, he rendered what he saw, what it felt like to walk about, experiencing structures almost tactilely from many different sides rather than from a single, overall vantage point. The medieval artist viewed his world quite subjectively; he was absorbed *within* the visual world he was representing, in contrast to the Renaissance painter who depicted the space around him from without, from a single, removed viewpoint through a picture plane.

Among Western children (Vernon 1970, citing Piaget), a real grasp of linear perspective (as measured in the reproduction of drawings) is not complete until about eight years of age, and concepts of total Euclidean space, with objects located in a landscape that recedes gradually into the distance, develop only in older children. But the experiments on which this conclusion was based used photography, itself a derivative of the very conventions of perspective drawing!

17. This documentation of moves is not unique to the Rendille, nor does it convey the entire picture because, even in fully nomadic societies, men also move across the landscape in the course of herding their animals, while a camp remains temporarily anchored in space. A similar pattern obtains among all the fully nomadic societies in Africa. However, not all nomadic societies are fully nomadic. In seminomadic situations (such as those described by some of the contributors to this volume), women, children, and old men will often remain behind in the camp while men move far afield with their animals or in caravan trade.

18. See Prussin 1987 for a more detailed discussion.

3. THE CREATIVE PROCESS

1. The same principle of gravity and balance is expressed in the Classical contrapposto stance of both the Greek women supporting the porch of the Erechtheum on the Parthenon in Greece and the African women who carry head loads. The posture of the African nomad as he balances himself on his long herding staff reflects this principle as well.

2. See Haberland 1963:pl. 69 for two-pole saddles used by the Borana in southern Ethiopia, and Bulliet 1975:51 for a description of their use in Jubaland (southern Somalia) and northeastern Kenya.

3. This Téda camel saddle (*basuur* in Arabic) was described more than a century ago by Nachtigal (1971–87, 1:415): "The saddle used in Tibesti (i.e., among the Téda) . . . is made of two forks of acacia wood, placed like a clamp before and behind the camel's hump; the prongs of the fork are bound together on either side by rods fastened crosswise. The whole structure, the separate parts of which are fastened to each other with little strips of leather instead of the less durable ropes, rests on a thick cushion of plaited straw or palm bast." (The cushions in fig. 3.4d are shown on one side only for clarity.)

4. The *adofa* is in general a mark of prosperity, so not every woman has one, and only relatively few women know how to decorate it. Fuchs estimates that less than half the Tubu households have one at their disposal (personal communication, 1992). Le Coeur (1950:60) points out that among the Daza the framework is overlaid with cow or antelope hides sewn together; in Tibesti it is overlaid with cotton cloth. Leather cushions *(oderi)*, the rectangular sheets of leather decorated with cowries *(dela)*, and red and green striped rugs or blankets from Fezzan are placed within it.

5. Nachtigal (1971–87, 2:344–45) recorded that the women of the wealthier families and their small children are carried by camels; if they possess horses, the men travel on horseback, but if they are old, on camels:

Among the more distinguished families, great care is taken with the construction of the basket-like frames which Awlad Sulayman women ride in. It is stained black, and covered and hung with woolen quilts and silk cloths, the diversity of which is a matter of pride for the women. The princesses, that is, the women born of the chief's family, have the privilege of putting up, on the side walls of the *karmat,* slender attachments made of wooden poles to the height of about a meter; these are also decorated with colored silk cloth.

6. Du Puigaudeau wrote (1980–81:179):

The riding saddle with its padding is placed on the slope of the back, between the hump and the withers, in such a way that all the weight rests on the shoulders. Nothing must push against the hump, in order to prevent incurable lesions. The saddle that leans too far forward would put the rider in danger of toppling over, head first, when his mount kneels abruptly. It must by no means lean backwards, since the rider's feet would be unable to easily hit the shoulder of the camel with the light heel taps that are a secret code between man and animal. A badly balanced saddle is a cause of fatigue for the animal as well as for the rider, and moreover throws off the harmony of their togetherness.

7. The equilibrium of the saddle is essential. The pack saddle carrying the litter may shift dangerously: if the belly girth is not firmly attached to the saddle by its buckle and counterstraps, the saddle will slip around and topple over under the belly. There is the further risk of having the saddle topple over to the right or left by the unequal weight of the baggage.

8. See Monteil 1952 and Monod 1967 for alternate historic interpretations.

9. This same classic Tuareg design distinguishes the hilt of Tuareg swords as well as Tuareg women's jewelry. Its presence in these various contexts is itself an interesting avenue to follow in the pursuit of Tuareg history.

10. Labat wrote (1728, 1:262): "it is the work of the women; they spin the hair and the wool which makes up this cloth, they work it on the loom and do all the other work of the house including the currying of horses, searching for wood and water, preparing bread and meat." He subsequently added that "all the women in general work very much . . . in a word, they are charged with all the work of the house" (vol. 2:301).

11. Caillié (1830, 1:154) wrote: "The Zenague women, laborious through necessity, spin and weave the hair of the sheep and camels, to form covering for their tents; they also sew them together; tan leather, make the *varrois* [the large leather velums of tanned sheepskins which are used during the winter season] and everything, except iron work."

12. Duveyrier noted (1864:187): "The women . . . occupy themselves weaving burnous, and during the great heat of the day, at the time men are taking their siestas, one hears, in almost all the houses, the noise of moving shuttles."

13. According to Pallme (1844:63):

As a general rule, the women are far more industrious than the men; for, besides attending to their domestic occupations, they employ themselves more especially with plaiting straw mats, making baskets to hold milk, and funnels for filtering *merissa.* They perform, moreover, other business, which should more properly be considered as the duty of the men. I have even seen them tanning leather, whilst their husbands were quietly looking on, smoking their pipes, and indulging in idleness.

14. Rio (1961) makes the same point in his discussion of the leatherworkers in the oasis of Tamentit, southern Algeria, a historic capital of the Touat region. The few men leatherworkers there, in comparison to the many found among the nomads, are almost exclusively engaged in embroidery on leather. The term by which they are known derives from the word for silk.

4. HASSANIYA-SPEAKING NOMADS

1. Hassaniya orthography is difficult to compile. Some authors have used Arabic script, while others have used an orthography based on their own language, so that systems of transliteration vary considerably. Furthermore, the language has multiple dialects and includes many Berber and Soninke terms in its vocabulary. For the Tekna, I have followed Andrews' preference; for the extracts from Du Puigaudeau, I have observed her transcription, even though it differs considerably from the currently accepted practice followed in Creyaufmüller 1983.

2. The Hassaniya word *harratin* designates a free man who is in the service of a nomadic family as an artisan or an agriculturalist. The term is also used in reference to the southern agriculturalists, the Soninke or Sarakole descendants of slaves bought or brought from the Sudan who live in the oasis cities.

3. The origin of the word Moor would be parallel to that of the Arabic term *Maghreb* = "man of the West." According to Andrews (personal communication, June 1992), the term Moor comes from the Greek *Mauros* = an inhabitant of ancient Mauretania in North Africa. There is considerable confusion in the literature because the French language uses the term *Maures* to designate the inhabitants of present-day Mauretania, though this too is derived from the Greek.

4. According to oral tradition, these castes of skilled craftspeople are reputed to have evolved out of Islamized tribes of Jewish origin. A number of scholars have attempted to address the question, but even though the possibility is tempting in the light of tent history, the ephemeral evidence requires considerably more supporting documentation and interpretation to make it convincing.

5. It is particularly important to distinguish between tanning and leatherworking. In Dakar today, it is the former slaves *(harratin)* who appear to have a monopoly on the tanning industry, but the leatherworking industry remains in the hands of a caste of women artisans.

6. The fieldwork on which Andrews' study is based was done during a detailed investigation of Moroccan tent types in 1968. The study was generously sponsored by the Social Science Research Council and the Royal Institute of British Architects.

7. A comprehensive survey of North African tents (*Cahiers des arts et techniques d'Afrique du Nord,* vol. 4 [Paris: Horizons de France, 1955]) contains articles on Moroccan, Algerian, Tunisian, and Libyan tents. The most detailed study and linguistic interpretation of Moroccan tents can be found in Laoust 1930 and in an architectural account by Rackow and Caskel 1938.

8. See Caro Baroja 1955 for a similarly illustrated velum in Western Sahara.

9. By 1967 almost no woodworking skills had survived in the Oued Noun. The wrapped peak is most probably an old form once used for multipeaked tents, but now reduced to a single piece. It was not influenced by the long Berber ridge found on other Moroccan tents.

10. A description of Trarza and Brakna travel, written more than a century and a half ago (Caillié 1830, 1:67–68), is almost identical with those of Du Puigaudeau:

At sunrise, the slaves took down the tents, and loaded them upon camels, together with the stakes, each camel carrying a tent; the rest of the goods were borne by oxen, and the women were conveyed on camels appropriated to that office. The saddles for this purpose are furnished with a sort of oval "pannier," large enough for two persons to sit in, and lined with a handsome carpet; that the journey may be more agreeable to the Moorish ladies, their seat is shaded by an awning of their finest manufactures.

The queen's saddle was adorned with scarlet and yellow cloth, and her cloth housing embroidered with many colors in silk. Her bridle was enriched with three pieces of copper, which rose like pyramids from the nose of the animal. The camels of the princesses were also much ornamented; and they sit in their saddles cross-legged like so many tailors.

Caillié's description of tents (1830, 1:92–93) is equally relevant:

The king's tent has nothing to distinguish it from those of his subjects; it is twenty feet long and ten wide, and covered like all the others with a stuff made of sheep's hair; at each end are eight leather straps and as many stakes, upon which it is stretched. Two upright poles ten or twelve feet long, crossing at the top and fitting into a crosspiece a foot long and six inches wide, are placed in the center to raise it; this crosspiece rises above the uprights and prevents their ends from piercing the awning. A carpet of sheep's hair, manufactured in the country, surrounds the interior of the tent; four stakes are driven in at one end, supporting two crossbars, over which a cord or string is passed in the form of a net, and upon this is placed their baggage. Their things are stowed in square leather sacks shaped like portmanteaus with an opening at the end; and these bags have a lid secured by a padlock. . . .

The harness of the horses and camels hangs up round the tent. . . . The king's bed is after the same fashion as that of the Blacks, consisting of a wattle covered with mats and raised by stakes and crossbars about a foot off the ground. . . . A matting is put round the goods at the end of the tent. . . . The store of water is kept in skins upon stakes in the inside of the tents.

11. Among the Tekna, the chief's tent was formerly flanked on the right and the left by a small tent of trusty servants. Set back a little, on a low rise if possible, it

opened onto the row of tents which the chief could then watch over.

12. Dubié (1953), on the other hand, observed that the orientation adopted by Mauretanian nomads for the most part was along a southeast-northwest axis; the entrance was on the west-northwest in the direction of the fresh wind coming from the ocean, and sheltered against the dry, hot winds as well as the tempests of sand accompanying the tornados arriving most often from the east-northeast.

13. The largest tent recorded in Mauretania (10 × 11 m) was in an emir's encampment consisting of sixty-eight tents at Boutilimit (Dubié 1953).

According to Du Puigaudeau, the tent of Sheik Abdallahi u. sheik Sidiya at Ain Salama was 10 × 10 m: made of fifteen strips, it had six wood crosspieces on each transverse side, plus one in each corner. The cords were short and attached to tall, forked sticks instead of ordinary stakes in order to avoid having long lines crossing those of neighboring tents at ground level. It was the only example of this type of attachment that she had occasion to witness.

14. The tent of Caïd Amharoc of the Zaïane at Khenifra, Morocco, for example, had a ridgepiece 10.60 m long, 35 cm wide × 17 cm thick, supported on three poles 9 m long. The tent, composed of twenty-five strips, was approximately 35 m long and 18 m wide (personal communication, Peter A. Andrews, June 1992, measured in 1968).

15. Laoust (1930) suggests that this strip may derive from the *triga* of Moroccan tents, but Andrews (above) disagrees.

16. The way in which the two poles are used suggests the creation of a saddle in its simplest form and by extension the interrelationship between tent and transport. It recalls the way in which structural poles are used by other nomads farther east to reconstitute the transport structures with each move.

17. A copy of the reception tent of the emir of Tagant, Abd-el-Rahman u. Bakar, it is now at the Musée de l'Homme, Paris.

18. The Sudanese blankets that Du Puigaudeau illustrates are the various kinds of *arkila kerka,* commonly known as Niafounke or Goundham blankets, woven by Songhay and Fulbe weavers.

19. Du Puigaudeau, in commenting on the shelf, noted that the *'amchchagab* means "that which supports" (personal communication, Peter A. Andrews).

20. A comparison of the difference in design and construction of the two types of sacks raises some interesting questions for further thought, particularly in the light of the square plan of a Mauretanian tent. Why should the square design, which calls for so much more material, be so essential to a woman's repertoire in contrast to the normal sack, whose design derives from making full use of a skin?

21. The most impressive and extensive documentation of designs on the sacks and pillows, based on field and archival research, can be found in Creyaufmüller 1983.

22. The calabashes in the archives of the Musée de l'Homme, Paris, are of particular interest.

23. When Gabus visited Walata (1955), he found ten women embroiderers still working. This same embroidery was first described by Dupuis-Yakouba at Timbuktu (1921). He noted that it was the tailors, all men of letters, who created it, but that the large tunics were worn by men and women alike. Indeed, Du Puigaudeau suggests that the use of these embroideries seems to have been imported from the Sudan where they are generally executed by men. However, when I was in Djenné, Mali, in 1970–71, these same tunics were being worn only by old women, and I was told that it is only they who have the right to wear them. According to more recently recorded information by Bernard Gardi, a mother will order a white gown and give it to her daughter. She, as a bride, will give it to her husband as a marriage gift, and he will then either embroider the gown himself or commission the embroidery from a tailor. Mostly men will wear these embroidered gowns, but women wear them too, although it is not clear to Gardi how a woman gets her personal embroidered gown (personal communication, January 1994). The implications of what seems to be a shift or reversal in both gender-discrete skills and literacy suggest an intriguing avenue of future inquiry.

24. What is of particular interest, however, is that among the Mauretanian nomads the newlywed's tent was traditionally made of white cotton. Put up in the evening, it was taken down every morning. Now, the lack of servants, the high cost of cloth, in a word, the general shrinking of modern life, has led families to simplify and abbreviate customs. The new household may be given one of the brown wool tents of the camp, and it is put up once and for all (Du Puigaudeau 1972).

5. THE TUAREG

1. Tuareg mythology attributes their origin to a woman of high rank whom they call Tin Hinan, and whose tomb is reputed to be at the citadel of Abalessa, Algeria (Reygasse 1950).

2. The ancestry of the Tuareg artisan guilds has long

intrigued scholars. Jemma (1972:269–70) has documented a matrilineal origin for one of the artisan lineages. Another myth of origin refers to the forty-four artisans from the Adrar-des-Iforas, enslaved by the Kel Rela, a noble clan, then liberated and moved to the Ahaggar, from where they subsequently returned. Others claim that the ancestors of the Tuareg artisans were Jews who had fled from Touat in 1492 (Rio 1961; Lhote 1944, 1984b; Gabus 1955–58; Jacques-Meunié 1982).

3. To compile a glossary of Tuareg terms is difficult because authors have used various orthographic conventions over time and dialects vary geographically. For purposes of simplification, Nicolaisen 1963 has been used wherever possible in the first part of the chapter for the Kel Ahaggar and Kel Dennek, and Casajus's transcription has been honored for the Kel Ferwan.

4. Chapelle (1949:34), for instance, claims that the vassal Kel Inteser are actually Mauretanian nomads who have become Tuaregized, whereas, on the other hand, settlements neighboring on the Berabich and extending as far west as Lake Faguibine and Goundham would be ancient Tuareg who have adopted the language and customs of the Mauretanian nomads.

The Kuntas, originally from Touat, are englobed in two main branches: one is installed in Mauretania, and the other has pushed up to the region of Bourem, Mali. Small Kunta fractions can be found everywhere among the Tuareg, particularly among the Adrar-des-Iforas, the Iwllemmeden, and the Ahaggar. Bilingual, they exercise a great influence over the Tuareg but are rarely Tuaregized and wear Moorish costume.

5. In the case of divorce, the woman takes the tent, leaving her husband without shelter. Occasionally in a camp one encounters a bed out in the open, sheltered from the wind by the long mat *(éseber)* but unprotected by a tent cover. This makeshift set-up is the lodging of a recently divorced man who has not been able to procure a new tent and has not yet remarried. Among the warriors and nobles *(imajeren)*, where each man has his own personal tent, this shelter is not found.

6. More recently Lhote (1984a:166) pointed out that the memory of woodworking among women is perpetuated in the Ahaggar: they continue to fashion wooden bowls and spoons out of wood for their personal use and as gifts: "I have seen in the Ahaggar camps a multitude of small utensils, certainly more than a century old, the work of the wives of celebrated nobles whose names are piously guarded, all of which are venerably conserved. This custom is even more remarkable when one considers the hatred which the Tuareg attach to manual work."

7. Benhazera (1908:11) noted:

. . . at each step, one finds the influence of the woman in Tuareg society. In history, in heredity, in life, in thought, in the conduct of the Tuareg, everywhere her influence is felt. It is from the woman that the Tuareg claim descent. In inheritance, one knows that it is transmitted through the woman. It is from his mother that a son acquires the right to command . . . and his station in life, noble, vassal, or serf. In life, the woman has a freedom unseen in Muslim life. She moves freely, and monogamy has been preserved. Her camels carry their own distinctive mark, she camps close to her own family after marriage, almost all women have a camel and a special saddle. In the tent, she reigns as mistress. It is she who is the most instructed, because she knows, better than the man, to read and write *tifinar*.

8. Photographs of this part of the marriage ceremony can be found in Nicolaisen 1963 and Göttler 1989.

9. Nicolas (1950) illustrates a similar type of two-pole ridgepiece used by the Arab Dermchaka who migrated from the north. A similar ridge cap is also used by the Ulad-Sa'id nomads in southern Tunisia (Rackow and Caskel 1938).

10. A similar Kel Ahaggar ceremony was described by Benhazera (1908:14):

Once the contract is signed . . . it is necessary to prepare the couch for the newlyweds. The women build up a sort of mattress of sand or earth, called *adebel*, and it is covered with a blanket *(haik)*. Above it, one will build the skin tent on two wooden arches *(igegan)* and the customary pickets. But at this moment, the men intervene: they strike the velum of the tent. Two on one side, two on the other, they rush the tent and rush it again, three times.

Then the tent is erected definitively. The men lead the bridegroom to the tent. Three times round it he is led, and he then enters it, taking care to set his right foot first, always, because that brings good luck.

The bridegroom is in the tent with his friends. The women now accompany the bride, who has remained hidden in either her maternal aunt's tent or in the tent of a relative along the maternal line. At some meters from the tent, the son of the maternal aunt of the bride advances and attempts to retain the bride, demanding as a gift a pair of sandals. When the sandals are given, there is an interchange of male and female choruses, and the bride enters the tent.

For seven days the bride's relatives provide food. During this time, the newlyweds cannot leave the tent.

11. A similar single-pole ridgepiece was collected from southern Libya among the Ulad 'Ali, but it is used in duplicate (Rackow and Caskel 1938). Although there are two poles under the tent, they do not converge into a single apex. Each pole has its own ridge cap, and these work in conjunction with two reinforcing girths.

12. *Éhakit* is a masculine word in *tamachek* in contrast to the term *éhen*. Duveyrier (1864) noted that this term was used by the Kel Ahaggar for the skin tent as a whole, whereas the term *éhen* was used in reference to a mat-covered tent. The etymology implies a gender distinction between leather tents and mat-covered tents. Parenthetically, Duveyrier also recorded a Tuareg term for a wool velum *(aberdjen)*.

13. The most beautiful *éseber* (*shitek* among the Iwllemmeden Kel Dennek) in the Niger region have another name attached to them: *ikadammatan* (Bernus 1985). The *ikadammatan* women have a reputation for creating the most beautiful mats. At the same time, their husbands are equally renowned for the fabrication of leather-encased talismans with particularly virile remedial and pharmaceutical powers which are then sold over a vast region.

14. For reasons of brevity rather than import, Casajus's very detailed discussion of the various plaiting techniques has been omitted from this extract. The reader is referred to the description in the original text (Casajus 1987:45–47) for further details.

15. *Aljin* derives from the Arabic *jinn*. In fact, the *kel esuf* have many points in common with the Arabic *jinn* as they are described in the Koran and the classics.

16. Nicolaisen (1963:391) has already called attention to the differences in orientation between northern groups using T-shaped posts and leather velums and southern groups using bentwood armature, mat-covered tents. He too suggests that this ninety degree rotation in space is not accidental.

17. According to Islamic doctrine as expressed in the Sufist tradition, and in keeping with the designs found on many amulets and much of the West African Islamic design gestalt (see, for example, Chap. 4 above), the five pillars of the faith are represented by the four corners plus the center of a square.

6. THE TUBU

1. The term Tubu has passed into general usage as a result of nineteenth-century European references. Explorers who traversed this region, such as Lyon (1821), Barth (1857), and Nachtigal (1971–87), all used the term, or a variant of it, in their accounts (e.g., Tibboo or Toubou). More recent writings (Rodd 1926; Cline 1950; Le Coeur 1950) use the term Téda, Téda-Daza, or Toda.

The substantive parts of this chapter draw heavily on Chapelle 1957 and Fuchs 1961, 1991. I am deeply grateful to Dr. Peter Fuchs for comments on a preliminary version of this chapter.

2. Chapelle (1957) chose to subsume the Kreda and the Bideyat who inhabit the Ennedi, and the Zaghawa of Wadai and Darfur under the generic Tubu term, but Fuchs (personal communication, 1992) believes that there is a clear cultural, ethnic, and language boundary between the Tubu, the Bideyat, and the Zaghawa.

3. In the late sixteenth century the Arabic term "Goran" was used in reference to the cattle herders in the southern plains of the Tibesti range (Chapelle 1957:5, 9, citing Leo Africanus).

4. For a more detailed historical overview of both Tubu history and the complexities of its ethnic composition, the reader should refer to Chapelle 1957:25–65 and Fuchs 1971.

5. At Kanem, the Arabic term for blacksmith *(haddad)* is used, rather inexactly, to designate the Azza (Le Coeur 1953).

6. Similar ones are found not only from the banks of the Niger to Bahr-el-Ghazal northeast of Lake Chad but throughout what has been termed the Bantu-speaking regions of Africa. Chapelle (1957:228) also points out that the area of the mat tent is even more extensive to the east since it is found in East Africa among the Issa and the Danakil under the name *ari,* among the Somalis under the name *aqal,* and among the Hama under the name *gurgi.*

Le Coeur (1937:29–45, citing Sallust in *Bellum Jugurthinum,* XVIII) insists that "its area seems to have extended previously to North Africa, if one believes the description that Sallust gives of the dwelling of the Numidians: 'They turn over the hulls of their ships and make huts of them.' . . . Still today, the dwellings of the Numidians, or as they say their *mapales,* by their oblong form and their curved roofs, look much like the hulls of boats." It was on the basis of this particular similarity that Le Coeur chose to suggest that the *mapalia* were the ancestors of Téda-Daza housing (see Chap. 1 above).

7. On the mountain, the dwelling house *(yaobi)* consists of an enclosure made of stones cemented with clay, and topped with a rounded roof *(yididahoo)* made of reeds or palm leaves placed over a framework of *tefi* wood and tied with palm fiber ropes (Le Coeur 1950: entry for *yaobi*). When one compares stone housing and mat-covered armature tents, what strikes one are the similarities, not in construction, but in spatial organization and etymological ascriptions.

8. See Chapelle 1957:227. The same hypothesis has been

cited (and supported) by various authors as an explanation for the prevalence of Tuareg mat-covered armature tents (see Chap. 5 above).

9. Le Coeur (1950) mentions that it is made of cowskins. If so, it is apparently the only Tubu leather artifact, apart from rope, which is made of cowskin.

10. In Tibesti, the *dela,* also called *kubu* or *odri* according to the form and the degree of ornamentation, is replaced by a large blanket of goat hides with the hair still on them. It is often accompanied by a large leather rectangle made of finely plaited strips which covers the bed.

11. The skins of male animals are not tanned because they are too stiff or hard. Sandals are made with the neck, the thickest part.

12. The practice that Le Coeur describes (1950) is merely a variant: The day the couple comes out, a pestle and a wood mortar full of millet are placed in front of the door on a sheepskin. The newlyweds together strike three blows with the pestle. Then the husband and wife each try to get the mortar away from the other. With the grain gathered after the sham battle, the young wife cooks her first conjugal meal.

7. MAHRIA TENTS

1. I am indebted to Hartmut Lang with whom I did fieldwork with the Mahria, who has helped to complete my work with his own observations and information, and never tires in his support and encouragement; and to Dr. Peter A. Andrews for his expert help and corrections regarding tents and their construction. I would also like to extend thanks to my friend Laurie Engel who polished my English, and to my husband, Jup Holter, for the sketches without which the drawings could not have been made.

2. Persson et al. 1979 has been used for the transcription of terms in this chapter because it is widely used for teaching and learning Sudanese Arabic and is especially adapted to the Sudanese phonetic system. For legibility, however, the International Phonetics Association symbol ħ has been substituted for H and ʻ for 9, even though they do not accurately reflect the Sudanese Arabic phonetic system. Baumer 1975 and Tubiana and Tubiana 1977 were used to identify the botanical names for plants.

3. Although *daʾira* means "circle," in this context circle is an abstract term similar to "domestic circle" and does not mean a proper circle. Tents are not arranged in a physical circle.

4. Although they wanted to remain permanent, many nomads still kept their tents and also lived in them, so that when the situation arose (e.g., in times of drought) they would be able to migrate again. Even some of the nomadic families who had settled in a town (Kutum) still had their tents built up next to their mud houses.

5. Although churning camel's milk is not a problem, it requires a temperature between 12 and 18 degrees centigrade, which means that milk cannot be churned during the heat of the day and during hot seasons. Camel's milk cannot, however, be made into cheese.

6. There was one exception, however, of an old woman weaving, but it should be seen as a loan from another group. She wove 80 cm-wide rugs (*shamla*; pl.: *shumaal*) of goat's hair on a backstrap loom and sold them in order to meet part of her living expenses. When such a rug is used by the Mahria as a cover for the litter that constitutes part of the woman's riding saddle, it is called a *kedaana*.

7. Another type of large bag *(mukhlaaya)* is used as a container for a man's utensils and clothes when he goes on a long journey. Although it too is made from camel or cowhide, it is more finely worked.

8. See Holter 1983:117–18 for a more detailed description.

9. One woman purposely buried her last son's placenta on the southern side because, she said, her previous male child had died and she wanted this one to survive.

10. A mother is glad when her daughters reach an age at which they can lend a hand and share in the many daily duties, so that the mother can enjoy a little more free time. In an earlier stage, when all her children are still small, she has to perform all the daily tasks alone. As a rule, households are big, with more than seven children. Of course, a mother is also proud when a daughter gets married; she then also needs the free time to manufacture the dowry (while the marriageable daughter takes over part of the housework). But the mother also loses a helper when the daughter gets married.

11. A grandmother not only plays a key role in the socialization of the loaned child, but also in that of her other grandchildren, especially those of the son to whose household she belongs.

8. RENDILLE HABITATION

1. Spencer's description of Rendille social structure (1973) has been much enhanced by more recent fieldwork. Anne Beaman's dissertation on the Rendille age-set system (1981) remains at the same time a model for the recording, description, and analysis of women's aspects, notably the

marriage ceremony; Gunther Schlee's works on the Rendille and on the historic interaction of culture and ethnicity in the camel country between Lake Turkana and the Horn of Africa (summarized in Schlee 1989) provide a fascinating new approach.

2. There is no standardized spelling for Rendille orthography, but Schlee's various publications provide the most knowledgeable resource. Rendille spellings below are guided by his suggested usage.

3. The Rendille calendar is based on a seven-day week and twelve named lunar months (uncoordinated with a solar year) beginning with the *almado* celebrations at the onset of the spring rains. The years are named after the days of the week; two times seven years make a named age set of fourteen, while forty-two years make an (ideal) male generation. The *sorriyo* ceremony takes place four times in twelve months, on the ninth (actually the tenth) day of the first, second, sixth, and seventh months, called Sondere One, Sondere Two, Harafa, and Daga.

The first group ritual of an age set (*manti wahar lagoraha* = "the day the goat is sacrificed") is performed by uncircumcised boys on a full moon night of a *sorriyo* month shortly after the previous age set has entered elderhood, and two and a half years before the boys are officially established as an age set. The boys of all ten clans take a selected goat and sacrifice it in the inaccessible bush on a rocky lava plateau, far from houses, enclosures, people, or camels.

The second ritual, one and a half years later (*manti her ladura* = "the day the ox is danced") is a similar ritual, similarly performed in the bush and by uncircumcised boys, but this time the sacrificed animal is a bovine ox. The ox, symbolizing the important alliance between the two tribes, is given by the Logol lineage of the Samburu to every age set.

A year later, the circumcision *(khandi)* itself takes place in the first *sorriyo* month of a Friday year. One of the most important of all Rendille rituals, it takes place in the *goob*, with the participation of all relatives. This ritual entails building a large special structure and an enclosure.

4. The only wood never used in house construction is Grewia tanax [Forsk.] Fiori Tiliceae *(mulehenyu)*, which has a distinctly unpleasant smell.

5. Like the Gabra, the Somali, and many other African cultures, numbers are of significance to the Rendille. While the number three represents female, the number four represents male. Numbers such as two and four are looked upon as being propitious and fertile, and the old Arnirkh Bulyar, when asked about the significance, related these numbers to the two breasts of a woman, the two tits of a goat, and the four tits of a cow and a camel. To everyone's surprise, he even included eights as being the number of tits of a dog, and when asked if the Rendille really considered the dog propitious, quietly smiled and said, "God created it" (Anders Grum, field notes, April 1975).

6. The description of a Rendille marriage during which a new house is created is based primarily on Anne Beaman's dissertation (1981).

7. As a consequence, it is tempting to speculate that the typical Rendille house form is at least four hundred years old, perhaps more (Schlee 1989:235).

8. Grum, field notes, March 1, 1975.

9. HANDICRAFTS OF THE SOMALI NOMADIC WOMEN

1. The Somali Democratic Republic was formed July 1, 1960, uniting the former British Somaliland Protectorate in the north with the former Italian trust territory of Somalia in the south. There were marked differences in the crafts produced within these two colonies, but there was also clearly a convergence because of the nomadic nature of society.

Much of the research for this paper was carried out in northern areas such as Hargeisa and its environs, but work was also done in Mogadishu. The artifacts represented in the photographs and drawings are from the collections of the museums of Hargeisa and Mogadishu as well as from private collections.

This paper was researched and written between 1985 and early 1987: it was a very different Somalia to the one that exists today. Since then, tragically, the country has been torn asunder by civil strife. The north has removed itself from the Republic. There has been a power struggle and interclan fighting in the south, wholesale destruction of life and property, and a serious threat of starvation to much of the population.

2. The notable exceptions to this broadly sketched picture are the mountainous range in the north of the country, where cold weather prevails in the winter months, and the "green belt" or cultivated farmlands between the two permanently flowing rivers, the Shebelli and the Juba in the south, where agriculture and sedentary farming is practiced and dwellings are fixed on the terrain.

3. Somali pronunciation and spelling follow the conventions used by B. W. Andrzejewski in his translation of Cawl (1982:100). The letter *c* should simply be ignored, since it represents a sound which a foreign speaker normally can-

not perceive at all, so that he will hear a name like Cali as Ali. The nearest sound to the consonant *x* is the English *h,* pronounced with some measure of emphasis, and thus Xasan would be pronounced as Hassan. The pronunciation values of vowel letters in Somali are much the same as those in Spanish or Italian; the doubling of these letters does not substantially change their quality but is merely a sign of length. The sequence of letters *aw,* as in Hawd, is always pronounced to rhyme with the English word "how."

4. In all fairness, mention should be made of the excellent, well-illustrated, and recently published book, which also served as a catalogue to a traveling exhibition of Somali crafts (Loughran et al. 1986). This publication may at first belie the authors' contention that Somali crafts have been neglected by foreign scholars, but Johnson reaffirms this in his introduction when he writes: "The study of Somali art has been neglected, as has its customary and gestural folklore." In her contribution to this book, Mary Jo Arnoldi states: "Among pastoral peoples the richness and variety of their oral arts overshadow their visual art production," and she quickly dismisses the *aqal* and its contents in two short paragraphs. The authors of this chapter have chosen to focus attention on the merits of the crafts of Somali nomadic women, as found in the *aqal,* its coverings, and its contents.

On the Somali side, the authors received enormous help from the Academy of Science and Arts (Akadeemiyada Cilmiga Iyo Fanka) and in particular from three outstanding scholars: Axmed Cali Abukir, Axmed Cartan Xaange, and Cabdi Daahir Afey. Cabdi Daahir Afey is a walking encyclopedia of Somali crafts and is always ready to share his knowledge. Axmed Cali Abukir most generously gave his time and expertise and also very kindly referred questions to his female relatives. Axmed Cartan Xaange is the author of a very useful book, *Dalkii Udgoonaa* [The Land of Spices] (Mogadishu: Akadeemiyada Cilmiga Iyo Fanka, 1984), which is devoted to various aspects of Somali culture, including the house and its coverings and related work songs.

The traditional handicrafts of Somalia were on display in museums in both Mogadishu and Hargeisa, and the authors had access to all the items in these collections. We are indebted for the assistance given to us by the Director of Hargeisa Museum, Zamzam Abdi, and her coworkers, and to the Director Ahmed Farah Warsame of the new National Museum of Mogadishu, for all his help. It is hoped that in time these displays will be better attended and more fully explained. (Unfortunately, the collections in both museums were heavily damaged, if not totally destroyed, in the course of recent conflicts.)

5. Abdi Arte (1978:15–16) writes: "The woman makes the mobile *guri* (house), mounts and dismounts it, carries water and firewood, cooks food, churns milk and makes *ghee.* The man sits under the shade and makes decisions on where to graze, where to settle, and if and when to move from one camp to another." Another source, Yusuf Hagi Adan, said: "Men's work is digging wells and bringing the water from the wells to the *aqal* by camel, arguing and fighting with other tribes, rearing, watering and grazing camels, making fences around the camp and arranging for the security against wild animals, unfriendly people and thieves. Women's work is everything else." But the male position is defended by Laurence (1963:63) who notes: "The division of labour was not as unfair as it sounded. The men protected the tribe with their spears, and led the herds to new grazing grounds, often going ahead to find the way. Men had to reserve their strength for their own demanding work."

6. Andrzejewski and Lewis (1964:49) noted that "although the range of the subject matter resembles that of the *gabay,* most *buraambur*s have a lighter touch, with less stylization and restraint in the actual recital. But the greatest difference lies in the fact that the *buraambur* is a poem composed by women for women—although men have been known to make interested listeners."

7. The plural of *saab* in Somali is *saabyo,* not *saab*s as found in the text of this chapter. In the interest of simplification, the authors have used the Somali singular form with the Anglicized plural suffix "s" throughout the text. Thus more than one *aqal* is referred to as *aqal*s, more than one *dhiil* as *dhiil*s, etc. It is also important to point out that *caws* is not the plural of *caw. Caws* is the Somali word for "grass" and also is sometimes used to refer to the woven mat made of grass, while *caw* is the Somali word for palm and is a material used to make a very different type of woven mat.

8. The term *aqal,* like *guri,* carries meaning full of implication as well. The question *aqal gal* (literally, "When are you going to enter the house?") in fact means "When will the wedding take place?" Both *guri* and *aqal* evolve out of the marriage context, in which a new lineage, a new camp, a new house come into being.

9. See Glover 1947 for more details on these acacias.

10. With no written sources, the authors relied heavily on interviews with women who could supply useful data on the technical side of craftmaking, and we are deeply indebted to them for their help: Habiba Ahmed Muhamed, Asha Ali Abukir, Faduma Ali Abokor, Dahabo Ainub Liban,

Muumino Hufane, Xawo Cabdi, Yusur Cali Abdalla, and to Mako Haji Awad who was our guide in all the Hargeisa research.

11. Adan (1981:116), on the basis of research conducted in the cities of Hargeisa and Burao, northern Somalia, notes: "Somali women compose poetry, but it is a special type of poetry which is not considered serious enough for the taste of the nomadic man (poetry has always been considered a man's domain). Called *buraambur*, it is shorter and lighter than those considered in the male domain. It can be accompanied by drums, clapping or stepping. Among the categories are lullabies *(hoobeyo)*, work songs *(salsal)* such as those sung while loading a camel, and *hoyal*, sung while weaving mats. There are also religious songs and healing songs."

12. The importance of *kebed* making, and the exciting songs that emerge from them, are described in detail in Adan 1981.

13. The Acacia bussei is a tree that grows over a considerable part of Somalia, between 650 and 1,500 m altitude, and is happiest in the red soil of the Haud. It is a tree known to all Somalis and features in much of their poetry. The tree provides them with much more than the shade of its spreading umbrella shape: its fibers are used for the weaving of the *kebed*, its roots are used to make the *qabax*, its bark for the *asal* solution which helps to seal the woven fiber containers, to produce a deep red dye, and to cleanse medicinally. It is also used in the treatment of cholera and dysentery. Its dense wood makes an excellent charcoal, and thus, sadly, it is becoming an endangered species in Somalia (Glover 1947:xxiv).

14. The size of the house is less a matter of whim or fancy, and more in direct proportion to the availability of house-building materials. In the Haud, the area around Burao, and the northwest Nugaal district, where euphorbia bushes, acacias, and grasses are plentiful, the houses tend to be larger. West of Hargeisa, Boroma district, the highlands, and the coastal areas, where these materials are scarce, the houses are correspondingly smaller. A big house also requires good grazing to support the many pack (male) camels needed to transport it.

In the northeastern district of the country, around Bosaso, Qarbo, and Bari region, where palms grow in abundance, the covering of the *aqal* is made primarily of *caw* or woven palm fronds. The color and designs are reputed to be very beautiful, and the women vie with each other for decorative effect. In this region, the *kebed* is not used because the Acacia bussei is not found, and even the *harrar* is rare.

15. No description of the *aqal* and its decoration would be complete without mention of the *lammo* or *jarco*, the cow skin tanned until it is beautifully soft and possesses a lovely patina. The covering of the house should start with the *lammo*, and it is a cherished item. It is the one covering that is entirely the work of men, and therefore not included in the main body of this article. It was a common practice in the north to sew two or three similar skins together with decorative stitches or shells at their seams. In addition to its use as decoration, the decorated cow skin was used to provide shade for a sick person or baby transported in the center of a loaded burden camel.

16. *Hadhuub geel* is the vessel used when milking camels and holds about four liters, while the *hadhuub adhi* is a much smaller milking cup for goat's or sheep's milk and can hold about one liter.

17. This explanation was given by Faduma Ali Abokor and Asha Ali Abukir.

18. What the *sibraar* is filled with depends on where the men are coming from and where they are going. If they are leaving the camel camp and traveling to a distant place, the *sibraar* is filled with milk; if they are coming from a well to a camel camp, it is filled with water. For a very long journey, it may be used for a mixture of milk and water *(badhax)*, which is both nourishing and thirst-quenching. Each time the container is used for a different liquid, it must be cleaned thoroughly. This is done by filling it with the *asal* solution, then turning it inside out to dry and refilling with the solution when it is back to its original shape.

19. Anonymous 1955.

20. To prepare the *muqmud*, long thin shreds of meat are put on clotheslines between two poles and allowed to dry. If the process is not completed in one day, salt is added to the uncooked meat to preserve it. When thoroughly dried, the meat is cut into small, narrow lengths and deep-fried in clarified butter made from goat's milk. When white bubbles form, the meat is removed. The herbs, cardamom, spices, onions, garlic, and salt (if the meat was left unsalted) are all fried in new butter, and when drained, this fragrant butter is added to the meat and solidifies around it. Dates and spices are crushed to form a stiff paste, and four small cylinders of this date mixture are injected into the mixture and allowed to protrude slightly above it. Finally, a dome cover made of the date paste is fitted over the meat and butter, held up by the protruding date cylinders so that it leaves a little space above the meat. This date cover is firmly sealed against the edges of the enamel bowl. So packed, the dish could stay untouched for several months.

BIBLIOGRAPHY

There are a number of extensive bibliographies for some of the peoples in this book and the geographical regions they move in, and they include scattered references to nomadic material culture. The inclusion of all the works that have been consulted would result in a vast compilation, so only those directly related to the particular concerns of this book are given here. What ultimately governed the inclusion of a particular entry was its relevance to nomadic architecture in the mind of the authors. Some general entries, while not referenced in the text, have been included primarily as an additional guide for the interested reader.

In addition, the bibliography also includes some references to nomadic cultures that are related to those considered by the authors. Thus references to the Hadendowa, the Kababish, and the Beni Amer have been included in addition to those for the Beja. Some relevant architectural references to the Afars and Danakils have also been included, since many authors address the entire Horn of Africa rather than the Somalis per se. Entries on botanical resources are limited to those containing information on the ethno-botanical and historico-botanical uses of particular trees, shrubs, and plants or on the processing and production technologies used in the creation of the nomadic built environment.

ABBREVIATIONS

BA Baessler-Archiv
Bull.CEHSAOF Bulletin du Comité des Études Historiques et Scientifiques de l'Afrique Occidentale Française
Bull.IFAN Bulletin de l'Institut Français d'Afrique Noir
CEA Cahiers d'Études Africaines
CNRS Centre Nationale de la Recherche Scientifique
CUP Cambridge University Press
HRAF Human Relations Area Files
JAH Journal of African History
JRAI Journal of the Royal Anthropological Institute
JRAIGBI Journal of the Royal Anthropological Institute of Great Britain and Ireland
JSA Journal de la Société des Africanistes
ORSTOM Office de la Recherche Scientifique et Technique Outre-Mer
OUP Oxford University Press
PUF Presses Universitaires de France
SNR Sudan Notes and Records
SOAS School of Oriental and African Studies
Trav.IRS Travaux de l'Institut de Recherches Sahariennes

Aafif, Mohamed. 1980–81. "Les harkas hassaniennes d'après l'oeuvre d'A. Ibn Zidane." *Hespéris-Tamuda* 9, 1: 153–68.

Abir, M. 1968. "Caravan Trade and History in the Northern Parts of East Africa." *Paideuma* 4: 103–20.

Acland, P. B. E. 1932. "Notes on the Camel in the Eastern Sudan." *SNR* 15, 1: 119–49.

Adams, William Y. 1977. *Nubia, Corridor to Africa*. Princeton: Princeton University Press.

Adan, Amina H. 1981. "Women and Words." *Ufahamu* 10, 3: 115–42.

Adu Bobie, Gemma J. 1981. "The Role of Rendille Women." *IPAL Technical Report Number F-2. UNESCO-MAB FRG Integrated Project in Arid Lands*, pp. 113–57. Nairobi: UNESCO.

d'Alverny, Lt. F. 1950. "Vestiges d'art rupestre au Tibesti oriental." *JSA* 20: 239–72.

Andrews, Peter Alford. 1971. "Tents of the Tekna, Southwest

Morocco." In Paul Oliver, ed., *Shelter in Africa,* pp. 124–42. New York: Praeger.

Andrzejewski, B. W., and Lewis, I. M. 1964. *Somali Poetry: An Introduction.* Oxford: Clarendon Press.

Anonymous. 1955. "The Hedo." *War Somali Sidihi* 59. Hargeisa: The Information Department Somaliland Protectorate.

Anquetil, Jacques. 1977. *Niger: L'Artisanat créateur.* Paris: Dessain et Tolra.

Archer, John, and Lloyd, Barbara. 1985. *Sex and Gender.* Cambridge: CUP.

Ardener, S., ed. 1975. *Perceiving Women.* London: Dent.

———. 1981. *Women and Space: Ground Rules and Social Maps.* London: Croom Helm.

Arkell, Anthony John. 1961. *A History of the Sudan to 1821,* rev. ed. London: Athlone Press.

Arnoldi, Mary Jo. 1984. "The Artistic Heritage of Somalia." *African Arts* 17, 4: 24–33.

Arte, Abdi. 1978. *Basic Education for Nomads.* Report of a Seminar held in Mogadishu, 1–9 April, 1978. Mogadishu: UNESCO/UNICEF.

Asad, Talal. 1970. *The Kababish Nomads (Northern Kordofan).* New York: Praeger.

Aubert de la Rue, Edgar. 1939. *La Somalie française.* Paris: Gallimard.

Aubréville, André. 1949. *Climats, forêts et désertification de l'Afrique tropicale.* Paris: Société d'Éditions Géographiques, Maritimes et Coloniales.

———. 1950. *Flore forestière soudano-guinéenne AOF-Caméroun.* Paris: Société d'Éditions Géographiques, Maritimes et Coloniales.

Ausenda, Giorgio. 1987. "Leisurely Nomads: The Hadendowa (Beja) of the Gash Delta and Their Transition to Sedentary Village Life." Ph.D. dissertation, Columbia University.

Aymard, Le capitaine. 1911. *Les Touareg.* Paris: Hachette.

Ayoun, R., and Cohen, B. 1981. *Les Juifs d'Algérie. 2000 Years of History.* Paris: J. C. Lactes.

Bachelard, Gaston. 1969. *The Poetics of Space,* trans. Maria Jolas. Boston: Beacon Press.

Barker, G. 1981. "Early Agriculture and Economic Change in North Africa." In J. A. Allen, ed., *The Sahara: Ecological Change and Early Economic History.* London: SOAS.

Barth, Heinrich. 1957. *Travels and Discoveries in North and Central Africa, 1849–1855,* 5 vols. New York: Appleton.

Baumer, Michel. 1975. *Noms vernaculaires soudanais utiles à l'écologiste.* Paris: Éditions CNRS.

———. 1983. *Notes on Trees and Shrubs in Arid and Semi-arid Regions.* Rome: United Nations Food and Agriculture Organization.

Beaman, Anne W. 1977. "Nomadic Womanhood: The Rendille's Other Half." Manuscript.

———. 1981. "The Rendille Age-set System in Ethnographic Context: Adaptation and Integration in a Nomadic Society." Ph.D. dissertation, Boston University, Boston, Mass.

———. 1983. "Women's Participation in Pastoral Economy: Income Maximization among the Rendille." *Nomadic Peoples* 12: 20–25.

Béart, Charles. 1955. *Jeux et jouets de l'Ouest africain,* 2 vols. Mémoire 42. Dakar: IFAN.

Beck, Pierre, and Huard, Paul. 1969. *Tibesti, carrefour de la préhistoire saharienne.* Paris: Arthaud.

Becker, Howard S. 1982. *Art Worlds.* Berkeley and Los Angeles: University of California Press.

Beckingham, C. F., and Huntingford, G. W. B., eds. 1954. *Some Records of Ethiopia, 1593–1646.* London: Hakluyt Society.

Bellin, P. 1963. "L'Enfant saharien à travers ses jeux." *JSA* 33, 1: 47–103.

Benhazera, Maurice. 1908. *Six mois chez les Touareg du Ahaggar.* Algiers: Adolphe Jordan.

Berkeley, Ellen Perry, ed. 1989. *Architecture: A Place for Women.* Washington, D.C.: Smithsonian Institution Press.

Bernatz, J. M. 1852. *Scenes in Ethiopia,* 2 vols. London: F. G. Moon.

Bernus, Edmond. 1967. "Cueillette et exploitation des resources spontanées du Sahel nigérien par les Kel Tamasheq." *Cahiers ORSTOM,* Sciences humaines 4, 1: 31–52.

———. 1974. *Les Illabakan (Niger): Une Tribu touaregue sahélienne et son aire de nomadisation.* Paris: ORSTOM.

———. 1979. "L'Arbre et le nomade." *Journal d'agriculture traditionelle et de botanique appliquée* (Musée National d'Histoire Naturelle, Paris) 26, 2: 103–28.

———. 1980. "L'Arbre dans le nomad's land." *Cahiers ORSTOM,* Sciences humaines 17, 3–4: 171–76.

———. 1981a. *Touaregs nigériens.* Mémoires ORSTOM 94. Paris: ORSTOM.

———. 1981b. "Points cardinaux: Les critères de désignation chez les nomades touaregs et maures." *Bulletin des Études Africaines de l'INALCO* 1, 2: 101–6.

———. 1985. "Colporteurs de charmes magiques: Les Ikadammatan." *Journal des Africanistes* 55, 1–2: 16–27.

Berry, John. 1992. *Cross-cultural Psychology.* Cambridge: CUP.

Bidault, Jacques, and Giraud, Pierre. 1946. *L'Homme et la tente.* Paris: J. Susse.

Boddy, Janice. 1982. "Womb as Oasis: The Symbolic Context of Pharaonic Circumcision in Rural Northern Sudan." *American Ethnologist* 9, 4:682–98.

Born, Martin. 1965. *Zentralkordofan, Bauern und Nomaden in Savannengebieten des Sudans*. Marburg: Geographisches Institut der Universität. Marburger Geographische Schriften 25.

Bovill, E. W. 1970. *The Golden Trade of the Moors*. London: OUP.

Brandt, Henry, 1956. *Nomades du soleil*. Lausanne: Clairefontaine.

Brett, M. 1981. *Les maures*. Paris: Édition Atlas.

Briffault, Robert. 1977. *The Mothers*, abridged, with an introduction by Gordon Rattray Taylor. New York: Atheneum.

Briggs, Lloyd Cabot. 1960. *Tribes of the Sahara*. Cambridge, Mass.: Harvard University Press.

Bril, Blandine. 1979. "Analyse des nombres associés à l'homme et à la femme en Afrique de l'Ouest." *Africa* 49, 4: 367:76.

Brosset, Lt. Charles Diego. 1928. "La Rose des vents chez les nomades sahariens." *Bull.CEHSAOF* 11, 4: 666–83.

Bruce, James. 1812. *Travels between the Years 1765 and 1773 through Part of Africa, Syria, Egypt and Arabia into Abyssinia, to Discover the Source of the Nile*. London: Albion Press.

Brugsch, Émile. 1889. *La Tente funéraire de la princesse Isimkheb provenant de la trouvaille de Déir el-Baharî*. Cairo: by the author.

Brugsch, Heinrich Karl. 1891. *A History of Egypt under the Pharoahs*. London: John Murray.

Budge, E. A. Wallis. 1928. *A History of Ethiopia, Nubia and Abyssinia*, 2 vols. London: Methuen.

Bulliet, Richard W. 1975. *The Camel and the Wheel*. Cambridge, Mass.: Harvard University Press.

Burckhardt, John Lewis. 1819. *Travels in Nubia*. London: John Murray.

Cahiers des arts et techniques d'Afrique du Nord, vol. 4. 1955. Paris: Horizons de France.

Cailliaud, M. Frederic. 1823. *Voyage à Méroé, au fleuve Blanc, au-delà de Fâzoql dans le midi du royaume de Sennâr, à Syouah et dans cinq autres oasis*. Paris: Rignoux.

Caillié, René. 1830. *Journal d'un voyage à Tembouctou et à Jenné dans l'Afrique Centrale pendant les années 1824–1828*, 4 vols. Reprint 1965. Paris: Éditions Anthropos.

Camps, Gabriel. 1987. *Les Berbères: Mémoire et identité*, 2nd ed. Paris: Éditions Errance.

Caro Baroja, Julio. 1955. *Estudios saharianos*. Madrid: Instituto de Estudios Africanos.

Casajus, Dominique. 1981. "La Tente et le campement chez les Touaregs Kel Ferwan." *Revue de l'Occident Musulman et de la Méditerranée* 32: 53–70.

———. 1982a. "Autour du ritual de la nomination chez les Touaregs Kel Ferwan." *Journal of the Anthropological Society of Oxford* 13, 1: 57–67.

———. 1982b. "Le mariage préférentiel chez les Touaregs Kel Ferwan." *Journal des Africanistes* 52, 1–2: 95–117.

———. 1983. "The Wedding Ritual among the Kel Ferwan Tuaregs." *Journal of the Anthropological Society of Oxford* 14, 2: 227–37.

———. 1987. *La Tente dans la solitude (Kel Ferwan)*. Cambridge: CUP.

Cassanelli, Lee V. 1982. *The Shaping of Somali Society: Reconstructing the History of a Pastoral People: 1600–1900*. Philadelphia: University of Pennsylvania Press.

Castries, H. de. 1923. "La conquête du Soudan par el Mansour." *Hespéris* 3, 4: 433–88.

Cauneille, Capitaine A. 1950. "Les Nomades Regueïbat." *Trav.IRS* 6: 83–100.

Cauneille, A., and Dubief, J. 1955. "Les Regueïbat Legouacem, chronologie et nomadisme." *Bull.IFAN* 17 (B): 528–50.

Cauvet, Gaston. 1925–26. *Le Chameau*, 2 vols. Paris: J. B. Baillière et Fils.

Cawl, Faraax M. J. 1982. *Ignorance Is the Enemy of Love*. London: Zed Press.

Cerulli, Enrico. 1957. *Somalia: Scritti vari editi ed inediti*, 3 vols. Rome: Amministrazione Fiduciana Italiana.

Chailley, M. 1952. "L'Habitation à la côte française des Somalis." *Bull.IFAN* 14, 4: 1490–1511.

Chapelle, F. de la. 1933–34. "Les Tekna du Sud Marocain." *L'Afrique française* 43:587–96, 633–45, 791–99; 44: 42–52.

Chapelle, Jean. 1948. "Les Nomades du Sahara méridional. Les Maures." *Tropiques* 304: 5–15.

———. 1949. "Les Nomades du Sahara méridionial." *Tropiques* 308: 25–38.

———. 1950. "Les Toubous." *Tropiques* 318: 29–38; 319: 16–24.

———. 1957. *Nomades noirs du Sahara*. Paris: Plon.

———. 1980. *Le Peuple Tchadien*. Paris: L'Harmattan.

Christides, V. 1980. "Ethnic Movements in Southern Egypt and Northern Sudan: Blemmyes-Beja in Late Antiquity and Early Arab Egypt until 700 A.D." *Listy Filologycka* 103: 129–43.

Chudeau, R. 1910. "Note sur l'ethnographie de la région du Moyen Niger." *L'Anthropologie* 21: 661–66.

Cipriani, Lidio. 1940. *Abitazioni indigene dell'Africa Orientale Italiana*. Naples: Tirennale d'Oltremare.

Clark, W. T. 1938. "Manners, Customs and Beliefs of the Northern Beja." *SNR* 21, 1: 1–29.

Cline, Walter. 1950. *The Teda of Tibesti, Borku and Kawar in the Eastern Sahara*. General Series in Anthropology 12. Menasha, Wisc.: George Banta.

Cole, Doris. 1973. *From Tipi to Skyscraper*. Boston: I Press, Inc.

Colomieu, Le Commandant V. 1863. "Voyage dans le Sahara algérien." *Le Tour du Monde* 8, 2: 161–99.

Corral, José. 1985. *Ciudades de las caravanas*. Madrid: Hermann Blume.

Costa, Carolo. 1933. "Le Abitazioni dei Somali." *Le Vie d'Italia* (Touring Club Italiano) 39, 3: 185–93.

Creyaufmüller, Wolfgang. 1979. *Völker der Sahara—Mauren und Twareg*. Stuttgart: Staatliches Museum für Völkerkunde.

———. 1983. *Nomadenkultur in der Westsahara: Die materielle Kultur der Mauren*. Hallein, Austria: Burgfried-Verlag, H. Nowak.

Cribb, Roger. 1991. *Nomads in Archaeology*. Cambridge: CUP.

Cuoq, Joseph. 1975. *Recueil des sources arabes concernant l'Afrique Occidentale du VIIème au XVIème siècle (Bilad al-Sudan)*. Paris: CNRS.

Dahl, Gudrun. 1987. "Women in Pastoral Production." *Ethnos* 52, 1–2: 246–79.

Dale, Ivan Robert, and Greenway, P. J. 1961. *Kenya Trees and Shrubs*. Nairobi: Buchanan's.

Dalzel, Archibald. 1793. *The History of Dahomy*. London: Spilsbury.

Daniels, Charles M. 1970. *The Garamantes of Southern Libya*. London: Oleander Press.

Dauber, Maximilien. 1983. *Nomades du Sahara: Regards sur le passé et le présent des peuples du désert*. Paris: Presses de la Cité.

Daumas, Melchior J. E. 1971. *The Ways of the Desert*, trans. Sheila M. Ohlendorf. Austin: University of Texas Press.

Delarozière, Marie-Françoise. 1969. *Désert, ma citadelle*. Paris: Le Livre Africain.

———. 1985. *Les Perles de Mauritanie*. La Calada: Edisud.

Demougeot, Émilienne. 1960. "Le Chameau et l'Afrique du Nord romaine." *Annales, Économies, Sociétés, Civilisation* 2: 209–47.

Dinges, Norman G., and Albert R. Hollenbeck. 1978. "Field Dependence-Independence in Navajo Children." *International Journal of Psychology* 13, 3: 215–20.

Dolan, R. 1980. "Migration Patterns in the Rendille, 1923–78." In *IPAL Technical Report Number A-3*, pp. 124–31. Nairobi: UNEP.

Domenech, Lafuente Angel. 1946. *Algo sobre Rio de Oro*. Madrid: Selecciones Graficas, Diagonal 23.

Douls, Camille. 1888. "Cinq mois chez les Maures nomades du Sahara occidental." *Le Tour du Monde* 55: 177–224.

Drake-Brockman, R. E. 1912. *British Somaliland*. London: Hurst and Blackett.

Drew, Philip. 1979. *Tensile Architecture*. Boulder, Colo.: Westview Press.

Drysdale, J. G. S. 1954. "Self sufficiency—Somali Milk and Water Vessels." *War Somali Sidihi* 26. Hargeisa: The Information Department Somaliland Protectorate.

Dubié, Paul. 1953. "La Vie matérielle des Maures." *Mélanges ethnologiques*. Mémories IFAN 23: 111–252. Dakar: IFAN.

Dudot, Bernard. 1969. "Les 'sigittawen' ou poteaux de mariage d'Agadès." *Notes africaines* 123: 89–91.

Dunbabin, Katherine. 1978. *The Mosaics of North Africa*. Oxford: Clarendon Press.

Du Puigaudeau, Odette. 1957. "Contribution à l'étude du symbolisme dans le décor mural et l'artisanat de Oualata." *Bull.IFAN* 19 (B), 1–2: 137–83.

———. 1967; 1968; 1970; 1972; 1975; 1980–81. "Arts et coutumes des Maures." *Hespéris-Tamuda* 8: 111–96; 9: 329–427; 11: 5–82; 13: 183–224; 16: 185–211; 19: 169–220.

Dupuis-Yakouba, A. 1921. *Industries et principales professions des habitants de la région de Tombouctou*. Paris: Émile Larose.

Duveyrier, Henri. 1864. *Les Touareg du Nord*. Paris: Challamel Ainé.

Edgerton, Samuel Y. 1976. *The Renaissance Rediscovery of Linear Perspective*. New York: Harper & Row.

El Bekri, Abou-Obeid. 1965. *Description de l'Afrique septentrionale*, trans. Mac Gluckin de Slane. Paris: Adrien-Maisonneuve.

Epstein, H. 1971. *Origin of the Domestic Animals of Africa*, 2 vols. New York: Africana Publishing Co.

Erikson, E. H. 1968. *Identity, Youth and Crisis*. New York: W. W. Norton.

Fadl Hasan, Y. 1973. *The Arabs and the Sudan*. Khartoum: Khartoum University Press.

Faegre, Torvald. 1979. *Tents: Architecture of the Nomads*. Garden City, N.Y.: Anchor Press.

Feilberg, C. G. 1944. *La Tente noire*. Copenhagen: Glyndalske Boghandel.

Ferrand, Gabriel. 1903. *Les Çomalis*. Paris: Leroux.

Ferree, Barr. 1889. "Primitive Architecture. 1: Sociological Factors." *American Naturalist* 23: 24–32.

———. 1890. "Climatic Influence in Primitive Architecture." *American Anthropologist* 3, 2: 147–58.

Fitch, James Marston, and Branch, Daniel P. 1960. "Primitive Architecture and Climate." *Scientific American* 203, 6: 134–44.

Fleming, G. J. 1919. "Beni 'Amer Marriage Custom." *SNR* 2: 74–76.

Foucauld, Père Charles de. 1951–52. *Dictionnaire Touareg-Français: Dialecte de l'Ahaggar,* 4 vols. Paris: Imprimerie Nationale de France.

Foucher, Louis. 1963. *La Maison de la procession dionysiaque à El Jem.* Paris: PUF.

Fradier, Georges. 1976. *Mosaïques de Tunisie.* Photographs by André Martin. Tunis: Cérès.

Fratkin, Elliot. 1987. "The Organization of Labor and Production among the Ariaal Rendille." Ph.D. dissertation, Catholic University of America: Washington, D.C.

Fuchs, Peter. 1956. "Über die Tubbu von Tibesti." *Archiv für Völkerkunde* (Vienna) 11: 43–66.

———. 1961. *Die Völker der Südost-Sahara.* Vienna: Wilhelm Braumüller.

———. 1971a. "Tubu (Ostsahara, Tibesti). Errichten und Abbrechen eines Zeltes." *Encyclopaedia Cinematographica.* E1210/1968. Göttingen: Institut für den Wissenschaftlichen Film.

———. 1971b. "Satteln und Beladen eines Kamels bei den Tubu (Ostsahara, Tibesti)." *Encyclopaedia Cinematographica.* W770/1966. Göttingen: Institut für den Wissenschaftlichen Film.

———. 1991. *Menschen der Wüste.* Braunschweig: Westermann.

Fullerton, Arlene, and Adan, Amina. 1987. "Handicrafts of the Nomadic Women of Somalia." Manuscript. Mogadishu.

Gabus, Jean. 1951. "Les Sources magico-religieuse de l'art maure." *Bibliothèques et Musées de la Ville de Neuchâtel.* Neuchâtel: 86–107.

———. 1955–58. *Au Sahara: Arts et symboles,* 2 vols. Neuchâtel: Édition de la Baconnière.

———. n.d. *Guide du Musée d'Ethnographie.* Neuchâtel: Paul Attinger.

Galand-Pernet, P. 1978. "Images et image de la femme dans les poésies touaregues de l'Ahaggar." *Bulletin de littérature orale arabo-berbère* (Paris) 9: 5–52.

Gallais, Jean. 1975. *Pasteurs et paysans du Gourma: La Condition sahélienne.* Paris: CNRS.

Garcia, Le lieutenant. 1955. "Moeurs et coutumes des Teda du Tou." *Bulletin d'Institut d'Études Centrafricaine* 10: 167–209.

Gardi, René. 1970. *Sahara.* Berne: Kümmerly & Frey.

———. 1973. *Indigenous African Architecture.* New York: Van Nostrand Reinhold.

Gast, M. 1959. *Collections ethnographiques, Touareg Ahaggar.* Album 1. Museé d'Ethnographie et de Préhistoire du Bardo. Paris: A.M.G.

———. 1962–63. "Les Mesures en Ahaggar. I. Mesures de temps." *Trav.IRS* 21, 1: 207–14. "Les Mesures en Ahaggar. II. Mesures de longeurs." *Trav.IRS* 22, 1–2: 195–201.

———. 1963. "Aspect de l'artisanat chez les Kel Ahaggar en 1963." *Libyca* 11: 221–33.

Gauckler, P. 1896. Le Domaine des Laberii à Uthina (Oudna)." *Monuments et mémoires,* Académie des Inscriptions et Belles-Lettres, Fondation E. Piot, vol. 3.

Gauthier-Pilters, Hilde, and Dagg, Anne Innis. 1981. *The Camel.* Chicago: University of Chicago Press.

Genevière, J. 1950. "Les Kountas et leurs activités commerciales. *Bull.IFAN* 12, 4: 1111–27.

Gerteiny, Alfred G. 1967. *Mauretania.* New York: Praeger.

Glover, P. E. 1947. *A Provisional Checklist of British and Italian Somaliland Trees, Shrubs and Herbs.* London: Crown Agents for the Colonies.

Goldsmith, J. H. 1920. "Marriage Customs among the Beni 'Amer Tribe." *SNR* 3, 4: 293–95.

Göttler, Gerhard, ed. 1984. *Die Sahara.* Cologne: Du Mont. New edition 1987.

———. 1989. *Die Tuareg.* Cologne: Du Mont.

Grall, Le lieutenant. 1945. "Le secteur nord du cercle de Gouré." *Bull.IFAN* 7, 1–4: 1–46.

Griffiths, J. F., ed. 1972. *Climates of Africa.* New York: Elsevier.

Grottanelli, Vinigi L. 1947. "Asiatic Influences on Somali Cultures." *Ethnos* 4: 153–81.

———. 1968. "Somali Wood Engraving." *African Arts* 1, 3: 8–16.

Grum, Anders. 1976. "Rendille Habitation: A Preliminary Report." Manuscript. Nairobi.

———. 1977. "The Rendille Calendar." Manuscript.

———. 1979. "When the Flies Once Owned the Camels, and 81 Other Stories of the Rendille." Manuscript.

———. 1990. "Arnirkh Bulyar's Narrative of Rendille Moves 1903–1971." Manuscript. Blantyre, Malawi.

Gsell, Stéphane. 1915. *Hérodote.* Algiers: University of Algiers.

Guillain, M. 1856. *Documents sur l'histoire, la géographie et le commerce de l'Afrique Orientale,* 3 vols. + folio. Paris: Arthur Bertrand.

Haberland, Eike. 1963. *Galla Süd-Äthiopiens.* Stuttgart: W. Kohlhammer.

Hallowell, A. Irving. 1955. *Culture & Experience.* Philadelphia: University of Pennsylvania Press.

Hamidoun, Mokhtar. 1952. *Précis sur la Mauritanie*. Études mauritaniennes 4. St. Louis, Senegal: IFAN.

Harris, William Cornwallis. 1844. *The Highlands of Ethiopia*, 3 vols. London: Longman, Brown, Green and Longmans.

———. 184–? *Illustrations of the Highlands of Ethiopia*. London: Dickenson and Son.

Hasan, Yusuf Fadl. 1967. *The Arabs and the Sudan from the Seventh to the Early Sixteenth Century*. Edinburgh: University Press.

Hearn, M. F., ed. 1990. *The Architectural Theory of Viollet-le-Duc*. Cambridge, Mass. MIT Press.

Heine, Bernd, and Brenzinger, Matthias. 1988. *Plant Concepts and Plant Use. Part IV: Plants of the Borana (Ethiopia and Kenya)*. Fort Lauderdale: Breitenbach.

Hillelson, S. 1925. *Sudan Arabic. English-Arabic Vocabulary*. London: Education Department, Sudan Government.

Hirschberg, Haim Zeev (J. W.). 1974. *A History of the Jews in North Africa*, vol. 1. Leiden: E. J. Brill.

Holter, Uta. 1983. "Craft Techniques Used by Mahria Women of Darfur." *Folk* 25: 97–128.

Huard, Paul. 1960. "Contribution à l'étude du cheval, du fer et du chameau au Sahara oriental." *Bull.IFAN* 22 (B), 1–2: 134–78.

Ibn Battuta. 1853–58. *Voyages d'Ibn Batoutah*, 4 vols., trans. C. Defrémery and B. R. Sanguinetti. Paris: Imprimerie Nationale.

Ibn Khaldun. 1927. *Histoire des Berbères*, 4 vols., trans. Baron de Slane. Paris: Paul Geuthner.

———. 1958. *The Muqaddimah*, 3 vols., trans. Felix Rosenthal. London: Routledge & Kegan Paul.

Introduction à la Mauritanie. 1979. Paris: CNRS.

Jackson, James Grey. 1809. *An Account of the Empire of Morocco*. Reprint 1968. London: Frank Cass.

Jacques-Meunié, Dj. 1982. *Le Maroc saharien des origines à 1670*, 2 vols. Paris: Klincksieck.

Jemma, D. 1972. "Les Artisans de l'Ahaggar." *Libyca* 20: 269–90.

Johnson, Douglas L. 1969. *The Nature of Nomadism: A Comparative Study of Pastoral Nomadism in North Africa and Southeast Asia*. Department of Geography Papers 118. Chicago: University of Chicago Press.

———. 1978. "Nomadic Organization of Space: Reflections on Pattern and Process." In Karl W. Butzer, ed., *Dimensions of Human Geography*. Chicago: University of Chicago Geography Department.

Jones, David Keith. 1984. *Shepherds of the Desert*. London: Elm Tree Books.

Knuffel, Werner E. 1973. *The Construction of the Bantu Grass Hut*. Graz: Akademische Druck.

Kowalski, T. T. 1971. *Growth and Development of Trees*, 2 vols. New York: Academic Press.

Kronenberg, Andreas. 1958. *Die Teda von Tibesti*. Wiener Beiträge zur Kulturgeschichte und Linguistik 12. Vienna.

Kubler, George. 1962. *The Shape of Time: Remarks on the History of Things*. New Haven: Yale University Press.

Kuper, Adam. 1980. "Symbolic Dimensions of the Southern Bantu Homestead." *Africa* 50, 1: 8–23.

Labat, Père Jean-Baptiste. 1728. *Nouvelle relation de l'Afrique Occidentale*, 5 vols. Paris: Cavelier.

Laoust, E. 1930. "L'Habitation chez les transhumants du Maroc central." *Hespéris* 10, 2: 151–253.

Laugel, Lt. M. 1957. "Évaluation des distances par les nomades du Sahara occidental." *Bulletin de Liaison Saharienne* 8, 26: 84–88.

Laurence, Margaret. 1963. *The Prophet's Camel Bell*. London: Macmillan.

Leach, Edmond. 1976. *Culture and Communication*. Cambridge: CUP.

Lechtman, Heather, and Steinberg, Arthur. 1979. "The History of Technology: An Anthropological Point of View." In George Bugliarello and Dean B. Doner, eds., *Symposium on the History and Philosophy of Technology*. Urbana: University of Illinois Press.

Le Coeur, Charles. 1937. "Les Mapalia numides et leur survivance au Sahara." *Hespéris* 24, 1–2: 29–45.

———. 1950. "Dictionnaire ethnographique Téda-Daza." *Mémoires IFAN* 9: 1–213. Dakar: IFAN.

———. 1953. "Technique, art et point d'honneur." *Études nigériennes* 1: 17–34.

———. 1969. *Mission au Tibesti: Carnets de route 1933–34*. Paris: CNRS.

Le Corbusier. 1946. *Towards a New Architecture*. New York: Brewer, Warren and Putnam.

Leriche, Albert. 1949. "L'Islam en Mauritanie." *Bull.IFAN* 11, 3–4: 458–70.

———. 1951. "Mesures maures, note préliminaire." *Bull.IFAN* 13, 4: 1227–56.

———. 1953. "Notes pour servir à l'histoire maure: Forgerons, Kunta, Maures du Hodh." *Bull.IFAN* 15, 2: 737–50.

———. 1955a. "Notes sur les classes sociales et sur quelques tribus de Mauritanie." *Bull.IFAN* 17 (B), 1–2: 173–203.

———. 1955b. "Terminologie géographique maure." *Études mauritaniennes* 6. St. Louis, Senegal: IFAN.

Leschi, L. 1942. "Rome et les nomades du Sahara central." *Trav.IRS* 1: 47–62.

Levtzion, Nehemia, and Hopkins, J. F. P., eds. 1981. *Corpus of*

Early Arabic Sources for West African History. Cambridge: CUP.

Lewicki, Tadeusz. 1962. "L'État nord-africain de Tahert." *CEA* 11, 4: 513–35.

———. 1965. "Animal Husbandry among Medieval Agricultural People of Western and Middle Sudan (according to Arabic Sources)." *Acta Ethnographica Academiae Scientiarum Hungaricae* 14, 1–2: 165–78.

———. 1974. *Arabic External Sources for the History of Africa to the South of Sahara*. London: Curzon Press.

Lewis, I. M. 1955. *Peoples of the Horn of Africa*. London: IAI.

———. 1960. "The Somali Conquest of the Horn of Africa." *JAH* 1: 213–29.

———. 1962. "Marriage and the Family in Northern Somaliland." *East African Studies* 15: 1–51.

———. 1981. *Somali Culture, History and Social Institutions: An Introductory Guide to the Somali Democratic Republic*. London: London School of Economics and Political Science.

Lhote, Henri. 1944. *Les Touaregs du Hoggar (Ahaggar)*, rev. ed. 1955. Paris: Payot.

———. 1947. *Comment campent les Touaregs*. Paris: J. Susse.

———. 1984a. *Les Touaregs du Hoggar*. Paris: Armand Colin.

———. 1984b. *Le Hoggar. Espace et temps*. Paris: Armand Colin.

Loughran, Katheryne and John L., Johnson, John William, and Samatar, Said, eds. 1986. *Somalia in Word and Image*. Bloomington: Indiana University Press.

Lucas, A. 1926. *Ancient Egyptian Materials and Industries*, 3rd ed. 1948. London: Edward Arnold.

Lyon, Captain George Francis. 1821. *A Narrative of Travels in Northern Africa in the Years 1818, 1819, 1820*. London: John Murray.

Maclaren, J. F. P. 1927. "The Nomad Tent of Northern Kordofan." *SNR* 10: 235–40.

MacMichael, H. A. 1912. *The Tribes of Northern and Central Kordofan*. Cambridge: CUP.

Marçais, Georges. 1946. *La Berbérie Musulmane et l'Orient au Moyen Age*. Paris: Aubier.

Marcy, G. 1937. "Introduction à un déchiffrement méthodique des inscriptions 'tifinagh' du Sahara central." *Hespéris* 24, 1–2: 89–118.

———. 1942. "Remarques sur l'habitation berbère dans l'antiquité." *Hespéris* 29, 1: 51–85.

Mariano, Anthony. 1956. "Somali Betrothal and Marriage Customs." *Somaliland Journal* 1, 3: 169–76.

Martinié, Jean. 1949. "À propos de mappalia." *Hespéris* 36, 3–4: 446–47.

McMichael, M. A. 1922. *A History of the Arabs in the Sudan*. Cambridge: CUP.

Meiggs, Russell. 1982. *Trees and Timber in the Ancient Mediterranean World*. Oxford: Clarendon Press.

Mercer, John. 1976. *Spanish Sahara*. London: Allen & Unwin.

Mikesell, Marvin W. 1955. "Notes on the Dispersal of the Dromedary." *Southwestern Journal of Anthropology* 11, 3: 231–45.

Moholy-Nagy, Sibyl. 1957. *Native Genius in Anonymous Architecture*. New York: Horizon Press.

Moldenke, Harold N. and Alma L. 1952. *Plants of the Bible*. Reprint 1986. New York: Dover.

Monod, Théodore. 1938. *Contribution à l'étude du Sahara Occidental*. Paris: Larose.

———. 1967. "Notes sur le harnachement chamelier." *Bull.IFAN* 29 (B), 1–2: 234–74.

———. ed. 1975. *Pastoralism in Tropical Africa*. London: OUP.

Monteil, Vincent. 1948. *Notes sur les Tekna*. Institut des Hautes Études Marocaines, Notes et documents 3. Paris: Larose.

———. 1949. "Note sur la toponymie, astronomie et l'orientation chez les Maures." *Hespéris* 36, 1–2: 189–220.

———. 1952. "Essai sur le chameau au Sahara occidental." *Études mauritaniennes* 2. St. Louis, Senegal: IFAN.

Moore, Henrietta L. 1988. *Feminism and Anthropology*. Oxford: Polity Press.

Moraes 'Farias, P. F. de. 1967. "The Almoravids: Some Questions concerning the Character of the Movement during Its Periods of Closest Contact with the Western Sudan." *Bull.IFAN* 29 (B), 3–4: 794–878.

Morgenstern, Julian. 1942–43. "The Ark, the Ephod, and the 'Tent of Meeting'." *Hebrew Union College Annual* 17: 153–265; 18: 1–52.

Mounier, Lt. 1942. "Le Travail des peaux chez les Touareg Hoggar." *Trav.IRS* 1: 133–70.

Munroe, Robert L. and Ruth H. 1971. "Effect of Environmental Experience on Spatial Ability in an East African Society." *Journal of Social Psychology* 83: 15–22.

Murray, G. W. 1927. "The Northern Beja." *JRAI* 57: 39–53.

Nachtigal, Dr. Gustave. 1971–87. *Sahara and Sudan*, 4 vols., trans., intro., and notes Allan G. B. Fisher and Humphrey J. Fisher. London: C. Hurst.

Nachtigall, Horst. 1966. "Zelt und Haus bei den Beni Mguild-Berbern (Marokko)." *BA* (Berlin), N.F. 14: 269–329.

Nadel, S. F. 1945. "Notes on Beni Amer Society." *SNR* 25, 1: 51–94.

Nasr, Seyyed Hossein. 1976. *Islamic Science*. London: World of Islam Festival Publishing Company.

Nerlove, Sara B., and Munroe, Ruth H. and Robert L. 1971. "Effect of Environmental Experience on Spatial Ability: A Replication." *Journal of Social Psychology* 84: 3–10.

New, T. R. 1984. *A Biology of Acacias.* Melbourne: OUP.

Nicolaisen, Johannes. 1961. "Essai sur la religion et magie touaregues." *Folk* 3: 113–62.

———. 1963. *Ecology and Culture of Pastoral Tuareg.* Copenhagen: National Museum.

Nicholas, Francis. 1938. "Les industries de protection chez les Twareg de l'Azawagh." *Hespéris* 25: 43–84.

———. 1950. *Tamesna.* Paris: Imprimerie Nationale.

Nicolas, Guy. 1968. "Un Système numérique symbolique: Le quatre, le trois et le sept dans la cosmologie d'une société hausa (vallée de Maradi)." *CEA* 8, 4: 566–616.

Noel, P. 1920. "Étude ethnographique et anthropologique sur les Tédas du Tibesti." *L'Anthropologie* 30: 115–35.

Norberg-Schulz, Christian. 1971. *Existence, Space & Architecture.* New York: Praeger.

Nordman, Daniel. 1980–81. "Les Expéditions de Moulay Hassan." *Hespéris-Tamuda* 19, 1: 123–52.

Norris, H. T. 1961. "The Early Islamic Settlement in Gibraltar." *JRAIGBI* 91, 1: 39–51.

———. 1962. "Yemenis in the Western Sahara." *JAH* 3, 2: 317–22.

Oberle, Philippe. 1971. *Afars et Somalis.* Paris: Présence Africaine.

Owen, T. R. H. 1937. "The Hadendowa." *SNR* 20, 2: 183–208.

Ozenda, P. 1958. *Flore du Sahara septentrional et central.* Paris: CNRS.

Pallme, Ignatius. 1844. *Travels in Kordofan.* London: J. Madden & Co.

Pankhurst, Richard. 1982. *History of Ethiopian Towns from the Middle Ages to the Early 19th Century.* Wiesbaden: Franz Steiner.

———. 1983. "The Tents of the Ethiopian Court." *Azania* 18: 181–95.

Parkyns, Mansfield. 1853. *Life in Abyssinia,* 2 vols. London: John Murray.

Parris, David. 1984. *Seasonal Mosaics of Roman North Africa.* Rome: Giorgio Bretschmeider.

Paul, A. 1950. "Notes on the Beni Amer." *SNR* 31: 223–45.

———. 1954. *A History of the Beja Tribes of the Sudan.* Cambridge: CUP.

Paulitschke, Dr. Philipp. 1893–96. *Ethnographie Nordöst-Afrikas,* 2 vols. Berlin: Dietrich Reiner. Reprint 1967. London: Johnson Reprint Co.

Persson, A. and J., and Hussein, A. 1979. *Sudanese Colloquial Arabic for Beginners.* Summer Institute for Linguistics, Horsleys Green, High Wycombe, England.

Phillipson, David W. 1985. *African Archaeology.* New York: CUP.

Préchaur-Canonge, Thérèse. 1962. *La Vie rurale en Afrique romaine d'après les mosaïques.* Paris: PUF.

Pritchard, James Bennett. 1959. *The Ancient Near East in Pictures Relating to the Old Testament,* 2nd ed. Princeton: Princeton University Press.

Prunes, Mateus. 1559. *Chart of the Mediterranean Sea.* Washington, D.C.: Library of Congress.

Prussin, Labelle. 1986. *Hatumere.* Berkeley and Los Angeles: University of California Press.

———. 1987. "Gabra Containers." *African Arts* 20, 2: 36–45.

Puccioni, Nello. 1960. *Risultati scientifici delle Missioni Stefanini Paoli (1913) e Stefanini-Puccioni (1924) in Somalia,* trans. Kathryn A. Looney. New Haven: HRAF.

Quantrill, Malcolm. 1987. *The Environmental Memory.* New York: Schocken.

Quézel, Pierre. 1965. *La Végétation du Sahara, du Tchad à la Mauritanie.* Stuttgart: Gustav Fischer.

Rackow, Ernst von. 1934. "Sattel und Zaum in nordwest Afrika." *BA* 17: 172–86.

———. 1958. *Beiträge zur Kenntnis der materialen Kultur Nordost-Marokkos.* Wiesbaden: Harrassowitz.

Rackow, Ernst, and Caskel, Werner. 1938. "Das Bedouinenzelt." *BA* 21, 4: 151–84.

Rätzel, Dr. Friedrich. 1887. *Völkerkunde,* 2 vols. Leipzig: Verlag des Bibliographisches Institut.

Rayne, H. A. 1921. "Somal Marriage." *Journal of the African Society* 21, 81: 23–30.

Revoil, Georges. 1885, 1886, 1888. "Voyage chez les Benadirs, les Çomalis et les Bayouns en 1882–1883." *Le Tour du Monde* 49: 1–80; 50: 129–208; 56: 385–416.

Reygasse, Maurice. 1950. *Monuments funéraires préislamiques de l'Afrique du Nord.* Paris: Arts et Métiers Graphiques.

Rhodes, Captain Godfrey. 1858. *Tents and Tentlife from the Earliest Ages to the Present Time.* London: Smith, Elder and Company.

Rio, Capitaine. 1961. "L'Artisanat à Tamentit." *Trav.IRS* 20: 135–83.

Robecchi-Bricchetti, Luigi. [1899]. *Somalia e Benadir.* Milan: Carlo Aliprandi.

Rodd, Francis Rennell. 1926. *People of the Veil.* London: Macmillan.

Ross, Helen Elizabeth. 1974. *Behavior and Perception in Strange Environments.* London: Allen and Unwin.

Rykwert, Joseph. 1982. *The Necessity of Artifice.* New York: Rizzoli.

Saad, Hamman Tukur. 1987. "Reflections on Fulfulbe Toponymy: A Study of Fulbe Towns in Old Adamawa Emirate." *Annals of Borno* (Maiduguri) 4: 7–24.

Sato, S. 1980. "Pastoral Movements and the Subsistence Unit of the Rendille of Northern Kenya with Special Reference to Camel Ecology." *Senri Ethnological Studies* 6: 1–78.

Scarin, Emilio. 1934. *Le Oasi del Fezzan,* 2 vols. Bologna: Nicola Zanichelli.

Schiffers, Henri. 1957. "Le Borkou et ses habitants." *Trav.IRS* 15, 1: 65–88.

———. 1971–73. *Die Sahara und ihre Randegebiete,* 3 vols. Munich: Afrika-Studien 60–62.

Schlee, Gunther. 1985. "Interethnic Clan Identities among Cushitic-Speaking Pastoralists." *Africa* 55, 1: 17–37.

———. 1989. *Identities on the Move.* Manchester: Manchester University Press.

Schneider, Capitaine J. 1939. "Le Tibesti." *Bulletin de la Société des Recherches Congolaises* 27: 5–93.

Seiwert, Wolf-Dieter. 1985. "Die Völker Äthiopiens in den Sammlungen des Museums für Völkerkunde zu Leipzig." *EAZ Ethnographische-Archäologische Zeitung* 26: 152–65.

Seligman, Brenda. 1918. "Sacred Litters among the Semites with Reference to the Utfa of the Kababish." *SNR* 1: 268–82.

Seligman, C. G. and Brenda Z. 1918. "The Kababish, a Sudan Arab Tribe." *Varia Africana* II. *Harvard African Studies,* ed. Oric Bates, 2: 105–85.

———. 1930. "Note on the History and Present Condition of the Beni Amer (Southern Beja)." *SNR* 13, 1: 83–97.

Showalter, Elaine. 1986. "Piecing and Writing." In Nancy K. Miller, ed., *The Poetics of Gender.* New York: Columbia University Press.

Shuuriye, Helga. 1975. "Das Nationalmuseum in Mogadishu." *Bildende Kunst* 23, 11: 531–35.

Simmel, George. 1984. *On Women, Sexuality, and Love,* trans., ed., and intro. Guy Oakes. New Haven: Yale University Press.

Smith, W. Robertson. 1903. *Kinship and Marriage in Early Arabia.* London: Adam and Charles Black.

Sobania, Neal W. 1979. "Background History of the Mt. Kulal Region of Kenya." *IPAL Technical Report Number A-2. UNESCO-MAB FRG Integrated Project in Arid Lands.* Nairobi: UNESCO.

———. 1980. "The Historical Traditions of the Peoples of the Eastern Lake Turkana Region, c. 1840–1925." Ph.D. dissertation, School of Oriental and African Studies, University of London.

Spencer, Paul. 1973. *Nomads in Alliance: Symbiosis and Growth among the Rendille and Samburu of Kenya.* London: OUP.

Stein, Lothar. 1981. "Ethnographische Sammelreise nach Kordofan und Darfur. 1973." *Jahrbuch des Museums für Völkerkunde zu Leipzig* 33: 91–100.

Striedter, Karl Heinz. 1984. *Felsbilder der Sahara.* Munich: Prestel-Verlag.

Tablino, Paolo. 1978. "The Traditional Celebration of Marriage among the Gabbra of Northern Kenya." *Africa* (Rome) 33, 4: 568–78.

———. 1980. *I Gabbra del Kenya.* Bologna: E.M.I.

———. 1985. "The Feast of Kolompte." Manuscript. Marsabit, Kenya.

Tallam, K. C. Arap. 1984. "Ethnoarchaeology of the Gabbra." Master's thesis, University of Nairobi, Nairobi, Kenya.

Teel, Wayne. 1984. *A Pocket Dictionary of Trees and Seeds in Kenya.* Nairobi: KENGO.

Theophrastus. 1916. *Enquiry into Plants and Minor Works on Odours and Weather Signs,* 2 vols., trans. Sir Arthur Hort. London: Heinemann.

Thorndyke, Perry W. 1981. "Spatial Cognition and Reasoning." In John H. Harvey, ed., *Cognition, Social Behavior and the Environment.* Hillsdale, N.J.: Lawrence Erlbaum.

Torry, William I. 1973. "Subsistence Ecology among the Gabra." Ph.D. dissertation, Columbia University, New York.

Toupet, Charles, and Pitte, J. R. 1977. *La Mauritanie.* Paris: PUF.

Tristam, H. B. 1860. *The Great Sahara.* London: John Murray.

Tubiana, Marie-José and Joseph. 1977. *The Saghawa from an Ecological Perspective.* Rotterdam: A. A. Balkema.

Turner, Victor. 1974. *Dramas, Fields, and Metaphors.* Ithaca and London: Cornell University Press.

———. ed. 1982. *Celebration.* Washington, D.C.: Smithsonian Institution Press.

Turton, E. R. 1970. "The Pastoral Tribes of Northern Kenya: 1800–1916." Ph.D. dissertation, University of London.

Urvoy, Le capitaine Y. 1934. "Chronique d'Agadès." *Société des Africanistes* 4, 2: 145–77.

Van Leeuwen, Mary Stewart. 1978. "A Cross-Cultural Examination of Psychological Differentiation in Males and Females." *International Journal of Psychology* 13, 2: 87–122.

Verity, Paul. 1971. "Kababish Nomads of Northern Sudan." In Paul Oliver, ed., *Shelter in Africa.* New York: Praeger.

Vernon, M. D. 1970. *Perception through Experience.* London: Methuen & Co.

Vitruvius. 1914. *Ten Books of Architecture,* trans. Morris Hicky Morgan. Cambridge, Mass.: Harvard University Press.

Webster, Grahame. 1969. *The Roman Imperial Army of the First and Second Centuries A.D.* London: Adam and Charles Black.

Wente-Lucas, Renate. 1988. *Afrika*. Katalog 3, Deutsches Ledermuseum. Offenbach-am-Main: Gutenberg.

Wenzel, Marian. 1972. *House Decoration in Nubia*. Toronto: University of Toronto Press.

White, F. 1983. *The Vegetation of Africa*. Paris: UNESCO.

Witkin, Herman A., and Berry, John W. 1975. "Psychological Differentiation in Cross-Cultural Perspective." *Journal of Cross-Cultural Psychology* 6, 1: 4–87.

Xaange, Axmed Cartan. 1984. *Dalkii Udgoona* [The Land of Spices]. Mogadishu: Akadeemiyada Cilmiga Iyo Fanka.

Yates, Frances A. 1966. *The Art of Memory*. Chicago: University of Chicago Press.

Zaborski, Andrzej. 1965. "Notes on the Medieval History of the Beja Tribes." *Folio Orientalis* 7: 289–307.

———. 1972. "Beja and Tigre in the 9th–10th Century Period." *Pocznik Orientalistyczny* 35: 17–30.

ILLUSTRATION CREDITS

All line drawings and photographs not otherwise credited are by Labelle Prussin.

Figures

1.1: Drawing by Richard Mino.

1.2a–b: Drawings by Richard Mino.

1.3a–c: Photographs by Karl-Heinz Striedter.

1.4a–b: Barth 1857, 5:126, 162.

1.4c: Photograph by Claudio Pollini.

1.5a, c: Drawings by Richard Mino.

1.6: Gauckler 1896, 3:pl. XXII. New York Public Library, Art and Architecture Collection, Miriam and Ira D. Wallach Division of Art, Prints and Photography, Astor, Lenox and Tilden Foundations.

1.7a: Cailliaud 1823:pl. III. New York Public Library, General Research Division, Astor, Lenox and Tilden Foundations.

1.7b: Dalzel 1793:opp. p. 135.

1.8: Guillain 1856:folio pl. 16. New York Public Library, General Research Division, Astor, Lenox and Tilden Foundations.

1.9: Drawing by Richard Mino.

1.10: Foucher 1963:fig. 16. Presses Universitaires de France.

1.11: Bernatz 1852, 1:pl. XIII New York Public Library, General Research Division, Astor, Lenox and Tilden Foundations.

1.12: Harris 1844:frontispiece.

1.13: Photograph by Karl-Heinz Striedter.

1.14a: Drawing by Richard Mino.

1.14b: Colomieu 1863:177. New York Public Library, General Research Division, Astor, Lenox and Tilden Foundations.

2.1: Drawing by Richard Mino.

2.2: Photograph by Peter Fuchs.

2.3: Drawing by Richard Mino.

2.4a–b: Drawings by Richard Mino.

2.5a–d: Drawings by Barbara Paxson.

2.6a–d: Drawings by Barbara Paxson.

2.7a–b: Drawings by Barbara Paxson.

2.10: Drawing by Richard Mino.

2.11: Gardi 1970: 98.

2.12a–b: Drawings by Richard Mino.

2.13: Drawing by Richard Mino.

2.14: Drawing by Richard Mino.

2.15: Drawing by Richard Mino.

3.1a: Revoil 1888: 397. New York Public Library, General Research Division, Astor, Lenox and Tilden Foundations.

3.2: Drawing by Richard Mino.

3.3a: Photograph by Joy Adamson. National Museums of Kenya.

3.4d: Drawing by Richard Mino.

3.6a–d: Drawings by Richard Mino.

3.7b–c: Drawings by Richard Mino.

3.8a: Photograph by Aubert de la Rue, 1938. Musée d'Ethnographie, Geneva.

3.9a–e: Drawings by Richard Mino.

3.10a–e: Drawings by Richard Mino.

3.11: Drawings by Richard Mino.

3.12b: Photograph by Anders Grum.

4.1: Photographs by Peter Andrews.

4.2: Drawings by Peter Andrews.

4.3: Drawings by Peter Andrews.

4.5a–d: Drawings by Peter Andrews.

4.6a–b: Drawings by Peter Andrews.

4.7: Drawings by Peter Andrews.

4.10: Drawing by Barbara Paxson.

4.11: Drawings by Richard Mino.

4.12: Drawings by Richard Mino.

4.13: Photograph by Raymond Mauny, IFAN Dakar.

4.14a–b: Drawings by Barbara Paxson.

4.16a–b: Drawings by Richard Mino.

4.17: Photographs by Victor Edelstein.

4.18: Drawings by Barbara Paxson.

5.1: Drawing by Richard Mino.

5.2a–b: Gardi 1970:99, 100.

5.3a–c: Drawings by Richard Mino.

5.7a: Drawing by Richard Mino.

5.8: Barth 1857, 3:423.

5.9: Musée du Niger, Niamey.

5.10a–c: Drawings by Richard Mino.

5.11: Drawings by Richard Mino.

5.12: Drawings by Richard Mino.

5.13: Brandt 1956:81.

6.2: Le Coeur 1950:fig. 69. Éditions du Centre National de la Recherche Scientifique, Paris.

6.3: Photograph by Peter Fuchs.

6.4: Photograph by Peter Fuchs.

6.6: Drawing by Richard Mino.

6.7: Drawings by Barbara Paxson.

6.8: Drawing by Barbara Paxson.

6.9a–e: Drawings by Barbara Paxson.

6.10a, c: Drawings by Richard Mino.

7.1: Photograph by Uta Holter.

7.2: Drawing by Jup Holter.

7.3: Photographs by Uta Holter.

7.4: Drawing by Jup Holter.

7.5: Drawing by Jup Holter.

7.6: Photograph by Uta Holter.

7.7a–c: Drawings by Jup Holter.

7.8: Drawings by Jup Holter.

7.9a–c: Drawings by Jup Holter.

7.10: Drawing by Jup Holter; photograph by Uta Holter.

7.11: Drawings by Jup Holter.

8.1: Photograph by Anders Grum.

8.2: Photograph by Anders Grum.

8.3a–c: Drawings by Anders Grum.

8.4: Drawing by Anders Grum.

8.5: Photographs by Anders Grum.

8.6: Drawing by Anders Grum.

8.7: Drawing by Richard Mino.

8.8a–c: Drawings by Richard Mino.

8.9: Photograph by Anders Grum.

8.10a–c: Drawings by Richard Mino.

8.11: Photograph by Anders Grum.

8.12: Photograph by Anders Grum.

8.13a–d: Drawings and photograph by Anders Grum.

8.14: Photograph by Anders Grum.

9.1: Drawings by Richard Mino.

9.2a: Drawing by Richard Mino.

9.2b–c: Photographs by Arlene Fullerton.

9.3: Photographs by Arlene Fullerton.

9.4: Photographs by Arlene Fullerton.

9.5: Drawings by Richard Mino.

9.6: Photographs by Arlene Fullerton.

10.1: *The Standard Library of Natural History, Embracing Living Animals and Living Races of Mankind. Vol. V: Africa-Europe-America* (New York: The University Society, 1911), vol. 5, p. 375.

10.3 (right): Drawing by Barbara Paxson.

10.4 (below): Photograph by Aubert de la Rue, 1938. Musée d'Ethnographie, Geneva.

10.5b–c: Drawings by Richard Mino.

10.8: Corral 1985:180.

10.9: Photograph by Peter Fuchs.

Plates

1: Photograph by André Martin. Fradier 1976:n.p.

2: Prunes 1559. Library of Congress.

3: Drawing by G. F. Lyon. Engraving by D. Dighton, 1821. National Museum of African Art, Eliot Elisofon Archives, Smithsonian Institution.

8: Photograph by Peter Fuchs.

9: Photograph by Uta Holter.

10: Photograph by Peter Fuchs.

12: Deutsches Ledermuseum, Offenbach-am-Main.

13: Département recherche et conservation, Musée National du Bardo, Algiers.

14: Photograph by Peter Fuchs.

15: Photograph by Peter Fuchs.

16: Photograph by Uta Holter.

17: Photograph by Uta Holter.

18: Photograph by Anders Grum.

19: Photograph by Anders Grum.

20: Photograph by Arlene Fullerton.

21: Photograph by Arlene Fullerton.

22: Photograph by Ulrich Braukämper.

23: Photograph by Barbara A. Worley.

INDEX

A

Abdallahi u. sheik Sidiya (sheik), 216n13
Abd-el-Rahman u. Bakar, 216n17
'Abdul-Mu'min, 10
Abu Simbel bas reliefs, 7
Acacia albida, 25, 105, 212n7
Acacia arabica, 212n7
Acacia bussei, 172, 176, 182, 222n14
Acacia ehrenbergiana, 25
Acacia faidheriba albida, 139
Acacia gummifera, 25
Acacia mellifera, 133, 136–37, 172
Acacia nilotica, 25, 81, 102, 105, 138, 172
Acacia senegal, 142
Acacia seyal, 139
Acacia sp.: disappearance of, 25; distribution of, 25, 29; dyes from bark, 30, 117, 178, 182, 194, 222n11; shade provided by, 24; use of, 27, 28–29, 30, 59, 112, 114, 117, 137, 172–73, 201
Acacia spirocarpa, 172
Acacia tortilis (A. raddiana), 25, 26, 53, 70, 72, 76, 78, 101, 105, 117, 133, 136, 212n7
Adam, 103
Adi-foor (Rendille stock satellite camp), 154
Adofa (Téda palanquin), 51
Agades, Tuareg sultanate of, 11, 19, 203
Ahennaka (Tuareg palanquin), 97, 98, 107
Alakakkad (Tuareg tent mat), 102
Aleya, Sidi u., 80
Aljinan (Tuareg spirits), 103

Almeida, Manoel de, 11
Almoravid *jihad,* 9–10, 11, 15, 66
Altars, 194–95
Anawal (Hassaniya camps), 74
Annals (Egyptian), 7
Anonymity, of African artists, xix
Antelope skins, 116
Anthropometry, 40–42
Aqal (Somali portable house), 170, 172–74, 178, 186
Arab caravans, 8–9, 34–35
Arabic language, 110
Arabs, in Chad, 110
Architectonic, xx
Architecture: balance in, 46, 47, 53–54, 198, 199–200; gendered value system of, xvii, 58–60, 198, 205; interior versus exterior of, 43, 190–93; permanence of, x, xvi, 42, 62; protective symbolism in, 68, 76, 87, 195; structural principles of, 46; value of, xix
Ardener, Edwin, xvii
Argania spinosa, 25, 71
Arkila kerka (Sudanese blankets), 216n18
Ark of the Covenant, 17, 19
Armature tents: building technology of, 54–58; of the Daza, 111–12, 114–15; prototypes for, 5–6, 55; of the Somali, 13; transport of, 47
Art, versus craft, xix–xx
Arte, Abdi, 170
Asala (Tuareg mats), 102
Asparagus acutifolius, 212n7
Asparagus sp., 28, 160
Assyrian architecture, 6, 8
Astronomy, 24, 34–35

Augustus (Roman emperor), 8
Awlad Sulayman nomads, 52
Ayou (Tibesti) rock paintings, 17
Azmuthal compass, 35
Azuner (Tubu marriage), 119
Azza (ethnic group), 110, 112, 116

B

Bachelard, Gaston, 191, 193
Bait (Berber tents), 10
Balanites aegyptiaca, 25, 27, 76, 78, 82, 102, 105, 128, 212n7
Balanites glabra, 182
"Bantu" (ethnic group), 55
Baraka (Tuareg benediction), 103
Barth, Heinrich, 19, 36, 88, 93–94, 99, 207n6, 210n29, 210n35
Basketmaking: by Azza artisans, 118, 119; bark for, 29; grasses for, 28; by Mahria nomads, 130; by Mahria women, 141–43; by Somali women, 178–85, 197; by Tuareg nomads, 90
Bassur (palanquin), 80
Bauhinia rufescens, 133, 136
Beaman, Anne, 162, 169
Beet (Mahria tent), 124
Beidan (aristocrats, "white"), 66, 80
Beja architecture, 6, 8, 17
Benhazera, Maurice, 88
Beni Amer, 189, 195
Beni Hassan, 11
Benin (Dahomy), 12
Berabich (ethnic group), 93
Berber Sanhaja, 88
Berber tribes: Arabization of, 66; architecture of, ix–x, 10; resistance to foreign invasions, 8, 15, 19; saddles used by, 49
Bernatz, J. M., 16, 207n6
Bernus, Edmond, 88, 91, 98
Bethune, Louise Blanchard, xvii
Bible: Exodus, 2
Birthing: among Hassaniya-speaking nomads, 86–87, 92, 93; among Mahria nomads, 146–47; among Rendille pastoralists, 162; among Tuareg nomads, 98
Blacksmithing: by Azza artisans, 110, 118; by Tuareg nomads, 92, 102, 198
Blemmye (Beja) architecture, 6
Boddy, Janice, 192
Boscia senegalensis, 25, 128
Boundaries, 33, 34, 40, 188

Brakna (ethnic group): architecture of, 64, 73–80; emirate of, 66; environment and vegetation of, 74; transport technology of, 78, 80–84
Branch, Daniel P., 20
Brideprice, 144
Bridewealth, xix, 61, 163, 165
Briffault, Robert, xvii
Brosset, Lt. Charles Diego, 35, 36, 41
Building technology, 53–58. *See also* Architecture
Bulyar, Arnirkh, 38
Bulyar, Kawab, 169
Buraambur (Somali poetry), 170, 222n11
Burckhardt, John Lewis, 6, 17, 52
Buroro (Tubu saddle), 122
Burton, Sir Richard Francis, 13
Bushlands, 26

C

Cadaba heterotricha/mirabilis, 182
Caesar, Julius, 14
Caïd Amharoc, 216n14
Cailliaud, M. Frederic, 12
Caillié, René, 34, 73
Calendar, lunar, 24
Calotropis procera, 25, 97
Camel hair, for weaving, 68–69
Camels and camel-riding technology, 13–19, 47, 80–84. *See also* Litters and palanquins; Saddles
Capparis decidua, 25, 128
Capparis sp., 25
Caravan routes, 8–9, 16
Caro Baroja, Julio, 66
Casajus, Dominique, 88, 101, 103–5, 106, 189
Cauvet, Gaston, 47
Celebrations, 60–61
Centricity, of human body, 42, 189
Chapelle, F. de la, 66
Chapelle, Jean, 51–52, 111
Charlemagne, 6
Charles IX (king of France), 209–10n28
Charles V (Holy Roman emperor), 209–10n28
Chevalier, Auguste, 36
Chudeau, R., 94, 97
Circumcision: of Mahria nomads, 146, 147; of Rendille brides, 163; of Rendille warriors, 154, 169; Sudanese, 192
Clitoridectomy, 163
Cognitive styles, 32–33
Cole, Doris, xvii

Collocynthis citrullus, 138
Colors: black, 194; blue, 194; favored by Hassaniya-speaking nomads, 84; red, 10, 30, 72, 76, 81, 119, 141, 145, 194, 213n12; used by Somali nomads, 178, 182; white, 194; yellow, 81
Commiphora africana, 25, 97, 105
Commiphora sp., 128
Containment, 191–93
Continuity, of space, 32, 42
Contrapposto stance, 213n1
Cooper, James Fenimore, ix
Cordia sinensis Lam. Boraginaceae, 156
Corippus, 6, 209n24
Cosmological space, 2
Cosmology: of Hausa, 198; of Tuareg nomads, 103
Crafts, versus art, xix–xx
Creativity, xix, 190
Creyaufmüller, Wolfgang, 73
Croix d'Agadès, 53
Crusader tents, 6
Cubits, 207n3
Cultural ecology, 188
Cultural interaction and borrowings, xxi
Culture, gendered definition of, xvii–xviii
Cymbopogan proximus, 136
Cypress, 212n7

D

Daa'ira el beet (Mahria campsite), 124
Dalbergia molanonylon, 82
Dalzel, Archibald, 12
Damra (Mahria stationary camp), 124
Danakil (ethnic group), 55, 57
Date palms (Phoenix dactylifera), 25, 28, 73, 141, 212n7
Daza (ethnic group): architecture of, 111–12, 114; relationship to Tubu, 108; transport technology of, 214n4
Death, among Mahria nomads, 148. *See also* Funerary architecture
Deir el-Bahri (Thebes), 7–8
Dela (Tubu leather curtain), 116, 119, 121, 122, 123, 195
Delarozière, Marie-Francoise, 200
Delobi (Tuareg riding saddle), 53
Dermchaka Arabs, 93, 217n9
Desertification, 22, 25, 212n7
Dionysian iconography, and camels, 14
Distance-time correspondences, 34
Domenech, Lafuente Angel, 66
Domestic environment, xix. *See also* Space, gendered divisions of

Donkeys, as pack animals, 49
Douls, Camille, 58
Dowry, xix, 58–60, 61, 219n10 (chap. 7)
Drew, Philip, 1
Drought resistance, of plants, 26–28
Drysdale, J. G. S., 179, 182
Dum palms (Hyphaene thebaica), 25, 26, 28, 53, 90, 101, 112, 114, 141, 147, 159, 212n7
Du Puigaudeau, Odette, 47, 52, 73, 85, 86, 99, 195
Duveyrier, Henri, 35, 58, 88, 106

E

Echinochloa colonum, 130
Ecological adaptation, 33
Éduben (Tuareg marriage), 91
Egg metaphors, 192
Egyptian architecture: funerary, 7–8; materials used in, 212n7; military, 7, 8
Éhakit (Tuareg skin tent cover), 96
Éhen (Tuareg marriage), 91–92, 218n12
Embroidery: by Hassaniya-speaking nomads, 85; by men, 59
Emi Kussi volcano, 110
Enclosures, geometry of, 42–43, 194
Environment: and anthropometry, 40–42; and boundaries, 33, 34, 40, 188; and continuity in space, 32, 42; and geometry of spatial enclosure, 42–43, 194; impact of, 20–22; light and shadow, 24; and measure and representation of space, 34–37; and mobility, 37–40; and nomadic spatial ability, 32–34; perception of, 23, 30–32; plant utilization, 26–28; rainfall, 24; and space, 186–90; topography, 22, 24, 34; vegetation, 24–26, 28–30; winds and sandstorms, 22–24
Eragrostis sp., 142
Erikson, E. H., 63, 190
Éseber (Tuareg tent screen), 98
Eskimo (ethnic group), 33
Ethiopian government, 11
Ethnic identity, xxi
Ethnicity, xxi
Euclidean geometry, 35, 213n16
Euphorbia sp., 179, 182
Explorers, tents used by, 13

F

Fariig (Mahria camp), 124
Fatima, hand of, 85
Feilberg, C. G., 1

Fellata-Baggare (ethnic group): architecture of, 56, 57, 193; marriage ritual of, 189
Field dependence-independence, 32–33
Field of the Cloth of Gold, 6, 209n27
Fitch, James Marston, 20
Focal points, 194
Foor (Rendille camel camp), 154
Foucauld, Père Charles de, 88, 95, 97
Francis I (king of France), 6, 209n27
Frīg (Hassaniya camp), 74
Fuchs, Peter, 111, 120
Fulani artisans, xxi
Fulfe architecture, x
Fuller, Buckminster, xviii
Funerary architecture: Egyptian (tents), 7, 8; of explorer Burton, 13; of Mahria nomads, 148; of Rendille pastoralists, 167; tombs of the kings of Ghana, 9; of Tuareg nomads, 104–5

G

Gaaloora clan (Rendille ethnic group), 155, 166
Gabra (ethnic group): architecture of, x, xi, 42, 55–56, 198, 204–5; building technology of, xxi; marriage ritual among, 61–62, 189, 194, 198; spatial organization of, 167; transport technology of, 48, 49, 50; women's work among, 58
Gabus, Jean, 73, 88, 98
Galgulame (Rendille "camel stampede"), 154
Gal-i-foor (Rendille mobile satellite camp), 154
Gast, M., 41
Geble-tell axis, 36, 41
Gender, xi; and architecture, xx–xxi, 58, 92, 205; and culture, xvii–xviii, xxi; division of labor by, 46, 58–59, 112, 118, 124, 129–30, 170; spatial divisions of, 42, 46, 59, 60, 72–73, 79–80, 85, 98–99, 103–5, 138, 158, 162–63, 196–98; and spatial perception, 33–34, 190; and symbolism, 84, 85; and transport technology, 47
Gender polarities, 196–98
Gender specificity, xv
Genghis Khan, 6
Ghana, empire of, 9
Goat hair, for weaving, 68–69, 75
Gommo (Tubu pack saddle), 122
Goob (Rendille settlement), 150–54
Goranes (ethnic group): architecture of, 111, 115; distribution of, 108
Government, itinerant, 11–13

Grall, Le lieutenant, 111
Grasslands, 25–26, 28
Grewia bicolor, 83
Grewia tanax [Forsk.] Fiori Tiliceae, 220n4
Groundwater, 24
Guillain, M., 13, 34
Gum arabic, 29
Gusii (ethnic group), 33

H

Hadendowa (Beja) architecture, 6, 8, 56, 195
Hadrian (Roman emperor), 14
Harka (Almoravid court), 11
Harmattan (sandstorms), 23
Harmony, 200
Harnesses, 47
Harratin ("blacks"), 66, 74, 76
Hassani (Hassaniya warriors), 66
Hassaniya-speaking nomads: architecture of, xxi, 56–58, 64–80, 195, 202–3; birthing among, 86–87, 92, 93; building technology of, xxi; camp of, 74–75; distribution of, 64; household furnishings of, 71–73, 78–80; imagery of, 84–86; place names of, 37; transport technology of, 47, 52, 80–84
Hatshepsut (queen of Egypt), temple of, 7
Hausa artisans, xxi
Hausa cosmology, 198
Hebrew architecture, x, 2, 212n7
Henry VIII (king of England), 6, 209n27
Herding, 58
Herodotus, 5, 6
Hodological perspective, 35
Hoggar rock engravings, 97
Horses, Arab, 15–16
House of Isguntus mosaics (Hippo Regius), 8
House of Laberii mosaics (Oudna), 8
House of Silenus mosaics (El Djem), 210–11n.38
House of the Dionysus Procession mosaics (El Djem), 14
Howdah (palanquin), 19
Hyphaene sp., 25
Hyphaene thebaica. *See* Dum palms

I

Iberre families, among Rendille, 160, 162
Ibn Battuta, 10, 34
Ibn Khaldun, xviii, 7, 10, 18–19, 59, 208n13

Ibn Yasin, 209n26
Igdalan (ethnic group), 102, 105
Imagery, of Hassaniya-speaking nomads, 84–86
Inner space, 43, 190–93
Institutional tents, 6–13
'Iris (Mahria marriage), 144
Isimkheb (Egyptian princess), 7–8, 13
Isma'il Pasha, 12

J

Jackson, Michael, 185
Jakhfa (Berber palanquins), 19
Juba (king of Numidia), 14
Juniperus procera, 26
Juniperus sp., 25

K

Kababish (ethnic group): architecture of, 56; building technology of, xxi; spatial acumen of, 213n11; transport technology of, 17, 51
Kachimbet (Tubu tent opening), 115
Kanembu hamlets, 207n6
Kanem kingdom, 110
Kantarki (Tuareg riding saddle), 53
Kanuri (ethnic group), 108
Khaīmat (Hassaniya tent), 75
Kibla (direction for Muslim prayer), 36
Kobode (Tubu palanquin), 122–23, 195
Kolompte feast, 62
Kowe (Tubu mats), 114
Kubba (a round tent), 10, 52, 211n44
Kubler, George, xix
Kunta (ethnic group), 93, 94

L

La Kahena, 19
Laoust, E., 97
Leach, Edmond, 2, 42, 190–91
Leather clothing, 116
Leather tanning, 30, 117, 119, 138, 215n5
Leatherworking: by Azza artisans, 116, 117–19; division of labor in, 59, 138; by Hassaniya-speaking nomads, 66, 73, 84; by Mahria nomads, 130, 138–41; by Somali nomads, 182–83; by Tuareg nomads, 90, 96, 198
Le Coeur, Charles, 108, 111, 115, 119, 120, 207n7

Le Corbusier (Charles-Édouard Jeanneret), x, 2, 186
Lewis, I. M., 170
l-ḥaima (Hassaniya tent), 67
Lhote, Henri, 88
Libyan architecture (ancient), 7
Light. *See* Sun and light
Lin, Maya, 190
Linear perspective, 32, 35, 213n16
Literacy, 194
Litters and palanquins: as container surrogates, 195; definitions of, 47; of Gabra, 49; and gender-divided space, 198; of Hassaniya-speaking nomads, 52, 72, 80–81, 83–84; history of, 17–19; as interior space, 43, 190; of Kababish, 17, 51; of Mahria nomads, 141, 146; relationship to house form, 44–46; of Rendille pastoralists, 49; of Somali nomads, 49; of Téda, 51–52; of Tekna nomads, 72; of Tuareg nomads, 50, 106–7; of Tubu nomads, 116–17, 122–23
Logoli (ethnic group), 33
Louis IX (king of France), 209n27
Lunar calendar, 24
Luxor bas reliefs, 7
Lyon, Capt. George Francis, 52, 88, 110, 118

M

Mā'allemin (Hassaniya artisan caste), 66
Maerua crassifolia, 25, 26
Maerua sp., 25
Mahlmal (palanquin), 17, 19, 52
Mahr (Mahria brideprice), 144
Mahria (ethnic group): architecture of, x, xxi, 130–37, 147, 195; building technology of, xxi; camps of, 124–29; distribution of, 124; divisions between public and private domains among, 124, 148; household furnishings of, 137–44, 148; marriage rituals of, 144–45; spatial division of the sexes among, 138, 148; transport technology of, 134–36, 138, 141, 143, 146; women's daily tasks among, 129–30, 148–49; women's life cycle among, 144–48
Maksar (palanquin), 19
Mansa Musa, 11
Mansur, al- (Sa'adian sultan), 15
Mapalia (tent), 5–6
Ma'qil (ethnic group), 64
Maqrizi, al-, 17, 19
Marcy, G., 207–8n9
Markab (palanquin), 19
Marriage rituals: and creation of architecture, 58–59,

Index   241

60–62, 91–92, 101; creation symbolism in, 43; and definition of space, 188; of Gabra, 61–62, 189, 194, 198; of Hassaniya-speaking nomads, 86–87; of Mahria nomads, 144–45; and pseudo-tanning, 30; of Rendille pastoralists, 160, 162, 163–65, 189, 198–99; and sedentarization, 202–5; of Somali nomads, 172, 176–78, 184–85, 197; of Tuareg nomads, 19, 91–107, 189; of Tubu nomads, 119–22. *See also* Dowry

Masinissa (king of Numidia), 8

Mas'udi, al-, 10, 60

Mecca: direction of, 36; Kaaba at, 60, 103; *kubba* used by pilgrims to, 52; rituals associated with, 60

Medicinal plants, 29

Mediterranean climate, 25

Mellen (Azza vassals), 110

Memory, 62–63

Menopause, 147

Mesa Verde, x

Metalworking, 59

Metragyne inermis, 76

Migrations. *See* Mobility

Min (pl. *minan*) (Rendille house), 155–58

Min discho (Rendille wedding or "house building"), 163

Min-ki-dakhan (Rendille "white house"), 165, 169

Min-ki-meerat (Rendille killer's house), 169

Mirages, 24

Mobility, xi, xvi, xx–xxi, 37–40, 188

Mock combat, in Tubu marriage ritual, 120

Moholy-Nagy, Sibyl, xvi

Montane growth (vegetation), 25

Monteil, Vincent, 66

Moore, Henrietta L., xix, xx, 59

Moors, etymology of, 66

Morgan, Julia, xvii

Moses, x, 2

Mothers, The (Briffault), xvii

Moulay Hassan, 11, 209–10n28

Muhammad 'Ali Pasha, 12

Muhammed, Askia, 19

Multifunctionalism, 44

Muqmud (a Somali dish), 184, 185, 222n20

Murabitin (Hassaniya holy men), 66

N

Nabo (Gabra sacred enclosure), 62

Nachtigal, Dr. Gustave, 52

Nagayati: Arts and Architecture among the Gabra Nomads of Kenya (film), xi

Name-giving, among Mahria nomads, 146, 147

Nature, versus nurture, xx

Navajo (ethnic group), 33

Nicholas, Francis, 93

Nicolaisen, Johannes, 88, 90, 91, 92–93

Nicolas, Francis, 88

Nizar Ma'ad, 10

Nomadic architecture: ignored by scholars, xviii; as mediation between culture and environment of the desert, xx

Nomads: aesthetic of, 186–205; and camels, 13–17; cultural values of, xx; as elusive, xvi–xvii; environment for, 20; ethnicity of, xxi; etymology of, 209n24; mobility of, xi, xvi, xx–xxi, 37–40, 188; spatial ability of, 32–34; spatial perception of, 30–32

Nonverbal communication, 188

Nubian architecture, 7, 203–4

Numerology, 85, 198–99, 200, 220n5

Numidian architecture, 5, 6, 8

Nurture, versus nature, xx

O

Oak forests, 25

Oasis vegetation, 25

Odoola clan (Rendille ethnic group), 154, 155, 159–60, 166–67

Odri (Tubu palanquin cover), 116

Okba b. Nafi, Sidi, 15

Olea sp., 26

Omari, al-, 53

Oral traditions, xviii, 3, 170

Oromo (ethnic group), 167

Osman Digna, 211n3

Ostrich eggs, 191–92, 195

Otfa (Kababish palanquin), 17

Otto, Frei, xviii

Ottoman Turkish architecture, 6

P

Palanquins. *See* Litters and palanquins

Pallme, Ignatius, 58

Palm trees, utilization of, 28. *See also* Date palms; Dum palms

Panicum milliaceum, 212n7

Panicum sp., 28

Panicum turgidum, 25, 27, 98, 99, 102, 137

Pankhurst, Richard, 11

Papilio (tent), 8, 209n24

Parasol tents, 10, 11, 12–13

Parkyns, Mansfield, 12
Pastoral compounds: illustrated in Tassili rock paintings, 4; of Rendille, 150–55
Pastoralism, xxi; of the Rendille, 150; in the Sahel, 25
Pennisetum sp., 129
Perception, 30–32
Phoenician architecture, 5
Phoenix dactylifera. See Date palms
Pillars of Islam, 103
Pine forests, 25
Place names, 37
Plains Indian architecture, xvii
Plant utilization, 26–30, 59
Play, and motor development, 63
Poetry: of Somali nomads, 170; of Tuareg nomads, 200
Pont Neuf (Paris), 193
Portolan sea charts, 35
Pottery, by Azza artisans, 118
Praeneste, Temple of Fortuna at, 5
Prester John, 210n31
Prestige. See Tents, institutional tradition of
Private domain, versus public domain, xx, 158
Procopius, 15
Prunes, Mateus, 10
Psychosis, and spatial disorientation, 34
Ptolemy II Philadelphus, 14
Public domain, versus private domain, xx, 158

Q

Qabo plant, 179, 182
Quilt metaphor, 189–90

R

Rainfall, 24
Rakuuba (Mahria shelters), 128
Ramesseum bas reliefs, 7
Red color, 194; of acacia dyes, 30, 117, 145, 178, 182, 194, 222n11; of Arab *kubba* tents, 10; of Azza *oru,* 119; in Mahria leatherworking, 141, 195; in Mahria marriage rituals, 145; nomadic preference for, 213n12; of Rendille and Gabra cow skins, 195; of Somali basketry, 178, 182, 195; used by Hassaniya-speaking nomads, 72, 76, 77, 81, 195; used by Tuareg, 195; used by Tubu, 195
Reguibat (ethnic group), 36, 67
Rekkey (Rendille widow's house), 167
Rendille (ethnic group): architecture of, x, xxi, 55, 155–58, 163–69, 195; distribution of, 150; gendered divisions of space in, 158, 162–63; household furnishings of, 159–63; marriage ritual of, 160, 162, 163–65, 189, 198–99; men's life-cycle in, 154–55; settlement pattern of, 150–55; transhumance of, 38–40, 46; transport technology of, 48, 49, 50, 159, 169
Rhus oxyacantha, 49
Ritual: and architecture, xi, xv, xxi, 60–62; associated with Rendille age-sets, 154–55; as conservative, 62; and environmental memory, 2; and movement, 60–62. See also Marriage rituals
Roland, 6
Roman architecture: materials used in, 25, 212n7; tents, 5–6, 8, 209n24
Roman colonization, 8, 14–15
Ronchamp, Le Corbusier's chapel at (1955), x
Root systems, 27, 29–30
Ropemaking: bark for, 29; gender division of labor for, 119; by Tekna nomads, 70
Royal entourages, 10–12, 40, 74
Ruala (ethnic group), 52
Rykwert, Joseph, 62

S

Saari (Somali house coverings), 174–78
Saddles: of Berbers, 49; definition of, 47–50; as gendered technology, 198; of Hassaniya-speaking nomads, 80–83; of Mahria nomads, 136, 141, 143, 146; of Rendille pastoralists, 48, 50, 52; of Somali and Gabra nomads, 48, 50, 52; Sudanese, 52–53; of Tekna nomads, 49; of Té nomads, 50, 52; of Tuareg nomads, 49, 50, 53; of Tubu nomads, 122
Sahel: etymology of, 35–36; vegetation of, 25–26
Salvadora persica, 25, 27
Sandstorms, 22–24, 74
Sansevieria robusta N.E. Br. Agavacea, 156
Schiffers, Henri, 111
Sedentarism, xvi
Sedentarization, xviii, 200–205
Seligman, Brenda, 17, 52
Seminomads, mobility of, 213n17
Sennacherib, 6
Settlement patterns: environmental influences on, 24; of Rendille pastoralists, 150–55
Severus, Lucius Septimius (Roman emperor), 14
Seyal acacia, 97
Shade and shadows, 24
Shahali (sandstorms), 23
Sheep's wool, 75

Index   243

Simmel, George, xvii
Sina'ah (technology/art), 44
Skin tents: prototypes for, 6; of Tuareg nomads, 90, 91
Skoura, towers at, x
Smith, W. Robertson, 207n2
Somali (ethnic group): architecture of, x, xxi, 13, 55, 170, 172–74, 178, 186, 193, 195; building technology of, xxi; distribution of, 170; gendered division of labor in, 170; household furnishings of, 174–85; marriage rituals of, 172, 176–78, 184–85, 197; sedentarization of, 201; transport technology of, 48, 49, 50; women's work among, 58
Somi architecture, x
Songs, of Somali weavers, 176, 177–78
Soninke place names, 37
Space: and anthropometry, 40–42; boundaries of, 33, 34, 40, 188; continuity in, 32, 42; and environment, 186–90; gendered divisions of, 42, 46, 59, 60, 72–73, 79–80, 85, 98–99, 103–5, 138, 158, 162–63, 196–98; geometry of spatial enclosure, 42–43, 194; inner space, 43, 190–93; measure and representation of, 34–37; and mobility, 37–40; perception of, 23, 30–32, 190; pseudo-fixed, 189; and spatial ability, 32–34; and surfaces, 193–94. *See also* Environment
Spatial ability, 32–34
Spatial enclosures, geometry of, 42–43, 194
Spinning, 59, 75
Strabo, 6
Structuralism, 2
Style, and reason, 44
Sudan: *Arkila kerka* (Sudanese blankets), 216n18; circumcision in, 192; government of, 11–12; saddles in, 52–53; white cotton tents of, 77–78
Sun' (creation), 44
Sun and light, 24
Surfaces, 193–94
Symmetry, 199–200

T

Tabernacle, 2–4, 6, 17
Tabernaculum (tent), 209n24
Tahyast (Tuareg riding saddle), 53
Tailoring, 59
Tamankayt (Tuareg ridge pole), 95, 96–97
Tamarindus indica, 212n7
Tamarix articulata, 25, 212n7
Tamazgut (ochre powder), 106

Tannin, 30, 59, 194
Taos, x
Tarik (Tuareg riding saddle), 53
Tariq b. Ziyad, 10
Tassili n' Ajjer rock art, x, 4, 6, 97
Tea ceremony, 86
Technological style, elements of, xix
Téda (ethnic group): architecture of, 111, 114; relationship to Tubu, 108; transport technology of, 50, 51, 52
Tekna (ethnic group): architecture of, 64, 66–73, 215–16n11; distribution of, 64; environment and vegetation of, 66–67; sociopolitical organization of, 64–66; transport technology of, 49, 72
Temne (ethnic group), 33
Temple of Solomon, 2
Tensile tents, 54–57
Tentorium (tent), 209n24
Tents: as architecture, 1–2; design of, 20; distribution of, 54–55; etymology of, 209n24; evolution of, 1, 55; history of, 1; institutional tradition of, 6–13; layered construction of, 2–3; military use of, 1, 6, 7, 8, 13; pitching and striking of, 56, 71, 76–77, 105, 106, 130, 132–34; prototypes for, 5–6; and the Tabernacle, 2–4, 6; vernacular tradition of, 4–6. *See also* Armature tents; Skin tents; Tensile tents; Woven tents
Tents of Meeting, 2–4, 6, 12, 13
Terké (Tubu riding mounts), 52, 53
Terminalia parvula, 182
Thapsus, battle of, 14
Theophrastus, 212n7
Tifinar inscriptions, 90, 92, 97, 194
Tifnit, painted ceilings at, x
Tigettewin (Tuareg forked poles), 96, 97
Time, measurement of distance by, 34
Toda (ethnic group), 108
Tolba (Hassaniya holy men), 66
Tombs, of kings of Ghana, 9
Tonkoh (Kababish palanquin), 17
Topography, 22, 24, 34
Toponymy, 37
Trajan (Roman emperor), 6
Trajan's column (Rome), 209n22
Transhumance, xxi, 20
Transport technologies, 2, 46–53
Trarza (ethnic group): architecture of, 64, 73–80; emirate of, 66; environment and vegetation of, 74; toponymy of, 66; transport technology of, 78, 80–84
Tristam, H. B., 50

Tropical climate, 25
Tuareg (ethnic group); architecture of, x, xxi, 6, 56–58, 90, 91–107, 193–94, 195, 212n7; building technology of, xxi, 60; directional terms used by, 36, 95, 102–3; distribution of, 88; funerary rites of, 104–5; gendered division of albor among, 90; household furnishings of, 97–98; and La Kahena myth, 19; marriage ritual of, xxi, 19, 91–107, 189; oral and written traditions of, 90; origins of, 88; sociopolitical organization of, 88–90; spatial precautions of, 105–7; transport technology of, 50, 53, 106–7
Tuareg Dag Rali, 49
Tuareg Kel Ahaggar: anthropometry of, 41; architecture of, 56–57, 90, 91, 94, 95–96, 97; distance-time correspondences among, 34; marriage ceremony of, 92–95; transport technology of, 50, 107; use of donkeys by, 49; women's work among, 58
Tuareg Kel Ajjer, 110
Tuareg (Iwllemmeden) Kel Ataram, 98
Tuareg Kel Ayr, 110
Tuareg (Iwllemmeden) Kel Dennek, 57, 91, 94, 96–101
Tuareg Kel Ferwan, 57, 90, 91, 97, 99, 101–5, 202
Tuareg Kel Inteser, 91, 93
Tubu: household furnishings of, 116–17
Tubu (ethnic group): architecture of, x, xxi, 56, 110–17, 195, 207n7; distribution of, 108–10; marriage rituals of, 119–22; sexual division of labor among, 112, 118–19; subsistence of, 110; transport technology of, 52, 53, 122–23, 214n4
Tuburbo Maius mosaics, 15
Tugurium (tent), 209n24
Turner, Victor, 60–61

U

Ulad 'Ali (ethnic group), 94, 217n11
Ulad-Sa'id nomads, 217n9
Urbanization, xviii
Utubu boru (Gabra tent arch), 55

V

Vandals, 15
Vegetation: description of, 24–25; and plant utilization, 26–30, 59; and root systems, 27, 29–30; types of, 28–30; and use of tannin, 30; zones of, 25–26
Vernacular architecture, xx
Vietnam War Memorial (Washington, D.C.), 190
Viollet-le-Duc, Eugène-Emmanuel, 44
Vitruvius, x, xvi

W

Wadis, 24, 25
Walata, decorated architecture of, 84, 85
Water absorption, 27
Waw (Arabic letters), 85
Weaving, 59; and field dependence-independence, 33; by Mahria women, 130, 136–37; by Somali women, 174–78; by Tekna women, 69; by Trarza and Brakna women, 75
Wind, 22–24, 66–67, 74, 156, 198
Women: as builders, xx–xxi, 58–60; pitching of tents by, 56, 58, 71, 130–37. *See also* Gender
Woodworking: division of labor in, 59, 197; by Somali nomads, 170, 197; by Tekna nomads, 215n9; by Tuareg nomads, 90, 92
Woolf, Virginia, xvii
Woven tents; prototypes for, 6; of Tekna nomads, 68–69; of Tuareg nomads, 90, 101–5; of Tubu nomads, 111, 114

X

Xeedho (Somali storage container), 184–85

Y

Yaobi (Tubu houses), 111

Z

Zara (Mahria bivouacs), 128
Zawiya (Hassaniya settlements), 66, 74, 84
Zemmour tent architecture (Morocco), 2
Zenaghe (ethnic group), 58
Zizyphus jujuba, 212n7
Zizyphus lotus, 25, 212n7
Zizyphus mauritiana, 25, 27
Zizyphus spina christi, 212n7

COLOPHON

The typefaces used in this book are Romeo Condensed and Columbus. The capitals of Romeo Condensed reflect the construction of many of the tents described in this book. As text face, Columbus complements these letterforms. The book was typeset by Paul Hotvedt of Blue Heron, Inc., in Lawrence, Kansas. Jean Lamunière, of Frederick, Maryland, produced the mechanicals. The book was printed on 70-lb. Moistrite Matte at Thompson-Shore, Inc., in Dexter, Michigan.